本书为限量发行 999 套的第　　648　　号

This book is copy number _____

in a limited edition of nine hundred and ninety-nine copies.

藏美

九如堂古陶瓷收藏 50 年

I

Collecting a Museum

50 Years of the Jiurutang Collection

九如堂　编著

文物出版社

图书在版编目（ＣＩＰ）数据

藏美：九如堂古陶瓷收藏50年 / 九如堂编著. --

北京：文物出版社, 2018.11

　　ISBN 978-7-5010-5383-4

　　Ⅰ.①藏… Ⅱ.①九… Ⅲ.①瓷器(考古) – 中国 – 图

集 Ⅳ.①K876.32

中国版本图书馆CIP数据核字(2017)第275899号

藏美——九如堂古陶瓷收藏 50 年
——————————————————————————

编　　著：九如堂

九如堂网址：http:// www.jiurutangcollection.com

责任编辑：谷艳雪　王　媛

责任印制：张道奇

中文校对：陈　婧　赵　宁

英文校对：[美] Justin Daniel Holcombe

出版发行：文物出版社

社　　址：北京市东直门内北小街2号楼

邮　　编：100007

网　　址：http:// www.wenwu.com

邮　　箱：web@wemwu.com

经　　销：新华书店

印　　刷：雅昌文化（集团）有限公司

开　　本：635mm×965mm　1/8

印　　张：86.75

版　　次：2018年11月第1版

印　　次：2018年11月第1次印刷

书　　号：ISBN 978-7-5010-5383-4

定　　价：2000.00元

藏美

九如堂古陶瓷收藏 50 年

I

Collecting a Museum

50 Years of the Jiurutang Collection

目　录

Contents

序　言

香港经济发达，文化荟萃，商贾文人云集。作为东方自由商埠，它又是中国国粹文物的流散之地，历朝历代由此流出的文物星罗棋布地散落于世界各地。20 世纪以来，迭有学识渊博、财力雄厚的在港同胞，热衷于保护祖国古老文化遗产，尽其所能搜藏各类文物，使国宝免遭流落，功不可没。

通常世人多喜爱精工细作、色彩缤纷之明清官窑瓷，因其显有皇家气派而争相购藏，品类广泛的高古之器却乏人问津。九如堂主人身处诸多奇异消闲之地的香港，却唯独钟情于祖国的远古文化遗存，寻古探幽，返朴求真，可谓独具慧眼。

九如堂主人悉心探研陶的产生、发展与用途，陶与青铜相互的影响，古代帝王礼器与典章以及由陶到瓷的演变等问题，从中领悟陶瓷文化的深奥所在。历代名师艺匠的智慧和别出心裁在陶艺中一一得以体现，造型、纹饰、釉色都韵味无穷。

九如堂按中国陶瓷发展史的脉络，由新石器时代到元代，以美学为主导进行陶瓷收藏，藏品之丰在东方收藏家中实属罕有，识者不胜羡佩。且九如堂主人收藏非以私利为目的，而更着重与公众分享，曾多次借出藏品到国外以及香港等地博物馆展览，弘扬中国古陶瓷文化艺术，实是令人敬佩。

为纪念九如堂收藏 50 周年，堂主重新出版图录为收藏做一总结。本人作为堂主之友，曾有机缘于香港及美国尽情鉴赏其收藏，兹应约略缀数语，为其藏品图录作序志念。

耿宝昌
2018 年初春于北京

Foreword

Hong Kong is a financial center and cultural hub that attracts both entrepreneurs and intellectuals alike. As a free port in the Orient, it has also been a transit point for many Chinese cultural artifacts before they get dispersed around the world. Since the 20th century, a number of learned and well-to-do Chinese in Hong Kong have tried their best to collect what they can to prevent these national treasures from disappearing into oblivion. Their contribution to this cause deserves all the recognition in the world.

While many fight to pay more for the decorative brilliance and royal grandeur of polychrome porcelains from the Ming and Qing dynasties, early pottery and ceramics have enjoyed a relatively lower profile. This is probably due to differences of interests, tastes and connoisseurship. The owner of the Jiurutang Collection is one of the happy few who have chosen to dedicate themselves to collecting these early pieces. His dogged pursuit for these early wares and his preference for ancient elegance speak to his discriminating taste and unique point of view. This is why the Jiurutang Collection is so special.

For the owner of the Jiurutang Collection, the first emergence and development of pottery, the important relationship between pottery and ritual bronzes and the evolution from pottery to porcelain are subjects that needed to be delved into before the complete story of Chinese ceramics can be understood. The genius of the potters can be seen in the form, the decorations, the glaze color of these early wares. Their charm delights and captivates the heart of all those who love ancient Chinese ceramics.

Objects from the Jiurutang Collection, spanning from the Neolithic to the Yuan dynasty are organized chronologically and collected from an aesthetic point of view. The owner collects only for the love of beautiful objects and art itself but also makes a point to share his passion for these ancient ceramics with the wider public through loans to major museums in Hong Kong and abroad.

Few ceramic collections in the Orient can match the richness and depth of the Jiurutang Collection. As a friend of its owner, I have been able to view these unusual treasures to my heart's content. I'm writing this foreword to introduce readers to this new catalogue and to celebrate the 50th anniversary of this remarkable collection.

Geng Baochang
Beijing
Spring 2018

前　言

自 1966 年购买第一件陶瓷器物开始收藏之路，匆匆不觉已是五十载。开始时，是它们古拙的造型、优美的线条深深吸引了我，那时没有窑口概念，但凡感觉美、合心意的就买。后来随着收藏知识的丰富和市场货品来源的增加，选择变多了，购买也变得谨慎，都是选择一些品位较高的陶瓷器物。后来到国外的博物馆参观后，我发觉它们都有一个共同点——都收藏有数量相当丰富、规格相当高的古代文物，包括古代陶瓷器物。高古陶瓷器虽然所占比例不多，但其质朴浑厚、粗犷雄伟的风格，以及器物内蕴藏的文化艺术内涵和时代的独特性，都令我深深着迷，也让我思考为何不按博物馆序列收藏一间自己的"博物馆"。

中国古陶瓷的出现、发展、成熟是与中国历史息息相关的，是中国古代历史信息的载体，而收藏完整的中国高古陶瓷系列藏品，就是收藏了一部中国古代史。所以之后每到博物馆参观，我都把自己既当作一个参观者，也当作一个博物馆馆长，思考我的博物馆藏品应该有哪些器物，才能以其艺术性、独特性和趣味性结合历史时代背景来吸引大众的目光。我列出一张长长的购买名单，包括必需的、首要和次要的，尽力去收藏。而我自小就喜爱"漂亮"的物品，于是便以"美学"为主导，按中国陶瓷发展史的脉络来进行收藏，并确立了五条标准：第一，线条柔和流畅，造型素朴简约，比例和谐协调；第二，釉质莹润细腻，釉色清雅脱俗；第三，各个朝代比较罕见；第四，具有纪年，有较高研究价值；第五，表现民族文化特征。

由于收藏始于 60 年代，时间较早，有机会接触到许多不同朝代、不同窑口、不同品种的陶瓷器，也把握时机购买到了自己认为值得收藏的器物。当时不管什么窑口，只要符合美的要求就买。有几次碰到南宋官窑器物，但都因太咸，釉面脱落，且有破损，没有购藏。有一些不错的器物，只是有一点缺陷，认为以后仍有机会碰到完美的而没有购入，结果昙花一现后便再没有在市场见到。回想起来，至今仍感到有些失落。

随着考古发掘资料日益丰富，收藏知识日益增加，有些 2003 年出版的《九如堂古陶瓷藏品》图录内的器物说明、窑口和断代，今次都做了修改。近十余年除了补充一些缺少的类型器物外，我将全部藏品，包括自购藏后从未开启的器物，逐一进行了审视和整理，重新筛选出 500 件藏品，分陶器部和瓷器部，下设九个馆，每个馆展示一个不同历史时期、有代表性的陶器或瓷器器物，形成完整的、有连贯性的、以"美"为中心的中国高古陶瓷收藏系列。每件藏品除了有详细说明、清晰的图片外，还尽可能附上相关的历史背景资料，让读者对中国的陶瓷历史、文化艺术有概括的认识，找到民族的自豪感和归属感。

本书是笔者以收藏家和鉴赏家的角度和语言撰写。除了纪念和总结九如堂五十载的收藏历程，也希望能作为中国高古陶瓷爱好者的指南，启发更多读者对中国古代历史和古陶瓷的兴趣，加入收藏历史和美的行列。

李喾鸣
九如堂
2018 年 11 月

Preface

Time flies. Fifty years have passed since I first embarked on my long journey of collecting and acquired my first piece of ceramic ware in 1966. At the beginning, I was deeply drawn to their archaic forms and elegant silhouettes. Without too much knowledge of kilns or kiln sites, I collected with my instincts and bought only what I thought was beautiful. As time went by and my knowledge base grew, the collection gradually focused on finer and finer grade of ceramic wares. Whenever I get a chance to visit museums abroad, I'm always struck by the remarkable quality of their Chinese collections that almost always included ceramics. Although ancient Chinese ceramics only make up a fraction of the artifacts in these collections, I found myself drawn to their boldness, creativity and artistic and cultural significance within the history of Chinese art. As these thoughts went through my mind, I asked myself, "Why not collect a 'museum' of your own?"

In the ensuing years that followed, I would wear two hats both as spectator and curator when contemplating and acquiring the kind of objects that I would like to include in the "museum". I even drew up a long shopping list of must-have representative pieces that would help me focus on building a coherent and comprehensive collection. I always knew what I liked and disliked so it was natural for me to start collecting based on aesthetics. This gradually developed into a very personal system of collecting. The artifact must, first and foremost, have an elegant shape, fluid silhouette and balanced proportions; second, a lustrous and refined glaze and a charming glaze color; third, a rarity of its kind within a dynastic period; next, dated inscriptions and scientific research value and last but not least, distinct cultural or ethnic features.

The advantage of starting my collection in the 60s meant exposure to a very diverse range of ceramic wares across many dynastic periods and kilns. I relied on my instincts and simply bought what I thought was right at each point in time without over thinking it. I do remember coming across some Southern Song Guan wares several times but backed away because of some flaws on the piece. I have let go of other equally good finds for the same reason thinking that something better will eventually turn up. They never did and I still think about these lost chances to this day.

For the past decade, I've set myself the task of organizing, editing, updating the item descriptions, kilns, sites and dates in the 2003 catalogue and refining the collection in its entirety so that the history of ancient Chinese ceramics can be told through the 500 objects that are in this catalogue. The two sections of this chronologically arranged catalogue – Pottery and Porcelain – are the cornerstones of the "museum". These two wings of the "museum" are made up of nine "rooms" each representing a specific period in ancient Chinese ceramic history. The illustrations and bilingual descriptions are supplemented by historical background information where possible to contextualize the objects on display in each "room".

On this most auspicious of occasions, the 50th Anniversary of the Jiurutang Collection, we would like to take this opportunity to celebrate our very personal journey of collecting with our readers. Written from the perspective of a collector-connoisseur, we hope this catalogue will kindle your passion for and increase your knowledge of Chinese ceramic art and history. Better yet, let this be an inspiration for you to join us in collecting your very own "museum" of ancient Chinese ceramics.

Lee Lurk Ming
The Jiurutang Collection
November 2018

新石器时代陶器

Neolithic Pottery

新石器时代陶器：

万物有灵

根据考古发掘资料显示，中国的陶器出现在距今 1 万年左右。广西桂林庙岩遗址出土的陶片经过科学测定距今 1.5 万年左右，这是中国目前发现的年代最早的史前陶片。河北徐水县南庄头早期新石器时代遗址发现有 13 片使用过的陶器残片，是圜底钵、圜底罐等造型极为简单的器物，陶质为夹砂深灰陶、夹云母褐红陶，年代距今 10000—9000 年。在江苏省溧水县、江西省万年县、河北省阳原县、北京市怀柔区、湖南省道县都发现有距今 1 万年左右的陶片。

大约在距今 7000 年左右的新石器时代，制陶工艺取得巨大成就，陶器品种多，艺术水平高，且兼具实用性与美观性。早期原始陶器是泥质素陶（软陶），利用河谷沉积土、普通泥土做原料，有红色、橙黄色的红陶，灰陶，以及相应的夹砂陶，后来又出现了白陶、彩陶、彩绘陶。制陶方式由手捏泥片成型、泥条盘筑、模制成型、范制成型、慢轮制作到快轮成型等。烧法由露天架火烧到陶窑烧制。这些陶器在日常生活中用于饮食、汲水、盛水、储藏、烹饪、祭祀和陪葬（图录 1 号、2 号、9 号、10 号、15 号）。

新石器时代早期，原始先民不但发展了制作陶器的工艺技术，还掌握了多种美化陶器的手法。他们从实用的角度出发，把生活中的理想、信念，大自然的美景变化，想象中的神灵，生产活动和繁衍后代的两性关系，在练好的泥团上塑造为各种器形，并加以美化。不论器形的设计，还是装饰或细节的处理，都兼顾了实用与美观。

在各个原始文化中，具有代表性的陶瓶、罐、瓮、甂、壶等器物，口较细小，从肩开始向外张侈，上腹圆鼓、丰满，中腹以下渐成弧线形收成平底，变得很清秀，既实用，又美观。有的器物做成动物形象，动物嘴做流，整件作品憨态可掬。有盖子的器物，将盖子上的提手做成鸟头、兽头，或是昂首、瞪眼、张嘴的巫师头像，表现出生命的活力。有足的器物只安三足，符合三点一面的力学原理，又表现出质朴浓郁的美学修养。

陶器上的几何图案和植物画面与人们的日常采集经济、耕作农业密不可分，是人对自然的感悟中抽象出来的艺术，表达了氏族社会人们的某种文化思想。它们有的追求节奏起伏、上下排列的变化，有的上下叠压、对称均衡，展现出跌宕起伏或是平稳和谐的感觉，绚丽多姿。这些图案或画面，无论简单的或复杂的，都表现了氏族中发生的情景或是远古流传下来的故事。

彩陶是制陶工艺技术发展到一定阶段以后才出现的，条件包括了较高的烧成温度、对颜料的使用和对陶泥的淘洗等等。彩陶在坯体成型以后，晾干到一定程度，或施上陶衣，经过打磨，再画上图案，再次打磨、晾干，经火焙烧成为陶器。颜料与陶胎融为一体，虽历经数千年依然不脱落。泥质陶的烧成温度在 750℃—850℃之间，夹砂陶在 850℃—950℃左右。绘陶原料是以天然矿物经研磨而成。黑彩是铁锰结核，红彩是赭石或红土，白彩是白黏土或瓷土。在陶器上进行修刮时使用的是石刀或陶刀等，打磨时用骨、竹、石等坚硬光滑的工具顺着一个方向进行，打磨后的陶器表面闪闪发亮。有些精美的彩陶，不但陶胎很薄，而且器表经精心打磨，造型流畅，纹饰丰富，色彩缤纷，风格典雅（图录 40 号、41 号、54 号、56 号）。彩陶在新石器时代文化陶器中所占比重很少，在当时即是为数不多的珍贵物品。

彩陶兴盛于氏族社会晚期，这也是图腾艺术繁盛的时期。原始先民对大自然变幻无常的现象无从捉摸，从而敬而畏之，认为自然界的一切都处于精灵的控制下，认为神灵无处不在，由此产生"万物有灵"的原始宗教观念，认为人和自然万物是可以通过神灵相互沟通的。图腾是记载神的灵魂的载体，以一种超人的形象作为氏族祖先、标志，把氏族成员团结在一起，是人与自然万物沟通的媒介。不同的氏族有不同的图腾崇拜。

新石器时代早中期是以母系为中心的母系社会，妇女是婚姻生活的中心。男女双方分属各自的氏族，生下的子女则按照母亲一方的血缘来计算，女儿是氏族的继承者，人们只知有母，不知其父。女性在氏族中享有崇高的威信，地位远远高于男人。这是因为当时的农业生产主要由妇女承担，更重要的是妇女肩负着氏族繁衍的重任。新生命的增添使氏族人口更繁盛，而人口资源是氏族赖以生存的根本。由此形成的祖先崇拜和母体崇拜，反映了先民对女体神生殖力的恐惧和崇敬。在陶器上一般以象征、夸张等手法来强化和突出女性性别特征和生殖部位，如巨腹、丰乳和突出刻画的生殖部位，把原始先民朴素的生殖崇拜表现得淋漓尽致（图录 11 号、29 号、55 号）。

大汶口文化是黄河下游地区新石器时代中晚期的一种文化，因 1959 年在山东泰安大汶口发现而得名。其时间跨度达 1800 多年，后发展为山东龙山文化。山东龙山文化的蛋壳黑陶器，无论在制作工艺上，还是陶色和器形上，都具有明显的大汶口文化痕迹（图录 14 号、16 号）。

蛋壳黑陶的陶土选择比较严格，要经过粉碎、精细淘洗和较长时间的陈腐，用快轮成型，精心修刮和打磨。其胎体精薄致密，造型规整，轻巧秀致，线条简练，通体黑色，熠熠发光，代表了整个新石器时代制陶工艺的最高水平。蛋壳黑陶主要在山东地区的大汶口和龙山文化遗址的大、中型墓葬中发现，河南龙山文化遗址和墓葬中也有发现。龙山文化以后黑陶仍有一些生产，只是胎体变厚，艺术水平远远不及龙山文化的黑陶。

良渚文化陶器以泥质黑陶最具代表性，但绝大部分都属于灰胎黑皮陶，烧成温度较低，胎质较软，陶衣呈黑色，较易脱落（图录 8 号）。

Neolithic Pottery :

Spirited Animism

Archaeological research and excavations have revealed that the history of Chinese pottery can be traced back to around ten thousand years before present. Tests have confirmed that potsherds excavated from the Miaoyan site in Guilin (Guangxi) are around 15000 years old. They are the earliest prehistoric potsherds known in China. Teams from Peking University and Hebei University discovered an early Neolithic site in Nanzhuangtou (Xushui, Hebei province) and found thirteen potsherds of large bowls and jars. They were categorized as sand-tempered dark gray pottery and mica-tempered brownish red pottery dated to 10000–9000 years before present. Potsherds dated to around ten thousand years ago have also been unearthed from Sushui county in Jiangsu, Wannian county in Jiangxi, Yangyuan county in Hebei, Huairou district in Beijing and Dao county in Hunan.

Around 7000 years ago in the Neolithic Age, pottery making saw rapid progress and a wide range of wares fulfilling both functional and decorative purposes were produced. Early pottery was made from earthen clay obtained from mud or alluvial silt deposited on riverbeds. Red pottery of red or buff color, gray pottery and black pottery were produced alongside sand-tempered pottery, white pottery, polychrome pottery, and painted pottery. Shaping methods included pinching, slab building, coiling and wheel throwing. Bonfires, and later on, kilns were used for firing. The vessels were daily utensils made for cooking, serving and storing foods and drinks, as well as being used as sacrificial and mortuary objects (Cat. Nos. 1, 2, 9, 10, 15).

Primitive people of the early Neolithic Age had not only developed the technology of pottery production but also mastered various skills to embellish the pottery they made. Aesthetics and practicality were given equal weight.

The vase, the jar, the urn, the tripod steamer (*yan*) and the flask are typical examples from the Neolithic period. They have a small mouth, sloping shoulders and a bulbous belly that tapers to a flat base. Legged vessels are affixed with three legs, which is in line with the three point contact principle.

The geometric and vegetal motifs on Neolithic pottery were closely associated with a foraging and agricultural economy. They were artistic expressions of the natural world, representing certain culture and ideology of the tribal societies. They displayed a range of rhythmical and compositional variations. The diversity of compositions bespeaks harmony, perpetuity and rhythm. These patterns or paintings, whether simple or elaborate, illustrate episodes occurring in the tribal society or a legend being passed down through generations.

Painted pottery emerged after production reached a certain stage of development. It required a higher firing temperature, the use of color pigments and levigated clay. First, the vessel shaped from moist clay is left to dry. Then the surface, sometimes coated with a slip, is burnished. Next, decorative motifs are painted onto the surface. The vessel will be burnished a second time, left to dry and finally hardened by firing. The firing temperature for earthenware is 750℃–850℃ and around 850℃–950℃ for sand-tempered pottery. Black pigments are derived from ferromanganese nodules, red ones from ochre or red clay and white ones from white clay or china clay. Pottery and stone blades are used for trimming while hard and sharp tools made with bones, bamboo or stones are used for burnishing. The gloss is a result of burnishing the surface of the vessel in one direction. The finest painted pottery are not only thinly potted but also meticulously burnished. They are noted for their fluid lines, rich decorations, contrasting palette and elegant style (Cat. Nos. 40, 41, 54, 56). Painted pottery is scarce among Neolithic pottery.

Painted pottery was prevalent during the late stage of tribal society, which coincided with the period of totemism. People believed that an omnipresent spirit controls everything in the natural world. As the guardian deity of a tribe, the totem was also seen as the common ancestor of the tribe in the form of a superhuman spirit. This tribal emblem served as a medium through which all things in Nature can communicate with one other and different tribes have different totems.

Mid-Neolithic societies are largely matriarchal. A child with parents from different clans would only trace the descent on the maternal side. Daughters were regarded as heirs of the family. People knew who their mother was but had no knowledge of their father. Women enjoyed a higher prestige in the clan and their status far exceeded that of men. The mysterious reproductive power of the maternal body is both feared and revered. Pregnant bellies, breasts, female genitalia are seen as symbols of fertility and abundance (Cat. Nos. 11, 29, 55).

The Dawenkou culture was a culture developed in the lower Yellow River basin through the mid to late Neolithic Age. It was first discovered in 1959 at Dawenkou (Tai'an) in Shandong province and spanned a period as long as 1800 years. The ending

phase of this culture developed into the Longshan culture of Shandong. The shape, color and production techniques of the Longshanoid black eggshell pottery are reminiscent of Dawenkou pottery (Cat. Nos. 14, 16).

The clay for making black eggshell pottery was carefully selected and processed. It was finely crushed and levigated. The vessels were turned on a fast wheel, meticulously trimmed to obtain a thin, dense body and burnished to a lustrous finish. Eggshell black-wares represent not only the finest Neolithic pottery but also the finest artifacts in the Neolithic repertoire. The majority of black eggshell pottery was found in large and medium-sized tombs, mainly from Longshanoid sites in Shandong. Examples have also been unearthed from other Longshanoid sites and tombs in Henan. Production of black wares still continued after the Longshan culture but never regained its former quality.

Black earthenware is the most characteristic of the Liangzhu culture pottery. They are relatively low-fired black carbonized pottery with a rather soft gray paste covered with black slip (Cat. No. 8).

1

红陶水波纹尖底瓶

新石器时代
仰韶文化半坡类型
约公元前 5000—前 4500 年
高：45.5 厘米
口径：6.8 厘米

Red pottery amphora with wave motif

Neolithic period
Banpo type, Yangshao culture
Circa 5000 – 4500 B.C.E.
Height: 45.5 cm
Mouth diameter: 6.8 cm

泥质红陶。直口，束颈，颈上端加厚，使口部呈蘑菇状，斜肩，长圆腹，腹下渐敛，尖底。腹两侧置环耳。上腹部饰斜向水波纹。全器经打磨，光滑黝亮。此器双耳系上绳子，在日常生活中用于汲水。打水时，瓶口部先进入水里，水往内灌时，重心慢慢移到瓶的下部，瓶口会倒转向上，这样就可把已盛载水的瓶拉上来。也可以将尖底插在洞里使之立起来。此种尖底瓶是典型的仰韶文化半坡类型器物。

半坡类型文化遗址集中分布在渭河中下游地区，北起河套地区，南到汉水中上游，东至豫西、晋南，西达陇东地区，以西安半坡遗址的早期遗存为代表。

本品经热释光测定最后烧制年代距今约5100 年。

Red earthenware. The jar has a straight mouth above a constricted neck with a thickened top that resembles the cap of a mushroom. Just below the sloping shoulders is an ovoid belly that tapers towards a pointed bottom. A pair of loop-lugs is located below the shoulders.

The upper belly is covered with oblique wave pattern. The entire vessel has been burnished to a smooth and lustrous surface. These jars are specially designed for drawing water. When the jar is lowered into water, it would tip over on its side and water would flow in through the mouth. As more and more water enters the jar, gravitational force would cause the jar to return gradually to its upright position. Then, the vessel is ready to be pulled out of water. At home, these jars are inserted upright into holes on the ground. These kind of jars are representative examples of Banpo type wares.

The Banpo sites in Xi'an, Shaanxi province spread over the middle and lower drainage area of the Wei River, a major tributary of the Yellow River. Geographically, it is bordered by the Ordos to the north, the upper Han River basin to the south, western Henan and southern Shanxi to the east and eastern Shaanxi to the west.

Thermoluminescence (TL) dating shows that the last firing date of this jar was approximately 5100 years before present.

2

红陶水纹碗

新石器时代
仰韶文化
约公元前 5000—前 3000 年
高：7.8 厘米
口径：16.3 厘米

Red pottery bowl with wave motif

Neolithic period
Yangshao culture
Circa 5000 – 3000 B.C.E.
Height: 7.8 cm
Mouth diameter: 16.3 cm

夹砂红陶。口微撇，碗身约呈 45 度角收到底，底平。碗身四周拍印斜向水纹，外底留有席纹印痕。胎泥较粗和疏松，混有砂粒，烧成温度较低。陶泥内加入石英砂粒，增强了器物的硬度，令器物牢固耐用。本品外形不甚规整，口部不圆、器身歪斜，应是用作盛器或食器，显示了早期陶器以实用性为主的原始性，弥漫着质朴、古拙、粗犷的美感。

仰韶遗址因 1921 年于河南渑池县仰韶村发现而得名，仰韶文化主要分布于黄河中游地区的陕西、河南、山西等省区，在甘肃、湖北、河北及内蒙古等邻近中原的边缘地区也有分布。

本品经热释光测定最后烧制年代距今 4800—3800 年。

Sand-tempered red earthenware. The bowl has a slightly flared mouth and sides tapering towards the base at a 45-degree angle. The exterior wall is decorated with oblique wave motif. The imprint of a woven mat fabric is visible on the flat base. The low-fired sand-tempered paste is rather coarse and porous. Adding quartz sand to the paste increases the hardness and durability. This bowl is not very neatly potted. The body is lopsided and the rim uneven. The bowl was probably used as an eating utensil.

The Yangshao culture was first discovered in 1921 in Yangshao village in Mianchi county, Henan province. The culture existed along the upper and middle reaches of the Yellow River in the Gansu, Qinghai, Ningxia, Shaanxi and Henan provinces.

Thermoluminescence test shows that the last firing date of this bowl was 4800 to 3800 years before present.

3

红陶鸟形壶

新石器时代

仰韶文化

约公元前 5000—前 3000 年

高：12.2 厘米

Bird-shaped red pottery jar

Neolithic period

Yangshao culture

Circa 5000 – 3000 B.C.E.

Height: 12.2 cm

泥质红陶。腹呈椭圆形，平底，底呈五角形。筒形壶口上昂作鸟首，相对下方饰一上翘短尾, 鸟背贴压条状堆纹二条。器体满布方向不同、刀刻的斜纹线，寓作羽毛、翅膀和爪，塑造出一只在水中畅游的水鸟形象。胎泥呈褐红色，较细腻，胎骨坚硬，烧成温度较高。刻工凌厉、深邃、利落。本品可能是用于盛水。本品制作精美，极富艺术性，是一件十分珍贵的史前文物。

Red earthenware. The jar has an ovoid body and a pentagon-shaped flat base. The up-tilted cylindrical mouth resembles a bird's head. A tail is affixed to the widest part of the belly at the opposite end. Two appliqué clay strips are attached to the back. The entire vessel is carved with oblique striations running in different directions to represent the feathers, wings and claws of the bird. The brownish-red paste is hard and refined. The vessel was fired to a rather high temperature. The carving is sharp and deep. This vessel was probably used as a water container.

4

白陶环耳杯

新石器时代

大汶口文化

约公元前 4300—前 2500 年

高：15.2 厘米

底径：7.3 厘米

**White pottery cup with
loop handle**

Neolithic period

Dawenkou culture

Circa 4300 – 2500 B.C.E.

Height: 15.2 cm

Base diameter: 7.3 cm

细泥白陶，质松软。口外撇、高颈、扁球形腹、喇叭状高圈足、边缘微隆。腹一侧置扁圆形耳。白陶以白色坩子土作胎，因其胎中氧化铁含量低（1.6% 左右），所以烧成后胎呈白色。胎泥均经多次淘洗，陶质细腻。本品精巧实用，表现出大汶口文化高超的工艺技巧。

白陶是珍贵的器物，在遗址和墓葬中出土的比例很低。

大汶口文化因在山东泰安大汶口发现而得名，范围东达黄海之滨，北至渤海南岸，西到鲁西平原的东部和河南东部部分地区，南及苏、皖北部。

White earthenware with a soft and refined paste. The cup has a flared mouth, a high neck, a bulbous belly and a trumpet-shaped ring-foot with slightly raised edges. On one side of the belly is a loop handle. Since white earthenware is fabricated from white clay with iron content as low as around 1.6 percent, the paste appears white after firing. The clay had been repeatedly levigated to obtain a very fine texture. The cup's exquisite shape attests to the superb artistry of the Dawenkou potters.

White earthenware is exceedingly rare and constitutes only a few percent of all the finds from archaeological sites and tombs.

The Dawenkou culture is named after the Dawenkou site which is located in Tai'an, Shandong province. Geographically, it is bordered by the Yellow Sea to the east, the southern shore of Bohai Gulf to the north, the plain of western Shandong to the west and Huaibei in northern Jiangsu to the south.

5

白陶三足鬶

新石器时代

大汶口文化

约公元前 4300—前 2500 年

高：25.2 厘米

White pottery *gui* tripod jug

Neolithic period

Dawenkou culture

Circa 4300 – 2500 B.C.E.

Height: 25.2 cm

泥质白陶。圆口深腹、口流合一，槽形流长且扁狭、颈呈漏斗形。颈、肩分界明显，裆的弧度很大，附三个中空袋足，二前一后，三足距离较大。颈、足间安绳索状柄。腹部饰链状堆纹一周，连接于柄的底部。颈下正前方饰一小圆饼。

三足鬶是炊具，为黄河下游大汶口文化晚期的典型器物。本品造型优美、制作精细、体态生动传神，塑造出一只昂首欲飞的禽鸟形象。

本品与图录 6 号为同期、同类物品，只是本品以白黏土作胎，而图录 6 号以红陶为胎。

White earthenware. The vessel has a circular mouth that tapers into an up-tilted, long and narrow beak. The junction between the funnel neck and the shoulders is clearly defined. The lower section of the belly branches out into three hollow legs tapering to conical points. The legs are set wide apart forming a big arch in between them. A cord-shaped handle connects the bottom of the neck to the top of the hind leg. A band of chain-like appliqué runs around the lower belly. Underneath the neck is a small boss appliqué.

The jug is characteristic of the pottery of the latter phase of the Dawenkou culture and the Longshan culture in the lower Yellow River basin. The vessel was used as a cooking utensil.

This item is similar in shape and period to Cat. No. 6 except that it is fabricated from white earthen clay while the latter is made from red earthen clay.

6

红陶三足鬶

新石器时代
大汶口文化
约公元前 4300—前 2500 年
高：29 厘米

Red pottery *gui* tripod jug

Neolithic period
Dawenkou culture
Circa 4300 – 2500 B.C.E.
Height: 29 cm

泥质红陶。口呈圆形，外侈。槽形流狭长向上斜翘，颈呈漏斗状。颈、肩分界明显，分档，下置三袋足，二前一后。颈、足间置双股泥条扭成藤条形柄，柄底两侧围绕腹部饰一圈链状堆纹。颈下正前方贴一小圆饼。本品构思巧妙、制作精美、泥料加工细致、造型规整优美。

Red earthenware. The vessel has a flared circular mouth, a long and narrow up-tilted beak and a funnel-shaped neck. The edge of the neck and the shoulders is well demarcated. The lower section of the vessel branches out into three hollow legs. A rattan-like handle comprising two entwining rolls of clay arches from the base of the neck to the belly. The lower end of the handle is connected to a chain-like appliqué encompassing the lower belly. A small boss is applied to the center front of the body below the neck.

7

蛋壳黑陶镂孔竹节柄杯

新石器时代

大汶口文化

约公元前 4300—前 2500 年

高：27.6 厘米

底径：7.3 厘米

Black pottery goblet with eggshell-thin body

Neolithic period

Dawenkou culture

Circa 4300 – 2500 B.C.E.

Height: 27.6 cm

Base diameter: 7.3 cm

泥质黑陶。侈口，深腹，圜形底，接高直柄。高柄空心，粗壮，呈七级竹节形，上有三条连珠状镂孔，每条七孔。圆拱形足，足边刻凹弦纹一周。器壁薄，但稍厚于龙山蛋壳陶。器表打磨乌黑发亮。本品造型严谨规整，装饰简单有力，器形高挑，亭亭玉立，为大汶口文化晚期精品。

薄胎磨光黑陶最早出现在大汶口文化时期，表现了大汶口文化超卓的制陶工艺。

Black earthenware. The goblet has a flared mouth, a deep belly and a rounded base connected to a tall and hollow stem in the shape of a bamboo with seven internodes. Each internode is pierced with three openings, forming three columns of apertures down the sides. A groove runs around the edge of the arched foot. The vessel is thinly potted but slightly thicker than typical Longshan eggshell pottery. The glossy black surface is a result of fine burnishing. The tall stem adds a touch of elegance to the overall design. It is a fine example of late Dawenkou culture pottery.

Burnished black eggshell pottery first appeared during the Dawenkou culture period.

8

黑陶柱足盉

新石器时代

良渚文化

约公元前 3100—前 2200 年

高：18 厘米

Black pottery *he* tripod jug

Neolithic period

Liangzhu culture

Circa 3100 – 2200 B.C.E.

Height: 18 cm

泥质黑皮陶。口呈椭圆形，前部上翘呈弧形流，粗短颈，椭圆形腹，下置三圆形实柱足，两前一后，背饰环形柄。所用陶土极为讲究：器身采用灰色陶泥，质细腻，胎体上施一层黑色陶衣，打磨乌黑光亮；柄、腹底部和三足用夹砂灰陶，以提高耐火性能，增强承托力，不易破裂。本品造型优美，盛水、酒兼作温煮器。

良渚文化是中国长江下游新石器时代文化，主要分布在今上海市、浙江省北部和江苏省南部的太湖周围地区。良渚文化黑皮陶十分精美，本品为其代表作品。

本品经热释光测定最后烧制年代距今5000—3500 年。

Gray earthenware with carbonized slip coating. The front end of the oval mouth is slightly raised and shaped into a pouring lip. The short thick neck sits on a squat and bulbous belly supported by three solid cylindrical legs. The choice of material is sophisticated. Refined gray earthen clay is used for the body, which has been coated with a layer of black slip and then meticulously burnished to a lustrous jet-black surface. The loop handle, base and legs are fabricated from sand-tempered gray clay to increase their fire resistance, load bearing capacity and durability. Vessel of this shape is known as *he*. It was used as a water or wine container.

The Liangzhu culture is a Neolithic culture developed in the lower Changjiang (Yangtze) River basin. Major sites are found in the drainage area of Lake Tai, reaching as far south as Qiantang River and as far north as around the city of Changzhou in Jiangsu. Pottery with carbonized black slip coating is typical of the Liangzhu culture period.

Thermoluminescence test shows that the last firing date of this piece was 5000 to 3500 years before present.

9

红陶大瓮

新石器时代
马家窑文化半山类型
约公元前 2600—前 2300 年
高：63.5 厘米

Large red pottery jar

Neolithic period
Banshan type, Majiayao culture
Circa 2600 – 2300 B.C.E.
Height: 63.5 cm

夹砂红陶。口平外翻、鼓肩、深腹、斜收，下腹部呈锥状，底平。胎体薄、全器重量颇轻。器身外壁拍印编织纹，肩腹交接处和腹中贴附加泥条两圈。本品用于盛水或储物，造型规整，左右对称，比例和谐，弧度优雅。如此大型器物烧成而无变形，可知几千年前的窑工已熟练掌握了制陶工艺，而且该大瓮历经数千年仍保存完整，实在难能可贵。

本品经热释光测定最后烧制年代距今5000—3300 年。

Sand-tempered red earthenware. The jar has a flat mouth with everted rim, broad shoulders and a deep, tapering belly and a flat base. The paste is thin and the vessel is rather lightweight. The exterior surface is impressed with woven mat pattern. A roll of clay reinforces the body between the shoulders and the belly and another encircles the mid-section of the body. The sand-tempered paste and additional clay strips are used to reinforce the vessel. The vessel was used for holding water or as containers. It's short of a miracle that a vessel of this size and age had survived intact at all.

Thermoluminescence test shows that the last firing date of this jar was 5000 to 3300 years before present.

10

红陶三足鬶

新石器时代

山东龙山文化

约公元前 2500—前 2000 年

高：34.5 厘米

Red pottery *gui* tripod jug

Neolithic period

Longshan culture, Shandong

Circa 2500 – 2000 B.C.E.

Height: 34.5 cm

泥质红陶，质颇细滑。整体造型优美，如一昂首引颈高歌的禽鸟。口呈圆形，边缘外卷，上附槽形流，流端尖而微弯曲，如鸟喙。粗筒状颈，颈上槽形流两侧贴半月形耳组各一个，寓意禽鸟的眼睛。颈腹分界不明显，以棱状扁条形柄相连。下置袋足三个，袋足圆浑丰满，末端成锥形。袋足外形类似女性的乳房，是新石器时期母系社会生育崇拜的体现，同时本品作为炊具，袋足可增大与火的接触面，缩短煮食时间。

Red earthenware with a rather fine paste. This vessel has a circular mouth with an outward-rolling rim that extends into a pointed and slightly curved tip resembling a bird's beak. The junction between the cylindrical thick neck and the belly is indistinct. A crescent-shaped lug is affixed to both sides of the neck to represent the eyes. A strap handle joins the neck to the belly. Below the belly are three baggy legs tapering to conical points. The design is practical because the baggy legs allowed a much larger surface area of the vessel to be exposed to the fire thus shortening the cooking time. This jug was used as a cooking utensil.

11

绳纹大母神三足瓮

新石器时代

陕西龙山文化

约公元前 2500—前 2000 年

高：62.7 厘米

口径：26 厘米

"The Great Mother" jar

Neolithic period

Longshan culture, Shaanxi

Circa 2500 – 2000 B.C.E.

Height: 62.7 cm

Mouth diameter: 26 cm

夹砂灰陶。颈微束，深腹，分裆，下承三袋状足。器体上部饰乳房两个，袋足丰盈。背后颈上贴扁系一个，系上有凸纹五条，上下端各挖四条凹纹，寓意五指。除颈部刻划方格纹外，全器拍印粗绳纹，绳纹规整，做工精细。整体造型别致，把体态健硕的少女和少妇的乳房以夸张手法表现在同一器物上——青春少女双乳圆浑坚挺，产后少妇乳房丰盈肥满（袋足）——构思独特，创意非凡，显示了远古先民对"母体"和生殖的神秘崇拜。本品体形巨大，纹饰刻划细致，制作精美，很可能具祭祀用途，是陕西龙山文化稀有的艺术珍品。

人类最初追求的是生存，接着是繁衍后代，并由此形成了对母体神秘生殖力的崇拜。中国神话中造人的是女娲，而希腊神话中大地之母和众神之母是"嘉娅"（希腊文写作"aia"，英文写作"gaia"）。所以女性是人类的祖先，故称"大母神"。本品是远古先民祈求人口繁盛和母体崇拜的上好实物资料。

Sand-tempered gray pottery. The jar has a slightly constricted neck and a deep belly that branches out into three udder-shaped legs. Below the mouth rim on the back is a strap handle. The handle is decorated with four grooves on both ends and five vertical ribs running from top to bottom. The entire vessel is neatly and finely impressed with thick cord motif except for the neck that is decorated with check motif. This jar was probably used as ritual ware. It is a rarity among rarities.

Chinese legend has it that the first human was created by the goddess Nuwa. In Greek mythology, Gaia was the Mother of Earth and Mother of All Gods. Women are the mother of all living beings, and therefore also referred to as "The Great Mother".

12

灰陶三足大瓮

新石器时代

陕西龙山文化

约公元前 2500—前 2000 年

高：63 厘米

口径：27 厘米

Large gray pottery jar with three legs

Neolithic period

Longshan culture, Shaanxi

Circa 2500 – 2000 B.C.E.

Height: 63 cm

Mouth diameter: 27 cm

夹砂灰陶。大口，平缘，颈肩不分。深腹，最大径在下腹部。圆裆，下承三乳状足，足中空。器身满饰由上而下的绳纹。上腹部两侧置扁状实耳各一，耳横向，微下斜，便于拿举搬运。本品为大型炊具，大口易于注入和倾出，中空乳足增加了器物与火的接触面，令食物更快被煮熟，是黄河中游陕西龙山文化精品。

1983 年山西汾阳出土有相似器物，现藏山西省考古研究所。

Sand-tempered gray earthenware. The jar has a wide mouth with flat rim, hardly distinguishable neck and shoulders, a deep and bulbous belly and a rounded bottom supported by three hollow udder legs. The exterior surface is densely covered with vertical cord motif. The upper belly has a flattened and downward-sloping lug on both sides. This large pot was used as a cooking vessel.

A similar jar was unearthed in 1983 from Fenyang, Shanxi province. It is now in the collection of the Shanxi Provincial Institute of Archaeology.

13

鸟形埙

新石器时代

龙山文化

约公元前 2500—前 2000 年

高：8.5 厘米

长：11.8 厘米

Bird-shaped *xun* ocarina

Neolithic period

Longshan culture

Circa 2500 – 2000 B.C.E

Height: 8.5 cm

Length: 11.8 cm

灰陶。鸟双眼突出，头向前伸，背脊较平，腹体圆鼓肥硕，体内空，小平底。全器打磨细滑、光亮，器表面留刮削痕。鸟背中央有一较大圆形吹孔，孔径约 0.9 厘米。体左侧置较小圆形调音孔四个，较高两个孔径约 0.6 厘米，下面两个孔径约 0.45 厘米。此器物简洁传神，小鸟引颈向前探望，欲走又停，憨态可爱。埙为乐器，龙山文化陶埙较罕见。

Gray earthenware. This is an ancient Chinese musical instrument known as *xun*, a type of ocarina. It is shaped like a bird with bulging eyes, a craning neck, an almost leveled back and a hollow body on a small flat base. The entire instrument has been finely burnished to a smooth and lustrous surface. Scrape marks are visible in some areas. The relatively large opening (0.9 cm diameter) on the spine is the blowhole. Four finger holes appear on the left. The diameter of the upper two holes is approximately 0.6 cm and the two smaller holes approximately 0.45 cm. *Xun* is rather rare among Longshan pottery.

14

蛋壳黑陶杯

新石器时代

山东龙山文化

约公元前 2500—前 2000 年

高：17.6 厘米

底径：4.9 厘米

Black pottery goblet with eggshell-thin body

Neolithic period

Longshan culture, Shandong

Circa 2500 – 2000 B.C.E.

Height: 17.6 cm

Base diameter: 4.9 cm

泥质黑陶。口缘外侈。全器分为三部分，上为杯体，中为手柄，下为台形底座，由两段筒形管把三部分连接。三部分均内空，但并不相通。杯体下半部满饰凸弦纹，手柄满刻凹弦纹和交替镂竖直纹。竖直镂纹除了起装饰作用外，在烧制时可疏导热气。杯体上部与底座光素无纹，上下对称。器表经极精细打磨，漆黑发亮。胎骨细密、坚硬，薄如蛋壳，杯身最薄处不足 0.5 毫米，故称"蛋壳陶"。本品造型轻巧、秀丽，色泽素雅，为典型山东龙山文化器物。

Black earthenware. This vessel with a flared mouth is made up of three hollow and internally disconnected sections, namely the cup, the stem and the pedestal, joined by two narrow tubes. A thick rib encompasses the middle of the cup. The lower half of the cup and the entire stem are incised with closely spaced horizontal grooves. The stem is further pierced with short staggered vertical slits. These decorative openings are probably vents through which heat was allowed to escape during firing. The entire vessel has been meticulously burnished to a jet-black surface. The body is hard and refined and the wall of the cup is less than 0.5 mm at the thinnest. This piece is noted for its exquisite design, delicate workmanship and elegant color. This is a typical example of Longshan pottery from Shandong.

15

蛋壳黑陶杯

新石器时代

山东龙山文化

约公元前 2500—前 2000 年

高：15.2 厘米

底径：5 厘米

Black pottery goblet with eggshell-thin body

Neolithic period

Longshan culture, Shandong

Circa 2500 – 2000 B.C.E.

Height: 15.2 cm

Base diameter: 5 cm

本品与藏品 14 号无论胎泥、生产工艺、还是装饰都相似，只是器壁更薄一点。

薄胎黑陶是作祭祀或陪葬用的。

蛋壳陶的原料取自河流沉积土，经过多次精细淘洗，制成器坯，再经仔细修刮和打磨，以接近 1000℃ 的高温烧成。在窑中焙烧时，先用氧化焰使胎体硬结，快将结束时把火焰控制为还原焰，并用浓烟熏翳，经过相当时间的渗碳（浓烟内的碳微粒跑到胎体里去）即烧成黑陶。因为经过精细打磨，泥料中的云母、石英等反光物质由散乱排列变成有序、顺势排列，所以照射到器物表面的光线由漫反射变成平行反射，形成蛋壳黑陶熠熠发光的特点。

The paste, crafting technique and decorative motif of this vessel is similar to Cat. No. 14 except that the body is even thinner.

Black eggshell pottery was used as ritual and mortuary ware.

The clay for fabricating eggshell pottery was obtained from silt sediments deposited on riverbeds. The material had to be repeatedly levigated before shaping. After working out the desired shape, trimming and burnishing would take place to perfect its appearance. Then, the vessel is fired to almost 1000°C, beginning with an oxidized flame to harden the clay and finishing off with a reduction atmosphere with thick smoke and soot to obtain the characteristic black color. Fine burnishing helps to pack down the scattered mica quartz and other reflective materials in the clay which gives the vessel its luster.

16

蛋壳黑陶阔缘杯

新石器时代

山东龙山文化

约公元前 2500—前 2000 年

高：11.3 厘米

底径：5 厘米

Black pottery goblet with eggshell-thin body

Neolithic period

Longshan culture, Shandong

Circa 2500 – 2000 B.C.E.

Height: 11.3 cm

Base diameter: 5 cm

泥质黑陶。口缘宽广上翻，呈浅盘状。腹深，微敛，下腹速收接台形底足。器身呈筒状，中部刮凹环带一周，环带上下满饰纤细凹弦纹。腹下部镂刻菱形纹和小圆孔纹。在镂空部分上下各置一底，故镂孔除了装饰美化外，也是烧造时热气体排出之通道。器身打磨光滑，乌黑光亮。本品制作精巧、造型优美、体轻壁薄，最薄处仅约 0.5 毫米。

Black earthenware. The vessel has a broad everted rim in the shape of a dish, a cylindrical body with a small belly and a contracted foot on a pedestal. The belly is incised with closely spaced horizontal lines. The lower belly is pierced with lozenge shapes and circles. The pierced section forms an individual compartment cut off from the cavity of the cup and the pedestal by two horizontal partitions. The decorative openings are also vents through which heat was allowed to escape during firing. The entire vessel has been highly burnished to a lustrous jet-black surface. It is delicately potted, elegantly shaped and exquisitely crafted. The thinnest part is only about 0.5 mm thick.

17

黑陶单耳杯

新石器时代

龙山文化

约公元前 2500—前 2000 年

高：14.3 厘米

口径：7.8 厘米

Black pottery cup with handle

Neolithic period

Longshan culture

Circa: 2500 – 2000 B.C.E.

Height: 14.3 cm

Mouth diameter: 7.8 cm

泥质黑陶。口微外侈、阔长颈、腹急斜收到底、底平、微内凹。颈肩间起凸棱一周、肩腹置扁状圈耳一个、四周围以双凹竖纹带七组。胎细滑。器体外表经打磨、器内留有拉坯旋纹痕。本品线条高低错落有致、造型清爽可爱。

Black earthenware. The cup has a slightly flared mouth and a tall wide neck. A ridge encircles the bottom of the neck. The body has a strap handle and seven groups of vertical double grooves. The lower belly tapers sharply towards a flat base with a slightly recessed center. The paste is smooth and refined. The exterior surface of the vessel has been burnished. Wheel marks are visible on the interior surface.

18

黑陶三足鬲

新石器时代
龙山文化
约公元前 2500—前 2000 年
高：7.8 厘米
口径：12.8 厘米

Black pottery *li* tripod cauldron

Neolithic period
Longshan culture
Circa 2500 – 2000 B.C.E.
Height: 7.8 cm
Mouth diameter: 12.8 cm

泥质黑陶。敞口，体薄，颈腹近乎垂直，下置三袋形空心尖足。口缘与足中部置扁状拱形把手。口缘把手阴刻弦纹数条。全器打磨光亮，黝黑。本品造型夸张，极富艺术感，为龙山文化的杰作。

按地域区分，龙山文化可分为河南龙山文化、陕西龙山文化和山东龙山文化，本品当属山东龙山文化遗物。

Black earthenware. The vessel has a wide mouth, a straight neck and body supported by three hollow baggy legs with pointed ends. The body is thinly potted. A strap handle incised with grooves joins the mouth rim and the mid-section of each leg. The entire vessel has been burnished to a lustrous jet-black surface. The vessel is a masterpiece of Longshan culture pottery.

There are regional variants between the Longshan culture in Henan, Shaanxi and Shandong. The present tripod should be from Shandong.

19

黑陶环足盘

新石器时代

龙山文化

约公元前 2500—前 2000 年

高：10 厘米

口径：19 厘米

Black pottery basin with looped feet

Neolithic period

Longshan culture

Circa 2500 – 2000 B.C.E.

Height: 10 cm

Mouth diameter: 19 cm

泥质黑皮陶。侈口，器体由上向下微斜，起棱骨三道，下置三扁圆足。器身内、外壁打磨光滑，内、外底有明显轮旋痕。胎细滑，稍厚。此器纹饰简单，但外翻的口沿、凸起的棱骨、向内斜收的下沿配上环形的足，既豪放又优美。

器身下部和扁圆足呈浅灰色，系表面渗碳造成的黑色被泥土侵蚀褪色所致。

Earthenware with black slip coating. The basin is thickly potted from a smooth and refined paste. It has a wide mouth and a body that tapers towards a base supported by three looped feet with ovoid cross-sections. Three ribs encircle the exterior wall. Both the exterior and interior surfaces have been highly burnished to a smooth and lustrous finish. Wheel marks are clearly visible inside the basin and on the base.

Discolorations due to burial have turned the color of the legs and the lower body light gray.

20

黑陶背壶
新石器时代
龙山文化
约公元前 2500—前 2000 年
高：14.6 厘米
口径：7 厘米

Black pottery travelling flask
Neolithic period
Longshan culture
Circa 2500 – 2000 B.C.E.
Height: 14.6 cm
Mouth diameter: 7 cm

泥质黑陶。口微外侈，平直颈，平底。
器体一侧呈圆弧状，相对侧扁平。靠近
扁平侧左右方腹间置扁圆耳各一，圆弧
侧体中线近底处贴向下倾斜成 45 度角的
尖突一个。胎细滑。本品造型别致，双
耳和尖突用于系绳，可以把壶挂在腰间。

Black earthenware. The flask has a slightly
flared mouth, a straight neck and a flat
base. The paste is smooth and refined. The
shape of the vessel is unique. One side of
the flask is convex and the other flat. A pair
of tubular lugs flanks the belly. The convex
face is marked by a pointed protuberance
that pitches downward at a 45-degree
angle. The flask can be worn around the
waist (the flat side against the body) on a
cord that is attached to the loop lugs.

21

性器官纹黑陶甗

新石器时代
陕西龙山文化
约公元前 2500—前 2000 年
高：41 厘米

Black pottery *yan* tripod

Neolithic period
Longshan culture, Shaanxi
Circa 2500 – 2000 B.C.E.
Height: 41 cm

夹砂黑陶。甗由上部的甑和下部的鬲相接而成，甑和鬲之间由带孔洞的泥质薄层分隔。食物放在泥质薄层上，然后在三足下架柴生火，加热鬲下部，水沸腾产生蒸气将甑中的食物蒸熟，原理类似现代的隔水蒸锅。甗外壁拍印细绳纹、三足作乳房状，双足交接处各贴一横突，寓意女性阴户。

那时尚未出现抹草泥的加工地面，器物最稳固的支撑方式就是三足和圜底，这也与现代物理学理论一致，可窥见远古先民的聪明才智和无限创意。

Sand-tempered black earthenware. The shape of the *yan* vessel is a hybrid of a *zeng* cauldron and a *li* tripod, partitioned by a perforated grate made of clay. First, firewood is placed between the tripod legs to light a fire after water is poured in. Then, the food is placed on the grate at the bottom of the *zeng* cauldron and cooked by steaming. The principle is very similar to that of the modern steamer. The exterior of the vessel is impressed with fine cord motif. Between each pair of legs is a horizontal appliqué protuberance denoting the female genitalia.

Since the method of plastering the ground surface with grass-tempered mud has yet to appear during the Neolithic Age, a rounded base or three-leg construction are the best designs for a vessel to sit or stand stably on a rugged ground. The design tallies with the theory of modern physics, demonstrating the ingenuity and infinite creativity of our remote ancestors.

22

浅红陶三耳罐

新石器时代晚期

齐家文化

约公元前 2200—前 1600 年

高：10.8 厘米

底径：7.8 厘米

Reddish pottery beaker with three handles

Late Neolithic period

Qijia culture

Circa 2200 – 1600 B.C.E.

Height: 10.8 cm

Base diameter: 7.8 cm

泥质浅红陶。口大外侈，颈腹分界明显，下腹阔大，底平。口缘与下腹部置环状扁平大耳三个，口缘和底部可见粘贴痕迹。肥大的下腹部和夸张的大耳令器物呈现稳重和豪放的气势。

Reddish earthenware. The cup has a flared wide mouth, a bulbous belly and a flat base. The junction between the neck and the belly is clearly defined. Three large strap handles arch from the mouth rim to the lower belly. Luting marks are visible at the top and bottom of the handles.

浅红陶三耳罐

23

双耳摇铃杯

新石器时代晚期
齐家文化
约公元前 2200—前 1600 年
高：13.2 厘米
底径：4.6 厘米

Red pottery rattle cup with double handles

Late Neolithic period
Qijia culture
Circa 2200 – 1600 B.C.E.
Height: 13.2 cm
Base diameter: 4.6 cm

夹砂红陶。侈口，高颈，颈、腰皆折，平底。口与腹间贴弧形长耳。下腹近底部四侧镂雕三角形孔各两个。杯内镂孔上方另贴一平底，上、下两底间置陶珠数粒，摇动时发出响声。外底中央有孔一个。此杯造型别致，线条玲珑，外形优美。

齐家文化因首先发现于甘肃省广河县齐家坪而得名，主要由马家窑文化、常山下层文化发展而来，为河西走廊新石器时代晚期文化，已开始使用铜器，它预示着青铜时代即将到来。

Sand-tempered red earthenware. The cup has a flared mouth, a tall neck that joins the body at an angle, a sharp turn between the belly and the foot and a flat base. The lower body is pierced with four pairs of triangular openings. The cavity of the cup terminates at the flat partition just above the pierced section. Inside the pierced section are several pottery beads, which produce a rattling sound when the cup is shaken. This cup was probably used for serving wine during rituals or festivities.

The Qijia culture was first discovered at the Qijiaping site in Guanghe, Gansu province. The Qijia culture was a late Neolithic and early Bronze Age culture that developed around the Ordos and the upper Yellow River basin.

24

红陶人首纽盖罐

新石器时代晚期

齐家文化

约公元前 2200—前 1600 年

高：17.2 厘米

Red pottery lidded jar with human-head knob

Late Neolithic period

Qijia culture

Circa 2200 – 1600 B.C.E.

Height: 17.2 cm

泥质红陶。口平，鼓腹，腹中部两侧贴钩状乳突各一个，底平。上置人首形纽盖，人首面部清晰端正，相貌威严，是从盖内把胎泥拉出捏成，再用工具加工刻划五官。胎细腻，颇坚硬，烧成温度较高。全器经仔细打磨光滑。盖边缘和罐口部各有一竖直划线，以确定盖与罐身的相对位置，这是因为盖是从近椭圆形球体切割出来的，与罐身并非分开制造。

从造型和生产工艺观察，本品大气端庄，线条简练，含蓄高雅，是不可多得的齐家文化艺术珍品。

Red earthenware. The jar has a flat mouth, a bulbous belly and a flat base. An udder-like lug is attached to each side of the body. The lid is surmounted by a knob in the shape of a human head with a solemn expression. The human head is formed by poking and pulling the clay up from the underside of the lid. The facial features were sculpted with tools. The fine-grained paste of considerable hardness was fired to a rather high temperature. The entire vessel has been highly burnished to a smooth and lustrous finish. The lid was not made separately but simply cut away from the ovoid body. A vertical match line at the joint indicates the exact location of where the lid should fit on the jar.

Judging from the shape and craftsmanship, this vessel probably belonged to a chieftain or shaman. It is a rarity among Qijia culture pottery.

25

红陶性爱双体罐

新石器时代晚期

齐家文化

约公元前 2200—前 1600 年

高：14.2 厘米

总阔（口部）：20.7 厘米

Red pottery conjoined jar

Late Neolithic period

Qijia culture

Circa 2200 – 1600 B.C.E.

Height: 14.2 cm

Overall width (mouth): 20.7 cm

夹砂红陶。罐体相连，口缘外翻，圆鼓腹。顶部相连处有一缺口，有如口对口。罐身左右两侧各有一条状泥条相接，有如两臂相拥。罐底部有扁圆锥状泥把两罐底部连接。扁圆锥状泥块寓意男性阴囊，前端长条状泥条示意男性性器官。罐身和底部扁圆锥状泥条四周刻直线纹和斜线纹，寓意体毛。罐下各有锥形实足两只。

Sand-tempered red pottery. Each of the conjoined jars has an everted mouth and a bulbous belly. There is a gap at the point where the two mouths meet. A clay strip connects the bellies on each side like embracing arms. Conical clay strips representing the male genitalia connect the jars at the bottom. Each jar is supported by two solid conical legs. Vertical and oblique striations are visible on the lower half of the vessel.

26

红陶鸮首罐

新石器时代晚期
齐家文化
约公元前 2200—前 1600 年
高：19.7 厘米

Red pottery jar with owl head design

Late Neolithic period
Qijia culture
Circa 2200 – 1600 B.C.E.
Height: 19.7 cm

夹砂红陶，较粗糙。罐上部塑成鸮首状，束颈，鼓腹渐收到底，底平。额上和下颚各贴一周窝状附加堆纹作羽毛，中间有竖直堆纹作喙，喙两侧各穿一孔为眼，刻画出一只昼伏夜出、凶恶威猛的鸮鸟形象。虽经清洗，本品底部仍有火炙后的炭烟残留物，说明是用于煮食的炊具。新石器时代的陶工多以大自然景象、所见所闻的事物作为创作来源，由此可以想见当时鸮的形象。

Sand-tempered red earthenware. The paste is rather coarse. The jar has an upper section in the shape of an owl's head, a constricted neck and a swelling belly that tapers towards a flat base. The toothed appliqué molding on the forehead and the chin represent the owl's feathers and the vertical one its beak. The hole on each side of the beak represents the eyes. The vessel has been cleaned but soot residues are still visible on the base, indicating that it was probably used as a cooking utensil. This jar gives us a glimpse of what owls might looked like at that time.

橙黄陶水纹大罐

新石器时代晚期
齐家文化
约公元前 2200—前 1600 年
高：40.4 厘米

Large buff pottery jar with wave motif

Late Neolithic period
Qijia culture
Circa 2200 – 1600 B.C.E.
Height: 40.4 cm

泥质橙黄陶。口缘外翻，圆唇，束颈，宽肩，肩腹分界明显，向下斜收，平底。质细腻，坚致，胎体颇薄。全器打磨光滑，颈部光素，留有用骨或竹磨划的打磨痕。腹部拍印斜向水波纹饰到腹底部，水波纹生动形象，如在微风吹拂下荡漾，也说明此罐可能是用于储水。本品造型圆浑硕大，线条简洁优美，是美学的典范。齐家文化遗留不少这类素陶罐，大小不一，但造型和制作如此精美者极罕有，是十分珍贵的史前艺术品。

Buff earthenware with a dense fine paste and a rather thin body. The jar has an everted mouth with rounded lip, a constricted neck, broad shoulders that join the belly at a distinct turn and a belly that tapers towards a flat base. The entire vessel has been highly burnished to a smooth and lustrous finish. The neck is devoid of decorative motif but bears scraping marks left by bone or bamboo tools. The entire belly up to the edge of the foot is impressed with oblique lines reminiscent of waves, suggesting that the vessel was used for storing water. The sites of Qijia culture have yielded a considerable amount of this type of undecorated pottery jars but examples with such refined shape and craftsmanship are few and far between. This jar is an exceedingly rare piece of prehistoric art.

28

橙红陶船形扁壶

新石器时代晚期
齐家文化
约公元前 2200—前 1600 年
高：45 厘米
口径：9.3 厘米

Boat-shaped orange-red pottery jar

Late Neolithic period
Qijia culture
Circa 2200 – 1600 B.C.E.
Height: 45 cm
Mouth diameter: 9.3 cm

泥质橙红陶。喇叭形口，折颈，小平底。器身中央起弓形脊棱到底，左右两端呈流线型。肩腹呈扁圆状，交接处贴附加堆纹一周，肩部光素无纹，腹部满饰斜向绳纹。器身横切面和底部形状呈菱形。从侧面看像一艘在水中航行的船，而腹部斜向的绳纹则像被船的龙骨分割后向两侧后方翻滚而去的水流。

本品造型极具创意，流线型的船身，凸出的龙骨，吃水线的设置（肩腹间的一周堆纹），均与现代船只结构相似。本品可能是模仿当时船只的外形，对此值得进一步研究探讨。

Orange-red earthenware. The jar has a trumpet mouth, a notched neck and a small flat base. The base and the cross-section of the vessel are diamond-shaped. A bow-shaped ridge runs from the shoulder down to the base on both sides. A round of appliqué clay strip reinforces the intersection between the shoulder and belly. The shoulder is undecorated while the belly is covered with oblique cord motif. Seen from the sides, the vessel resembles a boat. The oblique cord motif on the belly represents the waves.

The shape of the jar is unique. The streamlined "hull", the protruding "keel" and the "waterline" (the appliqué clay strip) are similar to the features of modern boats. It remains to be studied whether or not the form was modeled after Neolithic boats.

29

橙黄陶贴人形纹罐

新石器时代晚期
齐家文化
约公元前 2200—前 1600 年
高：17.4 厘米

Buff pottery jar with humanoid figures

Late Neolithic period
Qijia culture
Circa 2200 – 1600 B.C.E.
Height: 17.4 cm

泥质橙黄陶。口平外侈，短束颈，罐呈长圆锥形，小圜底。颈周有三条泥条线，罐体满饰竖直纹。颈腹对称贴四个以泥条塑造的人形图案，有笔直的身体、弯弯的双手和双足，在罐颈间贴双眼，眼球圆、大而凸出，眼下方刻印一周倒置三角形。胎泥为橙黄色，外表经浓烟熏翳处理后呈灰黑色，底部未经烟翳处露橙黄色胎。

四个人形图案贴在一个圆锥体上，令人遐想这个圆锥形物体象征母体的腹部，寓意胎儿在母体内成长，是生育崇拜和母体崇拜的体现。

Buff earthenware. The jar has a slightly flared mouth with flat rim, a short constricted neck, an elongated ovoid body and a small rounded base. Three clay strips encircle the neck. The body is densely covered with vertical striations. Four humanoid figures made with clay strips adorn the neck and the belly. Their bulging eyes are represented by clay appliqués. An inverted triangle is carved below each pair of eyes. The color of the buff paste except for the base has turned grayish black due to the exposure to thick smoke and soot.

The humanoid figures can be interpreted as fetuses growing inside the womb of the vessel.

30

橙黄陶双耳连体杯

新石器时代晚期

齐家文化

约公元前 2200—前 1600 年

高：11 厘米

总阔（连耳）：15.7 厘米

Buff pottery conjoined jar with double handles

Late Neolithic period

Qijia culture

Circa 2200 – 1600 B.C.E.

Height: 11 cm

Overall width (with handles): 15.7 cm

泥质橙黄陶。侈口，斜直颈，球形腹，平底。器呈两杯并列状，颈腹分界明显。口缘以扁平泥板相接，腹部相连但不相通。口缘与上腹部间置扁平弧形双耳。器表打磨光滑，但仍可见修削痕迹。

Buff earthenware. Each jar has a flared mouth, a straight tapering neck, a bulbous belly and a flat base. The junction between the neck and body is clearly defined. The two jars are joined by a tubular piece of clay at the belly. The two cavities are not actually connected. A pair of strap handles arches from the mouth rim to the upper belly. The vessel has been burnished to a smooth and lustrous surface but trimming marks are still visible.

31

黄陶锥刺纹单耳杯

新石器时代晚期

齐家文化

约公元前 2200—前 1600 年

高：14 厘米

底径：7.8 厘米

Buff pottery cup with strap handle and pecked motif

Late Neolithic period

Qijia culture

Circa 2200 – 1600 B.C.E.

Height: 14 cm

Base diameter: 7.8 cm

泥质橙黄陶。口椭圆而外侈，有短槽形流，深腹微鼓，平底外撇。宽柄到底，两侧起脊，脊上满刻锯齿纹，柄身刻划交叉纹线。颈腹间和近底缘处各阴刻弦线一圈，底弦线上下方分别饰锥刺纹两周和一周。

Buff earthenware. The cup has an ovoid mouth that is shaped into a spout to one side, a belly with slightly bulging sides and a flared flat base. A wide strap handle extends from below the rim to the base. Serrate edges and feather-like oblique incisions are visible down the center of the handle. An incised line runs around the intersection of the neck and the belly and another near the base. Three rows of pecked motif encompass the base, two of which above the incised line and one below it.

32

黄陶盉

新石器时代晚期

齐家文化

约公元前 2200—前 1600 年

高：19 厘米

底径：5 厘米

Buff pottery *he* jug

Late Neolithic period

Qijia culture

Circa 2200 – 1600 B.C.E.

Height: 19 cm

Base diameter: 5 cm

泥质橙黄陶。口颈高，微束，折颈，圆形腹，腹下渐收，平底。器身作壶形，前半部置微隆挡水板，上接朝天管状流，后半部为心形开口。口缘内侧前半部刻竖纹带，近流端加贴泥条一周，把流端加固。颈、腹间安带状把手。器壁较薄，全器打磨光滑、造型新颖有趣。

Buff earthenware. The jug is quite thinly potted. The front part of its mouth is covered by a water shield that links to an upright tubular spout. The back of the water shield forms a heart-shaped opening. Vertical striations are visible around the inner rim of the mouth. The outer rim of the spout is reinforced by a strip of clay. The trumpet-shaped neck joins the shoulders at an angle. The rounded belly tapers smoothly towards a flat base. A strap handle arches from the mouth rim to the belly. The entire vessel has been burnished to a smooth and lustrous surface. The design is unique and interesting.

33

灰陶双耳罐

新石器时代晚期
齐家文化
约公元前 2200—前 1600 年
高：8.2 厘米

Gray pottery jar with double handles

Late Neolithic period
Qijia culture
Circa 2200 – 1600 B.C.E.
Height: 8.2 cm

泥质灰陶。高颈扁腹，平底。口缘和腹间有大弧度曲耳一对，耳上部儿与口缘平行。胎泥细滑，器壁薄而坚硬。器由颈和腹两部接合而成，可见接合痕迹。器表打磨光滑，制作精细。本品造型素朴简约，比例和谐。齐家文化遗存大量双耳罐，但如本品般秀美的不多。

双耳配置方式与图录 34 号相近。

Gray earthenware. The jar has a tall neck, a compressed belly and a flat base. A pair of large handles arches from the mouth rim to the belly. The top of the handles is almost leveled with the mouth rim. The paste is smooth and refined and the body thin and hard. The neck and the belly were separately made and then joined together. Luting marks are visible along the junction. The surface of the vessel has been burnished to a smooth and lustrous finish. A large number of jars with double handles have been excavated from Qijia culture sites but very few are as elegant as the present piece.

The position of the double handles on this vessel is similar to that of Cat. No. 34.

34

灰陶束颈双耳罐

新石器时代晚期

齐家文化

约公元前 2200—前 1600 年

高：7.8 厘米

Gray pottery jar with double handles

Late Neolithic period

Qijia culture

Circa 2200 – 1600 B.C.E.

Height: 7.8 cm

与藏品 33 号的外形及制作方法相同，只是双耳位置在口缘下方，腹部较扁圆、同样表现出简约的美感。与图录 33 号和 36 号似是在同一时间、同一地点烧制。

This pot is similar to Cat. No. 33 in shape and production method except that the top ends of the handles are set below the mouth rim and the belly is more compressed. This jar is likely produced at the same kiln during the same peried alongside Cat. Nos. 33, 36.

35

灰陶双耳弦纹高足杯

新石器时代晚期
齐家文化
约公元前 2200—前 1600 年
高：19.8 厘米

**Gray pottery goblet with
double handles**

Late Neolithic period
Qijia culture
Circa 2200 – 1600 B.C.E.
Height: 19.8 cm

泥质灰陶。口平，唇外翻。由两个正、反漏斗形的杯状体连接组成。全器满饰平行弦纹线，口端有阶梯状扁平双耳与腹中部相接，耳表面刻竖纹。口缘内和双耳残留有朱砂红色。胎细滑，坚致。器物造型新颖漂亮，应为酒具。

本品经热释光测定最后烧制年代距今 4000—3000 年。

Gray earthenware. The vessel has a mouth with a leveled and out-rolling rim. The paste is smooth and refined. The goblet is made up of a funnel-shaped body on top of an inverted funnel-shaped stand. The entire exterior surface is decorated with parallel horizontal grooves. A pair of strap handles with a stepped detail at the top arches from the mouth rim to the mid-section of the body. The surface of the handles is marked with vertical striations. Traces of cinnabar pigment are found inside the mouth and on the handles. This cup was probably used as a wine vessel.

Thermoluminescence test shows that the last firing date of this piece was 4000 to 3000 years before present.

36

灰陶双耳带流壶

新石器时代晚期

齐家文化

约公元前 2200—前 1600 年

高：7.8 厘米

**Gray pottery jug with
double handles**

Late Neolithic period

Qijia culture

Circa 2200 – 1600 B.C.E.

Height: 7.8 cm

泥质灰陶。口大微侈、颈粗微束、肩阔广、折腹、平底。肩装上翘漏斗形管状流、流两侧置扁环状耳、其中一耳已无、有一种残缺美。胎泥细腻纯净、器壁薄而坚硬、全器打磨光滑。用作酒具或用于盛水。本品制作精细、线条利落、是一件珍贵的史前艺术品。

Gray earthenware. The jug has a mildly flared wide mouth, a slightly constricted thick neck, smooth broad shoulders joining the belly at an angle, and a flat base. A funnel-shaped spout rises high between the loop handles with ovoid cross-sections. One handle is missing but there is a sense of beauty in the asymmetry. The paste is pure and refined and the body thin and hard. The entire vessel has been highly burnished to a smooth and lustrous finish. This jug was used as a wine or water container. This jug is a rare piece of prehistoric art.

37

灰陶人形纹罐

新石器时代晚期

齐家文化

约公元前 2200—前 1600 年

高：21.3 厘米

底径：6.6 厘米

Gray pottery jar in humanoid form

Late Neolithic period

Qijia culture

Circa 2200 – 1600 B.C.E.

Height: 21.3 cm

Base diameter: 6.6 cm

夹砂灰陶，质较疏松。束颈，颈弯曲，昂肩，平底。肩腹部满饰绳纹，罐口内侧可见轮旋痕。颈肩部有椭圆形孔三个，作双眼和口；腹下部有一圆孔，作肚脐。本品虽然造型简单，却表现出一位昂首而立、仰望苍穹的先人形象，极具神韵和美感。

Sand-tempered gray pottery. The paste is rather porous. The jar has a constricted and craned neck, steep shoulders and a flat base. The neck and shoulder are pierced with three holes to represent the eyes and the mouth. Another hole on the lower belly denotes the navel. The neck and shoulders are densely covered with cord motif. Wheel marks are visible around the interior of the mouth. The image of a prehistoric man gazing at the skies is vividly portrayed.

38

灰陶绳纹双耳罐

新石器时代晚期

齐家文化

约公元前 2200—前 1600 年

高：33.7 厘米

底径：10.3 厘米

Gray pottery jar with cord motif

Late Neolithic period

Qijia culture

Circa 2200 – 1600 B.C.E.

Height: 33.7 cm

Base diameter: 10.3 cm

泥质灰陶。侈口、卷缘、直颈、斜肩、折腹、平底。侈口外缘贴泥条一周，用以加固口缘之强度。上腹左右置环系各一。颈肩部打磨光滑，腹部饰绳纹到底。

齐家文化器物以泥质红陶和夹砂红陶为主，灰陶较少，本品为齐家文化的典型器物。

Gray earthenware. The jar has a flared mouth with rolling lip, a straight neck, steep shoulders that meet the belly at an angle and a flat base. The outer rim of the mouth is reinforced with a round of appliqué clay strip. A pair of loop handles is set just below the shoulders. The neck and shoulders have been highly burnished to a smooth and lustrous surface. The belly is covered with cord motif down to the edge of the foot.

Red and buff earthenware make up the majority of Qijia culture pottery. Gray earthenware is relatively scarce.

39

白衣彩陶罐

新石器时代

仰韶文化大河村类型

约公元前 4500—前 3000 年

高：22.6 厘米

Painted pottery jar with white slip

Neolithic period

Dahecun type, Yangshao culture

Circa 4500 – 3000 B.C.E.

Height: 22.6 cm

泥质红陶。平口，直短颈，斜肩，鼓腹急收，小平底。器身施白化妆土作地。肩部以红、黑彩绘六组变体鸟纹和太阳纹，组间以网纹相隔。腹部画八组变体鱼纹，组间以竖条纹带分隔。肩、腹部纹饰之间有一道白化妆土纹带分隔，纹间等距饰四个黑彩长方块。本品线条柔和，构图精美，色彩艳丽，富有时代特色，是大河村类型典型器物。

Red earthenware. The jar has a flat mouth, a short constricted neck, sloping shoulders and a drum belly that tapers rapidly to a small flat base. The upper section of the body is coated with a layer of white slip. The shoulders are painted with six groups of bird and sun motif separated by mesh design. The belly is painted with eight groups of stylized fish motif separated by vertical stripes. A round of white slip decorated with four black rectangles at equal intervals runs between these two decorative zones. This jar is a typical example of Dahecun type pottery.

40

白彩鱼纹彩陶罐

新石器时代

大汶口文化

约公元前 4300—前 2500 年

高：18.3 厘米

Painted pottery jar with fish motif

Neolithic period

Dawenkou culture

Circa 4300 – 2500 B.C.E.

Height: 18.3 cm

泥质红陶。广口、微外侈、束颈、短肩。颈肩两侧置耳突各一。腹上、中部施黑彩，在黑彩上再以白彩描画五尾互相追逐的大鱼，圆点作鱼眼和头部，鱼身搅起波涛汹涌的连续旋纹。下腹近底处有一周黑彩纹带，带上饰连续的白圆点。旋纹为本品主题纹饰，图案生动流畅，像转动着的轮辐，表现出运动和力量的美。

Red earthenware. The jar has a wide mouth, a constricted neck and short shoulders. A pair of lugs is attached to the shoulders. The upper and middle sections of the belly are painted in white against a black ground with five spirals, each representing the eye and the head of a fish. The bodies of the fish interlock to form a series of continuous spiral. They resemble rotating spokes, suggesting beautiful movement and dynamism.The lower belly features a band of white circular motif against a black ground.

舞蹈纹彩陶罐

新石器时代

仰韶文化庙底沟类型

约公元前 4000—前 3500 年

高：24.6 厘米

底径：9.6 厘米

Painted pottery jar with winged-dancer motif

Neolithic period

Miaodigou type, Yangshao culture

Circa 4000 – 3500 B.C.E.

Height: 24.6 cm

Base diameter: 9.6 cm

泥质橙红陶。口缘外侈，束颈，扁圆腹，平底。颈部有刮削痕，器身上部和口内侧经磨光处理。内口缘有黑彩带纹一周。外壁以黑彩绘画鸟纹舞人三圈，每圈有手拉手立于弧线上翩翩起舞的舞人十个，像在进行巫术礼仪。本品是庙底沟类型彩陶中罕见的精美艺术品。

原始舞蹈往往是先民祭祀的组成部分。舞人的底部画有三至五条短竖线示意鸟足，有别于双足的鸟。将鸟的双足变为多足，在人形纹的关节处添加肢节等，是表明这些动物或人形是非凡的，具有神化的力量，是人与神灵沟通、互动的媒介。本品纹饰将鸟人格化，"寓人于鸟"，具有祖先崇拜之含义。

庙底沟类型彩陶以鸟纹为主要花纹之一。本品应是早期作品，中期鸟纹仅以圆点和弧形三角纹来表示，晚期则完全演变为几何形花纹。所以这一地区仰韶文化彩陶上的大量鸟纹可能具有图腾性质。

1973 年在青海大通县上孙家寨新石器时代遗址墓葬中出土的"舞蹈纹彩陶盆"与本品有异曲同工之处。

Orange-red earthenware. The jar has a flared mouth, a constricted neck, a compressed belly and a flat bottom. Trimming and scraping marks are visible around the neck. The upper section of the body and the interior of the mouth have been burnished. A black stripe runs around the interior mouth rim. The shoulders and upper belly are decorated with three rows of bird-shaped humanoid figures, ten figures to a row, connected at the hands. They seemed to in the middle of a shamanic dance or ritual. This jar is a rarity among rarities.

Dancing was often part of the religious and sacrificial rituals in primitive societies. There are three to five short squiggly vertical lines right under each figure representing the tails and/or legs. The human-like birds or the bird-like humans are idols of worship and believed to have divine power to communicate with Heaven. The personification of the birds is also a form of ancestor worship as the human image reminds the people of their ancestors.

Birds are one of the main decorative motifs. The present jar should be from the early stage of Miaodigou type culture. Bird motifs from the middle stage are typically represented by dots and triangles with arched sides. Those from the late stage are strictly geometric. It is possible that the bird motifs on Yangshao painted pottery were related to totem worship.

This jar is similar to a painted pottery basin unearthed in 1973 from a Neolithic tomb at Sunjiazhai in Datong, Qinghai province.

42

红陶鸟纹彩陶罐

新石器时代
马家窑文化石岭下类型
约公元前 3800—前 3000 年
高：16.6 厘米
口径：11.4 厘米

Painted red pottery jar with bird motif

Neolithic period
Shilingxia type, Majiayao culture
Circa 3800 – 3000 B.C.E.
Height: 16.6 cm
Mouth diameter: 11.4 cm

泥质橙红陶。侈口，口缘外卷，短颈，广肩、圆扁腹，腹下内收，小平底。腹两侧附小耳突。在褐红色胎上施黑彩。口缘和颈部绘宽带纹，腹上部前后两侧绘展翅鸟纹各一组，每组三鸟，以圆形花纹表示头部、黑点作眼，头部后方的波浪纹线代表翅膀。左右两鸟体形较大，有大而长的喙，两喙相接，中间的鸟较细小，小鸟的喙与大鸟的喙相接，看似大鸟给小鸟喂食，温馨无比。两组鸟纹间隙填以斜网纹。

石岭下遗址因在甘肃武山石岭下发现而得名。石岭下类型是从仰韶文化晚期分离出来发展为马家窑文化的初期阶段，主要分布在甘肃东部、中部和青海东北部。

1956 年甘肃天水出土有相同器物，现藏甘肃省博物馆。

Orange-red earthenware. The jar has a flared mouth with rolling lip, a short neck, broad shoulders and a compressed bulbous belly that tapers rapidly to a small flat base. A tiny stud is affixed to both sides of the belly. Motifs are painted in black on a brownish-red body. Thick black stripes encircle the exterior mouth rim and the neck. The front and the back of the vessel are decorated with a group of birds with outspread wings. Each group consists of three birds. The birds on the left and right are larger in size compared to the bird in the middle. The position of the bills suggests that a baby bird is being fed by its parents. The space between the two groups of bird motif is filled with a lozenge-shaped mesh.

Shilingxia type culture was first discovered at Shilingxia in Wushan, Tianshui prefecture. The Shilingxia type was a branch of the late Yangshao culture. It mainly developed in Tianshui in southeast Gansu, central Gansu and northeast Qinghai.

A similar vessel was unearthed in 1956 from Tianshui, Gansu province. It is now in the collection of the Gansu Provincial Museum.

43

白彩尖底瓶

新石器时代
仰韶文化西王村类型
约公元前3500—前2900年
高：38.8 厘米
口径：6.9 厘米

Painted pottery bottle with white decoration

Neolithic period
Xiwangcun type, Yangshao culture
Circa 3500 – 2900 B.C.E.
Height: 38.8 cm
Mouth diameter: 6.9 cm

橙黄陶。喇叭形口、细长颈、尖底。腹两侧置扁平环系各一。颈、肩和下腹部分别画白彩弦纹三组。肩部以白彩画"×"形旋纹三个，再在旋纹组成的区域内分别饰以单、双圆圈纹。肩和上腹部有细斜纹，中、下腹部和系有细竖纹。尖底部分打磨光滑。本品纹饰素雅，造型清秀，为西王村类型典型器物。此件器物加彩，有可能作为祭器使用。

仰韶文化分布地域很广，时间跨度很长，大致分为早中晚三期，第一期以半坡类型为代表，第二期以庙底沟类型为代表，第三期以西王村类型（或半坡晚期类型）为代表。各期各个类型的陶器都别具特色。

Buff earthenware. The bottle has a trumpet mouth, long neck and a pointed base. A pair of strap handles flanks the sides of the belly. The neck, the shoulders and the lower belly are respectively painted in white with cord motif. The shoulders are decorated in white with single and double circles separated by X-shaped marks. The shoulders and upper belly are covered with fine oblique striations, while the middle and lower belly and the handles bear fine vertical striations. The pointed bottom has been burnished. This vessel is a representative example of Xiwangcun type pottery. This bottle was probably used as ritual ware.

The Yangshao culture existed across an extensive region and for a long period of time. It can be roughly divided into three phases, namely Banpo type (Phase one), Miaodigou type (Phase two) and Xiwangcun type (Phase three), each with its own characteristics.

44

水波纹彩陶大罐

新石器时代
马家窑文化马家窑类型
约公元前 3100—前 2700 年
高：41.1 厘米
底径：14.8 厘米

Painted pottery jar with wave motif

Neolithic period
Majiayao type, Majiayao culture
Circa 3100 – 2700 B.C.E.
Height: 41.1 cm
Base diameter: 14.8 cm

橙黄色泥质陶。平底。肩下两侧置环形耳各一，耳脊饰堆纹。颈肩和腹部上下各有黑彩弦纹数道。下肩部绘三个以水波纹、弧线三角纹、十字纹组成的图案，有可能是变体鸟纹。器体硕大、全身打磨亮滑，为马家窑类型彩陶的典型器物。

马家窑文化因最先发现于甘肃临洮马家窑而得名。马家窑文化彩陶的水波纹色彩单纯明快，线条优美流畅，构图变化丰富，具有强烈的动感，极富艺术感染力。

Buff earthenware. The jar has a flat base and a pair of loop lugs with serrate ridges. The neck, shoulders and belly are painted with rounds of cord and wave motifs, curvilinear lines and triangles with rounded bottoms. The design could be a stylized bird motif. The entire surface has been burnished. It jar is a representative example of Majiayao painted pottery.

The Majiayao culture was first discovered in Majiayao, Lintao, Gansu province. The wave motif on the painted pottery of the Majiayao culture is considered the most distinctive motif of the prehistoric period. The motifs are noted for their simple and

elegant geometry and spontaneous and diverse patterns. The design has a strong artistic appeal and suggests a vivid sense of movement.

45

齿纹彩陶壶

新石器时代

马家窑文化半山类型

约公元前 2600—前 2300 年

高：41.3 厘米

底径：11.9 厘米

Painted pottery jar with sawtooth motif

Neolithic period

Banshan type, Majiayao culture

Circa 2600 – 2300 B.C.E.

Height: 41.3 cm

Base diameter: 11.9 cm

泥质橙黄陶。平底。口缘外两侧贴附加堆纹各一，腹置双环耳。胎薄、施黑红复彩。口缘内侧饰水波纹一周，颈绘倒置齿纹二周。器体上部绘齿纹三组，分别以弦纹带和细齿纹分间。纹饰底部挂垂弧纹一周。

在中国境内史前时期考古学文化中，半山类型陶器中彩陶所占比例最高，而黑红彩加锯齿形的图案可说是半山时期彩陶最鲜明、最独特的标志。彩陶齿形纹饰可能是对猛兽强而有力、锋利无比的牙齿崇拜的体现，也可能有辟邪以求吉祥的含义。

Buff earthenware with a thin paste. A pair of loop lugs is attached to the belly. The base is flat. The exterior mouth rim is decorated on each side with an appliqué motif. The painted decorations are executed in contrasting red and black pigments. The inner mouth rim is adorned with a round of wave motif. Two rows of upward-pointing sawtooth motif encircle the neck. The upper half of the body is painted with three groups of sawtooth motif separated by black stripes and serrate motif and bounded by a scallop

edge at the bottom.

Banshan type painted pottery constitutes the largest share of prehistoric archeological finds in China. Red and black painted pottery with sawtooth motif is one of the most representative examples of Banshan type painted pottery.

46

旋涡纹彩陶大罐

新石器时代

马家窑文化马家窑类型

约公元前 3100—前 2700 年

高：43 厘米

Painted pottery jar with spiral motif

Neolithic period

Majiayao type, Majiayao culture

Circa 3100 – 2700 B.C.E.

Height: 43 cm

橙黄色泥质陶。口平，缘外侈，微束颈，宽肩，肩腹分界明显，平底。肩两侧装环状耳各一，耳上贴附加堆纹。器身有彩部分经打磨光滑。颈有黑彩弦纹五道，肩腹画旋涡状水波纹和十字纹，纹饰底部有弦纹三周。上下弦纹相呼应，水波纹流畅，极具动感。

本品经热释光测定最后烧制年代距今 5500—4000 年。

Buff earthenware. The jar has a flared mouth with a leveled rim, a slightly constricted neck, broad shoulders that meet the belly at a distinct angle and a flat base. A loop lug is affixed to both sides of the belly. The painted parts of the body had been burnished to a smooth and lustrous finish. The neck and lower belly are painted with rounds of black stripes while the shoulders and belly are decorated with wave spirals and crosses.

Thermoluminescence test shows that the last firing date of this piece was 5500 to 4000 years before present.

旋涡纹带盖彩陶罐

新石器时代

马家窑文化马家窑类型

约公元前 3100—前 2700 年

高：30 厘米

底径：11.7 厘米

Painted pottery lidded jar with spiral motif

Neolithic period

Majiayao type, Majiayao culture

Circa 3100 – 2700 B.C.E.

Height: 30 cm

Base diameter: 11.7 cm

泥质橙色陶，质地细密。平口，平底。蒂状纽盖，饰水纹。颈部有四个对称鼻形纽，腹部两侧置环形耳。施赭黑色彩。纹饰分三层，颈肩部位饰锯齿纹两周，腹中部绘旋涡纹，腹下部绘变体鸟纹。此器造型优美，花纹变化多姿，全器满施彩，在新石器时代器物中颇稀少，而带盖者则更罕见。

Orange earthenware with a fine paste. The jar has a flat mouth and base. A lid with a stem-knob is painted with spirals radiating from the center. Four nose-shaped protuberances are evenly distributed around the neck. A pair of loop lugs is affixed on the belly. The body is decorated with three bands of painted motifs. Between the double rows of sawtooth pattern around the shoulders and the band of feather motif near the foot is a broad band of spirals. This vessel is noted for its beautiful shape and rich motifs. The entire surface of the vessel is adorned with painted motifs, which is quite rare among Neolithic wares. Ones with a matching lid are even more rare.

48

网纹单耳彩陶罐

新石器时代

马家窑文化马家窑类型

约公元前 3100—前 2700 年

高：22.5 厘米

底径：10.3 厘米

Painted pottery jar with net motif

Neolithic period

Majiayao type, Majiayao culture

Circa 3100 – 2700 B.C.E.

Height: 22.5 cm

Base diameter: 10.3 cm

泥质橙黄陶。腹体中部呈圆球形，平底。
器表磨光。口缘与肩部置竖环耳一个。
口缘内绘齿纹一周。外壁以黑彩围成三
个椭圆形装饰区，内画菱形网格纹，间
以雷电纹和竖带纹。此器造型圆浑饱满、
纹饰丰富，相当典雅。

Buff earthenware. The jar has a bulbous
body and a flat bottom. The surface is
highly burnished. A loop handle arches
from the mouth rim to the shoulders. The
interior rim bears a round of sawtooth
pattern. The exterior wall is painted in
black with three oval panels filled with net
motif separated by lightning pattern and
vertical striations.

49

黑彩绳纹尖底瓶

新石器时代
马家窑文化马家窑类型
约公元前 3100—前 2700 年
高：30.7 厘米
口径：5.4 厘米

Painted pottery amphora with cord motif

Neolithic period
Majiayao type, Majiayao culture
Circa 3100 – 2700 B.C.E.
Height: 30.7 cm
Mouth diameter: 5.4 cm

泥质红陶。口外侈，唇缘外折，长颈、宽肩、尖底。腹部置两环形耳，耳上饰附加堆纹。全器打磨光滑。施黑彩，除环形耳之间和底部无彩外，全器绘平行条纹，最下条纹上有开叉黑线纹。条纹代表绳子，而开叉黑线纹代表绳结。

马家窑文化彩绘尖底瓶发现不多。本品经热释光测定最后烧制年代距今约3900 年。

Red earthenware. This bottle has a flared mouth with everted rim, a long neck, broad shoulders and an elongated belly that tapers to a pointed base. A loop lug with an appliqué serrate ridge is affixed to both sides of the belly. The entire vessel has been burnished to a smooth and lustrous surface. The whole body is painted with black horizontal stripes to look like ropes. The last coil of rope is tied into a loose knot.

Pointed-bottom amphorae with painted decorations are rare among Majiayao pottery. Thermoluminescence test shows that the last firing date of this piece was around 3900 years before present.

水纹彩陶小罐

新石器时代
马家窑文化马家窑类型
约公元前 3100—前 2700 年
高：7.5 厘米
口径：7.3 厘米

Small painted pottery jar with wave motif

Neolithic period
Majiayao type, Majiayao culture
Circa 3100 – 2700 B.C.E.
Height: 7.5 cm
Mouth diameter: 7.3 cm

泥质红陶。口外侈、颈短而束、体中部外鼓、斜收到底，底平。胎细腻。器体外部经打磨抛光，以黑彩绘带状水波纹九道，口沿绘鸟纹十个，如鸟儿以“一”字形在水面上空飞行。

本品纹饰简单、构思巧妙，显现了彩陶艺术的魅力。

Red earthenware. The jar has a flared mouth, a short constricted neck, and a belly that swells in the mid-section and tapers towards a flat base. The paste is refined. The exterior is well burnished and encircled by horizontal wave motif. The inner mouth rim is painted with bird motif. The image of birds flying in a straight line over water is vividly depicted.

Deceptively simple yet highly original, this jar exemplifies the charm and genius of painted pottery.

51

黑白彩鸟纹钵

新石器时代
马家窑文化马家窑类型
约公元前 3100—前 2700 年
高：7.5 厘米
口径：15.5 厘米

Painted pottery bowl with bird motif

Neolithic period
Majiayao type, Majiayao culture
Circa 3100 – 2700 B.C.E.
Height: 7.5 cm
Mouth diameter: 15.5 cm

泥质橙红陶。敛口，圜底。全器以黑彩饰弧线纹、弧边三角纹和钩形纹，以白弧线和白彩圆点作饰，绘变体鸟纹。胎泥细腻，体薄坚致，烧成温度较高，器身内外经仔细打磨光滑。

新石器时代带白彩的器物较少。

Orange-red earthenware. The vessel has an incurved mouth and a rounded base. The design features a stylized bird composed by arcs, curved triangles and hook-like shapes in black. White arcs and dots are used to highlight the details. The thin and dense body is fired to a rather high temperature. The paste is refined. The interior and exterior of the bowl have been highly burnished to a smooth and lustrous finish.

Vessels with white painting are rare among Neolithic pottery.

52

彩陶双耳罐

新石器时代

马家窑文化半山类型

约公元前 2600—前 2300 年

高：18.9 厘米

口径：16.8 厘米

底径：10.2 厘米

Painted pottery jar with double lugs

Neolithic period

Banshan type, Majiayao culture

Circa 2600 – 2300 B.C.E

Height: 18.9 cm

Mouth diameter: 16.8 cm

Base diameter: 10.2 cm

浅黄陶，胎薄。颈微束，鼓腹急收，平底。颈两侧置环耳。器表稍经打磨处理，满布草根纹。全器施黑、红彩到腹下。口内缘画弦纹一周，上有短竖纹，下挂垂帐纹。颈外围以曲折纹和绳纹。器身绘齿状竖纹带六条，在黑彩的底色上满饰胎本色齿纹。

半山类型因 1923 年首次发现于甘肃省广河县半山遗址而得名。半山类型彩绘内容丰富，复杂图案的主体常用黑、红两彩相间的锯齿纹构成，色彩鲜明、形式多变。

Buff earthenware. The jar has a flat mouth, a slightly constricted neck with double lugs and a bulbous belly that tapers to a flat base. The surface of the jar is lightly burnished and covered with grass-root marks. Black and red motifs adorn the exterior surface from the mouth to the lower belly. The interior mouth rim is decorated with a band of short vertical striations and a band of scallop design. A round of zigzag and cord motifs adorns the neck. The body of the jar is decorated with a dense toothed motif separated by six vertical stripes with serrate edges.

Banshan type painted pottery was first discovered in 1923 at Banshan in Guanghe, Gansu province. Banshan-type painted pottery is usually decorated with rich and elaborate saw-tooth motif of diverse styles and vibrant colors, painted alternately in black and red.

53

彩陶网纹双耳罐

新石器时代

马家窑文化半山类型

约公元前 2600—前 2300 年

高：18.5 厘米

Painted pottery jar with net motif and loop-lugs

Neolithic period

Banshan type, Majiayao culture

Circa 2600 – 2300 B.C.E.

Height: 18.5 cm

泥质橙黄陶。侈口，短颈、溜肩、鼓腹、
小平底。胎细滑，颇薄和坚致。腹两侧
附扁环耳。以红、黑两色相间施彩。口
内饰垂帐纹、颈和肩部两侧绘网纹，腹
部画垂弧纹和锯齿纹。本品造型丰满、
线条优美、色彩鲜艳，为半山类型彩陶
精品。

Buff earthenware. The jar has a flared
mouth, a short neck, steep shoulders, a
swelling belly and a small flat base. A pair
of tubular lugs is attached to the sides. The
vessel features a red and black contrasting
design. The neck and the shoulders are
decorated with crosshatched motif and
the belly is painted with curvilinear design
and sawtooth motif.

54

性器官纹彩陶壶

新石器时代
马家窑文化半山类型
约公元前 2600—前 2300 年
高：22.8 厘米

Painted pottery jar with female genitalia motif

Neolithic period
Banshan type, Majiayao culture
Circa 2600 – 2300 B.C.E.
Height: 22.8 cm

泥质橙黄陶。短颈微侈、腹向两侧圆鼓。胎泥细腻，质坚，胎体细薄。器表经细心打磨光亮。颈部以黑彩画变体鸟纹。器腹以红、黑彩绘相连女性器官纹饰，周边饰以锯齿纹，最下方以一周黑弦纹把各个纹饰连在一起。下腹两侧贴扁环耳各一。本品造型优雅、颜色鲜艳，丰富的图案与饱满的造型浑然一体，是十分精美的史前艺术品。

Buff earthenware. The jar has a slightly flared mouth, a short neck and a swelling belly. The paste is thin, hard, dense and refined. The exterior of the vessel is highly burnished to a smooth and lustrous finish. The neck is painted in black with stylized bird motif. The belly is decorated with a female genitalia design with serrate edges in contrasting red and black pigments. A pair of tubular lugs is attached to the sides. This jar is an exceedingly fine piece of prehistoric art.

55

雌雄同体神鸟彩陶壶

新石器时代

马家窑文化半山类型

约公元前 2600—前 2300 年

高：23.5 厘米

底径：7.8 厘米

Painted pottery jar in the shape of a hermaphrodite bird

Neolithic period

Banshan type, Majiayao culture

Circa 2600 – 2300 B.C.E.

Height: 23.5 cm

Base diameter: 7.8 cm

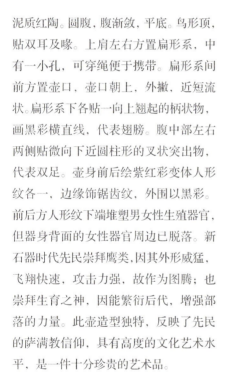

泥质红陶。圆腹，腹渐敛，平底。鸟形顶，贴双耳及喙。上肩左右方置扁形系，中有一小孔，可穿绳便于携带。扁形系间前方置壶口，壶口朝上，外撇，近短流状。扁形系下各贴一向上翘起的柄状物，画黑彩横直线，代表翅膀。腹中部左右两侧贴微向下近圆柱形的叉状突出物，代表双足。壶身前后绘紫红彩变体人形纹各一，边缘饰锯齿纹，外围以黑彩。前后方人形纹下端堆塑男女性生殖器官，但器身背面的女性器官周边已脱落。新石器时代先民崇拜鹰类，因其外形威猛，飞翔快速，攻击力强，故作为图腾；也崇拜生育之神，因能繁衍后代，增强部落的力量。此壶造型独特，反映了先民的萨满教信仰，具有高度的文化艺术水平，是一件十分珍贵的艺术品。

萨满教是世界上存在时间最长、最原始的宗教，最早出现在亚洲北部、中亚以及中国河西走廊和西亚一带，信仰男女同体可以延续后代。目前中国的鄂伦春族仍有信奉萨满教的人群，并有萨满。北美爱斯基摩人和南美洲一些部落人群信仰的宗教与萨满教相似。

Red earthenware. The jar has a rounded belly that tapers gently towards a flat base. The top of the jar is in the shape of a bird's head with appliqué ears and beak. The perforated lugs are used for tying a rope to the vessel. The mouth of the jar has a slightly flared rim and is set at an oblique angle to resemble a short spout. Below the lugs is a pair of up-tilting protuberances painted in black with crosshatches to suggest the wings of the bird. A pair of bifurcated protuberances representing the bird's feet is found further down. The front and back of the jar are painted in maroon with a highly stylized humanoid figure bordered by a sawtooth motif against a black ground. Below each of the figures is an appliqué with hybrid genitalia. Hermaphrodites unite both genders in one being and are revered by the cults of fertility and primitive religions like Shamanism. It is a unique object of high artistic and cultural value.

Shamanism is one of the most longstanding and primitive religions in the world. It first appeared in North Asia, Central Asia, West Asia and the Gansu Corridor of China. There are still believers and shamans among the ethnic people known as the Oroqen in northern China today. Similar religions are found among the Eskimos of North America and certain native tribes in South America.

鸟形彩陶壶

新石器时代

马家窑文化半山类型

约公元前 2600—前 2300 年

高：27.7 厘米

底径：14.3 厘米

Bird-shaped painted pottery jar

Neolithic period

Banshan type, Majiayao culture

Circa 2600 – 2300 B.C.E.

Height: 27.7 cm

Base diameter: 14.3 cm

泥质橙红陶。腹呈扁圆形，平底。器口在腹部前方上侧，斜置，作禽鸟之头颈。器口外饰齿状花边小耳，耳上穿孔。腹部左右两侧置扁状环耳，作禽鸟之羽翼。胎薄，器体表面打磨光滑，施黑红彩。头颈绘黑彩网纹和锯齿纹。器身上半部以黑红复彩描画六尾在水中翻腾的大鱼，鱼身隐于水下，只冒出鱼头，黑圆点为鱼的大眼。器顶部饰一同心圆纹饰，为水鸟和大鱼嬉戏追逐时搅动的旋涡。纹饰下方以一周弧线连接六个鱼纹，弧线下挂一周垂帐纹。

鸟形壶在半山时期出现不多，却是半山类型的典型器物之一。本品造型丰满，线条流畅，纹饰富丽，动感极强为不可多得的艺术珍品。

Orange-red earthenware. The jar has a bulbous belly and a flat base. The mouth is set off-center and at an angle to simulate the head and neck of a bird. The neck is decorated with mesh and sawtooth patterns. A pair of floret-shaped perforated lugs is affixed on the sides of the mouth rim. The pair of tubular lugs flanking the body represents the wings of a bird. The entire surface of the vessel was burnished before painting was done. The painted motifs are executed in black and red pigments. The upper section of the body is decorated with six large fish frolicking in the water with big black eyes showing above water. The concentric rings just below the neck are wave swirls created from the spinning movement of the fish.

Bird-shaped jars are scarce among Banshan finds. This vessel is a rarity among Banshan type pottery.

57

网纹单耳彩陶鸭形壶

新石器时代

马家窑文化半山类型

约公元前 2600—前 2300 年

高：15.8 厘米

Duck-shaped painted pottery jar

Neolithic period

Banshan type, Majiayao culture

Circa 2600 – 2300 B.C.E.

Height: 15.8 cm

泥质红陶。器身扁圆，作水鸟状。斜直口，颈肩间贴环状单竖耳，鼓腹，短尾，小平底。施褐黑彩。颈饰双层锯齿纹，腹左右画翅膀一对，伴以锯齿纹，背部绘一大圆圈，内填方格纹和网纹，圈周围以锯齿纹。造型憨态可掬，十分可爱。

Red earthenware. The jar in shape of a duck has a straight neck, a loop lug between the neck and shoulders, a drum body, a short tail and a small flat base. The decorative motifs are painted in dark brown pigment. The neck is adorned with double rounds of sawtooth motif. A pair of wings with serrate edges is painted on the sides of the body. The back of the vessel is decorated with check and mesh patterns.

58

双颈彩陶壶

新石器时代

马家窑文化半山类型

约公元前 2600—前 2300 年

高：22.2 厘米

阔（连耳）：20.5 厘米

底径：9.3 厘米

Painted pottery bottle with twin necks

Neolithic period

Banshan type, Majiayao culture

Circa 2600 – 2300 B.C.E.

Height: 22.2 cm

Width (with lugs): 20.5 cm

Base diameter: 9.3 cm

泥质橙黄陶。双圆筒形长颈，颈下部相连，唇口、球形腹、平底。颈上饰黑彩带三圈，肩和腹中部各有黑纹带一道，纹带间绘圆圈纹一周共十个，圆圈纹之间填黑彩。器中部两侧置环形竖耳，竖耳间有黑彩带纹一圈与下方垂帐纹连接。双颈的彩陶壶发现较少。

Buff earthenware. The bottle has two long necks with lipped mouths and adjoining bases, a bulbous belly with a pair of loop lugs and a flat base. There are three black stripes on each neck and two around the shoulders and the belly. The upper body is adorned with ten circular motifs against a black ground bounded by a black scallop edge. Painted pottery with twin necks are very rare.

59

绳纹彩陶壶

新石器时代

马家窑文化马家窑类型

约公元前 3100 – 前 2700 年

高：40.2 厘米

底径：12.5 厘米

Painted pottery jar with cord motif

Neolithic period

Majiayao type, Majiayao culture

Circa 3100 – 2700 B.C.E.

Height: 40.2 cm

Base diameter: 12.5 cm

泥质橙黄陶。腹置双环耳。口缘内侧划水波纹一周，颈周满绘网状纹。器身上半部饰绳纹四组，间以黑色和红褐色粗带纹。纹饰最下方以垂弧纹收结。此器体硕大，胎薄，黑、红褐彩与橙黄胎地相映成趣。绳纹装饰显示了绳索在先民日常生活中的重要性。

1977 年甘肃省兰州出土有相似器物，现存甘肃省博物馆。

Buff earthenware. A pair of loop lugs flanks the jar at the belly. The interior mouth rim is painted with a round of wave motif and the neck with crosshatches. The upper half of the jar is decorated with alternating cord motif and black and red stripes bounded by a scallop edge.

A similar vessel was unearthed in 1977 from a tomb in Lanzhou, Gansu province. It is now in the collection of the Gansu Provincial Museum.

60

彩绘双鸮纹罐

新石器时代

马家窑文化马厂类型

约公元前 2200—前 2000 年

高：11.8 厘米

底径：5 厘米

Painted pottery jar with double-owl motif

Neolithic period

Machang type, Majiayao culture

Circa 2200 – 2000 B.C.E.

Height: 11.8 cm

Base diameter: 5 cm

泥质红陶。平口，球形腹，小平底。器身施白色陶衣，上绘紫红彩。口缘外有两圈阔带纹，前后侧带纹上各饰小孔两个，左右两侧贴小锥突各两个。器身绘网纹、十字纹和竖纹作饰。此罐装饰方法独特，以双小孔为眼、双锥突作耳、白陶衣三角形为喙，刻画出两只双眼圆睁、竖起双耳、细察八方动静的鸮鸟形象。

马厂类型因 1924 年首次于青海省民和县马厂原遗址发现而得名。

Red earthenware. The jar has a flat mouth and a bulbous belly and a small flat base. The surface is painted with maroon patterns on a white-slipped ground. Two maroon bands encircle the exterior mouth rim. The front and back of these maroon bands are respectively pierced with two small holes. Two small studs are attached to both sides of the mouth opening. The body is painted with mesh motif, cross shapes and vertical stripes. The jar is ingeniously designed. The perforations and studs denote the eyes and ears and the triangular shapes under the eyes the beaks.

Machang type pottery was first discovered in 1924 at Machangyuan in Minhe, Qinghai province.

61

人形纹彩陶罐

新石器时代

马家窑文化马厂类型

约公元前 2200—前 2000 年

高：21.5 厘米

底径：10.5 厘米

Painted pottery jar with humanoid figures

Neolithic period

Machang type, Majiayao culture

Circa 2200 – 2000 B.C.E.

Height: 21.5 cm

Base diameter: 10.5 cm

泥质橙黄陶。口缘外侈，直颈、球形腹，小平底。施紫红、黑两彩。口缘内壁上端绘一周齿纹、紫红带纹及水波纹。口外缘上方饰弦纹五道，颈围垂直水波纹一周。口肩部置双耳。腹部画连续变体人形纹两组，上方间隙呈四个倒置等边三角形，下方呈八个直角三角形。在等边三角形内各绘人物形体一个，头发竖起，面部一点代表五官，手臂弯屈上举，手指张开，双脚外撇，脚趾清晰可见。在直角三角形内各饰一黑彩圆点，两个平行相对的直角三角形看上去又是一个抽象的人面，中以紫红、黑彩竖带为鼻梁，二黑彩圆点作眼睛，十分有趣。此彩陶表现了马厂人高度的艺术抽象和创造才能。

本品所绘人形可能是要表现"巫师"口念咒语、手舞足蹈，替族人"驱邪治病"。

Buff earthenware. The jar has a flared mouth, a straight neck, a globular belly and a small flat base. The decorations are painted in black and maroon. The inner rim has a band of sawtooth design above a solid band of maroon and a row of wave motif. The outer rim is encompassed by five rounds of fine cord motif while the neck is painted with vertical wavy stripes. A pair of loop lugs arches from the mouth rim to the shoulders. The belly is adorned with two groups of abstract human figures. The decoration is divided into eight right-angled triangles and four equilateral triangles. Inside each of the equilateral triangles is a humanoid figure with spiky hair, facial features represented by a dot, half-raised arms, outspread fingers, outstretched legs and feet with toes clearly visible. Inside each of the right-angled triangles is a black dot. Each pair of these right-angled triangles can be interpreted as an abstract human head, the dots representing the eyes and the column down the middle the nose. The visual effect is very interesting and eye-catching.

The humanoid figures with raised arms are probably sorcerers dancing and chanting incantations to ward off evil spirits and cure diseases.

62

人形蛙纹双流彩陶壶

新石器时代

马家窑文化马厂类型

约公元前 2200—前 2000 年

高：29.8 厘米

底径：10.2 厘米

Painted pottery bottle with double spouts and frog motif

Neolithic period

Machang type, Majiayao culture

Circa 2200 – 2000 B.C.E.

Height: 29.8 cm

Base diameter: 10.2 cm

泥质橙黄陶。壶顶并排置大小流口各一，流口缘外翻，口内缘饰齿纹带。短颈，上绘网状纹。肩腹特别夸张，腹部呈球形，中腹以下急收，小平底。腹中部饰环形耳一对。肩腹上部画变体人形蛙纹两组，间饰圆圈纹两个，圈内填圆弦纹及网纹，大流口一侧所绘蛙体较大。腹下部绘一圈带纹及垂弧纹。施紫红、黑色两彩。纹饰绘画精细，色彩明艳。

此器造型别致，颇罕见，顶部伸出的流口如引颈张大的青蛙嘴巴，大、小流口可能分别代表雄性与雌性，而圆圈纹则为夸大表现的青蛙眼睛。

Buff earthenware. The bottle has two spouts on top, one larger and one smaller. The interior rim of the spouts is decorated by a row of sawtooth design. Both spouts have a slightly flared rim and a short neck with mesh pattern. The body has steep shoulders above a swelling belly that tapers towards a small flat base. A pair of loop lugs is attached to the belly. The upper body is painted with two stylized frogs divided by two oversized circles with concentric rings and a core of mesh pattern. The frog below the bigger spout is slightly larger in size. The decoration is bounded by a black band with a scallop edge. The decorations are painted in black and maroon.

The painted patterns are exquisitely executed, vividly colored and uniquely designed. The openings of the spouts resemble wide open mouths, probably the bigger one representing the male and the smaller one the female. The two big circles between the frogs are likely to be a pair of eyes in exaggeration. The overall design is very special and rare.

63

人形蛙纹彩陶大罐

新石器时代
马家窑文化马厂类型
约公元前 2200—前 2000 年
高：45 厘米
口径：19.5 厘米

Large painted pottery jar with frog-shaped humanoid figures

Neolithic period
Machang type, Majiayao culture
Circa 2200 – 2000 B.C.E.
Height: 45 cm
Mouth diameter: 19.5 cm

泥质橙黄陶。侈口，短颈，球形腹，下腹收敛较瘦，小平底。施红、黑两彩。口内边缘绘锯齿纹和双勾五角形，颈部饰折角纹。腹上部画双"W"状变体人形蛙纹两组，圆圈形纹饰作头部，上方之"W"纹为前腿，下方为后腿，中间之竖带纹作躯体。前后两组变体人形蛙纹以网格圆圈纹相间。腹中部贴双竖耳。腹下部绘黑色带纹和连续垂弧纹。

此器个体较大，纹饰精致，色彩鲜艳，紫红、黑色彩与橙黄色地衬托得宜，是马厂类型彩陶的精品。

本品与图录 62 号的变体人形蛙纹肢节上都长出了爪指，有"寓人为蛙"之意，祈望能有蛙之生殖力，具图腾崇拜含义。

Buff earthenware. The jar has a flared mouth, a short neck and a bulging belly that tapers to a small flat base. The painting is done in black and maroon. The interior rim of the mouth is bordered by sawtooth pattern above a band of maroon and a double-lined pentagon design. The outer neck is decorated with short folded lines. The upper body features two highly stylized frogs with heads represented by concentric circles. The forelimbs and hind limbs resembling two W-shapes are connected by the vertical torso of the frog. Three circlets filled with mesh pattern are contained within each of the large circular motifs that separate the frogs. A pair of loop lugs is affixed to the belly. The decoration is bounded by a black band with a scallop edge.

This vessel is generously sized, exquisitely painted and vividly colored. The maroon and black patterns contrast delightfully with the buff ground.

Frogs are a symbol of fecundity and fertility. The elbows and the tips of the hands and feet of the humanoid figures have froglike webbed claws similar to Cat. No. 62. The zoomorphic representation alludes to humans endowed with froglike reproductive powers.

蛇纹彩陶罐

新石器时代

马家窑文化马厂类型

约公元前 2200—前 2000 年

高：36.5 厘米

底径：9.2 厘米

Painted pottery jar with snake motif

Neolithic period

Machang type, Majiayao culture

Circa 2200 – 2000 B.C.E.

Height: 36.5 cm

Base diameter: 9.2 cm

泥质橙黄陶。侈口，直颈，胎薄，平底。口缘内侧以黑彩画双线五角纹饰。颈饰黑彩雷电纹。腹以黑红彩绘团蛇五条，其中一条有长方形呈哑铃状的蛇头。纹饰绚丽对称，优美流畅，极具动感。

Buff earthenware with a thin paste. The jar has a flared mouth, a straight neck and a flat base. The interior mouth rim is painted in black with a double-lined pentagon. The neck is decorated with lightning motif. The belly is painted in black and red with five coiling snakes, one of which has a rectangular head resembling a dumbbell.

65

人首彩陶壶

新石器时代

马家窑文化马厂类型

约公元前 2200 年—前 2000 年

高：30.2 厘米

口径：10.6 厘米

底径：10 厘米

Painted pottery jar with human-head design

Neolithic period

Machang type, Majiayao culture

Circa 2200 – 2000 B.C.E.

Height: 30.2 cm

Mouth diameter: 10.6 cm

Base diameter: 10 cm

泥质橙黄陶。底平，腹中下部置双耳。器口饰紫红彩带纹、黑彩连弧纹和垂滴纹。肩部堆塑人首像一个，五官清晰，描画细致，大眼、高鼻、阔耳、张口、留须，栩栩如生。面部及脑后满施黑彩直线纹，以示头、面被头发覆盖，而发式是区别古代部族的重要标志。器身绘黑色和紫红色彩带数道，间以三角形直线纹、哑铃纹、水滴纹、网纹和人形纹。颈和腹下分别画曲折纹和垂叶纹饰。器身满布草根痕迹。

以雕塑手法做出人头装饰的彩陶很少，这是一件体现祖先崇拜的珍贵艺术品。

本品经热释光测定最后烧制年代距今 5300—3400 年。

Buff earthenware. The jar has a flat base and a pair of loop lugs affixed to the lower belly. Inside the mouth is a band of maroon with a scallop edge and a row of water drops. A human head with distinct facial features stands on the shoulder. It is finely sculpted with big eyes, high nose, broad ears, open mouth and beard. The facial expression is extremely vivid. The face and the back of the head are covered with hair-like black lines. Hairstyle was a symbol of identification and tribal affiliation. The body of the jar is painted with horizontal stripes of black and maroon between rows of triangles, dumbbell shapes, water-drop motif, net pattern and stylized humanoid figures. The neck and the lower belly are decorated with zigzag design. The surface of the vessel is covered with grass-root marks from burial.

Painted pottery with sculpted human head is very rare. This vessel is an object used in rituals of ancestor worship.

Thermoluminescence test shows that the last firing date of this piece was 5300 to 3400 years before present.

彩陶豆

新石器时代

马家窑文化马厂类型

约公元前 2200—前 2000 年

高：7.3 厘米

口径：16.3 厘米

底径：10.5 厘米

Painted pottery *dou* stem-dish

Neolithic period

Machang type, Majiayao culture

Circa 2200 – 2000 B.C.E.

Height: 7.3 cm

Mouth diameter: 16.3 cm

Base diameter: 10.5 cm

泥质橙黄陶。口平缘，微向内倾斜，豆呈浅盆状，足阔短，呈喇叭状。口外缘下和足缘上约 1.5 厘米处各有一周泥条接痕，说明口缘和足缘是在坯体完成后再粘上去的。器内壁施黑彩，间以深褐红彩纹带。内壁上半部以一周黄泥色圆点作饰，底心以黄泥色画双线十字纹饰一个。外腹壁上部绘褐红、黑彩纹带和一周波浪纹。足缘饰黑彩。足两侧有圆孔各一个。腹、足露胎处有器表磨光处理痕迹。

Buff earthenware. The vessel has a shallow dish with a slightly inward-slanting flat rim, supported by a short and broad stem with a splayed foot. Luting marks are visible under the exterior mouth rim and about 1.5 cm above the foot, indicating that the mouth rim and the flared base of the stem were made separately. The interior wall is decorated with alternating black and maroon bands and a ring of buff dots. The center of the bowl features a double-lined cross shape in buff color. The exterior wall is painted with alternating bands of maroon and black and a round of

wave motif. A hole is pierced on both sides of the stem. Burnishing marks are visible

on the belly and the stem where the paste is exposed.

67

叶纹单耳彩陶罐

新石器时代晚期

齐家文化

约公元前 2200—前 1600 年

高：14.3 厘米

底径：6.5 厘米

**Painted pottery jar with
mountain motif**

Late Neolithic period

Qijia culture

Circa 2200 – 1600 B.C.E.

Height: 14.3 cm

Base diameter: 6.5 cm

泥质橙黄陶。大口、高颈、口微撇、平底。颈间安环耳一个，上饰锥刺凹圆圈纹。颈、肩间有锥刺凹圆圈纹带一周。腹上部以黑彩绘三层山形纹，纹饰上下以黑彩弦纹各一道收结。器壁较薄，全器外壁和颈内壁打磨光滑发亮。

Buff earthenware. The jar has a wide mouth with slightly flared rim, a tall neck and a flat base. The strap handle and the joint between the neck and the shoulders are decorated with pecked circular motif. The upper belly is painted in black with three layers of inverted triangles. The decoration is bounded by black cord motif. The jar is quite thinly potted. The entire exterior of the jar as well as the inside of the neck have been highly burnished to a smooth and lustrous finish.

夏商周陶器

Pottery of the Xia, Shang and Zhou

夏商周陶器：
创意非凡

夏是中国史书中记载的第一个世袭制朝代，一般认为是多个部落联盟或复杂酋邦形式的国家。商周是奴隶制发达的时期，青铜文化光辉灿烂，甲骨文、铜器铭文出现，社会文化教育逐渐开展。春秋战国时期，由于青铜器制作工艺难度很大、成本较高，加上各国的兼并战争消耗社会财富，青铜器日渐式微，陶器手工业的发展加快。陶制的礼器、陈设艺术品深受社会各阶层喜爱，既满足王侯贵族、庶民百姓日常生活、祭祀、殉葬的需要，同时给人的美学享受也不亚于青铜器，如本书收录的陶鼎、豆、壶、簋、甗以及燕下都瓦当等，都与同时代的青铜器艺术风格完全一致。

这一时期，中原周边地区也存在一些具有地方特色的文化，包括夏家店文化下层、寺洼文化和辛店文化等，它们已步入青铜文化时期。

陶器有泥质灰陶、夹砂灰陶、夹砂灰褐陶、黑陶、黑皮陶、棕灰陶、泥质红陶、夹砂红陶、白陶、印纹硬陶等。这些陶器主要作为饮食器、储盛器、炊器和礼器等。在商周时期还出现了专门用于殉葬的明器。

泥质陶作为日常生活中使用最多的器皿，造型古拙典雅，结构棱角分明，表面打磨光滑，喜欢用绳纹、穿带耳进行装饰，简洁明朗，质量相当高。有些器形仍带有新石器时代生育崇拜和母体崇拜的遗风。如图录68号白陶三足盉，除了高尖拔挺如乳房状的三足外，还有一个向外张开的圆形大孔，寓意女性的阴户，其结构之巧妙令人叹服。

白陶是用白黏土或坩子土制作，在夏商周时期生产数量很少，只在贵族大墓中才有出土。本图录68号白陶三足盉和69号白陶带盖三足盉是这一时期白陶的代表作。

新石器时代晚期，相当于中原地区夏或早商时期，南方地区出现印纹硬陶器，西周、春秋、战国时期得到飞跃发展。印纹硬陶在长江以南地区和东南沿海地区出土较多。陶土是一种含铁量很高、含砂、能耐高温的黏土，这种原料在江南地区广泛出产。印纹硬陶的胎质比一般泥质或夹砂陶器细腻、坚硬，烧成温度也比一般陶器高，在950℃—1100℃左右，陶色为灰褐色、紫褐色、黄褐色和红褐色，莫氏硬度4—5度，较一般泥质陶器更坚固耐用。纹饰有云雷纹、曲折纹、菱格纹、菱格填线纹、方格纹、方格填线纹、米字纹、山纹、水纹、回字纹等。江南地区的印纹硬陶器应是承袭当地用陶土烧制的一般印纹陶器（软陶）发展起来的。如图录98号春秋印纹扉棱罐、99号春秋印纹陶瓶、100号春秋印纹双系扁壶与95号西周几何印纹硬陶罍比较，纹饰基本相同，只是印纹硬陶烧制温度更高。

大多数印纹硬陶采用泥条盘筑法成型，成型时用刻划各种图案花纹的陶拍子拍打胎体表面，使坯体牢固结实，同时陶拍子上的各种花纹纹路拍破湿润陶坯表层的薄膜，使水分在焙烧时可以顺畅排出，保证了陶器在烧成时表面不破裂、不变形。而陶器表面排列有序的花纹，也使普通的日用陶器变得质朴典雅、庄重优美、风格独特。

原始先民生活简单，思想纯朴，对事物和大自然各种现象观察入微，有丰富的想象力和创新意识，在制陶过程中会把日常生活所见所闻和大自然的变化反映到器物上。例如图录93号和94号，只是在系上加了一些简单的堆纹，就大大提升了器物的艺术水平，给人以美和愉悦的感受。

春秋战国时期，思想自由开放、经济快速发展，在艺术和工艺技术上可说是一个真正百花齐放、百家争鸣的时代。独立手工业作坊

大量涌现，制陶手工业发达，以财雄势大的
官府作坊为首的大小作坊纷纷采取措施改进
工艺技术、提高质量，生产出一些创意非凡、
精美绝伦、有极高欣赏价值的艺术精品。图
录 96 号西周印纹硬陶罐、111 号络绳纹罐、
116 号战国印纹硬陶槽形长流罐等都极其代
表性，是美的极致。

根据考古学者的调查，浙江等地一些窑址中
同时烧制印纹硬陶和原始瓷。印纹硬陶的烧
制成功是制陶工艺的一大突破，为陶器向瓷
器的转化创造了条件。

建筑艺术在战国至汉时迅速发展，民族传统
中的瓦木结构完备起来。《楚辞·招魂》有云：
"高堂邃宇，槛层轩兮，层台累榭，临高山兮。
网户朱缀，刻方连兮，冬有突厦，夏室寒兮。"
本书收录的战国到汉代瓦当反映了这种文化
现象，从中可以感悟到时代精神。

Pottery of the Xia, Shang and Zhou:

Creativity Unbound

Xia, the first hereditary dynasty recorded in Chinese history, is believed to be a complex chieftain state made up of a number of tribal alliances. The Shang and Zhou dynasties were highly developed slave societies and part of a brilliant bronze culture. The emergence of the Chinese writing system (inscriptions on oracle bones and bronzes) also furthered cultural and educational progress. During the Spring and Autumn and Warring States periods, bronze ware production declined due to cost and an impoverished society caused by frequent warfare between feudal states. The gradual fading out of bronzes made way for the development of pottery. People from all sections of society embraced both decorative and ritual pottery. They were used as everyday utensils in households, decorations in stately homes, sacrificial wares on altars and grave goods in tombs. The pottery *ding* tripods, the *dou* stem-bowls, the *hu* jars, the *gui* bowls, the *yan* steamers and the eaves tiles from Yanxiadu in this catalogue are artistically on a par with contemporaneous bronzes.

During the Xia and Shang dynasties, some cultures with distinct regional characteristics existed in the periphery of the Central Plain. Among them were the Lower Xiajiadian culture, Siwa culture and Xindian culture of the Bronze Age period.

Pottery of this period consists of gray earthenware, sand-tempered gray or grayish-brown pottery, black pottery, carbonized black pottery, brownish-gray pottery, red earthenware, sand-tempered red pottery, white pottery and high-fired stamped pottery. Mortuary objects made for burial emerged for the first time during the Shang and Zhou dynasties.

The majority of household utensils used during the Shang and Zhou periods were earthenware decorated with cord motifs and loop lugs. The overall design was simple and the surface highly burnished.

Some of them are reminiscent of Neolithic pottery as exemplified by the white pottery tripod jug with three udder-shaped legs (Cat. No. 68).

White pottery was fabricated from white clay or an earthen material known as *ganzitu*. Production was scarce during the Xia, Shang and Zhou dynasties. Examples were only found in large aristocratic tombs. The white pottery jug with lid (Cat. No. 68) and white pottery jug with female genitalia design (Cat. No. 69) are representative examples.

Stamped pottery (pottery with impressed motifs) emerged in southern China during the late Neolithic period, which coincided with the Xia and early Shang dynasties. High-fired stamped pottery saw rapid development during the Western Zhou, Spring and Autumn and Warring States periods. These vessels were mainly produced in the southern regions. The paste of high-fired stamped pottery is usually finer and harder then that of earthenware or sand-tempered pottery. They were fired to 950℃ –1100℃, which is higher than the temperature used to produce ordinary pottery. The biscuit came in different colors ranging from grayish-brown to purplish-brown, yellowish-brown and reddish-brown. High-fired stamped pottery has a hardness of 4–5 degrees on Mohs scale, which makes it harder and more durable than ordinary pottery. Typical decorative motifs include cloud and thunder pattern, zigzag bands, hatched lozenge shapes, check and hatched check design, eight-point stars, mountains, waves and key frets, etc. They were fabricated from high-fired and sand-tempered clay with high iron content. Iron was obtained in large quantity around the lower Changjiang River basin. The high-fired stamped pottery produced in Jiangnan region was probably a sophisticated version of the indigenous low-fired stamped pottery made from local clay. The decorative motifs on the Spring and Autumn jar with serrate flanges and impressed motif (Cat. No. 98), the Spring and Autumn vase with impressed motif (Cat. No. 99) and the Spring and Autumn flask with double lugs and impressed motif (Cat. No. 100) are essentially the same as the high-fired stamped jar of the Western Zhou period (Cat. No. 95) except that the high-fired stamped pottery are fired to a higher temperature.

Most vessels were built by using the coiling method. The vessels are then beaten into shape with a pottery paddle to make the clay more compact. This process also helped break the surface tension of the moist clay and remove air bubbles, thus avoiding cracking and deformation during firing. A paddle is also used to impress a repeated pattern of identical motifs onto the vessel.

Prehistoric people lived simply and were fascinated by natural phenomena. The objects that they made were characterized by themes drawn from everyday life and imbued with a fascination for the natural world (Cat. Nos. 93, 94).

During the Spring and Autumn and Warring States periods, people enjoyed freedom of thought and economic progress. It was an era that saw a rapid growth in the arts and crafts. The pottery industry thrived and independent workshops multiplied. To compete with government workshops with deep pockets, the private ones had to streamline their methods of production and elevate the standards of products. As a result, a large number of exceedingly beautiful works of art were created. Examples include the high-fired stamped pottery from the Western Zhou period (Cat. No. 96), the *lei* jar with appliqué net and impressed motif (Cat. No. 111) and the high-fired pottery jar with long open spout (Cat. No.

116).

Archaeologists from Zhejiang have concluded that high-fired stamped pottery was produced in the same kilns as proto-porcelain. The successful production of this genre of pottery is a major breakthrough in Chinese ceramic history and laid the foundation for the advent of porcelain.

The architecture and building industry saw immense growth from the Warring States to the Han periods. Traditional tile-and-timber structures grew in sophistication. *Zhaohun* (Summons of the Soul), one of the verses in *Chuci* (Verses of Chu State), contains these lines: "High hall, profound mansion, multistoried building; pavilion on tall terrace, overlooking high mountains; lattice windows with red painting and rectangular openwork. Profound houses [are suitable] for winter. They are cool [to live] in summer." The Warring States and Han eaves tiles in this catalogue are representative examples of the architectural styles and conventions of this period.

68

白陶三足盉

夏

约公元前 2070—前 1600 年

高：31 厘米

White pottery *he* tripod jug

Xia dynasty

Circa 2070 – 1600 B.C.E.

Height: 31 cm

夹砂白陶，质颇细腻。口部有上翘的短管状流，流口后方有一大一小两个圆孔。与流相对一侧安带状宽把手，上刻斜十字纹。把手与器体间有三柱状条相接，以加强把手强度。筒形身，下承三袋足，在两个袋足会合处起凹棱直达器身上部。正面两袋足间有一上方凸起呈拱状的圆孔。

本品特别之处在于流口后方较小圆孔和下方袋足间圆孔之间有一根圆管相连（附图 1），其作用可能是加热时让火直接进入圆管内，以加快升温的速度并使温度更高。至于圆管下方周边外翻的圆孔，从其位置和外形来看，应寓意女性阴户，与生育崇拜、母体崇拜有关。

Sand-tempered white pottery with a refined paste. The mouth of the vessel is furnished with an up-tilted short spout that is pierced with one larger and one smaller hole in the back. A strap handle incised with crosshatching is affixed to the back. It is reinforced by three struts connected to the wall of the jug. The cylindrical body is supported by three baggy legs.

Judging from its shape and position on the vessel, the female genitalia is represented by a circular opening with a raised and everted rim between the two front legs. The most unusual feature of this vessel is the internal tube that connects this circular opening with the smaller hole at the back of the spout (Fig. 1). The tube probably allowed the fire to reach deeper into the vessel to speed up the heating.

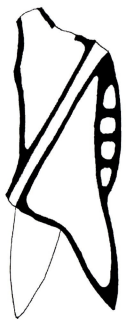

附图 1　剖面

Fig. 1　Cross section

69

白陶带盖三足盉

夏

约公元前 2070—前 1600 年

高：29.5 厘米

White pottery *he* tripod jug with lid

Xia dynasty

Circa 2070 – 1600 B.C.E.

Height: 29.5 cm

泥质白陶。圆形顶，小口，短流，粗直颈，扁平宽把手，袋足。流后方有半圆形口，口上覆半圆形盖，盖上置弯纽。盖后方与顶部交接处有一小圆孔。颈部上下各饰锯齿形花边一周。流外侧下方两袋足间贴乳丁一个。宽把手左、右侧各起竖凹弦纹两道，中间由上而下刻箭镞头纹饰十个。胎质细腻，薄胎，最薄处约 1 毫米。

夏代以白陶数量最少。本品以杂质较少的坩子土做原料，造型优美，纹饰丰富，制作精细，器经打磨光滑，为夏代白陶代表作品。

White earthenware. It has a circular top with a small mouth and a short spout, a thick straight neck, a broad strap handle and three baggy legs. The back of the spout turns into a circular opening with a semi-circular lid surmounted by a bridge knob. A small round opening straddles the edge of the lid and the cirular top near the handle. A band of serrate design encircles the upper and lower parts of the neck. A stud is attached to the exterior wall between the baggy legs under the spout. Two grooves run down each side of the strap handle while ten arrowhead patterns are arrayed down the center. This jug has a hard and fine paste and a thin body measuring about 1 mm at the thinnest.

Among the pottery from the Xia dynasty, examples of white pottery are scarce. The present piece is fabricated from a type of earthen clay with fewer impurities known as *ganzitu*. The vessel is noted for its beautiful lines, elaborate decoration, exquisite workmanship and smooth and lustrous finish. This vessel is a representative example of the finest white pottery from the Xia dynasty.

70

青灰陶鬲

夏家店下层文化

约公元前 2000—前 1500 年

高：27.8 厘米

口径：16.5 厘米

Greenish-gray pottery *li* tripod jar

Lower Xiajiadian culture

Circa 2000 – 1500 B.C.E.

Height: 27.8 cm

Mouth diameter: 16.5 cm

泥质青灰陶。敞口、口缘外撇成喇叭状、深腹束腰、矮裆，下承以三个乳状矮实足。全器打磨光滑、无纹饰。此器造型秀丽、比例特殊，以矮小三足承托高挑的鬲体。

夏家店下层文化是北方草原地区早期青铜文化，因内蒙古赤峰夏家店村遗址而得名。夏家店下层文化陶器以夹砂灰陶和褐陶为主，手制，泥条盘筑成型，烧成火候普遍较高。此器为夏家店下层文化最具代表性的作品。敖汉旗大甸子遗址出土有相似器物。

Greenish-gray earthenware. The vessel has a wide trumpet mouth and a deep body with a constricted waist supported by three short and solid udder-legs. The entire surface is unadorned and burnished to a smooth and lustrous finish.

The lower stratum of Xiajiadian culture is an early Bronze Age culture developed in the northern steppes. It was discovered at Xiajiadian village in Chifeng, Inner Mongolia. Greenish-gray earthenware makes up the majority of pottery from the lower stratum of Xiajiadian culture. They were handmade, built by coiling method and fired to a relatively high temperature. This jar is the most representative example of the pottery from the lower stratum of Xiajiadian culture. Similar vessels have been excavated from the Dadianzi site in Aohan Banner county.

71

云雷纹彩绘尊

夏家店下层文化

约公元前 2000—前 1500 年

高：22.8 厘米

Painted pottery *zun* pot with cloud-and-thunder motif

Lower Xiajiadian culture

Circa 2000 – 1500 B.C.E.

Height: 22.8 cm

泥质灰陶。喇叭形口，束腰，腰约占器身的五分之四，腹急收到底，平底。胎泥较粗，胎体厚重。体表以红、白彩绘勾连纹，纹饰生动流畅，鲜艳夺目。口缘内侧绘如眼睛般的椭圆形纹饰一周，以横线连接。

由于彩绘是在器物烧成后才画上去的，所以易脱落。这类彩绘陶器很可能是用于祭祀。本品造型优美、线条流畅，是一件十分珍贵的艺术品。

Gray earthenware. The pot has a trumpet mouth, a waisted body that is about four-fifths of the overall height and a carinated lower body that tapers rapidly to a flat base. The paste is rather coarse and the body thick and heavy. The surface is painted in red and white with scrolling motifs. A string of eyelike oval shapes encircles the inner mouth rim.

The painted motifs were applied after firing and thus prone to flaking. This type of painted pottery was probably used as ritual ware.

72

黑陶簋

商

公元前 1600—前 1046 年

高：11.5 厘米

口径：16.3 厘米

Black pottery *gui* bowl

Shang dynasty

1600 – 1046 B.C.E.

Height: 11.5 cm

Mouth diameter: 16.3 cm

泥质黑陶。口平，圆唇外翻，胎体较厚重，腹弧形内收到底，大圆饼足。肩腹以两周凸弦纹分隔，凸弦纹上方刻山形纹一周。构图和纹饰简单，但粗厚的唇缘、腹间的粗弦纹线和圆饼形圈足相配得宜，很有欣赏价值。本品为食具。

美国旧金山亚洲艺术博物馆收藏有相似器物。

Black earthenware with a rather thick and heavy body. The bowl has a flat mouth with a flared rim and rounded lip, a convex belly and a splayed foot. Two grooves run between the shoulders and the belly. A band of incised mountain motif decorates the area above the grooves. This bowl was used as a food utensil.

A similar vessel is in the collection of the Asian Art Museum of San Francisco, USA.

73

灰陶三足斝

商

公元前 1600—前 1046 年

高：13.5 厘米

口径：15.2 厘米

Gray pottery *jia* tripod vessel

Shang dynasty

1600 – 1046 B.C.E.

Height: 13.5 cm

Mouth diameter: 15.2 cm

泥质灰陶。平口，口内敛，外斜，直腹。口缘上两侧置提手各一，微向下倾斜。腹上部贴堆纹一周，下贴圆饼形鼓丁装饰六个，腹下斜收到底。下腹部有空心袋形尖足三个，上贴附加堆纹。器身满饰由上而下的细绳纹。造型规整，制作严谨。

Gray earthenware. The vessel has a flat mouth and cylindrical body. A lug is affixed to both sides of the mouth rim. An appliqué border encircles the upper belly. Below it are six equally spaced appliqué bosses. The lower belly is supported by three hollow baggy legs. An appliqué border adorns the top of each leg. The exterior of the body is covered with fine cord motif. The vessel is neatly potted and meticulously crafted.

74

泥质灰陶贴花鼎

商

公元前 1600—前 1046 年

高：12 厘米

Gray pottery *ding* tripod with appliqué design

Shang dynasty

1600 – 1046 B.C.E.

Height: 12 cm

泥质灰陶，质坚硬。唇外翻，呈槽形，鼓腹，下承三袋足。口缘下和肩腹交界处各有一周凹弦纹带，纹带上下和袋足饰绳纹，袋足上的绳纹较粗。三足上方由肩部开始，贴竖扉棱各一，扉棱之间，间以圆饼状乳突。器形和装饰与同时期的青铜器一致。

Gray earthenware with a hard paste. The vessel has an everted rim with a grooved surface and a bulbous belly supported by three baggy legs. A groove encircles the body under the rim and another around the junction of the shoulders and the belly. The areas above and below the grooves and the surface of the legs are adorned with cord motif. The cord motif on the legs is broader in width. Vertical serrated flanges decorate the shoulders. A disc-like stud is attached midway between the flanges. This vessel is similar to contemporaneous bronzes in shape and decoration.

75

黑陶觚

商

公元前 1600—前 1046 年

高：17.4 厘米

口径：14.2 厘米

Black pottery *gu* vessel

Shang dynasty

1600 – 1046 B.C.E.

Height: 17.4 cm

Mouth diameter: 14.2 cm

泥质黑陶。口大外侈，深腹，平底，底内凹。腹下以一粗唇状圆棱束腹，把器身分成两部分。上部呈喇叭形；下部呈梯形，上饰凸弦纹两道。质松，较粗糙，厚胎。此器虽然素身，但外撇的喇叭形口与凸圆唇、凸弦纹以及外撇的底足线条优美和谐，是一件值得收藏的艺术品。此器形在夏商时期较为流行，是陪葬用的礼器。

Black earthenware. The vessel is thickly potted from a rather coarse and porous paste. It has a wide and flared mouth, a deep belly and a flat and slightly recessed base. A ring-like ridge encircles the lower belly, dividing the body into a trumpet-like upper section and a trapezoidal lower section decorated with rib design. This vessel was probably used as funerary ware.

76

青灰陶觚

商

公元前 1600—前 1046 年

高：20.6 厘米

口径：14.4 厘米

Greenish-gray pottery *gu* vessel

Shang dynasty

1600 – 1046 B.C.E.

Height: 20.6 cm

Mouth diameter: 14.4 cm

本品与图录 75 号在时代、生产工艺、装饰等方面都极相似，只是胎泥呈青灰色且无唇状圆棱。

美国旧金山亚洲艺术博物馆收藏有相似器物。

This vessel is comparable to Cat. No. 75 in terms of period, production technique and decoration except that the paste is greenish-gray in color and the body has no ring-like ridge.

A similar vessel is in the collection of the Asian Art Museum of San Francisco, USA.

77

黑陶贯耳壶

商

公元前 1600—前 1046 年

高：25.6 厘米

底径：6.9 厘米

Pottery *hu* pot with tubular lugs

Shang dynasty

1600 – 1046 B.C.E.

Height: 25.6 cm

Base diameter: 6.9 cm

泥质黑陶，陶胎为灰色，表层为黑色。圆口，略外侈，微束颈，腹深稍鼓，圈足较高、外撇。口上覆插盖，盖呈滑轮状。颈附双竖耳，颈、腹饰弦纹数道，腹下部与圈足界限明显。器壁较薄，内外壁留有明显的轮制旋削和手工批削痕迹。造型规整秀丽、端庄典雅，为商代晚期典型器物。

本品经热释光测定最后烧制年代距今4100—2700 年。

Black earthenware with a gray paste underneath a black surface. The vessel has a flared mouth with a pulley-shaped stopper, a slightly constricted neck flanked by a pair of vertical tubular lugs, a deep belly and a splayed ring-foot. The neck and the belly are encircled by several rounds of incised lines. The wall is rather thin. Distinct wheel marks and scrape marks are visible on both the interior and exterior walls. This vessel is a representative example of the pottery from the late Shang period.

Thermoluminescence test shows that the last firing date of this piece was 4100 to 2700 years before present.

78

灰黑陶大口山形纹尊

商

公元前 1600—前 1046 年

高：26.5 厘米

**Grayish-black pottery *zun* vessel
with mountain motif**

Shang dynasty

1600 – 1046 B.C.E.

Height: 26.5 cm

泥质灰黑陶，质细腻。大口外卷，深腹，
器呈直筒形，腹下内收，高圈足。腹体
上、中、下刻三组连续的三角山形纹带，
山形纹上下方各以弦线相连，纹带内相
对各贴六组圆突和竖泥条作饰。

本品与同类青铜器器形相似（附图 2），
是商代晚期陶器精品。

河南安阳出土有相似器物，现藏安阳市博
物馆。

美国纽约大都会博物馆收藏有一件年代、
外形和纹饰与本品相似的器物。

Grayish-black earthenware with a fine
paste. The vessel has a wide and flared
mouth and a deep cylindrical belly and
a tall ring-foot. The body is decorated
by three bands of mountain motif. The
top and bottom bands are affixed with
alternating disc-like studs and vertical clay
strips with serrated edges.

This shape of this vessel is similar to
contemporaneous bronzes (Fig. 2). It is a
fine example of late Shang pottery.

A similar vessel has been unearthed from
Anyang, Henan province. It is now in
the collection of the Anyang Municipal
Museum.

A vessel of similar period, shape and
decoration is in the collection of the Asian
Art Museum of San Francisco, USA.

附图 2　河南安阳郭庄出土亚址尊（商）

Fig. 2 *Yazhi* bronze *zun* unearthed at Guozhuang in Anyang,
Henan (Shang dynasty)

79

绳纹黑陶甗

商

公元前 1600—前 1046 年

高：34.3 厘米

口径：21.3 厘米

Black pottery *yan* steamer with cord motif

Shang dynasty

1600 – 1046 B.C.E.

Height: 34.3 cm

Mouth diameter: 21.3 cm

灰黑陶。口缘微外撇，颈内凹，深腹细腰，附三袋状空足。器由上部的甑和下部的鬲相接而成，甑、鬲相通，外壁相接处以一圈泥条加固。外壁满饰绳纹，内壁满布修刮时留下的细密刷纹。胎质坚硬，烧成火候较高。本品线条优美、做工规整、稳重得体、有很高的艺术价值。

Grayish-black earthenware with a rather high-fired hard paste. The vessel has a slightly flared mouth, a constricted neck, a narrow waist and a deep belly supported by three hollow baggy legs. The shape is formed by fitting a *zeng* cauldron on top of a *li* tripod, the joint being luted and reinforced on the outside by clay strips. The exterior surface is densely covered with cord motif while the interior shows fine brush marks from scraping and trimming. This vessel is noted for its harmonious shape, elegant lines, meticulous craftsmanship and bold construction.

绳纹三足瓮

商

公元前 1600—前 1046 年

高：40.8 厘米

口径：22.2 厘米

Three-legged pottery jar with cord motif

Shang dynasty

1600 – 1046 B.C.E.

Height: 40.8 cm

Mouth diameter: 22.2 cm

夹砂灰陶，坚硬致密。口缘贴一圈附加堆纹。中腹圆鼓呈球形，腹下内收成圆裆，承以三实足。器身遍饰绳纹，绳纹细密规整。器体中部刮削出宽条纹带两道，增添了装饰效果。全器体大、圆浑、比例适中，说明陶工对材料的选择及对烧造技术的掌握已达很高水平。

Sand-tempered gray pottery with a hard and dense paste. The exterior mouth rim is reinforced with a strip of clay. The body has a drum belly and a rounded bottom supported by three solid legs. The entire surface is impressed with cord motif. Two broad bands have been scraped out as decoration. The size and proportion of the vessel are proof that the potters' skills in material selection and firing technique had already reached a high level of sophistication.

81

绳纹单柄壶

商

公元前 1600—前 1046 年

高：14.1 厘米

阔：13.9 厘米

长：17.2 厘米

Pottery jug with overhead-handle and cord motif

Shang dynasty

1600 – 1046 B.C.E.

Height: 14.1 cm

Width: 13.9 cm

Length: 17.2 cm

浅灰白陶。胎薄，质坚硬。大喇叭形口与壶腹相通，相对一侧置小喇叭形口，与壶腹并不相通，大小口以扁平拱形柄相连。短颈，圆鼓腹，腹和柄上拍印绳纹。右侧腹中偏下方刻一"◻◻"形云雷纹饰。

云雷纹可能是由旋涡纹发展而来。夏、商早、中期，西周，春秋，战国的灰陶、印纹硬陶和原始青瓷上，云雷纹是主要纹饰。

1961 年湖北汉阳出土一件夹砂红陶雷电击人纹陶拍，其方形雷纹与本品之云雷纹相似。

Grayish white pottery with a thin and hard paste. A strap-handle arches overhead between two trumpet-shaped mouths above short necks. Only the larger mouth is connected to the cavity of the vessel. Impressed cord marks are found on the handle and the bulbous belly. A squared spiral is incised on the lower belly on the right side of the jug. The design first appeared in the late Neolithic period and is probably a variation of the spiral motif.

Commonly referred to as *yunleiwen* (cloud-and-thunder pattern), it is the main motif on gray pottery, high-fired stamped pottery and proto-celadon of the Xia, early Shang, mid Shang and Western Zhou dynasties as well as the Spring and Autumn and Warring States periods.

In 1961, thunder pattern similar to the cloud-and-thunder pattern on this jug is found on a pottery paddle in Hanyang, Hubei province.

82

红陶双耳大口罐
寺洼文化
约公元前 1350 年前后
高：45 厘米

Red pottery jar with large mouth
Siwa culture
Circa 1350 B.C.E.
Height: 45 cm

夹砂红陶。马鞍形大口，束颈，上腹圆鼓，向下急收，小平底。口肩间置弧形竖耳一对。全器光素无纹，打磨光滑。器身沾有数块黑彩斑。胎泥颇细腻，器壁较厚。寺洼文化罐出土甚多，但多为小件器物。本品造型优美、线条流畅，为寺洼文化艺术珍品。

寺洼文化因首先发现于甘肃省临洮县寺洼山遗址而得名，其双耳罐以马鞍形器口最具代表性。可将本品与图录 85 号对照了解。

Sand-tempered red earthenware. The jar has a large saddle-like mouth, a constricted neck and a bulbous belly that tapers drastically to a small flat base. A pair of vertical loop handles arches from the neck to the shoulders. The entire vessel is devoid of decorative motif. The surface has been highly burnished to a smooth and lustrous finish. There are several dark patches on the vessel. It has a refined paste and a thick body. Many jars have been uncovered from the Siwa sites but the majority of them are quite small. This jar is a rarity among Siwa pottery.

The Siwa culture was first discovered at the Siwa site in Lintao, Gansu province. Saddle-like mouths are a characteristic of these jars with double-handles. This jar and Cat. No. 85 can be studied side by side.

83

灰陶双耳鬲

辛店文化

公元前 1000 年前后

高：10.4 厘米

Gray pottery *li* tripod

Xindian culture

Circa 1000 B.C.E.

Height: 10.4 cm

夹砂灰陶。侈口，束颈，颈腹分界不明显，小圆底，下承三个袋足。颈腹间置环状耳两个，口缘下、耳上和颈间贴附加堆纹。袋足上有火炙残留痕迹。此类器物是先民广泛使用的炊具，遗址出土较多，但造型朴实典雅且保存完好的较少。

辛店文化因发现于甘肃临洮辛甸而得名（1924 年由瑞典考古学家安特生发现，后其《甘肃考古记》一书中将辛甸误译为辛店，其后沿用"辛店文化"之名），是西北地区青铜时代一支重要的文化遗存。

Sand-tempered gray earthenware. The vessel has a flared mouth, a constricted neck that joins smoothly with the belly and a small rounded base supported by three baggy legs. A pair of loop handles arches between the neck and the belly. The exterior mouth rim, the handles and the neck are decorated with appliqué motifs. Fire marks are visible on the baggy legs. This type of vessels was probably used as cooking utensils.

The Xindian culture was first discovered by the Swedish archaeologist Johan Andersson in 1924 at Xindian in Lintao, Gansu province. The Xindian culture is a Bronze Age culture that developed in Gansu and Qinghai in northwest China.

84

红陶双耳鬲

辛店文化

公元前 1000 年前后

高：14.7 厘米

Red pottery *li* tripod

Xindian culture

Circa 1000 B.C.E.

Height: 14.7 cm

夹砂红陶。广口、口缘外侈、束颈。颈腹分界不明显，颈腹间两侧装环耳一对。下装袋足三个，袋圆鼓、丰盈如乳房，足端呈圆锥状，如乳头。口缘外侧、双耳、袋足腹间均贴附加堆纹作饰。在灯光照射下，器表可见金色的闪光。用肉眼或 10 倍放大镜观察，可发现一些深色和黑色的物质，应是有意混入夹砂胎泥内的珍珠贝的细末和颗粒，经光线照射后发出反射光。本品制作精细，器形古朴典雅，有很高的艺术和欣赏价值。

Sand-tempered red earthenware. The vessel has a wide mouth with flared rim, a constricted neck that joins smoothly with the belly, a pair of loop handles arching between the neck and the belly and three udder-shaped baggy legs. The exterior mouth rim, the handles and the neck are decorated with appliqué motifs. Under 10x magnification, the golden sparkles on the surface are actually made up of dark black particles. They are probably pulverized or granular mother-of-pearl purposely mixed into the sand-tempered paste to make it glitter.

85

马鞍形口双耳罐

辛店文化

公元前 1000 年前后

高：44.7 厘米

底径：10.6 厘米

Painted pottery jar with saddle-shaped mouth

Xindian culture

Circa 1000 B.C.E.

Height: 44.7 cm

Base diameter: 10.6 cm

橙红陶。马鞍形口，束颈，球形腹，下腹收敛，小平底。口、肩间置弧形竖耳一对。颈部饰紫红黑纹带一周，下绘红地黑边双勾曲纹和太阳纹直达上腹部，双勾曲纹中间有下垂波纹两道。此罐色彩鲜艳，体形硕大又不失秀丽，为不可多得的辛店文化遗物。

本品描画的双勾曲纹代表羊的双角，太阳纹是羊的眼睛，下垂的波纹是羊的胡子、颈周的红黑带是围在羊脖子上的编织带。羊是羌族崇拜的主要神灵，对于古代居于甘肃和四川北部的羌族人来说可能带有族徽的意义。辛店文化遗址出土的很多陶器，包括大双耳罐上都有这种双勾纹和太阳纹装饰。

Red earthenware. The jar has a constricted neck, an undulated mouth rim, a swelling belly that tapers to a small flat base and a pair of handles arching from the rim to the shoulders. Bands of maroon and black encircle the neck. The upper body is painted with sun motifs enclosed by sickle-shaped motifs in black on red ground and parted by two vertical wavy lines. This jar is a rarity among Xindian pottery.

The sickle-shaped motif represents the horns of a ram, the sun motifs the ram's eyes and the vertical wavy lines the beard. The red and black bands around the neck of the jar represent the braided collar around the ram's neck. The ram was among the major deities of tribal worship. This motif can be viewed as the tribal emblem of the Qiang people dwelling in Gansu and northern Sichuan. Many artifacts have been unearthed from Xindian culture sites including large jars with double handles and vessels with sickle-shaped and sun motifs.

86

旋涡纹彩陶大罐

辛店文化唐汪类型

公元前 1000 年前后

高：68.8 厘米

Large painted pottery jar with spiral motif

Tangwang type, Xindian culture

Circa 1000 B.C.E.

Height: 68.8 cm

泥质橙黄陶。大口微侈，微束颈，颈肩分界清晰，腹圆鼓深广，小圜底。肩、腹两侧各置扁竖环耳一对。胎体厚重。口缘到下腹施红色陶衣，以双描法用黑彩线在器身四周绘连续旋涡纹三组，颈部饰云纹和变体鸟形纹。由旋涡纹组成的图案生动严密、气势磅礴，如巨浪翻腾，有极强的律动感。本品造型粗犷雄伟，古朴浑厚，体形巨大，不破裂不歪斜，说明当时制陶工艺已达很高水平。

唐汪类型因 1956 年于甘肃省东乡族自治县唐汪川山神遗址首次发现而得名，其彩陶以生动凌厉的旋涡纹著称。

Buff earthenware. The jar has a wide and slightly flared mouth, a slightly constricted neck, a bulbous belly and a small rounded base. The body is thick and heavy. A pair of tubular lugs flanks the shoulders and a second pair the belly. The surface is coated with red slip from below the mouth to the lower belly. The neck is painted with cloud motif and stylized birds. Three registers of continuous spirals encompass the body. This colossal jar is a rarity among late Neolithic pottery.

Tangwang type culture was first discovered in 1956 at Tangwangchuan, in Dongxiang autonomous county, Gansu province. Tangwang type painted pottery is known for its spiral motifs.

87

动物纹彩陶罐

辛店文化姬家川类型

公元前 1000 年前后

高：31.5 厘米

底径：9 厘米

Painted pottery jar with animal motifs

Jijiachuan type, Xindian culture

Circa 1000 B.C.E.

Height: 31.5 cm

Base diameter: 9 cm

夹砂浅黄陶，质较粗糙。器身中部置双系，小平底。胎体厚重。施米黄色陶衣。口缘下、肩和腹部，以黑、红褐彩分别绘画曲折纹和菱纹，间饰动物纹两只、变体鸟纹和双短线纹。动物身细长，双耳，长尾，细长脚，似为马或鹿。下腹部以竖纹六组作饰。

辛店文化由于农业和畜牧业的产生和发展，器物上有些会带有动物纹样，如犬纹、鸟纹、羊纹、鹿纹、马纹、熊纹、蜥蜴纹等。

Sand-tempered buff pottery. The jar has a thick and heavy body and a small flat base. A pair of loop lugs is attached to the belly. The body is coated with buff slip. The outer mouth rim, the shoulders and the belly are decorated with zigzag and lozenge designs painted in black and red. The space between the decorative bands is adorned with two animals, a stylized bird and short double-striations. The animals look like they could either be horses or deer. The lower belly is painted with six groups of vertical stripes.

The depiction of animals on Xindian culture pottery appeared at the same time when agriculture and livestock raising began to develop.

88

黄陶几何纹杯

西周

公元前 1046—前 771 年

高：10.8 厘米

口径：17.4 厘米

Buff pottery cup with geometric motif

Western Zhou dynasty

1046 – 771 B.C.E.

Height: 10.8 cm

Mouth diameter: 17.4 cm

泥质橙黄陶。侈口、口缘外翻、上刻弦纹三道。微束腰、平底、底微内凹。口缘与腹下部置宽大扁形环耳，上饰弦纹八条。耳顶贴卷云纹饰四个。腹上部外壁刻回字纹几何图形一周。下腹部饰弦纹九圈，最下一圈出边，与环耳下端相接，可能用于承接外溢的酒水，以免弄污衣服和地面。本品造型古朴粗犷，纹饰丰富，为不可多得的西周遗物。

Buff earthenware. This cup has a flared mouth with a broad everted rim decorated with three rounds of incised lines, a waisted body and a flat and slightly recessed base. A wide strap handle with eight vertical incised lines connects the mouth rim to the bottom of the cup. The top of the handle is adorned with four appliqué *ruyi* patterns. The upper half of the exterior wall is incised with a band of geometric frets. The lower wall is encircled by nine ribs. The raised edge near the bottom probably helped to prevent liquids from dripping down the side of the cup. This cup is a rare example of Western Zhou pottery.

89

红陶鐎斗

西周

公元前 1046—前 771 年

高：11.8 厘米

口径：10.8 厘米

Red pottery jar with handle

Western Zhou dynasty

1046 – 771 B.C.E.

Height: 11.8 cm

Mouth diameter: 10.8 cm

泥质红陶，质颇坚。侈口、圆唇、束颈、
斜肩、鼓腹、小圜底。器身拍印绳纹，
肩腹间一侧置中空圆筒形柄。外底有
旋纹。底和下腹部有火炙痕迹，说明是
炊具。

Red earthenware with a rather hard paste.
The jar has a flared mouth with rounded
lip, a constricted neck, steep shoulders,
a bulbous belly and a small rounded
base. The body is impressed with cord
motif. A cylindrical handle is affixed on
the shoulder. Wheel marks are visible on
the base. The fire marks on the base and
the lower belly indicate that the jar was
probably used as a cooking vessel.

红陶鐎斗

90

印纹硬陶之字纹盂

西周

公元前 1046—前 771 年

高：8 厘米

High-fired pottery basin with zigzag motif

Western Zhou dynasty

1046 – 771 B.C.E.

Height: 8 cm

泥质灰陶。颈斜呈弧线状，宽肩，鼓扁腹，底宽大而平、呈圆饼状。肩腹拍印之字纹、颈周满饰弦纹。肩两侧置双圆条耳各一。胎坚硬、粗糙、厚重。烧成火候过高，器身内外和底部有气泡破裂形成的凹坑。本品造型优美、纹饰豪迈粗犷，是西周时期的典型器物。

西周印纹硬陶纹饰简约，只是在陶器表面以齿形工具刻划水波纹、弦纹、之字纹或其他几何图纹。

Gray earthenware. The vessel has a neck that slopes towards the shoulders, a compressed bulbous belly and a flat disc-like base. The neck is decorated with closely spaced incised lines. The shoulders and belly are impressed with zigzag motif. A pair of loop lugs flanks the shoulders. The paste is hard and coarse in grain and the body is thick and heavy. Pits are visible on the interior, the exterior and the base of the basin. This vessel is a typical example of Western Zhou pottery.

Western Zhou pottery is simply decorated. The exterior surface is usually incised with wave, zigzag or geometric motifs.

灰陶鬲

西周

公元前 1046—前 771 年

高：21.5 厘米

Gray pottery *li*

Western Zhou dynasty

1046 – 771 B.C.E.

Height: 21.5 cm

泥质灰陶。口圆，体呈方形，平肩，直腹到底、底平。底四方角呈圆锥状作足，外底呈内拱形。肩上画斜纹线，腹拍粗绳纹，下方绳纹较粗并凸起，由下向上交叉排列。上方绳纹由下伸向两侧，本品造型新颖、写实性强、应是炊具。

Gray earthenware. The *li* has a circular mouth, flat shoulders, a squarish body and a flat bottom supported at the corners by four conical legs. The legs are set wide apart forming a big arch in between them. The body of the *li* is impressed with a variety of cord marks. This jar was used as a cooking utensil.

92

红陶绳纹鬲

西周

公元前 1046—前 771 年

高：16 厘米

口径：18.8 厘米

Red pottery *li* with cord motif

Western Zhou dynasty

1046 – 771 B.C.E.

Height: 16 cm

Mouth diameter: 18.8 cm

泥质红陶。短颈外侈，鼓腹斜收到底，底部等距离隆起三个矮锥状突作底足。小圜底，底微内凹。腹中部起粗凸弦纹一道，把肩、腹部分隔。肩上满饰细弦纹线，腹部拍印竖向粗绳纹。

Red earthenware. The *li* has a short neck, steep shoulders, a bulbous belly and a small rounded base with a recessed center supported by three short conical legs. A thick rib around the mid-section of the body divides the shoulder from the belly. The shoulder is covered with closely spaced incised lines. The belly is impressed with thick vertical cord motif.

93

印纹硬陶水纹罐

西周

公元前 1046—前 771 年

高：17.2 厘米

High-fired pottery jar with impressed wave motif

Western Zhou dynasty

1046 – 771 B.C.E.

Height: 17.2 cm

泥质灰陶。小平口，小唇缘，斜肩，鼓腹，平底。上腹两侧贴双股扭绳纹耳一对。肩光素无纹，肩腹交接处剔出一周凹弦纹，使肩腹呈梯级状。腹满饰水纹线，纹线粗细不一，起伏不定。胎质细腻，坚硬，烧成温度较高。本品做工精细，口上的小唇缘、肩腹上的凹弦纹和腹部的水波纹共同构成了一件优雅的艺术品。

Gray earthenware. The vessel has a small flat mouth with slightly raised lip, sloping shoulders, a bulbous belly and a flat base. A pair of lugs formed by twisting together two rope-like clay strips is affixed to the shoulders. The junction between the shoulder and belly is gouged out to a stepped profile. The shoulder is devoid of decorative motif. The belly is decorated by undulating lines of uneven thickness. The paste is fine and hard and the firing temperature relatively high.

94

印纹硬陶大耳罐

西周

公元前 1046—前 771 年

高：17.4 厘米

High-fired pottery jar with lugs and impressed motif

Western Zhou dynasty

1046 – 771 B.C.E.

Height: 17.4 cm

泥质灰陶。整个罐可以看作一幅立体画作：腹中部粗水纹线下的纹饰寓意岸上景物在水中的倒影，相连的菱形纹是为山，菱形内相间的横和直纹线是树木。粗水纹线上方的细水波纹线是河流或湖泊，肩腹弦线上方是岸上陆地。弧状绳纹耳下端串成长条凹凸状，呈椭圆形，可能寓意一粒一粒的蟾蜍卵附着在水中的树枝上（蟾蜍产的卵是一串串连在一起的）。根据形状，也可能是寓意地球上最古老的生物之一"鲎"，也叫"马蹄蟹"，有椭圆的外形，连着一条小尾巴，中国长江口东南沿岸有分布。陶工就这样赋予了陶瓷生命力。

从胎泥、造型、装饰和画意来看，本品与图录 93 号相似。

Gray earthenware. The vessel depicts a scene on the seashore. Rows of undulating lines represent the ripples near the shoreline. The geometric patterns below it are the reflection of mountains and trees in the water. The lozenge-shaped pattern represents the mountains and the horizontal and vertical striations inside them the trees. The ends of the rope-like lugs have extensions that resemble long chains of toad eggs laid near the water's edge. The lug is shaped like a horseshoe crab (*Limulidae*), one of the oldest surviving sea creatures with a horseshoe-shaped carapace and a rigid and pointy tail that dwells in and around shallow waters. These creatures are found along the southeast coast of Changjiang Delta in China.

Judging by the paste, the shape and the decorative motifs, this vessel and Cat. No. 93 could have been produced during the same period, at the same kiln and possibly by the same potter.

95

几何印纹硬陶罍

西周

公元前 1046—前 771 年

高：50.5 厘米

High-fired pottery with impressed geometric motifs

Western Zhou dynasty

1046 – 771 B.C.E.

Height: 50.5 cm

泥质褐陶。口缘外翻，短颈、大圆腹，小圆底。肩腹部拍印三周云雷纹，除肩部饰曲折纹外，其余部分间以回纹到底。胎质较硬，胎体较重，器表呈紫褐和紫黑色。烧成温度较高。内壁留有拍印时用手抵着内壁的指痕和修刮痕。本品装饰华丽，印纹深邃，保存完整，是一件十分珍贵的艺术品。体形如此硕大的器物烧成而不变形，可见当时对胎泥的炼制和烧造技术的掌握已达相当高的水平。

本品经热释光测定最后烧制年代距今 2800—1800 年。

Brown earthenware. It has a mouth with everted rim, a short neck, a bulbous belly and a small rounded base. Three bands of impressed cloud-and-thunder motif encircle the area on the belly. The rest of the body, except for the shoulders that are decorated with zigzag motif, is covered with fret motif down to the edge of the foot. The vessel has a rather hard and heavy body fired to a relatively high temperature with a purplish-brown and purplish-black surface. Impression marks are visible on the interior wall formed by the supporting hand while patterns are paddle-stamped onto the exterior surface.

Thermoluminescence test shows that the last firing date of this piece was 2800 to 1800 years before present.

96

印纹硬陶罐

西周

公元前 1046—前 771 年

高：42 厘米

口径：19.5 厘米

High-fired pottery jar with impressed motif

Western Zhou dynasty

1046 – 771 B.C.E.

Height: 42 cm

Mouth diameter: 19.5 cm

泥质灰陶。侈口，唇缘外卷，缩颈，肩腹丰满圆鼓，小圜底。颈饰弦纹数道，肩、腹间饰三周曲折纹，外壁其余部分拍印回字纹到底部。印纹深邃，棱边锐利。胎呈黑褐色，外形工整，胎薄，烧结程度高，叩击时发出近乎金属的铛铛声，以当时的技术来说，极少数器物能达此境界。器表外壁可见凹凸不平及重叠的拍印痕，器内壁有拍印时支垫留下的印窝。本品为江南印纹硬陶的典型器物。

西周是印纹硬陶发展的繁盛期，烧成温度高，质硬，陶色紫褐或黑褐，多组合纹。

1974 年上海青浦墓出土有相似器物。

本品经热释光测定最后烧制年代距今约 2400 年。

Gray earthenware with a dark brown paste. The jar has an everted rim, a constricted short neck, rounded shoulders, a bulbous belly and a small rounded base. The neck is encircled by several ribs. The shoulder and the belly are densely impressed with key-fret motif interrupted by three bands of herringbone pattern. The vessel has a well-balanced shape, a highly vitrified paste and a thin body that gives a metallic sound when knocked with the knuckle. Given the technology of the time, vessels of such quality are extremely rare. The impressed motifs are rugged and overlapping in some places. Impression marks are visible on the interior wall formed by the supporting hand while patterns are paddle-stamped onto the exterior surface. This jar is a representative example of the high-fired stamped pottery found in the Jiangnan region.

Stamped pottery with geometric motifs flourished in southern China during the Western Zhou period. They have a hard paste of purplish-brown or dark brown color. The patterns or combination of patterns, are sharp-edged and deeply impressed onto the surface.

A similar artifact was unearthed in 1974 from a tomb in Qingpu, Shanghai.

Thermoluminescence test shows that the last firing date of this piece was around 2400 years before present.

灰陶水纹钵

春秋

公元前 770—前 476 年

高：10 厘米

Gray pottery pot with wave motif

Spring and Autumn period

770 – 476 B.C.E.

Height: 10 cm

泥质灰陶，胎质细腻。短颈、圆肩、鼓腹、底平微内凹。肩和腹部饰水波纹带三道，以两道素纹带分隔，下腹光素。内壁和内底有螺旋形纹线，外壁底留有绳条切割留下的弧形纹线。外底表层经磨损后露出的胎呈红色，是胎泥未烧熟所致。本器圆浑丰满、波纹如被风吹拂、起伏不定、极具动感。水波纹粗细有别，腹径最大的地方较粗，肩部的较细，合乎人类视觉观感，体现了先人敏锐的观察力。

Gray earthenware with a fine paste. The vessel has a short neck, rounded shoulders, a bulbous belly and a flat and slightly recessed base. The shoulders and belly are decorated with three bands of wave motif divided by two plain zones. The area above the foot is also devoid of decoration. The interior wall and bottom are lined with wheel marks. The outer base shows a curve mark resulted from severing the vessel off the wheel with a cord. A red paste resulted from under firing shows through the base where the surface is worn. The rounded form of the vessel imparts a sense of fullness.

The wavy lines suggest water waves rocking gently in a light breeze, generating a strong sense of momentum. The waves are uneven in thickness; thickest around the maximum diameter of the body and thinnest around the shoulders. This is in line with what we actually see in space as the waves curl more near the shore. A keen observation of nature underlies the ancient potter's creative process.

98

印纹陶扉棱罐

春秋

公元前 770—前 476 年

高：41 厘米

口径：10.3 厘米

底径：17.7 厘米

Pottery jar with serrate flanges and impressed motif

Spring and Autumn period

770 – 476 B.C.E.

Height: 41 cm

Mouth diameter: 10.3 cm

Base diameter: 17.7 cm

泥质褐红陶。小口斜向外翻，短颈微束，斜肩，罐体修长，造型酷似宋代的梅瓶。肩部等距堆塑三条扉棱直达下腹部，扉棱顶拱起成耳，耳上端左右贴 "S" 形纹饰。肩腹间饰云雷纹一圈，外壁拍印方格纹到底。胎体较厚重，表面呈紫褐色，烧制温度较低。

本品的扉棱特别长，呈曲节状，且在扉棱顶部贴 "S" 形纹饰，将扉棱塑造为一条身形长长、有两颗凸出的又圆又大眼球的蛇或爬虫，使器物除了实用价值外还增加了艺术性，突显了先民们无限的创意和丰富的想象力。

Brownish-red earthenware. The jar has a small mouth with an everted and beveled rim, a slightly constricted short neck, broad shoulders and an elongated body. This jar is in the shape of a *meiping* vase of the Song period. Three serrated flanges cascade down the side from the shoulders to the lower belly; their upper end arches into a loop lug decorated by an S-shaped ornament. The exterior surface is impressed with check motif except around the turn of the shoulders and the belly where it is impressed with cloud-and-thunder motif. This jar has a rather thickly potted body

fired to a relatively low temperature with a purplish-brown surface.

The unusual length of the serrate flanges and the S-shaped end ornaments on this jar probably carry some special implications. These flanges were apparently borrowed from contemporaneous bronzes but extra decorative details such as bulging round eyes were added to suggest a snake or reptile. The infinite creativity and rich imagination of the potters are exemplified in this superlative piece of art.

99

印纹陶瓶

春秋

公元前 770—前 476 年

高：21.5 厘米

口径：5.5 厘米

底径：9.3 厘米

Pottery vase with impressed motif

Spring and Autumn period

770 – 476 B.C.E.

Height: 21.5 cm

Mouth diameter: 5.5 cm

Base diameter: 9.3 cm

泥质褐红陶。小口，平沿外翻，短颈，丰肩，腹下部渐收成平底。器体间隔拍印多层纹饰，肩部有曲折纹和云雷纹，腹部满饰回字纹到底，以一周云雷纹带把回字纹分成上下两部分。灰胎，烧成温度较低。胎体较薄而均匀，内壁见轮旋纹痕。

本品经热释光测定最后烧制年代距今2500—1700 年。

Brownish-red earthenware. The vessel has a small mouth with flat everted rim, a short neck, broad shoulders and a flat base. The surface is decorated with bands of impressed patterns. The shoulders are adorned with zigzag and cloud-and-thunder motifs. The upper the belly is decorated with a band of key-frets above a broader band of cloud-and-thunder motif. The rest of the body down to the foot is covered with key-frets. The gray paste appears rather thin but even in thickness. Wheel marks are visible on the interior wall.

Thermoluminesence test shows that the last firing date of this piece was 2500 to 1700 years before present.

100

印纹陶双系扁壶

春秋

公元前 770—前 476 年

高：38 厘米

口径：10.7 厘米

底径：22 厘米

**Flat pottery flask with
impressed motifs**

Spring and Autumn period

770 – 476 B.C.E.

Height: 38 cm

Mouth diameter: 10.7 cm

Base diameter: 22 cm

泥质褐红陶。小口斜外翻、短颈微束、肩平、腹大于肩、圜底。体呈扁圆状、腹底分界不明显。肩两侧置绳纹系各一。器体拍印方格纹到底，腹中部置一周云雷纹，把方格纹分成上下两部分。胎呈褐红色、胎体厚重、烧成温度较低。

Brownish-red earthenware. The vessel has a small mouth with everted rim, a short and slightly constricted neck, leveled shoulders, a flat oval-shaped body and a rounded base. A pair of rope-like lugs is affixed to the shoulders. Except for the band of cloud-and-thunder motif around its mid-section, the entire exterior surface of the vessel is impressed with check motif. The paste is brownish-red in color. The thick and heavy body was fired to a low temperature.

101

印纹硬陶席纹罐

春秋
公元前 770—前 476 年
高：18.6 厘米

**High-fired pottery jar with
impressed mat motif**
Spring and Autumn period
770 – 476 B.C.E.
Height: 18.6 cm

泥质灰陶。大口，口缘边向内斜，腹圆鼓，
平底。口、腹间的肩窄且微凹，上饰水
波纹。肩部前后对称贴如"Ω"形纹饰
一对，模仿青铜器上的饕餮衔环。全器
拍印席纹到底。胎色泛青，质细腻、坚
硬。本品体形丰满规整，纹饰朴实大方，
为春秋时期典型器物。

Gray earthenware with a fine and hard
paste of greenish color. The vessel has a
large incurved mouth, narrow shoulders,
a bulbous belly and a flat base. The
shoulders are decorated with wave motif.
A pair of Omega-shaped appliqués adorns
the shoulders where the *taotie* ring-masks
would have been on bronze vessels. The
entire exterior surface is impressed with
mat motif. This jar is a typical example
from the Spring and Autumn period.

102

黑陶弦纹盖盂

战国

公元前 475—前 221 年

高：16.3 厘米

底径：9.1 厘米

Black pottery lidded bowl with grooved design

Warring States period

475 – 221 B.C.E.

Height: 16.3 cm

Base diameter: 9.1 cm

泥质黑陶。器由身和盖合成、子母口、圈足。全器满饰弦纹、弦纹棱边锐利、很有节奏感。全器打磨光滑亮丽，乍看之下宛如色泽明亮的漆器。整体匀称、和谐、造型简单但不失典雅。

Black earthenware. The entire exterior surface of the set is decorated with rounds of grooved design with sharp edges. The highly burnished surface is comparable to the smooth and lustrous surface of lacquerware. The symmetry of the overall vessel imparts a sense of balance and harmony.

103

灰陶匜
战国
公元前 475—前 221 年
高：8.5 厘米
长：22.5 厘米

Gray pottery *yi* basin
Warring States period
475 – 221 B.C.E.
Height: 8.5 cm
Length: 22.5 cm

泥质灰陶。浅椭圆形器身，底微拱，下承四足。口缘一侧有槽状流，相对一侧置兽首环柄。口缘下刻云雷纹一周，其下饰凹弦纹两道。本品与战国时期兽首青铜匜造型一致（附图 3）。

Gray earthenware. The oval-shaped vessel has a slightly domed base supported on four legs. One end of the mouth has a trough-shaped spout and the other a loop handle with animal-head design. The outer mouth rim is carved with a band of cloud-and-thunder pattern bounded by double incised lines. This vessel is similar in shape to the bronze *yi* from the Warring States period (Fig. 3).

附图 3　湖北擂鼓墩 1 号墓出土曾侯乙匜（战国）
Fig. 3　*Yi* basin unearthed from Marquis Yi of Zeng tomb No. 1 at Leigudun in Hubei (Warring States period)

104

灰陶兽耳三足壶

战国

公元前 475—前 221 年

高：20.4 厘米

口径：11.9 厘米

Three-legged gray pottery jar with animal design

Warring States period

475 – 221 B.C.E.

Height: 20.4 cm

Mouth diameter: 11.9 cm

泥质灰陶。口平外翻，粗颈微束，斜肩，圆鼓腹收到底，平底，下附三锥状足。肩对称贴回首立兽四只。腹上部起棱线纹四道，下腹以白彩绘倒置山形纹一周，间隙用红彩填以正山形纹。本品体形不大，但带有战国时期大型器的霸气。

本品器形与同期青铜器一致。美国旧金山亚洲艺术博物馆收藏有相似器物。

Gray earthenware. The vessel has a flat everted rim, a slightly constricted thick neck, sloping shoulders and a globular belly that tapers to a flat base supported by three conical legs. Four ribs encircle the upper belly while the lower belly is painted in white with a band of inverted mountain motif. The space between the mountains motif is painted in red with upward pointing peaks. Four animal-shaped handles are set on the shoulders. Despite its small size, the vessel has the majestic presence of a much larger jar like the grand vessels from the Warring States period.

This vessel is similar in shape to contemporaneous bronzes. A similar vessel is in the collection of the Asian Art Museum of San Francisco, USA.

灰陶荸荠尊

战国

公元前 475—前 221 年

高：23.8 厘米

Gray pottery *zun* vessel in the shape of a water chestnut

Warring States period

475 – 221 B.C.E.

Height: 23.8 cm

泥质灰陶。平缘外撇、粗颈、溜肩、直腹到底，器身似荸荠形，底平。颈肩间和肩腹间各饰一周箭头状锥刺纹。底边斜削一周，纹带棱边锐利整齐。腹中压印一方形印章，内印"田□私印"四字，应是物主姓名。整器丰满稳重，造型新颖。

Gray earthenware. The vessel has a mouth with flat everted rim, a thick neck, sloping shoulder, straight belly and a flat base. The body is shaped like a water chestnut. A band of pecked arrowhead motif encircles the junction of the neck and shoulders and a second band the upper belly. The vessel has a beveled base with sharp edges. The mid-section of the belly is impressed with a four-character square seal that reads, "*Tian X Si Yin*" which is likely the name of the owner of this vessel.

106

黑陶折腰钵

战国

公元前 475—前 221 年

高：13.6 厘米

口径：19.2 厘米

Black pottery basin of angular form

Warring States period

475 – 221 B.C.E.

Height: 13.6 cm

Mouth diameter: 19.2 cm

泥质黑陶。口平、束颈、溜肩、鼓腹急收到底。缘顶有凹棱一周，用于系绳。颈部磨光，肩上下刻双弦纹线两组，组间刻倒置山形纹饰八个。山形纹饰内和下腹部刻划竖直纹，寓意山上又高又笔直的林木。底平，上有席纹印痕。胎薄、细腻、坚硬，烧成温度较高。本品制作精美、线条流畅，质朴典雅，是难得的艺术珍品。

Black earthenware. The vessel has an everted mouth with flat rim, a constricted neck, sloping shoulders and a belly that tapers rapidly to the base. A grooved edge runs around the mouth rim. The undecorated neck is well burnished. The shoulders are decorated with a band of inverted mountain motif bounded on both sides by double lines. The vertical striations inside the mountain motif and on the belly represent trees. The imprint of a woven mat fabric is visible on the flat base. The refined, thin, dense and hard paste had been fired to a relatively high temperature.

107

黑陶山形纹罐

战国

公元前 475—前 221 年

高：38 厘米

口径：15.6 厘米

Black pottery jar with mountain motif

Warring States period

475 – 221 B.C.E.

Height: 38 cm

Mouth diameter: 15.6 cm

泥质黑陶。口平、颈微束、广肩缓收到底。缘顶四周起凹棱，用于系绳。肩部磨光，肩上下各有一组饰斜纹线的弦纹带，一窄一阔。两组纹带间刻倒置山形纹饰六个，山形纹内刻划斜直纹，寓意山坡上高高的林木。腹部到近底处压印短斜、直纹，寓意山腰下生长茂盛的灌木林和草本植物。底平，上有席纹印痕。胎薄，质坚、细腻，烧成温度较高。本品制作精细，是难得的艺术珍品。

本品胎泥、制作和装饰手法与图录 106 号近乎一致。

Black earthenware. The jar has an everted mouth with flat rim, a constricted neck, broad shoulders and a belly that tapers gradually to the base. A grooved edge runs around the mouth rim. The undecorated neck is well burnished. The top and bottom of the shoulders are decorated with a band of inverted mountain motif. The incised oblique striations inside the mountain motif represent trees. The entire belly down to the foot is impressed with short oblique striations to represent the

shrubs and lush vegetation found near the foot of the mountain.

Judging by the paste, workmanship and decorative style, this jar and Cat. No. 106 could have been produced during the same period, at the same kiln and possibly by the same potter.

108

弦纹三足茧形壶

战国

公元前 475—前 221 年

高：19.7—20.3 厘米

阔：15.8 厘米

长：27.8 厘米

Three-legged cocoon jar with vertical grooves

Warring States period

475 – 221 B.C.E.

Height: 19.7 – 20.3 cm

Width: 15.8 cm

Length: 27.8 cm

泥质灰陶，胎质坚硬。敞口、束颈，腹部较长，呈蚕茧形。底置三矮足，就算在不平的表面，三点一面也能保证壶身着地平稳。二前足较短，约在腹部中线前面，后足较高，在腹中线另一侧较后处，壶身向双足方约 15 度角倾斜。器身刻竖双弦纹六组，两端饰圆形弦纹数圈。全器打磨光滑，有明显垂直弦纹痕。

此器底足十分特别，可能是用于盛水或盛酒。壶身倾斜，则水或酒内的沉淀物会停留在一端，倾倒时不易随水或酒倒出。茧形壶出土很多，但此种造型比较少见。

Gray earthenware with a hard paste. The vessel has a flared mouth, a constricted neck and a cocoon-shaped belly. The belly is supported by three tiny legs, two shorter ones aligned on one side and a longer one on the other side. The three-leg design ensures the stability of the vessel even on uneven surfaces. The body of the jar effectively slopes forward about 15 degrees. The body is decorated with vertical grooves and the two ends concentric grooves. The entire jar is burnished and distinct wheel marks are visible on the surface.

The deliberately lopsided design allows the sediment in the water or wine inside the jar to settle at the lower end. A large number of cocoon jars have been excavated but examples of this kind are few.

109

红陶饕餮纹大瓦当

战国

公元前 475—前 221 年

高：17.7 厘米

直径：35.7 厘米

Large red pottery eaves tile with *taotie* motif from Yanxiadu

Warring States period

475 – 221 B.C.E.

Height: 17.7 cm

Diameter: 35.7 cm

泥质红陶，夹杂沙砾和贝砾。瓦当呈半圆形，瓦面模印双龙饕餮纹饰。双龙左右外翻作眉，龙口吐舌，眼大鼻大，狰狞威猛。纹深清晰，制作精美。顶有平凹槽一道。瓦当的直径通常是 15—25 厘米，本品则达到 35.7 厘米，可以想象承载这些大瓦的木椽构架多么巨大，燕国宫殿建筑物又是多么宏伟壮观。

战国时期，各诸侯国宫廷建筑大多使用瓦当，瓦当的造型和当面题材有明显的地方特色。有别于战国时期其他诸侯国，燕下都瓦当皆为半圆形，纹饰以饕餮纹最有代表性。商周时期，饕餮纹大量用于青铜器上，纹饰狰狞、凶恶、恐怖、神秘，象征奴隶主的绝对权威，用以震慑奴隶的反抗。贯穿整个燕国历史，饕餮纹一直被用作瓦当的主体纹饰，延续了商周青铜器饕餮纹遗风。尽管这些饕餮纹饰狰狞可怖，但仍表现出某种原始的、拙朴的美。

Pottery earthenware tempered with sand and shell grit. The semi-circular eaves tile has a *taotie* pattern on the front surmounted by a pair of dragons. Features of the mask include large eyes; stylized depictions of eyebrows, nose and ears; and the protuberant tongues of the dragons. The top of the eaves tile has a furrow with a flat bottom. The present example with a 35.7 cm diameter is a behemoth among Yanxiadu eaves tiles since the typical diameter is around 15 – 25 cm. One can imagine the size of the wooden rafters supporting them and the magnificence of the palatial architecture of the Yan State.

During the Warring States period, these tiles were widely used on the eaves of buildings of the aristocrats and feudal lords. Their shapes and decorative motifs have a regional distinctiveness. Unlike the eaves tiles found in other feudal states of this period, those from Yanxiadu are all semi-circular and mostly decorated with *taotie* motifs. The *taotie* motif is a type of monster mask. During the Shang and Zhou periods, they were widely used on ritual bronze vessels. These ferocious-looking and mysterious monster masks symbolized the absolute authority of the slave owners and were used to inspire fear in the hearts of the people. *Taotie* was the primary motif on eaves tiles throughout the history of the Yan State.

110

灰陶饕餮纹大瓦当

战国

公元前 475—前 221 年

直径：34 厘米

高：17.3 厘米

厚：3.9 厘米

Large grey pottery eaves tile with *taotie* motif from Yanxiadu

Warring States period

475 – 221 B.C.E.

Diameter: 34 cm

Height: 17.3 cm

Thickness: 3.9 cm

本品外形和纹饰与图录 109 号相同，只是本品为泥质灰陶。瓦顶上的平凹槽直达筒的尾部。体大，胎骨厚重，夹杂沙砾和贝砾。烧成温度较高，用指叩击瓦筒，发出铛铛响声。

燕下都是战国时期燕国的都城，遗址在今河北省易县都城东南 2.5 千米处。从燕下都瓦当可看到燕国与周王朝浓厚的历史渊源和文化艺术上的传承关系，也反映了燕下都都城建设的发达和经济文化的繁荣。其纹饰蕴藏的丰富内涵，对探索当时的文化艺术、审美情趣有重要的史料价值。

This piece is identical in shape and decoration to Cat. No. 109, except that it is fabricated from gray earthen clay and the furrow extends along the length of the semi-cylindrical form. The eaves tile is quite large, thickly molded and heavy. Sand and shell grits have been added to the clay to increase its strength. The firing temperature was relatively high. The semi-cylindrical form of the tile gives a clear sound when knocked with the knuckle.

Yanxiadu was the capital of the Yan State during the Warring States period. The site is located 2.5 km southeast of Yixian, Hebei province. Indications of the strong historical, artistic and cultural ties between the Yan State and the Zhou court can be gleaned from these artifacts. They are an important reference for studying the arts, the culture and the aesthetic conventions of the time period.

111

印纹硬陶绳络纹罍

战国

公元前 475—前 221 年

高：23.3 厘米

阔：30.3 厘米

口径：17.2 厘米

底径：17 厘米

High-fired pottery *lei* jar with appliqué net design

Warring States period

475 – 221 B.C.E.

Height: 23.3 cm

Width: 30.3 cm

Mouth diameter: 17.2 cm

Base diameter: 17 cm

附图 4　山西长治分水岭出土青铜绳络纹罍（战国）
Fig. 4 Bronze *lei* jar with net design unearthed at Fenshuiling in Chanzhi, Shanxi (Warring States period)

泥质灰陶。侈口，口缘外翻、薄唇、短颈、丰肩，肩和上腹向外鼓出，下腹渐收，大平底。胎薄而坚硬，高温烧成。在满饰拍印布纹的器体上覆以粗大绳索网纹。其粘贴网纹方法如下：先在颈肩及下腹近底处置凸弦纹线各一圈，然后用双股泥条扭成菱形纹及"十"字形接线，一个接一个粘贴上去，粘贴接口明显可见。这样把器身分为平行六周格，每周格之大小均按器身弧度比例和视觉感官而定，即上、下格较小，而腹中圆鼓部分格最大。比例之准确、手工之精细、造型之优美，可见两千多年前陶工之灵巧心思，有极高的艺术价值。

绳络纹盛行于春秋、战国。1972 年山西省长治县出土一件春秋青铜绳络纹罍，其造型及绳络纹饰与本器相似（附图 4 ）。

本品经热释光测定最后烧制年代距今约 2100 年。

大约 20 年前的一天，一间古玩店老板来电说有新货到，就是这件绳络纹罍。当我在古玩店内观看时，一位个子不高、瘦削、年约 60 多岁的男子一直在门外望着店内。后来古玩店老板告诉我，此人是一位日本著名的古玩商，在我离开后他就马上进店询问该绳络纹罍是否已售出，并提出转卖要求。古玩店老板跟他说这个藏家只买不卖的，不用问了。所以说购藏很讲运气，如果我迟到一步，这个罍或许已在日本藏家手里了。

Gray earthenware. The jar has a thinly potted and high-fired hard body, a flared mouth with a thin everted rim, a constricted neck, rounded shoulders and a bulging belly that tapers to a broad flat base. The vessel is decorated with an appliqué design of a knotted net against a ground of impressed textile motif. The net is created by piecing together vertical, horizontal and oblique segments of clay. The spacing of the net adjusts accordingly to its position on the jar to emphasize the contours of the vessel. The result is a tighter mesh at the top and bottom and a looser mesh in the middle.

A Warring States bronze *lei* jar of similar shape and decoration was unearthed in 1972 at Changzhi, Shanxi province (Fig. 4). Net motifs were popular among bronzes in northern China during the Spring and Autumn and Warring States periods.

Thermoluminescence test shows that the last firing date of this piece was around 2100 years before present.

One day around twenty years ago, the owner of an antique shop asked me to come by to see some new items. When I was examining this *lei* jar with net design inside his shop, I noticed that a lean, medium-height gentleman in his sixties was standing outside and gazing into the shop. Later, the owner told me this person was a famous antique dealer from Japan and after I left the shop he asked the owner whether the *lei* jar had already been sold to me and expressed his wish to purchase the jar from me. The owner told him that I only made purchases and never sold anything, and there was no use asking. The acquisition of antiques depends greatly on luck. If I had been late for a while, this *lei* jar would have gone into the hands of this Japanese collector.

112

印纹硬陶编织纹铺首罐

战国

公元前 475—前 221 年

高：27 厘米

底径：14.6 厘米

High-fired pottery jar with impressed wicker motif

Warring States period

475–221 B.C.E.

Height: 27 cm

Base diameter: 14.6 cm

泥质灰陶，呈浅紫褐色。口凹入成沟，可能为承放盖子。斜颈，丰肩，腹部上丰下渐收成小平底。肩两侧饰铺首，外肩到底足满饰拍印编织纹，纹饰清晰工整。通常此类罐不带铺首，纹饰精美的也较为少见。本品造型圆浑饱满、线条流畅秀美，根据胎和纹饰来看，当为战国晚期器物。

Gray earthenware of light purplish-brown color. The vessel has a sloping neck, broad shoulders and a bulbous belly that tapers gradually towards a small flat base. The groove surrounding the exterior mouth rim may have been used for holding a lid in place. A pair of animal-mask handles flanks the shoulders. The exterior surface is impressed with a highly detailed wicker motif. Animal-mask handles are quite rare on this kind of vessels. Judging from the paste and decorative motif, this jar should be dated to the late Warring States period.

113

印纹硬陶菊纹罐

战国

公元前 475—前 221 年

高：11 厘米

口径：10.1 厘米

High-fired pottery jar with impressed chrysanthemum motif

Warring States period

475 – 221 B.C.E.

Height: 11 cm

Mouth diameter: 10.1 cm

泥质浅红褐陶，质颇粗糙、坚硬。短颈、斜肩，鼓腹，平底。器由上下两部分黏合而成，内壁留有一周黏合痕。器身满拍印菊纹，纹饰规整。器表呈褐黑色，唇缘内外和腹下近底处呈深褐黑色，有龟裂纹，并有光泽，未知是否由于烧造时窑炉内空气中大量灰尘的颗粒粘附上去而成。腹中部有一大滴呈棕黑色的釉，釉面透明，玻璃质感重，很可能是与原始青瓷同炉烧造时溅到的釉滴。本品烧成温度高，扣之铿铿响，其硬度已达到原始青瓷标准，可以旁证原始瓷是由印纹硬陶发展而来的。

Light reddish-brown earthenware with a rather coarse and hard paste. The vessel has a flat mouth, a short neck, a bulbous belly and a flat base. The upper and lower part of the vessel were made separately and then joined together. Luting marks are visible along the interior wall. The entire exterior is impressed with chrysanthemum motif. The surface is brownish-black in color but the inside and outside edge of the mouth rim and the lowest part of the belly are deeper in tone. The dark surface could have been a result of dust particles in the air settling on the jar during firing. A drop of brownish-black glaze with a transparent and highly glassy surface is visible on the belly. The drop of glaze could have been from a proto-celadon piece that was fired together in the same kiln. This vessel was fired to a high temperature. It gives a clear sound when knocked with the knuckle. Its hardness has reached or even exceeded that of proto-celadon. It indirectly proves that proto-porcelain was evolved from high-fired stamped pottery.

114

印纹硬陶米字方格纹大罐

战国

公元前 475—前 221 年

高：39.3 厘米

口径：19.1 厘米

High-fired pottery jar with chrysanthemum motif

Warring States period

475 – 221 B.C.E.

Height: 39.3 cm

Mouth diameter: 19.1 cm

浅灰褐色陶，胎硬，颇粗糙。斜颈、丰肩、深腹、平底微内凹。颈外侈，口缘边向外斜削一周，口缘内壁有螺旋纹多道。颈光素无纹，器身外壁拍印米字方格纹到腹底。器身厚重，表面不够平整，烧成温度高，扣之有金属声。全器覆盖一层浅黑色物质，颈内外呈深黑色，有光泽，颈上黑色物质层有气泡。罐底有残留炉渣。本品很可能是黑釉器物创烧过程中的早期样本，与图录 113 号应是同一时期的遗物，有待学者作进一步研究。

Light grayish-brown earthenware with a rather coarse and hard paste. The vessel has a flared mouth with beveled rim, a tapering neck, broad shoulders, a deep belly and a flat and slightly recessed base. Spiraling lines run around the interior mouth rim. Except for the neck which is plain, the entire exterior down to the foot is impressed with chrysanthemum motif. The vessel is thick and heavy and the surface is uneven. The body was fired to a high temperature. It gives a metallic sound when struck. The entire surface is covered with a layer of material that is blackish and lustrous. Air bubbles are visible in this layer around the neck. Traces of kiln dregs can be seen at the base of the jar. It remains to be studied whether this vessel is an early example of black-glazed pottery. This vessel and Cat. No. 113 should belong to the same time period.

115

印纹硬陶双耳大罐

战国

公元前 475—前 221 年

高：51 厘米

底径：20.5 厘米

High-fired pottery jar with lugs and impressed motif

Warring States period

475 – 221 B.C.E.

Height: 51 cm

Base diameter: 20.5 cm

泥质灰陶，质坚硬，呈褐色。短颈外侈、丰肩、平底，肩两侧贴兽形系各一。器身拍印米字方格纹，印纹细密规整。烧结温度较高，叩之发出铿铿声。制作如此大型器物而不变形，可见当时的制陶工匠已掌握了很高的烧制技术。

Gray earthenware. The brown paste is hard. The jar has a short flaring neck, broad shoulders and a flat base. A pair of animal-shaped lugs flanks the shoulders. The vessel surface is impressed with chrysanthemum motif. The body was fired to a relatively high temperature. It gives a clear sound when knocked with the knuckle.

116

印纹硬陶槽形长流罐

战国

公元前 475—前 221 年

高：32 厘米

阔（连流）：51.5 厘米

口径：12.5 厘米

High-fired pottery jar with long open spout

Warring States period

475 – 221 B.C.E.

Height: 32 cm

Width (with spout): 51.5 cm

Mouth diameter: 12.5 cm

泥质灰陶，胎质坚硬。敛口，唇缘向外翻卷，直颈，丰肩，圆腹，平底。腹侧装槽形流，流口长、微弯，流与罐体相接处上方刻意保留一截罐体作挡水板，以防止倒水时水流太急。流相对一侧贴拱形绳索耳，耳上下端各置横 "S" 形纹饰一个。除颈部外，器表满印细方格纹。肩腹间和下腹部各刻凹弦纹一道，流切口周边饰凹弦纹，与肩腹弦纹相配。本品体形圆浑饱满，线条优美流畅，为不可多得的艺术珍品。

本品经热释光测定最后烧制年代距今 2700—2300 年。

Gray earthenware with a hard paste. This jar has a small mouth with everted rim, a straight neck, broad shoulders, a swelling belly and a flat base. Protruding from the side of the belly is a slightly curved open spout in the shape of a trough. There is a splashguard at the opening between the body and the spout. A rope-like loop lug adorned with double-S appliqué on both ends is attached to the other side of the belly. Except for the neck, the entire vessel is covered with tiny impressed check motif. The lower shoulders, the mid-section of the belly and the exterior rim of the spout are decorated with fine grooves. This jar is a rarity among rarities.

Thermoluminescence test shows that the last firing date of this piece was 2700 to 2300 years before present.

117

印纹硬陶布纹铺首桶

战国

公元前 475—前 221 年

高：12.9 厘米

底径：12.2 厘米

High-fired pottery pail with animal masks

Warring States period

475 – 221 B.C.E.

Height: 12.9 cm

Base diameter: 12.2 cm

泥质红陶。大撇口、体圆、上大下小、斜壁直下及底、底平。造型简单，适用于日常生活。器身满饰拍印斜布纹，近底部布纹不见。上腹两侧饰铺首环系各一，铺首纹饰简单，但形象凶猛、主题突出。器物内壁满布指压痕。外壁灰黑，但内壁和外壁腹下露红色胎骨，说明本品在烧成过程中曾用浓烟熏翳，胎壁表面颗粒空隙中充满了细小的黑色炭微粒，令器物表层变黑。新石器时代龙山黑陶就是这样烧成，战国时期仍广泛使用。

Red earthenware. The vessel has a wide mouth and straight sides that tapers to a flat base. The exterior surface is impressed with oblique textile motif. The textile motif near the base has worn off, probably due to heavy use. The upper belly is decorated on both sides with a ringed animal mask. Impression marks are visible on the interior wall formed by the supporting hand while patterns are paddle-stamped onto the exterior surface. The exterior surface is largely grayish-black but the interior and the lowest part of the exterior reveal a red paste. The vessel is blackened by the carbon in the heavy smoke

during firing. The carbonized surface of Longshanoid black pottery is produced in the same way. This method was still widely used in northern and southern China duirng the Warring States period.

秦汉六朝陶器

Pottery of the Qin, Han and Six Dynasties

秦汉六朝陶器：

视死如生

公元前 221 年，秦始皇建立了大一统的秦王朝，疆域东起辽东，西到陇西，南达南海，北至长城一带。秦朝虽只存在了十五年，但在政治、经济、文化艺术方面取得了很多成就。此时陶瓷艺术领域富有创造力，从生活用陶、建筑构件到仿生像生的陶塑，体现出深沉雄浑的现实主义气魄。兵马俑群代表了秦代陶塑艺术的最高成就。

图录118号磨划纹蒜头壶、119号灰陶"宛亭"铭蒜头壶、120号灰陶蚕形壶等，不仅造型端庄大方，且陶质细腻。

秦末农民起义推翻了秦王朝，经过楚汉战争，刘邦建立了大汉帝国。全国大一统的巩固推动了文化艺术高峰的出现，陶器、瓷器、釉陶的生产突飞猛进，陶瓷美学达到一个崭新的高度。

汉陶的时代性很强，能根据实用要求以简洁的线条造型。如将富有弹性的线条放在最显著的部位，使轮廓外突的部位表现出最强的立体感（图录155号），其高贵庄重的气派不亚于当时的青铜器、鎏金器。秦代以来宫廷贵族、社会上层爱用的茧形壶、蒜头壶、鹅形壶以及各类陶罐等器形也被继承下来，制作工艺有了很大的提高。图录158号鸟形灯，细长颈拼命前伸，鼓眼伏耳，昂首朝天，展翅翘尾，大有一飞冲天之势。

汉代人物雕塑比前代丰富。图录151号彩绘说唱俑，和中国国家博物馆收藏的说唱俑，以及四川各地博物馆珍藏的或说、或站、或唱的说唱俑本质上完全一致。陶工运用夸张的手法，选择了最能表达人物心理活动的一瞬间来达到传神的效果。这些陶俑以高度夸张的形体姿态，手舞足蹈的狂放气势，表现出运动、力量、气魄之美，是汉代陶瓷艺术的重要组成部分。

图录162号坞堡建筑形式的陶楼，下端是一个折沿陶盆，盆内有一只大鹅和五尾游鱼。主体建筑矗立盆中央，斜桥与盆沿相接，盆沿有六只鹅在"巡逻"。楼上有由斗拱托起的栏杆，武士们张弓搭箭、高度警惕，屋内有正在表演的歌舞伎和奢侈享受的主人。反映出汉代社会豪强大族拥兵自卫的社会现实。

汉代崇尚"黄老之学"，追求成仙和长生，形成了"死即永生"和"灵魂升仙"的观念，相信来生和转世，其厚葬之风为历代所惊叹。《墨子·节葬下》记载："棺椁必重，葬埋必厚，衣衾必多，文绣必繁，丘陇必巨……"墓葬争相奢华，以彰显身份和权力。汉代陶器以灰陶为主，除少部分作为日用器外，大部分作为殉葬的明器。明器包括衣食住行各方面的物品和器具，有博山炉、仓、灶、井、磨、楼阁以及猪、牛、羊、狗、鸡等动物偶像和各式各样的奴仆、歌舞杂技俑群等，应有尽有。有些灰陶器表面涂漆，是模仿当时的漆器，数量稀少，只在大墓才有出土（图录153号）。

铅釉陶在陕西关中地区首先出现，自汉宣帝（公元前91—前49年）以后开始获得较快的发展。由于主要流行于黄河流域和北方地区，所以也称"北方釉陶"。又由于釉药中含有大量的氧化铅，故也称"铅釉"。汉代釉陶的胎体多为砖红色，外敷浓厚的棕黄色、绿色、绿黑色、酱褐色的釉。大多数器施单色釉，也有部分施复色釉。铅釉在高温下流动性大，熔融性强，釉层不见气泡或其他残存结晶体，釉色清澈透明，釉面光泽感强。铅釉是一种在 700℃ 左右即开始熔融的低温釉，它的主要着色剂是铜和铁，在氧化气氛中烧成，铜呈现青翠的绿色，铁则呈现黄褐色和棕红色。当铅绿釉处于潮湿环境下被水和大气侵蚀，釉面会轻微溶蚀，溶蚀下来的物质连同水中的可溶性盐类在釉层表面析出、堆栈，当沉积物达到一定厚度时，对光线的反射就产生了绚丽的银白色光泽，所以许多釉陶有熠熠发光的银釉现象。

铅釉技术的发明和推广对汉以后的陶器生产影响深远，唐代的三彩陶器以及宋明时期的琉璃釉陶都是由此发展而来。

六朝承汉启唐，是江南陶瓷业获得迅速发展的时期。六朝时淘洗坯泥的技术比汉代更为进步，烧窑的火力更高，釉料的提炼也更精纯。灰陶和釉陶的制作都取得了长足的进步，出现了很多优秀的作品（图录 167 号和 168 号）。

北朝铅釉技术在汉代的基础上又有所改进，制胎材料除传统的陶土外还大量使用烧造瓷器的瓷土，铅釉的配方也更纯净。加上窑炉的改进和烧造技术的提高，胎体的烧造温度已大大高于传统釉陶，有些器物已经基本瓷化。这种原料和烧制温度上的改进，为北朝白瓷的烧制成功和唐三彩的出现奠定了一定的基础（图录 169 号、170 号和 171 号）。

Pottery of the Qin, Han and Six Dynasties:

The Cult of Immortality

After Emperor Qinshihuang unified China in 221 B.C.E., the territories of the Qin Empire reached as far as Liaodong in the east, southeast Gansu in the west, South China Sea in the south and the Great Wall in the north. Though short-lived, the Qin era saw great advances in politics, economy, arts and culture. There was tremendous creativity in the ceramic arts alone. Examples of this ingenuity are evident in everyday objects, building materials and the representational arts. The terracotta army of warriors and horses represents the height of artistic achievement for sculptural art.

The gray pottery bottle with garlic-shaped mouth (Cat. No. 118), the gray pottery bottle with garlic-shaped mouth and inscription (Cat. No. 119) and the gray pottery cocoon jar (Cat. No. 120) are representative examples.

The Qin dynasty was finally overthrown by peasant uprisings. Liu Bang, one of the rebel leaders, established the Han Empire. China saw its first cultural peak under this unified regime.

The production of cocoon jars, garlic-mouthed bottles, goose-shaped bottles and pottery vessels of various shapes favored by the Qin royalty and the elite continued into the Han dynasty but with increased sophistication. For example, details are placed to accentuate the three-dimensionality of the objects (Cat. No. 155). The monumentality and elegance of these artifacts are comparable to those of contemporaneous bronzes and gilt objects (Cat. No. 158).

Han pottery figurines are remarkably detailed. The pair of painted pottery singers in this catalogue (Cat. No. 151) is comparable to the figurines that are in the collection of the National Museum of China and the museums in Sichuan. They are an indispensable part of the Han ceramic repertoire.

Also in the catalogue are sculptures displaying military might and defense power as illustrated by the magnificent pottery watchtower with armed archers and patrolling geese (Cat. No. 162).

Concepts such as "eternity in death" and "the immortal soul" were widespread during the Han dynasty. People believed in the next life and rebirth, which helped lessen their fear of death. As a result, the Han dynasty had the most lavish funerary practices in Chinese history. Historical records revealed that wealthy burials often include heavy coffins, graves that are dug deep, elaborate grave goods and large burial chambers. People competed in funerary extravagance to show off their status and power. Gray pottery represents the majority of Han pottery. Apart from a small number of everyday utensils, most of them were used as mortuary ware. Among these objects are censers, granaries, stoves, wellheads, lifelike models of houses and animal and human figurines. Some gray pottery objects are painted with lacquer to imitate lacquerware but they are rare and can only be found in large tombs (Cat. No. 153).

Lead-glazed pottery first emerged in central Shaaxi and saw rather rapid development after the reign of Emperor Xuandi (91–49 B.C.E.) of the Han dynasty. They were found around the Yellow River basin and across northern China, hence also the name "Northern glazed pottery". Since the glaze contained a large amount of lead oxide, it is also called "lead glaze". Most glazed pottery of the Han period has a brick-red body under a thick brownish-yellow, green, greenish-black or soy-brown glaze. Most are monochrome but some are polychrome. Lead glaze is highly viscous when fired to a high temperature. Lead glaze is a low-fired glaze that melts and fuses when temperature rises to around 700°C. Its chief colorants are copper and iron, the former producing bright green and the latter amber and reddish-brown when fired in a reduction atmosphere. Burial in a humid environment or longtime exposure to water and atmospheric erosion will cause degradation of the glaze surface. The decomposed material and the soluble salts in the water will then ooze out onto the surface of the glaze. When the sediments accumulate to a certain thickness, light will be refracted to give a beautiful silvery sheen. This explains why many glazed pottery objects take on a silvery iridescence.

The evolution from unglazed to glazed pottery represents an enormous technological breakthrough and has a profound influence on later pottery production. The *sancai* pottery of the Tang dynasty and the glass-like *liuli*-glazed pottery of the Song and Ming dynasties were developed on this foundation.

The techniques of levigation during the Six Dynasties were far more advanced than those of the Han dynasty. The firing temperature was also higher and the glazes purer. The development of both gray and glazed pottery flourished during the Six Dynasties (Cat. Nos. 167, 168).

The lead glaze of the Northern Dynasties is built on the technology from the Han dynasty but more refined. China clay became widely used in addition to traditional earthen clay. Purer lead glazes were also formulated during this time. With the improvement of kiln design and firing technique, the paste could be fired

to a temperature that is much higher than that of traditional glazed pottery. Some of them are technically vitrified. Improvement of raw materials and firing temperature laid the foundation for the emergence of white porcelain of the Northern Dynasties and the *sancai* wares of the Tang dynasty (Cat. Nos. 169, 170, 171).

118

灰陶磨划纹蒜头壶

秦

公元前 221—前 206 年

高：28.5 厘米

阔：22.9 厘米

Gray pottery bottle with garlic-shaped mouth

Qin dynasty

221 – 206 B.C.E.

Height: 28.5 cm

Width: 22.9 cm

泥质灰陶。口部作蒜头形，细长颈，丰肩，圆鼓腹，平底。口缘上刻弦纹两周，颈、肩和腹部置凸弦纹各一周。以弦为界，肩部磨划斜网格纹和云雷纹各一周，上腹部满饰斜网格磨划纹。腹、底分界不明显。造型工整、稳重、饱满，在浑圆的器体上安排三周凸弦纹增加了形体的节奏感。秦时的陶壶多为平底，带圈足的很少。

磨划纹是用石器或骨器在已干燥的坯体上刻划出各种纹饰，流行于战国及秦汉时期。

Gray earthenware. The bottle has a garlic-shaped mouth, a narrow long neck and a globular belly that tapers towards a flat bottom. The shoulders are encircled by three ribs. The top row is decorated with a round of crosshatching followed by a layer of cloud-and-thunder pattern. The row below is adorned with crosshatching. The junction between the lower belly and the base is indistinct.

After the paste dries, the motifs are scraped onto the surface using stone or bone implements. This decorative technique was widely used throughout the Warring States period, the Qin dynasty and the Han dynasty.

119

灰陶"宛亭"铭蒜头壶

秦

公元前 221—前 206 年

高：28.8 厘米

底径：9.3 厘米

Gray pottery bottle with garlic-shaped mouth and inscription

Qin dynasty

221 – 206 B.C.E.

Height: 28.8 cm

Base diameter: 9.3 cm

泥质灰陶。顶作小扁壶状、长颈、平底。颈上部置凸棱一圈，将颈分为上下两部分，上部磨划菱格纹，上有长方格，内刻"宛亭"两字；下部饰芭蕉纹。肩有山形磨划纹。

由于私营制陶作坊的出现，战国时期多有在陶器上标示陶工的姓名、作坊名称、地名等现象，"宛亭"表明其是秦代"宛"地市府经营的制陶作坊的产品。秦时，宛县（今河南省南阳市）属南阳郡管辖。

Gray earthenware. The vessel has a garlic-shaped mouth, a long neck and a flat base. A rib encompasses the upper part of the neck, dividing the neck into two sections. The upper section is scraped with a band of lozenge design and a rectangular frame with two characters inscribed inside that read, "Wan Ting". The lower section is decorated with banana leaf motif. The shoulders are encircled by a round of scraped mountain motif.

Due to the emergence of privately run pottery workshops during the Warring States period, it was quite common for vessels to be inscribed with the names of the potters, the workshops or locations. "Wan Ting" refers to a government-run pottery workshop in Wan region. During the Qin dynasty, Wan county (present-day Nanyang city in Henan) was under the jurisdiction of Nanyang prefecture.

120

灰陶茧形壶

秦

公元前 221—前 206 年

高：26.4 厘米

阔：26.5 厘米

Gray pottery cocoon jar

Qin dynasty

221 – 206 B.C.E.

Height: 26.4 cm

Width: 26.5 cm

泥质灰陶。侈口圆唇，椭圆形腹，以腹着地，无底足。口缘内侧起弦纹两圈。束短颈，颈中央置凸弦纹一道。颈肩处刻褶叠纹带一周。壶体饰竖弦纹十八道，相间拍印绳纹和施磨划斜方格纹，绳纹带稍高于磨划纹带。应是在坯泥未完全干透时，先在器腹满拍印绳纹，接着刻上垂直弦纹，相间地把纹带内的绳纹轻轻刮去，当坯胎干燥后再施磨划纹。在磨划纹带内可见竖直刮痕及两端残留的绳纹。

除西安兵马俑坑外，秦代陶瓷艺术品发现不多，此件秦茧形壶胎质细腻，灰陶颜色纯正，烧成工艺水平很高。

1976 年秦始皇陵园鱼池遗址出土有相似器物。

Gray earthenware. The jar has a flared mouth and a rounded rim. The jar is in the shape of a barrel laid sideways with no feet attached to the base. Two indented lines run around the interior mouth rim. A rib and a band of incised vertical striations encircle the neck. The body is encompassed by eighteen grooves. The spaces between the grooves are filled with alternating bands of impressed cord motif and lozenge check pattern, the latter on a slightly recessed ground. The decorations are created by impressing the entire surface with cord motif before the vessel has completely dried out. Then, the vertical grooves and every other band of cord motif are scraped out. After it dries, lozenge check pattern is scraped onto the plain surface. Vertical scrape marks and vestiges of cord motif are visible along the edges.

Apart from the terracotta army found in the mausoleum of the Emperor Qinshihuang, pottery artifacts from this period are quite scarce.

A similar vessel was unearthed in 1976 at the fish pond site near the imperial mausoleum of the Emperor Qinshihuang.

121
绳纹大茧形壶

秦

公元前 221—前 206 年

高：56 厘米

阔：66.5 厘米

Large pottery cocoon jar with cord motif

Qin dynasty

221 – 206 B.C.E.

Height: 56 cm

Width: 66.5 cm

泥质陶。器呈蚕茧形，以腹为底。顶正中开一小口，双唇，唇间起凹槽。短颈，微束。器体满饰拍印横向绳纹，上饰竖向弦纹带七道。浅灰白胎，质坚，胎骨厚重。口小腹大，可能用于储水或盛酒。也有一说是作战时把壶体埋在地下，颈部露出地面，将耳朵贴在颈部孔上可以遥听敌人的马蹄声。

Gray earthenware. The jar is in the shape of a cocoon laid sideways. A small mouth with double lips divided by a groove is set on a short neck. The entire vessel surface is impressed with horizontal cord motif. The body is encircled by seven vertical grooves. The paste is grayish-white in color and the body is hard, thick and heavy. The small mouth and the massive belly suggest that the vessel was used for storing water or wine. Some say that this type of vessels may have been used as motion sensors during wars. The vessel would have been buried in the ground with only its neck sticking out. By placing one's ear close to the mouth of the jar, one could hear the sounds of galloping horses approaching.

122

灰陶"千万岁为大年"文字瓦当

汉

公元前 206—公元 220 年

直径：15 厘米

**Gray pottery eaves tile
with inscription**

Han dynasty

206 B.C.E. – 220 C.E.

Diameter: 15 cm

泥质灰陶。圆形，带筒瓦残存约 8 厘米。面内凹，模印"千万岁为大年"六字。

瓦当是古代建筑檐上筒瓦的瓦头，主要用于保护木制飞檐、排水防水、美化屋面轮廓。其式样主要有圆形和半圆形两种。瓦当出现在西周，发展于战国时期，盛行于秦汉，多用于宫殿、官署、苑囿、关隘、陵墓、祠堂、私舍等建筑。当面除画像图案、几何图像装饰外，自汉武帝起，文字的使用非常广泛。汉代流行黄老思想，人们追求长生不老和死后升仙，瓦文词语多以吉祥语、祷颂词为常见，如"千秋万岁""延年益寿""宜子宜孙""与天无极""长乐未央""汉并天下"等。

Gray earthenware. The circular eaves tile is attached to an 8cm long remnant of a cylindrical tile. The face of the eaves tile is molded with six characters that read, "*Qianwansui Weidanian*" (A thousand autumns and ten thousand years) on a recessed ground.

Eaves tiles are cylindrical tiles lining the front of eaves, mostly with a circular or semicircular face. They are mainly used for protecting the wooden eaves from rainwater and enhancing the contours of the facade. They were mainly used on palatial mansions, government buildings, gardens, gates at strategic mountain passes, tombs, ancestral halls and private residential buildings. Eaves tiles emerged during the Western Zhou period, developed during the Warring States period and became widely used during the Qin and Han dynasties. The quest for immortality and the belief in life after death is prevalent during the Han dynasty and so the inscriptions on the tile-ends are mostly sayings that convey auspiciousness and well wishes. Examples include: "*Qianqiu wansui*" ([To live] a thousand autumns and ten thousand years); "*Yannian yishou*" (Extend life and enjoy longevity); "*Yizi yisun*" (Good for the sons and grandsons); "*Yutian wuji*" (As infinite as Heaven); "*Changle weiyang*" (Long-lasting and endless happiness); and "*Hanbing tianxia*" (The Han dynasty unifies the nation).

123

灰陶"菑川武库"文字瓦当

汉

公元前 206—公元 220 年

直径：19.4 厘米

Gray pottery eaves tile with inscription

Han dynasty

206 B.C.E. – 220 C.E.

Diameter: 19.4 cm

泥质灰陶。圆形，带 9.5—11.5 厘米长的筒瓦残存。当面下凹，内以"十"字形半椭圆泥条分成四份，泥条中央相汇处贴乳突一个，周边和泥条上模印连续箭镞头作饰。当面模印"菑川武库"四字。

"菑川武库"说明该瓦当是菑川地区存放武器的官府建筑物上所用，武库文字的瓦当存世十分稀少。菑川国，一作甾川国，是中国汉代王国。西汉初年置，菑川国治所在剧县（今山东省寿光市南），属青州刺史部。

Gray earthenware. The circular eaves tile is attached to a 9.5–11.5cm long remnant of a cylindrical tile. The face of the tile features a recessed surface divided into four quadrants by four clay strips connected by a stud in the center. The circular border of the eaves tile and the clay strips are decorated with molded arrowhead motif. The four quadrants are molded with four characters that read, *"Zhichuan wuku"* (Zhichuan arsenal) indicating that the eaves tile was made for an arsenal. Eaves tiles inscribed with the names of government arsenals are exceedingly rare.

Zhichuenguo was the name of a vassal kingdom of the Han dynasty, established in the early Western Han period, south of present-day Souguang city in Shandong. It was governed by the Provincial Governor of Qingzhou.

124

大灰陶立马

汉

公元前 206—公元 220 年

高：76 厘米

长：67.5 厘米

Large gray pottery standing horse

Han dynasty

206 B.C.E. – 220 C.E.

Height: 76 cm

Length: 67.5 cm

泥质灰陶。马四蹄稳踏、扬尾、挺胸、张口、
含衔、露齿、圆睁眼、竖耳。剪鬃，背
置鞍鞯。马为雄性，带性器官，躯体圆浑，
劲健凶猛。

汉代雕塑艺术水平相当高超，塑造的各种
马形象生动逼真，具有较高的审美情趣。

Gray earthenware. Horse standing foursquare with upright tail, bulging chest,
cropped mane, wide-open eyes, pricked
ears and gaping mouth. Its back is
decorated with a saddle on a blanket.

Han pottery horses are noted for their
various styles and poses and their realistic
and lively expressions.

125

灰陶禽畜俑一组五件

汉

公元前 206—公元 220 年

高：9.5—17.4 厘米

长：10.9—16.7 厘米

A group of gray pottery livestock figurines

Han dynasty

206 B.C.E. – 220 C.E.

Height: 9.5 – 17.4 cm

Length: 10.9 – 16.7 cm

泥质灰陶。包括大、小牛各一，羊、公鸡和犬各一，各俑面部清晰、神情各异，趣味盎然。成形方法为先模印，再刻划切削成形。除犬外，其余各俑绘有红彩。牛腹部洞开。羊和犬体内中空，有排气孔。公鸡为实体烧制。

此组禽畜俑是殉葬用的明器。专为随葬而制作的器物一般用竹、木或陶土制成，竹木因年代久远而易腐朽，只有陶制明器能留存于后世。

Gray earthenware. The group of livestock includes: a larger and a smaller ox; a goat; a rooster; and a dog. Each figurine is sculpted with a different facial expression. They were first molded out of clay and then the details added on by carving, incising, trimming and scraping. Except for the dog, all figurines are partially painted with red pigment. The underside of the oxen figurines is hollow and open. The goat and the dog have a hollow body with ventilation holes for air to escape during firing. The rooster has a solid body.

These figurines are grave goods buried along with the dead. Objects used as burial goods were usually made of bamboo, wood or clay. Only the pottery ones can survived until today because of its relative durability.

126

红陶庖厨俑

东汉

公元 25—220 年

高：49.3 厘米

Red pottery figurine of a cook

Eastern Han dynasty

25 – 220 C.E.

Height: 49.3 cm

泥质红陶。俑中空，器壁厚度适中，左右两侧中部有夹模痕。俑跪坐，头戴山形帽，身穿斜襟右衽三层衣，束腰带，挽袖到手肘部。膝前置小案儿，几上平放鲜鱼一尾，鱼头、身、尾和鳍清晰。庖厨左手按鱼，右手放在腰腿间，右手拇指和食指间有一孔洞，应原用于插放木制刀具，惜刀具已腐烂。

这类陶俑通常五官模糊，而本俑五官清晰，形象生动，充满浓厚的生活气息，自然可亲，是四川陶俑珍品之一。

1979 年四川新都东汉遗址出土有相似器物。

Red earthenware. The figurine has a hollow body and walls of moderate thickness. Luting marks are visible along its sides. The figurine is seated on his heels. He wears a hill-shaped cap and three layers of right-fastened garments held by a waist belt. The sleeves are rolled up to the elbows. In front of him is a fish with clearly defined head, body, tail and fins on a small low table. His left hand is holding down the fish. There is a hole between his right thumb and index finger where a wooden

knife may have been inserted.

The facial features of this type of figurines are usually indistinct. The present example is noted for its delicate and realistic detailing. It is among the finest pottery figurines from Sichuan.

A similar artifact was unearthed in 1979 from an Eastern Han site in Xindu, Sichuan province.

127

红陶舞俑

东汉

公元 25—220 年

高：48 厘米

Red pottery figurine of a dancer

Eastern Han dynasty

25 – 220 C.E

Height: 48 cm

泥质红陶。俑中空，以对模接合法制作，再施以刻纹。俑头部微上扬、中梳高髻，两侧有小髻，高额长脸，耳朵前后穿圆形饰物，五官清晰。内穿交领长袖舞衣，外罩右衽三层衣，袖口宽大，上饰摺叠纹，腰束带，右手上举，左手叉腰，双足张开，呈表演舞蹈姿态。其柔软的身姿、纤细的腰肢、贯注的神情、飘逸的长袖、轻盈的舞步，构成了极具旋律的画面。

在中国历史上，大量制作"像人"的陶俑是在氏族社会崩溃、封建制兴起的春秋战国时代，即废除人殉制之后。到汉代作为殉葬之用的陶俑制作和使用达到巅峰，陶俑完全写实或稍作夸张，反映社会生活，其中以四川陶俑最有代表性。本品当为四川所出。

Red earthenware. The hollow figurine is created by joining two molded pieces together. The details are then worked out by carving. The figurine has a slightly raised head with a high topknot flanked by smaller buns, a long face and ears with ornaments in the front and back. The facial features are delicately rendered. The dancer wears a long-sleeved dancing robe with overlapping lapels under three layers of garments with wide sleeves bordered with ruffles held up by a waist belt. The right hand is raised while the left hand is placed at the waist.

Mass production of human figurines in China began in the Spring and Autumn and Warring States periods when the practice of human sacrifice was abolished and the feudal system succeeded the clan society. The practice of using pottery figurines as grave goods reached its height during the Han dynasty. These figurines are characterized by their highly realistic expressions and stylized details. Pottery figurines from Sichuan, like the present piece, are the most representative examples.

128

黑陶盖豆一对

战国—西汉

公元前 475—公元 8 年

高：30.2 厘米

Pair of black pottery lidded *dou* stem bowls

Warring States period –
Western Han dynasty
475 B.C.E. – 8 C.E.
Height: 30.2 cm

泥质黑陶。豆与盖子口，扣合成圆球形，器座和盖纽呈相对喇叭形。全器经打磨和施磨划纹。盖纽中空，上有圆孔，围以水波纹三周，纽柄有凸弦纹一道。盖上依次有水波纹两周、三层山纹一周，山纹之间隙置云气纹，再下有弦纹两周，最下方是斜线纹。豆身满饰弦纹。上下倒置的喇叭形衬托出圆鼓的肩腹，弧度线条柔和完美，令人赞叹。

Black earthenware. The top and bottom halves are nearly identical. The entire surface has been polished and adorned with scrape motif. The hollow stem-knob lid has a circular opening at the top surrounded by three rounds of wave motif. A ridge encircles the neck of the stem on the outside. The lid is decorated with two bands of wave motif, three bands of mountain motif (the spaces between the mountain shapes are filled with cloud motif), two rounds of incised lines and then a border of oblique striations. The spaces between the mountain peaks are decorated with cloud motif. Further down are two rounds of incised lines and then a band of oblique striations. The entire surface of the stem foot is decorated with incised lines.

129

黑陶鼎

战国—西汉

公元前 475—公元 8 年

高：29 厘米

Black pottery *ding* tripod

Warring States period –
Western Han dynasty

475 B.C.E. – 8 C.E.

Height: 29 cm

泥质黑陶。直腹，底近平，下附三方足。
圆鼓顶盖立三扁纽。口缘附两个方形竖
耳。全器经打磨和施磨划纹，磨划纹划
工草率。盖顶有放射状圆圈纹，外围有
一周连续 "W" 形纹，盖下半部有连续
四层山形纹，山形纹之间隙置云气纹。
豆体四周满布竖直纹。

鼎为食器，盖倒置可盛物。

Black earthenware. The vessel has a belly
with straight sides supported by three
legs. The top of the dome-shaped lid has
three slab-like upright flanges. A pair of
rectangular upright lugs flanks the mouth
rim. The entire vessel has been polished
and adorned with scraped motif. The top
of the lid is decorated with concentric
circles within a border of W-shaped motif.
The decorative band around the lower part
of the lid features four layers of continuous
mountain motif and the spaces between
them filled with cloud motif. The entire
surface of the bowl is covered with vertical
striations.

Ding tripods were used as food vessels.
The lid doubles as a bowl when turned
upside down.

黑陶弦纹唾壶

西汉

公元前 206—公元 8 年

高：20.3 厘米

口径：26.8 厘米

Black pottery spittoon with grooved design

Western Han dynasty

206 B.C.E. – 8 C.E.

Height: 20.3 cm

Mouth diameter: 26.8 cm

泥质黑陶，胎细腻。上部如斗笠碗，短直颈。下部如水丞、宽肩、圆鼓腹、平底。器表打磨光滑。上、下腹以一周齿纹分界，上腹饰双弦纹三道，下腹光素无纹。大外撇的斗笠形上部、扁而圆鼓的腹部、肩腹上的弦纹线、齿纹和急斜收的下腹部，构成线条优美、端庄大气的外形，具有很高的艺术和欣赏价值。

Black earthenware with a refined paste and a highly burnished surface. The upper section resembles a conical bowl. The basin-shaped vessel below has broad shoulders, a bulbous belly and a flat base. A band of sawtooth motif divides the belly into the upper and lower sections. The upper section is encircled by three grooves. The lower section is plain.

131

灰陶带盖双系壶

西汉

公元前 206—公元 8 年

高：13.2 厘米

阔：15.5 厘米

Gray pottery lidded pot with double lugs

Western Han dynasty

206 B.C.E. – 8 C.E.

Height: 13.2 cm

Width: 15.5 cm

泥质灰陶。口平，上置插盖，呈倒置杯状，圈足，整体呈椭圆状。肩腹分界明显，以一周凹棱分隔。长边两侧贴横向贯耳各一。本品造型饱满，线条柔和，侧面看像一艘在水中航行的船。从胎和造型看，本品当为西汉早期遗物。

美国旧金山亚洲艺术博物馆藏有相似器物。

Gray earthenware. The vessel has an ovoid body, a flat mouth supporting a lid that resembles an inverted cup and a ring foot. The sharp junction between the shoulders and the belly is accentuated by a groove. A pair of tubular lugs flanks the body. The shape of the vessel looks like a boat when viewed from the side. Judging from the paste and the shape, this pot should be dated to the early Western Han period.

A similar artifact is in the collection of the Asian Art Museum of San Francisco, USA.

132

灰陶甗

西汉

公元前 206—公元 8 年

通高：26.7 厘米

Gray pottery *yan* steamer

Western Han dynasty

206 B.C.E. – 8 C.E.

Overall height: 26.7 cm

泥质灰陶。由上部的甑和下部的釜组合而成。甑呈碗状，内底部有米粒形孔洞数个。釜口有矮直唇，以承接甑足底部、底平，呈圆形，下承三兽足。釜肩部两侧贴兽面铺首各一。胎灰白，细滑。全器打磨光滑。本品造型规整，制作精细，线条流畅，是一件精美的艺术品。

Gray earthenware. The vessel is formed by fitting a *zeng* cauldron on top of a *fu* tripod. The base of the bowl-shaped *zeng* has several pits about the size of rice grains. The mouth of the tripod has a short straight lip which slots into the foot of the cauldron. The tripod has a circular flat base supported by three animal feet. The shoulders of the *fu* tripod are flanked by a pair of appliqué animal masks. The grayish-white paste is refined. The entire vessel has been well burnished to give a smooth and lustrous surface.

133

灰陶弦纹茧形壶

西汉

公元前 206—公元 8 年

高：31.9 厘米

阔：34.2 厘米

Gray pottery cocoon jar with incised grooves

Western Han dynasty

206 B.C.E. – 8 C.E.

Height: 31.9 cm

Width: 34.2 cm

泥质灰陶。折沿，颈粗短，腹大，呈椭圆形，圈足外撇。颈起三道弦纹，器身由上而下饰十一组圆圈纹，每组由三条弦纹组成。圈足有弦纹一道。颈和圈足相呼应。

本品造型别致，如蚕茧和鸭蛋，故称茧形壶、鸭蛋壶或大腹尊。

Gray earthenware. The jar has a mouth with an angular everted rim, a short thick neck and an ovoid belly. The neck is encircled by three ribs. The body is adorned with eleven bands of triple grooves. The neck and the ring foot mirror each other in shape. A rib encircles the splayed foot.

This vessel is uniquely shaped like a cocoon or duck's egg and commonly referred to as a "cocoon jar", "duck's egg jar" or "big bellied jar".

134

灰陶兽足樽一对

西汉

公元前 206—公元 8 年

高：25.5 厘米

Pair of gray pottery *zun* containers

Western Han dynasty

206 B.C.E. – 8 C.E.

Height: 25.5 cm

泥质灰陶。樽为筒形身，下承熊形兽足
三个。口缘下和腹下各有弦纹两道，纹
线内刻连续垂帐纹。腹中部饰弦纹三周。
拱形盖，子口，上起凸弦纹两圈。盖面
等距贴圆突三个，盖顶置半圆环，上附
铜环一个。胎细腻，全器经打磨光滑。
本品外形与图录 160 号樽相同，只是一
无釉一有釉。

本品经热释光检测最后烧制年代距今
2400—1500 年。

Gray earthenware with refined paste.
Each container has a cylindrical body
supported by animal-shaped legs. The
exterior mouth rim and lower belly are
respectively decorated with a scallop
design bounded by two rounds of incised
lines. Three incised lines encircle the mid-
section of the belly. The dome-shaped
lid is decorated with two concentric ribs.
The upper part has three equally spaced
appliqué studs. Each bridge knob is
furnished with a movable bronze ring.
The entire surface has been burnished to
a smooth and lustrous surface. This vessel

is similar in shape to Cat. No. 160 except
that this is unglazed.

Thermoluminescence test shows that the
last firing date of this piece was 2400 to
1500 years before present.

135

彩绘镂空熏炉

西汉

公元前 206—公元 8 年

高：13.6 厘米

Painted pottery censer with openwork design

Western Han dynasty

206 B.C.E. – 8 C.E.

Height: 13.6 cm

泥质灰陶。形似豆，子母口，细柄，倒置碗状足。扁圆盖，上附喇叭形纽。盖和炉身刻划三角和方格纹，盖有镂孔。盖纽、扁圆盖、斜收的下腹和喇叭形足搭配和谐，是一件造型优美的艺术品。

1972 年湖南长沙马王堆一号墓出土有相似器物，现藏湖南省博物馆。

Gray earthenware. The censer resembles a *dou* stem bowl in shape. The stem foot resembles an inverted bowl. The flattened circular lid has a small trumpet-shaped knob on top. The surfaces of the censer and the lid are decorated with triangular and square openwork design.

A similar vessel was unearthed in 1972 from Mawangdui tomb No. 1 in Changsha, Hunan province. It is now in the collection of the Hunan Provincial Museum.

136

灰陶鸟形器

汉

公元前 206—公元 220 年

高：12.8 厘米

Gray pottery object with bird-head design

Han dynasty

206 B.C.E. – 220 C.E.

Height: 12.8 cm

泥质陶。长喙、长颈、扁圆腹、圜底。中空，顶和底部正中各有一圆孔。颈肩部有批削痕。此器可能为手把件。

Gray earthenware. The hollow object is in the shape of a bird with a long beak, a long neck, a squat belly and a rounded base. The top is pierced with a hole that aligns perfectly with another hole that is located at the bottom. Scrape and shaving marks are visible around the neck and shoulders. This object may have been used as a grip handle.

137

白陶篦纹双耳罐

汉

公元前 206—公元 220 年

高：22 厘米

口径：9.2 厘米

底径：9.2 厘米

White pottery jar with combed motif

Han dynasty

206 B.C.E. – 220 C.E.

Height: 22 cm

Mouth diameter: 9.2 cm

Base diameter: 9.2 cm

白陶。侈口，圆唇，短颈微束，斜肩，下部内收，平底，底径和口径相当。腹上部两侧置环形耳，环耳中部内凹。腹部刻凸篦纹带十周，肩饰弦纹一周，颈肩间一侧刻箭头形符号"↑"一个。胎白，细腻，质坚。烧造温度较高，叩之声音清越。造型工整，精美。

White earthenware. The jar has a flared mouth with rounded lip, a slightly constricted short neck and shoulders that taper towards a flat base. The mouth and the base are almost identical in diameter. A pair of ring handles is attached to the sides of the upper belly. The belly is decorated with ten bands of raised combed motif.

A round of cord motif encompasses the shoulders. An upward-pointing arrowhead appears between the neck and the shoulder on one side. The refined paste is white and hard. It was fired to a relatively high temperature and gives a pleasant sound when knocked with the knuckle.

138

灰陶鱼鸟动物纹锤

汉

公元前 206—公元 220 年

高：38.6 厘米

Gray pottery jar with zoomorphic design

Han dynasty

206 B.C.E. – 220 C.E.

Height: 38.6 cm

泥质灰陶。侈口，束颈、斜肩、鼓腹、圈足。腹中部起凸弦纹一道，把锤分成上下两部分。凸弦纹处对称贴铺首两只。颈肩间饰竖水波纹带一周，纹带上方到口沿刻连续山纹和云气纹，纹带下方到腹中凸弦纹间连续刻游鱼。凸弦纹下方到腹底刻划凤凰、雀鸟和奔跑的动物。本品造型饱满、线条流畅、纹饰丰富、刻工精细、鱼鸟动物、生动传神，是一件十分珍贵的艺术品。

Gray earthenware. The jar has a flared mouth, a constricted neck, sloping shoulders, a bulbous belly and a ring foot. A rib encircles the mid-section of the belly, dividing the body into upper and lower parts. A pair of appliqué animal masks is affixed to the sides. The neck and the shoulders are decorated with a band of water wave motif. The area above it up to the mouth rim is incised with continuous mountains and cloud motif. A frieze incised with swimming fish decorates the area just above the rib. The entire surface below the rib is incised with phoenixes, birds and other animals lining up one after the other. The entire vessel is lavishly covered with meticulously incised motifs. This jar is a rarity among rarities.

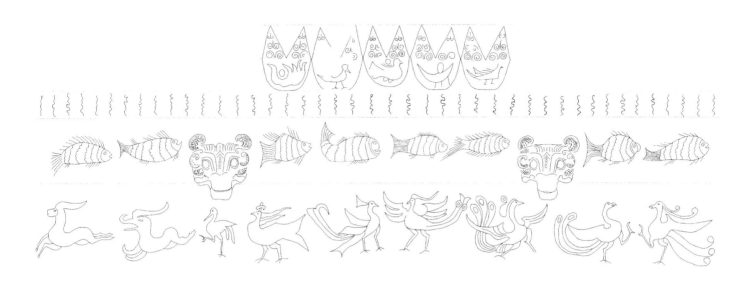

139

黑陶白彩双耳大壶

汉

公元前 206—公元 220 年

高：41 厘米

底径：12 厘米

Large black pottery jar with white painted motif

Han dynasty

206 B.C.E. – 220 C.E.

Height: 41 cm

Base diameter: 12 cm

磨光黑陶，胎细腻。口呈菱形、短束颈、斜肩、球形腹、内敛、假平底、底刻 "Ｙ" 形符号、四周围以绳纹。颈刻斜直纹带一周。肩腹两侧扁弧形柄连接口缘和器体中部，柄上各饰凹圆涡纹三个。口缘另两侧中部各起一锐利棱线，由口缘尖端直达腹部。双耳下端两侧由下而上切削旋涡状弦纹两圈，中央呈火山状锥形突起。器体和柄满绘白彩网纹。本品体型巨大，棱角流畅锋利，造型生动威猛，异常优美，应为部落族长或巫师才能拥有的。

此种壶是居住在中国西部地区的羌人用器，很可能是用于祭祀，其夸张的羊头形状有鲜明的民族特点，羌人称之为 "羊头罐"。羌人生活和羊密切相关，吃、穿、用都离不开羊，以羊为图腾以及祭祀天神。

本品凌厉夸张的弧线、凸眼大耳的独特造型和表现手法透露出广汉三星堆器物的遗风，那么这些居住在四川的羌人跟3000 多年前居于成都平原、有高度文明的古蜀人是否有传承关系呢？这是值得进一步探讨的。

1926 年四川省出土有类似器物，1982 年四川省宝兴县东汉墓群也出土有相似器物。

Burnished black pottery with a refined paste. The jar has a flared lozenge-shaped mouth, a constricted neck, sloping shoulders and a bulbous belly that tapers towards a slightly concave base incised with a "y" mark. Two strap handles with rounded edges connect the two sides of the mouth rim to the belly. The surface of each handle is decorated with three grooved spirals. The two corners of the lozenge-shaped mouth turn into sharp ridges that scale down the center of the jar. A pair of large up-curved spirals, resembling the horns of a ram, is carved on to the front and back of the vessel. Volcano-like conical protrusions mark the center of these spirals. The body and the handles are adorned with crosshatching painted in white.

These kinds of jars were among the vessels used by the ancient Qiang people of western China. This jar is probably a sacrificial vessel belonging to a chieftain or shaman. The Qiang people called this type of jars "ram-

head jars". They depended heavily on these animals as a source of food, fiber and skins. The ram was their totem and the god to whom they offered sacrifices.

Jars like this are reminiscent of the artifacts unearthed from Sanxingdui site in Guanghan, Sichuan province. Whether there is any connection between the Qiang people and the ancient Shu civilization remains to be studied.

Similar artifacts were unearthed in 1926 from Sichuan and also in 1982 from the Eastern Han tombs at Baoxingxian in the same province.

140

黑陶双耳壶

汉

公元前 206—公元 220 年

高：16 厘米

底径：8 厘米

Black pottery jar with double handles

Han dynasty

206 B.C.E. – 220 C.E.

Height: 16 cm

Base diameter: 8 cm

本品造型与图录 139 号相似，只是本品为平底。罐腹部前后两侧磨划两个相连向内弯曲如弹簧的羊角，壶体中部由上而下的棱作胸骨，壶口缘尖为口，左右双耳作羊耳，颈部纹带为挂在羊脖子上的羌绣编织带。以夸张的手法将羊头面部主要特征生动地刻画了出来。

This vessel is similar to Cat. No. 139 except that the base is flat. A pair of spirals resembling the horns of a ram is scraped on to the front and back of the vessel. The ridge down the center of the jar represents the ram's sternum, the beak of the jar the ram's mouth, the handles the ram's horns and the decorative bands around the neck of the jar the ram's collar. The essence of a ram is vividly captured.

141

黑陶羽纹双耳壶

汉

公元前 206—公元 220 年

高：17.2 厘米

底径：8.3 厘米

Black pottery jar with feather motif

Han dynasty

206 B.C.E. – 220 C.E.

Height: 17.2 cm

Base diameter: 8.3 cm

本品造型和纹饰与图录 139 号基本相同。双耳上刻羽毛，中间棱脊为羽骨，两侧斜纹作羽毛，顶部以双勾线刻出较粗长的拨风羽毛两条。在近口缘一侧扁圆耳上有一小圆孔，应是在胎体仍未干透时，用细小的圆条硬物由外面内戳成，圆孔周边可见胎泥堆积。新石器时期，先民用戳孔来记载发生的某些大事。

在羊头罐上加上鸟类羽毛，赋予了羊更高的生命力，把羊神化，寓意其像鹰类自由飞翔并与天上神灵沟通。

This ram-head jar is similar in shape to Cat. No. 139, except that the handles are incised with feather motif. The rib down the center of the handle represents the shaft of the feather and the oblique striations on either side the vane. A small hole is pierced near the mouth rim on top of the loop handle. It was poked from the outside in using a small rod before the paste was dried. Traces of clay have accumulated around the hole. Piercing a hole in an object was a method used by

Neolithic people to record an important event.

The image of a ram with wings capable of communicating between heaven and earth is vividly depicted.

黑陶文字动物纹双耳壶

汉

公元前 206—公元 220 年

高：21.7 厘米

底径：8.8 厘米

Black pottery jar with inscription and zoomorphic design

Han dynasty

206 B.C.E. – 220 C.E.

Height: 21.7 cm

Base diameter: 8.8 cm

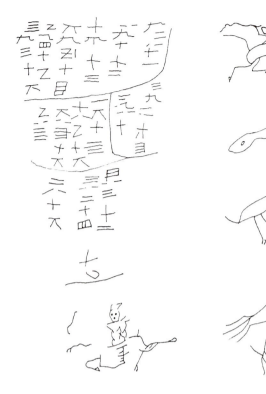

底微内凹，上刮交错弦纹带。器身前后刻四个对称突起的旋涡纹，涡纹顶部和口缘内侧施红彩。颈上刻垂直纹两周，上留有草根纹和白色沉渍物。其中一耳上方刻数目字四组，好像是乘数的九因歌，也可能是记录一些事情；下方刻划人骑马奔跑，人面部有眼和口。另一耳由上而下依次刻划一个左手御马、右手挥鞭策马飞驰的人，一条爬行中的蛇，一只昂首、竖耳、翘尾的动物，一只羽冠高耸、长尾散开的大鸟，以简约线条勾勒轮廓，生动传神，与汉代禽兽铜镜上的羽人物像相似。通常这类壶颈上仅饰羌绣编织带一周，而本壶有两周，再加上双耳刻有数字、人和动物形象，其含义值得进一步研究。

The base of the vessel is scraped with crosshatching. Each face of the vessel is carved with a pair of symmetrical spirals. The crests of the spirals and the interior of the mouth are painted red. Two bands of vertical striations encircle the neck. Traces of grass-root marks and white sediments are visible on the surface. The top of one handle is incised with four groups of numerals suggesting the multiplication table or recording of events using numerals. The lower part of the handle is incised with a figure galloping on horseback. The figure's face is depicted with eyes and mouth. The upper part of the other handle is incised with a rider holding a rein in his left hand and a whip in his right on horseback. Below this is a crawling snake, a creature with raised head, pricked ears and upright tail and a large bird with a high crest and a long outspread tail, bearing resemblance to the images of the winged figures on Han dynasty bronze mirrors with zoomorphic design. This type of jars usually has one collar around its neck but this one has two. The double collars, the numeral markings as well as the human and zoomorphic designs indicate the great importance of this jar.

黑陶双耳壶一对

汉

公元前 206—公元 220 年

高：16.5 厘米

Pair of black pottery jars with double handles

Han dynasty

206 B.C.E. – 220 C.E.

Height: 16.5 cm

泥质黑陶。全器打磨光滑。双耳上刻有羽毛纹饰，脖子挂羌绣编织带。本品其中一壶的柄上戳有小孔一个。本品圆润丰满、弧度优雅、棱角分明，散发出迷人魅力，有很高的艺术和欣赏价值。

Black earthenware. The entire surface of each vessel has been burnished to a smooth and lustrous finish. The handles are incised with feather motif. The necks are adorned with decorative bands reminiscent of the traditional Qiang woven collars. One of the jars has a small hole pierced onto the handle.

144

黑陶饕餮纹双耳壶

汉

公元前 206—公元 220 年

高：12.1 厘米

Black pottery jar with *taotie* motif

Han dynasty

206 B.C.E. – 220 C.E.

Height: 12.1 cm

本品为喇叭形圈足，颈部四周挂饕餮纹编织带、双耳上刻箭头纹。耳下左右刻双线角形纹绕到左右腹，寓意又大又弯的山羊角由头顶向下伸展。箭头纹、饕餮纹编织带和羊角划纹边缘凹凸不平、大小不一，应是在器物烧成后才刻上去的。本品应是作为礼器于祭祀时使用的。

虽然其中一耳已破损，但无碍壶的美态，反而增添了一种残缺美。

This jar is similar in shape to other ram-head jars except for the trumpet-shaped ring foot. A band of *taotie* motif representing a woven collar encircles the neck. The surface of the handles is incised with arrowhead design. The front and the back of the vessel are decorated with spirals incised with double outlines to suggest the horns of a ram. The jagged edges and uneven thickness of the arrowhead motif and the decorative *taotie* collar suggest that these motifs were incised onto the vessel after firing. This jar was used as ritual ware.

Instead of dampening its beauty, the broken handle actually makes the vessel even more alluring by imbuing it with a sense of imperfect beauty.

145

彩绘三足陶鼎

西汉

公元前 206—公元 8 年

高：21 厘米

口径：24 厘米

Pottery *ding* tripod with painted motifs

Western Han dynasty

206 B.C.E. – 8 C.E.

Height: 21 cm

Mouth diameter: 24 cm

泥质灰陶。子口，扁圆腹体，圜底，三兽足。口缘附双耳。拱形盖，盖上置三小孔，用以插入木质纽耳，但纽耳已腐烂。盖边、双耳、鼎口缘及三兽足均施白粉彩，盖及腹侧四周在黑彩地上满绘红、白和紫色云气纹，具有很强的装饰性。

汉代是中国历史上一个稳固的大一统时代，经济发达，教育文化昌盛，各方面的艺术都取得很高的成就。制陶工艺方面，不但在制作和烧成上取得很多的成就，在色彩的运用上也很有水平。本品图案布局很有章法，线条流畅，色彩鲜明，是汉代彩绘陶的代表作。汉彩绘陶很不容易保存，因此此件作品比较珍贵。

Gray earthenware. The vessel has a shallow belly decorated with a pair of upright lugs and a rounded base supported by three animal legs. A wooden knob, now missing, should have been affixed to the top of the lid. The edge of the cover, the handles, the rim and the legs are coated with white slip. The lid and the sides of the vessel are painted with cloud motif in red, white and purple against a ground of black to create a highly decorative effect.

The motifs on this vessel are well composed, fluently delineated, brilliantly colored and the painted colors properly preserved. It is a representative example of the painted pottery from the Han dynasty.

彩绘三足陶鼎

146

彩绘方壶

西汉

公元前 206—公元 8 年

高：49 厘米

底：14 厘米 ×14 厘米

Square pottery lidded jar with painted motifs

Western Han dynasty

206 B.C.E. – 8 C.E.

Height: 49 cm

Base: 14 cm × 14 cm

泥质灰陶。口、颈、腹和圈足皆呈方形，束颈、鼓腹，腹、足分界明显，足上窄下阔，呈倒斗状。壶盖四面起坡，呈金字塔形。盖四角各穿一孔，以插木戟，但戟已失。颈、足、盖和两面腹壁满绘红、白、黄、蓝色云气纹和三角纹；另两侧腹部描画饕餮衔环纹饰，饕餮露出獠牙，凶恶威猛。器物棱线凌厉，造型优美。线条勾连交错、婉转流畅，与漆器纹饰风格相近。

此种方壶在汉代是一种量器，圆的名锺，方的名钫。

Gray earthenware. The jar has a squarish cross-section throughout. It has a flared mouth, a constricted neck and a drum body supported by a tall splayed foot. The junction between the belly and the foot is distinct. The pyramidal lid has four holes on top where wooden shafts would have been inserted. The entire vessel is lavishly painted with cloud scrolls and triangular shapes in red, white, yellow and blue except for the two sides that are painted with a *Taotie* mask with a yellow face and protruding fangs. The curving and fluid patterns are reminiscent of the motifs on lacquerware. Square jars of this style were used as measuring containers during the Han dynasty.

They are known as *fang* in Chinese while circular ones are called *zhong*.

147

彩绘茧形壶

西汉

公元前 206—公元 8 年

高：31 厘米

阔：37.5 厘米

Painted pottery cocoon jar

Western Han dynasty

206 B.C.E. – 8 C.E.

Height: 31 cm

Width: 37.5 cm

泥质灰陶。小口外翻，束颈，腹大，呈椭圆形，小圈足外撇。颈有弦纹一道，腹饰弦纹数匝。腹体以朱彩、白粉彩和紫彩勾绘出云气纹四组，以三道朱彩竖直纹带分隔。纹饰鲜艳，气势磅礴，流畅自如，极为生动，反映了西汉时期彩绘水平之高。

Gray earthenware. The jar has a small mouth with everted rim, a constricted neck, a cocoon-shaped belly and a splayed ring foot. A rib encircles the neck. Several vertical grooves encompass the belly. The body is painted with red and purple pigments and white chalk. Four groups of cloud motif are divided by three vertical stripes of red color. This vessel is representative of the highest standards of pottery making in the Western Han dynasty.

148

灰陶龙柄魁

汉

公元前 206—公元 220 年

高：7.1 厘米

口径：18.7 厘米

Gray pottery ladle with dragon-handle

Han dynasty

206 B.C.E. – 220 C.E.

Height: 7.1 cm

Mouth diameter: 18.7 cm

灰陶。圆形、大口、直壁微敛、矮玉璧底。口缘下有弦纹一道、一侧置龙头把手、把手高度与口缘齐平。龙头刻划精细、睁眼、张口、伏角、形态可爱。龙头和魁身内外满涂朱砂红彩、可惜大部分已脱落、但内壁保留较完整。魁身质坚、壁薄、线条流畅、玉璧底部修坯十分精细。

Gray earthenware. The circular ladle has a wide mouth and straight sides that tapers towards a base in the shape of a jade disc. A groove runs around the exterior mouth rim. One side of the body is furnished with a handle in the shape of a dragon's head leveled with the mouth rim. The dragon is finely rendered with open eyes, gaping mouth and backward-thrusting horns. The ladle was originally painted with red pigment. Cinnabar red pigment that used to cover the entire ladle can be seen only on the inside of the ladle. The ladle has a hard and thin body. The jade-disc base has been meticulously trimmed.

149

彩绘人物谷仓

汉

公元前 206—公元 220 年

高：21 厘米

底径：11.2 厘米

Painted pottery granary jar with human figures

Han dynasty

206 B.C.E. – 220 C.E.

Height: 21 cm

Base diameter: 11.2 cm

泥质灰陶。锥形顶上置半圆状瓦脊，筒形体，下承三兽足，平底。仓身上部开一正方形窗。通体涂白粉为地，施红、黑彩。窗下仓腹两侧绘对向穿华丽服饰的妇女各二，窗四周和腹下端饰菱格纹。仓背描桌几一张，上置花瓶及罐。兽足现切削痕迹。此器色彩鲜艳，纹饰丰富，在研究汉代风俗习惯、人物和服饰方面有参考价值。

Gray earthenware. The granary jar has a conical lid with radiating ribs representing the cylindrical roof tiles, a square-shaped opening on the upper part of the body and a flat base supported by three animal legs. The entire surface is coated with white slip; decorative motifs are painted in red and black. The window is flanked on each side by two splendidly dressed ladies facing towards the window. A band of lozenge pattern encompasses the top and bottom of the vessel. The back of the granary is decorated with a low table displaying a vase and a jar. Vestiges of trimming and shaving are visible on the animal legs. The vessel is an excellent reference for studying the customs as well as the appearance and costumes of the Han people.

150

彩绘人物屋

汉

公元前 206—公元 220 年

高：22.3 厘米

底长：22.3 厘米

Painted pottery house with human figures

Han dynasty

206 B.C.E. – 220 C.E.

Height: 22.3 cm

Base length: 22.3 cm

泥质灰陶。单檐悬山顶、正面开窗、门各一。通体涂白粉为地、施红、黑彩。正面绘妇女二人、上饰门框和窗花。背面在矮儿上描画花瓶、碗、盖碗及灯笼等物。一侧面绘网状连线纹、另一侧画衣服。汉代厚葬之风盛行，本品显示了子孙希望去世的亲人在阴间仍能过着谷物满仓、童仆成群的舒适生活。

Gray earthenware. The pottery house has a gable roof with overhanging eaves. The facade is pierced with a window and a door. The walls are coated with white slip; decorative motifs are painted in red and black. Two ladies are depicted on the facade. The doorframe and lattice windows are outlined in black. The back wall is painted with a low table displaying some objects including a vase, a bowl, a covered bowl and a lantern. The sidewalls are decorated with check pattern on one side and a dress on the other. Furnishing the graves of the dead with an abundance of burial material was a common practice during the Han dynasty. People believed that by doing so the deceased would live comfortably in the afterlife.

151

灰陶彩绘说唱俑一对

汉

公元前 206—公元 220 年

高：14.7 厘米、18.5 厘米

Two painted pottery singers

Han dynasty

206 B.C.E. – 220 C.E.

Height: 14.7 cm, 18.5 cm

泥质灰陶。坐地者头梳高髻，身穿中长衣，束腰，双腿弯屈，双臂放在膝盖上，手指张开向前伸。张口，似高声歌唱。头发及鞋绘黑彩，面部、手脚绘红彩，衣服绘白彩。下肢见刀工批削痕，明快利落。站立者头梳高髻，身穿中长衣，束腰，双腿右前左后张开，双臂外展成 90 度角，握拳。口微张，似在讲话或低声歌唱。头发绘黑彩，面部及双手绘红彩，衣服绘白彩，裤为灰黑本色。下肢也有刀工批削痕。

汉墓中常出土田园、仓库、庐舍、车马、家畜、庖厨、伎乐百戏、奴婢劳作等模型，表现富贵人家的生活状况和社会关系，是汉代历史的真实写照。这对说唱俑是研究汉代文化生活的重要资料。

Gray earthenware. The figurine is seated with his knees bent, arms resting on the knees, palms open and fingers stretched. His hair is tied into a topknot and he wears a knee-length belted tunic. His wide-open mouth suggests that he is singing aloud. His hair and shoes are painted in black. His face, hands and legs are painted in pink and his clothes in white. Shaving marks from brisk trimming are visible around the exposed legs. The standing figurine also has his hair tied into a topknot. He wears a hip-length belted tunic and a pair of trousers. His feet are wide apart, his outstretched arms at a right angle to each other and his fists clenched. The slightly open mouth suggests that he is either talking or singing softly. His hair, face and hands are painted in pink and his upper garment in white. The dark gray color of his trousers is the original color of the paste. Shaving marks are visible around the trousers.

Lifelike models of granaries, houses, horses and wagons, domestic animals and figurines of cooks, jugglers, support staff and other attendants at work are burial objects commonly found in Han tombs. This pair of figurines is an important reference for studying the culture and the way of life of the people of the Han dynasty.

152

彩绘陶鸭形壶

汉

公元前 206—公元 220 年

高：25.5 厘米

底径：10.5 厘米

Duck-shaped painted pottery bottle

Han dynasty

206 B.C.E. – 220 C.E.

Height: 25.5 cm

Base diameter: 10.5 cm

灰陶。鸭长颈，顶有一方孔，嘴长而扁，嘴端略薄，左右刻眼，可见纯熟的刀削痕。身呈扁球形，整体造型像荸荠，生动地表现出鸭子肥美的憨态。壶体在黑彩地上满绘红、白彩纹饰，但不及底。颈、肩间堆隆起白彩圆点数周，红、黑、白彩对比鲜明，异常艳丽。造型别致，线条柔和。

Gray pottery. The bottle is in the shape of a duck with a long neck. There is a square opening on top of the head. The beak is flat and relatively thin at the tip. The shaving marks bespeak the proficient trimming technique of the potter. The flattened bulbous belly and the curved neck combined to resemble a water chestnut. Motifs are painted in red and white on a black ground. Several rounds of raised white dots encompass the lower neck. The contrasting colors combined to create an alluring visual effect.

153

加彩漆陶壶一对

西汉

公元前 206—公元 8 年

高：53.5 厘米（带盖），

 48.2 厘米（不带盖）

底径：24 厘米

Pair of black-lacquered pottery jars with painted motifs

Western Han dynasty

206 B.C.E. – 8 C.E.

Height: 53.5 cm (jar with lid),

 48.2 cm (jar without lid)

Base diameter: 24 cm

泥质灰陶。敞口，长颈，溜肩，圆腹，圈足。其一带圆拱形盖，另一不带盖。肩两侧贴兽面铺首。全器外表磨光髹黑漆，在漆面上用红、黄、白彩描绘流动的云气纹、水波纹、菱形纹和三角纹，运笔流畅，具有很高的技巧。

带盖的壶经粗暴冲洗，彩绘大部分被冲掉，露出器表的漆层，在黝黑光亮的漆层上仍可清楚见到彩绘痕迹。

另一不带盖的壶经轻微清洗，留下彩绘较多，器表被泥渍遮盖，未露出黑漆。

汉代漆陶是高档产品，出土数量很少。

Gray earthenware. Each jar has a wide mouth, a long neck, sloping shoulders and a bulbous belly. One has a domed lid and the other without. A pair of animal masks has been affixed to the shoulders. The entire outer surface is lacquered and decorated with cloud scrolls, wave motif, lozenge pattern and triangle design painted in red, yellow and white.

The painted motifs have mostly come off on the jar with a lid that has undergone heavy rinsing but some colors can still be seen over the glossy black lacquered surface.

Partial rinsing of the other jar has preserved a larger area of painted motifs but revealed less of the glossy black surface still covered by soil residues.

Lacquered pottery was a luxury item during the Han dynasty. Vessels like these are few and far between.

154

黑陶折腰壶

汉

公元前 206—公元 220 年

高：41 厘米

口径：24.5 厘米

Black pottery carinated jar

Han dynasty

206 B.C.E. – 220 C.E.

Height: 41 cm

Mouth diameter: 24.5 cm

泥质灰陶。斜高领、广斜肩，颈肩急缩，腹下急收到底，底平。器肩饰箭头状锥刺纹三道，其余光素无纹。本品纹饰简单，但口缘线、锥刺纹线、肩腹折纹线和足底缘的弦纹线配合器物外形凌厉的折线，对比鲜明，极具创意。

图录 155 号与本品外形极为相似，只是有施釉。

Gray earthenware. The vessel has a high collar. The slanting shoulders makes a sharp turn at around the mid-section of the body and then contracts drastically towards a flat base. Apart from three bands of pecked arrowheads encircling the shoulders, the vessel surface is devoid of decorative motifs.

Cat. No. 155 is very similar to this jar except that it is glazed.

155

绿釉高领折腰壶

东汉

公元 25—220 年

高：40.5 厘米

口径：21.5 厘米

Green-glazed pottery carinated jar

Eastern Han dynasty

25 – 220 C.E.

Height: 40.5 cm

Mouth diameter: 21.5 cm

泥质褐红陶。喇叭形口，阔斜肩、扁腹，腹下部急内斜收到底，底平。施绿色釉，之后再上一层透明釉，釉色光亮莹润，开细纹片。绿釉流淌，在壶的颈、肩和腹部形成一条条斑纹，与褐红胎色相间，色彩艳丽，装饰效果极强。底无釉，近底足露胎处可见旋纹痕。造型新颖别致。

参照汉墓出土陶壶，此种造型的陶壶应该是东汉晚期的制品。

Brownish-red earthenware. The jar has a trumpet-shaped mouth, sloping shoulders, carinated belly and a small flat base. The jar is glazed green under a layer of clear glaze with a smooth and lustrous surface covered with crackles. Streaks of running glaze appear around the neck, shoulders and belly that contrast sharply with the brownish-red shown through the thin glaze. The base and the area around the foot are without glaze. Circular wheel marks are visible on the unglazed foot.

Based on the examples excavated from Han tombs, jars of this shape should be dated to the late Eastern Han period.

156

绿褐釉朱雀纹壶

汉

公元前 206—公元 220 年

高：34.8 厘米

底径：16 厘米

Pottery vase with Vermilion Bird design

Han dynasty

206 B.C.E. – 220 C.E.

Height: 34.8 cm

Base diameter: 16 cm

侈口，束颈，斜肩，腹体中部圆鼓，下腹内敛，圈足外撇，平底。由颈部到腹部饰弦纹带四道。器外壁施褐黄釉。底部无釉，露红色胎。肩和上腹部相对两侧各刻振翅飞翔的朱雀一只，双翅及身体刻网状纹，刀法流畅自然，形态生动逼真。朱雀呈银绿色，是低温铅釉在潮湿环境下析出沉积后的现象。本品朱雀之刻工及呈色为汉代陶器雕刻艺术的佼佼者。

1995 年陕西甘泉县城汉墓出土有相似器物。

在同一件器物上施两种以上反差较大釉色的汉代低温铅釉陶器，全国有三个地区分布较为集中，一是河南济源地区；二是陕西宝鸡地区；三是陕北南部地区。

The vase has a flared mouth, a constricted neck, sloping shoulders and a globular belly that tapers towards a splayed foot with a flat base. Four bands of cord motif encircle the neck and the upper body. The exterior surface is covered with a yellowish-brown glaze. The unglazed base reveals a red paste. The vase is decorated on both sides with a Vermilion Bird with crosshatching on the body and the wings. The iridescent green glaze on the birds is the result of burial and is typical of low-fired lead glaze. The engraving and coloring are among the finest in Han pottery.

A similar artifact was unearthed in April 1995 from a Han tomb in Ganquan, Shaanxi province.

Han dynasty low-fired lead-glazed ceramics with two or more contrasting glaze colors on the same vessel are found in three areas in China: Jiyuan in Henan province; Baoji in Shaanxi province; and Ganquan in southern Shaanxi.

157

绿釉弦纹三足罐

汉

公元前 206—公元 220 年

高：28.4 厘米

底径：19.8 厘米

Green-glazed three-legged jar

Han dynasty

206 B.C.E. – 220 C.E.

Height: 28.4 cm

Base diameter: 19.8 cm

小口，短直颈，阔肩，腹部圆鼓，中腹以下收敛较急，平底，底置三矮足。肩刻单弦纹一周，腹饰双凸弦纹两组，棱线流畅有力。罐体断面胎呈红色。底露胎，呈浅黄色。器外壁满施釉，釉厚薄不均匀，腹中部有泪痕。肩呈绿色，腹中部为绿色、褐色及绿褐色交错，腹下半部呈深褐色到近黑色。肩和腹中部釉有部分脱落，但残存釉色极为翠绿和光亮，腹下半部釉色保存良好，晶莹柔润。内壁无釉，胎表面呈灰色。本品胎较薄，叩之声音较清脆，烧成温度应较一般釉陶高。

The jar has a small mouth, a short straight neck, broad shoulders and a bulging belly that narrows towards a flat base supported by three short legs. An incised line encompasses the shoulders while two groups of double ridges encircle the belly. The exterior surface is decorated with a variety of glaze colors. The upper section is covered with patches of brilliant green intermixed with brown and brownish-green. The glaze is uneven in thickness and tear marks are visible around the middle part of the belly. The lower section of the body is green and dark brown. The glaze on the lower belly is well preserved. Its smooth surface takes on a soft luster. The glaze near the base looks almost black. Broken edges reveal a red paste. The unglazed bottom appears pale yellow and the unglazed interior gray. This jar has a relatively thin body that gives a pleasant sound when struck. Its firing temperature is probably higher than the average glazed ware.

158

绿釉鸟形灯

汉

公元前 206—公元 220 年

高：31.4 厘米

底径：10.4 厘米

Bird-shaped pottery lamp in green glaze

Han dynasty

206 B.C.E. – 220 C.E.

Height: 31.4 cm

Base diameter: 10.4 cm

四方柱体，上顶四方平台，台上置三足鸟形油灯，下为半圆山纹底座。鸟细长颈，睁眼、伏耳、昂首朝天，翅膀外展、翘尾，有冲天之势。灯盘作鸟体，向下分级渐敛，外侧及翅膀饰圆圈和条状纹。泥质红陶胎。除内底座外，满施绿釉。造型大气，线条简练、优美传神，有很高的艺术水平。汉代青铜灯也有此类造型。

From a mountain-shaped semi-spherical pedestal rises a square pole surmounted by a square platform and a three-legged oil dish in the shape of a bird. The bird has a long and slender neck, wide-open eyes, fold-back ears, raised head, stretching wings and an upright tail. The abdomen of the bird serves as the oil dish. The tiered base and the underside of the wings are decorated with circular and stripe motifs. Red earthenware. The entire surface except the base of the pedestal is in green glaze. The shape is similar to the bronze lamps from the Han period.

159

黑釉陶都树

汉

公元前 206—公元 220 年

高：58.8 厘米

底：15.4 厘米 × 15.4 厘米

Pottery tree with black glaze

Han dynasty

206 B.C.E. – 220 C.E.

Height: 58.8 cm

Base: 15.4 cm × 15.4 cm

泥质红陶。底平。树干呈圆锥形，立于正四方形底座中央，上贴蝉四组，每组三只，对称围伏于树干上，上小下大，比例协调。顶置天鸡两只，头、爪相接成菱形，上穿三孔，中间大两侧小。底座四角塑双角卧兽各一，两兽中间各置一坐熊。坐熊头立小兽，前腿伏于树干，树干刻菱格纹、山纹和斜直纹，兽和蝉体印圆圈纹，鸡体饰直线纹，方座刻草叶纹及印圆圈纹。通体施黑褐色釉，釉泛青，满开细碎纹片。

桃都树语出《括地图》："桃都山有大桃树，盘屈三千里，上有金鸡，日照则鸣。"古人视桃都树为神树，可通天。道教以桃木剑为降妖伏魔的法器。蝉被古人视为能获得超脱和再生的神虫，在祭典中可用于通神。

Red earthenware. The pole-like conical trunk of the tree rises from the center of a square pedestal. Four groups of incrementally sized cicadas, three per group, diminishing in size as it goes up, encircle the trunk of the tree. On the top of the tree stand two facing roosters. The top is pierced as well as the tails of the roosters. Four sculpted animals with double horns crouch at the corners of

the pedestal. A bear decorates each of the four sides of the base. On the bear's head stands an animal. The trunk is engraved with peak motif, oblique hatching and crosshatching. The bodies of the animals and cicadas are stamped with circular motif while the bodies of the roosters are incised with vertical hatching. The square pedestal is carved with leafy motif and stamped with dots. The entire sculpture is coated with a brownish-black glaze with a greenish tint and numerous crackles.

This kind of tree is called a Taodu tree.

According to *Kuoditu*, a book on mystic geography compiled in the Han dynasty, "In Taodu Mountain there is a huge peach tree that covers an area of three thousand *li* (Chinese mile). On top of the tree stands a golden rooster that crows at sunrise." The ancient Chinese considered the peach tree a divine tree that can rise up to Heaven. Daoist priests use peach wood swords to perform exorcism rituals. The ancient Chinese saw the cicada as a sacred symbol of resurrection and it was used as a medium during sacrificial rituals.

绿釉铺首凤纹盖樽酒具一套

汉

公元前 206—公元 220 年

高：19.2 厘米（樽）

长：13 厘米（勺），10.5 厘米（耳杯）

径：20.1 厘米（樽），11.9 厘米（盘）

Green-glazed wine set
with *zun* container

Han dynasty

206 B.C.E. – 220 C.E.

Height: 19.2 cm(*zun* container)

Length: 13 cm(ladle), 10.5 cm(ear-cup)

Diameter: 20.1 cm(*zun* container),
　　　　　 11.9 cm(tray)

樽与长柄勺、耳杯（羽觞）组成一套完整的汉代酒具。

樽直口平唇，筒式体、平底，三兽足。自口部至底足刻弦纹三组，口缘下两侧对称贴兽耳衔环铺首。盖子口，顶饰三圈凸弦纹线，纹间模印飞凤衔环、双勾山形纹、水纹和叶纹。全器内外满施翠绿釉，光彩夺目，由于坯为泥质红陶，薄釉处呈现褐红色，产生色彩变幻效果。盖面和樽体内底泛银白色。三兽足底部各有细条形顶烧钉一个。

勺为椭圆形，外壁印水纹，龙首柄。耳杯为船形，外壁印水纹、山纹和菱纹，两侧贴长圆形折耳。盘为侈口，浅腹，平底。用于放置勺。

樽为盛酒器，汉代釉陶、唐代三彩釉陶均有生产。李白《行路难》："金樽清酒斗十千，玉盘珍羞直万钱。"说的就是这类器物。

此套器物纹饰清晰、细腻、流畅，釉色艳丽，体薄工整，为同类器物之精品。

A complete wine set during the Han period would include a wine container (*zun*), a ladle and ear-cups (*yushang*).

The wine container has a straight mouth and a base supported by three animal legs. The *zun* container is decorated with three groups of cord motif encircling the upper, middle and lower body. A pair of appliqué ringed-masks is affixed on the sides. The lip is rabbeted to hold the lid in place. On the top of the lid stands a flying phoenix holding a ring in its mouth enclosed by a round of double-lined peak motif and a round of wave motif bounded by serrate leaves. Both the exterior and interior of the vessel are coated with a lustrous emerald-green glaze. The reddish-brown color of the paste comes through the glaze where it runs thin, producing a fascinating visual effect. The top of the lid and the inner bottom of the vessel show a beautiful silvery iridescence. A tiny spur is found attached to the underside of each animal foot.

The ladle is oval-shaped with stamped wave motif on the outside and has a long handle in the shape of a dragon's head. The boat-shaped ear-cup has an oval wing-ear on both sides. The exterior is impressed with wave, peak and lozenge designs. The tray has a flared mouth, shallow sides and a flat base.

Vessels of this shape have been found among Han glazed pottery and Tang *sancai* (tricolored) wares. In his poem, *Xinglunan* (A Difficult Journey), the Tang poet Li Bo writes, "The golden *zuns* are filled with ten catties of wine; the foods served on the jade plates are worth ten thousand *qian* (a monetary unit)." The *zun* mentioned in this poem refers to this kind of vessel.

This wine set is noted for its exquisite craftsmanship and brilliant glaze color. It is a superlative example of its kind.

161

绿釉狩猎纹壶

汉

公元前 206—公元 220 年

高：38.4 厘米

底径：19.8 厘米

Green-glazed pottery vase with hunting scene

Han dynasty

206 B.C.E. – 220 C.E.

Height: 38.4 cm

Base diameter: 19.8 cm

盘口，长颈，斜肩，腹部圆鼓下敛，近底直向下垂，平底。肩腹上下饰三线弦纹两组，对称贴衔环铺首一对，围以狩猎纹带一周，有人骑马弯弓待射，山野有奔逃中的虎、羊、鹿、马等走兽与飞禽，模印纹饰深邃清晰，动物形态栩栩如生，充满动态美感。颈和下腹部光素无纹。泥质红陶胎。器身施深翠绿色釉，器体满布釉料流淌的浆痕。釉光均匀亮泽。

The vessel has a plate-mouth, a long neck, sloping shoulders, a globular belly that narrows to a straight foot and a flat base. An appliqué ringed-mask is affixed to both sides of the shoulders. A frieze of carved motif bounded on both sides by triple grooves decorates the body. A horse rider with a bow in his hands and a number of birds and animals including a tiger, a goat, a deer and a horse are depicted in the hunting scene. Both the neck and the lower belly are undecorated. Red earthenware. The exterior surface is covered with an even and lustrous layer of emerald-green glaze. Streaks of running glaze are visible on the vessel surface.

162

绿釉望楼

东汉

公元 25—220 年

高：58.5 厘米

阔（盆）：40.4 厘米

Pottery watchtower with green glaze

Eastern Han dynasty

25 – 220 C.E.

Height: 58.5 cm

Width (basin): 40.4 cm

泥质红陶。庑殿顶两层楼，下承四曲尺形足柱，立于圆形水池内。屋顶和平台均以一斗三升斗拱承担。上层平台栏杆四角有张弩控弦的武士向四周戒备。下层较高大，为密闭式，饰砖形纹，开一小门，门与池岸之间架有素胎小桥，体现碉楼坚固、易守难攻。水池周边堆贴昂首素胎鹅六只，水池内置鹅一只、青蛙一只、游鱼五条，栩栩如生。鹅群警觉性高，可能是用于防卫。通体施绿釉，釉色清澈明亮，泛银色光。

水亭、望楼和碉楼均为汉代坞堡的保卫设施。

Red earthenware. Two-storied watchtower with hipped roof supported by four pillars. The projecting eaves of the hipped roof and the balcony overhang are supported by corbel bracket sets comprising one block and three arms. An archer with a bow in his hand guards each corner of the balcony. The lower story has a higher ceiling. The absence of openings on the walls except a half-opened small door suggests the defensive nature of this tower. The bridge that links the front entrance to the other side of the pond is without glaze. Six unglazed sculpted geese perch on the outer edge of the pond while the seventh one swims inside it, accompanied by one frog and five fish. The squadron of geese by the waterside has defensive implication because these birds are known to fan their wings and shriek at the sight of intruders. The entire sculpture is coated with a lucid green glaze with silvery iridescence.

Waterside pavilions, watchtowers and fortresses are all part of the formidable defensive works of the Han dynasty.

163
绿褐釉兽足谷仓

西汉

公元前 206—公元 8 年

高：31.3 厘米

Pottery granary jar with green and reddish-brown glazes

Western Han dynasty

206 B.C.E. – 8 C.E.

Height: 31.3 cm

泥质红陶。小平口，圆肩，筒形体，上阔下微敛，平底，下承三熊足。带山形平盖，呈褐绿色。三组三重弦纹把器体分为四部分，上部施绿釉，其余施褐红釉。造型稳重，褐、绿釉色对比鲜明。

本品是刻意烧成两色，要令绿、褐色分界明显，需对釉的配比、浓度以及烧制温度掌握十分准确。

Red earthenware. The jar has a small flat mouth, rounded shoulders and a cylindrical body that tapers slightly to a flat base supported by three bear-shaped legs. The lid is shaped into a mountain and glazed brownish-green. The body is divided into four horizontal sections by three bands of triple grooves encompassing the body. The uppermost section is glazed green while the rest is coated with reddish-brown glaze.

This jar was designed to display two contrasting glaze colors. In order to achieve such a clean demarcation line between the two glazes, the amount of iron oxide and copper oxide in the two glazes as well as the consistency of the glazes and the firing temperature had to be flawless.

164

绿釉熊足谷仓

汉

公元前 206—公元 220 年

高：37.8 厘米

底径：19.3 厘米

**Green-glazed pottery granary jar
with bear-shaped legs**

Han dynasty

206 B.C.E. – 220 C.E.

Height: 37.8 cm

Base diameter: 19.3 cm

泥质红陶。平口，带山形纹扁平状盖。
伞形顶，上有放射状凸起伞骨状瓦脊。
筒形体，平底，下承以三熊足。盖的底
部贴三个圆柱状突出物，用以把盖固定
在谷仓口上。仓体以三组四重弦纹装饰，
给单调的筒状腹增添了美感。全器满施
绿釉，聚釉处呈翠绿色，釉薄处呈褐黄色。
造型稳重，熊足生动精细。

Red earthenware. The jar has a flat mouth.
The top resembles an umbrella with
radiating ribs representing roof tiles. The
lid is decorated with mountain motif. The
cylindrical body is supported by three
bear-shaped legs. The underside of the lid
has three cylindrical appliqué struts for
holding the lid in place. The body of the
granary is decorated with three bands of
quadruple grooves. The entire vessel is
covered with a green glaze that takes on
a dazzling emerald hue where it pools and
appears brownish-yellow where it runs thin.

165

褐绿釉陶灶

汉

公元前 206—公元 220 年

高：21.8 厘米

长：29 厘米

Pottery stove in brownish-green glaze

Han dynasty

206 B.C.E. – 220 C.E.

Height: 21.8 cm

Length: 29 cm

泥质红陶。灶前端为圆弧形，后端平直，四熊足承托。烟囱顶塑成博山形，后有火门。两灶眼置一大一小两釜，四周置镂铲、勺子等厨具，以及鱼、肉、主食和碟装的菜肴。面周边饰回字纹带，火门两侧模印一人及一个大水缸，平板有火云气纹，以示正在烧火煮食，而司厨站在一旁，随时调整火候和添水。全器满施褐绿釉。此器造型新颖别致、纹饰丰富、雕塑及印工均极精细，甚为罕见。

Red earthenware. This lifelike model of a stove is a rectangular block with rounded edges in front. It is supported by four bear-shaped legs. The chimney is in the shape of a mountain. The rear wall has a vent opening and an extended work platform. There are two cauldrons, a stirrer, a ladle and various foodstuffs on the stovetop. The walls flanking the vent are molded with a figure and a large water jar and the extended base patterns of flames and billowing smoke. The raging flames suggest cooking in progress. The entire surface is covered with an brownish-green glaze.

绿釉银光陶井

东汉

公元 25—220 年

高：23.6 厘米

口径：17.6 厘米

Green-glazed pottery wellhead with silvery iridescence

Eastern Han dynasty

25 – 220 C.E.

Height: 23.6 cm

Mouth diameter: 17.6 cm

泥质红陶。井栏口呈圆形，方折缘，身微斜，平底微内凹。上竖弧形井架，屋顶形盖顶，屋顶下两支柱之间置滑轮。盖顶和井架两侧贴小鸟各一，顶鸟朝前，两侧小鸟相背。井内安放平底瓶，用以汲水。器内外满施绿釉，呈美丽的银绿色。通常低温釉的胎釉结合不牢固，釉很易剥落，但本品保存极好，应是烧造温度较高及墓室干燥所致。用手指击叩时，器物发出清脆的铛铛声。

唐代称井栏为"床"。《韵会》称床："井干，井上木栏也。"李白《答王十二寒夜独酌有怀》："怀余对酒夜霜白，玉床金井冰峥嵘。"《静夜思》："床前明月光，疑是地上霜。"诗中的"床"都是指井栏。

Red earthenware. The circular well is enclosed by parapets with angular overhang and straight sides that tapers towards a flat base with a slightly recessed center. Arching over the well is a wellhead surmounted by a small pavilion with a pulley. On top of the roof stands a front-facing bird. Halfway down the arch on either side of the wellhead rests a small bird facing sideways and away from each other. Inside the well lies a flat-bottomed jar for drawing water. The entire piece is covered with green glaze with rainbow and silvery iridescence. Low-fired glaze usually does not sinter well with the paste and is prone to flaking. However, the glaze on this piece is extremely well preserved, probably a result of high firing temperature and low humidity in the tomb chamber. When knocked with the knuckle, the body gives a clear and melodious sound.

During the Tang dynasty, the parapet around the mouth of the well was called chuang, a word that commonly means "bed". In his poem, Da Wang Shi'er hanye duzhuo youhuai (In reply to Wang Shi'er's Reflections on Drinking Alone in a Cold Night), the Tang poet Li Bai writes, "You thought of me being alone with my wine in a frosty night when water has gone frozen in the well with jade parapet and golden railing." Another poem Jingyesi (Contemplation in a Quiet Night) also by Li Bai reads, "The moon shines brightly over the parapet (around the well), creating the illusion of a frosty ground. I raise my head to watch the moon and lower my head to contemplate my hometown."

167

黑陶鱼纹盘

六朝

公元 222—589 年

高：13.1 厘米

口径：40.8 厘米

Black pottery dish with fish design

Six Dynasties

222 – 589 C.E.

Height: 13.1 cm

Mouth diameter: 40.8 cm

黑陶，胎细腻。口缘外折，微斜，斜腹壁，平底。内口缘有凹弦纹一周。盘内底刻鱼三尾，鱼头重叠呈"品"字形。内壁两侧对称刻大鱼各一尾，鱼身饰锥刺鱼鳞纹，锥刺尖锐突起；另两侧各刻一个用于捕捉鱼虾的竹篓。鱼纹勾勒生动流畅，自然逼真。本品刻工精美绝伦，为六朝同类器物中的精品。

《三国志·魏书·王肃传》裴松之注引《魏略》："（董）遇言：'当以三余。'或问三余之意。遇言：'冬者岁之余，夜者日之余，阴雨者时之余也。'"后以"三余"泛指空闲时间。如晋陶渊明《感士不遇赋序》："余尝以三余之日，讲习之暇，读其文，慨然惆怅。"而中国的私塾也有以"三余斋"为名。由于"三鱼"与"三余"谐音，故本品可能是勉励人们要好好利用空闲时间去学习和提升自己。

Black pottery with a refined paste. The vessel has a slightly outward-slanting everted rim and a straight side that tapers towards a flat base. A groove runs under the inner mouth rim. The middle of the dish is decorated with three fish with their heads overlapping each other in trefoil-like arrangement. The inner wall is carved with two large fish with pecked scales. There are two wicker baskets used for catching fish and shellfish between them. The tactile quality of the decorations brings the entire vessel to life. This vessel is a superlative example of its kind.

"Three fish" (sanyu) is homophonous with the expression known as "three surplus times" (sanyu). In Weilue (Brief History of the Wei State [of the Three Kingdoms Period]), the Han dynasty scholar, Dong Yu, writes, "Winter is the surplus time of the year; the night is the surplus time of the day; overcast and rainy days are the surplus time of sunny days". He urged his followers to make sure of the "three surplus times" to read and educate themselves. Later on, "sanyu" became a generic term for "surplus times". In the Preface to Ganshibuyu fu (Melancholy over Unrecognized Talent), the Eastern Jin scholar, Tao Yuanming, says, "I read [similar] works [written by some earlier scholars] in my 'three surplus times' and after teaching hours. They made me feel heavy-hearted." Some private academies in China called themselves Sanyuzhai (Sanyu studio). Since "three fish" and "three surplus times" share the same pronunciation in Chinese, the three-fish motif could have been a pun encouraging people to make good use of their surplus time to study and enrich their minds.

168

灰陶磨划纹长颈大瓶

北魏

公元 386—534 年

高：48.4 厘米

底径：13.3 厘米

Large gray pottery vase with scraped motifs

Northern Wei dynasty

386 – 534 C.E.

Height: 48.4 cm

Base diameter: 13.3 cm

灰陶，质细腻坚致。口缘外翻，圆唇，长颈，斜肩，缩腹，平底。颈腹起凸弦纹四道。上、下两道弦纹较粗大，沿弦线满雕锥刺纹。颈部满饰垂直磨划纹，肩和腹部分别置斜向与直向交叉磨划纹。此器纹饰简单大方，线条清爽脱俗，具有很高的艺术和欣赏价值。

河南偃师北魏墓出土有相似器物。1998 年山西大同市南郊区水泊寺乡北魏墓出土有相似器物。

Gray pottery with a hard and fine paste. The vase has a flared mouth with everted rim and rounded lip, a narrow long neck, sloping shoulders and a belly that tapers gently towards a flat base. The ribs marking the top and bottom of the shoulders are lined with pecked motif. Two more ribs encircle the middle part of the shoulders. The shoulders and the belly are decorated with crosshatching and check pattern.

A similar vessel has been unearthed from a Northern Wei tomb in Yanshi, Henan province. Another similar vessel has also been unearthed in 1998 from a Northern Wei tomb at Shuiposixiang in the southern suburb of Datong, Shanxi province.

169

黄绿釉碗

北齐

公元 550—577 年

相州窑

高：9.2 厘米

口径：12 厘米

底径：5.5 厘米

Bowl with yellow-green glaze

Northern Qi dynasty

550 – 577 C.E.

Xiangzhou kilns

Height: 9.2 cm

Mouth diameter: 12 cm

Base diameter: 5.5 cm

碗呈杯状，实足，底足微外撇，足边缘斜削一周。外底心微内凹，留有三个细小呈品字形分布的长条状支烧痕，痕平滑，呈浅红色。内底心留有一大二小规整呈 "品" 字形分布的圆形叠烧痕。胎薄，触之有粉质感。修胎精细规矩。施黄绿色釉，外壁施釉半截，露出洁白微泛红、打磨光滑细腻的胎骨，内、外壁釉面满布细密开片纹，呈水银光泽。本品又名金钟杯，线条柔和，制作精细，当为供皇室使用的器物。

1968 年河北平山县上三汲村崔昂墓出土有相似器物。

The bowl has the shape of a cup with a slightly splayed foot and a solid flat base. The base has a beveled rim and a slightly recessed center bearing three tiny strip-like spur marks of light red color with a smooth surface. The inside of the bowl bears marks left by one larger and two smaller fireclay spacers neatly positioned at the points of a triangle. The entire interior is covered with a yellow-green glaze but the glaze covers only the upper half of the exterior wall, exposing a fine and highly burnished thin paste of white color with a reddish tint and a powdery touch. The body has been meticulously and neatly trimmed. The glaze on the interior and exterior surfaces has crackles and a silvery iridescent luster. This bowl is also called *jinzhongbei* (golden bell cup). This bowl is noted for its delicate lines and exquisite craftsmanship. This bowl was likely made for imperial use.

A similar vessel was unearthed in 1968

from the tomb of Cui Ang at Sanji village in Pingshan, Hebei province.

170

白釉绿彩四系盖罐

北齐

公元 550—577 年

相州窑

高：20 厘米

底径：17 厘米

White-glazed lidded jar with four lugs and green splashes

Northern Qi dynasty

550 – 577 C.E.

Xiangzhou kilns

Height: 20 cm

Base diameter: 17 cm

罐口平缘，直颈，斜长肩。口上附伞形盖。底平、微外撇，底边缘斜削一周。腹中部起凸缘，将腹部分成两部分。肩上方贴尖形系四个，系以弦纹相连。白胎微泛黄，瓷土经过淘洗提炼。器外壁施淡黄色釉，釉不及底，釉层较薄，釉面起细碎纹片，满布水银光。罐身有三块绿彩斑。凸缘上和盖面聚釉处留有大量虹化沉积物。本品应为釉陶器。

相州窑窑址在河南安阳，因隋唐时称相州而得名，也称安阳窑。

1971 年河南省安阳县洪河屯村发现的北齐骠骑大将军范粹墓出土有与本品造型相近并带绿彩的罐。

The jar is fabricated from white paste with a yellowish tint. The refined china clay has been levigated. The jar has a parasol-shaped lid, flat mouth, straight neck, tall slanting shoulders, and a flat base with a beveled rim. The flange encircling the mid-section of the jar divides the belly into two parts. Four equally spaced lugs with pointed tips are affixed to the shoulders and connected by rounds of indented lines. The exterior surface of the vessel is covered with a relatively thin layer of pale yellow glaze that stops short of the base. Three green splashes appear on the glaze around the body. The glaze is covered with tiny crackles and iridescent luster. Large amount of rainbow deposits are visible on the flange and the lid where the glaze accumulates. This jar should belongs to the category of glazed pottery.

The Xiangzhou kilns were located in Anyang, Henan province. The region was called Xiangzhou during the Sui and Tang dynasties, hence the name. These kilns are also known as Anyang kilns.

A jar of similar shape with similar green splashes was unearthed in 1971 from a tomb at Honghetun village in Anyang, Henan province. The tomb belonged to Fan Cui, a general of the Northern Qi dynasty, posthumously honored as "Great General of Chariots and Cavalry".

171

绿釉唾壶

北朝

公元 386—581 年

相州窑

高：12.8 厘米

底径：8 厘米

Pottery spittoon with green glaze

Northern Dynasties

386 – 581 C.E.

Xiangzhou kilns

Height: 12.8 cm

Base diameter: 8 cm

泥质红陶。盘口、束颈、斜扁圆腹、圆饼状平底微外撇、外底心微内凹。底有弦纹一周。体薄、质颇坚硬。全器内外满施绿釉、施釉不均、釉薄处呈现胎骨的褐红色。器身釉面满布开片纹，尤以薄釉处更明显。底部留有十分工整呈"品"字形分布的细小支烧痕三个、支钉断面呈红色、支钉大小和排列方法与图录160号汉绿釉铺首凤纹盖樽酒具相同。

釉陶到东汉末年衰落，十六国时期北方恢复生产、至北朝时期有所发展。

Red earthenware. The paste is thin and rather hard. The vessel has a plate mouth, a constricted neck, sloping shoulders, a rounded belly and a disc-like flat base with a slightly recessed center. The interior and exterior surfaces are covered with green glaze of uneven thickness. The brownish-red color of the paste comes through where the glaze runs thin. The surface of the glaze is full of crackles, and in particular, the areas where the glaze runs thin. The bottom is grooved once near the edge and has three very neat and equally spaced spur marks. The size and position of the spur marks are similar to those found on Cat. No. 160.

Production of glazed pottery declined in the late Eastern Han period, resumed in northern China during the Six Dynasties and made considerable progress during the Northern Dynasties.

172

三彩凤首壶

北齐—隋

公元 550—618 年

巩义窑

高：36.5 厘米

底径：9.8 厘米

Pottery phoenix-head ewer with *sancai* glaze

Northern Qi – Sui dynasty

550 – 618 C.E.

Gongyi kilns

Height: 36.5 cm

Base diameter: 9.8 cm

附图 5　宁夏固原李贤夫妇墓出土鎏金银银胡瓶（北周）

Fig. 5　Gilt silver ewer of Persian origin unearthed from the tomb of Li Xian and his wife in Guyuan, Ningxia (Northern Zhou)

小口，口上围以圆珠十二颗。口、颈交界处作凤首状，细颈斜溜肩，胆状圆腹，上腹左右贴浮雕联珠纹团花。前方饰绶带，由颈直落中腹部，端点贴菱形花。绶带相对一侧，由口缘到腹中部置曲形把柄。柄堆塑成葡萄枝状，上挂葡萄两串，呈棕黄、紫黑色。柄下端贴联珠纹团花一个，上下置云气纹各一。胎色白中泛红，胎质细腻，有粉质感。遍身施绿色釉为地，兼施棕黄釉和白釉，绿色有如嫩柳新荷，淡雅宜人，显得格外鲜艳可爱，这种鲜嫩的绿色为北齐和隋三彩器所独有。器表釉面和皮壳呈彩虹光泽。圆高足外撇，边缘上卷，上有砖红色呈"品"字形分布的支钉三个，其一已破损，支钉大小和排列方法与图录 171 号北朝绿釉唾壶相同。足底内凹成漏斗形，露胎。此壶形制特别，造型优美，雍容华贵，为凤首壶之珍品。

凤首壶工艺造型受波斯萨珊王朝金银器有盖鸟首壶（胡瓶）的影响，充满异国情调（附图 5）。反映了北朝和隋唐时通过陆上和海上丝绸之路与中东和中近东各国的文化交往，显示了中国陶瓷艺术对外来文化的吸收。

The flared mouth of the ewer is crowned with twelve large-sized beads. The upper part of the narrow neck is in the shape of a phoenix's head. The ewer has a pyriform belly decorated on both sides with an appliqué floral medallion bordered by small beads. A raised garland runs down the front of the body from under the beak of the phoenix and terminates in an appliqué diaper. The handle arching between the mouth and the belly is modeled as a grapevine laden with two bunches of grapes, one in amber and the other in purplish-black. Two scrolling clouds are attached to the sides of the handle. A floral medallion encircled by beads conceals the junction between the end of the handle and the belly. The pale pink paste is refined. The surface of the vessel is covered with a soft green glaze highlighted with amber and white splashes. The tall splayed foot has roll-up edges bearing three spur marks (one missing). The size and position of the spur marks on the vessel are similar to those found on Cat. No. 171. The base of the foot is unglazed and has a funnel-shaped interior. This vessel is a rarity among phoenix-head ewers.

The design of the phoenix-head ewers was influenced by Persian metal ware, namely the lidded bird-head ewer of the Sassanian Empire (Fig. 5). Ideas and elements from foreign cultures that were part of the transcontinental and maritime Silk Routes during the Northern Dynasties, Sui dynasty and Tang dynasty were readily assimilated into Chinese culture.

唐宋辽元陶器

Pottery of the Tang, Song, Liao and Yuan

唐宋辽元陶器：

绚丽多彩

唐文化博大精深，唐代陶瓷艺术也反映了"盛唐气象"。唐朝陶器的品种很多，应用很广，有灰陶、红陶和彩绘陶，从日常生活用具到陈设艺术品，乃至人物、动物俑等墓葬随葬品，都有很高的艺术性。

此时最具代表性的陶器是唐三彩。唐三彩属于低温釉陶，用红色陶土或白色坩子土作胎，釉中大量加入铅作助熔剂，以含铁、铜、钴等元素的矿物为呈色剂。一般来说唐三彩要先素烧胎，然后施釉再烧，烧釉的温度要低于第一次烧胎的温度，烧胎的温度一般在850℃—1000℃左右，烧釉的温度在750℃—850℃之间。

不同颜色的釉需要加入不同的呈色剂，而白釉则不需要。铅釉中加入氧化铁，釉色呈黄色、赭褐色、棕色、黑色等颜色；加入铜的氧化物，釉色呈老绿色、浅绿色、翠绿色等；加入钴，可烧出蓝釉，有深沉的藏蓝色、纯正的天蓝色等。所以唐三彩并非只有三种颜色。因为在中国人心目中，"三"表"多"的意思，所以称多彩陶器为三彩。

工匠施釉看似随意，但其实还是有所设计的。比如图录 190 号三彩兽足炉，有白釉、褐黄釉和蓝釉等，其肩部有一周美丽的褐黄釉围成的宽体白色莲瓣纹，每瓣的中心还有一条浅黄线代表瓣心。入窑焙烧时釉层熔融、流动、浸漫、中和，釉彩灿烂夺目，让人无法数清究竟有多少色彩。

烧制三彩的窑场有河南巩义窑，河北邢窑，陕西铜川黄堡窑，西安醴泉坊窑，四川邛窑等等。除传统器形外，很多生活用具的原型来源于波斯及中东地区的金银器、玻璃器、铜器，反映出唐朝和外面世界的交往活动，以及胡汉融合的多元文化。

如图录 178 号和 179 号类型的陶塔，在唐墓尤其官僚贵族墓出土较多，与南亚印度等国的佛塔有相似之处。初唐为一个侈口罐加上一个塔尖形状的盖；盛唐时罐体加高，除塔尖形的盖以外，罐底向下延伸成喇叭形底座；中晚唐时底座和罐身分开制作。摆设时盖、罐、底座相配，气派壮观，本身线条就很优美，加上华美的彩绘更加不同凡响。

唐三彩釉陶工艺在唐以后继续存在，宋、辽、西夏、金、元都继续生产，元代以后发展为琉璃釉陶。辽代陶器受唐三彩釉陶工艺的影响，生产大量精美的铅釉陶器，其中不乏深具民族特色的器物，如图录 203 号皮囊壶等。辽三彩也有粗细之分，粗者胎质松软呈红色，釉色混浊不透明，施釉不到底，釉层易剥落。细者如图录 204 号三彩摩羯壶，胎薄、质细滑呈淡红色，施釉讲究，除底外全身挂釉，釉色娇艳夺目，可与唐三彩媲美。邻国日本、朝鲜以及中东地区的波斯、非洲的埃及受唐三彩工艺的影响，先后烧出带有自身特点的低温多彩陶器，如日本奈良彩、朝鲜新罗三彩、波斯三彩、埃及三彩等等。

唐宋时期，居于云南南诏国（公元 738—902 年）和大理国（公元 937—1253 年）的白族，由于大乘佛教的传入而产生火葬制度。火葬最有代表性的是其葬具——火葬罐。当时殡葬崇尚简朴，并无太多陪葬品，一般只有贝币、铜钱、铜镯、铜片、小杯、碟、碗和料器等。火葬罐内安放死者骨灰和未烧尽、经贴金或涂朱砂并书梵文的余骨。以材质来看，火葬罐有陶、瓷、铜和石制，以陶器最多、最普遍。葬式规格视死者身份而定，普通者用单罐，富者用外罐套装内罐。纹饰方面，绝大多数是素面。一部分罐面朱书梵文经咒，饰莲瓣纹或贴塑模印莲瓣纹、十二生肖等，象征高洁清净的西方极乐世界。小部分罐面阴刻梵文经咒和亡者佛名，应是上层阶级所用。经咒多是《佛顶尊胜陀罗尼经》中的《陀罗尼》部分，这一部分又称为"陀罗尼咒"或"陀罗尼神咒"，用来超度死者亡灵（图录180号、181号和182号）。宗教信仰和火葬习俗是南诏、大理国最重要的文化遗存，具有鲜明的时代、地域和民族特色。

Pottery of the Tang, Song, Liao and Yuan:

Resplendent Brilliance

Tang ceramics are known for its boundless splendor. It also boasts a variety of pottery types that include gray pottery, red pottery and painted pottery that are used as daily utensils, decorative objects as well as mortuary wares.

Sancai, or tri-colored glazed pottery, is the most representative of the pottery from the Tang dynasty. It is a type of low-fired glazed pottery fabricated from red earthen clay or a white earthen material known as *ganzitu*. The glaze is formulated from china clay, earthen clay, plant ash and lime. Substantial amount of lead ash and dregs were added as flux agents while iron oxide, copper oxide and cobalt oxide were employed as colorants. *Sancai* pottery is usually fired twice, to a temperature of 850℃ –1000℃ before glazing and then to a lower temperature of 750℃–850℃ after glazing.

Various metallic oxides are incorporated into the glazes to obtain different hues, but no metallic oxide was required for white glaze. Yellow, reddish-brown, amber and black are produced by adding iron oxide into the lead glaze. Green is derived from copper oxide. The amount of copper in the glaze determined whether the green appeared deep, pale or bright. Blue is obtained from cobalt. It might vary from dark blue to pure sky blue. *Sancai* is a broad term for multiple colors. Tang *sancai* just means a type of polychrome glazed pottery. Therefore, pieces with only one or two typical *sancai* colors can still be referred to as *sancai*.

The application of glazes appears arbitrary at first glance, but upon closer examination, reveals a certain order. The tripod censer in white, amber and blue *sancai* glazes (Cat. No. 190) is a fine example. The shoulder is adorned with lotus petals reserved against a blue ground. The tip of the midrib of each petal is highlighted by a vertical splash of brown. During firing, the glaze will run, melt and fuse to result in a seemingly infinite variety of hues and patterns. The importance of fire in the development of ceramic art is profound.

Sancai pottery was produced at the Gongyi kilns in Henan, Xing kilns in Hebei, Huangbao kilns (in Tongchuan) and Liquan Fang kilns (in Xi'an) in Shaanxi, and Qiong kilns in Sichuan. Many daily utensils were modeled after the metal ware, glassware and copper ware from Persia and the Middle East and the altar utensils associated with Buddhism in South Asia. They reflect the thriving trade and exchanges between the Tang dynasty and outside world and the integration of Han and non-Han cultures.

Pagoda-shaped jars (Cat. Nos. 178, 179) came largely from the tombs of Tang aristocrats or royalties. Their shape resembles that of the Buddhist stupa in India and other South Asian regions. Early vessels have wide mouths and lids in the shape of a stupa. High Tang examples have elongated bodies and trumpet-shaped pedestals in addition to the stupa-shaped lids. Mid and late Tang pieces have detached pedestals.

Pottery of the Liao dynasty was heavily influenced by Tang *sancai* pottery. Objects with strong ethnic features such as the leather pouch flask (Cat. No. 203) were produced. Liao *sancai* pottery came in two groups, the fine ones and the coarse ones. The latter has a soft red paste and a cloudy glaze that comes off easily. The Makara jar (Cat. No. 204) in this catalogue is an illustrative example of the fine group of Liao *sancai* pottery. The entire vessel, except for the base, is covered with amber and green glaze. Its beauty rivals that of Tang *sancai* pottery. After the Tang and the Liao dynasties, production of *sancai* pottery continued under Song, Xixia and Jin rule until it was overtaken by the glass-like *liuli* glazed pottery in the Yuan dynasty. Under the influence of *sancai* ware, various types of low-fired polychrome pottery with distinct regional characteristics also emerged in neighboring countries such as Japan and Korea, but also as far as Persia in the Middle East and Egypt in Africa. The most notable are Nara *sancai* from Japan, Silla *sancai* from Korea, Persian *sancai* and Egyptian *sancai* ware.

During the Tang and Song periods, cremation was practiced by the Bai ethnic group in the Nanzhao Kingdom (738–902 C.E.) and the Dali Kingdom (937–1253 C.E.) in Yunnan due to the influence of Mahayana Buddhism. The most representative burial object associated with cremation was the cinerary urn. Simple funerary practice was the custom of this period. Mortuary objects were few and consisted only of cowries, copper cash, copper bracelets, copper plaques, small cups, dishes, bowls and glassware. Ashes and cremated bone fragments are placed inside the urns. The bone fragments were applied with gold leaves, painted with cinnabar and inscribed with Sanskrit script. These cinerary urns were made of pottery, porcelain, copper or stone. The design of these urns is determined by the social status of the deceased. The elite would have a larger urn enclosing a smaller one. The surfaces of these urns are mostly undecorated. Some lids are inscribed in cinnabar with Sanskrit mantras and lotus petals and some decorated with appliqué lotus petal motif or twelve zodiacs. A small number of urns probably belonging to the elites are incised with Sanskrit mantras and the Buddhist names of the

deceased. The most often used mantras are the Dhāraṇī taken from The Uṣṇīṣa Vijaya Dhāraṇī Sūtra. These chantings are used to redeem the soul of the dead (Cat. Nos. 180, 181, 182). These religious and cremation practices are among the most important cultural heritages of the Nanzhao Kingdom and Dali Kingdom.

173

灰陶鳖形穿带壶

唐

公元 618—907 年

高：8.3 厘米

长：29 厘米

Turtle-shaped gray pottery flask

Tang dynasty

618 – 907 C.E.

Height: 8.3 cm

Length: 29 cm

灰陶，胎细滑，质坚。小口外翻，短颈。
体呈扁圆形，正面微鼓，底面平而微内凹。
两侧面各饰寓意足部的扁形系两个，便
于穿绳携带，下端贴一小尾巴。腹正底
面分别饰细密和较疏同心圆旋纹。缩头、
小口、短尾、四足微伸，形似爬行中的鳖，
造型生动。

Gray pottery with a fine and smooth paste.
The vessel has a small mouth with everted
rim, a short neck and a flattened circular
body with a slightly convex front and
concave back. Each side is furnished with
two lugs to denote the feet of the tortoise.
The tubular lugs are used for tying a rope
to the vessel. The bottom of the vessel has
an appliqué tail. Both the front and back
of the vessel are decorated with concentric
grooves.

174

灰陶花瓣形口带座壶

唐

公元 618—907 年

通高：55.2 厘米

Foliate-mouthed gray pottery ewer with stand

Tang dynasty

618 – 907 C.E.

Overall Height: 55.2 cm

灰陶。壶三叶花瓣形口、颈细稍束、溜肩、鼓腹、下腹渐敛、近底处刻弦纹一周、平底。口缘下饰波浪形凸缘两道、口、肩一侧置圆条形短錾手、錾手与肩接合处表面平削。座中空、呈两砵相对而置状、以圆筒形柄相连。上方砵外缘拍印八个宝相花纹、下方砵中部贴一周棘刺纹、圆筒状柄中部最窄处束一周棘刺纹。

花瓣形口为西亚银器胡瓶的口形、但本品短颈、壶体饱满、轮廓线圆、带有明显的唐文化造型特点、是吸收外来文化的优秀作品。

Gray pottery. The vessel has a trefoil mouth, a constricted narrow neck, steep shoulders and a bulbous belly that tapers towards a flat base. Two ridges encircle the mouth rim. A groove encompasses the lower belly near the base. A short handle with circular cross-section arches from the mouth to the shoulders. The surface of the joint between the handle and the shoulders has been scraped flat. The hollow pottery stand resembles two bowls placed base to base and connected by a cylindrical shaft. The top edge of the stand is impressed with eight *baoxiang* flowers, a type of Buddhist floral motif. The narrowest part of the shaft and the mid-section of the lower half of the base are decorated with a round of appliqué spikes design.

The short neck and overall shape of the piece is typical of Tang wares but the foliate mouth design is borrowed from West Asian silverware. This piece is a fine example of the synthesis of foreign and Chinese elements.

175

灰白胎战马一对

唐

公元 618—907 年

长治窑

高：52.2 厘米，51.9 厘米

长：50.7 厘米，51 厘米

Pair of gray pottery warhorses

Tang dynasty

618 – 907 C.E.

Changzhi kilns

Height: 52.2 cm, 51.9 cm

Length: 50.7 cm, 51 cm

马其一颈披鬃，另一剪鬃、缚尾。马耳内侧和剪鬃挂红彩。灰白胎，胎体结实。马腿和马尾露出生锈的铁线。带鞍，鞍可取下。马各部比例适度，骨肉匀称，造型雄健有力，线条优美。

唐长治窑的陶马以突出表现马匹强壮的肌肉和矫健的体态为特点，因马腿瘦长，故腿部需用铁线支架来支撑身躯。

Grayish-white pottery with a dense paste. The horses are furnished with removable saddles. One horse has a long mane around the neck and another has a cropped mane. The tails of both horses are knotted. The inner side of the ears and the cropped manes are painted red. Rusted wires are exposed from within the legs and tails.

Pottery horses produced by the Changzhi kilns during the Tang dynasty are noted for their sinewy muscles and sprightly carriage. Iron wires are added for reinforcement to support the long and slender legs.

176

灰陶四系穿带瓶

辽

公元 907—1125 年

高：27.5 厘米

底径：12 厘米

Gray pottery jar with four loop lugs

Liao dynasty

907 – 1125 C.E.

Height: 27.5 cm

Base diameter: 12 cm

灰陶。口微外侈，束颈，丰肩，底阔，肩、底周长几乎相等，平底微向内凹。肩和腹部两侧置四系，用以系绳穿带。系并非粘贴上去的，而是把胎体拉出而成，这样可加强系的承受力，更为耐用。全器磨光，近底部饰两周耙齿纹。器内外有明显的轮旋纹，外壁留有很多竹篦修刮痕。造型粗犷，表现出草原民族的特性。

Gray pottery. The jar has a slightly flared mouth, a constricted neck, bold shoulders, a cylindrical body and a flat base with a slightly recessed center. The lugs are used for tying a rope to the vessel. The lugs are not attached onto the body but pulled out from the paste for greater load-bearing capacity and durability. The entire surface has been burnished. The area around the base is decorated with two bands of rake motif. Distinct wheel marks are visible around the interior and exterior walls. Extensive trimming and scraping marks are found on the exterior. The vessel has a strong nomadic influence.

177

灰陶龟驮四猴炉

辽

公元 907—1125 年

高：12 厘米

底径：9.7 厘米

Gray pottery censer with monkey and tortoise design

Liao dynasty

907 – 1125 C.E.

Height: 12 cm

Base diameter: 9.7 cm

泥质浅灰陶。底座呈龟形、底平。龟体俯伏，龟首微伸出体外，双目圆睁，面部清晰，前后足缩在壳缘，每足有五爪，有尾。龟背上驮香炉一个，香炉内凹成圆钵状。香炉顶部依龟首前、后、左、右各塑坐猴一只，面向四方。猴子眼、耳、口、鼻、眉毛清晰，乳房丰满，乳头突出，上腹有肚脐，屈腿而坐。龟壳刻三角形纹、猴子头、身和龟下体满饰细密条纹。

此器造型特别，可能为祭器。

Light gray earthenware. The base of the censer is in the shape of a crouching tortoise with a small head, glaring eyes, clawed limbs and short tail. The censer on top of the tortoise is a quatrefoil receptacle sculpted with four seated monkeys. Each monkey has delicately rendered eyes, ears, mouth, nose, eyebrows and torso. They are seated with knees flexed. The surface of the tortoise is decorated with triangular design. The head, body and abdomen of each monkey are covered with dense and fine striations.

This uniquely shaped censer was probably used as ritual ware.

178

灰陶红彩透雕塔式罐

唐

公元 618—907 年

高：88.2 厘米

底径：27.5 厘米

Gray pottery reliquary pagoda with openwork and red pigment

Tang dynasty

618 – 907 C.E.

Height: 88.2 cm

Base diameter: 27.5 cm

灰陶塔，用于存放舍利子或骨灰。塔由盖、舍利罐、托和底座四部分组成。顶为七层相轮宝珠莲瓣盖，下为灰黑色圆形舍利罐，外罩透雕连环金钱纹壳，上满饰红彩，承于莲花形托上。莲花托上贴仰莲瓣十六片，每片中部塑涂以红彩的小孩一个，寓意年年有子。最下层为塔座，上下大，中间小，上部为满饰红彩的球状体，外罩透雕连续"卍"字纹饰的壳，下为倒置碗状，中束扭绳一圈为饰。塔座覆碗状外壁隐约可见满布不同颜色的彩绘纹饰。全器体形高大，气势不凡，表现了唐代雕塑艺术的精湛。

舍利子为得道高僧圆寂后，金身经火化遗留下的粒状物。

"卍"或"卐"字纹饰是典型宗教纹样，源于新石器时期中近东地区，用来表示对灵魂再生的崇拜。后世佛教用其代表"轮回"，可以给人们带来新生、吉祥。黄河流域上游甘肃、青海地区的马家窑文化马厂类型彩陶曾将其用作为装饰纹样之一。武则天时期将该符号读作"万"，意为"吉祥万德之所集"（李志钦：《黄河彩陶纹饰鉴赏》，安徽美术出版社，2009 年）。

Gray earthenware. The reliquary in the shape of a pagoda houses the ashes of the dead or sacred *śarīra*. The pagoda is made up of four segments: a lid, a jar, a stand and a pedestal. The lid has a foliate rim, an oblate body and a finial with seven vertically stacked rings. The globular *śarīra* jar with a dark gray body is enclosed by a spherical structure painted in red and pierced with interlocking coin motif. The jar is supported by a lotus stand sculpted with sixteen upward-facing petals. Each petal is painted in red and decorated with an image of a child. The upper section of the dumbbell-shaped pedestal is pierced with a band of Buddhist swastikas, inside which is a spherical structure also painted in red. A rope-like girdle encircles its narrow waist. Multi-colored painting is visible on the lower section of the pedestal.

Śarīra refers to the sacred relics or bead-shaped objects that are found in the cremated ashes of Buddhist monks.

The swastika "卍" is an ancient religious symbol in the Neolithic period. It was venerated as a symbol of rebirth and later adopted by Buddhism as a sign of transmigration, signifying new life and good fortune. According to historical records, the "卍" or "卐" sign was pronounced as wan (a word that means "ten thousand") during the reign of Empress Wuzetian to symbolise the "gathering of ten thousand fortunes." They can be found on Machang-type pottery of the Majiayao culture.

红黑彩陶塔

北宋

公元 960—1127 年

高：112 厘米

底宽：22.3 厘米

Pottery reliquary pagoda with red and black painting

Northern Song dynasty

960 – 1127 C.E.

Height: 112 cm

Base width: 22.3 cm

这是一座三层陶塔。第一层、第二层为六角形仿木结构楼阁式塔，第三层为六边形台座之上的宝瓶式塔，塔刹三层相轮，上为尖形宝珠。壶门式塔座六转角处贴塑六位以肩拱托塔的力士。

塔通体雕琢富丽。仿木结构腰檐、檐下斗拱、平座斗拱、斗尺龟纹栏板、板门、倚门而立的持莲蕾供养人、龟纹格扇窗以及腰檐屋顶脊兽均刻画塑作具足、生动。塔通体涂白，仿木结构木柱、门窗、栏杆、脊兽局部涂朱。宝瓶塔下部朱绘仰莲瓣，相轮涂朱。力士发涂墨色，身白，局部衣饰涂朱。本品除顶部宝瓶式塔为质坚的白胎外，其余均为浅红色陶胎，质轻，较疏松。

是一件难得的宋辽金时期的陶塔或者塔形器精品。

This is a three-storied pagoda. The hexagonal first and second stories are imitating wood-structured Chinese pagoda while the third story is made up of a stupa in the form of a reliquary jar upon a hexagonal core unit, topped by a spire supporting a tear-shape gem. Each corner of the hexagonal base is supported by a strongman.

The entire reliquary pagoda is elaborately sculpted with lavish details. The outside of the pagoda is coated with a white slip throughout except for the hairs on the built figures around the base, the eaves, pillars, doors, windows, parapets and the tiny creatures on the eaves which are all partially painted red on a white slip ground. The entire reddish earthenware sculpture is light weight and porous except for the reliquary jar which is made with a hard and fine white clay.

This is a rare example of a pottery pagoda or pagoda-shaped vessel produced during the Song, Liao and Jin periods.

180

陀罗尼经咒火葬罐

大理国

公元 937—1253 年

高：26.2 厘米

底径：12 厘米

Cinerary urn engraved with Buddhist mantras

Dali Kingdom

937 – 1253 C.E.

Height: 26.2 cm

Base diameter: 12 cm

泥质黑陶。出土时被红土覆盖，表面没有清理干净的地方呈红色。拱形盖上贴一塔状锥形柱，沿柱旁一周顺时针方向（沿柱旁一周由右向左顺时针方向）刻白文"佛顶尊胜陀罗尼神咒"，外侧刻梵文。罐外体满刻梵文经咒。罐中腹由右向左刻白文"追为亡妇赵药师綺神识"。罐下腹由右向左刻白文"当愿托生净土证弥陀尊亲睹无量光佛前蒙胎于莲花授记"。字体锋棱深邃、苍劲有力，甚具美感。外形和用途与图录 181 号和 182 号相同。

大理国时佛教极盛，流行冠姓双名制，其组成方式为"姓＋佛名＋俗名"。上至王室段氏，下到一般平民百姓，无论男女老少大都有佛名。

根据所刻文字，亡妇姓赵，佛号"药师"，俗名"綺"。

Black earthenware. The urn was covered with red soil in its original condition. Red color is visible where it had not been cleaned. The domed lid is surmounted by a pagoda-shaped knob. Engraved around the knob in clockwise direction are nine Bai-Han characters reading "*Foding zunsheng tuoluoni shenzhou*" (*The Uṣṇīṣa Vijaya Dhāraṇī Sūtra*). The rest of the lid is engraved with Sanskrit characters. The entire exterior of the urn is engraved with Sanskrit mantras. Running from right to left around the mid-section of the belly are ten Bai-Han characters that read, "*Zhuiwei wangfu Zhao-Yaoshi-Qi shenzhi*" (for the soul of my deceased wife Zhao-Yaoshi-Qi). Another line of Bai-Han characters running right to left around the lower belly reads, "Wish to take rebirth in the Pure Land, behold Amitabha the Buddha of Infinite Light, be reborn from a lotus, and receive a prediction from the Buddha." The form and function of this urn is similar to Cat. Nos. 181, 182.

Buddhism was prevalent during the period of the Dali Kingdom. It was customary to have a Buddhist name in addition to a formal given name. A full name is composed of three parts, in this order: surname, Buddhist name, and personal name. People of all genders and ages, from all sections of society, had a Buddhist name.

Based on the engraving, the deceased woman's surname was Zhao. Yaoshi (Medicine Buddha) was her Buddhist name and Qi her personal name.

181

白族文经咒火葬罐

大理国

公元 937—1253 年

高：27.8 厘米

底径：14 厘米

Cinerary urn with Buddhist mantras engraved in Bai characters

Dali Kingdom

937 – 1253 C.E.

Height: 27.8 cm

Base diameter: 14 cm

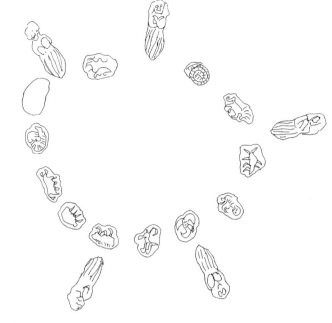

附图 6a　内壁十二生肖和佛像手绘图

Fig. 6a Sketch of the zodiac animals and Buddha images around the interior wall

灰陶胎，质坚，胎体较薄。罐平底。拱形盖，顶贴荷叶抱宝珠纽。盖刻八瓣莲花，伴以八颗莲子纹，周边衬以莲瓣纹。器外壁满刻直行白文经咒，字体流畅、工整、有力，刀工深邃、凌厉。器内下腹壁四周贴椭圆形十二生肖，在十二生肖上方贴长方形佛像五个（附图 6a ）。

火葬罐是用来盛放亡者骨灰的。出土的火葬罐刻经文的不多，大多是素身，部分用朱砂书写或是模印烧出"卍"字、十二生肖等图案。罐上的经咒一般是"陀罗尼经"，又称"陀罗尼咒"或"陀罗尼神咒"，以此来超度死者亡灵（附图 6b）。

白文是白族仿照汉字创造的一种文字，在明代以前使用广泛，后近失传。有刻字的火葬罐多刻梵文经咒，目前所知，除本品外未发现其他刻汉字或白文经咒的火葬罐，而内壁贴十二生肖和佛像的火葬罐也甚少。

因本品所刻经咒上没有出现白族人的冠姓双名，所以有可能为当时大理国的一位大宋官员亡者所有。

本品经热释光测定最后烧制年代距今1000—700 年。

Gray pottery with a hard and relatively thin paste and a flat base. The lid is surmounted by a jewel-in-the-lotus knob. The domed lid is engraved with an eight-petalled lotus flower. A lotus border encircles the rim of the lid. The urn is engraved with Buddhist mantras in Bai characters. The characters are skillfully carved and fluently executed. Appliqués of the twelve zodiac animals are found along the inside wall of the vessel near the bottom. Above them are appliqués of the Five Dhyani Buddhas (Fig. 6a).

Cinerary urns were made for storing the ashes of the dead. Very few excavated cinerary urns are engraved with mantras. Most inscribed urns are either plain or with mantras written in cinnabar; some are molded with Buddhist swastikas or the twelve zodiac animals. The most often used mantras are the *Dhāraṇī*, ritual speeches believed to have the power of redeeming the souls of the deceased (Fig. 6b).

Bai characters are based on Han characters and new words are created on modified Han characters. It was widely used before the Ming dynasty and then faded out. The inscriptions on most inscribed urns are Buddhist mantras originally written and chanted in Sanskrit. No other urns inscribed with mantras in Han or Bai characters have been documented previously. Examples with appliquéd zodiac animals and Buddha images are rarer still.

Since no typical Bai name (a surname preceding double personal names) is found among the inscription, this urn could have been intended for a non-Bai deceased official dispatched by the Song dynasty to the Dali Kingdom.

Thermoluminescence test shows that the last firing date of this piece was 1000 to 700 years before present.

附图 6b　罐面白文经咒拓本

Fig. 6b　Rubbing of the mantras on the surface of the urn

182

梵文经咒火葬罐

大理国

公元 937—1253 年

高：26 厘米

底径：10.8 厘米

Cinerary urn engraved with Buddhist mantras in Sanskrit characters

Dali Kingdom

937 – 1253 C.E.

Height: 26 cm

Base diameter: 10.8 cm

灰白胎，质坚，较薄。罐平底。拱形盖，顶贴荷叶抱宝珠纽。盖顶外圈等距离分布八颗星宿，每两颗星宿线条组成一个三角形，相连后呈放射八角状，象征宇宙八方。盖边和罐口缘四周饰莲瓣纹。盖外壁刻梵文十三个，涂以朱砂。盖内壁和罐肩分别以朱砂书梵文十四个和十八个，但罐肩上有些字已不能辨认。罐外壁以梵文和汉字满刻经咒，部分梵文和白文汉字仍留有涂上的朱砂，其中白文汉字为"追为何般若接神道"。

The urn has a hard and thin grayish white paste and a flat base. The lid is surmounted by a jewel-in-the-lotus knob; the surface is decorated by an eight-pointed star symbolizing the four cardinal points and the four sub-cardinal directions in the universe. A lotus border encircles the rim of the lid. Thirteen Sanskrit letters are engraved over the triangles and filled with cinnabar. The underside of the lid and the shoulders of the urn are respectively written in cinnabar with fourteen and eighteen Sanskrit characters but some around the shoulders are now illegible.

The exterior wall is fully engraved with rows of mantras, mainly in Sanskrit and some in Chinese characters. Traces of cinnabar can still be seen. Amid the mantras are eight Han Chinese characters that read, *"Zhuiwei He-Bore-Jie shendao"* (To send [the soul of] He-Bo're-Jie onto the divine path). He-Bo're-Jie was the name of the deceased.

183

三彩黑釉骆驼

唐

公元 618—907 年

高：52.8 厘米

长：41 厘米

Pottery camel with black
sancai **glaze**

Tang dynasty

618 – 907 C.E.

Height: 52.8 cm

Length: 41 cm

颈上扬，昂首朝天，双目圆睁，四足直立，作张口嘶鸣状。双峰分向左、右倾斜，尾巴弯曲附于臀部。口、耳和眼部两侧施白彩，头、颈、驼峰、腿及下腹部鬃毛施黑彩，背部饰棕黄、白、绿点彩作披毯，其余部分饰棕黄色彩。胎呈粉白色，质细滑。

三彩施黑釉较为少见，本品以黑釉和棕黄釉衬托背部之棕黄、白、绿点彩，对比鲜明，效果相当突出。

The camel has an up-curved neck supporting a raised head with eyes and mouth wide open and humps that are pointing away from each other. A short curly tail is attached on the backside. The forelock, the mane, the front of the neck, the humps, upper legs and abdomen are highlighted in black. The blanket on the back is mottled with amber, white and green glazes. The mouth, ears, eyes and temples are decorated in white while the rest of the body is covered with amber glaze. The ivory-colored paste is refined.

Sancai pottery with black glaze is relatively rare. The amber and black glaze on the camel's body provide a contrasting background for the amber, white and green mottling around the humps. The flamboyant hues produce a highly dramatic visual effect.

184

贴花三彩马

唐

公元 618—907 年

巩义窑

高：49.8 厘米

长：47.5 厘米

Pottery horse with *sancai* glaze with appliqué decorations

Tang dynasty

618 – 907 C.E.

Gongyi kilns

Height: 49.8 cm

Length: 47.5 cm

马颈微弯、张口作鸣叫状，双耳直立，耳间鬃毛左、右分梳，鬃呈白色。前腿直立，后腿微弯，立于长方形踏板上。鞍披束腰毯，毯绘红彩，安放于白彩鞯下。口含镳、面部络头饰蟾蜍杏叶纹四枚、胸前和股后革带上分别挂攀胸五枚和六枚。股后有一洞，用于插尾，尾已失落。体施琥珀色釉，镳饰琥珀及白色相间釉。蟾蜍绘绿彩，杏叶填白彩。胎呈粉白色，质细滑。马体态矫健、骨肉匀称、釉色明亮。

1965 年洛阳关林出土有相似器物。

The horse has a slightly bent neck, a gaping mouth, a split forelock between pricked ears and a white mane. It stands foursquare on a rectangular plinth, with forelegs upright and hind legs flexed. The saddle rests on a piece of saddlecloth highlighted with white and wrapped by a red blanket. A bit mouthpiece is fitted to the horse's mouth. The halter around its head is adorned with four ornamental medallions featuring a green toad crouching on a white apricot leaf. Five similar medallions are suspended from the

chest strap, and six more from the crupper straps. There is a hole at the backside where the tail once has been. Its body is covered with amber glaze throughout while the harness straps are decorated with alternate amber and white glazes. The ivory-colored paste is refined.

A similar artifact was unearthed in 1965 from Guanlin, Luoyang, Henan province.

185

三彩镇墓兽

唐

公元 618—907 年

高：103 厘米

底阔：27.2 厘米

Pottery tomb guardian with *sancai* glaze

Tang dynasty

618 – 907 C.E.

Height: 103 cm

Base width: 27.2 cm

人面兽身，长发竖立似角盘旋而上，兽耳宽大横立，阔鼻大口，双目圆睁，微向下视，颌下胡须呈齿轮状。肩贴双翼，昂首挺胸，前肢直撑，后肢弯曲，蹲坐在崖形台座上。头发、眼、眉毛、胡子画黑彩，口、面部和耳绘红彩，腹、肩、颈前和后肢施棕黄釉，颈前到下腹部有长条形白釉带，与施白釉的前肢相配。肢端呈牛蹄状，施绿釉，翅膀、颈背部和台座饰绿、棕黄、白色点彩釉。胎呈粉白色，质地较细密。从正面看，华而不奢；从背面看，雍容华丽。

The tomb guardian is in the shape of a mythical beast with a human face, fan-shaped ears and outstretched wings. Its long hair rises from the forehead and turns into flame-like projections. With its chin held high and chest puffed, the beast sits elegantly on its haunches on a cliff-like platform. Its hair, eyebrows, eyes and beard are highlighted with black; its lips, ears and face with red; and its neck, shoulders, abdomen and hind legs with amber. A white stripe runs from under the chin to the lower body to mirror the white forelegs. The legs terminate in cattle hoofs glazed in green. The wings, the back and the pedestal are mottled with green, amber and white pigments. The ivory-colored paste is refined.

186

三彩天王俑

唐

公元 618—907 年

高：89.5 厘米

底阔：19.5 厘米

Pottery Lokapala with
sancai **glaze**

Tang dynasty

618 – 907 C.E.

Height: 89.5 cm

Base width: 19.5 cm

俑瞪眼张口，头戴展翅翘尾鹘冠，外披铠甲，两肩覆膊甲，身附护胸、护心和护腹。双臂微上提，右手作握剑状；左手大拇指和中指竖起，作法印状。双足着靴，踏于褐色卧牛上，牛下为崖形台座。除鹘尾及眼、口部绘红彩，颈、面和手部露胎外，其余部位施绿、褐、白三彩和交错点彩。胎色白中泛红，质细腻。俑身体各部比例匀称，肌肉发达，蹙眉怒目，有一种凶神恶煞、气势迫人的感觉。

唐三彩陶俑主要是用作陪葬的明器，唐代盛行厚葬，典章中有明确规定不同等级的官员死后可陪葬明器的数量和尺寸规格，但达官贵人往往使用比规定数量多许多倍的三彩器物。三彩器在武则天至唐玄宗开元天宝年间（公元 7—8 世纪）进入极盛期，之后逐渐减少。本品和图录 185 号和 187 号均应为该时期遗物。

The Lokapala, or Buddhist Heavenly King, is portrayed with a bulging eyes and gaping mouth. His cap features a pheasant with outstretched wings and an upright tail with red highlights. His armor is furnished with protective plates over the shoulders, chest and abdomens. His forearms are raised, his right fist clenched and left hand held in shuni mudra. He wears a pair of long boots and stands above a brown bull crouching on a cliff-like platform. Except for the eyes and lips that are painted in red and the neck, face and exposed hands the original color of the paste, the entire sculpture is mottled with green, brown and white. The white paste with a reddish tint is refined.

The majority of Tang *sancai* figures are burial objects but the common people were forbidden from using them. The quantity, size and specification of burial objects allowed for the deceased officials of different ranks were clearly stipulated in Tang institutions. However, these rules were often ignored and people were buried with funerary wares that are beyond their rank and status. *Sancai* ware enjoyed popularity from the reign of Empress Wuzetian to the Kaiyuan and Tianbao periods of Emperor Xuanzong (7th–8th century) before fading out. This present example, Cat. Nos. 185, 187 are artifacts from this period.

187

三彩射箭武士俑

唐

公元 618—907 年

高：90.5 厘米

底阔：21 厘米

Pottery warrior archer with *sancai* glaze

Tang dynasty

618 – 907 C.E.

Height: 90.5 cm

Base width: 21 cm

俑瞪眼闭口，头戴鹞冠帽，帽身向下外张到颈，鹞鸟展翅翘尾。外披铠甲，两肩覆膊甲，身附护胸和护腹。侧身扭腰作弯弓射箭姿势，左手横伸与身体呈 90 度角，中指、无名指及尾指紧握，大拇指和食指弯曲前伸，眼微向下望着左手；右手横向提起，弯臂握拳，大拇指夹紧食指。双足着靴，踏于褐色卧牛上，牛下为崖形台座。除鹞尾及眼、口绘红彩，颈、面和手露胎外，其余部位施绿、褐、白三彩和交错点彩，色彩配搭得宜，斑驳绚烂，华而不乱。胎粉白泛红，质细腻。

俑高大威猛，虎背熊腰，面目狰狞，仿佛随时准备驱赶入侵者，是墓主人的忠实守护者。

The warrior wears a pheasant cap with a flap extending over his nape. The pheasant has outstretched wings and an upright tail highlighted in red. The warrior has a solemn face with bulging eyes and pursed lips. His armor is featured with protective plates over the shoulders, chest and abdomen. His body is twisted at the waist, forming the *tribhanga* curve. The gesture of the arms strongly suggests that he is holding up a bow. He wears a pair of long boots and stands on a brown bull crouching on a cliff-like platform. Except for the eyes and lips that are painted in red, and the neck, face and exposed hands the original color of the paste, the entire sculpture is mottled with green, brown and white. The white paste with a reddish tint is refined.

The warrior is modeled with a stocky and powerful build and an awe-inspiring face. He is a faithful guard to his dead master in the after life, ready to ward off evils and intruders.

188

三彩武士俑

唐

公元 618—907 年

高：109 厘米

Pottery warrior with *sancai* glaze

Tang dynasty

618 – 907 C.E.

Height: 109 cm

俑头束髻，咧嘴，怒目圆睁望向前方。
左手张开放于腰间，右手握拳抬起至肩
上。身穿盔甲到膝，腰板直挺，脚踏方台，
雕造出唐代将军凶悍的形象。胎色粉白，
质细腻。

The warrior has a topknot on his head, a
gaping mouth and a pair of bulging eyes.
He is standing on a rectangular platform
with his left hand on the waist and his
right arm raised to shoulder level. The
ivory-colored paste is refined.

189

三彩双龙耳壶

唐

公元 618—907 年

巩义窑

高：37.8 厘米

底径：9.3 厘米

Sancai-glazed pottery amphora with dragon-handles

Tang dynasty

618 – 907 C.E.

Gongyi kilns

Height: 37.8 cm

Base diameter: 9.3 cm

盘口，颈饰弦纹，丰肩，长圆腹，平底，近底处稍束。口、肩部置双股条状龙形柄，龙张口入瓶汲液，柄上贴圆珠三个。上半部交错施褐、绿、白三彩釉，釉色斑驳艳丽。腹下部露胎，胎体细滑，呈米白色，微泛红。

双龙耳瓶在鸡头壶的基础上吸收了外来的胡瓶的特点，盛行于初唐时期。

1966 年河南洛阳关林出土有相似器物。

The vessel has a plate mouth, an ovoid body that tapers towards a slightly splayed foot and a flat base. A pair of dragon-shaped handles rises from the shoulders and curves downward to the mouth rim. The mouths of the dragons are holding onto the mouth rim as if trying to drink from the vessel. The handles are each decorated with three pearls. The upper part of the vessel is adorned with bold splashes of brown, green and white. The white paste with a reddish tint is refined.

Amphoras with dragon-handles were basically rooster-head ewers but with features that were characteristic of Central Asian ewers. The shape was in vogue during the early Tang period.

A similar vessel was unearthed in 1966 from Guanlin, Luoyang, Henan province.

190

蓝釉三彩兽足炉

唐

公元 618—907 年

巩义窑

高：12.1 厘米

口径：11.9 厘米

Pottery censer with blue *sancai* glaze

Tang dynasty

618 – 907 C.E.

Gongyi kilns

Height: 12.1 cm

Mouth diameter: 11.9 cm

卷缘，扁圆腹，小平底，下承三兽形足。肩腹间饰弦纹两道，肩、腹分界明显。口及兽足施棕色釉，肩腹部施蓝、琥珀、白三色釉，釉彩自然流淌，相互浸润。器内施薄褐黄釉，荡釉不匀。肩部蓝釉围成宽肥莲瓣纹，瓣纹中央有棕色竖纹一条。蓝釉向下流淌，舒畅自如，变幻莫测，有如泼墨。胎呈粉白色，质细滑。此器身矮腹丰，浑厚庄重，且蓝釉有很好的装饰效果。

蓝釉的原料为氧化钴，巩义黄冶窑为最早使用氧化钴的窑场。

The censer has a rolling mouth rim, a squat belly and a small flat base supported by three animal legs. Two grooves run around the distinct turn between the shoulders and the belly. The mouth and animal legs are coated with amber glaze while the shoulders and belly are decorated with blue, amber and white glazes that run freely into each other. The interior is coated with a thin and uneven layer of brownish-yellow glaze. The shoulders featured broad lotus petals reserved against a blue ground. The tip of the midrib of each petal is highlighted by a vertical splash of brown. The blue glaze runs freely down the body among other glazes to produce a dramatic visual effect reminiscent of Chinese splashed-ink painting. The ivory-colored paste is refined.

The blue glaze derives its color from cobalt oxide. The Huangye kilns in Gongyi were the first to make use of this mineral.

191

蓝釉三彩五足炉

唐

公元 618—907 年

巩义窑

高：9.5 厘米

口径：13.5 厘米

Pottery censer with blue
sancai **glaze**

Tang dynasty

618 – 907 C.E.

Gongyi kilns

Height: 9.5 cm

Mouth diameter: 13.5 cm

炉作圆形，外折宽平缘，器身内收呈四级阶梯状，平底，下承以五条龙首足，足踏环形扁条状座。口缘和器外壁以蓝釉为地，间以褐黄釉，器内侧和底无釉。釉满布细碎开片纹。胎白细腻、体薄，较坚硬。口缘内折缘处留有三点支烧痕。本品外形新颖、精巧玲珑、釉浓郁艳丽，油润亮泽、为蓝釉器佳作。

1969 年河南洛阳李楼下庄出土有相似器物。

本品经热释光测定最后烧制年代距今 1400—1000 年。

The circular censer has a broad and flat everted rim. The body of the vessel tapers to a four-stepped profile and a flat base supported by five dragon-head legs resting on a circular stretcher with a flat top. The rim and the exterior surface of the censer are splashed with amber glaze against a ground of blue while the inner sides of the base of the stretcher are without glaze. Tiny crackles are found on the glazed surface. The unglazed areas revealed a fine white paste. The body is relatively thin but hard. Three spur marks are found inside the rim. This censer is a fine example of blue *sancai* ware.

A similar vessel was unearthed in 1969 from Xiazhuang at Lilou, Luoyang, Henan province.

Thermoluminescence test shows that the last firing date of this piece was 1400 to 1000 years before present.

192

绿釉带盖兔耳罐

唐

公元 618—907 年

高：25 厘米

底径：11.3 厘米

Green-glazed lidded jar with rabbit-shaped lugs

Tang dynasty

618 – 907 C.E.

Height: 25 cm

Base diameter: 11.3 cm

口缘外卷，短颈，丰肩，圆鼓腹，腹以下渐敛，平底，底微外撇。上覆圆形盖，中央饰扁圆宝珠状纽。肩部一侧有圆柱短流，两侧和与流对称一侧的腹中部分别贴一兔形系。胎呈白色，坚硬。施墨绿色釉，釉薄而明亮，呈玻璃透明状。施釉厚薄不匀，釉不到底。

本品釉料以铅化合物为助熔剂，主要呈色剂是氧化铜，使釉呈现绿色。

The jar has a rolling mouth rim, a short neck, bold shoulders and a bulbous belly that tapers towards a slightly splayed flat base. The top of the domed lid has a pearl-shaped knob. A cylindrical spout is set on the shoulders. Two appliqués rabbit-shaped lugs adorn the shoulders and a third on the back of the jar. The white paste is dense. The vessel is covered with a transparent and dark green glaze with a lustrous surface. The thin and unevenly applied glaze stops around the lower belly.

Lead compound has been used as the flux agent of this glaze. The green color of the glaze is derived from copper oxide.

193

三彩穿带壶

唐

公元 618—907 年

高：22.1 厘米

底径：9.8 厘米

Sancai-glazed pottery jar with loop lugs

Tang dynasty

618 – 907 C.E.

Height: 22.1 cm

Base diameter: 9.8 cm

半圆花瓣形口，束颈，溜肩，体呈扁壶状。圈足外撇，底内凹。颈起凸弦纹两级，肩上覆盖三层叶纹，两侧置半环形系。系与下腹间堆塑双条状花茎，茎内凹成槽，两侧边缘呈棘状凸起成脊，凹槽下的圈足置相对应的系孔，以便穿绳提携。胎白中泛红，质坚细滑。施琥珀色釉，肩以下间以绿釉作点缀，近底处可见流釉现象。

The jar has a semicircular mouth with foliate rim, a constricted neck, sloping shoulders, an elongated body, a splayed ring foot and a base with a recessed center. Two ribs encircle the neck. The shoulders are surrounded by three layers of overlapping leaf motif and flanked by a pair of semicircular lugs. A pair of appliqué floral stalks decorates each side. The loop lugs and the two holes on the ring foot allow a rope to be tied around the vessel. The white paste with a reddish tint is refined. The jar is covered with brown agate glaze and adorned with green splashes below the shoulders. The area around the base is partially covered with glaze that ran freely down the body.

琥珀釉盖罐

唐

公元 618—907 年

巩义窑

高：17.5 厘米

底径：7.3 厘米

Pottery lidded jar in brown amber glaze

Tang dynasty

618 – 907 C.E.

Gongyi kilns

Height: 17.5 cm

Base diameter: 7.3 cm

罐口略向外卷，短颈，丰肩，肩以下渐收敛，宽圈足，平底外撇。足缘边斜削一圈。口上置尖顶状盖，盖出边，上有凸弦纹四道，与肩上三道凹弦纹相呼应。全器外壁施薄琥珀色釉，釉色莹润明亮，釉层有细密小开片，施釉不及底。器体四周留有上釉时由上而下的刷纹，刷纹精细，排列有序。胎色白中泛红，胎质坚、细腻，触之有糯米粉质感。足内底露胎，见轮旋痕。本品制作精细，线条优雅流畅。

The jar has a slightly rolling mouth rim, a short neck, bold shoulders and a bulbous belly that tapers towards a broad splayed ring foot with a beveled edge. The rim of the conical lid hangs over the mouth of the jar. The concentric ribs on the lid mirror the grooves that are on the shoulders. The entire exterior surface of the jar and lid except the area around the base is thinly coated with a smooth and lustrous layer of brown amber glaze showing dense tiny crackles. Fine vertical brushing marks from glaze application are visible on the jar. The white paste with reddish tint is refined and compact. Wheel marks are visible around the unglazed interior of the ring foot.

195

琥珀釉龙柄壶

唐

公元 618—907 年

巩义窑

高：12.5 厘米

底径：5.3 厘米

Amber-glazed pottery jar with dragon-handle

Tang dynasty

618 – 907 C.E.

Gongyi kilns

Height: 12.5 cm

Base diameter: 5.3 cm

壶口略向外卷、大口、直长颈、丰肩、肩以下渐收、平底。颈与肩腹间立圆曲柄。柄上下两端刻简化龙头，相对一侧肩部置一圆管状短流。腹中饰弦纹两道。胎色白中泛红、胎质坚硬、细腻、滑、不拉手、有糯米粉质感。烧成温度较高、扣之铛铛发响。施琥珀色釉、釉色明澈温润、釉面满布细密开片纹。下腹垂釉、形成美妙的装饰效果。本品造型古朴典雅、修坯精细规整、一丝不苟。

The jar has a broad mouth with slightly everted rim, a straight neck, bold shoulders and a belly that tapers towards a flat base. A handle carved with stylized dragon motif arches between the shoulders and the neck. A cylindrical spout is set on the shoulders. Two narrow grooves encircle the belly. The white paste with a reddish tint is dense and smooth. Since the firing temperature was rather high, the body gives a pleasant sound when knocked with the knuckle. The surface is coated with a smooth and lustrous amber glaze bearing tiny crackles. The glaze streaks around the foot are highly decorative.

196

绿釉龟背筹筒

唐

公元 618—907 年

高：22.2 厘米

阔：18.7 厘米

Pottery tally container on tortoise back with green glaze

Tang dynasty

618 – 907 C.E.

Height: 22.2 cm

Width: 18.7 cm

附图 7　江苏丹徒银器窖藏鎏金龟负论语玉烛银酒筹器（唐）

Fig. 7　Gilt silver tally container on tortoise back with the inscription Lunyu yuzhu, unearthed from a hoard of silverware at Dantu, Jiangshu (Tang dynasty)

由盖、身、座组成。盖为圆拱形，与身可分开，刻弦纹四周，顶饰宝珠形盖纽，上部开圆孔四个。身作圆筒形，饰弦纹一道。粗大的筹筒重重压在龟形底座上，龟背与筒底粘贴在一起。龟身上部以两周圆圈纹作龟甲，足刻阴直线纹。龟颈较粗，头上扬，小眼圆睁，嘴唇紧闭，似乎鼻孔冒着粗气，肥臀曲尾，浑身是劲，四足着地，匍匐前进。胎质灰白、疏松、较粗。全器施绿釉，釉分布不均，底无釉。此种釉质、釉色和器物造型搭配协调，突出了龟的憨态。

以往鉴赏家们总是称赞唐代陶塑中的马、骆驼、牛等大型动物，没想到像龟这样的小动物在形和神方面也塑造得如此生动，这也从侧面反映出唐代雕塑艺术的高度成就。

龙首龟身的碑座称为碑趺，名字叫赑屃，是传说中龙的儿子，其力大无穷，好负重。

1982 年江苏丹徒丁卯桥发现一处大型唐代银器窖藏，内有一鎏金龟负"论语玉烛"银酒筹器（酒筹是行酒令的工具）。本品很可能是仿该种金银器的明器（附图 7）。

The vessel comprises a lidded container and a base. The dome-shaped lid with a pearl-knob is decorated with four rounds of concentric grooves and perforated with four holes around the top. A grooved line encompasses the cylindrical body. The sturdy container sits on an inseparable base in the shape of a tortoise. The carapace of the tortoise is denoted by two rounds of circular motif. The feet have incised lines representing the claws. The tortoise has a rather thick neck, a raised head, small circular eyes, pursed lips, round nostrils, a plump hip and a curly tail. The underside of the tortoise is unglazed, exposing a rather coarse and porous grayish white paste. The entire vessel is glazed in green but the glaze is unevenly distributed.

Connoisseurs of Tang sculptures have always appreciated larger animals such as the horse, the camel and the ox. Few were aware of the expressive and sculptural potential of smaller animals like the tortoise.

Tortoises modeled with a dragon's head were commonly used as the base of steles. Legend has it that a tortoise with a dragon's head was the first of nine sons of the Dragon.

In 1982, a Tang dynasty cache that yielded a large number of silverware was discovered near Dingmaoqiao in Dantu, Jiangsu province. Among the finds was a rectangular gilded silver container for holding tallies for the drinkers' wager game. It was supported by a tortoise bearing the inscription, "Lunyu yuzhu" (The Analects and jade candle). The present artifact is probably a ceramic version of that vessel (Fig. 7).

197

绿釉莲瓣贴花注子

唐

公元 618—907 年

高：23.2 厘米

底径：7.9 厘米

Green-glazed ewer with appliqué lotus motifs

Tang dynasty

618 – 907 C.E.

Height: 23.2 cm

Base diameter: 7.9 cm

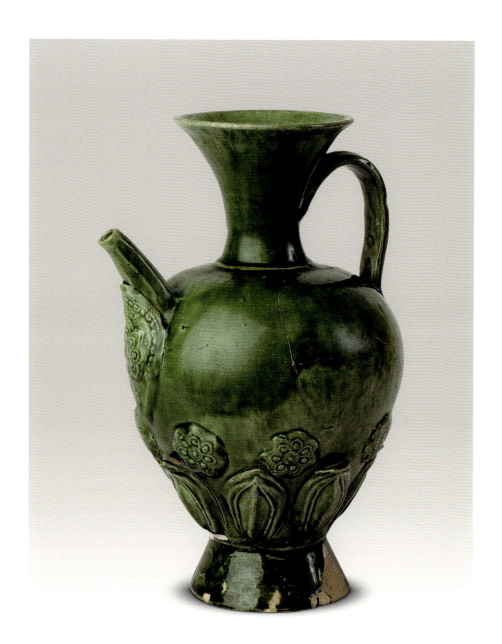

喇叭形口，长颈，斜肩，鼓腹，下腹内敛，高圈足外撇。颈、肩间以凸弦纹一道分界，肩上阴刻弦纹三周。肩、腹间安六棱直流，相对侧有扁条形把手。下腹底部贴仰莲瓣纹饰，瓣间贴带莲子的莲蓬，流下方置宝相团花一朵。足底内凹，露胎。粉红色胎，细滑。满施翠绿色釉，釉色明亮，玻璃质感强。器物造型和贴花工艺具明显唐代风格。

本品经热释光测定最后烧制年代距今 1100—900 年。

The ewer has a trumpet mouth, a long neck, sloping shoulders and a bulbous belly that tapers to a tall splayed ring foot. A ridge runs around the junction between the neck and the shoulders. Three rounds of incised lines encircle the shoulders. A spout with six vertical ribs is set on the shoulders. A strap handle arches from the shoulders to the neck. The lower belly is decorated with appliqué lotus petals. The spaces between the petals are adorned with appliqué *baoxiang* flowers. A larger *baoxiang* flower is attached to the lower part of the spout. The recessed base is unglazed. The pink paste is fine and smooth. The entire surface is covered with a lustrous emerald-green glaze. The shape of the ewer and the appliqué motifs are characteristic of Tang pottery.

Thermoluminescence test shows that the last firing date of this piece was 1100 to 900 years before present.

198

绿釉铁绘刻花梅瓶

辽

公元 907—1125 年

高：25.2 厘米

底径：7.9 厘米

Green-glazed *meiping* vase with ferruginous painting

Liao dynasty

907 – 1125 C.E.

Height: 25.2 cm

Base diameter: 7.9 cm

瓶口外撇、圆唇、短颈、溜肩、肩腹丰满，肩以下渐敛，平底。胎呈浅红褐色，质细滑，较疏松。施绿釉到下腹部。瓶身前后侧先以单勾法刻花卉纹轮廓各一组，另两侧划竖双弦弧线，像开光图案，把两组花卉分隔，然后以剔花技法把轮廓内的绿釉剔出，再填以铁锈色。梅瓶在辽代不多见，而铁绘刻花的则更少。

南宋吉州窑、金代耀州窑和金、元磁州窑等瓷器上普遍使用开光技法，元、明、清景德镇瓷器上更是大量使用，起到突出主题纹饰的作用。

The vase has a flared mouth with rounded lip, a short neck, steep shoulders and a bulging belly that narrows towards a flat base. The unglazed area exposes a smooth, fine and relatively porous paste of pinkish color. The lower body is unglazed. The front and back of the vessel is incised with floral motif set between double-lined upright arcs. The arcs served to highlight the thematic motif and can be seen as the forerunner of the decorative panel. The green glaze within the outlines has been shaved away and a russet pigment applied in its place. *Meiping* vases are scarce among Liao finds and those with ferruginous painting are even fewer.

Decorative panels are seen on Jizhou ware of the Southern Song dynasty, Yaozhou ware of the Jin dynasty, Cizhou ware of the Jin and Yuan dynasties and most prevalent on Jingdezhen ware of the Yuan, Ming and Qing dynasties.

199

三彩人首莲花座

辽

公元 907—1125 年

高：26.2 厘米

底径：12.8 厘米

Sancai-glazed pottery pedestal with lotus and human head motif

Liao dynasty

907 – 1125 C.E.

Height: 26.2 cm

Base diameter: 12.8 cm

鼓形底座上塑一双面怪物头部。束颈，上刻竖纹。头顶仰莲花瓣碗状物。怪物浓眉如绳状，怒目圆睁，鼻大、口大，双唇紧闭，两耳竖起，头侧出角，双额贴螺旋堆纹，面目狰狞，令人望而生畏。胎色米黄，较疏松。怪物脸部施褐黄色釉，其余部位为绿釉，施釉不均。此器体内上下相通，可能只是用来承托物件。本品造型十分特别，未见类似器物发表。胎质、釉色、施釉情况类似辽三彩器。

The pedestal in the shape of a waist drum is molded with a twin-face monster. It has a glowering stare, bulging eyes, rope-like eyebrows, pricked ears and horns protruding from the side of its head. Its neck is carved with vertical striations. The head is surmounted by a bowl-shaped receptacle decorated with lotus petals in relief. The glazes are uneven in thickness and color. The pale yellow paste is rather porous. The hollow pedestal is presumably used as a base for some vessel. No other pedestal of its kind have been documented.

Judging from the paste, glaze color and glaze application, this pedestal is similar to Liao *sancai* wares.

三彩戏狮卧枕

宋

公元 960—1279 年

高：13.8 厘米

长：30.8 厘米

Sancai-glazed pottery headrest with tiger and children motif

Song dynasty

960 – 1279 C.E.

Height: 13.8 cm

Length: 30.8 cm

枕体两侧塑男、女小孩各一。后置一狮子，双眼圆睁，张开血盆大口咬着女孩后脑部。女孩左手顶着狮口，竭力把狮头推开，右手抓着狮毛向右拉。 另一侧的男孩用手拉着狮尾，不让狮子吞下女孩。女孩左、右耳旁结发髻，额前刘海左右分，手戴玉镯。男孩束发于后脑，戴宝珠颈圈和手镯。两孩头顶如意形向下微弯枕面，上刻一只在荷塘畅游的天鹅，荷叶间饰珍珠地，刻工流畅有力。淡红色胎，细滑。枕面施绿釉，器体施褐、绿、黄白釉，胎、釉结合紧密，开细片纹，釉色美丽，色泽对比鲜明。底平，露胎，墨书"张置"两字。狮鼻孔与内体相通，烧造时用于排气。

孩儿枕通常为一个小孩，两个小孩的甚少见。

The headrest features a boy and a girl in front and a lion with bulging eyes in the back. The lion has its mouth over the girl's head; the girl pushes away the lion's head with her left hand while pulling on a tuft of the lion's fur with her right hand. The boy is tugging at the tail of the lion to prevent the beast from swallowing the girl. The top of the headrest is in the shape of a cloud-head with a slightly pitched surface carved with a swan amid lotus leaves against a ground of pearl motif. The girl has a bun on each side of her head and bangs parted in the middle. She wears a jade bracelet around her right wrist. The boy has his hair tied up at the back of his head; he wears a jeweled necklace and a bracelet. The top of the headrest is glazed green. The sides are painted with amber, green and yellowish white glazes. The paste and the glazes sinter perfectly and crackles are found on the surface. The pinkish paste is fine and smooth. The unglazed flat base is inscribed in ink with two characters, "*Zhang zhi*" (Acquired by Zhang). The nostrils of the lion are connected to the cavity of the headrest, which allowed the hot air inside the headrest to escape during firing.

Most headrests with child motif feature only one child. Examples with two children are quite rare.

201

三彩皮囊壶

辽

公元 907—1125 年

缸瓦窑

高：32.8 厘米

底径：7.7 厘米

Sancai-glazed flask in the form of a leather pouch

Liao dynasty

907 – 1125 C.E.

Gangwa kilns

Height: 32.8 cm

Base diameter: 7.7 cm

小口卷缘，直颈，皮囊形扁腹、体细长，圈足。造型仿皮囊式样。颈至肩部装半环执手，颈肩交界处贴环状圈，圈足。粉红色胎，质较粗且疏松。施酱黄釉，肩部挂绿色彩条。釉色明亮，玻璃质感重。釉不到底，器身下部可见施釉前敷上的白粉化妆土。

The flask has a small mouth with rolling lip, a straight neck, a long and slender body, a belly resembling a leather pouch and a ring foot. An appliqué ridge encircles the bottom of the neck. The upper two-thirds of the vessel is covered with soy-yellow glaze while the shoulders are decorated with green splashes. The glaze is lustrous. The unglazed area revealed a paste coated with white slip. The pink paste is coarse and porous.

202

绿釉铆钉皮囊壶

辽

公元 907—1125 年

缸瓦窑

高：26.7 厘米

底径：7.7 厘米

Leather-pouch flask with boss design and green glaze

Liao dynasty

907 – 1125 C.E.

Gangwa kilns

Height: 26.7 cm

Base diameter: 7.7cm

扁圆颈、体扁长、上部略收、下部圆鼓、圈足微外撇。颈一侧有直立小口，与后方绞索状提梁相连接。口缘下颈周饰凸弦纹两道、弦纹上下交错排列铆钉纹。腹两侧及正面分别贴有三道和一道仿皮囊缝线凸棱，凸棱上置铆钉纹。泥质淡红色胎。施淡绿釉、釉薄、不到底。造型及装饰均模仿北方游牧民族的皮囊。

Light red earthenware. The flask has a flattened and elongated body with a narrow top, an ovoid neck, a bulbous belly and a slightly splayed ring foot. Set on one end of the neck is a small upright mouth that is connected to the loop handle in the form of entwined ropes. A double ridge studded with boss design runs around the mouth rim and lower neck. The sides of the vessel are decorated with three appliqués clay strips studded with boss design. The strips and the bosses are made to imitate the seams sewn on a leather pouch. The vessel is thinly covered with a light green glaze that stops short of the foot. The shape and decoration of the flask are modeled after the leather pouches used by the northern nomadic people.

203

绿釉刻花皮囊壶一对

辽

公元 907—1125 年

缸瓦窑

高：29.8 厘米

底阔：6.8 厘米

Pair of leather-pouch flasks with incised floral design under green glaze

Liao dynasty

907 – 1125 C.E.

Gangwa kilns

Height: 29.8 cm

Base width: 6.8 cm

体高身扁，上窄下阔，底平微内凹。塔式盖，尖圆纽，上贴凸棱八条。管状口，圆唇，管后置片状马鞍两个，上有圆孔，用以系绳。马鞍后部各贴塑一作骑马状的小孩（有说是猴子，但从脸形和前臂有衣袖来看应为小孩）。壶身周边饰皮囊缝合线，腹壁两侧刻卷草纹，纹饰柔和流畅。红陶胎，胎薄。壶外壁、管状流内壁和壶底满施深绿色釉，施釉均匀，釉上覆盖美丽的水银光层，开细碎纹片。底部残留细小长形支烧钉痕和用绳切割坯底时留下的绳纹。

此类皮囊壶通常工粗厚重，且底部大多不上釉，做工如此精细的甚少。此外，壶上蹲骑小孩的皮囊壶很少，蹲骑两个小孩的更少，而成对且盖、壶俱全且保存完整的，目前所知仅此一对而已，是极为珍贵的辽代艺术品。

Each flask has an elongated and flat body that is narrower at the top and wider at the bottom. The lid is in the shape of a pagoda with a conical knob with eight appliqué ribs. The cylindrical mouth has a rounded lip. The upper part is notched and flanked by two suspension holes each decorated with a child figurine in the posture of riding a horse. The figures on the flasks are said to be monkeys but the faces and the sleeves over the forelimbs suggest that they are children. The pouch-like body is outlined by pronounced seams and carved on the two broad sides with tendril scrolls.

The exterior wall, the inside of the mouth and the base are evenly coated with a dark green glaze with beautiful iridescence. Fine crackles are visible in the glaze. The flat base has a slightly recessed center; spur marks and cord marks are visible on the base. The red earthen paste is rather thin.

Leather-pouch flasks decorated with child figurines in the posture of riding a horse are rare and ones with twin figures are fewer still. This present example is the only known intact pair of its kind. It is a rarity among rarities from the Liao dynasty.

三彩摩羯壶

辽

公元 907—1125 年

高：22.6 厘米

阔：31 厘米

Pottery Makara jar with *sancai* glaze

Liao dynasty

907–1125 C.E.

Height: 22.6 cm

Width: 31 cm

壶身作鱼形、昂首、口为流、脊上设荷叶形壶口。背两侧置翅膀、尾部上翘。以扭结纹状提梁连接背和尾、提梁前端贴如意纹。形体肥美、充满活力的鱼龙伏于莲花座上、整体刻划细腻流畅。器体施浓艳褐、绿釉、开细纹片、釉色晶莹、润泽、褐绿交错、斑驳绚丽、宝光四射。淡红色胎、薄而细滑、体薄处不足 2 毫米。圆饼状实足、底平、露胎、四周有残留垫烧砂粒块。

摩羯本是印度神话中的河水之精、生命之体，公元 4 世纪末传入中国。历经隋、唐，摩羯的形象融入了龙、鱼的特征。辽代三彩陶器中尚见摩羯形壶。辽摩羯壶发现的数量不多，从造型、制作、釉色和完整度来看，本品堪为代表。

本品经热释光测定最后烧制年代距今 1100—800 年。

The vessel is in the shape of a fish with a raised head on a lotus plinth. The mouth of the fish serves as the spout and an opening in the shape of a lotus leaf the mouth of the jar. A pair of wings protrudes from the back. An overhead handle in the form of entwined ropes connects the opening and the up-turned tail fin, its front end decorated by appliqué S-spirals. The entire vessel is meticulously carved with elaborate details and covered with rich amber and green glazes with crackles on the smooth and lustrous surface. The glazes run into each other freely. The pinkish paste appears fine and thin; the thinnest part measures less than 2 mm. The pedestal has a disc-like solid foot with an unglazed flat base. Sand particles left by the spacers are found around the base.

According to Indian myths, Makara is a mythical sea creature and the embodiment of life. The image was first introduced to China in the late 4th century. During the Sui and Tang dynasties, it had the body of a fish and the head of a dragon. Makara jars in *sancai* glaze are prevalent during Liao dynasty but gradually faded out by the end of the Song dynasty. Only a small number of Makara jars from the Liao dynasty have been found. The present jar is the finest of its kind in terms of shape, craftsmanship, glaze color and intactness.

Thermoluminescence test shows that the last firing date of this piece was 1100 to 800 years before present.

205

褐绿彩莲鱼纹盘

元

公元 1206—1368 年

长治窑

高：2.6 厘米

口径：15.4 厘米

Pottery dish with aquatic motif with green and amber glaze

Yuan dynasty

1206 – 1368 C.E.

Changzhi kilns

Height: 2.6 cm

Mouth diameter: 15.4 cm

撇口，浅壁，矮圈足。胎浅褐，较粗糙。施白色化妆土。盘内刻游鱼莲花纹、白地、鱼身浅褐，余为绿彩，外绕一圈浅褐釉和一圈绿釉带，刻画出一幅鱼儿戏于莲花水草之间的动感画面。盘外施绿釉，不及底。

The dish has a wide mouth, shallow sides and a short ring foot. The brownish paste is rather coarse. The center is engraved with a fish amid lotus blossoms and aquatic plants. The decorative motifs are encircled by a band of amber glaze and a broader band of green glaze. Except for the body of the fish, which is in amber, the rest are painted in green on white ground. The exterior wall is coated with green glaze that stops short of the foot.

206

花卉纹盘

元

公元 1267 年

长治窑

高：3.3 厘米

口径：14.7 厘米

Pottery dish with floral motif

Yuan dynasty

1267 C.E.

Changzhi kilns

Height: 3.3 cm

Mouth diameter: 14.7 cm

敞口、浅壁、矮圈足。胎呈浅褐，稍粗。盘内壁口缘下施绿釉和白釉各一圈。盘心刻菊纹，白花、红蕊衬以绿彩枝叶。盘外壁施绿釉，不及底。盘底墨书"至元四年李七斤置"。

至元（公元 1264—1294 年）是元世祖忽必烈的年号，取自《易经》"至哉坤元"之意。

盘主人可能在出生时体重七斤，故名李七斤。把小孩出生体重作名字的习俗在山西颇为流行，笔者一位山西朋友的朋友名字叫赵八斤，便是如此。元代一斤合现在的 596.82 克（吴承洛：《中国度量衡史》，上海商务印书馆，1957 年），元七斤即 4177.74 克。

This dish has a wide mouth, shallow sides and a low ring foot. The brownish paste is rather coarse. The center is engraved with a chrysanthemum blossom featuring white petals and red stamens borne on a green stem surrounded by green leaves. The decorative motifs are encircled by a narrow band of white glaze and a broad band of green glaze. The exterior wall is coated with green glaze that stops short of the foot. The bottom is inscribed with characters that read, "[Made in] the 4th year of the Zhiyuan period (1267 C.E.) for Li Qijin".

This dish was probably made in the Zhiyuan period (1264–1294 C.E.) of Kublai Khan's reign. The reign title Zhiyuan came from the phrase *"zhizai kunyuan"* (ultimate earthly primal force) from *Yijing* (Classics of Changes).

"Qijin" literally means "seven catties". The owner of the dish probably weighed seven

catties when he was born. According to Wu Chengluo's *Zhongguo Duliangheng Shi*, seven catties in Yuan times was equivalent to 4177.74 g or 4.1774 kg (Wu Chengluo's *History of Measuring Units in China*, The Commercial Press, 1957).

本书为限量发行 999 套的第 _648_ 号

This book is copy number _____

in a limited edition of nine hundred and ninety-nine copies.

藏美

九如堂古陶瓷收藏 50 年

II

Collecting a Museum

50 Years of the Jiurutang Collection

九如堂　编著

文物出版社

藏美

九如堂古陶瓷收藏 50 年

II

Collecting a Museum

50 Years of the Jiurutang Collection

原始瓷器

Proto-Porcelain

原始瓷器：

豪迈霸气

经过几千年制陶工艺经验的积累，江南地区一些生产印纹硬陶的作坊终于生产出中国最早的瓷器，这就是原始瓷。早在 20 世纪 30 年代，在河南安阳殷墟商晚期文化遗址就出土了原始瓷瓷片。20 世纪 50 年代，考古工作者陆续在河南郑州二里岗商代中期文化遗址发现原始瓷瓷片，在铭功路、人民公园商代墓葬发现完整的原始瓷大口尊等器物。

原始瓷用瓷石作胎，表面施石灰质玻璃釉，经过 1200±30℃ 高温烧成，基本达到瓷器的标准。胎体基本烧结并有莫来石结晶，呈灰白色或浅褐色，气孔率和吸水性很低，莫氏硬度达 7 度，叩之能发出清越的声音。釉用高岭土加适量的石灰石粉末、草木灰和黄土配成，以 Fe_2O_3 为着色剂，在还原火焰中烧成，釉色呈青绿色、黄绿色或灰青色，依据烧成火焰气氛的变化而有不同。

原始瓷出现于夏代晚期，成熟于商代早期，发展于西周早期，兴盛于战国早期，衰落于战国中期，在长江流域的南方和黄河流域的北方广大地区出土较多。成熟瓷器是在原始瓷的基础上逐渐发展起来的。和成熟瓷器相比，原始瓷处于瓷器刚刚发明的阶段，器物品种少，胎体较粗，杂质很多，吸水率和气孔率比成熟瓷器高很多；釉层很薄，显色不美，由于釉色基本是青绿色调，故又称为"原始青瓷"。此时的龙窑又短又小，有的瓷器烧成温度偏低；由于没有垫饼等窑具，坯件直接放在窑床上，底部没有烧结。

商代和西周的原始瓷生产数量很少，十分珍贵，这从商周遗址出土原始瓷数量极少可见一斑（图录 207 号、210 号）。商周原始瓷兼有贵族专用和祭祀器物的用途，从随葬品的安排来看，原始瓷器和青铜器处于同等尊贵的地位。以世界各大博物馆来说，商周原始瓷藏品相当缺乏。

商代的原始瓷使用泥条盘筑、慢轮、手工捏塑等成型工艺，在器物内部形成比较粗糙的轮制修坯痕迹。器形以罐、盆、钵、豆、壶、罍为主。胎色呈灰白、青灰、灰褐。施釉较薄。装饰以素面为主，间有少量弦纹、三角纹、菱格纹、云雷纹等。

西周时原始瓷数量增加，除了豆、盂、钵、罐等常见造型外，已有尊、簋、盉、鼎、灯具等。胎釉特征变化明显，釉面玻化程度较高，但釉层仍比较薄。纹饰上打破了较早前的素面，开始出现水波纹、弦纹和"S"形纹、绳纹系等贴塑纹饰（图录 213 号、214 号）。

春秋时期原始瓷生产水平提高，开始使用快轮成型，胎体厚薄均匀，器物内部可看到快轮拉坯成型的螺旋纹痕迹，器物外底部留有以绳切割胎泥的偏心旋纹。此时纹饰出现了席纹、窃曲纹（鸟纹）、锥刺纹、扉棱等仿青铜器的纹饰，而大量云气纹和"S"形纹饰堆塑的使用是这时期的突出特征（图录 215 号、216 号、217 号）。

战国早期，奴隶制度逐渐解体，生产力得到解放，工商业发展，除了独立的陶瓷手工业作坊外，也出现了财雄势大的官办作坊（此类官办作坊具有早期官窑的性质），在竞争下成就了非凡的战国原始瓷产品，有极高的艺术和历史价值。目前所见高规格的战国原始瓷遗物，大多应出自此时的官办作坊，可说是战国时期的官窑器物。这一时期的原始瓷器物，造型雄伟古拙、圆浑粗犷兼而有之，仿青铜礼乐器制品数量增多，出现蟠螭纹、夔纹、饕餮纹、铺首衔环等纹饰。

战国中晚期，中国社会处在由奴隶制转向封建制的激烈动荡时期，社会生产力受到极大影响，原始瓷烧造工艺一度下降，产品釉色偏暗，广泛出现麻癞现象，釉层极易剥落。经过汉初的休养生息，原始瓷又快速发展起来。

汉朝时期的原始瓷主要分布在浙江、江苏和安徽等地，多为灰胎，釉面为褐绿色，特征为釉不及底、露胎处呈褐红色。纹饰多为水波纹、麻布纹、云气纹、神兽飞鸟、狩猎图。壶、洗、盆、罐等常贴铺首衔环（兽面衔环）和叶纹横系等。

本书收录的原始瓷相当丰富，它们把从原始瓷到成熟瓷器进化的历程清楚地展现了出来，相信读者在欣赏、分析这些极具代表性的各个时期的原始瓷时，定会有所收获。

Proto-Porcelain:

Boldness Incarnate

Based on millennia of experience, the workshops that were making high-fired stamped pottery in Jiangnan region (lower Changjiang River basin), finally gave rise to proto-porcelain, the earliest porcelain ever produced in China. Shards of proto-porcelains can be found as early as the 1930s, from the late Shang cultural layer at the old Shang capital in Anyang, Henan province. Some were excavated from the mid Shang cultural layer at the Erligang site in Zhengzhou. Proto-porcelains including an intact wide-mouthed *zun* pot from a Shang tomb were also discovered at the People's Park on Minggong Road.

Proto-porcelain is fabricated from china stone and coated with a transparent lime glaze. The paste contains mullite crystals. When fired to a high temperature of 1230±30ºC, the body becomes vitrified. It has a low porosity, a low permeability and a hardness of 7 on the Mohs scale, which is consistent with the basic features of porcelain. The grayish-white or light brown body makes a pleasant sound when knocked with the knuckles. The glaze was formulated from a mixture of *kaolin*, lime powder, plant ash and loess. Ferric oxide was used as colorant and firing was done in a reduction atmosphere. Change of kiln atmosphere results in a variety of glaze colors ranging from brilliant green to yellowish-green or grayish-green.

Proto-porcelain laid the foundation for the development and perfection of later porcelain. At this early stage of porcelain production, the paste was relatively coarse with impurities and vessels were often under-fired because the dragon kilns were short and small. Due to the absence of spacers and other kiln equipment, the vessels had to be placed on grates inside the kiln, which resulted in a poorly vitrified base. The porosity and water permeability of proto-porcelains were also much higher than that of mature porcelains. The glaze was also thin with poor color consistency. Since the objects are glazed green, they are also called "proto-celadons". Proto-porcelain first appeared in the late Xia dynasty, developed from the early Shang dynasty to the early Western Zhou, thrived during the early Warring States period and declined in the middle of this same period. Artifacts are found predominantly in the region south of the Changjiang River basin and north of the Yellow River basin.

Production of proto-porcelains was very limited during the early stages of the Shang and Western Zhou periods. These vessels are considered exceedingly rare especially ones from the Shang period. Artifacts found at Shang and Zhou sites are few and far between (Cat. Nos. 207, 210). The arrangement of burial objects found in tombs revealed that porcelains occupied the same venerable position as bronzes and are used by the elites in rituals. Proto-porcelains of the Shang and Zhou periods are scarcely found even in the major museums around the world.

Proto-porcelains of the Shang dynasty were either hand-built by using coiling and pinching methods or thrown on a slow wheel. Coarse wheel marks are visible around the interior of the thrown vessels. Major types include the jar, the basin, the bowl, the *dou* stem-bowl, the *hu* jar and the *lei* jar. The body appears grayish-white, greenish-gray or grayish-brown. The glaze is relatively thin. The surfaces are mostly plain but some are decorated with cord motif, triangular patterns, lozenges or cloud-and-thunder pattern.

The number of proto-porcelains during the Western

Zhou period increased manifold. New shapes include the *zun* pot, the *gui* pot, the *he* jar, the *ding* tripod and the lamp. The paste and the glaze are distinctly different from earlier examples. The glaze is still quite thin though more vitrified. Plain surfaces are decorated by wave motif, cord motif, S-spirals and appliqué rope-like lugs (Cat. Nos. 213, 214).

Fast wheels began to be used during the Spring and Autumn period which made the thickness of the vessel walls more consistent. Rings of wheel marks can be seen on the interior wall. The form is removed from the wheel by cutting it loose with a piece of string. The decorative motifs of this period include impressed mat design, S-shaped dragon motif or bird motif (*qiequ* motif adopted from bronzes), pecked motif, flanges, appliqué clouds and S-spirals (Cat. Nos. 215, 216, 217).

Due to the disintegration of the slave system, the early Warring States period saw great advance in production and commerce. In addition to private ceramic workshops, there were also large, well-financed, government-run workshops, which operated not unlike the early imperial kilns. The best of these Warring States proto-porcelains were produced at such government workshops. They are seen as the imperial pottery of its time. During this period, vessels imitating ritual bronzes increased in number. Stylized dragon motifs, *taotie* masks and ringed-masks were used.

The mid to late Warring States period and the Qin dynasty witnessed the transformation of a slave society to a feudal society amidst intense political and social unrest. Warfare greatly lowered the productivity and quality of proto-porcelains. It is not until the Han dynasty that the pottery industry regained its momentum.

Proto-porcelain of the Han dynasty was produced around Zhejiang, Jiangsu and Anhui. Most vessels have a gray body and a brownish-green glaze. The glaze stops short of the base revealing a brownish-red color where it is unglazed. Decorative motifs include waves, hemp fabric marks, clouds, mythical animals and birds and hunting scenes. Jars and basins are often adorned with appliqué animal masks with rings and horizontal leaf-shaped lugs.

The development from proto-porcelain to mature porcelain will be covered extensively in this catalogue.

207

青釉弦纹豆

商—西周

公元前 1600—前 771 年

高：7 厘米

口径：10.8 厘米

底径：5.3 厘米

Celadon *dou* stem-bowl with cord motif

Shang – Western Zhou dynasty

1600 – 771 B.C.E.

Height: 7 cm

Mouth diameter: 10.8 cm

Base diameter: 5.3 cm

原始青瓷。唇外翻，折肩，斜腹壁，喇叭形圈足。颈和口沿内侧各饰弦线纹带各一组，腹部内外满布不规则细小弦纹多组。胎浅灰白，细腻。除圈足底外，全器施石灰釉，釉泛褐色，施釉不均，圈足釉收缩成细碎点状。釉色明亮，玻璃质感较强，颈肩部可见窑变乳浊釉。釉开细碎纹片，尤以乳浊釉为甚。器心留有坚硬的、呈"品"字形分布的长条状物三块，应为支烧残留物，对研究叠烧的起源和工艺有极大的研究价值。

原始瓷在商代处于初创阶段，产量不多，十分珍贵，只在贵族墓才有发现。

1966 年山东省青州市苏埠屯遗址 M2 以及 1998 年滕州市前掌大遗址 M4、M119 的商晚期至西周早期墓葬群出土有相似器物，现藏山东省博物馆。

2011—2012 年浙江萧山柴岭山商至西周墓葬群出土有相似器物。

Proto-celadon. The vessel has an everted mouth rim, angular shoulders, a tapering belly and a trumpet ring-foot. A band of cord motif runs around the neck and inside the mouth rim. The interior and exterior of the belly are extensively covered with groups of irregularly spaced fine striations. The light gray paste is refined. Except for the area enclosed by the ring-foot, the entire vessel is covered with an uneven layer of brownish lime glaze with a lustrous surface. Contraction of glaze during firing has resulted in numerous pockmarks around the ring-foot. Opalescent streaks as a result of kiln transmutation appear in the glaze around the neck and the shoulders. Tiny crackles are also visible amid the opalescent areas. The interior of the bowl still retained three tiny strips of materials forming the three points of a triangle. These could be the remnants of the spacer placed between fired objects. This bowl is an important reference for studying the origin and development of stacked firing in Chinese ceramic history.

Proto-celadon was at its early stage during the Shang dynasty. Since output was scarce, examples are very rare and could only be found in the tombs of feudal lords.

Similar examples have been unearthed from late Shang to Western Zhou dynasty tombs in 1966 at site M2 in Subutun (Qingzhou city, Shandong province) and in 1998 at site M4 and site M119 in Qianzhangda (Tengzhou city, Shandong province). They are now in the collection of the Shandong Provincial Museum.

Some are also found at the Shang and Western Zhou dynasty tombs from 2011 – 2012 at Chailingshan, Xiaoshan, Zhejiang province.

208

青釉钵

商—西周

公元前 1600—前 771 年

高：6.7 厘米

口径：13.2 厘米

底径：5.5 厘米

Celadon bowl

Shang – Western Zhou dynasty

1600 – 771 B.C.E.

Height: 6.7 cm

Mouth diameter: 13.2 cm

Base diameter: 5.5 cm

原始青瓷。口沿内伸，小圆肩，平底，底微内凹。器形颇规整。口沿和肩间以细密弦纹带作装饰。胎灰白、较厚重。除外底外，全器内外施石灰釉，施釉厚薄不均，釉呈褐色，上浅下深。釉色亮泽，开纹片。外壁腹下部有乳白和蓝色的窑变乳浊釉。腹下半部釉层收缩，呈麻癞状并有许多棕眼。器内、外壁和外底部分被泥浆覆盖。

浙江萧山柴岭山商代至西周遗址出土有相似但没施釉的硬陶器物。

Proto-celadon. The bowl has an incurved mouth rim, small rounded shoulders and a flat base with a slightly recessed center. The shoulder is decorated by a group of closely spaced fine cord pattern. The grayish paste looks rather thick and heavy. Shaping is neatly done. Except for the external base, the entire vessel is covered with a lustrous but uneven layer of crackled lime glaze. The brownish glaze appears darker on the lower half of the body. Milky white and opalescent blue streaks as a result of kiln transmutation are visible on the lower belly. The pockmarks, streaking and pinholes around the lower belly are the result of the contraction of glaze during firing. The interior of the bowl, part of the lower belly and the external part of the base are covered with mud.

Similar but unglazed high-fired pottery have been unearthed from the Shang to Western Zhou dynasty sites at Chailingshan in Xiaoshan, Zhejiang province.

209

青釉三耳弦纹罐

西周

公元前 1046—前 771 年

高：22.6 厘米

阔：30.3 厘米

底径：20.3 厘米

Celadon jar with three loop lugs and cord motif

Western Zhou dynasty

1046 – 771 B.C.E.

Height: 22.6 cm

Width: 30.3 cm

Base diameter: 20.3 cm

原始青瓷。直口、肩腹丰满圆鼓、底足外撇、大平底。肩贴双云气纹拱形耳三组。全器满刻弦纹，予人动感的旋律和生生不息的感觉。胎浅灰色，质坚，胎釉结合紧密，烧成火候较高，叩之铿铿作响。满施青褐色釉，釉色均匀、润泽、明亮。该器造型圆浑稳重，线条优美，为西周原始青瓷佳品。

本品仍保留着底边外突的"大平底"风格，这是流行于西周早期的一种工艺特征（见王屹峰：《中国南方原始瓷窑业研究》，中国书店，2010 年）。

Proto-celadon. The jar has a straight mouth, bold shoulders and a bulbous belly that tapers towards a slightly splayed broad base. Three loop lugs with cloud-head design are equally spaced around the shoulders. The entire exterior is carved with dense cord motif, imparting a strong sense of motion and movement. The glaze sintered well with the hard and refined paste. As the firing temperature was relatively high, the vessel gives a clear sound when knocked with the knuckles. The surface is coated with an even layer of greenish brown glaze with a smooth and lustrous surface. This jar is a fine example of Western Zhou proto-celadon.

This jar has a broad flat base, a feature that is prevalent during the early Western Zhou period (See Wang Yifeng, *Zhongguo nanfang yuanshi ci yaoye yanjiu* [A Study of the Proto-Celadon Industry in Southern China], Cathay Bookstore Publishing House, 2010).

210

青釉敞口尊

西周

公元前 1046—前 771 年

高：8 厘米

口径：10.5 厘米

底径：6.7 厘米

Celadon *zun* pot with flared mouth

Western Zhou dynasty

1046 – 771 B.C.E.

Height: 8 cm

Mouth diameter: 10.5 cm

Base diameter: 6.7 cm

原始青瓷。敞口，圆唇，口缘外翻，直颈，折肩，腹壁弧形下收，喇叭形圈足。内口缘刻细凹弦纹六周，下篦刻不连贯斜水波纹十一组。外口缘下方与肩满饰弦纹。夹砂灰白胎，质坚硬，叩之铿铿响，烧造温度较高。除足底外，器内外施石灰釉，釉青绿，泛微黄，聚釉处呈翠绿。釉薄，釉层比较均匀，玻璃质感强，开片。胎釉结合紧密，无剥釉现象。腹及圈足釉薄处呈猪肝红色。圈足内底斜削成 45°，留有垫烧物残渣。腹与底足交接处可见不规则夹痕，说明是造好器体后再黏上底足。本品胎釉结合紧密，釉色纯正，为西周原始青瓷之佳品。

据 1998 年《文物》第 9 期《河南平顶山应国墓地八十四号墓发掘简报》一文介绍，该墓出土文物共 130 余件 / 组，其中铜器 90 余件，玉石 30 余件 / 组，陶鬲和原始青瓷簋各 1 件，其余为金、骨和料器等。墓葬年代推定为西周恭王后期。其中出土的青瓷簋，外形、纹饰和大小与本品相似。

1983 年杭州市余杭区临平山出土有相似器物，现藏于杭州市余杭博物馆。

Proto-celadon. The vessel has a wide mouth with rounded lip and everted rim. The straight neck makes an angular turn to join the bulbous belly that tapers towards a trumpet-shaped ring foot. Six rounds of incised lines and oblique hatching encircle the inner mouth rim. The neck and the shoulders are covered with grooves. The sand-tempered grayish white paste is rather hard. It gives a clear sound when struck, suggesting that the firing temperature was rather high. Except for the area enclosed by the ring foot, the exterior and interior of the vessel are coated with a thin and rather even layer of pale green lime glaze with a yellowish tint and a glassy surface filled with crackles. A bright hue is noted where the glaze pools. The glaze sinters well with the paste and no flaking is visible. Patches of reddish-brown appear around the belly and the ring foot where the glaze runs thin. The rim of the ring foot has been beveled at a 45-degree angle; fireclay marks are found around it. Since an irregular seam is visible between the lower belly and the foot, the latter was probably separately finished. The excellent sintering of the paste and the celadon glaze as well as the perfect tone of the glaze make this vessel a fine example of Western Zhou proto-celadon ware.

A proto-celadon *gui* pot similar in shape, decoration and size was unearthed among some 130 items/sets of artifacts from a tomb at Pingdingshan in Henan. The proto-celadon *gui* pot is dated to the latter years of the Duke of Gong of the Ying State during the mid Western Zhou period. Other artifacts among the finds include over 90 pieces of bronzes, over 30 pieces of jades, a pottery *ge* cauldron as well as artifacts made of gold, bone and glass (See "Excavation Report of Tomb No.84 from the Cemetery of the Ying State at Pingdingshan", *Wenwu* 1998:9).

A similar pot was unearthed in 1983 at Linpingshan (Yuhang district) in Hangzhou, Zhejiang province. It is in the collection of the Yuhang Museum in Hangzhou.

211

青釉塔形盉

西周

公元前 1046—前 771 年

高：14 厘米

底径：9.2 厘米

Pagoda-shaped celadon *he* jug

Western Zhou dynasty

1046 – 771 B.C.E.

Height: 14 cm

Base diameter: 9.2 cm

原始青瓷。呈塔形，尖顶，顶以下渐广，近底处内收。圈足，微外撇。肩部一侧置圆形短流，流的左侧贴一扁平上翘手柄。器顶塑展翅小鸟一只。手柄顶部和小鸟足下各贴小圆点四粒，流顶三粒作饰。灰白胎，含一定数量细沙，质坚，胎体较薄。施石灰釉，釉呈淡青黄色，釉薄而均匀，满布细碎纹片。器内壁和足底无釉。底内缘向外斜削成 45 度。通体满饰细密弦纹，造型新颖。全器由顶、颈肩、上腹、下腹和圈足五部分黏合而成，可见黏合痕。西周器物造型如此精细工整，十分难得，是一件优秀的艺术品。

1982 年浙江衢县出土一件西周青釉盉壶，与本品相同，现藏衢州市博物馆。

1965 年安徽屯溪西郊西周墓葬出土与本品相似器物。

Proto-celadon. The jug is shaped like a pagoda with a conical top. The lower third of the body tapers towards a slightly splayed ring foot. A short cylindrical spout is set on the shoulders; there is an up-tilted handle to its left. A small bird sits at the top of the vessel. Four circular nodes decorate the end of the handle where it joins the body. Another four nodes appear below the bird's feet and three more at the top of the spout. The unglazed inner rim has been trimmed at a 45-degree angle. Fine grooves encircle the entire body. The grayish white paste appears hard and relatively thin and contains considerable amount of sand particles. The exterior is thinly covered with an even layer of pale green lime glaze with tiny crackles. The inner walls and the bottom of the vessel are unglazed. The body is formed by joining together five separate sections, namely the top, neck and shoulders, upper belly, lower belly and ring foot. Luting marks are visible. Vessels demonstrating such beautiful glaze color and meticulous workmanship are rare among Western Zhou pottery.

A similar celadon jug from the Western Zhou period was unearthed in 1982 from Quxian, Zhejiang province. It is now in the collection of the Quzhou City Museum.

Another example was unearthed in 1965 from a Western Zhou tomb in the western suburb of Tunxi, Anhui province.

212

青釉弦纹盉

西周

公元前 1046—前 771 年

高：10 厘米

底径：9 厘米

Celadon *he* jug with grooved design

Western Zhou dynasty

1046 – 771 B.C.E.

Height: 10 cm

Base diameter: 9 cm

原始青瓷。盖、腹粘连，腹中部折收到底。圈足，外缘突出于底部。盖、腹间以一道凸缘分隔，上腹一侧置扁圆流，流与腹部相通，流口呈心形。流后方和相对一侧各贴云雷纹饰两组。全器满饰弦纹。外底微凸，露灰白胎。胎质致密，胎体颇厚重。施石灰釉，釉泛青黄色，釉色明亮，开细碎纹片。

本品造型新颖、线条流畅、造工精细规整，是一件难得的艺术品。

Proto-porcelain. The lid is non-functional and fixed to the body. The belly makes an angular turn midway and tapers to a rimmed foot. A spout with a heart-shaped mouth is set on the shoulders. The edge of the lid is decorated with a pair of appliqué cloud-and-thunder design. The entire vessel is encircled by grooves and covered with a lustrous lime glaze with a greenish-yellow tint and tiny crackles. The slightly convex base reveals a grayish-white paste that is fine and compact. The jug is quite thickly and heavily potted.

This jug is noted for its unique shape, sleek lines and exquisite workmanship.

213

青釉灯具一对

西周

公元前 1046—前 771 年

高：5.2 厘米

口径：18.5 厘米

底径：10.2 厘米

Pair of celadon oil lamps

Western Zhou dynasty

1046 – 771 B.C.E.

Height: 5.2 cm

Mouth diameter: 18.5 cm

Base diameter: 10.2 cm

原始青瓷。喇叭形圈足，上承双口缘浅盘，盘中置小盂一个。小盂外壁饰弦纹，肩上横贴三个"S"形纹饰，呈"品"字形，浅盘内壁饰弦纹，间以水波纹，口缘棱边等距贴"S"形纹饰四个。胎灰白，质硬。器身内外施石灰釉，釉呈深豆青色。施釉不均，聚釉处成块状，有开片纹和剥釉现象。圈足内外无釉，露胎处呈火石红色。小盂用于装灯油，浅盘用于装水。本品也可能是作祭祀用途的礼器。

此器造型特别，设计精巧，纹饰丰富，制作精细。

Proto-celadon. Each oil lamp is in the shape of a double-rimmed shallow dish supported by a trumpet foot. The center is furnished with a miniature basin whose rim is decorated with three appliqué S-spirals. The interior of the dish is alternately decorated with cord motif and wave motif. The groove between the double rims is adorned with four equally spaced appliqué S-spirals. The interior and exterior are covered with a deep pea-green-colored lime glaze. The glaze has been unevenly applied; lumps are visible where it runs thick. Crackles and flaking are visible. The grayish-white paste has a high degree of hardness. Both the inside and outside of the ring foot are unglazed, exposing a biscuit of burnt orange color. The basin was used for holding oil and the dish for holding water. These lamps could also be utensils used in sacrificial rituals.

This pair is noted for its delicate design, rich decorations and exquisite workmanship.

214

青釉索耳折腰盂

西周

公元前 1046—前 771 年

高：7.1 厘米

阔：21.2 厘米

底径：13.7 厘米

Celadon basin with rope-shaped lugs and angular sides

Western Zhou dynasty

1046 – 771 B.C.E.

Height: 7.1 cm

Width: 21.2 cm

Base diameter: 13.7 cm

原始青瓷。宽口，直颈，斜肩，折腰，平底。肩上、下饰弦纹数道，中饰水波纹带，两侧置竖绳纹系，另两侧由上而下排列三个"S"形纹饰。腰、腹分界明显，腹下斜收到底。胎浅褐色，颇坚硬、细滑。内外施石灰釉，釉发黄褐色，釉色明亮柔润。

折腰盂为西周原始瓷器之典型器物。本品线条硬朗、造型华美、釉层保存完整，甚为难得。

Proto-celadon. The basin has a wide mouth, a straight neck, sloping shoulders that join the belly at an acute angle and a flat base. The shoulders are decorated with a frieze of wave motif between grooved borders and a pair of vertically placed loop lugs in the shape of entwining ropes. Halfway between the lugs on both sides of the shoulders are three stacked appliqué S-spirals. The shoulders turn sharply to join the belly, which then tapers to a narrower base. The light brown paste is refined and hard. Both the interior and exterior are covered with a smooth and lustrous lime glaze of yellowish-brown color.

The shape is typical of Western Zhou proto-porcelain. This vessel is noted for its dramatic contours, elegant shape and well-preserved glaze.

215

青釉窃曲纹双系罐

春秋

公元前 770—前 476 年

高：21.5 厘米

底径：17.5 厘米

Celadon jar with S-shaped dragon motif

Spring and Autumn period

770 – 476 B.C.E.

Height: 21.5 cm

Base diameter: 17.5 cm

原始青瓷。小口微敛、短颈、斜肩、鼓腹、平底。肩两侧贴绳纹系各一，系侧各置云气纹饰一个。器身拍印仿铜器窃曲纹（有说是鸟纹）到底，共八周。胎质坚致，通体内外施石灰釉、釉呈绿褐色，均匀明亮。胎釉结合紧密，全器满布细碎纹片。器外底中部及边缘处可见开片青釉，边缘留有支烧残物。此类器物外底部通常不施釉，此器外底部施釉说明其当时应十分珍贵。

本品与图录 209 号相比，西周时期之 "大平底" 外凸部分已进行削边处理，颈肩也抹光一周，是春秋中晚期的一种工艺特征（见王屹峰：《中国南方原始瓷窑业研究》中国书店，2010 年）。

1976 年江苏高淳永宁苗圃春秋墓出土有相似器物，现藏镇江市博物馆。

Proto-celadon. The jar has a small and slightly incurved mouth, a short neck, steep shoulders, a swelling belly and a flat base. A pair of loop lugs in the shape of entwining ropes with S-spirals flanks the shoulders. The body is impressed with eight rounds of highly stylized S-shaped dragon motif (or bird motif) adopted from bronzes. The glaze sintered well with the refined paste. Both the interior and exterior surfaces are evenly coated with a brownish-green lime glaze covered with tiny crackles. The center and the edge of the base are also covered with crackled celadon glaze. Fireclay marks are found on the edge. Since glaze was a precious material, the base of these jars was usually left unglazed. The glazed base indicates that this jar was an object of considerable value of its time.

The base of this vessel is trimmed as opposed to the "broad flat base" style that was prevalent during the Western Zhou period (Cat. No. 209). This feature and the articulation between the neck and shoulders are characteristic of the mid-late Spring and Autumn period (See Wang Yifeng, *Zhongguo nanfang yuanshi ciyaoye yanjiu* [A Study of the Proto-Celadon Industry in Southern China], Cathay Bookstore Publishing House, 2010).

A similar jar was unearthed in 1976 from a tomb dated to the Spring and Autumn period at Yongling Nursery in Gaochun, Jiangsu province. It is now in the collection of the Zhenjiang Municipal Museum.

青釉锥刺纹三足鼎

春秋

公元前 770—前 476 年

高：14.4 厘米

阔：27.8 厘米

口径：17.6 厘米

Celadon *ding* tripod with pecked motif

Spring and Autumn period

770 – 476 B.C.E.

Height: 14.4 cm

Width: 27.8 cm

Mouth diameter: 17.6 cm

原始青瓷。束颈，翻缘圆唇，宽肩，扁鼓腹，圜底，三扁形足，造型与同时代的青铜器相同。器腹部满饰锥刺纹。腹贴扉棱四个，把器腹分为四等份。其中两个扉棱上方置绳索状环系，其中一系旁塑有两条蛇，正追赶前方的两只青蛙；相对的系旁立昂首雀鸟两只，等待机会把青蛙或蛇捉来饱腹。古语有谓"螳螂捕蝉，黄雀在后"，本品可说是"蛇捕青蛙，黄雀在后"。胎呈灰白色，胎质坚致。通体内外施石灰釉，釉呈青褐色，薄而均匀。

Proto-celadon. The vessel has a mouth with rounded lip and everted rim, a constricted neck, broad shoulders, a compressed globular belly and a rounded base supported by three strap legs. The shape is also found among contemporaneous bronzes. The body is decorated with rows of pecked motif resembling rice seedlings sprouting in paddy field. Halfway between the ears on both sides of the body is a vertical flange, dividing the body into four sections. A pair of loop lugs in the form of plaited ropes is attached to the shoulders. Above one of the lugs are two frogs carved in the round, and below it two snakes chasing after the frogs. The other lug is flanked by two standing birds with their eyes set on their preys. An old Chinese proverb says, "The mantis stalks the cicada, unaware of the oriole behind" (one covets the gains ahead without being aware of the danger behind). In this case, the snakes are the hunters and the hunted. Both the interior and exterior are evenly coated with a thin layer of greenish-brown lime glaze. The grayish white paste is dense.

217

青釉双耳三足鼎

春秋

公元前 770—前 476 年

高：9.1 厘米

口径：16.4 厘米

Celadon *ding* tripod with double S-spiral lugs

Spring and Autumn period

770 – 476 B.C.E.

Height: 9.1 cm

Mouth diameter: 16.4 cm

原始青瓷。颈短、稍外撇、短斜肩、腹急收到底、平底、承以三扁圆足。肩满印方格纹，腹壁光素。肩两侧饰如意组纹耳，另两侧贴云气纹各一。内底中心有一周螺旋同心圆直达壁上。胎质坚硬，呈浅灰白色。全器内、外壁均施青黄色釉，施釉较均匀，聚釉处釉色晶莹润亮，满布开片纹，有缩釉现象。在腹、底交界周边，可见蓝白色呈失透状的窑变釉色。底露胎。

商周时期对于原始瓷器胎、釉和温度之控制十分困难，本品釉色佳，烧结程度高，胎、釉结合紧密，无明显剥落现象，在当时的技术条件下已是十分难得。

Proto-celadon. The censer has a slightly flared mouth, a short neck, narrow sloping shoulders and a belly that tapers towards a flat base supported by three legs. The shoulders are densely covered with check pattern; the belly is plain. A pair of lugs in the shape of S-spirals is set on the shoulders while an appliqué S-spiral appears halfway between the lugs on both sides. Except for the base, the interior and exterior of the vessel are coated with a rather even layer of yellowish-green crackled glaze. Where the glaze pools, the color appears particularly bright and clear. Retraction of glaze occurs in some areas. The unglazed base reveals a grayish-white paste. Wheel marks are visible along the interior wall. The blue and white opalescent hues around the base are a result of kiln transmutation.

Control over paste, glaze and firing temperature was still a challenge during the Shang and Zhou periods. It is quite an achievement for this vessel to have such a beautiful glaze that also sintered well with the paste with no visible flaking.

218

青釉席纹罐

春秋

公元前 770—前 476 年

高：26.8 厘米

Celadon jar with mat motif

Spring and Autumn period

770 – 476 B.C.E.

Height: 26.8 cm

原始青瓷。大口、斜短颈，颈周饰波浪纹，鼓腹，平底。肩相对两侧贴矩状环形堆纹各一，寓意饕餮衔环，以示器物之尊贵。器体拍印席纹到底。灰白胎，质坚致。体内外施石灰釉，釉色青黄。底露胎。体态圆浑、线条流畅，纹饰朴实大方，为春秋时期典型储器。

图录 101 号无论器形和时代都与本品相似，只是没施釉，说明原始瓷是由印纹硬陶发展而来的。

1975 年江苏金坛出土有相似器物，现藏镇江市博物馆。

Proto-celadon. The jar has a large mouth, a gently sloping short neck, a swelling belly and a flat base. The neck is surrounded by wave motif. The shoulder is affixed with a pair of rectangular appliqués where the ringed masks would have been on bronzes, which suggests the importance of this jar. The entire vessel surface down to the foot rim is impressed with mat motif. The grayish-white paste is hard and refined. Both the interior and exterior are covered with a lime glaze of greenish-yellow color. The base is unglazed. The jar is noted for its robust shape, sleek lines and a restrained decorative motif. This vessel is characteristic of the pottery of the Spring and Autumn period. It was used as a storage container.

Cat. No. 101 is similar to this item in shape and time period but unglazed, suggesting that proto-porcelain is evolved from high-fired stamped pottery.

A similar vessel, now in the collection of the Zhenjiang Municipal Museum, was unearthed in 1975 from Jintan, Jiangsu province.

219

青釉双耳水波纹小罐

春秋

公元前 770—前 476 年

高：9.4 厘米

底径：9.8 厘米

Celadon jar with loop lugs and wave motif

Spring and Autumn period

770 – 476 B.C.E.

Height: 9.4 cm

Base diameter: 9.8 cm

原始青瓷。平底，底边缘稍向外突出。肩和上腹部满饰水波纹，两侧置对称绳纹耳各一，上贴如意形纹饰。内壁下半部有明显轮旋纹。灰白胎，质坚、厚重。器体内、外壁施石灰釉，釉呈灰青色。下腹部釉已大部分脱落，有缩釉和开片现象。底露胎。

Proto-celadon. The unglazed flat base has a slightly splayed foot rim. The shoulders and the upper belly are densely decorated with wave motif. A pair of rope-like lugs with appliqué *ruyi* design is affixed to the shoulders. Wheel marks are visible around the lower part of the interior. The interior and exterior surfaces are covered with a grayish-green lime glaze. The glaze around the lower belly has mostly come off. Crackles and retraction of glaze are visible. The grayish white paste is hard and heavy.

220

青釉豆

战国

公元前 475—前 221 年

高：5.5 厘米

口径：11.7 厘米

底径：4.8 厘米

Celadon *dou* stem-bowl

Warring States period

475– 221 B.C.E.

Height: 5.5 cm

Mouth diameter: 11.7 cm

Base diameter: 4.8 cm

原始青瓷。撇口卷唇，斜折腹，腹下急收，与喇叭形圈足相接。豆内壁上腹部饰弦纹一组，余光素无纹饰。浅灰白胎、胎薄、坚硬、颇细滑、烧结程度较好。内壁仍见闪闪发亮、呈点状的残留青釉，外壁青釉已全部脱落。器心残留呈"品"字形分布的长条状支烧痕。器形不甚规整，器身歪斜，口部不圆，显示出其原始性。此器古拙质朴，令人喜爱。

南京溧水七里岗出土有相似器物。

Proto-celadon. The vessel has a flared mouth with rolling rim, a shallow body, slightly tapering sides that join the belly at an angle and a high splayed trumpet foot. Apart from the cord patterns encircling its upper interior, the entire vessel is devoid of decorative motif. The light gray paste appears thin, hard, smooth, refined and well vitrified. The celadon glaze on the exterior wall has come off but traces of it are still visible on the interior surface. Spur marks forming the points of a triangle are visible

around the center of the bowl. The shape of the bowl lacks symmetry and the mouth rim is uneven. These features are typical of early proto-celadon. The bowl imparts a

sense of rustic beauty and primitive charm.

A similar vessel was unearthed at Qiligang, Lishui in Nanjing.

221

青釉提梁盉

战国

公元前 475—前 221 年

高：19.9 厘米

Celadon *he* tripod with overhead handle

Warring States period

475 – 221 B.C.E.

Height: 19.9 cm

原始青瓷。直口，鼓腹，圜底，下承以三兽足，造型仿青铜盉。腹背置夔龙提梁，肩部一端有兽首流，流与腹不相通。与流对称一端贴一脊棱作兽尾。圆盖，中央饰半圆扁纽，上有一孔。盖面和器身满印"S"形云气纹饰（有说是变体鸟纹），以多道弦纹将云气纹分隔。浅粉红色胎，胎质细腻。施石灰釉，釉呈青黄色。

战国时期提梁盉之足较春秋时期为短。

1987 年浙江绍兴皋埠镇上蒋村出土有相似器物。

Proto-celadon. The vessel has a straight mouth, a bulbous belly and a rounded base supported by three animal legs. From the shoulders rises an overhead-handle in the shape of a *kui* dragon. An animal-head spout is set on the shoulders and an animal's tail is affixed to the opposite side. A semi-circular slab-knob perforated with a hole is set in the center of the circular lid. The lid and the body are impressed with S-shaped cloud motif (or stylized bird motif) divided by several horizontal grooves. The vessel is covered with a greenish-yellow lime glaze. The pale pink

paste is refined.

The legs of the *he* tripods from the Warring States period are shorter than those of the Spring and Autumn period.

A similar vessel was unearthed in 1987

from Shangjiang village at Gaobuzhen, Shaoxing, Zhejiang province.

222

青釉云雷纹提梁盉

战国

公元前 475—前 221 年

高：20.9 厘米

Celadon *he* tripod with cloud-and-thunder motif

Warring States period

475 – 221 B.C.E.

Height: 20.9 cm

原始青瓷。直口、短颈、丰肩、扁圆腹、圜底、三兽蹄足、足较高长。兽首流与腹并不相通。虎形尾、半圆形提梁、梁上贴齿状棱脊、锥状堆纹和挂勾纹。盖作圆形子口、上饰凸弦纹两道、中央立一鸟形纽。肩和腹部满印云雷纹、以弦纹一道相界。浅灰胎、胎质略微泛黄。全器满施石灰釉、釉呈青褐色、有缩釉及剥落现象。该器造型美观、刻划细腻、与战国青铜盉造型一致。

Proto-celadon. The vessel has a straight mouth, a short neck, bold shoulders, a squat bulbous belly and a rounded base supported by three tall animal legs. A false sprout with dragon head design is attached to the upper belly. A tiger-shaped lug is affixed to the opposite side. The outer edge of the semi-circular overhead handle is decorated with two flanges with serrated edges, a conical motif and a hook-like motif. The lid is held in place by the rabbeted rim of the mouth. It has a bird-shaped knob encircled by two concentric ribs. The entire body is impressed with cloud-and-thunder motif divided by two horizontal grooves, one around the shoulders and the other around the upper belly. The grayish paste has a yellowish tint. The vessel is coated with a greenish-brown lime glaze throughout. There appears to be retraction and flaking of glaze. This vessel is noted for its beautiful shape, exquisite workmanship and finely rendered decorations. The shape is consistent with the bronze tripods from the same period.

223

青釉镂孔熏炉

战国

公元前 475—前 221 年

高：51.3 厘米

口径：12 厘米

Celadon censer with openwork

Warring States period

475 – 221 B.C.E.

Height: 51.3 cm

Mouth diameter: 12 cm

原始青瓷。口微外侈，广肩，鼓腹，平底，下附三乳丁足，肩中竖立一管状囱。囱口缘起凸环带一道，上饰云雷纹，囱由上而下至颈端间饰竖棱纹和素纹带，棱纹高于器表，具浅浮雕感。肩、腹镂雕三角形气孔三周，镂孔上、下较细小，中间较大，以四周云雷纹带相隔。腹两侧安环形系各一。胎质坚，细腻。施石灰釉，釉呈青黄色，釉色润亮，分布不均，有麻癞现象。釉面有细碎开片纹。底无釉，底和乳丁足胎呈粉红色。囱内缘露胎，满布细密轮旋痕。本品造型优美，雄伟霸气，是一件十分珍贵的艺术品。

烧制此类大型器物，尤其还带有三角形镂雕，需要对炉体结构和高温负重有正确计算，要烧成不变形，难度极高。

熏炉的出现可追溯到春秋战国时期，当时已有烧炭取暖的容器，材质以青铜、陶、瓷为主。将一些带有特殊气味或芳香味的植物撒在炭火上，利用焚烧时产生的烟气来驱逐蚊蝇、僻潮湿、净化室内空气和熏香衣物。

浙江省博物馆收藏有相似器物。

Proto-celadon. The censer has a cylindrical chimney with a slightly flared top, broad shoulders, a globular belly and a flat base attached with three tiny udder feet. The outer mouth rim of the chimney is encircled by a band of raised cloud-and-thunder motif, underneath which are two bands of vertical striations in relief. The shoulders and the belly are pierced with three rows of triangular openings, parted by narrow bands of cloud-and-thunder pattern. A pair of loop-lugs is set above the belly. The vessel is covered with a lustrous greenish-yellow crackled lime glaze. Since the glaze is unevenly distributed, spotting and streaking are visible. The paste is hard and refined. The unglazed base and the udder legs have burnt to a light pink. The inner rim of the chimney is covered with fine wheel marks. The vessel imparts a sense of monumentality. It is a rarity among rarities.

The firing of such a huge vessel with triangular openwork involves precise calculation of the weight-bearing structure of the vessel and the firing temperature of the kiln.

The origin of censers can be traced back to the Spring and Autumn and Warring States periods when braziers with burning charcoals were already in use. The smoke generated from sprinkling aromatic herbs on the charcoals is used to repel pests, purify indoor air, remove dampness and fumigate clothing. These vessels were mainly bronze, pottery or porcelain wares.

A similar example is in the collection of the Zhejiang Provincial Museum.

224

青釉饕餮纹三耳盖尊

战国

公元前 475—前 221 年

高：32.5 厘米

底径：15 厘米

Celadon lidded *zun* vessel with animal masks

Warring States period

475 – 221 B.C.E.

Height: 32.5 cm

Base diameter: 15 cm

附图 8　湖北擂鼓墩一号墓出土曾侯乙大尊缶（战国）

Fig. 8　*Zun* vessel unearthed from a tomb belonging to the Marquis Yi at Leigudun in Hubei (Warring States period)

原始青瓷。子母口，斜肩，腹体中部鼓出，下腹和底部比较宽肥，平底。颈肩间刻弦线两道，腹中部饰云雷纹带一周，纹带稍高出器表，具浮雕感。两侧贴饕餮衔环纹饰，环可自由转动。盖中部和近边缘处有双弦纹两组，盖上置竖耳三个。粉红胎，胎质细滑、坚硬。腹上部和盖施石灰釉，釉不均匀，呈青黄色，有麻癞现象。下腹体光素无釉，有明显轮旋痕。该器造型华美，饕餮纹饰刻划精细。

陶瓷在高温烧造过程中，器物的装饰垂环易与器表粘连成为死环。这种活环烧造工艺自春秋、战国时期后便消失，直到明代重现，失传近两千年，可以想见当时陶瓷烧造技术之高超。

中国历史博物馆陈列的湖北随州擂鼓墩一号墓出土巨型青铜尊，造型和装饰与此件基本相同，只是青铜器的盖和尊体用链相连，腹部多两个圆环耳，底足略外撇（附图 8）。该墓是战国曾国墓，青铜尊是曾侯乙王室所用的大型储酒器。

Proto-celadon. The vessel has a rabbeted rim, steep shoulders, a swelling belly and a flat base. A slightly raised frieze with cloud-and-thunder motif in low relief encircles the body. A *taotie* animal mask fitted with a movable ring is affixed to the two sides of the frieze. Halfway between the frieze and the mouth are two parellel indented lines. The lid is decorated with two groups of double indented lines, one closer to the edge and the other near the center. Three equally spaced loop lugs are set around the lid. The pink paste is hard and refined. The upper body and the lid are covered with greenish-yellow lime glaze but the glaze is unevenly distributed; spotting and streaking are visible on the surface. There are wheel marks on the unglazed lower body.

During the course of high-temperature firing, the once movable rings would sometimes get stuck onto the surface. The technique of producing movable rings vanished for 2000 years after the Spring and Autumn period and the Warring States period and was not seen again until the Ming dynasty. The exceptional level of ceramic firing technique of this period is fully manifested in this vessel.

The National Museum of China has in its collection a huge bronze vessel unearthed from Leigudun Tomb No.1 in Hubei province. Its shape and decoration are identical to this one except that the lid is connected to the body by a chain, the belly has two additional loop handles and the foot is slightly splayed (Fig. 8). The tomb belonged to the Marquis Yi of the Zeng State of the Warring States period. The bronze vessel was a wine container used in the household of the Marquis.

225

青釉弦纹兽耳大尊

战国

公元前 475—前 221 年

高：30.6 厘米

口径：25.2 厘米

底径：19.5 厘米

Large celadon *zun* vessel with animal-shaped handles

Warring States period

475 – 221 B.C.E.

Height: 30.6 cm

Mouth diameter: 25.2 cm

Base diameter: 19.5 cm

原始青瓷。侈口，直颈，鼓腹，平底。肩、腹刻弦纹四道，弦纹间满印云雷纹。肩上对称饰回首立兽形耳及扉棱各一对，兽耳带活垂环。橙黄胎，细滑，胎薄，较坚硬。内外施石灰釉，釉呈褐色。本器体型圆浑丰满，古朴中显灵秀，粗犷中见雅致，造型极优美，艺术价值极高。

此器的造型以及回首张望的立兽形耳、扉棱、云雷纹等特征在战国时期灰陶、青铜器上出现较多。

尊是盛酒器，其造型从实用角度考虑而设计，侈口便于注入，也便于倾出，鼓腹则可增大容量。

Proto-celadon. This vessel has a flared mouth, a straight neck, a bulbous belly and a flat base. Four grooves encompass the shoulders and the belly. The spaces in between are impressed with cloud-and-thunder motif. A pair of standing animals with heads turned and a pair of vertical flanges are affixed to the shoulders. Each animal-shaped handle is fitted with a movable ring. The buff paste is smooth, thin and rather hard. Both the interior and exterior are covered with a brownish lime glaze. The vessel looks simple yet elegant, bold yet refined. The artistic value of this vessel is immeasurable.

The shape of the jar, the handles, the vertical flanges and the cloud-and-thunder motifs are characteristic features of gray pottery and bronzes from the Warring States period.

As a wine container, the vessel was mainly designed from a functional perspective. The flared mouth facilitates the pouring of wine into or out of containers while the deep belly allows for greater storage capacity.

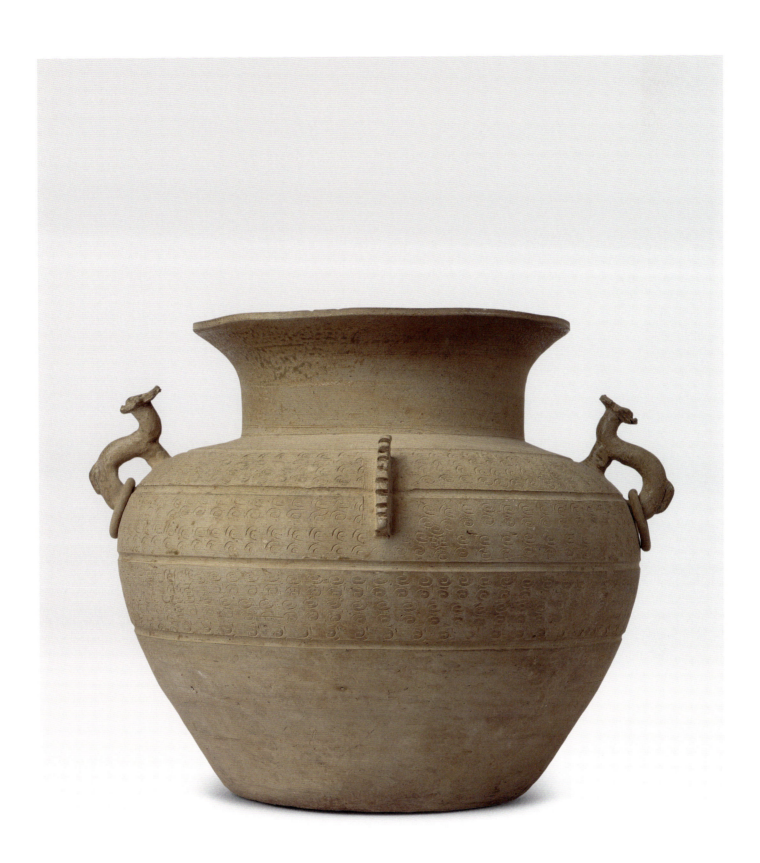

226

青釉云雷纹尊

战国

公元前 475—前 221 年

高：27 厘米

口径：23.8 厘米

底径：17.5 厘米

Celadon *zun* vessel with cloud-and-thunder motif

Warring States period

475 – 221 B.C.E.

Height: 27 cm

Mouth diameter: 23.8 cm

Base diameter: 17.5 cm

原始青瓷。喇叭形侈口，颈长而粗，扁腹圆鼓，高圈足，足缘平折外撇。腹体拍印云雷纹，腹上、下约两厘米处划弦纹各一道，上弦纹内刻山形纹，下弦纹内拍印云雷纹，上下相对。胎灰黄，质坚。全器内外施石灰釉，釉呈青黄色，施釉不均，有缩釉现象。造型雄伟霸气、庄重古朴兼而有之，纹饰集中在器体中部，上、下光素，对比鲜明。器形与同时代的青铜礼器一致（附图 9）。

Proto-celadon. The vessel has a trumpet mouth, a long thick neck and an oblate belly resting on a tall ring foot with splayed and angular rim. The belly is impressed with cloud-and-thunder motif. There is a band of zigzag lines incised above the belly and a band of cloud-and-thunder pattern underneath it. The grayish yellow paste is hard and dense. Both the interior and exterior are covered with a lime glaze of greenish yellow. The glaze is unevenly distributed and retraction is noted in some areas. The three bands of decorative motifs stand out nicely against the plain surface of the vessel. The shape of this vessel is similar to the bronze ritual wares of the same period (Fig. 9).

附图 9　丹徒出土云雷纹独耳尊（西周）

Fig. 9 *Zun* vessel with single ring handle and cloud-and-thunder motif unearthed at Dantu (Western Zhou dynasty)

227

青釉兽耳钫

战国

公元前 475—前 221 年

高：40.8 厘米

底径：17.5 厘米

Celadon *fang* jar with animal-shaped handles

Warring States period

475 – 221 B.C.E.

Height: 40.8 cm

Base diameter: 17.5 cm

原始青瓷。口、颈、腹皆呈方形，鼓腹，平底。盖盝顶，四角置鸟形组各一。盖上满饰云雷纹。腹部四面刻"日"字形凹框，纹间满拍印云雷纹，贴带活动环耳的双角立兽各一。颈、肩及下腹部无纹饰。橙黄胎，胎细滑，质较硬。全器施石灰釉，釉色青中泛褐。此器纹饰丰富，体态雄浑霸气，钫身四周棱边锋利，线条流畅，刚劲有力，是珍贵的艺术品。

战国时期青铜器流行此种造型。

Proto-celadon. The jar has a square mouth, a square neck and a faceted body that tapers towards a flat base. The lid has four trapezoidal facets and a truncated top surmounted by four bird-shaped knobs, each occupying a corner of the top square. The lid is densely decorated with cloud-and-thunder motif. Each of the four faces of the belly features a grooved rectangular frame with a horizontal incision across the middle resembling the Chinese character "日". The spaces within are covered with impressed cloud-and-thunder motif. On each of its sides stands a horned animal figure fitted with a movable ring. The buff paste is refined and compact. The entire surface is covered with a brownish-green lime glaze. The turns between the four facets of the body are sharply angled. This jar is an exceedingly fine piece of sculptural art.

This shape is typical among Warring States bronzes.

青釉铺首三足盘

战国

公元前 475—前 221 年

高：10 厘米

口径：38 厘米

Celadon three-legged basin with animal masks

Warring States period

475 – 221 B.C.E.

Height: 10 cm

Mouth diameter: 38 cm

原始青瓷。宽平缘内折，边缘下凹，可能用于承托盘盖。直腹壁，口、底大小相若，下承以三足。外壁贴饕餮衔环纹饰四个，眼、耳、口、鼻和角等清晰，鼻环可转动。饕餮间各刻一阴竖纹，把外壁分为八等份。盘口和外壁满拍印云雷纹，纹饰细腻。施石灰釉，釉呈青褐色。底及内壁无釉，露浅黄色胎，胎质细滑。盘心中央有十字排列小圆孔五个，直穿透到底。盘可能为炭盘或用于承载炭盘，圆孔用于透气。造型与商周青铜器一致。

Proto-celadon. The basin has a flat broad rim that hangs over the interior of the vessel. The rabbeted inner edge is probably used for holding the lid in place. The straight sides descend to an equally wide base supported by three animal legs. Three *taotie* masks with distinct eyes, nose, mouth and horns are affixed to the sides. The rings hanging from the noses are movable. Two vertical lines are incised halfway between each pair of animal masks, dividing the exterior wall of the basin into eight equal sections. Both the rim and the outer side are impressed with delicate cloud-and-thunder motif. The entire vessel except the interior wall and the base are covered with a greenish-brown lime glaze. The pale yellow paste is refined. The five small holes arranged in cruciform in the center of the vessel suggest that this basin may have been a brazier or a charcoal holder; the holes are probably vents. The shape is very similar to the bronzes from the Shang and Zhou periods.

229

青釉盘口鼎

战国

公元前 475—前 221 年

高：18.5 厘米

口径：21.6 厘米

Celadon *ding* tripod with plate-shaped mouth

Warring States period

475 – 221 B.C.E.

Height: 18.5 cm

Mouth diameter: 21.6 cm

原始青瓷。大盘口、釜形器身、底内凹、下承三扁条形实足，足高微外撇，造型简单、圆浑、别致。胎薄而细滑，呈淡灰色。内外施石灰釉，釉呈青褐色。釉层薄，施釉不均，有麻癫现象。

此器形的青铜器名为"越式鼎"，常见于浙、闽、粤一带。

Proto-celadon. The cauldron-like body is furnished with a large plate mouth and a recessed base supported by three splayed solid legs with a flat inner face. The light gray paste is smooth and refined. Both the interior and exterior are coated with a thin layer of greenish-brown lime glaze. The uneven distribution of glaze has resulted in spotting and streaking. The shape is simple, unique and imparts a sense of fullness.

Bronze vessels with this shape are called "Yue-style *ding* tripod" in Chinese. They are found in the provinces of Zhejiang, Fujian and Guangdong.

230

青釉大兽首三足瓿

战国

公元前 475—前 221 年

高：34.4 厘米

阔：39 厘米

底径：23.7 厘米

Celadon three-legged jar with large animal-shaped handles

Warring States period

475 – 221 B.C.E.

Height: 34.4 cm

Width: 39 cm

Base diameter: 23.7 cm

原始青瓷。平唇，短直颈，广肩，鼓腹，平底。下腹部近底处置兽状三足。肩部两侧贴兽首各一，兽首刻划精细、夸张，巨角、长面，兽角和头部远高出口缘。兽口衔活动圆环，环大、圆而规整，上起棱线数条。胎呈橙黄色，胎质细腻。全器外壁满施石灰釉，釉色青中泛绿；施釉不均，釉面有麻癞现象。本品体形硕大、线条圆浑优美，做工极为精细。

Proto-celadon. The jar has a leveled rim, a short straight neck, bold shoulders, a globular belly and a flat base. Three animal feet are affixed to the lower belly near the base. Two large animal heads with movable rings hanging from their noses are affixed to the two sides of the vessel. The entire exterior is coated with a bluish lime glaze with a greenish tint. Since the glaze is unevenly distributed, spotting and streaking are visible on the surface. The buff paste is refined. The jar is uniquely shaped with a pair of exaggerated animal-shaped handles that extends pass the level of the mouth rim. The large movable rings are perfectly circular.

231

青釉弦纹带盖三足瓿

战国

公元前 475—前 221 年

高：37.2 厘米

阔：38.8 厘米

底径：21 厘米

Celadon three-legged lidded jar with rib motif

Warring States period

475 – 221 B.C.E.

Height: 37.2 cm

Width: 38.8 cm

Base diameter: 21 cm

原始青瓷。子母口、短直颈、斜肩、圆深腹、平底、下承三足，足下端凸出呈圆饼状。肩部两侧贴兽耳，耳挂活环。口上附鼻纽梯级形圆盖，盖上饰凸弦线三周。器身饰凸弦纹五道，纹间满拍印云雷纹。胎褐黄、较坚硬。全器施石灰釉，釉色青中带绿、釉薄、较均匀。体形硕大饱满、古朴浑厚，身、盖俱全，保存完整，弥足珍贵。

Proto-celadon. The jar has a rabbeted mouth, a short straight neck, slanting shoulders, a deep bulbous belly and a flat base supported by three legs with disc-like ends. A pair of animal-shaped ears fitted with movable rings is attached to the shoulders. The lid is surmounted by an arch knob encompassed by three concentric stepped ribs. Five ribs encircle the body. The spaces in between are filled with impressed cloud-and-thunder pattern. The brownish-yellow paste has a relatively high degree of hardness. The celadon-colored lime glaze is thin and relatively even. This jar is noted for its robust shape and intactness.

232

青釉棱纹曲柄盖壶

战国

公元前 475—前 221 年

高：20.7 厘米

底径：10.5 厘米

Celadon lidded jar with S-shaped handle and fluted body

Warring States period

475 – 221 B.C.E.

Height: 20.7 cm

Base diameter: 10.5 cm

原始青瓷。小直颈、溜肩、筒形腹、平底。带拱形盖，上贴蒂状纽。口径和底径大小相近。壶体四周满刻竖棱纹，棱不及底，棱骨高而锐利。肩至下腹部间置一扁状曲把，上饰竖弦纹，与壶身竖棱相配合。相对一侧肩部贴锥突一个。浅灰胎，胎薄，较坚硬。施石灰釉到棱纹下端，釉色褐黄，有明显麻癞现象。颈部四周承托盖子的部分无釉，上有多个垫饼残留痕，与盖缘的垫饼痕相吻合，推断盖是放在壶体上一起烧造的，反映出原始青瓷烧造工艺的提高。本品造型圆浑饱满、华丽，构思奇特，艺术效果极佳。

Proto-celadon. The jar has a narrow straight neck, sloping shoulders, a barrel-shaped body and a flat base. The slightly domed lid has a knob in the shape of a stalk. The width of the mouth and the base are similar. The upper and middle parts of the belly are decorated with sharply edged fluted design. An S-shaped strap handle arches between the shoulder and the bottom edge of the flutings. The handle surface is engraved with vertical grooves to mirror the fluted design on the body. A tiny stud is affixed to the shoulders on the opposite side. The grayish paste is thin and relatively hard. The entire vessel is coated with a brownish-yellow lime glaze with visible spotting and streaking. The neck is bare of glaze and the rim shows fireclay marks. Similar residue is found adhering to the rim of the lid, suggesting that the lid and the jar were fired together. This jar is noted for its robust and elegant shape.

233

青釉直纹单把壶

战国

公元前 475—前 221 年

高：15 厘米

底径：11.8 厘米

Celadon jar with single handle and combed motif

Warring States period

475 – 221 B.C.E.

Height: 15 cm

Base diameter: 11.8 cm

原始青瓷。小口、直颈、平肩、圆筒形器身，腹下部较肩稍阔。平底，下承三乳状足。方棱曲把，顶饰卷云纹，相对一侧肩下贴简化饕餮衔环纹饰一个。腹中部刻垂直梳齿纹带一周。胎浅黄、细腻、质颇坚硬。通体施石灰釉，呈青褐色，釉薄而不均匀。造型饱满、线条优雅。

上海博物馆收藏有一件同类器，只是器身饰平行弦纹。

浙江余杭潘板桥大溪出土有相似器物。

Proto-celadon. The jug has a small mouth, a straight neck, leveled shoulders, cylindrical sides and a flat base supported by three udder feet. The S-shaped handle has a cloud spiral on its upper end. A *taotie* mask with a ring is attached on the other side of the vessel. A band of vertical striations decorates the belly. The pale yellow refined paste has a rather high degree of hardness. The lime glaze covering the vessel is thin and uneven and brownish-green in color.

A vessel of similar shape but with grooved design around the entire body is in the collection of the Shanghai Museum.

A similar vessel has also been unearthed from Daxi in Panbanqiao, Yuhang, Zhejiang province.

234

青釉梳齿纹匜

战国

公元前 475—前 221 年

高：8.4 厘米

底径：7.8 厘米

Celadon *yi* basin with vertical combed motif

Warring States period

475 – 221 B.C.E.

Height: 8.4 cm

Base diameter: 7.8 cm

原始青瓷。敛口，腹圆鼓，下腹渐收，底小微圜。内壁有明显轮旋纹痕。口缘一端饰椭圆形斜朝上扁流。口缘下划阴弦纹一周，下刻竖直梳齿纹到腹下部。与流相对一侧弦纹上贴卷云纹饰一个。胎微黄、质坚硬。全器内外施石灰釉，釉色青中泛褐。造型工整、优美。

本品与战国时期青铜匜造型一致。

浙江绍兴漓渚镇大兴村出土有相似器物。

Proto-celadon. This vessel has a slightly incurved mouth and convex sides tapering to a small and slightly rounded base. Distinct wheel marks are visible on the inside of the basin. One side of the mouth is shaped into an up-tilted semicircular beak. An indented line runs under the rim on the exterior, marking the top edge of a broad band of vertical combed motif. A small spiral appliqué is attached onto the indented line on the other side of the beak. The yellowish paste has a rather high degree of hardness. Both the interior and exterior are coated with a green lime glaze with a brownish tint. The vessel is neatly and elegantly shaped.

The shape is consistent with the bronze water basins from the same period.

A similar artifact has been unearthed from Daxing village at Lizhuzhen, Shaoxing, Zhejiang province.

235

青釉槽形流匜

战国

公元前 475—前 221 年

高：13 厘米

底径：11 厘米

Celadon *yi* basin with open spout

Warring States period

475 – 221 B.C.E.

Height: 13 cm

Base diameter: 11 cm

原始青瓷。撇口，呈不规则圆形，尾部较阔大，微圜底。口缘一侧置半圆形槽形流，相对一侧口缘下有简化饕餮衔环纹一个，环可自由转动。浅黄胎、坚硬。全器内外施石灰釉、釉带青褐色、施釉不均，有麻癞现象。本品造型饱满、线条流畅。

陶匜由新石器时代至汉代均有制作，本品与战国时期青铜匜造型一致（附图 10）。

江苏无锡鸿山邱承墩出土有相似器物。

Proto-celadon. The vessel has a broad mouth and a rounded base. The mouth has an undulating rim and extends to form a trough-like open spout. The exterior wall on the other end features a simplified *taotie* mask with a movable ring. The light yellow paste is hard and dense. The entire interior and exterior are covered with a greenish-brown lime glaze. The glaze has been unevenly applied with spotting and streaking. The vessel is noted for its rounded form and sleek lines.

Pottery basins were produced throughout the Neolithic period to the Han dynasty. The present example is similar in shape to the bronze basins of the same period (Fig. 10).

A similar vessel has been unearthed from Qiuchengdun, Hongshan, Zhejiang province.

附图 10　山西太原金胜村出土线刻狩猎纹匜（春秋晚期）

Fig. 10　*Yi* basin with incised hunting motif unearthed at Jinshengcun in Taiyuan, Shanxi (Late Spring and Autumn period)

青釉贯耳连体罐

战国

公元前 475—前 221 年

高：6.7 厘米

长（连耳）：22.5 厘米

Celadon twin jars with tubular lugs

Warring States period

475 – 221 B.C.E.

Height: 6.7 cm

Length (including lugs) : 22.5 cm

原始青瓷。直口，短颈，丰肩，鼓腹，平底，底微内凹。器呈两罐并列状，腹部相连但并不相通。罐外侧各置一微向内斜贯耳。器腹饰竖向粗棱纹。灰白胎，细密，质坚。器身施石灰釉到棱纹下端，釉色青中带褐，釉薄，有麻癞现象。底部露胎，露胎处留有制作时用绳子切割胎泥造成的偏心旋纹痕。此器造型别致，较为罕见。

Proto-celadon. The vessel has a dense and hard paste of grayish-white color. Each jar has a straight mouth, a short neck, bold shoulders, a bulbous belly and a flat base with a slightly recessed center. The cord mark on the unglazed base is the result of removing the form from the wheel by pulling a piece of cord under it. The two jars are conjoined at the belly on the outside but they are not internally connected. Each jar is furnished with an inward-inclining tubular lug. The belly is decorated with fluted design. The entire vessel surface down to the lower edge of the fluted belt is covered with a lime

glaze of green color with a brownish tint. Spotting and streaking are found in the glaze. The shape of this vessel is unique and quite rare.

237

青釉楞纹双系罐

战国

公元前 475—前 221 年

高：22 厘米

底径：18 厘米

Celadon jar with loop lugs

Warring States period

475 – 221 B.C.E.

Height: 22 cm

Base diameter: 18 cm

原始青瓷。直口，丰肩，底平。肩和上腹饰竖瓦楞纹，以一道阔带纹分隔。肩部瓦楞纹较细，腹部较粗疏。肩上左右对称贴环状系各一，系四周围以长方形框，框内满拍印"S"状云雷纹。胎色灰白，较坚硬。施石灰釉到底，釉色泛黄褐。

Proto-celadon. The jar has a straight mouth, bold shoulders and an unglazed flat bottom revealing a rather hard paste of grayish-white color. The shoulders and upper belly are decorated with corrugated motifs parted by a broad band. The motifs around the shoulders are finer and denser. The shoulders are flanked by a pair of appliqué rings set within a rectangular frame with impressed S-shaped cloud-and-thunder motif. The entire surface is covered with a green lime glaze with a brownish tint.

238

青釉乳突席纹罐

战国

公元前 475—前 221 年

高：26 厘米

口径：18.8 厘米

Celadon jar with boss design and mat motif

Warring States period

475 – 221 B.C.E.

Height: 26 cm

Mouth diameter: 18.8 cm

原始青瓷。圆唇，矮颈，斜肩，造型丰满，肩和上腹部圆鼓，中腹以下逐渐缓收成平底。颈部置弦纹两道，肩周等距贴圆突三颗，肩下拍印连续组合席纹近底。浅红胎，质坚硬，较厚重，扣之发出清脆声。外施石灰釉，不及底，釉薄，呈黄绿色，收缩不均匀，成颗粒状。应是战国晚期作品。

Proto-celadon. The jar has a mouth with rounded lip, a short neck, sloping shoulders and a bulbous belly that tapers to a flat base. Two rounds of cord motif encircle the neck. Three studs are equally spaced apart on the shoulders. The body below the shoulders down to almost the foot is impressed with mat motif. The light red paste is hard and relatively heavy. The body gives a pleasant sound when knocked with the knuckles. The exterior surface is coated with a thin layer of yellowish-green lime glaze that stops short of the base. Uneven contraction of the glaze has resulted in a granular surface. This jar should be dated to the late Warring States period.

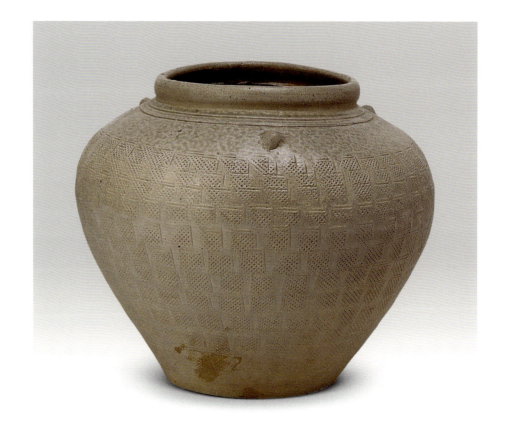

239

青釉錞于

战国

公元前 475—前 221 年

高：38 厘米

底径：19 厘米

Celadon *chunyu* bell

Warring States period

475 – 221 B.C.E.

Height: 38 cm

Base diameter: 19 cm

原始青瓷。短直颈，肩部丰满，肩和上腹微鼓，深腹，下腹成直圆筒形，近底处稍外撇。盖与颈内缘黏合，上置弦纹两道。盖中央贴一弓形纽，突出口缘，拙实牢固。肩和上腹部满刻卷云纹，下饰弦纹两道。与弓形纽同向的两侧肩上贴竖凸棱线直到底足。腹下另两侧刻横长方形框各一，内刻卷云纹和镂空大米粒形小孔五个。浅黄胎，细腻、颇坚硬。盖和器身外壁施石灰釉，釉呈黄褐色，施釉不均，有麻癞现象。此器中空无底，与战国青铜錞于造型相似。

2003 年浙江长兴县鼻子山战国墓出土有相似器物，现藏于长兴县博物馆。

江苏无锡市邱承墩墓出土有相似器物。

Proto-celadon. The object is shaped with a short straight neck, rounded shoulders, a swelling upper belly, deep cylindrical sides and a slightly flared foot. The lid adhering to the inner edge of the mouth is decorated with two concentric grooves. A bow-shaped knob flanked by two tiny studs is attached to the lid from which a rope can be suspended. The shoulders and upper belly are densely incised with curly cloud motif and bounded by two rounds of grooves at the bottom. A rib runs down from the neck to the foot on the two sides of the body. A squarish frame is incised halfway between the ribs near the bottom. Within the frames are five tiny rice-shaped openings against a ground of incised curly motif. The refined paste of light yellow color is rather hard. The lid and the entire outer surface are covered with a lime glaze of yellowish-brown color with spotting and streaking due to the uneven distribution of glaze. The body is hollow and has no base. This shape is modeled after the bronze bells of the same period.

A similar artifact was unearthed in 2003 from a Warring States tomb at Wufeng village in Zhichengzhen, Wuxi, Jiangsu province.

Others have been unearthed from the tomb of Qiu Chengdun in Wuxi, Jiangsu province.

240

青釉乳丁纹甬

战国

公元前 475—前 221 年

高：24.6 厘米

底长：17.7 厘米

Celadon *yongzhong* bell with boss design

Warring States period

475 – 221 B.C.E.

Height: 24.6 cm

Base length: 17.7 cm

原始青瓷。甬呈双面拱形，上窄下阔，内空。腰鼓形干，上有一扁纽，用于悬挂。钲部无铭文。前、后、左、右篆间各有九枚四周饰云纹和折角纹的圆柱状乳突，共计三十六枚。舞、篆、隧部均饰云纹和折角纹。胎灰白，坚硬。外施石灰釉，釉青褐色。造型仿西周铜编钟。

甬为敲击乐器，以槌叩之而鸣。

Proto-celadon with a hard grayish-white paste. The surface of the bell is covered with a greenish-brown lime glaze. The bell has a hollow body with an almond-shaped cross-section, a narrower top and a wider bottom. There is a slab handle on top of the dumb-bell shaped stem. Each side is decorated with two segmented panels framed by borders with cloud and arrowhead motifs. Each panel is furnished with nine pillar-like bosses, totaling a number of thirty-six bosses. The top, middle and lower sections of the bell are decorated with cloud and arrowhead motifs. This shape is modeled after the bronze chime bells of the Western Zhou dynasty.

This bell was a percussion instrument played with a hammer.

青釉镇

战国

公元前 475—前 221 年

高：9.1 厘米

底径：11.2 厘米

Celadon bell-shaped weight

Warring States period

475 – 221 B.C.E.

Height: 9.1 cm

Base diameter: 11.2 cm

原始青瓷。外形呈馒头状、平底中空。顶、腹划弦纹各一道，顶部弦纹内和腹部弦纹下方饰云雷纹。器体中部有上、下两周左右倒置的"S"形纹饰，每周五个，纹饰上下相间，呈"品"字形。顶端置带环半圆纽一个，环黏在顶部，不能转动。胎浅黄，质坚。器体外壁施石灰釉，釉呈青褐色，上有开片纹和麻癞现象。本品造型饱满，线条优美。

浙江长兴鼻子山和亭子桥窑址出土有相似器物。

Proto-celadon. The pottery weight is in the shape of a steamed bun with a hollow body and a flat base. An incised line encircles the top and the lower belly. The area above and below the incised lines is decorated with cloud-and-thunder motif. The mid-section of the body is decorated with two rows of five vertically oriented S-spirals. The top has an arched knob fitted with a fixed ring that is stuck onto the surface. The pale yellow paste is hard. The surface of the weight is coated with a crackled greenish-brown lime glaze with spotting and streaking.

Similar vessels have been unearthed from

Bizishan in Changxing and the kiln site at Tingziqiao, both in Zhejiang province.

242

青釉棱纹铺首罐

战国—西汉

公元前 475—公元 8 年

高：26.8 厘米

Celadon jar with fluted design and animal masks

Warring States period–Western
Han dynasty
475 B.C.E. – 8 C.E.
Height: 26.8 cm

原始青瓷。短直颈，广肩，鼓腹，平底。肩上两侧刻竖棱纹带两段，以"S"形云雷纹相连，云雷纹带上贴扁状微上翘铺首。铺首刻划精细。腹四周以竖棱纹带作饰，器身其余部分留空。粉红胎，胎体颇厚重。施石灰釉，釉浅褐色，微泛青，釉收缩不均，有麻癫现象，施釉只到腹棱下。器体圆浑饱满。应为战国晚期至西汉初期的作品。

Proto-celadon. The jar has a short straight neck, broad shoulders and a bulbous belly upon a flat base. The opposing sides of the shoulders are each incised with a belt of vertical ribs, connected by S-shaped cloud-and-thunder design topped with slightly up-tilted and flattened appliqué animal mask showing distinct and exquisite features. The belly of the jar is surrounded by a belt of fluted design while the rest of the surface is left plain. The pink paste is rather thick and weighty. The light brownish lime glaze with a greenish tint shows spotting and streaking effect resulted from uneven shrinkage. The glaze stops short of the base. The jar should be dated to the late Warring States period to the early Western Han dynasty.

243

灰釉云气纹钟

西汉

公元前 206—公元 8 年

高：44.5 厘米

Gray-glazed jar with cloud motif

Western Han dynasty

206 B.C.E. – 8 C.E.

Height: 44.5 cm

原始青瓷。夹砂硬陶胎。圆口外侈，长颈，斜肩，深腹，腹向下敛，平底。肩两侧置拱形叶纹耳，耳上端贴如意纹饰。颈上、下饰水波纹带各一周。肩腹置凸弦纹三道，弦纹间刻鸟纹和云气纹。纹饰生动活泼，仿战国时期漆器的笔法。器身上部施灰釉，厚薄不均，呈褐红和青褐色。腹中、下部无釉，呈火石红色，刻有动物或形似文字等图案。造型稳重优美，风格浑厚古朴。

台北"中央研究院"所藏一件殷墟小屯出土的灰陶罐上有相似的图案。

浙江省博物馆收藏有相似器物。

Proto-celadon and sand-tempered high-fired pottery. The jar has a flared mouth, long neck, and a flat base. A pair of lugs in the shape of an arched leaf surmounted by a *ruyi*-shaped appliqué is attached on the shoulders. The neck is engraved with two bands of wave motif. Three ribs encircle the upper body and the spaces in between are filled with bird and cloud motif. The decorative motifs are reminiscent of those found on lacquerware from the Warring States period. The upper body is covered with gray glaze but the glaze is unevenly distributed, appearing brownish-red and greenish-brown in color. The unglazed lower body revealed a burnt orange color. The surface is engraved with animal motif or designs resembling Chinese characters.

The motif is similar to that on a gray earthenware jar unearthed from Xiaotun in Yinxu and it is now in the collection of the Academia Sinica in Taipei.

A similar vessel is in the collection of the Zhejiang Provincial Museum.

青釉带流三足罐

西汉

公元前 206—公元 8 年

高：16.6 厘米

口径：10.2 厘米

长（连流）：32 厘米

Three-footed celadon spouted jar

Western Han dynasty

206 B.C.E. – 8 C.E.

Height: 16.6 cm

Mouth diameter: 10.2 cm

Length (including spout) : 32 cm

原始青瓷。短直颈，丰肩，扁圆腹，平底下承三矮足。肩部一侧置前阔后窄的槽形流，前端三分之二处开口，流上翘，略高于罐口。槽形流面刻连续菱形纹，上印圆圈纹。流相对一侧贴双股绳纹耳，上贴垂环和云气纹，仿商周时期青铜器的饕餮衔环纹饰。垂环与罐体黏结，不能转动。胎呈浅灰色，胎体较薄，质坚而细滑。器上半部施褐黄色釉，釉色光亮润泽，上刻划水波纹带三周，分别以圆圈纹和弦线纹相间。腹下部和底露胎部分呈褐红色。

本品造型优美，做工精细，设计合理，是十分精美的盥洗用具。

Proto-celadon. The jar has a small mouth, a short straight neck, broad shoulders and a squat bulbous belly supported by three short feet. A slightly splayed spout with two-thirds of its upper side open is set on the shoulder. The tip of the spout extends slightly beyond the level of the mouth rim. The upper part of the spout is engraved with continuous lozenges and stamped with circles. On the other side is a loop lug in the shape of two entwined

ropes decorated with cloud spirals. The appliqué ring and cloud motif above it is a faithful imitation of the ringed *taotie* mask on Shang and Zhou bronzes. The ring fitted to the handle has stuck to the body making it immovable. The interior of the jar is unglazed, exposing a thinly potted and refined paste of light gray color. The upper half of the jar is covered with a lustrous greenish-yellow glaze. A round of circle motif runs between two rounds of wave pattern just beneath the shoulders. The unglazed lower part and the base are burnt to a brownish-red color.

This jar was a utensil used to hold water for washing.

245

青釉弦纹双唇罐

西汉

公元前 206—公元 8 年

高：28.2 厘米

口径（外唇）：21.7 厘米

Celadon jar with double mouth rims and grooved motif

Western Han dynasty

206 B.C.E. – 8 C.E.

Height: 28.2 cm

Mouth diameter (outer rim): 21.7 cm

原始青瓷。双口缘、短颈、溜肩、鼓腹、平底。两侧对称置竖耳、上饰叶脉纹。器身满布弦纹。施青釉、釉已大部分脱落。胎橙黄色，坚硬。造型新颖、庄重、秀丽。双唇中置水，可防止虫蚁爬到罐内，是十分巧妙及实用的设计。

时至今日、中国四川地区居民仍使用此类双唇罐贮放酱菜、泡菜。

Proto-celadon. The jar has double mouth rims, a short neck, steep shoulders, a bulbous belly and a flat base. A pair of loop lugs with leaf vein motif is set vertically on the shoulders. The body is encompassed by closely spaced grooves throughout. The celadon glaze on the body has mostly come off. The pale yellow paste is compact. The double rim is an ingenious and practical device: the space between the two rims can be filled with water to prevent insects from crawling into the jar.

Even nowadays, jars of similar designs are still widely used for storing pickles and other preserved vegetables in households throughout the province of Sichuan.

青釉水波纹双耳盖瓿

西汉

公元前 206—公元 8 年

高：23.5 厘米

Celadon lidded jar with wave motif and double handles

Western Han dynasty

206 B.C.E – 8 C.E.

Height: 23.5 cm

原始青瓷。直口，广肩，鼓腹，平底，下承四扁足。盖纽作塔式，顶立小鸟，开有四个三角形气孔。肩左右侧贴铺首耳一对。盖面和肩部饰弦纹数道，弦纹间饰连续水波纹。灰白胎，质坚硬。上腹部施石灰釉，呈黄褐色。下腹部无釉，呈褐红色，是含铁量高的胎土烧造时析出的铁结晶。

水波纹是汉代流行的装饰纹样。

Proto-celadon. The jar has a straight mouth, broad shoulders, a bulbous belly and a flat base supported by four flattened feet. The pagoda-shaped knob is surmounted by a small bird. The top of the lid is pierced with four triangular ventilation holes. A pair of animal masks flanks the shoulders. The lid and the shoulders are decorated with bands of continuous wave motif divided by several rounds of cord motif. The grayish white paste has a high degree of hardness. The upper belly is covered with a yellowish-brown lime glaze. The unglazed lower belly revealed a brownish-red color. This is a result of the diffusion of crystallized iron

from a paste with high iron content during firing.

Wave motif was a popular decorative element of the Han dynasty.

青釉双耳瓿

西汉

公元前 206—公元 8 年

高：20.8 厘米

底径：16 厘米

Celadon lidded jar with handles

Western Han dynasty

206 B.C.E. – 8 C.E.

Height: 20.8 cm

Base diameter: 16 cm

原始青瓷。短直颈、斜肩、扁圆腹、平底下承三矮足，底微向内凹。肩上刻双弦线纹三道，两侧贴铺首状耳，耳面翘起呈扁平状。铺首的眼、耳、口、鼻、角刻划精细。口上附缓坡状圆顶小纽盖。灰胎，质坚。施青绿色釉，釉流淌，在器身四周中下方形成一条条下垂的泪釉痕。下半部及底部露胎处呈紫红色。本品造型丰满、线条柔和、纹饰清晰，是西汉时期的典型器物。

由于胎中杂质较多，烧结后胎中气体膨胀，故在器体内外形成许多大小不一的隆起。又由于釉料配制简单，窑炉结构尚不够合理，因此釉色不稳定、不均匀及有泪釉痕。这是西汉原始青瓷的一个特征。

Proto celadon. The jar has a short straight neck, slanting shoulders, a squat bulbous belly and a flat base supported by three short feet. Three engraved double lines encompass the shoulders. A pair of handles affixed to the shoulders is sumounted by upright animal masks wih finely carved eyes, ears, mouth and nose in low relief. The slighty domed lid has a small knob attached to its relatively flat top. The upper half of the vessel and the lid are covered with a greenish glaze that runs down in streaks. The effect is highly decorative. The grayish paste has a high degree of hardness. The unglazed lower belly and the slightly recessed base have burnt to a purplish red color.

Since the paste contains a relatively high degree of impurities, irregular expansion of air within the paste during firing has resulted in numerous bumps of various sizes on the surface. Due to the primitive formulation of glaze, inadequate kiln structure and firing technique, the glaze is unstable in color, uneven in distribution and rife with glaze streaks. These limitations are characteristic of Western Han proto-celadons.

248

灰褐釉铺首弦纹瓿

东汉

公元 25—220 年

越窑系

高：30.2 厘米

底径：14.3 厘米

Jar with animal masks with grayish brown glaze

Eastern Han dynasty

25 – 220 C.E.

Yue-type kilns

Height: 30.2 cm

Base diameter: 14.3 cm

原始青瓷。口缘向下倾斜成一凸起台阶，腹下部收敛，平底。上腹置弦纹三组，把上腹分为三部分。上部刻飞鸟纹饰，划线利落，纹饰清晰。其余两部分光素无纹。肩相对两侧贴铺首扁环耳各一。胎质颇坚。施石灰釉，釉呈青褐色。腹下部无釉，呈红褐色。本品造型圆浑，线条优雅，时代特点突出。

浙江上虞博物馆收藏有相似器物。

Proto-celadon. The mouth rim is surrounded by an outward-slanting step. The lower part of the bulbous belly tapers towards a flat base. Three groups of indented lines encircle the upper belly, dividing the upper body into three sections. The top section is engraved with flying birds with crisp outlines. The other two sections are devoid of decorative motifs. A pair of flattened lugs with appliqué animal mask flanks the shoulders. The paste is hard and dense. The upper part of the vessel is covered

with a greenish brown lime glaze. The unglazed belly shows a paste that has burnt to a reddish brown color.

A similar vessel is in the collection of the Shangyu Museum in Zhejiang.

249

青釉镂孔熏炉

东汉

公元 25—220 年

高：19.8 厘米

阔：26.5 厘米

Unglazed censer with openwork

Eastern Han dynasty

25 – 220 C.E.

Height: 19.8 cm

Width: 26.5 cm

原始青瓷。短颈，口缘微内斜。外形如两只互盖的大碗，碗边重叠成凸缘，分成上、下两部分。上部呈三层阶梯状，上层横向交替置如意纹和龟各两只、中层交替戳圆形和三角镂孔各四个，下层有圆形镂孔四个，与中层圆形镂孔上下相对。上、中层和突缘上饰水波纹带。腹下承三蹄形足。器中空，底有圆形开口，大小与口径相同。灰白胎，泛浅黄色，胎体坚实厚重。上部施釉，釉薄，呈褐黄色，惜大部分已脱落。器身下半部呈褐红色。本品器形别致、做工精细、纹饰仍带战国晚期风格。

杭州大观园汉墓出土有一件相似的熏炉，只是没有蹄形足。

Proto-celadon. The top of the censer is in the shape of an inverted bowl. A broad ledge divides the vessel into an upper and lower section. The upper section is divided into three tiers with a stepped profile. The top tier is decorated with *ruyi* and tortoise appliqués. The middle tier is pierced with alternating circular and triangular openings and the lower tier with only circular ones. The upper tier, middle tier and the ledge are incised with bands of wave motif. The vessel is supported on three hoof feet. The vessel has a circular cut-out at the base which is approximately the same size as the mouth opening. The grayish white paste with a light yellowish tint is dense, hard and heavy. The upper part has been thinly covered with a brownish-yellow glaze but the glaze has mostly come off. The lower half of the vessel is a brownish red color. The decorative motifs are reminiscent of those from the late Warring States period. The censer is a fine example of Han proto-celadon.

A similar censer without hoof feet was unearthed from a Han tomb in Daguanyuan in Hangzhou.

250

青釉五联罐

东汉

公元 25—220 年

高：25 厘米

Five-mouthed celadon jar

Eastern Han dynasty

25 – 220 C.E.

Height: 25 cm

原始青瓷。罐形体，上立五个盆口小瓶，中间的小瓶较大。圆鼓腹，高足，足外撇，平底微内凹。大、小罐体饰弦纹数道。胎质坚硬，呈褐红色。施石灰釉，釉色泛黄，釉收缩不均。从外形、釉色和胎土来看，本品为东汉早期作品。

五联罐流行于东汉时期，是富者的陪葬明器，象征着财富和权势。五联罐多流行于广东、广西、湖南、福建一带。东汉早期时体形较矮，只是在大罐肩部四周附堆起四个小罐，没有其他装饰。其后器身加长，还堆塑各种瑞兽、飞禽，在三国以后演变为堆塑楼阁的谷仓罐。

相传五罐是模仿神话中昆仑山为中央，周边围以四座神山的造型，作为安顿亡者灵魂之所，可以引领平安到达极乐世界。

浙江上虞博物馆收藏有相似器物。

Proto-celadon. The jar has a bulbous belly and a splayed tall flat foot with a slightly recessed center. The neck of the jar is fashioned as a miniature bottle surrounded by four additional bottles on the shoulders. The five miniature bottles are decorated with cord motif. The brownish red paste is hard and dense. The entire vessel is covered with a lime glaze with a yellowish tint. Shrinkage of glaze is uneven. The shape, paste and glaze color suggest that this jar was from the early Eastern Han period.

Five-mouthed jars symbolizing wealth and power were used as burial objects for the affluent during the Eastern Han period. Five-mouthed jars were popular around the Guangdong, Guangxi, Hunan and Fujian area. Early Eastern Han pieces are shorter with only four mouths affixed to the broad shoulders and no decorations. Later examples have an elongated body adorned with appliqué animals and birds. From the Three Kingdoms period on, they took the form of granary jars with elaborately sculpted architectural motifs.

According to Chinese mythology and folklore, five-mouthed jars (with Mount Kunlun in the center surrounded by four sacred mountains) not only serve as a repository for the remains of the dead but also a guide to a smooth journey to Paradise.

A similar vessel is in the collection of the Shangyu Museum in Zhejiang.

251

青釉兽首船形器

东汉

公元 25—220 年

高：22.9 厘米

长：38.6 厘米

Celadon boat-shaped vessel with animal head

Eastern Han dynasty

25 – 220 C.E.

Height: 22.9 cm

Length: 38.6 cm

原始青瓷。船首饰兽头、张口、口与船体内相通。船身呈流线型，尾部垂直，微内斜，底平。船面上置宝珠顶四柱凉亭一座。船戳印连续圆圈纹，船面满刻菱形十字纹。胎厚重、色浅灰。兽头、亭顶、船面和船缘四周施青釉，其余部分呈紫褐色。

汉代南方地区盛行船形陶质艺术品，但外形像这样的船很少见，是研究水上交通工具极好的资料。

Proto-celadon. The bow of this pottery boat is decorated with an animal head whose mouth is connected internally to the streamlined hull. The stern is perpendicular to the horizon. The bottom is flat. On the deck stands a pavilion with four pillars supporting a pyramidal roof. The top edge of the shipboard is stamped with continuous bead motif while the deck is densely carved with lozenge grids. The boat is heavily potted and the paste is light gray in color. The animal head, the roof of the pavilion, the deck and the top edge of the shipboard are all coated with celadon glaze and the rest with purplish brown slip.

Boat-shaped vessels were prevalent in

southern China during the Han dynasty but ones like this are rare. This vessel is an excellent reference for studying early water transport.

252

青釉鸱鸮尊

东汉

公元 25—220 年

高：31.6 厘米

阔：16 厘米

Owl-shaped celadon *zun* vessel

Eastern Han dynasty

25 – 220 C.E.

Height: 31.6 cm

Width: 16 cm

原始青瓷。尊盖塑成猫头鹰形，子口。弯喙，前端尖锐。双目置脸部两侧，圆而凸，望向前方，炯炯有神，凶恶、威猛兼而有之。尊体作腹，下承双足和尾。双足微弯，短小粗壮，扁形尾微向后斜，挺胸而立，睥睨一切。鸮首及胸部施青釉，满印条状羽毛。鸮首羽毛呈放射状，面部呈凹陷的盆状。胸部左、右各饰两道斜向后的弦纹，刻划出鸮的翅膀。胸两侧各横贴叶纹双环耳一个，用以穿带。胸下饰弦纹三道，把胸、腹分隔。腹、双足和尾部无釉。

猫头鹰被视为吉祥鸟，能保护主人平安。史前仰韶文化陶器和商周青铜器都有鸮尊的造型。

本品经热释光测定烧制年代距今约1700 年。

Proto-celadon. The owl-head lid is held in place by the rabbeted rim of the vessel. The owl has a hooked beak set between a pair of circular eyes. The short and stout legs are slightly flexed while the fan-shaped tail slopes to the ground. Its head and chest are covered with celadon glaze and engraved with feather motif. The plumage on the head is arranged in radiated form. Two grooved lines run down the sides at an angle to denote the wings. A pair of horizontal loop handles is set on the shoulders. Three grooves encompass the body below the chest, separating it from the unglazed abdomen. The legs and tail are unglazed.

Owls are considered auspicious birds in ancient China and believed to have magical powers. Examples of this shape can be found among the pottery of the Neolithic Yangshao culture and the bronzes of the Shang and Zhou periods.

Thermoluminescence test shows that the last firing date of this piece was around 1700 years before present.

东汉瓷器

Eastern Han Porcelain

东汉瓷器：

成就超卓

一般说，瓷器需符合以下三条件：第一是原料的选择和加工，主要表现在 Al_2O_3 的提高和 Fe_2O_3 的降低，使胎质呈白色；第二是经过1200℃以上的高温烧成，使胎质烧结致密、不吸水分、击之发出清脆的金石声；第三是在器表施有高温下烧成的釉，胎釉结合牢固，厚薄均匀（中国硅酸盐学会:《中国陶瓷史》，文物出版社，1982 年）。

中国瓷器由于"白云母、绢云母及还原气氛的影响"，"不但有可能在较低温度下烧结，而且仍具有与硬质瓷相等强度和硬度"，因而虽然烧成温度较低，"但化学物理性能均与欧洲硬质瓷胎釉限度接近"（江西省轻工业厅景德镇陶瓷研究所:《中国的瓷器》，中国财政经济出版社，1963 年）。西方学者把中国在公元 10 世纪前经 1150℃—1300℃烧成的瓷器统称为炻器。

东汉中、晚期，青瓷摆脱了原始状态。在绍兴、上虞、慈溪、宁波等地东汉瓷窑都发现有青瓷，且风格一致。绍兴和慈溪上林湖东汉青瓷烧成温度在 1200℃ 以下，坯体尚未达到烧结的水平；上虞帐子山东汉青瓷烧成温度在 1200℃ 以上；上虞小仙坛东汉青瓷的烧成温度在 1260℃—1310℃。

汉瓷器以古越州地区的青瓷为最。小仙坛东汉晚期窑场的制品，胎釉结合紧密，釉层透明，光泽度强，釉面淡雅清澈，犹如一池清水。东汉青瓷器形以罐为多，纹饰以素面为主，少量有水波纹、弦纹、三角纹、叶纹或贴双系、四系等（图录 256 号、258 号）。

此外，在上虞、宁波的东汉窑址中还发现了酱色釉和黑釉瓷器，如图录 265 号和 266 号为东汉酱釉器的代表，267 号为东汉酱釉瓷的上佳作品。通常这类酱釉、黑釉瓷器的坯泥炼制不精，胎质较粗，釉中氧化铁含量较高，烧结温度较低。器表施釉一般不到底，釉层比较丰厚而富有光泽，器表多留有泪釉痕。由于在器表施以黑褐色的深色釉，粗糙而灰黑的胎体得到覆盖，为瓷器生产扩大原料范围开辟了一条新的途径。酱釉、黑釉瓷器的出现，同样是汉代瓷业的一项重大成就。

由原始瓷器发展为瓷器，是陶瓷工艺上的一大飞跃。青瓷品质高雅，坚固耐用，有玻璃釉层的保护，不易藏污纳垢，大大改善了人类的生活。所以随着三国两晋瓷器的发展，它很快就以绝对优势代替陶器、铜器、漆器而成为人们日常饮食起居的生活用品。青瓷的烧制成功是中国陶瓷史上的重要创新，代表了汉代瓷业的最高成就。

Eastern Han Porcelain:

An Enlightened Achievement

Generally speaking, porcelain must meet the following three conditions: Firstly, as far as the selection and processing of raw material is concerned, a higher AI_2O_3 and lower Fe_2O_3 composition is required to obtain a white paste. Secondly, the vessel has to undergo a firing temperature of over 1200℃ to result in a dense, vitrified and non-absorbent body that gives a metallic sound when struck. Thirdly, the surface of the vessel is coated with a high-fired glaze that is even in thickness and fuses well with the paste (Chinese Ceramic Society, *Zhongguo Taocishi* [History of Chinese Ceramics], Cultural Relics Press 1982).

"Due to the presence of white mica and sericite in the clay, and a reduction atmosphere in the kiln, it is not only possible for porcelain to vitrify at a lower temperature, but also possible to achieve the same durability and hardness as hard porcelain. Despite being fired to a lower temperature, Chinese porcelain has physiochemical properties resembling that of European hard porcelain." (See *Zhongguo de ciqi* [Chinese Porcelains] compiled by the Jingdezhen Research Institute of Ceramics, Bureau of Light Industry of Jiangxi, published by China Finance and Economics Publishing House, Beijing, 1963). Western scholars use the term "stoneware" to denote all types of Chinese porcelains fired to a temperature of 1150℃ –1300℃ prior to the 10th century.

Celadon from the mid and late Eastern Han period were unearthed from Eastern Han kiln sites in Shaoxing, Shangyu, Cixi and Ningbo in Zhejiang. The finds from Shaoxing and Lake Shanglin in Cixi were fired to below 1200℃ and not completely vitrified. Examples from Mount Zhangzi in Shangyu were fired to over 1200℃ while those from Xiaoxiantan in Shangyu were fired to a high temperature of 1260℃ –1310℃.

Yue celadons produced in the ancient Yuezhou region are the finest of Eastern Han porcelains. Examples unearthed from the late Eastern Han kilns at Xiaoxiantan revealed a perfect sintering of body and glaze. The transparent, lustrous, pure and refined glaze resembles a pool of clear water. The majority of the vessels were jars. Some are decorated with wave motif, cord motif, triangular design, leaf motif, and two or four appliqué lugs (Cat. Nos. 256, 258).

The Eastern Han kiln sites in Shangyu and Ningbo also yielded contemporaneous soy-glazed and black-glazed porcelains. Cat. Nos. 265, 266 are representative examples of soy-glazed ware and Cat. No. 267 represents the best from this period. The paste of this type of soy-glazed and black-glazed porcelains is often coarse in texture and higher in iron content but it can still vitrify to a satisfactory degree when fired to a relatively low temperature. The glaze is usually quite thick and lustrous and does not reach the base. Glaze streaks are often found on the surface. The emergence of this type of soy-glazed and black glazed porcelains is a great achievement for the Han porcelain industry.

The evolution from proto-porcelain to porcelain was a major breakthrough in Chinese ceramic technology and the successful production of celadon the highest achievement. Following its development during the Three Kingdoms period and the Western and Eastern Jin periods, porcelain rapidly gained advantage over pottery, bronze and lacquerware and replaced them as daily utensils.

253

褐釉五铢钱镳斗

东汉

公元 25—220 年

高：20 厘米

口径：8.6 厘米

Brown-glazed wine warmer with coin motif

Eastern Han dynasty

25 – 220 C.E.

Height: 20 cm

Mouth diameter: 8.6 cm

附图 11　五铢钱（汉）

Fig. 11　*Wuzhuqian* coin (Han dynasty)

口缘微内敛、束颈、斜肩。肩、腹交界处削纹带一圈，纹带上方饰凹弦纹一周，下方起凸棱一道，令肩、腹明显分界。腹下急收到平底，底贴柱形实足三只。梯形盖，上饰拱形纽。肩和盖上各印东汉时期流通的五铢钱币三个。腹凸棱上置六棱面扁柄，柄上翘。浅灰黄胎、质结实、细滑。由凸棱到盖顶施褐色釉，满布黑褐斑点。其余部位露胎，露胎处呈浅褐色。在凸棱上、下方和底、足交接处见蓝白色混浊的色彩。

本品用于温酒，形制与汉、晋同期青铜器相同。

五铢铜钱始铸于汉武帝，在中国货币史上占有十分重要的地位。钱纹在东汉陶瓷上相当流行（附图 11）。

按道家的说法，数字"三"为数之小终，大可包罗天地万物，而"三"的三倍数"九"是个位数中最大的"阳数"。因此，"三"和"三"的成倍数暗示着量之众，即以"三"寓多。三个五铢钱寓意财源广进。

The jar has an incurved mouth, a constricted neck, sloping shoulders and a carinated belly. The junction between the shoulders and the belly has been planed down to form a receding band bordered by a groove on both sides. The belly tapers towards a flat base supported by three solid cylindrical legs. The lid is in the shape of a truncated cone with an arched knob. The lid and the shoulders are stamped with three coin designs, recognizably the *wuzhuqian* of the Eastern Han period. An up-tilted handle with hexagonal cross-section is attached to the ridge around the belly. The light grayish yellow paste is hard, smooth and refined. The lid, the handle and the part of the body above the ridge are covered with a brown glaze with dark brown mottling. The rest of the body is unglazed. The unglazed part has burnt to a light brown color. Splashes of hazy blue and white glaze as a result of kiln transmutation appear on the ridge, the belly, and around the junction between the legs and the base.

This vessel was used as a wine warmer. The shape is modeled after contemporaneous bronzes.

Coins known as *wuzhuqian* (literally, "five *zhu* money") were first cast during the reign of the Western Han emperor Wudi. They are of great significance in the monetary history of China. Coin motifs are commonly found among Eastern Han ceramics (Fig. 11).

According to Daoist doctrines, "three" stands for "a small ending", but it could also denote all things big and small in the universe. Since "nine", the multiple of three, is the highest single-digit odd number, "three" and its multiples signify abundance. A motif with three *wuzhuqian* coins can be understood as "having abundant wealth".

254

褐釉平缘编织纹罐

东汉

公元 25—220 年

越窑

高：21.8 厘米

阔：34.7 厘米

口径：22.8 厘米

Brown-glazed jar with flat rim and mat motif

Eastern Han dynasty

25 – 220 C.E.

Yue kilns

Height: 21.8 cm

Width: 34.7 cm

Mouth diameter: 22.8 cm

口平缘，缘阔约 2.6 厘米，底平，微内凹。内、外缘起凸棱，外壁四周拍印席纹。灰胎，质坚，细滑。施浅褐色釉，釉明亮，有缩釉现象，釉不及底。底部露胎，呈火石红色。

本品纹饰与图录 238 号战国青釉乳突席纹罐相同，说明我国陶瓷烧制工艺技术和装饰手法是一脉相承的。

The flat mouth has a 2.6 cm wide rim with a ridge along both edges. The entire exterior is impressed with woven mat motif under a lustrous light brown glaze that stops short of the base. Retraction of glaze is noted. The slightly recessed base is unglazed, exposing a biscuit of burnt orange color. The gray paste is hard, smooth and refined.

The decorative motif of this jar is identical to Cat. No. 238 from the Warring States period, which goes to show that the firing and decorative techniques of each dynastic period succeed each other in a continuous lineage.

255

褐釉双系弦纹罐

东汉

公元 25—220 年

越窑

高：25.8 厘米

口径：12.3 厘米

底径：13.5 厘米

Brown-glazed jar with double lugs and cord motif

Eastern Han dynasty

25 – 220 C.E.

Yue kilns

Height: 25.8 cm

Mouth diameter: 12.3 cm

Base diameter: 13.5 cm

口略侈，短颈微束。肩部丰满，上腹特别圆鼓，下腹渐收，平底、底微内凹。肩部两侧置叶纹系各一，系下至罐体中部满饰平行弦纹。灰白胎，质坚、体薄。施褐色釉，不及底，露胎处呈褐红色。施釉不均，聚釉处呈深黑褐色，开细纹片。本品造型规整，线条优美，为瓷器成熟时期的代表作。

The jar has a slightly flared mouth, a short constricted neck, bold shoulders, a swelling upper belly and a lower part that tapers gradually to a flat base with a slightly recessed center. A pair of leaf-shaped lugs flanks the shoulders. Parallel cord motif encircles the body from below the lugs to the mid-section of the belly. The grayish white paste is thin and hard. The vessel surface is covered with a dark brown crackled glaze that stops short of the base. The unglazed part revealed a brownish red color. This vessel is a representative example of mature porcelain.

256

青釉双耳罐

东汉

公元 25—220 年

越窑

高：16 厘米

阔：21.3 厘米

口径：10.8 厘米

Celadon jar with double lugs

Eastern Han dynasty

25 – 220 C.E.

Yue kilns

Height: 16 cm

Width: 21.3 cm

Mouth diameter: 10.8 cm

侈口，短颈微束，丰肩，肩和上腹圆鼓，下腹渐收，平底，底微内凹。肩刻划弦纹三周，两侧置对称叶纹系。胎质灰白细腻。施青绿色釉，不及底。露胎处呈火石红色。此罐胎釉结合牢固，釉透明度高，色泽青翠，颈肩交接聚釉处呈深翠绿色，并见蓝色和乳白色的混浊釉色彩。釉有开片纹。近底处露接合痕，说明底是在罐体成型后黏接到一起的。本品釉色纯正、温润，是青瓷成熟时期的代表作。

造型结构上腹径大于通高，这是东汉、三国、西晋时期青瓷罐类器物规律性的特点。

The jar has a slightly flared mouth, a short and slightly constricted neck, broad shoulders, a bulbous upper belly and an unglazed flat base with a slightly recessed center. The grayish white paste is refined. The entire surface except around the foot is covered with a green celadon glaze that stops short of the base. The shoulders are encircled by three indented lines and adorned with two lugs with leaf motif. The highly translucent green glaze sinters well with the paste. It pools around the junction of the neck and the shoulders to give a deep emerald color with blue and milky white hues. Crackles are found all over the glazed surface. The luting marks around the foot suggest that the base was separately made. The unglazed areas revealed a burnt orange color. The glaze is rich and lustrous. This jar is a representative example of mature celadon.

The widest part of this jar measures taller than its height, a proportion typical of the

celadon jars of the Eastern Han, Three Kingdoms and Western Jin periods.

257

青釉弦纹双系罐

东汉

公元 25—220 年

越窑

高：10 厘米

阔：14.8 厘米

口径：9.8 厘米

Celadon jar with double lugs

Eastern Han dynasty

25 – 220 C.E.

Yue kilns

Height: 10 cm

Width: 14.8 cm

Mouth diameter: 9.8 cm

短颈微束、鼓腹、底平微内凹。肩两侧饰竖系各一，系间刻弦纹三道。胎灰白色，质坚细密。内口缘和外壁施青釉、釉不及底，近底沿有垂釉现象，聚釉处呈绿色，青翠可爱、开细小纹片。下腹近底边和器底露胎处呈浅褐色。胎釉结合牢固、烧成温度高、扣之铿锵作响。原始瓷自商代出现后，一直到东汉才完成向瓷器的过渡。本品瓷化程度之高、釉色之清彻艳丽、甚至较许多后期越窑青瓷器物更好、为东汉越窑青瓷成熟时期的优秀作品。

The jar has a slightly constricted short neck, a bulbous belly and a flat base with a slightly recessed center. A vertical lug is set on the shoulders. Three indented lines are incised between the lugs. The grayish white paste is hard and refined. The interior mouth rim and the exterior surface of the jar are covered with a greenish glaze that ends unevenly in welts. The glaze appears bright green where it pools. Small crackles are found in the glaze. The

unglazed area around the lower belly and the base appears light brown in color. The paste sintered well with the glaze. Since the firing temperature was high, the body makes a clear sound when struck. From its emergence during the Shang dynasty, proto-celadon has undergone a long period of growth and change before reaching the stage of mature porcelain in the Eastern Han dynasty. The glaze of this jar is more transparent, more vitrified and more beautiful than many Yue celadon wares of the later periods. This vessel is a fine example of Yue celadon from the Eastern Han period.

青釉山纹双系罐

东汉

公元 25—220 年

越窑

高：18.7 厘米

底径：13.8 厘米

Celadon jar with mountain motif and double lugs

Eastern Han dynasty

25 – 220 C.E.

Yue kilns

Height: 18.7 cm

Base diameter: 13.8 cm

直唇，短束颈，鼓腹，平底微内凹。口缘下和肩部饰山形纹各一周，以双线弦纹相间，肩置叶纹竖耳一对。胎灰白，细腻坚实。内外施青绿色釉，釉较厚，有泪釉现象，聚釉处呈墨绿色。釉不及底，开纹片。底露胎，呈橘红色，留有黑色支烧残渣。可能烧造时温度太高或釉汁太浓，罐体一侧出现橘皮棕眼，相连的露胎处也呈皱纹状。

The jar has a straight mouth, a short constricted neck, a bulbous belly and a flat base. A band of mountain motif encircles the collar and the shoulders, divided by double indented lines. A leaf-shaped vertical lug is affixed to the two sides of the shoulders. The grayish white paste is hard and refined. The interior and exterior surfaces are covered with a relatively thick grass green glaze with streaks. The glaze stops short of the base. There are crackles in the glaze and appears dark green where it pools. The unglazed and slightly concave base revealed an orange red paste with spur marks. Orange-peel effect and pinholes are visible on one side of the jar possibly due to firing at temperatures that are too high. The unglazed area adjacent to it is also affected and appears wrinkled.

259

黑釉四系水纹罐

东汉

公元 25—220 年

德清窑

高：13.6 厘米

口径：10.7 厘米

Black-glazed jar with wave motif and four lugs

Eastern Han dynasty

25 – 220 C.E.

Deqing kilns

Height: 13.6 cm

Mouth diameter: 10.7 cm

直口、短颈、溜肩、鼓腹、平底、底微内凹。肩部饰弦纹两道，纹间和颈上各刻划水波纹一周。肩部等距贴四横系。白色胎，质坚硬，叩之铿铿发响。器身内外施黑釉、釉厚，颇均匀，胎釉结合紧密、釉色润泽、釉面满布开片纹。足边和底露胎，见浅褐红色护胎釉。本品为德清窑瓷器成熟期的代表作。

The jar has a straight mouth, a short neck, sloping shoulders, a bulbous belly and a flat base with a slightly recessed center. The shoulders are decorated with two rounds of cord motif and four equally spaced apart horizontal lugs. The white paste is hard. It makes a ringing sound when struck. The surface is coated with a black glaze that stops short of the base. The thick and rather evenly distributed glaze sintered well with the paste. The glaze is smooth and lustrous and covered with crackles. The foot rim and the base are unglazed, revealing a paste coated with light brownish red slip. This jar is a representative example of mature porcelain from the Deqing kilns.

260

褐釉网纹罐

东汉

公元 25—220 年

越窑

高：32.5 厘米

Brown-glazed jar with net motif

Eastern Han dynasty

25 – 220 C.E.

Yue kilns

Height: 32.5 cm

口外侈，斜短颈，溜肩，肩以下渐收到底，底平。器身满拍印圆圈，内饰网格纹，腹近底处有弦纹数道。深灰胎，胎坚硬。釉呈褐色。器身四周有黑色泪釉痕和斑块，可能是烧制时火候偏高所致。

The jar has a flared mouth, a short neck, sloping shoulders and a belly that narrows to a flat base. The deep gray paste is hard. The body of the jar is stamped with circles filled with a net motif. Several grooves encircle the body near the base. The glaze is brown in color. The glaze streaks and dark patches around the body are possibly due to firing at temperatures that are too high.

261

青釉席纹罐

东汉

公元 25—220 年

越窑

高：29 厘米

Celadon jar with mat motif

Eastern Han dynasty

25 – 220 C.E.

Yue kilns

Height: 29 cm

口平、外侈，短颈，溜肩，腹部上丰、下渐收成平底。颈肩间饰凸弦纹一道，通体拍印席纹。胎灰白，质坚。上半部施釉、釉色发青、釉层薄。下半部无釉，呈火石红色。

The jar has a flared mouth with flat rim, a short neck, sloping shoulders, and a bulbous belly whose lower part narrows to a flat base. The grayish white paste is hard. A rib encircles the collar of the jar. The entire exterior surface is impressed with mat motif. The upper part of the body is covered with a thin layer of greenish lime glaze. The unglazed area revealed a burnt orange color.

青釉五联罐

东汉

公元 25—220 年

越窑

高：46.2 厘米

底径：13.3 厘米

Five-mouthed celadon jar

Eastern Han dynasty

25 – 220 C.E.

Yue kilns

Height: 46.2 cm

Base diameter: 13.3 cm

器分三节，由上面一个小罐和下面两个较大的罐体对接而成，三节相通。中部罐体四周置小瓶各一，与中罐并不相通。小罐及中罐肩上各饰小鸟四只。大罐肩上塑坐熊三只，左前腿抚嘴，右前腿下垂，三熊之间贴一鱼三鸟。罐体上各刻弦纹数道。胎灰白色，质坚，胎体较厚重。施青釉，呈淡青褐色，不均匀。大小罐的下腹部、底和罐体无釉处呈褐红色。

本品造型和装饰特别，是为陪葬、祭祀而制作的。

The vessel is made up of three interconnected sections – a small bottle resting on a jar that sits on top of a larger jar. Four miniature bottles are luted onto the shoulders of the middle jar but they are not connected to its cavity. Four birds carved in the round are attached onto the shoulders of the small bottle and the jar in the middle. Three bears with left forelegs over their mouths and right forelegs hanging down are sculpted around the shoulders of the bottom jar. The space between each pair of bears is sculpted with a fish and three birds. Each section is encircled with a number of grooves. The grayish white paste is rather thick and hard. The vessel is covered with an uneven layer of celadon glaze of greenish brown color. The lower part of each section, the base and some patches on the body are unglazed, exposing a paste that has burnt brownish red.

This vessel is noted for its unique shape and decorations. This jar was made for burial and ritual purposes.

263

青釉五联罐

东汉

公元 25—220 年

越窑

高：47.8 厘米

底径：16.5 厘米

Five-mouthed celadon jar

Eastern Han dynasty

25 – 220 C.E.

Yue kilns

Height: 47.8 cm

Base diameter: 16.5 cm

葫芦形相通罐体，平底。顶立一盘口小壶，与中部圆腹粘连，圆腹上塑小壶四个，小壶与罐体并不相通，壶间置小鸟各一。下罐体肩部堆塑熊三只，左、右前腿上弯抚下颌，间饰鱼各一。壶、罐通体各饰弦纹数道。胎灰白，质坚，胎体厚重。施青釉，呈灰黄色，施釉不均，有麻癞现象。腹下部和底露胎。在下罐肩部近鱼处各开气孔一个，用于排放烧造时罐内产生的气体，以防烧裂。本品器形圆浑、线条优美，为东汉青瓷成熟期的典型器物。

The gourd-shaped jar consists of a smaller upper bulb and a larger bulb below. The mouth of the upper bulb in the shape of a bottle is connected to the cavity of the jar whereas the four miniature bottles surrounding it are not. An appliqué bird is set in between the miniature bottles. The shoulders of the larger bulb are decorated with three bears and three fish. The entire vessel is covered with an uneven layer of grayish yellow celadon glaze with spotting and streaking. The grayish white paste is hard, thick and heavy. The lower belly and the flat base of the jar are unglazed. There is a ventilation hole next to each fish to allow hot air to escape during firing and prevent the vessel from cracking. This jar is a representative example of mature celadon from the Eastern Han period.

264

青釉九联罐

东汉

公元 25—220 年

越窑

高：56.8 厘米

阔：25.3 厘米

Nine-mouthed celadon jar

Eastern Han dynasty

25 – 220 C.E.

Yue kilns

Height: 56.8 cm

Width: 25.3 cm

器为三节葫芦形，平底，腹上各饰弦纹
数道。顶部正中和四周共置直立盘口小
壶五个，正中的壶较高大，壶间贴小鸟
各一只。中节罐体四周饰微向外斜盘口
小壶四个，壶间堆塑坐熊四只，坐熊下
方各贴小鸟两只。下节罐肩部间隔堆贴
熊三只、龟一只、鱼三条、鸟五只等动物，
手法简洁，动物表情生动。灰白胎，质
坚。施淡青色釉，釉色青翠，有开片纹。
釉不到底边，足底无釉。除正中小壶外，
其余小壶与三节罐体并不相通。

通常五联罐较为多见，七联罐已不多，
而九联罐则更少。浙江省博物馆近年曾
入藏一件相似的九联罐。

The gourd-shaped jar consists of three
main bulbs decreasing in size as it goes up.
The upper bulb is crowned by a miniature
bottle and surrounded by four miniature
bottles with a sculpted bird in between.
The middle bulb has four miniature bottles
each separated by a sculpted bear. Below
each bear are two birds carved in the
round. The shoulders of the lower bulb
are decorated with animals including

three sculpted bears, one tortoise, three
fish and five birds. Crackles are visible
on the surface of the pale green glaze.
The grayish white paste is rather hard.
The area around the foot and the flat
base is unglazed. Except for the bottle at
the very top, none of the other bottles
are connected to the cavity of the vessel.

While seven-mouthed jars are less often
seen than five-mouthed ones, nine-
mouthed jars are rarer still. The Zhejiang
Provincial Museum had acquired a similar
nine-mouthed jar in recent years.

265

黑釉五联罐

东汉

公元 25—220 年

越窑

高：46 厘米

底径：15.7 厘米

Five-mouthed jar in black glaze

Eastern Han dynasty

25 – 220 C.E.

Yue kilns

Height: 46 cm

Base diameter: 15.7 cm

本品造型与图录 263 号相似，只是全器
施黑釉。

1978 年浙江省余姚石堰翁家山（今属慈
溪市）有相似器物出土。

This jar is similar to Cat. No. 263 except
that it is glazed black.

A similar vessel was unearthed in 1978 at
Wengjiashan (now Cixi City) in Shiyan,
Zhejiang province.

黑釉盘口弦纹双耳罐

东汉

公元 25—220 年

越窑

高：15.4 厘米

口径：7.5 厘米

底径：7.3 厘米

Black-glazed jar with double lugs and plate-shaped mouth

Eastern Han dynasty

25 – 220 C.E

Yue kilns

Height: 15.4 cm

Mouth diameter: 7.5 cm

Base diameter: 7.3 cm

盘口，短颈，斜肩，平底。肩两侧贴叶纹环耳各一，肩下部至近底处满饰弦纹。器体施黑釉，布满开片纹，弦纹之间聚釉处呈黝黑色。底露胎，质细滑，呈浅红色。罐体内壁无釉，呈浅灰褐色，叩之声音清越。本品造型饱满，釉色光润，制作精美。

江苏镇江东汉永元十三年（公元 101 年）墓出土的一件黑釉盘口双耳罐与本品近乎一致，为年代判断提供了依据（上海博物馆：《上海博物馆藏瓷选集》，插图 7，文物出版社，1979 年）。

The jar has a plate-shaped mouth, a short neck, sloping shoulders and a flat base. A pair of lugs with leaf motif is attached to the shoulders. The whole body except the area above the lugs is densely encircled by grooves. The entire surface is covered with a crackled black glaze that appears jet-black where it pools along the grooves. The unglazed base revealed a smooth and refined paste of pink color. The unglazed interior appears grayish brown. When knocked with the knuckles, the vessel gives a clear sound.

An identical jar has been unearthed from an Eastern Han tomb dated to the 13th year of the Yongyuan period (101 C.E.) in Zhenjiang, Jiangsu province (*Shanghai Bowuguan cangci xuanji* [Selected Examples of Porcelains from the Collection of the Shanghai Museum], Cultural Relics Press, 1979, Plate 7). It is an excellent reference for the dating of the present jar.

267

酱釉双耳壶

东汉

公元 25—220 年

越窑

高：13 厘米

口径：5.5 厘米

底径：6.7 厘米

Soy-glazed jar with double lugs

Eastern Han dynasty

25 – 220 C.E

Yue kilns

Height: 13 cm

Mouth diameter: 5.5 cm

Base diameter: 6.7 cm

浅盘口、高颈、扁圆腹、圈足高而外撇。肩腹间饰弦纹两组，上置对称竖环耳。浅灰胎，质坚润滑。外壁和颈内侧施酱釉，烧造时釉料自由流淌，形成由上而下深浅交融的褐红色、褐色和酱红色，釉色晶莹柔润，艳丽可爱。底露胎，可见旋纹痕及褐红色。近足底边缘有三处不规则露胎，是烧造前蘸釉者用手拿着底足，将坯体头下底上浸入釉浆时手指所留下的痕迹。本品釉色斑驳灿烂而均匀，胎釉结合紧密，瓷化程度高，为东汉青瓷成熟期的代表器物，也可说是早期铁锈斑纹器物。

The jar has a shallow plate-shaped mouth, a tall neck and a squat bulbous belly resting on a tall splayed ring foot. Two groups of grooves encompass the body between the shoulders and the belly. A pair of lugs is vertically set on the shoulders. The grayish white paste is hard and smooth. The interior of the neck and the outer surface of the vessel are coated with a lustrous and translucent soy-colored glaze with variegated streaks of brownish red, brown and soy red colors. Wheel marks are visible on the unglazed brownish red base. The three unglazed patches distributed evenly around the foot near the edge are finger smudges from dip glazing. The paste sintered well with the highly vitrified glaze. This jar is a representative example of mature Eastern Han celadon as well as an early example of ferruginous decorations.

六朝瓷器

Porcelains of the Six Dynasties

六朝瓷器：

承上启下

从公元 3 世纪初到 6 世纪末，中国南方先后有孙吴、东晋和南朝的宋、齐、梁、陈 6 个汉族政权在南京（孙吴时称建业，东晋、南朝称建康）建都，史家称为"六朝"。六朝承汉启唐，创造了极其辉煌灿烂的"六朝文明"。当北方战争频繁，社会遭受严重破坏时，南方战争较少，社会相对安定，大批北人南渡，给南方增加了许多劳动力，还带来中原地区较为先进的生产技术，为南方特别是长江中下游地区社会经济的迅速发展创立了良好的社会环境。本书所指六朝瓷器还包括与南朝相对应的北朝（北魏、东魏、西魏、北齐和北周）瓷器。

吴黄龙元年（公元 229 年）秋九月，吴大帝孙权定都建业，江南沃野在水利、农业、手工业方面得天独厚，特别是青瓷手工业大力发展，烧制出不少较东汉青瓷更精彩的产品。这时的瓷器胎质坚致，胎呈白或灰白色，优质瓷的釉青亮光润，一部分仍有麻癞现象，露胎处仍带东汉器物样的褐红色。器物纹饰较少，只有划或印的网格纹、弦纹、水波纹等，贴塑、模印纹则比较丰富（图录 270 号）。

六朝青瓷器物无论在造型还是装饰上都与汉代陶瓷相通，特意为随葬而烧制的青瓷明器也与汉代上下贯通。六朝淘洗泥料的技术比汉代更为先进，窑炉火力更高，釉料的提炼也更先进，再加上高岭土的发现，瓷器的发展取得了长足的进步。

从窑址出土器物看，北朝晚期，相州窑、巩义窑和邢窑在烧制青瓷的过程中创烧出白瓷，所以早期白瓷都明显带有青瓷的特征，瓷器釉面往往呈现一种白中微闪青绿的颜色（图录 296 号、298 号）。北朝白瓷的出现改变了中国瓷器以青瓷为主导的发展方向，也为彩瓷的出现打下了基础。

晋瓷和南朝青瓷以往称为六朝青瓷，也称为早期青瓷，主要产地在浙江上虞、余姚、慈溪、绍兴等地，原为古越人聚居地。这里的制瓷手工业自商周、两汉、三国、两晋、南朝、隋唐五代到宋代，历时 2800 多年的发展，规模越来越大。由于唐代这个地区归越州都督府管辖，而唐代瓷窑以州命名，故称此地区所产瓷器为越窑。鉴于该地区瓷器生产一脉相承，部分陶瓷研究家把这个地区从原始青瓷到宋越窑青瓷的青瓷都称为"越窑"。

六朝佛教盛行，尤以南朝为甚，在梁武帝（公元 502—549 年）时达到鼎盛。据唐法琳《辩正论》记载，南朝至梁，有寺院 2846 所，僧尼 82700 余人。由于统治阶层和文人学士大都崇信佛教，所以陶瓷质地的礼佛用具以及反映追求永生和死后升仙的器物大量生产。此类器物大多以莲瓣纹、莲花纹、佛像或佛祖身上的物品作装饰（图录 290 号）。

青瓷谷仓罐（又名堆塑罐、魂瓶）流行于三国吴及两晋时期，由东汉五联罐演变而来，是最具时代特色的器物之一（图录 272 号、273 号）。塑造时把现实生活和神话相结合，各种装饰题材用不同的手法表现出来，既有现实主义的内容，又有抽象夸张的浪漫主义色彩，艺术价值毋庸置疑。尤其是豪门甲第祈求五谷丰登、六畜兴旺的主题，既表现了墓主人的财富和部族家丁的武装实力，又表现了子孙繁衍和死后升往极乐世界的愿望，装饰繁缛瑰丽，寓意深刻，有鲜明的时代特征和艺术风格。谷仓罐以越窑生产为多，婺州窑和瓯窑也有生产。

鸡首壶也是此时期甚具特色的器物（图录 289 号、293 号）。鸡首壶出现于三国末年，流行于晋至唐初，也称天鸡壶，因壶肩部塑鸡首形而得名。各类鸡首壶的鸡首有实心和空心之分，有的在日常生活中使用，有的则是陪葬用的明器。西晋时壶身、壶颈较矮，鸡首多无颈，鸡尾甚小。东晋时壶体加高，鸡首有了颈部，鸡尾消失，代之的是高于壶口的圆股形曲柄，晚期则在把手上端饰龙首和熊纹。烧制鸡首壶的主要有越窑、德清窑、瓯窑和北方一些瓷窑，如西安隋李静训墓出土的白瓷鸡头壶应该是北方瓷窑所产，而德清窑主要生产黑瓷鸡首壶。西安唐总章元年（公元668年）李爽墓出土一件青瓷鸡头壶，在此以后鸡头壶很少出现。

Porcelains of the Six Dynasties:

Enduring Lineage

From the 3rd century to the end of the 6th century, the Chinese regimes based in southern China, namely Wu, Eastern Jin, Song, Qi, Liang and Chen successively made Nanjing their capital (Nanjing was called Jianye under the Wu regime, and Jiankang under the Eastern Jin). These six regimes are collectively referred to as the Six Dynasties in Chinese history. The Six Dynasties also include in a broad sense the five northern regimes, namely Northern Wei, Eastern Wei, Western Wei, Northern Qi and Northern Zhou, collectively known as the Northern Dynasties. Having inherited the culture of the Han dynasty, the Six Dynasties created a brilliant culture of its own and laid a solid foundation for the Tang dynasty. Frequent warfare in northern China during this period impacted the economy and caused many northerners to move south. An increased labor force and advanced production technologies from the Central Plain contributed to the growth of socio-economic development in southern China especially around the mid and lower reaches of the Changjiang River.

In the 9th month of the 1st year of the Huanglong period (229 C.E.) of the Wu regime, Sun Quan the founder of Wu State made Jianye (Nanjing) his capital. Jiangnan region was richly endowed with fertile lands and abundant water resources, which favored the development of the agriculture and handicraft industries. The production of celadon in particular saw rapid growth. Many surpassed the quality of Eastern Han celadon. The grayish white paste is compact, the exposed area burnt to a brownish red color and the decorative motifs are restrained (Cat. No. 270).

Celadon of the Six Dynasties were by and large similar to Han ones in shape and decoration.

They were characterized by more sophisticated levigation methods, higher firing temperature and better glaze formulation. The discovery of *kaolin* also gave impetus for the development of porcelains. It was against this backdrop that the Xing kilns in the North and the Yue kilns in the South emerged.

Excavated examples suggest that the Xiangzhou kilns, Gongyi kilns and Xing kilns started operation during the late Northern Dynasties period. The earliest white porcelains were invented during the firing of celadon. These white porcelains still showed the characteristics typical of celadon. Their white glaze often displayed a bluish-green tint (Cat. Nos. 296, 298). It replaced celadon as the dominant type of ceramics and laid the foundation for the advent of painted porcelain.

Celadons of the Western Jin, the Eastern Jin and the Southern Dynasties are collectively referred to as the "Six Dynasties celadon wares" or "early celadon". They were mainly produced in Shangyu, Yuyao, Cixi and Shaoxing in Zhejiang. The region was originally inhabited by the ancient Yue people. Production in this region started in the Shang and Zhou dynasties and continued through the Han, Three Kingdoms, Western and Eastern Jin, Southern Dynasties, Sui, Tang, Five Dynasties and Song dynasty. During the Tang dynasty, this region was under the jurisdiction of the Yuezhou commandery. As Tang kilns were named after the prefecture to which they belonged, these kilns were called the Yue kilns. "Yue wares" have been used by some ceramic historians to denote the entire line of porcelains produced in this region, from proto-porcelains to Yue celadons of the Song dynasty.

Buddhism flourished during the Six Dynasties (in

particular the Southern Dynasties) and reached the height of influence during the reign of Emperor Wudi (502–549 C.E.) of the Liang regime. It is mentioned in the Tang dynasty monk Falin's *Bianzhenglun* (Defending the Right) that there were 2846 monasteries and over 82700 monks during the Liang regime of the Southern Dynasties. Most members of the ruling class as well as the scholar-gentry were followers of Buddhism. Lotus petals, lotus blossoms, Buddhist images or attributes associated with the Buddha outnumbered other decorative motifs (Cat. No. 290).

Celadon granary jars also called "soul urns" (a type of funerary urn with sculpted decorations) are one of the most representative examples of Six Dynasties wares (Cat. Nos. 272, 273). They were widely used in the Wu State of the Three Kingdoms and the Western Jin and the Eastern Jin dynasties. The shape is derived from the five-mouthed jars of the Eastern Han period. A variety of decorative techniques were used on these wares and the decorations were elaborate and highly symbolic. Scenes depicting clan members celebrating a bumper harvest surrounded by an endless supply of livestock combine realism with the wishes and desires of the clan. The artistic value of these jars is beyond question. Most granary jars came from the Yue kilns but some also from the Wuzhou and Ou kilns.

Rooster-head ewers or *tianjihu* (divine rooster ewer) are also characteristic examples of this period (Cat. Nos. 289, 293). They first appeared in the late Three Kingdoms and were prevalent throughout the Western Jin, Eastern Jin, Sui and Tang dynasties. Ewers of this style decreased in number after the Zongzhang reign. Western Jin ewers have shorter bellies, small tails and no necks. By the time of the Eastern Jin period, necks

appeared and the tails replaced by a thick round handle that rises above the mouth rim of the ewers. The rooster's head can be hollow or solid. Some of these ewers were used as daily utensils while others mortuary objects. Handles with dragon heads and bear motif are found on later examples. They were mainly produced in the Yue kilns, the Deqing kilns, the Ou kilns and some Northern kilns. These vessels were also being made in the Northern kilns as evidenced by the discovery of a white porcelain rooster-head ewer unearthed from the tomb of Li Jingxun of the Sui dynasty in Xi'an. The Deqing kilns produced mainly black-glazed rooster-head ewers. The celadon rooster-head ewer unearthed from the tomb of Li Shuang in Xi'an was dated to the 1st year of the Zongzhang reign period (668 C.E.).

268
青釉虎头罐

三国

公元 220—280 年

越窑

高：21 厘米

口径：13 厘米

Celadon jar with tiger-head design

Three Kingdoms period

220 – 280 C.E.

Yue kilns

Height: 21 cm

Mouth diameter: 13 cm

短直颈微束，鼓腹，平底微内凹。肩部饰弦纹四道，上贴塑虎头和虎尾，惜虎尾已断，相对两侧置竖叶纹系。虎头清晰，竖耳，张嘴鼓睛，鼻孔上翻，獠牙外露，造型生动，颇具神韵。胎呈灰白色，质坚，叩之声音清越。施青釉，不及底，施釉颇均匀，肩及上腹部有缩釉现象。内壁无釉。外壁近底处和外底呈褐红色。

The jar has a short and slightly constricted neck and a swelling belly. Four rounds of indented lines encompass the shoulders while a pair of lugs with leaf motif is placed vertically on the shoulders. Halfway between the handles on one side is a tiger head in high relief. The tail on the other side is missing. The head is vividly depicted with pricked ears, a wide-open mouth, bulging eyes, flared nostrils and protruding fangs. The surface of the jar is evenly covered with a celadon glaze that stops short of the base. Retraction of glaze is noted around the shoulders and upper belly. The interior wall is bare of

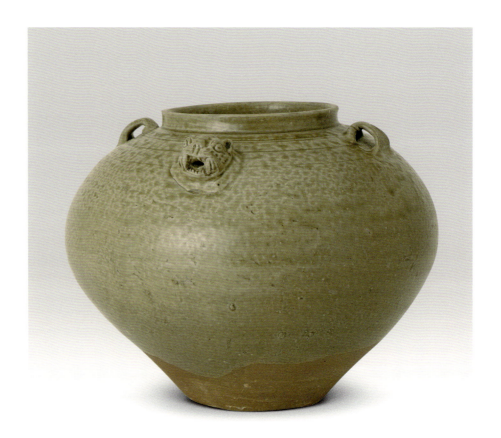

glaze, exposing the grayish white paste. It makes a ringing sound when struck. The unglazed area around the foot and the slightly recessed base have burnt brownish red.

269

青釉虎首双系罐

三国

公元 220—280 年

越窑

高：16.5 厘米

口径：10.6 厘米

Celadon jar with tiger-head design

Three Kingdoms period

220 – 280 C.E

Yue kilns

Height: 16.5 cm

Mouth diameter: 10.6 cm

本品与图录 268 号相似，只是体形较细小，虎尾完整。

This jar is similar to the last, Cat. No. 268, except that it is smaller and the tail is intact.

青釉三鸟钮盖盂

三国（吴）

公元 222—280 年

越窑

高：8.2 厘米

底径：8.1 厘米

Celadon lidded basin with knob in the shape of three birds

Three Kingdoms period (Wu)

222 – 280 C.E.

Yue kilns

Height: 8.2 cm

Base diameter: 8.1 cm

盂敛口，扁腹，圈足，底微内凹。口缘部分置对称四横系。器身饰菱形方格纹。伞形盖，以顶为中心竖向刻三组针刺纹线，把盖等分成三部分，依纹线方向堆塑三只头部相接触的小鸟作盖钮，三鸟扑翅交喙，手法简练，形象生动活泼，为整体造型起到妙笔点睛的作用。灰白色胎，质坚，细滑。通体施淡青釉。底部露胎，呈褐红色。

六朝时期陶瓷器上通常装饰的鸟，是与天上神灵沟通的媒介。此类盂的盖顶通常堆塑两只鸟，三只鸟的很少见。

偏安江南一隅的吴政权，社会、经济较稳定，陶瓷业得以发展，有不少精致细腻的作品，本品是其代表性的器物。

1979 年江苏省南京市幕府山三国吴墓出土有相似器物，现藏南京市博物馆。

The basin has an incurved mouth, an oblate belly and a ring foot. Four equally spaced loop lugs are set horizontally around the rim. The body is decorated with lozenge design. Three columns of small dots radiating from the tip of the parasol-shaped lid divide the lid into three segments. The knob features three birds with beaks touching, wings spreading and bodies straddling the upper ends of the dotted lines. The grayish white paste is fine, hard and smooth. The unglazed base with a slightly recessed center is brownish red in color. The entire exterior surface of the basin is covered with a light green glaze.

Six Dynasties ceramics are usually decorated with birds. They are seen as a medium between heaven and earth. Usually two birds are sculpted on the lid of this type of water basin. Lids with three birds are rare.

The Wu State enjoyed relative political, social and economic stability in the lower Changjiang River basin. Its ceramic industry made considerable progress and produced many exquisite works of art of which this piece is a representative example.

A similar vessel, now in the collection of the Nanjing Municipal Museum, was unearthed in 1979 from a tomb which belonged to the Wu State during the Three Kingdoms period in Mount Mufu in Nanjing, Jiangsu province.

青釉鸡首双系壶

西晋

公元 265—317 年

高：16.7 厘米

底径：10.5 厘米

Celadon jar with rooster-head design and double lugs

Western Jin dynasty

265 – 317 C.E.

Height: 16.7 cm

Base diameter: 10.5 cm

小口，短颈微束，上刻弦纹两道。圆球腹。高圈足外撇，上饰弦纹两周。口缘两侧置环形系一对。肩、腹间堆塑公鸡头，鸡冠高竖，圆目，张口作鸣叫状，相对侧贴鸡尾。罐作鸡身，造型新颖有趣。灰白胎。满施灰青釉，有缩釉现象。

鸡为古人所爱之物，以"鸡"为"吉"视之。

The jar has a small mouth, a short constricted neck with two rounds of indented lines, a globular body and a tall and splayed ring foot encircled by two grooves. A pair of loop lugs is set upon the shoulders. Halfway between them on one side of the upper belly is a rooster head with a high crest, circular bulging eyes and gaping mouth. On the opposite side is an appliqué rooster tail. The paste is grayish white in color. The entire surface is covered with a grayish green glaze. Retraction of glaze is noted.

Since the Chinese word for "rooster" (*ji*) is homophonous with the word for "good omen", the rooster is considered an auspicious bird in China.

272

青釉堆塑雀鸟家畜谷仓罐

西晋

公元 265—317 年

越窑

高：47.7 厘米

底径：16.8 厘米

Celadon granary jar with sculpted birds and animals

Western Jin dynasty

265 – 317 C.E.

Yue kilns

Height: 47.7 cm

Base diameter: 16.8 cm

器分上、下两部分，以一外侈折缘为分界。灰白胎，质坚。全器施青釉，釉色明亮青绿、润滑，腹下近底无釉。底平，露胎。器上部堆塑两层楼房，屋檐下两侧各贴一熊，用背顶着屋梁和斗拱，下层左右置门阙，四周堆塑吹笛、抚琴、吹笙、弹琵琶、击鼓、杂技等歌舞人物。在歌舞人物外侧，围以猪、牛、羊等家畜，或睡、或坐、或咬尾、亲昵、嬉戏，异常逼真，生动有趣，显示了当时的生活景象。楼房上方饰五小罐，正中罐高、口大，与下部器腹相通，周围四罐较短小，不通器腹。五罐四周满布群鸟，互相簇拥，引颈展翅，向上飞向罐口，争吃谷粮，表达了粮谷满仓、子孙繁衍、六畜兴旺、百鸟争食之美满幸福的愿望，有强烈的时代感。

器下部为一下窄上大之圆形腹，腹上部贴羽人乘神兽纹饰一周。

浙江西晋墓中谷仓罐出土较多。

The vessel is made up of two parts divided horizontally by a flared ridge. The upper part features a double-storied building with a pair of bears guarding the entrance on the ground floor and supporting the eaves with their napes. Another pair of bears are guarding the facade of the upper floor and supporting the bracket set under the projecting eaves with their napes. The front entrance of the house is flanked by pillars capped with a pyramidal roof. Clustering around the courtyard are musicians playing the flute, *qin-zither* (a plucking string instrument), *sheng* (a kind of reed pipe), *pipa* (also a plucking string instrument) and drum. There are also acrobats, singers and dancers. They are surrounded by domestic animals that are chasing or playing with each other. Above the building is a wide-mouthed jar with four miniature jars attached to its sides. Only the central jar is connected to the cavity of the vessel. A flock of birds is seen surrounding the five jars.

The lower part of the vessel features a bulbous belly that tapers down towards the base. The upper belly is encircled by appliqué figures of winged immortals riding on divine beasts. The grayish white paste displays a high degree of hardness. The entire upper section and the upper part of the lower section are covered with a smooth and lustrous bluish green celadon glaze. The lower belly and the flat base are bare of glaze.

Granary jars are quite common among grave goods excavated from the Western Jin tombs in Zhejiang.

273

青釉堆塑楼阁伎乐人谷仓罐

西晋

公元 265—317 年

越窑

高：47 厘米

底径：16.2 厘米

Celadon granary jar with sculpted house and performers

Western Jin dynasty

265 – 317 C.E.

Yue kilns

Height: 47 cm

Base diameter: 16.2 cm

器顶部雕塑一组多层亭台楼阁作盖，盖上四角置坞堡，开有瞭望孔。盖用泥团固定在五联罐正中罐上。正中罐较大，上方四周贴小罐四个。正中罐体一侧置另一两层楼房，中有庑殿式门楼，左、右饰肩檐，四周围以院墙。沿院墙堆塑一系列人物百戏，有奏乐的，有要技的，有狩猎的，五联罐四周堆贴雀鸟，百鸟云集，互相簇拥，引颈争食，一派谷粮盈廪、人丁兴旺的景象。器下部为一下窄上大之圆腹，满贴羽人乘神兽以及熊、龟、蛇、鱼、蟹、爬虫、铺首等，展示了一个神人杂处、光怪奇诞的世界。

谷仓罐上、下部以一道腰缘分隔开，好像是分开了不同的世界。腰缘以下为地下界，腰缘到中央五联罐口为人间界，而顶盖部分之亭台楼阁为人们追求的仙境一极乐世界。把天上与人间、空中的飞鸟、地上的动物和水中的游鱼、远古的神话和日常生活景象糅合在一起，反映了古人对死后羽化登仙的追求。胎灰白，质坚。全器施青釉。底平，露胎。

本品结构异常复杂、制作精巧、主次分明，错落有致，集模印、堆砌、塑、刻划、镂雕等多种技法，是当时成型最复杂、

装饰手法和表现内容最丰富的一种明器。

江西上虞市驿亭镇五夫西晋墓出土有相似器物，现藏上虞市文物管理所。

The upper section of the granary jar features a group of architectural structures. The lid is in the form of a fortress with watchtowers and loopholes in the enclosure walls. It is held in place by small lumps of clay resting on the rim of the jar. Below the rim are four miniature jars followed by a double-storied building behind a front gate flanked by two pillars capped with pyramidal roof. The courtyard within the enclosure wall is clustered with molded figures engaged in a wide range of activities including hunting, music playing and acrobatics. Together they evoke a vivid scene of bumper harvest. Above these figures is a flock of birds making their way up to the top of the granary. The lower section of the vessel has a bulbous belly and tapering sides. It is lavishly decorated with appliqué bears, tortoises, snakes, fish, crabs and reptiles, animal masks, and winged immortals riding on divine beasts.

A ridge above the shoulders acts as a demarcation between the upper and lower halves of the jar. The lower part, with the appliqué creatures, represents the afterlife. The section above the ridge but below the lid is the earthly domain and the architectural structures on top of the lid represents paradise. The grayish white paste is fine and hard. The entire vessel except the flat base is covered with celadon glaze.

This jar is a grand synthesis of various shaping techniques including molding, appliqué, pinching, sculpting, engraving and openwork. Of all the different kinds of grave goods from this period, granary jars are known to have the most elaborate shapes, most lavish decorations and richest narratives.

A similar jar has been unearthed from a Western Jin tomb at Wufu village in Yitingzhen, Shangyu, Zhejiang province. It is now in the collection of the Cultural Relics Administration Bureau in Shangyu, Zhejiang province.

青釉镂孔熏炉

西晋

公元 265—317 年

越窑

高：14.3 厘米

底径：14 厘米

Celadon censer with circular openwork design

Western Jin dynasty

265 – 317 C.E.

Yue kilns

Height: 14.3 cm

Base diameter: 14 cm

短颈，圆唇，鼓腹，平底，底心微凹。肩有弦纹四道，上置双系。腹部饰平行圆孔三周，每周十八孔，孔径按鼓腹大小而定，上、下两排较小，中间较大，每排圆孔以弦纹相间。胎质灰白，坚致。外壁施青釉，不及底，有泪釉痕。露胎处现浅褐色。近足底处有气泡向内、外侧隆起。制作工整，造型别致。在圆形、鼓腹的坯体上可以做出规律排列的圆孔，说明西晋时期镂孔技术已较为成熟。

The censer has a mouth with rounded lip, a short neck, a bulbous belly and a base with a slightly recessed center. The upper half of the body is covered with celadon glaze with streaks running down the belly. Four grooves encircle the shoulders; a pair of loop lugs is attached above. The belly is pierced with three orderly rows of openwork, each featuring eighteen holes separated by indented lines. The size of the holes is proportional to their position on the vessel. The largest holes are located at the widest part of the vessel. This goes to show that openwork technique was already quite mature during the Western Jin dynasty. The grayish white paste is hard and dense. The unglazed part revealed a light brown color. Air bubbles are visible near the outside and inside surface of the base.

275

青釉镂孔熏炉

西晋

公元 265—317 年

越窑

高：9.3 厘米

底径：10.2 厘米

Celadon censer with circular openwork design

Western Jin dynasty

265 – 317 C.E.

Yue kilns

Height: 9.3 cm

Base diameter: 10.2 cm

圆唇、短颈、鼓腹、底微内凹。肩饰弦纹两道，肩贴对称横耳一对。肩腹上下截平行圆孔三周，每周分别有孔 22 个、32 个和 32 个，周间以弦线纹分隔。胎灰白，坚致。外壁施青釉，施釉均匀。圈足露胎、微外撇。

The censer has a mouth with rounded lip, a short neck, a bulbous belly and a base with a recessed center. The exterior surface is covered with an even layer of celadon glaze. Two grooves encircle the shoulders; a pair of loop lugs is attached below. The shoulders and the upper belly are pierced with three rows of circular perforations divided by indented lines. The top row has twenty-two holes and the middle and bottom row has thirty-two each. The slightly splayed ring foot is unglazed. The grayish white paste is hard and dense.

青釉 "安成" 铭四系小盂

西晋

公元 265—317 年

高：5.8 厘米

底径：7.1 厘米

Small celadon basin with inscription

Western Jin dynasty

265 – 317 C.E.

Height: 5.8 cm

Base diameter: 7.1 cm

本品与图录 270 号外形和纹饰相同，但盖已失。外底内凹呈弧状，弧状底面上阴刻 "安成" 两字（查 "安成" 为西晋时郡名，位于今江西省新余市以西袁河流域）。除圈足底边和外底露胎处呈褐红色外，全器内外施青釉，釉色发黄泛青绿。

本品造型美观，系两侧与盂身接合处的胎泥上饰以爪纹，盂内也施青釉，制作精细并刻以地名，当为官家使用的器物，是一件很有历史价值的文物。

浙江省余姚市梁辉九顶山西晋太康八年（公元 287 年）墓出土有相似器物，但外底没有铭文，现藏余姚市文物保护管理所。

浙江省嵊州市浦口镇大塘岭西晋太康十一年（公元 290 年）墓出土有相似器物，但外底没有铭文，现藏嵊州市文物管理委员会。

This basin is similar to Cat. No. 270 in shape and decorative motifs except that the lid is missing. The entire vessel is covered with a yellowish celadon glaze with a greenish tint. The unglazed foot rim and base appear brownish red. The concave base is incised with two characters "Ancheng". It is the name of a county during the Western Jin dynasty. It is located in the present day Yuan River basin west of Xinyu City, Jiangxi province.

This basin is beautifully shaped. The area where the loop lugs meet the shoulders are embellished with claw motif. The interior of the basin is also coated with celadon glaze. The inscription identifying a specific location indicates that the vessel was made for government use. This is an artifact of great historic value.

A similar vessel but without inscription on the base was unearthed from a tomb at Mount Jiuding in Lianghui, Yuyao, Zhejiang province. The tomb is dated to the 8th year of the Taikang period (287 C.E.) of the Western Jin dynasty. It is now in the collection of the Yuyao Municipal Office of Cultural Relics Preservation and Administration.

Another example also without inscription on the base was discovered from a tomb at Datangling in Pukouzhen, Shengzhou, Zhejiang province. The tomb is dated to the 11th year of the Taikang period (290 C.E.). It is now in the collection of the Shangyu Municipal Office of Cultural Relics Preservation and Administration.

青釉辟邪烛台

西晋

公元 265—317 年

越窑

高：9.5 厘米

长：13.8 厘米

Pixie-shaped celadon candleholder

Western Jin dynasty

265 – 317 C.E.

Yue kilns

Height: 9.5 cm

Length: 13.8 cm

此器塑成狮头兽。兽头昂起、双目圆睁、双耳竖起、张口露齿。颌下有长须、项脊刻鬃毛、腹部两侧划羽翼、尾呈蕉叶状紧贴臀部、四足蜷于腹下。脊中部竖一管状插孔与腹部相通。灰白胎、质坚。施青釉、釉色淡绿泛黄、釉面滋润。

辟邪是古代传说中的一种神兽、形象凶猛、可避邪消灾。

浙江省余姚市梁辉九顶山西晋太康八年（公元 287 年）墓出土有相似器物、现藏余姚市文物管理所。

浙江省新昌县楼基西晋元康九年（公元 299 年）墓出土相似器物、现藏新昌县文物管理委员会。

The candleholder is in the shape of a lion-like beast. The tubular device inserted onto the back of the animal is connected to the hollow body. The grayish white paste is hard. The entire surface is covered with a smooth glaze of light green color with a yellowish tint.

The animal is called a *pixie*, a divine creature in Chinese mythology used to ward off evil and disasters.

A similar artifact was discovered in a tomb at Mount Jiuding in Lianghui, Yuyao, Zhejiang province. The tomb is dated to the 8th year of the Taikang period (287 C.E.) of the Western Jin dynasty. It is now in the collection of the Yuyao Municipal Office of Cultural Relics Preservation and Administration.

Another similar example was unearthed from a tomb at Louji, Xinchang, Zhejiang province. The tomb is dated to the 1st year of the Yuankang period (299 C.E.) of the Western Jin dynasty. It is now in the collection of the Cultural Relics Administrative Committee of Xinchang County.

青釉印纹簋

西晋

公元 265—317 年

越窑

高：11.8 厘米

口径：20.5 厘米

底径：14.4 厘米

Celadon bowl with molded motifs

Western Jin dynasty

265 – 317 C.E.

Yue kilns

Height: 11.8 cm

Mouth diameter: 20.5 cm

Base diameter: 14.4 cm

微折缘，扁腹，高圈足，足外撇，口和足下缘有弦纹数道。上、下腹部各模印联珠纹一周，中间饰以细斜方格纹，对称贴口衔环铺一对。内壁有弦纹数道，弦线间分别饰以联珠纹和星状水纹。灰白胎。内外施青釉，色调青中泛黄，釉面匀净光亮，满布开片纹。足内底部露胎。本品是西晋时期的代表作品。

浙江省上虞市蒿坝乡南穴村吴天纪元年（公元 277 年）墓出土有相似器物，现藏上虞市文物管理所。

The vessel has an angular rim, a squat belly and a tall ring foot. Several grooves encircle the mouth and foot rims. The belly is decorated with tiny lozenge checks and a band of continuous beads. A ringed animal-mask is set on both sides of the frieze. Bands of continuous beads and star-shaped wave motif encircle the interior wall of the vessel. The paste is grayish white in color. Both the interior and exterior surfaces are covered with a greenish celadon glaze with a yellowish tint. The glaze is smooth and full of crackles. The base enclosed by the ring foot is unglazed. This vessel is a typical example of Western Jin celadon.

A similar vessel has been unearthed from a tomb at Nanxue village in Haobaxiang, Shangyu, Zhejiang province. The tomb is dated to the 1st year of the Tianji period (277 C.E.) of the Wu dynasty. It is now in the collection of the Shangyu Municipal Office of Cultural Relics Preservation and Administration.

279

青釉褐斑四系罐

东晋

公元 317—420 年

越窑

高：19.5 厘米

底径：13.5 厘米

Celadon jar with brown spots and four lugs

Eastern Jin dynasty

317 – 420 C.E.

Yue kilns

Height: 19.5 cm

Base diameter: 13.5 cm

盘口，短直颈，斜肩，直腹，平底。盘口缘上饰对称褐斑六块。肩饰联珠纹两周，间以细斜方格纹带，贴四个对称系。灰白胎，质坚，细滑。通体施青釉，呈灰绿色，满布开片纹，有泪釉现象。釉不到底，底部露胎。本品继承西晋风格，只是稍有变化，应为东晋初期生产。

浙江省博物馆收藏有一件造型与本品相似的罐。

The jar has a plate-shaped mouth, a short straight neck, slanting shoulders and an almost cylindrical body. The shoulders are decorated with four loop lugs and two bands of continuous beads divided by a belt of tiny lozenge checks. The upper side of the plated mouth is adorned with six patches of brown mottling. The entire vessel is covered with a grayish green celadon glaze that stops short of the base. Crackles and tear marks are visible on the glaze. The grayish white paste is hard, smooth and refined. The flat base is unglazed. This jar should be dated to the early Eastern Jin period.

The Zhejiang Provincial Museum has a jar identical in shape to this one.

280

青釉卧羊

东晋

公元 317—420 年

越窑

高：16.2 厘米

长：13.2 厘米

Celadon crouching goat

Eastern Jin dynasty

317 – 420 C.E.

Yue kilns

Height: 16.2 cm

Length: 13.2 cm

羊作伏卧状，昂首鼓睛，眼睛上方刻眉毛，双角经耳后卷向近眼处。颌下有须，两耳横出，头上有一圆孔。背饰弦纹作脊，脊端贴短曲尾。腰部细小，突出腿臀部的丰满肌肉，手法夸张。整体匀称可爱。灰白色胎，致密坚实。通体施青釉，釉色莹润，釉面亮泽。此类器物自三国至东晋均有烧造。

羊是古人心目中的吉祥物，以"羊"为"祥"视之。

The sculpture features a crouching goat with a narrow waist and robust haunches. A hole is pierced on the top of the head. The grayish white paste is hard, dense and fine. The entire sculpture is coated with a translucent and lustrous celadon glaze. Goats in celadon glaze were made throughout the Three Kingdoms and Eastern Jin periods.

The Chinese word for "sheep/goat" is *yang*, which rhymes with the word for "auspicious", *xiang*. Thus, goats are considered to be lucky in China.

青釉蛙形双系壶

东晋

公元 317—420 年

越窑

高：15.6 厘米

口径：13.8 厘米

Celadon jar with double lugs and frog design

Eastern Jin dynasty

317 – 420 C.E.

Yue kilns

Height: 15.6 cm

Mouth diameter: 13.8 cm

直口、鼓腹、平底。颈和腹部饰弦纹数道、颈部对称贴竖系一对。器腹塑蛙首、蛙腿、蛙首阴刻弦纹二道为口。胎质灰白、质坚。施青釉、釉色青中带黄。口缘及蛙的两眼饰褐色斑点、增添了生命力、也使单一的青釉多了色彩变化。本品造型新颖有趣。

浙江省博物馆收藏有一件高 11.8 厘米、造型及褐斑与本品近乎一致的器物（浙江省博物馆：《青瓷风韵》、第 39 页、浙江人民美术出版社、1999 年）。

中国是一个传统的农业国家，南方地区有几千年栽种水稻的历史，青蛙在稻田里可以帮助农民消灭害虫，取得丰收；同时青蛙有极强的繁殖能力，与人们多子、多孙、多福的愿望相符，所以几千年来受到人们喜爱。

The jar has a straight mouth, a swelling belly and a flat base. Several incised lines encompass the neck and the belly and a pair of loop lugs is affixed vertically to the upper neck. The head, forelimbs and hind limbs of the frog are done with appliqués. The mouth rim of the jar and the eyes of the frog are highlighted in brown. The grayish white paste is hard. The entire surface is covered with a greenish celadon glaze with a yellowish tint. The shape is unique and interesting.

The Zhejiang Provincial Museum has a jar of identical shape with similar brown mottling but measures 11.8 cm in height (*Qingci fengyun* [The Charm of Celadons], Zhejiang Provincial Museum, Zhejiang People's Art Press, 1999, p.39).

China is an agrarian society where paddy cultivation has been practiced in the southern regions for millennia. Frogs help eliminate harmful pests in the fields, which is paramount to a good harvest. The Chinese revered the frog because it is a symbol of fertility and abundance.

282

青釉褐斑魂瓶

东晋

公元 317—420 年

越窑

高：39.8 厘米

阔：18.4 厘米

Celadon funerary urn with brown mottling

Eastern Jin dynasty

317 – 420 C.E.

Yue kilns

Height: 39.8 cm

Width: 18.4 cm

人字坡形屋顶为盖，与瓶身不相黏。屋脊两端置鸱头，褐斑点彩作眼，屋檐四周饰联珠纹。器身为三节葫芦形。瓶身上部呈直立内缩的长方形，下方底线印一列联珠纹，正中刻七级竖长方形门，由下而上刻数字一至七，门下贴拱形台阶一道，寓意踏上七级天阶便能到达极乐世界，显示出佛教对当时文化的影响。胎色灰白，胎质坚实润滑。平底露胎除底足外满施灰青釉，釉色明亮，釉面润泽，器身施褐彩斑点，极富装饰效果。此魂瓶造型新颖、端庄秀丽，颇为少见。

The lid in the form of a gabled roof can be detached from the body of the urn. A pair of owl heads with eyes highlighted by brown dots rises from the ends of the roof ridge. The edge of the eaves is engraved with continuous beads. The gourd-shaped urn has three bulbs. Except around the foot and the base, the entire surface is covered with a rich and lustrous grayish green glaze. The brown mottling adds variety to the otherwise monochrome palette. The structure on top has an oblong cross-section and tapering sides. The bottom of the structure is decorated with a frieze of continuous beads. The front door features seven rectangular frames engraved from bottom to top with the Chinese numerals "one" to "seven". There is a flight of steps in front of it. Paradise is just beyond the seven celestial steps marked on the wall. The influence of Buddhism is evident. The grayish white paste is hard and smooth. The flat base is unglazed. Funerary urn (or "soul urn") of such a unique and elegant shape is rare.

283

青釉羊首神鸟灯盏

东晋

公元 317—420 年

越窑

高（杯）：4 厘米

阔（连尾）：9.3 厘米

Bird-shaped celadon lamp bowl with goat head design

Eastern Jin dynasty

317 – 420 C.E.

Yue kilns

Height (cup): 4 cm

Width (including tail): 9.3 cm

直口，弧腹下斜收成平底。盏内底中央塑一昂首向左前望的羊头，羊角沿耳方向弯曲，合嘴，颔下长须。外壁口缘下饰弦纹一周。在与羊头同一方向的外壁上贴塑一带冠神鸟，头部高出口缘，张嘴睁眼向左望，双足上缩，羽毛下垂，展翅欲飞，生气盎然。神鸟头部相对侧外壁上饰高于口缘的翘尾为柄，盏体作身，构成鸟的整体。翅、尾刻直线纹，胸刻人字线纹，寥寥数道勾勒出鸟的羽毛。灰白胎，胎薄，质坚，细腻。内外施青釉，呈灰青色，外壁施釉不到底，施釉不均匀。

东晋时期，盏内、外同时塑贴动物的器物较少。

The lamp bowl has a straight mouth and convex sides that tapers towards a flat base. A goat with its head turned rises from the center of the bowl. An indented line runs around the outer wall below the rim. An appliqué of a celestial bird with circular eyes, open mouth, long neck and stretched wings decorates the exterior wall. A tail that is attached to the mouth rim on the opposite side serves as the handle. Incised striations and herringbone motif are visible on the tail and the wings respectively. The thinly potted cup has a hard and fine paste of grayish white color. Both the interior and exterior are coated with an uneven layer of grayish green glaze. The area around the foot is bare of glaze.

Vessels with sculpted or appliqué animals or birds on both the inside and outside are scarce among Easten Jin wares.

378　六朝瓷器　|　Porcelains of the Six Dynasties

青釉舞俑供盘

晋

公元 265—420 年

越窑

高（盘）：3.2 厘米

口径：15.5 厘米

Celadon tray with musicians and dancing figurines

Jin dynasty

265 – 420 C.E.

Yue kilns

Height (tray): 3.2 cm

Mouth diameter: 15.5 cm

圆形浅盘，圈足。盘内心刻莲花瓣纹五个，其上堆贴一猪、一羊和四个盛载鱼、糕点、蔬菜等食物的容器。盘内近边缘处堆塑十一个手持不同乐器以及歌唱的乐人，中心位置有两人在跳舞或在进行祭祀仪式。各人造型、动作均不相同，生动传神，可能是在进行祭祀或是庆祝丰收。灰白胎，质坚。除内底足外满施橄榄色青釉。

此器对研究晋人的生活习俗有参考价值，是一件十分珍贵的文物。

The circular tray with a ring foot has five lotus petals carved around its center. Miniature sculptures of a pig, a goat and four plates holding fish, pastries and vegetables are affixed to the center while eleven figurines stand near the edge of the tray. Some are singers while others are musicians holding different instruments. Closer to the center are two figurines in the act of dancing or performing a sacrificial ritual. All figurines are distinct from each other in appearance and posture. They are

probably worshipping their ancestors or celebrating a bumper harvest. The grayish white paste is hard. Except for the area enclosed by the foot, the entire vessel is covered with an olive green glaze.

The tray is an excellent reference for studying communal life in the Jin dynasty.

青釉博山炉

晋

公元 265—420 年

南台窑

高：17 厘米

阔（盆）：14 厘米

Mountain-shaped celadon censer

Jin dynasty

265 – 420 C.E.

Nantai kilns

Height: 17 cm

Width (basin): 14 cm

器分为盆托、腹和盖三部分，腹与托粘连。盖呈圆锥形，盖顶置锥形纽，下有圆孔四个，圆孔下盖面饰朝上的三角形凸起物三周，每周四个，相互交错相替，密而不乱。胎灰白，质硬。全器外壁施青釉，呈灰蓝色细碎雪花状。炉托平底露胎，部分呈火石红色，有旋纹痕。

博山炉是熏炉式样之一，仿汉代铜炉，流行于汉晋时期。秦汉时盛传东海有蓬莱等三座仙山，博山炉便是据此传说设计。炉盖高而尖，象征"三山"仙境。底盆可以盛水，象征海水。焚香时，烟从盖上圆孔冒出，云雾缭绕，有如仙境。

博山炉多在贵族墓中出现，反映了墓主人对长生不老的渴望。

The censer is made up of three sections, namely a tray, a body and a lid. The body and lid are attached to each other and inseparable. The mountain-like lid is surmounted by a nipple-shaped knob. There are four circular perforations surrounding the knob. The area below are decorated with twelve flame-like triangular protuberances arranged in three registers. The grayish white paste is hard. The entire exterior of the vessel is covered with a celadon glaze with grayish blue snowflake effect. The censer is supported by a tray with a flat base. The unglazed surface revealed a paste of burnt orange color.

Censers with mountain-shaped lids are prevalent during the Han and Jin periods. They are called *boshanlu*. The shape was modeled after the bronze censers of the Han dynasty. During the Qin and Han dynasties, it was widely believed that there were immortals living in the divine mountains of Penglai, Yingzhou and Fangzhang in the East Sea.

Boshanlu censers are mostly found in royal tombs and reflect the deceased's wish for everlasting life.

286

青釉虎子

晋

公元 265—420 年

南台窑

高：13 厘米

阔：12 厘米

Celadon pot in the shape of a mythical animal

Jin dynasty

265 – 420 C.E.

Nantai kilns

Height: 13 cm

Width: 12 cm

兽形器，昂首、张口、鼓目、耸耳、拱鼻、四足蜷于腹下，形似一只蹲伏的猛兽。器身饰圆条提梁，肩上部有一斜直筒口，素身。束腰圆筒形腹，前端较阔大、胸平，股微隆。灰白胎，质坚。通体施灰绿色釉，上满布灰蓝窑变釉色。

虎子，源于战国西汉时的铜虎子，用途说法不一，一为溺器，也有说为水器。

南台窑窑址在福建福州市。

The animal-shaped vessel has a wide-open mouth doubling as a spout, bulging eyes, pricked ears, a protruding snout and an overhead handle. The body resembles a dumb-bell with a constricted mid-section. Its wider end forms the broad, flat and slightly convex chest of the beast. Four limbs are tucked under the belly. The entire vessel is covered with a grayish green glaze with grayish blue mottling as a result of kiln transmutation. The grayish white paste is hard.

Pots of this shape were traditionally called *huzi*, literally "tiger". This pot is modeled after the bronze *huzi* pots of the Warring States period and Han dynasty. Their function is still contentious. They were probably used as chamber pots or water containers.

The Nantai kilns were located in Fuzhou, Fujian province.

287

青釉莲瓣烛台

南朝

公元 420—589 年

高：15.7 厘米

阔：14.2 厘米

Celadon candle stand with lotus design

Southern Dynasties

420 – 589 C.E.

Height: 15.7 cm

Width: 14.2 cm

底盘浅腹，侈口，直壁，平底。盘心起高台，上刻两层覆莲花瓣，顶立锥形八方形柱，柱中部两侧各贴一四瓣莲花，其上近柱顶两侧各置一环。柱顶立锥形花蕊。灰白胎，质硬。通体施淡绿色釉，底露胎无釉。此器刻工精细，花瓣体薄，整体造型优美，是南朝福建地区的青瓷产品，较长江下游的青瓷时代要晚一些。

The base of the stand is in the shape of a shallow dish with a flared mouth, straight sides and a flat base. From the center of the dish rises a tapering octagonal pillar with a circular base decorated with double layers of inverted lotus petals. The pillar is flanked by a pair of four-petalled lotus blossoms carved in the round and a pair of rings. The top of the pillar is adorned with a conical stamen. The entire surface is covered with a pale green glaze. The flat base is unglazed exposing a grayish white paste. The lotuses are exquisitely carved with thin and delicate petals. This belongs to the celadon tradition of the Fujian region during the Southern Dynasties which is preceded by the celadon tradition of the Lower Changjiang River basin.

288

青釉烛台

南朝

公元 420—589 年

高：16 厘米

阔：13 厘米

Celadon candle stand

Southern Dynasties

420 – 589 C.E.

Height: 16 cm

Width: 13 cm

本品造型与图录 287 号相似，只是盘中圆柱体顶上立的是一只展翅欲飞的鸟。

This candle stand is similar to the last, Cat. No. 287, in shape except that the pillar is surmounted by a small bird.

289

黑釉双鸡首龙柄壶

南朝

公元 420—589 年

德清窑

高：38.8 厘米

底径：13.1 厘米

Black-glazed ewer with dragon handle and double rooster-head design

Southern Dynasties

420 – 589 C.E.

Deqing kilns

Height: 38.8 cm

Base diameter: 13.1 cm

盘口、细颈、丰肩，直腹往下缓慢收束，下腹较瘦、平底，有垫烧痕。肩部竖立两直颈鸡首流，竖冠、圆嘴、睁眼，流与壶体不相通。鸡首相对一侧塑双股龙首柄，龙嘴咬着壶口。肩部另两侧置桥形系各一。浅灰色胎，质细滑，底呈褐红色。满施黑釉，釉色均匀，釉面明亮，有开片纹。器形拔挺、秀丽。

此类黑釉鸡首壶在浙江省德清窑烧造。德清窑同时烧青釉与黑釉瓷器，但以黑瓷著名。由于釉内所含氧化铁及钛成分不一，烧成气氛不同，烧成后呈青色或黑色。通常釉料中氧化铁含量较高（4%–9% 以上），釉层有一定厚度，烧成后呈黑色。

德清窑双鸡首壶存世不多，如本品釉色之佳、体型之高大者则更少。

1972 年南京化纤厂东晋墓出土了一件青瓷鸡首壶，底部刻"罂主姓黄名齐之"铭，可知晋时称此类器形为"罂"。

The ewer has a plate-shaped mouth, a slender neck, broad shoulders and a deep belly that tapers towards a flat base with fireclay marks. On the shoulders is a mock spout in the shape of twin rooster heads, each with a long neck, an upright crest, a circular mouth and wide-open eyes. The double-stranded handle features a dragon with its mouth holding onto the rim of the plate-shaped mouth. Halfway between the spout and the handle on each side of the shoulders is a bridge-shaped angular lug denoting the wings of the rooster. The surface is covered with an even layer of lustrous black glaze with crackles. The light gray paste is hard and refined. The base has burnt to a brownish red.

This kind of black-glazed ewer with rooster-head design was produced at the Deqing kilns in Zhejiang. These kilns began operation during the Han dynasty, became well developed in the Jin dynasty and gradually declined during the Sui and Tang periods. The Deqing kilns produced both celadon and black ware but the latter is better known. The amount of iron oxide and titanium oxide contained in the glaze as well as the kiln atmosphere determined whether the glaze appeared green or black. Black glaze can be achieved if the iron oxide content is relatively high (from 4 to over 9 percent) and the glaze is thick enough.

Examples of rooster-head ewers from Deqing kilns are scarce in number. Examples as massive as the present piece with such exquisite glaze color are very rare.

A celadon rooster-head ewer was unearthed in 1972 from an Eastern Jin tomb in Nanjing. The base is inscribed, "The owner of this *ying* vessel is called Huang Qizhi". Thus, this type of ewer was also known as *ying* during the Jin period.

290

青釉莲瓣纹带托碗

南朝

公元 420—589 年

洪州窑

通高：10.7 厘米

口径（托）：23.5 厘米

**Celadon cup and saucer with
lotus petal motif**

Southern Dynasties

420 – 589 C.E.

Hongzhou kilns

Overall height: 10.7 cm

Mouth diameter (stand): 23.5 cm

全器由莲瓣纹碗和托盘组成。碗平口微
敛，口缘下有凹弦纹两道，实足，足心
微内凹。碗外饰双托莲瓣纹六片，瓣纹
凸起。八棱托盘敞口，实圈足，底心微
内凹。盘内壁刻双托莲瓣纹八片，与棱
口相对，外壁光素无纹。盘心正中有一
凸起圆环，用以承托碗。碗和托盘是先
剔地再刻莲纹，具浮雕感。米黄色胎，
质坚、细腻，胎骨厚重。施黄绿色透明釉，
釉色金黄泛绿，釉层肥厚，釉面玻璃质
感强、晶莹通透、宝光四射，开细碎冰
裂纹片。碗和托盘底足无釉。本品制作
精细，造型、胎料、修坯、釉色、装饰、
烧制都一丝不苟，尽善尽美。

南朝佛法兴盛，统治阶层和一般文人学
士都信奉佛教，本品应是上层礼佛人士
使用的一件珍贵器物。

1975 年江西吉安出土有相似器物，现藏
江西省博物馆。

洪州窑位于江西省清丰山溪、药湖岸畔，
因此地唐代属洪州而得名。

Both the cup and the saucer are decorated

with lotus petal motif. The cup has a
slightly incurved mouth with two rounds
of grooves below the external rim. The
solid foot is slightly recessed in the center.
The exterior wall is decorated with six
lotus petals in low relief. The saucer has an
eight-lobed mouth and a solid foot with
a slightly recessed center. The interior
wall is decorated with eight lotus petals.
A ridge encircles the center of the saucer
for holding the cup in place. The exterior
wall of the tray is undecorated. The lotus
petals on the cup and saucer are engraved
on a planed ground. The rice yellow glaze
is hard, smooth and refined. The body is
thick and heavy. The cup and saucer are
covered with transparent yellowish green
glaze. The glaze is thick, transparent and

highly lustrous with tiny crackles. The base
of the cup and saucer is unglazed.

Buddhism enjoyed popularity during
the Southern Dynasties. Members of the
ruling class and the scholar-gentry were
keen followers. This present cup and saucer
set would have been among the precious
Buddhist ritual wares used by the elite.

A similar vessel, now in the collection
of the Jiangxi Provincial Museum, was
unearthed in 1975 from Ji'an, Jiangxi
province.

The Hongzhou kilns were located along
the shores of the Qingfengshan Stream
and Yaohu Lake in Jiangxi.

291

青釉莲瓣纹博山炉

南朝

公元 420—589 年

洪洲窑

高：15.9 厘米

阔：11.7 厘米

Mountain-shaped celadon censer with lotus petal design

Southern Dynasties

420 – 589 C.E.

Hongzhou kilns

Height: 15.9 cm

Width: 11.7 cm

浅腹平底盘，中起束腰圆柱座，上立层层叠叠、向上拔挺、微向内斜的莲瓣，寓意高耸入云的仙山，顶部立一只展翅欲飞的仙鸟。炉前开一梯形小孔。灰白胎，质坚。施青釉，釉色呈青黄，开冰裂纹片，玻璃质感强。

本品造型独特、设计巧妙，炉中冉冉上升的烟气可直达天庭，仙鸟则作为媒介向上苍传达人们的愿望。

The censer has a waisted pedestal and a tray with a flat base. Rising high from the pedestal are overlapping lotus petals. The top of the censer is decorated with a small bird with spreading wings. The front of the censer has a small trapezoidal opening. The grayish white paste is hard. The exterior of the censer is covered with a crackled greenish yellow glaze with a highly lustrous surface.

It was believed that the smoke emitted from a censer could reach up to the heavens and that the divine bird is a medium between heaven and earth.

292

青釉六系盆口壶

南朝

公元 420—589 年

洪州窑

高：40.5 厘米

Celadon jar with plate-shaped mouth and six lugs

Southern Dynasties

420 – 589 C.E.

Hongzhou kilns

Height: 40.5 cm

盘口，束颈，溜肩，平底。肩部贴六个桥形系，两对双系和两个单系相间。盆口下方有对称环坠耳系。浅灰色胎，质厚重。釉呈黄绿色，玻璃质感强，开细碎冰裂纹片。

一般来说，洪州窑烧成温度较低，胎釉结合不够紧密，出土器物多有脱釉现象，而本品体形硕大、线条优美、釉光莹润、弥足珍贵。

The jar has a plate-shaped mouth, a constricted neck, slanting shoulders and a flat base. The shoulders are decorated with a pair of double lugs and a pair of single lugs. The light gray paste is thick and heavy. The vessel is covered with a lustrous yellowish green glaze. Crackles are found on the surface.

Hongzhou wares were generally fired to a relatively low temperature. The paste did not sinter well with the glaze, which is prone to flaking. The present jar is noted for its majestic build, bold shape, elegant lines and lustrous glaze.

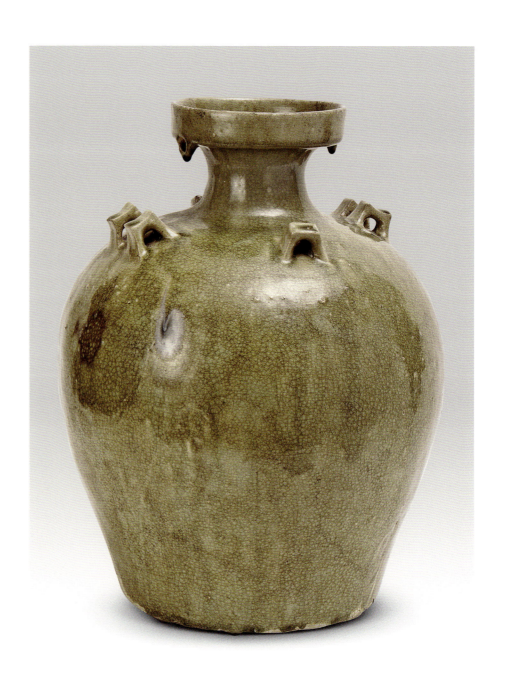

293
青釉莲瓣纹双鸡首壶

南朝

公元 420—589 年

洪州窑

高：34.2 厘米

底径：15.2 厘米

Celadon ewer with lotus motif and double rooster-head design

Southern Dynasties

420 – 589 C.E.

Hongzhou kilns

Height: 34.2 cm

Base diameter: 15.2 cm

浅盘口，细长颈，斜肩，肩和上腹圆鼓，下腹收束，到近底处外撇，平底。肩部并排斜立直颈鸡首一对，与壶身并不相通，相对一侧置龙首弧柄，另两侧饰桥形系。肩、腹间刻覆莲瓣纹一周。胎浅灰白色，质坚细滑。施釉到底，有流釉现象，釉色青绿，玻璃质感强，满布细密纹片。底露胎处呈淡红色，有垫烧残渣。青瓷双鸡首壶较为少见。

The ewer has a plate-shaped mouth, a long and slender neck, sloping shoulders, a bulbous upper belly, a tapering lower belly, a slightly splayed foot and an unglazed flat base exposing a pink paste with fireclay marks. Two mock spouts in the shape of rooster heads with long necks are affixed to the shoulders. A dragon's head handle connects the mouth to the shoulders. Halfway between the handle and the spout on either side of the shoulder is a bridge-shaped angular lug. The widest part of the body is carved with a round of lotus petals. The entire vessel including the foot is covered with a lustrous green crackled glaze. Running of glaze is noted on the surface. The grayish white paste is hard, smooth and refined. Celadon ewers with double rooster heads are quite rare.

294

青釉双鸡首龙柄壶

南朝

公元 420—589 年

洪州窑

高：40 厘米

底径：15.3 厘米

Celadon ewer with dragon handle and double chicken-head design

Southern Dynasties

420 – 589 C.E.

Hongzhou kilns

Height: 40 cm

Base diameter: 15.3 cm

盘口，长颈，溜肩，腹略鼓，下腹内收，近底处外撇，底平。颈肩交界处压弦纹一周。肩部竖立并排直颈鸡首两个，鸡首高冠、圆口，与壶不相通。肩部鸡首相对侧置龙首双柄，寓作鸡尾。肩左右贴桥形方系各一，寓作翅膀。胎呈灰白色，颇厚重。满施青黄色釉，釉面开纹片。器体下半部有脱釉现象，可能曾长期被泥土掩埋。本品体形丰满，形态活泼可爱，为洪州窑上乘之作。

The ewer has a plate-shaped mouth, a long neck, slanting shoulders, a rounded belly and a flat base. A groove encircles the lower part of the neck. On the shoulders stand two mock spouts in the shape of rooster heads with a high crest and a circular mouth opening. A double-stranded handle with a dragon's head on top denoting the tail of the rooster connects the mouth to the shoulders. Halfway between the handle and the spout on both sides of the shoulders is a bridge-shaped angular lug. The grayish white paste is relatively thick and heavy. The ewer is covered with a crackled greenish yellow glaze with flaking on the lower belly, probably due to burial. This vessel is a fine example from the Hongzhou kilns.

295

青釉莲纹碗

北朝

公元 386—581 年

高：7.6 厘米

口径：15.5 厘米

Celadon bowl with lotus motif

Northern Dynasties

386 – 581 C.E.

Height: 7.6 cm

Mouth diameter: 15.5 cm

灰白胎，稍粗糙坚硬。器内外施青釉，釉色泛浅青灰，满布细碎纹片。器身刻双层仰莲瓣纹。饼状足，底无釉、微内凹，造型规整。

The bowl has a rather hard and coarse paste of grayish-white color. The exterior and interior surface of the vessel is covered with finely crackled celadon glaze showing a greenish-gray tint. The exterior wall is carved with a double layer of lotus petal motif. The a disc-like solid foot and the slightly domed base are unglazed. The bowl is neatly potted.

296

白釉盘口壶

北朝

公元 386—581 年

巩义窑

高：32.3 厘米

口径：9.2 厘米

底径：11.8 厘米

Vase with plate-shaped mouth with white glaze

Northern Dynasties

386 – 581 C.E.

Gongyi kilns

Height: 32.3 cm

Mouth diameter: 9.2 cm

Base diameter: 11.8 cm

盘口，唇外卷，颈短，器体呈胆状。颈、肩和腹中部各刻弦纹三组，每组有弦纹三道。底平，外侧有凹弦纹一周，底中部内凹约 1 毫米。胎厚重，色灰白，质较粗。器身敷一层白色化妆土，全器内外满施乳浊釉。外壁满挂一条条由上而下的凝脂状泪釉痕，泪釉痕和釉厚处呈青绿色，釉薄处呈白色和米黄色。内壁釉层较薄，凝脂状滴痕较外壁少，由于未敷白色化妆土，故色泽偏青。釉开片，片纹较大。底施釉，有三支烧钉残痕，呈"品"字形的分布方法与图录 160 号东汉绿釉盖樽和 171 号北朝绿釉唾壶相同。

本品器形端庄，线条流畅，本为瑕疵的泪釉痕却起到了特殊的装饰效果，为早期白瓷的优秀作品。

The vase has a plate-shaped mouth with everted rim, a short neck and a bladder-shaped body. The thick and heavy grayish white paste is rather coarse in grain. The exterior surface is coated with a layer of white slip while the entire vessel including the interior is covered with an opalescent glaze. The glaze streaks on the outside have a greenish tint while the glaze appears white and yellowish where it runs thin. The glaze on the interior wall is relatively thin. It forms fewer globules than the exterior wall and looks greenish due to the absence of white slip. Large crackles are found in the glaze. The neck, shoulders and mid-section of the belly are encircled by three groups of cord motif. The base is flat and slightly recessed. A groove runs around the outer base. The arrangement of the spur marks forming the three points of a triangle on the glazed base is identical to Cat. Nos. 160, 171.

The vessel is noted for its elegant shape, fluid silhouette and the unique decorative effect of the glaze streaks. This vessel is a fine example of early white porcelain.

297

白釉鱼篓形罐

北齐—隋

西元 550—618 年

巩义窑

高：16.3 厘米

底径：14.9 厘米

White-glazed jar in the shape of a fish basket

Northern Qi – Sui dynasty

550 – 618 C.E.

Gongyi kilns

Height: 16.3 cm

Base diameter: 14.9 cm

口微外卷，短束颈，肩以下渐广到底，形似鱼篓。胎洁白细腻，有粉质感。器身外壁先敷薄薄一层白色化妆土，再罩透明釉。釉色洁白，釉面微泛银光，聚釉处见白中泛青和闪黄。底平无釉，底边缘斜削一圈。本器修坯精细，造型稳重，端庄优雅，是早期北方白瓷的代表作品。

本品口缘呈圆唇形，应该不带盖，很可能是皇室订制的礼佛用具。

巩义窑始烧于南北朝，发展于隋，兴盛于唐，式微于宋金。窑址主要分布在大、小黄冶、白河和铁匠炉等地。

The jar has a slightly out-rolling mouth rim, a short constricted neck and a body that gradually widens from the shoulders down to the base. Its shape resembles a fish basket. The glaze appears greenish or yellowish where it pools. The fine white paste has a powdery touch. The exterior surface is coated with a transparent glaze over a layer of white slip. The glaze is pure and white and has a faint silvery iridescent luster. The unglazed base has a beveled rim. The jar is finely trimmed and majestically shaped. This vessel is a representative example of early Northern white porcelain.

The lipped mouth suggests that this jar was not made with a lid. This jar could have been a Buddhist ritual utensil commissioned by the imperial houses.

The Gongyi kilns started production during the Northern and Southern Dynasties, progressed during the Sui dynasty, flourished during the Tang period and declined during the Song and Jin dynasties. The kiln sites were mainly distributed around the areas of Dahuangye, Xiaohuangye, Baihe and Tiejianglu.

298

白釉大罐

南朝

公元 420—589 年

洪州窑

高：34.8 厘米

口径：10.9 厘米

底径：13.7 厘米

Large jar with white glaze

Southern Dynasties

420 – 589 C.E.

Hongzhou kilns

Height: 34.8 cm

Mouth diameter: 10.9 cm

Base diameter: 13.7 cm

口缘微外侈、颈微束、斜肩、底足外撇、平底实足。胎褐、粗糙。全器覆盖一层白色化妆土、釉有光泽、呈乳浊的白色、淡青和米黄色、向底足流淌、肩和近底处有凝脂状泪釉痕。除滴痕处外、其余部分釉薄、见细碎冰裂纹。底无釉、留有垫饼残渣、与东汉釉陶底部的垫饼残渣相似。

The jar has a slightly flared mouth, a constricted neck, slanting shoulders, a solid splayed foot and a flat base. The brown paste is coarse in grain and the entire surface is coated with white slip. The opalescent glaze appears lustrous and takes on shades of white, pale blue and pale yellow. It runs thinly over the vessel surface and collects into thick globules on the shoulders and near the base. Tiny crackles are visible on the surface. The fireclay remnants on the unglazed base are similar to those found on Eastern Han glazed pottery.

隋唐五代瓷器

Porcelains of the Sui, Tang and Five Dynasties

隋唐五代瓷器：

高雅含蓄

公元 581 年，隋文帝定都大兴城，结束了自西晋末年以来近 300 年的分裂局面。为巩固统治，隋文帝推行了一系列发展经济、缓和社会矛盾的政策，南北各地经济文化及工艺技术交流频繁，社会安定繁荣。隋朝虽然只有 37 年，但青瓷、白瓷、酱黄釉瓷的生产远远超过三国两晋南北朝时期。

公元 618 年，唐朝立国。经过近一个世纪的治理，其农业、手工业、商业和海外贸易得到空前的发展，社会安定，经济繁荣，教育文化昌盛，国力强大。隋唐时期，陶瓷手工业出现繁荣局面，陶瓷艺术也以崭新的面貌展现在世人面前。

中国南方一直以生产青瓷为主，这与当地的地理条件、烧制工艺、文化传统、审美观念等有直接关系。南方青瓷秉持无欲淡泊、修身养性的传统，造型精巧玲珑，巧意雕琢，讲究青绿釉色和行云流水的纤细花纹装饰。北方则继承黄土文化的深厚传统，产品雄放壮美，色彩对比强烈，以白瓷占据主流，形成"南青北白"的局面。

唐时，南方以越窑为代表的青瓷生产蓬勃发展，除越窑以外还有婺州窑、瓯窑、岳州窑、寿州窑、洪州窑、衢州窑、长沙窑、成都青羊宫窑等都生产青瓷。越窑工艺居群窑之首，出现了为宫廷烧"秘色瓷"的贡窑，唐代诗人用"千峰翠色""嫩荷含露""古镜破苔"来形容它的美。

同时期，北方以邢窑为代表的白瓷在社会上产生广泛的影响，邢窑与越窑一道成为进献宫廷的贡品，陆羽在《茶经》中虽然褒越贬邢，但也以"如银类雪"来称赞邢窑。

白瓷在北朝时期开始出现，是在烧制青瓷的基础上发展而来的。北朝晚期已能烧制较为

成熟的白瓷器物，隋朝是白瓷的发展期，唐代进入繁盛期。隋唐时期的白瓷窑址有巩义窑、邢窑和曲阳窑，生产有不少灵巧清绮之作品（图录 302 号、303 号、304 号）。1982 年和 1984 年，考古工作者分别在河北临城县陈刘庄和河北内丘县城郊发现了隋代烧造白瓷的窑址，二者都属于唐代邢窑的前身。窑址资料显示，邢窑也分精粗。粗白瓷多施洁白的化妆土护胎。精细白瓷一般不施化妆土，白得纯净高雅，以端庄的造型、流畅的线条、精湛的工艺取胜。此外河南的相州窑、鹤壁集窑、西关窑、荥阳窑，山西的浑源窑、平定窑，陕西的黄堡窑，安徽的萧县窑等也生产白瓷。

除青瓷、白瓷外，青瓷釉下彩在湖南长沙窑、衡阳窑及四川邛崃窑中广泛生产，用以氧化铜、氧化铁为呈色剂的彩料在胎体上画出褐、绿彩画。长沙窑、邛崃窑釉下彩突破了青瓷的单一色调，为后来彩瓷的发展开了先河。

唐朝的青瓷、白瓷、花瓷、釉下彩瓷、黑瓷、酱黄釉瓷等品种蓬勃发展，大量生产和外销，瓷器在人们生活中的使用范围更加广泛。唐文化的遗址和墓葬，甚至一些规模不大的墓葬都出土有瓷器。沿海港口城市和岛屿也较常出土唐代瓷器。在东北亚的日本、朝鲜，南亚的巴基斯坦、印度、斯里兰卡，东南亚各国，中东各国，非洲东部和北部，以及欧亚之间的伊斯坦布尔，即陆上、海上丝绸之路沿线的文化遗址都发现有唐朝的瓷器。唐文化博大精深，瓷器艺术绚丽多姿，其继承性、传播性和对外来艺术的吸收性，充分体现出独特的时代特点。

五代十国时期（公元 907—960 年），社会经济发展到较高的层次，新兴城市涌现，商人和市民阶层势力较强，经济贸易和文化交流活跃，海外贸易、海船航行能力都远远超过

以前。虽然战争频繁，但新建的小国经济仍然在向前发展。例如钱镠建立的吴越国发展农业、商业和手工业，尤其注重发展以越窑为首的瓷器手工业。越窑青瓷在生产数量、器物种类以及精细刻花、镂空、划花和仿金银装饰方面都超过唐朝。秘色瓷的生产也较晚唐多。其他各个窑口的青瓷生产基本没有衰落，有的还有相当大的发展，如耀州窑受越窑工艺的影响烧出薄胎青瓷（图录337号），完全改变了唐时面貌。也就在此时，南方窑口突破"南青北白"的局面，南唐烧造出南方最早期的优质白瓷（图录344号）。

Porcelains of the Sui, Tang and Five Dynasties:

Elusive Elegance

In 581 C.E. Emperor Wendi of the Sui dynasty made Daxing (present day Xi'an) his capital, thus ending the fragmentation era that lasted for almost 300 years since the Western Jin dynasty. To consolidate his rule, Emperor Wendi implemented a series of policies to promote economic growth and ease social conflicts. This resulted in frequent economic, cultural and technological exchanges between the northern and southern regions. Despite the short span of the Sui dynasty, celadons, and soy-glazed wares that were produced within these thirty-seven years far surpassed those of the Three Kingdoms period, Western and Eastern Jin dynasties, and the Northern and Southern Dynasties.

Founded in 618 C.E., the Tang dynasty saw great progress in agriculture, commerce and overseas trade. This is one of the most glorious epochs in the history of China. Pottery making saw unprecedented growth and new aesthetics emerged during the Sui and Tang periods.

Celadon was the dominant type of ceramics in southern China. This is directly related to the unique geographical conditions, firing techniques, and the kiln structure as well as the lifestyle, customs and aesthetics of the people. Southerners who sought wellness and a tranquil way of life preferred the color green while Northerners favored white porcelains with their bold shapes and majestic presence.

During the Tang dynasty, Yue wares from southern China became more and more refined. Apart from the Yue kilns, celadons were also produced at these kilns: Wuzhou, Ou, Yuezhou, Shouzhou, Hongzhou, Quzhou, Changsha, and Qingyang (in Chengdu). The finest examples are from the Yue kilns that also produced a kind of tribute celadon known as *miseci* ("secret color porcelains"). Tang poets described the green glaze color of this tribute ware as "the green of a thousand peaks" or "tender lotus blossoms soaked with dew".

Meanwhile, the influence of Xing wares from northern China was widespread. In his book *Chajing* (Classic of Tea), the famous Tang scholar and tea connoisseur Lu Yu, described Xing wares as "like silver, like snow" although he did betrayed his preference for Yue wares. Both Xing and Yue wares were tribute items.

White porcelains developed on the foundation laid by celadons first appeared during the Northern Dynasties. The successful production of white wares was already achieved towards the end of the Northern Dynasties. They continued to develop during the Sui dynasty and flourished during the Tang period. During the Sui and Tang periods, white wares were made at the Gongyi kilns, Neiqiu kilns, Xing kilns (in Lincheng) and Quyang kilns in Hebei (Cat. Nos. 302, 303, 304). In 1982 and 1984, Sui kilns producing white wares were discovered at Chenliuzhuang in Lincheng county and in the suburbs of Neiqiu county, both in Hebei. These kilns are the forerunners of the Tang dynasty Xing kilns system. Archaeological records revealed that Xing white wares came in two categories – the coarse and the fine. The coarse ones usually have a body coated with a layer of white slip; the fine ones have no such coating. Other kilns that also produced white wares were the Xiangzhou kilns, the Hebiji kilns, the Xiguan kilns and the Xingyang kilns in Henan; the Hunyuan kilns and the Pingding kilns in Shanxi the Huangbao kilns in Shaanxi; and the Xiaoxian kilns in Anhui.

Besides celadons and white wares, painted underglaze wares were widely produced in the Changsha and Hengyang kilns in Hunan and the Qionglai kilns in Sichuan. Brown and green pigments derived respectively from copper and iron were used to sketch out designs directly on the body of the vessels, sometimes accompanied by a few lines of poetry. Painted underglaze wares from the Qionglai kilns and Changsha kilns are a breakthrough to the monochrome palette of celadons, clearing the path for the development of painted porcelains.

Celadons, white porcelains, polychrome porcelains, painted underglaze porcelains, and black-glazed and soy-glazed porcelains of the Tang dynasty saw rapid growth and many were produced and exported. Artifacts have been unearthed from Tang cultural sites and even some small tombs in the inland regions as well as coastal ports and offshore islands. They are also found in Japan and Korea in Northeast Asia; Pakistan, India and Sri Lanka in South Asia; Southeast Asia, Middle East, East Africa and North Africa; Istanbul at the junction of Asia and Europe, and even cultural sites along the transcontinental and maritime Silk Road.

The Five Dynasties (907–960 C.E.) is a period of sophisticated social and economic development. New cities sprung up, the merchant class rose in power and trade and commerce thrived. Overseas trade flourished because oceangoing ships were able to make much longer voyages. Despite frequent warfare, the newly founded states enjoyed an economic boom. Qian Miao, founder of the Wuyue State, devoted much of his attention to the development of agriculture, handicraft and commerce, and in particular the ceramic industry exemplified by the Yue kilns. Yue celadons surpassed its Tang predecessor in quantity, range and decorative techniques during this period. Output of *mise* porcelains outnumbered that of the late Tang period. Celadons produced in other kilns also made great advances. For example, the thinly potted celadon from the Yaozhou kilns (Cat. No. 337) changed the face of Tang ceramics. The earliest high-quality white porcelain from the Southern Tang dynasty also emerged during this time (Cat. No. 344).

白釉四系盖罐

隋

公元 581—618 年

巩义窑

高：32 厘米

底径：11.5 厘米

White-glazed lidded jar with four lugs

Sui dynasty

581 – 618 C.E.

Gongyi kilns

Height: 32 cm

Base diameter: 11.5 cm

短颈，最大腹径在器体中部。肩贴条状双系四个。平底，假圈足微外撇，底足边缘斜削一周。口上有倒置的浅碗状宝珠纽盖。灰白胎、质硬、胎体厚重。外壁施半截白泛淡青色釉，釉面开细纹片，内壁荡一层褐黄色釉。内壁施釉，说明本品是日用器具。本品线条优美流畅，器体上、下部配搭得宜。根据器体和系的形状、釉色和釉面开片纹，以及带有一点早唐的特征来判断，本品为隋晚期佳作。

北朝至唐代前期大型墓葬中发现的白釉大件器物往往只施半釉，这是北朝施釉方法的延续，到盛唐以后逐渐减少。

The jar has a short neck and a bulbous belly. Four equally spaced double-strand loop lugs are set around the shoulders. The slightly splayed foot has a flat solid base with a beveled rim. The lid resembling an inverted bowl is surmounted by a pearl knob. The grayish white paste is hard, thick and heavy. The upper half of the body is covered with a white glaze with a pale greenish tint and tiny crackles. The interior is coated with a layer of brownish yellow glaze. The glazed interior suggests that this jar was used as an everyday utensil. The shape of the jar, the design of the lugs, the glaze color and the pattern of the crackles already bear some of the features of early Tang wares. Therefore, this exquisite jar should be dated to the late Sui dynasty.

Large vessels unearthed from Northern Dynasties to early Tang tombs are often only half-glazed which is a glazing method passed on from the Northern Dynasties. This glazing style slowly faded out after the High Tang period.

300

青釉盘口四系壶

隋

公元 581—618 年

高：36 厘米

底径：9.5 厘米

Celadon vase with plate-shaped mouth and four lugs

Sui dynasty

581 – 618 C.E.

Height: 36 cm

Base diameter: 9.5 cm

盘口，长直颈，肩上贴四系，圆腹斜收到底。底平，底外缘微向外凸出。灰白胎。口内侧、器身外壁和外底先涂一层浅酱褐釉，再罩上青釉，釉不到底。釉呈青黄色，满布细碎开片纹。有泪痕，浅蓝色乳浊窑变釉随处可见，尤以盘口内侧和颈肩为甚。

中国陶瓷生产有"南青北白"之分，本品当为早期北方青瓷的佼佼者。

The vase has a plate-shaped mouth, a long straight neck and a bulbous belly that tapers to a flat base encircled by a slightly protruding flange. Four loop lugs are set around the shoulders. Grayish white paste. The interior mouth rim, the exterior surface of the vessel and the base are first coated with a layer of light soy brown glaze before applying a layer of celadon glaze. The greenish yellow celadon glaze stops short of the lower part of the body; tear marks are visible on the surface. Light blue opalescent hues as a result of kiln transmutation appear all over the glaze and in particular the inside of the plate-shaped mouth, the exterior surface of the neck and the shoulders.

There are two main ceramic genres in China – green ware in the South and white ware in the North. This vase is a fine example of early Northern celadon.

青釉四系盘口壶

隋

公元 581—618 年

寿州窑

高：41.5 厘米

口径：16.2 厘米

底径：12.8 厘米

Celadon vase with plate-shaped mouth and four lugs

Sui dynasty

581 – 618 C.E.

Shouzhou kilns

Height: 41.5 cm

Mouth diameter: 16.2 cm

Base diameter: 12.8 cm

盘口，肩和上腹圆鼓，平底。颈上起凸弦纹两组。颈肩交界处刻凹弦纹一周，周间堆贴四枚双股拱系，拱系顶部贴 "S" 形纹饰。盘口内有凹弦纹两圈，下方凹弦纹上对称饰团蛇四条。胎质灰白，坚硬，较粗糙，叩之声音清亮。内外施青灰釉至腹下，有麻癞现象。盘口内外以及颈和上腹部有蓝白色的乳光窑变釉。下腹和底露胎。此器外形规整、美观，是一件优秀的艺术品。

"S" 形及团蛇纹饰流行于西周及春秋战国时期，在以后的器物上甚少出现，故本品对研究隋代的风俗文化与前代之承继关系有相当大价值。

寿州窑窑址在安徽淮南市上窑镇、观家岗、余家沟、外窑等地。始烧于隋代，盛于唐，终于唐晚期，以烧青瓷为主，尤以黄釉为著。唐代属寿州，故名。

The vase has a plate-shaped mouth, rounded shoulders and a bulbous upper belly that tapers to a flat base. Double ridges encircle the upper and lower part of the neck. The border between the neck and the shoulders is demarcated by a groove and straddled by four equally spaced double-strand loop lugs surmounted by S-shaped appliqués. A groove runs under the interior rim and another appears further down, punctuated by four coiling snake appliqués. The unglazed area reveals a hard and relatively coarse grayish white paste. When knocked with the knuckles, the body gives a clear sound. Both the interior and exterior are covered with a greenish gray glaze that stops short of the lower belly. Spotting and streaking of glaze are visible. Blue and white hues as a result of kiln transmutation appear on the inner and outer mouth rim, the neck and upper belly.

The S-shapes and coiling snake appliqués were prevalent during the Western Zhou, the Spring and Autumn and Warring States periods, but seldom found on later vessels. This vase is an important reference for studying the scope of artistic influence from the past.

The Shouzhou kilns are located in the town of Shangyao in Huainan city, Anhui province. Production started in the Sui dynasty, reached its peak during the Tang dynasty and ceased in late Tang. These kilns produced mainly celadons and in particular yellow glazed ones. Shangyao was under the jurisdiction of the Shouzhou prefecture during the Tang dynasty, hence the name.

白釉圆唇罐

隋

公元 581—618 年

巩义窑

高：30 厘米

底径：21.5 厘米

White-glazed cylindrical jar with rounded lip

Sui dynasty

581 – 618 C.E.

Gongyi kilns

Height: 30 cm

Base diameter: 21.5 cm

唇外卷，溜肩，近直筒形腹，平底，底边斜削一圈。胎色白净，胎质坚、细腻，修坯规整。器身内、外施白釉，釉面晶莹通透如玉，玻璃质感强，满布细密冰片纹。颈部聚釉处，釉色白中泛微青及闪黄，这是隋代白瓷常见的现象。体型饱满，古朴浑厚，端庄高贵，气势非凡，为隋代白瓷代表作之一。

本品口缘呈圆唇状，应不带盖，可能是皇室订制的礼佛用具。

北京故宫博物院收藏有相似的器物。

The jar has a rounded lip above a short neck, steep shoulders, a cylindrical body and a flat base with a beveled edge. The paste is white, dense and rather thick. Both the interior and exterior are coated with a white glaze underneath a lustrous, clear and glassy glaze with crackles. The glaze shows a greenish or yellowish tint where it pools around the neck which is characteristic of Sui dynasty white ware. This jar is admired for its monumental size, well-rounded contours, graceful shape and stately presence. It is among the finest and most precious examples of Sui white ware.

The rounded lip of this jar suggests that it was not made with a lid. It could have been a Buddhist ritual utensil commissioned for imperial use.

A similar jar is in the collection of the Palace Museum in Beijing.

303

白釉束腰僧帽盖盅

隋

公元 581—618 年

巩义窑

高：18.8 厘米

底径：12.9 厘米

White-glazed waisted jar with "monk's cap" lid

Sui dynasty

581 – 618 C.E.

Gongyi kilns

Height: 18.8 cm

Base diameter: 12.9 cm

口带盖。盖如僧帽状，上宽下窄，周边饰 12 个呈阶梯状的扁棱凸起。盖呈圆拱形，中部饰弦纹两道，宝珠形纽贴于顶上的矮台上。口缘起凸棱一周，束腰、平底，底边起圆棱，微外撇。胎色洁白、纯净，胎质坚细，修胎精细规矩。器身内外满施白釉，釉微泛青，透明，玻璃质感强，亮泽、晶莹，十分可爱。釉面开冰裂纹，器身和盖聚釉处呈浅绿色。外底和盖内无釉。整体造型别致，做工精细，高贵华丽，气势不凡。僧帽状的盖将规格已极高的器物提升到宗教层面，增添了神圣色彩。本品为隋代白瓷最华美、最贵重的作品之一，这类器物也是近年来收藏界、特别是欧美收藏家争相追求的艺术珍品。

1954 年陕西西安郭家滩姬威墓出土有一件与本品相似的白釉罐，但盖之周边无僧帽的阶梯状凸起，现藏陕西历史博物馆。

中国国家博物馆收藏有一件与本品相似的器物，但盖外形并非僧帽状。

The domed lid of this jar has a flared and upturned brim with twelve peaks bordered by a stepped edge. The shape of the lid resembles a monk's cap. The lid is surmounted by a pearl knob resting on a disc. Two concentric grooves adorn the area between the knob and the brim. The jar has concave sides and a slightly flared flat base bounded by a rounded ridge. The white paste is pure, refined, thin and hard. The entire exterior surface and the interior of the vessel are coated with a green-tinted white glaze with a smooth, lustrous surface covered with ice crackles. The glaze appears pale green where it pools around the body and the lid. The flat bottom and the underside of the lid are unglazed. The monk's cap design imparts a sense of religious sacredness to the vessel. It is among the finest examples of early white ware from the Sui dynasty.

A similar white-glazed jar but without a stepped edge around the lid was unearthed in 1954 from the tomb of Ji Wei at Guojiatan in Xi'an, Shaanxi province.

Another similar example is in the collection of the National Museum of China but the lid is not in the shape of a monk's cap.

304

白釉莲瓣纹熏笼

隋

公元 581—618 年

相州窑

高：7.8 厘米

底径：11.6 厘米

White-glazed censer with lotus petal motif

Sui dynasty

581 – 618 C.E.

Xiangzhou kilns

Height: 7.8 cm

Base diameter: 11.6 cm

敛口，平肩，底平。笼身镂雕竖长方形孔四组，每组五条。镂孔上方和肩腹交接处置弦纹两道，上、下分别刻划覆莲花和卷草纹带。四组镂孔底部以一道平行弦线相连。近底边刻弦纹两圈。胎白，细滑，质坚。施白釉，釉略微泛青，聚釉处呈青绿色，有冰裂纹片。底中部有一大块圆形露胎，是在施满釉后把底心中部的釉刮走放支烧窑具，以防止烧制时器物底部与支烧器具粘连所形成。本品造型稳重，修坯精细，装饰华美，花纹细腻，为隋代白瓷代表作之一。

邢窑博物馆收藏有一件外形与本品相似的青釉熏炉，肩上也刻有一周覆莲瓣纹。

The censer has an incurved mouth, flat shoulders and an unglazed flat base. The sides are pierced with four groups of openings, each comprising five rectangular slits. Immediately above the slits is a band of scrolling tendrils carved between double grooved borders. The space around the mouth is engraved with lotus petals. The lower ends of the slits are joined by double grooves while two more grooves appear around the body near the base. The spotless white paste is hard, smooth and fine. The entire surface is covered with a crackled white glaze with greenish sparkles. The glaze appears green where it pools. A large circular unglazed spot appear in the center of the base. The glaze has been scraped away from this spot after the entire piece was covered with glaze to prevent the base from sticking to the supporting spurs during firing. This censer is a fine example of Sui white ware.

A similar celadon censer with identical inverted lotus petals is in the collection of the Xingyao Museum in Hebei.

305

黄釉戳纹壶

唐

公元 618—907 年

高：18.2 厘米

底径：7.8 厘米

Amber-glazed ewer with pecked design

Tang dynasty

618 – 907 C.E.

Height: 18.2 cm

Base diameter: 7.8 cm

直口，圆唇，高颈，直筒状腹，平底，足缘外边缘向外斜削一周。圆短流，流饰弦纹六道。双泥条柄，肩两侧置双环系。腹刻戳点纹。胎白、细滑，质坚实。施白化妆土，再覆褐黄釉，釉不及底。

河北省隆尧县文物保管所收藏有相似器物，只是腹部纹饰为席纹。

河南省的窑口以及邢窑、定窑也生产这类器物。

The vessel has a straight mouth with rounded lip, a tall neck, a cylindrical body, a bevel-rimmed foot and a flat base. A short circular spout surrounded by six grooves is set on the shoulders. A double-strand loop handle is attached on the other side of the shoulder. Halfway between the spout and the handle on the shoulders is a double-strand loop lug. The belly is decorated with rounds of pecked dots. The white paste is hard and refined. The body is coated with white slip underneath an amber glaze that stops around the lower belly.

A similar vessel but with mat motif is in the collection of the Cultural Relics Repository in Longyao, Hebei province.

Similar vessels were produced at the kilns in Henan as well as the Xing and Ding kilns.

306

黄釉席纹壶

唐

公元 618—907 年

高：15.4 厘米

底径：8.8 厘米

**Amber-glazed ewer with
mat motif**

Tang dynasty

618 – 907 C.E.

Height: 15.4 cm

Base diameter: 8.8 cm

圆唇、颈粗微敛、溜肩、圆鼓腹、饼状
足，足缘外边缘向外斜削一周。肩贴圆
短流，流饰弦纹多道。腹刻席纹，纹纤
细整齐。胎白、细滑、质坚。施黄褐色
釉，釉色泛青黄，釉下挂白色化妆土，
釉不及底。腹一侧留有两块烧制时窑沾
残痕。本品线条优美，器形饱满。

河南省的窑口以及邢窑、定窑都有生产
此类器物。

河北省临城县岗头村出土有相似器物，
腹部两侧也留有窑沾泥块，现藏临城文
物保管所。

The vessel has a mouth with rounded lip,
a slightly constricted thick neck, slanting
shoulders, a bulbous belly and a solid
disc-like foot with a beveled rim. A short
circular spout decorated with rounds of
grooves is set on the shoulder. The belly
is decorated with very fine and neatly
arranged mat motif. The white paste is
hard and refined. The vessel is covered
with a layer of white slip underneath an
amber glaze with a greenish yellow tint.
The glaze stops short of the lower part

of the belly. Two lumps of kiln residues
adhering to the body during firing are
visible on one side of the belly.

This type of vessels was produced at the
kilns in Henan as well as the Xing and
Ding kilns.

A similar vessel with lumps of clay
adhering to the sides of the body was
unearthed from Gangtou village in
Lincheng, Hebei province. It is now
in the collection of the Cultural Relics
Repository in Lincheng.

307

黄釉钵

唐

公元 618—907 年

寿州窑

高：10.2 厘米

阔：16 厘米

Bowl in yellow glaze

Tang dynasty

618 – 907 C.E.

Shouzhou kilns

Height: 10.2 cm

Width: 16cm

胎白，质坚，矮圆唇，鼓腹，圜底。腹上部施黄褐釉，釉下方边缘处再刷一周深褐黄色纹带，有泪釉痕由纹带流到素身的下腹部。全器光素无纹，但釉色深浅对比和泪釉痕形成很好的装饰效果。器物圆浑饱满，线条简单，优美流畅。

The bowl has a hard white paste, a short rounded lip and a rounded bottom. The upper part of the body is covered with yellowish-brown glaze whose lower extremity is bounded by a belt of brownish-yellow glaze with streaks running down the sides and stopping short of the base. The contrast of the colors and the glaze streaks creates a highly decorative effect. The entire vessel is devoid of other decorations. The vessel is full and rotund in shape. The lines are simple yet fluid and elegant.

308

黄釉盏

唐

公元 618—907 年

高：4.5 厘米

口径：16 厘米

底径：7.5 厘米

Shallow bowl with yellow glaze

Tang dynasty

618 – 907 C.E.

Height: 4.5 cm

Mouth diameter: 16 cm

Base diameter: 7.5 cm

敛口、浅斜腹、矮圆饼状足、底平微内
凹。足端边缘斜削一圈。胎洁白、质细
腻，胎体较厚重，内壁可见轮旋痕。内
外施蜡黄色釉，呈半失透状、釉不及底。
内外壁有垂釉、聚釉处呈黄褐色，釉面
满布条状开片纹。圈足和底露胎。腹下
近圈足四周无釉，上有五个支烧残留痕。
本品修坯规整、质朴厚重，是一件优秀
的作品。

安徽寿州窑和河南省的窑口也有生产此
类褐黄色盏。

河北省临城县文物保管所收藏有相似器
物，只是为玉璧底。

The bowl has an incurved mouth, tapering
sides, a disc-like solid foot with a beveled
rim and a flat base with a slightly recessed
center. The white paste is refined. The
body is relatively thick and heavy. Both the
interior and exterior are covered with a
translucent wax-yellow glaze that stops in
welts above the base. The glaze is covered
with strip-like crackles, and appears
yellowish brown when it pools. Rings of
wheel marks are visible on the interior
wall. The ring foot, beveled foot rim and
base are bare of glaze. The unglazed part of
the exterior wall bears five spur marks.

This type of brownish yellow bowls was
produced at the Shouzhou kilns in Anhui
and the kilns in Henan.

A similar vessel but with a jade-disc base
is in the collection of the Cultural Relics
Repository in Lincheng, Hebei province.

309

白釉碗

唐

公元 618—907 年

巩义窑

高：5.6 厘米

口径：14 厘米

底径：7.5 厘米

Bowl with white glaze

Tang dynasty

618 – 907 C.E.

Gongyi kilns

Height: 5.6 cm

Mouth diameter: 14 cm

Base diameter: 7.5 cm

敞口，口缘外侈，深腹，缓收到底，圈足外撇，足端外缘斜削一圈。胎白、细滑，胎骨较厚重。器内、外壁施白釉，釉不及腹底，釉面满布细碎纹片。圈足和底裸胎。本品虽光素无纹，但造型端庄，线条优美，修坯精细，为不可多得之佳作。

巩义窑生产白瓷应是从唐初开始，武则天至玄宗时期比较兴旺，陶器和瓷器品种增多，开元、天宝以后数量逐渐下降。

The bowl has a wide mouth, a flared rim and deep sides that taper smoothly towards a splayed ring foot with a beveled rim. Both the interior and exterior are covered with white glaze with tiny crackles. The glaze on the outside does not reach the bottom of the belly. The ring foot and the base are unglazed. The paste is white, refined and relatively heavy.

The Gongyi kilns started to produce white wares during the early Tang period. Production thrived during the reign of Empress Wuzetian and the reign of Emperor Xuanzong and declined after the Kaiyuan and Tianbao periods of Emperor Xuanzong.

310

白釉三足炉

唐

公元 618—907 年

邢窑

高：9 厘米

口径：8.6 厘米

Tripod censer with white glaze

Tang dynasty

618 – 907 C.E.

Xing kilns

Height: 9 cm

Mouth diameter: 8.6 cm

炉口外撇，底平露胎。腹压直棱四条，把腹分成四瓣，腹下承以三立足。胎洁白、细滑、质坚。器身内外施白釉，外壁釉不到底，釉面有细碎纹片。颈部和棱线聚釉处，釉色白中泛青。本品釉色和胎骨具典型唐代邢窑"类雪"的特征。

唐代邢窑三足炉较少见。

The censer has a flared mouth and a four-lobed body supported by three legs. The lobed body is divided by four vertical grooves. The flat base is unglazed. The immaculate white paste is fine, smooth and hard. Both the interior and exterior surfaces are covered with a white glaze that stops short of the base on the outside. The glaze bears tiny crackles and shows a greenish tint where it accumulates around the neck and along the grooves. The glaze color and paste of this censer are "as white as snow" which is characteristic of Xing ware from the Tang dynasty.

Tripod censers are relatively rare among Xing wares from the Tang dynasty.

白釉狮形柄龙首流盖壶

唐

公元 618—907 年

邢窑

高：18.2 厘米

底径：5.8 厘米

White-glazed lidded ewer with lion handle and dragon spout

Tang dynasty

618 – 907 C.E.

Xing kilns

Height: 18.2 cm

Base diameter: 5.8 cm

侈口，颈微束，丰肩斜收到底，底平外撇，足边缘斜削一周。肩上塑一狮子形柄。狮子后腿立在壶肩上支撑身体，前腿伸入壶口内壁，狮首向内探视。狮子各部位刻划清晰，五爪的前后腿，卷曲的尾巴，细窄的腰身，隆起的脊骨，呈团状并梳理整齐的鬃毛，圆睁的双眼，竖起的耳，突显了狮子发达的肌肉和威猛的气势。口上带盖，盖褶边上贴圆突三枚，盖后三分之一留空，以与狮首相配合。柄相对一侧贴朝天龙首流，流底部饰一周褶边纹，与盖上褶边相呼应。白胎，质坚致细密。施白釉，釉色泛青，呈失透状，釉不及底。本品造型和雕工精美绝伦，是十分珍贵的艺术品。

在此件壶出现以前，人们通常以为这类壶是不带盖的。

北京故宫博物院收藏有与本品相似的狮柄龙流壶，但没有盖，且施釉不及底。

陕西西安市文物保护考古研究所藏有一件类似的白釉螭柄执壶，但非龙首流，也没有盖，且施釉不到底。

The ewer has a flared mouth, a slightly constricted neck, broad shoulders and sides that taper towards the base. The handle is sculpted as a lion standing on its hind legs while stretching its forelimbs down the inner mouth rim and poking its head into the vessel. The back of the lid is trimmed to fit the lion's head. The lion is meticulously modeled with five claws to each limb, a curly tail, a narrow waist, arched spine, thick mane, wide-open eyes and pricked ears. A spout in the shape of an upright dragon's head is set on the shoulder. The ruffle encircling the base of the spout mirrors the ruffle skirting on the trimmed opening of the lid. The ruffle on the lid is adorned with three circular appliqué studs. The white paste is refined, hard and dense. The vessel is covered with an opaque white glaze with a greenish tint. The glaze stops short of the base. The slightly splayed foot has a beveled rim and a flat base. This vessel is a rarity among rarities.

This type of ewer was generally thought to be lidless until the discovery of this lidded ewer.

A similar ewer with lion handle and dragon spout is in the collection of the Palace Museum in Beijing but it does not come with a lid and the glaze does not reach the foot.

Another similar example with *chi* dragon handle is in the collection of the Cultural Relics Preservation and Archaeological Research Institute in Xi'an, Shaanxi province. It has no lid, no dragon head spout and the glaze does not reach the base.

312

白釉带盖罐

唐

公元 618—907 年

巩义窑

高：25.1 厘米

阔：28.7 厘米

Lidded jar with white glaze

Tang dynasty

618 – 907 C.E.

Gongyi kilns

Height: 25.1 cm

Width: 28.7 cm

敛口，圆唇，球形腹，小平底。口上带盖，盖贴宝珠形纽。胎质细腻，坚硬，洁白。罐身内外和盖面施白釉，聚釉处白中泛绿色。罐内壁和盖面有冰裂纹，罐外壁无纹片。釉层凝厚，有泪釉现象。盖内和罐底露胎。器形丰满，弧度优雅，盖、体配合完美，令人赞叹不已。

唐代瓷器给人以圆浑饱满的观感，小中见大，精巧而有气魄，单纯而有变化，糅合造型艺术的雍容大度和线条艺术的曲直有致，流利酣畅地表现时代风格，这些在本品一一体现出来。

本品俗称波斯罐，外形仿波斯器物。

本品经热释光测定最后烧制年代距今约 1000 年。

The jar has an incurved mouth with rounded lip, a globular body, a small flat base and a lid with a pearl knob. Both the interior and exterior of the jar as well as the upper side of the lid are coated with a white glaze that appears greenish where it pools. Ice crackles are found only inside the vessel and on the upper surface of the lid. The glaze is thick and glaze streaks are visible along the sides. The inside of the lid and the base of the jar are bare of glaze, revealing a fine, smooth, hard and spotless white paste. The curvature of the domed lid matches perfectly with that of the body.

The sense of fullness and abundance typical of Tang porcelains is fully manifested in this jar.

This type of jar is commonly referred to as "Persian jars". The shape was modeled after Persian vessels.

Thermoluminescence test shows that the last firing date of this piece was around 1000 years before present.

313

白釉带柄鸟形壶

唐

公元 618—907 年

巩义窑

高：22.6 厘米

White-glazed bird-shaped jar with handle

Tang dynasty

618 – 907 C.E.

Gongyi kilns

Height: 22.6 cm

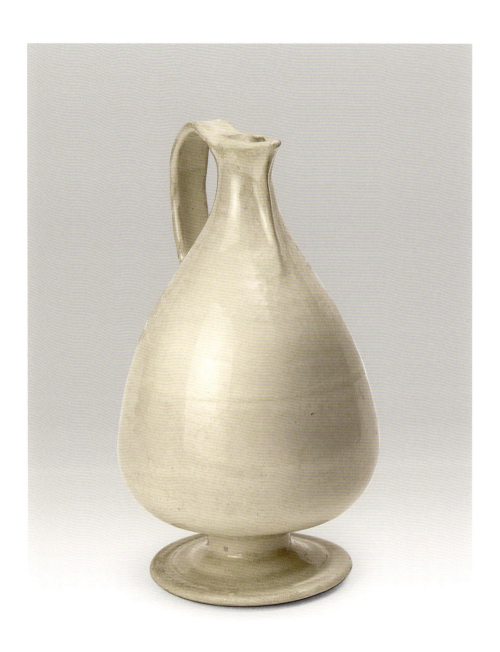

口窄长，呈鸟喙状，微束颈，溜肩，胆状圆腹，下承短筒形柄，大圆饼状足，足底内凹。口缘与肩间置扁曲柄流，圆饼足上饰一周弦纹。本当有鸟首形盖，可惜已无存。胎洁白、细腻。施乳白釉，釉色纯净，颈、腹底和足部开细碎纹片，足部聚釉处呈淡青绿色。本器线条流畅、优美、尖尖的喙、窄窄的颈、鼓鼓的腹、圆圆的足，刻画出一只憨直、可爱、四平八稳的鸟的形态，是一件非常优秀的作品。

本品造型受波斯萨珊王朝金银器鸟首壶的影响。

本品经热释光检测最后烧制年代距今1100—800 年。

The jar has an elongated mouth resembling the beak of a bird, a slightly constricted neck, slanting shoulders, a bladder-shaped belly supported by a cylindrical short stem and a disc-like foot with a concave base. A strap handle arches between the mouth rim and the shoulder. The foot is decorated with a round of groove. The lid in the shape of a bird's head is missing. The paste is white and refined. The vessel is covered with a milky white glaze. Crackles are found around the neck, the underside of the belly and the foot. The glaze appears pale green where it pools around the foot.

The shape of this jar was influenced by the metal bird head ewers of the Sassanid Empire of Persia.

Thermoluminescence test shows that the last firing date of this piece was 1100 to 800 years before present.

314

白釉皮囊壶

唐

公元 618—907 年

巩义窑

高：19.5 厘米

阔：14.9 厘米

底径：8.1 厘米

Leather pouch ewer with white glaze

Tang dynasty

618 – 907 C.E.

Gongyi kilns

Height: 19.5 cm

Width: 14.9 cm

Base diameter: 8.1 cm

提包式，深袋腹，假圈足，平底露胎。顶置拱形提梁，末端翘起成尾鋬。朝天短管状流，上绕绳带。壶两侧及正前方各饰一道仿皮革缝线凸棱，提梁下马鞍状背两侧模印背毯。胎骨洁白、细腻，带粉质感。器身施化妆土，外罩乳白色釉。釉色白净，釉质光润。本品造型美观、别致，形状模仿北方游牧民族的皮囊壶。

1956 年陕西西安莲湖区白家口出土有相似器物，现藏陕西历史博物馆。

This ewer is in the shape of a leather pouch with deep sides and an overhead loop handle, the end of which curls up to resemble a cantle. The body is supported by a low solid ring-foot enclosing an unglazed flat base. The cylindrical spout is short and upright surrounded by carved rope design. The ribs down the front and on the broad sides of the ewer are meant to imitate the seams of a leather pouch. The saddle-like back underneath the overhead handle is decorated with a molded design

featuring a saddle blanket. The white paste is refined with a powdery touch. The entire surface is coated with white slip underneath a milky white glaze. The glaze is lustrous and pure white. This vessel is modeled after the leather pouch flasks used by the nomadic tribes of northern China.

A similar vessel was unearthed in 1956 from Baijiakou in Lianhu, Xi'an, Shaanxi province. It is now in the collection of the Shaanxi History Museum.

315

白釉唾壶

唐

公元 618—907 年

巩义窑

高：10.5 厘米

口径：14.9 厘米

底径：7.5 厘米

Spittoon with white glaze

Tang dynasty

618 – 907 C.E.

Gongyi kilns

Height: 10.5 cm

Mouth diameter: 14.9 cm

Base diameter: 7.5 cm

上部似浅碗，下部如水丞，口径大于器腹。胎色洁白，胎质细密、坚硬。通体内、外施乳白色釉，釉色莹润纯净，开细密纹片，有泪釉痕。璧形足，底部无釉。

唾壶为古代贵族宴饮吐鱼骨或兽骨等的承器，故又有"渣斗"之称。唾壶自晋代开始使用，也见于唐朝之金银器。

The vessel is made up of a shallow bowl that sits on top of a water basin. The diameter of the mouth is wider than that of the belly. The paste is pure white, refined, dense and hard. Both the interior and exterior surfaces are covered with a smooth and lustrous milky white glaze with tiny crackles and glaze streaks. The foot is in the shape of a jade-disc and the base is unglazed.

The spittoon was a container used during banquets for holding food dregs such as fish bones. It is also called a *zhadou* (dreg container) in Chinese. It first appeared during the Jin dynasties. The shape is also found among metal wares of the Tang dynasty.

316

白釉镂空熏笼

唐

公元 618—907 年

巩义窑

高：12.8 厘米

底径：15.6 厘米

White-glazed cage-shaped censer with openwork design

Tang dynasty

618 – 907 C.E.

Gongyi kilns

Height: 12.8 cm

Base diameter: 15.6 cm

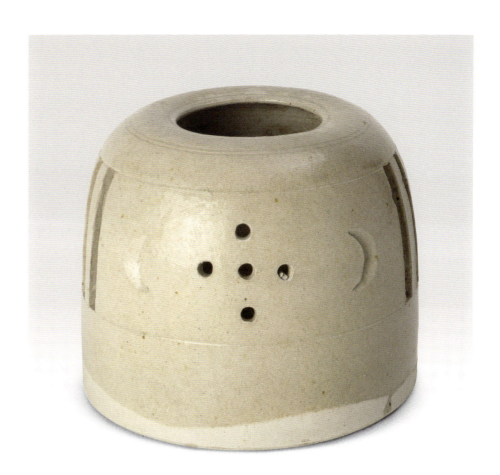

敛口，圆唇，无颈，浅底足，腹足交界处斜削一圈。肩上有双弦纹一道。腹部两侧镂雕竖长条形孔各一组，每组五条，两组长条形孔上下分别以弦纹连接。另两侧各置圆孔五个，排列成"十"字形，圆孔两侧镂刻月牙状纹饰两个。胎白泛浅灰，颇细滑。器外壁施白釉，釉不及底，釉面满布细碎纹片。内外底有明显轮旋痕。

The cage-shaped censer has an incurved mouth with rounded lip and no neck. The shallow foot has a beveled rim. Double indented lines encircle the shoulders. The wall of the censer is pierced with two groups of five rectangular vertical slits. The spaces between them are pierced with five small holes arranged in cruciform with a crescent-shaped carving on each side. An indented line joins the upper edges of all the slits and another connects the lower edges. The white paste with a grayish tint is rather fine and smooth. The exterior wall is covered with a white glaze with tiny crackles; the glaze stops short of the base. Distinct wheel marks are visible on the inner and outer base.

317

白釉镂空熏笼

唐

公元 618—907 年

巩义窑

高：11.2 厘米

底径：12.6 厘米

White-glazed censer with openwork design

Tang dynasty

618 – 907 C.E.

Gongyi kilns

Height: 11.2 cm

Base diameter: 12.6 cm

敛口，圆唇，无颈，由肩到腹以刚劲的弧形线条组成笼体，平底。肩、腹间镂雕竖长方形孔三组，每组三条，三组镂孔上下端分别以阴刻弦线连接。其中一组镂孔左、右置一窄长弯孔和一圆孔。方形镂孔作窗户，圆孔为太阳，窄长弯孔是月亮。施白釉，釉泛微黄，有开片纹，釉不到底。底露胎，胎洁白，质坚、细滑。

本品制作精细，外形圆浑饱满，为巩义窑精美的艺术品。

1957 年陕西西安李静训墓出土的青釉熏笼与本品外形相似。

笼状熏器流行于隋唐年间，唐壁画上有宫女手捧熏笼的形象。熏香是用沉香或香料等粉末加蜂蜜、梅粉捻成。

香料在人类生活上有着重要的地位，除了用于烹饪、储存食物和调味外，也作净化、防腐、治疗、化妆等用途。中世纪的欧洲，香料是最贵重的商品之一，其价值几与黄金相同。当时香料产地主要在马来群岛（今马来西亚、新加坡和印尼），香料要先经过中国，通过陆上丝绸之路到达欧洲，路途遥远。后来阿拉伯商人开拓了把香料从产地经印度洋到波斯湾沿岸再转往欧洲的航路，是为"香料之路"，也称作"海上丝绸之路"。

The censer has an incurved mouth with a rounded lip, sloping shoulders and no neck. The upper wall is pierced with three groups of three rectangular vertical slits. One of the groups has a crescent opening on its right and a circular opening on its left. An indented line joins the upper edges of all the slits and another connects the lower edges. The slits represent windows while the circular and crescent shapes are respectively the sun and the moon. The censer is covered with a yellow tinted and crackled glaze. The base and the area around the foot are unglazed, exposing a hard and fine white paste.

This censer is noted for its exquisite craftsmanship and robust shape. It is a fine example from the Gongyi kilns.

A censer of similar shape but in celadon glaze was unearthed in 1957 from the tomb of Li Jingxun in Xi'an, Shaanxi province.

This type of cage-shaped censer was popular during the Sui and Tang dynasties. The incense was made by kneading pulverized agarwood or spices with honey and plum. Images of court ladies holding cage-shaped censers are found on Tang murals.

The demand for spices played an important role in world history. Apart from being used as a cooking ingredient, food preservative and condiment, spices can also be used as purifier, antiseptic and cosmetic ingredient. Spices were among the most precious commodities in medieval Europe, nearly as much as gold in worth. At that time, spices were mainly from the Malay Archipelago (present day Malaysia, Singapore and Indonesia). To get these spices to Europe, they had to be shipped first to China and then transported overland via the Silk Route to reach their final destinations. Later, Arab merchants opened up the sea route that allowed spices to be shipped directly from their place of origin to Europe via the Indian Ocean and Persian Gulf. This route was thus known as the Spice Route. Since the Spice Route was similar in function to the overland Silk Route, it is also called the Maritime Silk Route.

318

白釉双龙柄贴花壶

唐

公元 618—907 年

巩义窑

高：55.2 厘米

底径：12 厘米

White-glazed amphora with appliqué design and dragon handles

Tang dynasty

618 – 907 C.E.

Gongyi kilns

Height: 55.2 cm

Base diameter: 12 cm

盘口，颈细长，上饰凸弦纹三道。丰肩，鼓腹，下腹渐敛，底平微外撇。盘口和肩部两侧塑衔瓶龙首柄一对。龙卷角，竖耳，鼓睛，望向壶内。柄下方各贴花卉纹饰一个。腹下部近底处有弦纹数道。壶身与颈部长度相若。胎白、细腻，胎骨坚硬、颇薄。外壁施白釉，釉不及底。本品高大端正，稳重敦实，为唐代典型器物。

本品经热释光测定最后烧制年代距今约 1000 年。

The vessel has a plate-shaped mouth, a long and slender neck, bold shoulders, a bulbous belly that tapers gradually towards a slightly splayed foot and a flat base. Three ribs encircle the neck. A pair of dragonhead handles rises from the shoulders to join the mouth rim. Each dragon is featured with curling horns, pricked-up ears and bulging eyes. The lower end of each handle is adorned with an appliqué floral design. Several indented lines encircle the area between the lower belly and the foot. The neck and the body of the vessel are similar in height. The paste is white, refined, thin and hard. The exterior surface is covered with a white glaze that does not reach the base. This amphora is a representative example of Tang dynasty ware.

Thermoluminescence test shows that the last firing date of this piece was 1000 years before present.

319

白釉双龙柄壶

唐

公元 618—907 年

巩义窑

高：52.5 厘米

底径：13.9 厘米

White-glazed amphora with dragon handles

Tang dynasty

618 – 907 C.E.

Gongyi kilns

Height: 52.5 cm

Base diameter: 13.9 cm

本品外形与图录 318 号大致相同，也是白胎，釉层薄而滋润，乳白色釉泛青，白度仍未达到成熟白瓷的标准，应为唐早期遗物。

此器形是在晋代鸡首壶的基础上吸收波斯文化的特点而创制的。

This vessel is similar to Cat. No. 318. It is covered with a thin and smooth layer of milky white glaze with a greenish tint. The paste is white. Since the degree of its whiteness has yet to reach the standard of mature white porcelain, this piece is dated to the early Tang period.

The shape of this amphora is modeled after the chicken-head ewers of the Jin dynasty but with a Persian influence.

320

黑釉白弦纹四系罐

唐

公元 618—907 年

巩义窑

高：14.3 厘米

底径：7.8 厘米

Black-glazed jar with four loop lugs and white grooves

Tang dynasty

618 – 907 C.E.

Gongyi kilns

Height: 14.3 cm

Base diameter: 7.8 cm

短颈，圆腹，腹下渐敛，饼状足外撇。肩部贴四竖系。腹部饰以三道平行白弦纹。胎洁白，质细，坚硬。器身内外施黑褐釉，釉不到底。本品造型圆浑饱满，黑白相映成趣。

The jar has a straight mouth above a short neck and a bulbous belly that tapers smoothly towards a splayed disc-like foot. Four vertical loop lugs are set on the shoulders while three equally spaced white grooves encompass the belly. The pure white paste is hard and fine. Both the interior and exterior are coated with a brownish black glaze but the lower belly and the foot are bare. This jar is noted for its rounded contours, robust shape and the sharp contrast of a white motif against a black ground.

321

黑釉白弦纹三系罐

唐

公元 618—907 年

巩义窑

高：14 厘米

口径：6.2 厘米

底径：6.6 厘米

Black-glazed jar with three loop lugs and white grooves

Tang dynasty

618 – 907 C.E.

Gongyi kilns

Height: 14 cm

Mouth diameter: 6.2 cm

Base diameter: 6.6 cm

本品与图录 320 号外形和结构都相似，只是肩部贴竖系三个、腹部装饰白弦纹两道。釉色黝黑明亮，讨人喜欢。

This jar is similar in shape and structure to the last, Cat. No. 320, except that it has only two white grooves around the body and three loop lugs on the shoulders.

322

蓝灰花釉彩斑壶

唐

公元 618—907 年

郏县窑

高：32.2 厘米

阔：17.2 厘米

底径：9.7 厘米

Ewer in grayish blue glaze with variegated splashes

Tang dynasty

618 – 907 C.E.

Jiaxian kilns

Height: 32.2 cm

Width: 17.2 cm

Base diameter: 9.7 cm

花瓣形口，细长颈，溜肩，丰腹，下腹渐内敛，平底。颈与肩之间置执柄，柄下端贴一圆突。胎色灰白，质坚，厚重。施灰蓝色乳光釉，釉不到底。釉厚，蕴含黑蓝、天蓝、月白、银白、紫斑多种色釉，层叠相间，深浅交错，多姿多彩，不同器物上的色釉斑纹无一相同。本品造型秀丽，色彩斑斓，白蓝釉面窑变自然舒畅、流淌自如，有如一幅中国泼墨画，又如一帧印象派画作，独具特色。

花瓣口壶的式样受波斯萨珊王朝时期金银器胡瓶影响。

郏县窑遗址于 1964 年在河南郏县黄道村发现，所以也称黄道窑，是唐代重要瓷窑。产品以白瓷为主，兼烧黄釉、黑釉、白釉绿彩器，并生产花釉瓷，即以黑色、月白或灰篮釉为地色，饰以天蓝色或灰黑色彩斑。

1956 年河南郏县会兴镇附近的一座墓葬中出土有一件与本品相似的器物。

The ewer has a floral-shaped mouth rising from a slender neck, sloping shoulders and a swelling belly that tapers gently towards a flat base. The lower end of the handle that arches between the upper neck and the shoulder is decorated with a circular protuberance. The vessel is thickly potted with a grayish white hard paste. It is covered overall with a thick and opalescent grayish blue glaze with dark blue, sky blue, moon white, silvery white and purple splashes that run freely into each other stopping just short of the foot. This ewer is noted for its elegant shape and resplendent color scheme. The spontaneous transmutation and merging of the blue and white glazes produce a unique effect reminiscent of Chinese splash-ink painting.

The foliate rim is adopted from the Sassanid metal ewers of Persia.

The Jiaxian kiln sites were discovered in 1964 at Huangdao village in Jia county, Henan province. Hence, these kilns are also called Huangdao kilns. They are among the important kilns of the Tang dynasty, producing mainly white porcelains. Other glazed wares produced at these kilns include yellow ware, black ware, white ware with green painting as well as polychrome vessels with sky blue or gray splashes against a ground of black, moon white or grayish blue glaze.

A vessel of similar shape and color was unearthed in 1956 from a tomb near Huixingzhen in Jiaxian, Henan province.

323

黑釉蓝斑双耳罐

唐

公元 618—907 年

鲁山窑

高：14.9 厘米

口径：7.4 厘米

底径：9.3 厘米

Black-glazed jar with blue splashes and double lugs

Tang dynasty

618 – 907 C.E.

Lushan kilns

Height: 14.9 cm

Mouth diameter: 7.4 cm

Base diameter: 9.3 cm

口缘外翻，短颈，饼状足，足稍外撇。肩间两侧贴拱形系各一。灰白胎，坚硬。器身外壁施黑釉到腹中部，釉面上饰蓝、白、褐色蝌蚪状斑纹三组，聚釉处釉高出器表。下腹露胎处见批削痕，足外侧斜削一圈。

The jar has an everted mouth rim, a short neck and a flat base. The slightly splayed disc-like foot has a beveled rim. An arched loop lug is set on the shoulders. The grayish white paste is hard. The exterior is covered with a black glaze that stops around the mid section of the belly. Three tadpole-shaped splashes of blue, white and brown adorn the glazed surface. The glaze is in relief where it accumulates. Scraping marks are visible around the unglazed lower belly.

324

黑釉球形壶

唐

公元 618—907 年

鲁山窑

高：16.6 厘米

底径：9 厘米

Spherical ewer with black glaze

Tang dynasty

618 – 907 C.E.

Lushan kilns

Height: 16.6 cm

Base diameter: 9 cm

壶口外卷、细颈、圆肩、短圆直流、球形腹、饼状足。流相对一侧置双股曲柄、连接口缘和上腹部，柄上、下端贴乳丁纹饰各一。灰白胎、质坚、颇细滑。器内外施黑釉，外壁釉不到底。本品器形浑圆饱满，各部分比例适中，为唐代壶典型式样之一。

根据胎和底足之修刮方式，本品应是鲁山窑器物。

The spherical ewer has a flared mouth with rolling rim, a short neck, rounded shoulders and a disc-like foot. A two-strand handle is set on the shoulders opposite a short straight spout. The upper and lower ends of the handle are each decorated with a stud. The grayish white paste is hard and refined. The interior and exterior are covered with a black glaze that stops short of the base on the outside. The vessel is noted for its rounded shape and balanced proportion. The shape of this vessel is typical of Tang ewers.

Based on the paste and the way that the bottom is trimmed, this vessel is from the Lushan kilns.

325

黑釉蓝斑壶

唐

公元 618—907 年

鲁山窑

高：19.5 厘米

底径：7.8 厘米

Black-glazed spouted ewer with blue splashes

Tang dynasty

618 – 907 C.E.

Lushan kilns

Height: 19.5 cm

Base diameter: 7.8 cm

口外卷，短颈，丰肩，斜腹，平底。肩一侧饰圆锥形短流，相对侧置执柄，连于颈肩之间。胎灰白，细滑。釉呈黑褐色，壶身施釉不到底。颈、肩、腹、柄和流部饰乳浊状蓝白斑纹，向下及四周流淌。壶形秀雅，是唐代执壶之典型。

The ewer has a flared mouth with outrolling rim, a short neck, rounded shoulders and a belly the tapers towards a flat base. A cylindrical spout is set on the shoulders opposite a handle that arches between the neck and the shoulders. The grayish white paste is smooth and refined. Opalescent blue and white splashes run freely amid a brownish black glaze. The lower third of the body is bare of glaze. This vessel is a representative example of Tang ewers.

326

长柄水壶

唐

公元 618—907 年

长沙窑

高：21 厘米

阔：21 厘米

底径：9.1 厘米

Spouted jar with lid and long handle

Tang dynasty

618 – 907 C.E.

Changsha kilns

Height: 21 cm

Width: 21 cm

Base diameter: 9.1 cm

宝塔形阶梯状圆盖，盖侧贴横向半圆系。壶体压直纹四道，使腹作瓜棱形。肩腹间置直身棱形流，相对侧肩上贴横向半圆系，与盖侧系相配，便于用绳把壶身和盖相连。流左侧置下圆上扁、粗壮结实的把柄。通体施青釉，呈褐黄色，满开细碎纹片。平底露胎，胎浅褐色，较粗糙。

考古资料显示，长沙窑在岳州窑最兴旺发达的时候逐渐兴起，之后受越窑工艺影响，发展较快。大约隋到唐中期，长沙窑工艺都不够成熟，质地粗糙、烧成温度不高，许多作品有生烧现象，自中晚唐以后工艺逐渐成熟，器物多有美丽的彩绘装饰，此外还烧一些低温铅釉陶器。

This vessel has a lid in the shape of a stupa with stepped profile. A semicircular loop is attached horizontally to its side. The body of the jar is impressed with four vertical grooves to resemble a four-lobed gourd. A spout with a lozenge shape cross-section protrudes from the belly. A loop similar to that on the lid is set horizontally on the opposite shoulder. A cord can be used to connect the lid to the body of the vessel. To the upper left of the spout is a handle with a cylindrical lower section and flattened upper end. The entire surface is covered with a celadon glaze of amber color with tiny crackles. The unglazed flat base reveals a relatively coarse paste of light brown color.

Archaeological discoveries revealed that the Changsha kilns emerged when the Yuezhou kilns were at the peak of their development. Later, under the influence of Yue wares, Changsha wares saw rapid progress. Due to technological limitations, Changsha wares produced during the Sui dynasty and the first half of the Tang dynasty were rather coarse. Firing temperature was not high enough and under-fired pieces were rife. From mid Tang onward, as production techniques became more sophisticated, items with polychrome painting and low-fired lead-glazed pieces began to emerge.

327

花鸟脉枕

唐

公元 618—907 年

长沙窑

高：7.9 厘米

阔：10.3 厘米

长：17.7 厘米

Wrist rest with bird-and-flower design

Tang dynasty

618 – 907 C.E.

Changsha kilns

Height: 7.9 cm

Width: 10.3 cm

Length: 17.7 cm

枕面微凹，圆角，底微弯，整体呈银锭形。枕背置气孔。胎灰白，质较细滑、坚致。通体敷淡土黄色薄釉，底露胎。枕面以白描手法勾绘绿、褐彩花鸟，即先在白坯上画出花鸟的轮廓，再用绿、褐彩填绘，然后施面釉烧成。枕四侧面画花草各一。枕面花左右饰飞翔的昆虫两只，长尾彩鸟立于花草上，昂首向前，聚精会神，像在等待丰盛晚餐的到来。笔法刚劲有力，线条流畅，画意益然。

本品是长沙窑成熟时期的代表作品，画意高超，简洁生动，有很高的艺术水平。

The wrist rest in the shape of a silver ingot with rounded corners and a slightly depressed top is covered with a thin layer of pale yellowish brown glaze. The top is decorated with bird-and-flower design in *baimiao* (plain drawing) style. Designs were directly painted on the surface before applying the green and brown pigments. Each of the four sides of the wrist rest is painted with a flower borne on leafy stem.

The flower on the top has two insects flying by its sides while a long-tailed bird perches on the foliage. The brush strokes are vigorously and fluently executed and the images are highly painterly in style. The grayish white paste is hard and rather refined. The slightly concave underside is bare of glaze. There is a small hole in the back to allow for air to escape during firing.

This is a representative example of mature Changsha kiln ware.

328

贴花水注

唐

公元 618—907 年

长沙窑

高：21.5 厘米

底径：14.8 厘米

Spouted jar with appliqué design

Tang dynasty

618 – 907 C.E.

Changsha kilns

Height: 21.5 cm

Base diameter: 14.8 cm

小口，口缘微卷，直颈，丰肩，腹体宽
呈筒形，腹壁向底部微敛，大平底，浅
圈足。六方形短流，相对一侧置三股藤
状把手连接肩腹，两侧肩上置三股横穿
式系两个。流与系下贴鸟纹葡萄花，上
覆盖大片斑块状褐彩，形成三个梨形彩
斑纹，突出堆贴团花的装饰效果。灰白
胎，质较细腻、坚致。通体施淡黄色釉，
釉不及圈足，有冰裂开片纹。

褐斑贴花壶是长沙窑代表性产品，大多
数为粗颈大口缘，出土数量很多，但绝
大部分有破损，特别是口缘部分。本品
釉色光洁、明亮，造型浑厚、饱满，完
整无缺，实为同类器之珍品。

1956 年湖南长沙窑窑址出土有相似器
物，现藏湖南省博物馆。

This jar has a small mouth with slightly
rolling lip, a straight neck, bold shoulders
and an almost cylindrical body that tapers
gently towards a broad flat base enclosed
by a shallow ring foot. A hexagonal spout
rises from the shoulder while a three-
strand rattan-like handle arches between
the shoulder and the belly. Halfway
between the spout and the handle on
each side of the shoulder is a vertically set
three-strand loop lug. Applied beneath
the spout and lugs are three grapevine
medallions highlighted in brown. The
grayish white paste is hard and rather fine.
The entire body except around the foot
is covered with a yellowish celadon glaze
with ice crackles.

Spouted jars with appliqué decorations

are typical among Changsha wares. Many
have been unearthed but most of them
damaged at the mouth or with thick necks
and broad rims. The present piece is noted
for its smooth and lustrous glaze, majestic
and robust shape, and in particular, its
intactness. This jar is the finest of it kind.

A similar jar was unearthed in 1956 from
the Changsha kiln site in Hunan. It is now
in the collection of the Hunan Provincial
Museum.

329

青釉花口唾壺

五代

公元 907—960 年

越窑

高：10.7 厘米

口径：14.9 厘米

底径：6.2 厘米

Celadon spittoon with quatrefoil mouth

Five Dynasties

907 – 960 C.E.

Yue kilns

Height: 10.7 cm

Mouth diameter: 14.9 cm

Base diameter: 6.2 cm

侈口，呈四瓣葵花口状，花口下刻四道垂直线纹。细颈、圆腹。上部近似坦腹浅碗，呈漏斗状，下部如水注。器内外施青釉、满布开片纹。底露胎、胎质坚细、呈浅灰色。造型工整、秀丽，如盛开的花朵。

The spittoon has a flared quatrefoil mouth, a narrow neck and a globular belly. The shape of the vessel consists of a funnel-shaped shallow bowl placed on top of a bottle. There are four vertical grooves coming down the exterior wall of the bowl from the notched mouth rim. Both the interior and exterior of the vessel are covered with a crackled celadon glaze. The unglazed base exposes a refined, hard paste of light gray color.

330

青釉"大中四年"铭墓志盖罐

唐

公元 850 年

越窑

高：19 厘米

底径：10 厘米

Celadon lidded jar with incised epitaph

Tang dynasty

850 C.E.

Yue kilns

Height: 19 cm

Base diameter: 10 cm

圆口、四方形体。圆底，圈足矮而浅，残留多个垫饼痕。圆拱形盖，中置山形纽，盖面刻莲花四枝。罐体近底足处有对称圆孔一对，与罐内相通。灰白胎，质坚、细滑。盖、罐体、圈足内外满施青釉，呈橄榄色，釉色滋润。盖内有一周垫圈残留痕，与口缘上的残痕吻合，说明盖是放在罐口上一起烧造的。

罐体满阴刻铭文，自右至左如下："唐务州兰溪县灵山乡，故藤府君墓志铭并序。府君则南阳人也，兄弟三人，君三祖讳以备，家戮直而不书。府君讳国兴，即达之长子也。府君凤承孝行，积习文使，为丈夫身，有君子气。寻山钓水，游泳自至。去名辞禄。蕴结含情，开怀风举，何言遘疾，奄至不起。呜呼！府君殁也，在大中四年五月。内奄颜高，万事云罢。夫人琅琊黄氏，育女二人，尚在童春。主丧过礼，以其年十月廿二日备葬礼，明州慈溪县梅州乡何村内，买得西原山之阳田之宾地，东至陈去镇约一里，西至陈墓，南至田，景向为坟。呜呼！自古有死，加君可伤。泉门深，路汇汇，恐地变，虑山异，刊名为墓志云：生遘高堂，死备棺椁。岁月兮庵，霜风兮易落，府君得兮永章。身殁名存兮可伤。"

查大中四年为唐宣宗李忱年号，时为公元 850 年。

新石器时代的原始先民认为死亡只是人体的暂时睡眠，人的灵魂会自由地游走，所以在陪葬的陶罐上敲开一个孔洞，让这些游魂能随时回到故乡。1974 年青海省乐都县柳湾出土一个彩陶罐，陶罐中装着一具小孩的尸骨，根据碳 14 考古测定，该陶罐和尸骨距今约 7000 年。陶罐上有一人为洞开的小孔，本品上的圆孔可能也是这一用意。

The jar has a rounded lip, an oblong body and a low ring foot. The domed lid has a mountain-shaped knob and four lotuses carved on top. Two symmetrically pierced holes, one on either side of the vessel, can be found near the ring foot. The light gray paste is hard and refined. The entire vessel is covered with a rich celadon glaze of olive green color. The ring of fireclay mark inside the lid matches that on the rim of the jar, indicating that the lid was placed over the mouth of the jar during firing.

A lengthy epitaph comprising columns of incised Chinese characters reading right to left occupies the entire exterior wall. The inscription was in memory of a man called Teng Guoxing, the eldest son of Teng Da and a native of Nanyang in Henan. He was said to be a dutiful son, a man of letters, and a dignified and virtuous person. He enjoyed exploring the mountains and waters and was fond of swimming. He was also known for his pleasant character and elegant demeanor. Unfortunately, he was struck down by illness and died in the 5th month of the 4th year of the Dazhong period (850 C.E.). His wife was

from a Huang family in Langya, Shandong. Their two daughters were still very young. The funeral was held on the 22nd day of the 10th month of the same year, and he was buried at Mount Xiyuan in Meizhouxiang, Cizi county, Mingzhou prefecture (now Zhejiang province), some distance away from the Lanxi county where he lived when he was alive. His death was deeply mourned.

Dazhong was the reign title of Emperor Xuanzhong (Li Chen) of the Tang dynasty. The 4th year of his reign corresponds to 850 C.E.

People from the Neolithic period believed that the body only takes a temporary sleep when one dies and that the human soul was free to wander around. Therefore, pottery funerary urns are perforated to allow the soul to return anytime. In 1974, a painted pottery urn with a small man-made perforation holding the skeleton of a child was unearthed from Liuwan in Ledu, Qinghai province. The jar and the skeleton had a carbon-14 date of around 7000 years before present. The holes on the present jar may have also served this purpose.

side 2

side 1

side 4

side 3

青釉凤鸟盏

唐

公元 618—907 年

越窑

高：3.2 厘米

口径：14.9 厘米

底径：6.8 厘米

Celadon cup with phoenix design

Tang dynasty

618 – 907 C.E.

Yue kilns

Height: 3.2 cm

Mouth diameter: 14.9 cm

Base diameter: 6.8 cm

盏浅腹，玉璧底。内壁刻飞翔的长尾凤鸟两只，间饰云气纹。盏心刻团花，四周绕以圈状纹。外壁光素，可见旋纹痕。胎灰白、细腻。盏内、外壁和外底心施釉，釉呈橄榄色，有开片纹。底足露胎，见残留垫饼痕。本品造型工整稳重，为中唐时典型饮食用具。

玉璧底也称作玉璧形圈足，形似玉璧，唐代中、晚期流行足式之一，唐代越窑、邢窑、定窑、长沙窑等各窑口烧制的碗、杯等制品上均有所见。一般不施釉，较精致的制品在底心内凹处施釉，只有圆环形底面露胎。

The shallow bowl has a base in the shape of a jade disc (*bi*). The interior and exterior as well as the center of the disc-shaped base are covered with a crackled olive glaze. Spur marks are found around the unglazed part of the base. The grayish white paste is smooth and refined. The interior wall is engraved with two long-tailed phoenixes flying amid clouds while the center displays a floral medallion surrounded by spirals. The outer wall is plain and wheel marks are visible. This bowl is neatly shaped. It is one of the typical food utensils from the mid Tang period.

The base in the shape of a jade disc is also called a "*bi*-shaped ring foot". They are prevalent on the bowls and cups produced at the Yue kilns, Xing kilns, Ding kilns, Changsha kilns and other kilns during the Tang dynasty. Usually, the entirely base is unglazed but the more sophisticated ones are glazed at the recessed center while the paste is exposed through the ring-shaped foot.

332

青釉双系罐

唐

公元 618—907 年

越窑

高：20.7 厘米

底径：11.3 厘米

Celadon jar with double lugs

Tang dynasty

618 – 907 C.E.

Yue kilns

Height: 20.7 cm

Base diameter: 11.3 cm

敞口，颈微束，溜肩，鼓腹，平底。肩置曲柄状双系，系一端成椭圆形，与肩粘连；另一端成环状，向上翘起，并不与罐体连接。颈腹间有弦纹数道。灰胎，质细滑。全器内外满施青釉，釉色青绿，有泪釉痕。胎釉结合紧密，一系上有一点开片纹。外底微内凹，外底边缘四周留有一圈垫饼痕。器身内底可见垫烧痕四个，呈正方形排列，可能底部曾放置小件器物一同入炉烧造。

The jar has a wide mouth, a slightly constricted neck, sloping shoulders, a bulbous belly and a flat base. The shoulder is flanked by a pair of lugs with angular turn, a semi-circular upright top and an oval-shaped bottom. Several indented lines encircle the neck and the belly. The grayish paste is smooth and refined. The entire interior and exterior are covered with a greenish celadon glaze with streaks. The glaze sinters well with the paste. No crackles are visible on the surface apart from a spot on one of the lugs. The base has a slightly recessed center. A ring of fireclay marks is found on the base around the rim. Four equally spaced spur marks are found on the inside bottom of the jar, suggesting that a smaller object might have been placed inside it and fired together in the kiln.

333

青釉双耳小罐

五代

公元 907—960 年

越窑

高：11.5 厘米

底径：5.6 厘米

Small celadon jar with loop-lugs

Five Dynasties

907 – 960 C.E.

Yue kilns

Height: 11.5 cm

Base diameter: 5.6 cm

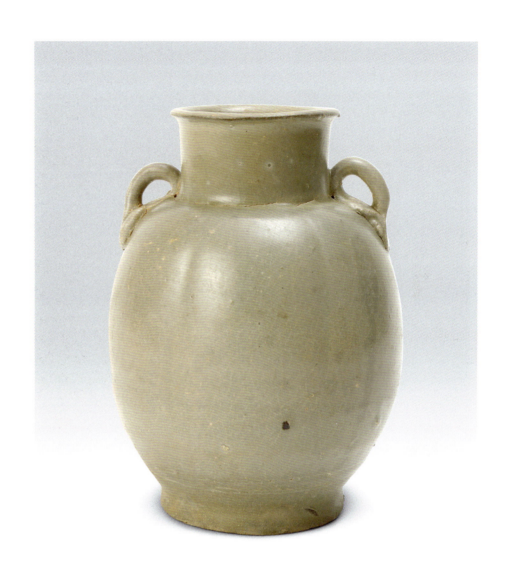

口微外翻，直颈，五瓣瓜棱状腹。颈肩两侧贴环耳各一，除下腹近底处刻弦纹一周外，全器光素无纹。灰白胎，胎细腻。器外壁施青绿色釉，呈失透状，满布冰裂纹。圈足微外撇，底足面平削，上有垫饼痕七个，足底墙微向内倾斜。器内壁布满细旋纹。

The jar has a slightly everted mouth, a straight neck and a five-lobed gourd-shaped body. The opposing sides of the neck and shoulders are each set with a loop-lug. The entire vessel except for a groove near the base, is devoid of decorative motif. The surface is covered with an opaque bluish-green glaze with crackles throughout. The rim of the slightly splayed ring-foot is trimmed flat. Seven spur marks are found around the foot rim. The interior wall of the foot slants slightly towards the base. The interior of the jar has fine wheel marks throughout.

334

青釉八棱双耳瓶

五代—北宋

公元 907—1127 年

越窑

高：15.2 厘米

底径：5.1 厘米

Celadon octagonal jar with double lugs

Five Dynasties – Northern Song dynasty

907 – 1127 C.E.

Yue kilns

Height: 15.2 cm

Base diameter: 5.1 cm

直口，高颈，耸肩，八棱形筒状腹，下腹微收，圈足内敛，足底有垫烧痕。颈刻弦纹两道，肩饰博山式小系两个，八棱面上刻花卉纹。胎呈灰白色，胎质坚细。通体施深绿色釉，釉面满布开片纹。造型新颖挺拔。

1980 年江苏镇江宋墓出土有相似器物（带盖），现藏镇江市博物馆。

The jar has a straight mouth, a tall neck, raised shoulders, an elongated octagonal body that tapers towards a ring foot and a base bearing fireclay marks. Two rounds of indented line encircle the neck. Two mountain-shaped small lugs are set on the shoulders. The grayish white paste is hard and refined. The entire vessel is covered with a crackled deep green glaze. The eight faceted sides of the body are carved with floral motifs. The tall and upright shape is unique and elegant.

A similar vessel with lid was unearthed in 1980 from a Song tomb in Zhenjiang, Jiangsu province. It is now in the collection of the Zhenjiang Municipal Museum.

335

青釉葫芦形执壶

五代—北宋

公元 907—1127 年

越窑

高：20.8 厘米

底径：6.6 厘米

Celadon ewer of double gourd shape

Five Dynasties – Northern Song dynasty

907 – 1127 C.E.

Yue kilns

Height: 20.8 cm

Base diameter: 6.6 cm

上部呈球形、小圆口。下部压竖直纹六道，呈瓜棱形。由筒状颈把上、下部连接，作葫芦状。肩一侧置曲管状流，相对侧贴竖条纹扁柄。圈足微外撇，足底四周残留垫烧痕迹。胎呈灰色，质细、致密、体薄。器身和底足满施深青绿色釉，釉层均匀，釉面光滑、晶莹、滋润，呈半透明状，无开片纹。

The ewer in the shape of a double gourd is fabricated from a thin, refined and dense paste of gray color. The entire surface including the foot and the base is coated with an even layer of lustrous, smooth and translucent deep green glaze with no crackles. The small bulb-shaped mouth is connected to the body by a cylindrical neck while the belly is impressed with six vertical grooves to imitate the lobed body of a gourd. A curved tubular spout is set on the shoulders opposite a strap-handle that connects the mouth to the shoulders. Fireclay marks are found around the rim of the slightly splayed ring foot.

青釉五棱碗

五代
公元 907—960 年
耀州窑
高：6.2 厘米
口径：16.2 厘米
底径：8 厘米

Celadon bowl with five-lobed rim

Five Dynasties
907 – 960 C.E.
Yaozhou kilns
Height: 6.2 cm
Mouth diameter: 16.2 cm
Base diameter: 8 cm

葵口外撇，斜壁，浅圈足。壁自口折缘处起五棱，棱外凹内凸。灰色胎，质坚。通体内外包括圈足满施青釉，釉色莹润，青绿可爱。釉面玻璃质感强，开冰裂纹片。圈足底可见数个支烧痕。

五代耀州窑仍以光素无纹饰的器物为主，设计着眼于造型的秀美。五代时多用木柴做燃料，器物在还原气氛中烧成，因而炉中所含一氧化碳较多，加上烧造技术等原因，成品多呈艾色。本品绿而青翠，釉面润泽，为当时的最佳呈色。

The bowl has a five-lobed mouth with a flared rim, slanting sides and a shallow ring-foot. The entire vessel including the ring-foot is covered with a smooth, lustrous celadon glaze. The highly glassy surface is covered with ice crackles. The grayish paste has a high degree of hardness. Several spur marks are found on the base.

Yaozhou wares of the Five Dynasties are mostly undecorated. The kilns of the

Five Dynasties were mainly fuelled by firewood, which sometimes result in a large amount of carbon monoxide being present in the kiln. This together with the given firing technology of the time will give a characteristic yellowish tint to the green celadon glaze. The smooth and lustrous green glaze of this bowl is considered the finest celadon green at the time.

337

青釉葵瓣碗

五代

公元 907—960 年

耀州窑

高：7.4 厘米

口径：17.9 厘米

底径：9.1 厘米

Celadon bowl with foliate mouth

Five Dynasties

907 – 960 C.E.

Yaozhou kilns

Height: 7.4 cm

Mouth diameter: 17.9 cm

Base diameter: 9.1 cm

葵花口，壁起凹棱，把碗体分为五瓣，高斜壁、大圈足、微外撇。灰胎，胎体薄，质坚。器内外均匀施青釉，釉面莹润，釉色青绿。胎釉结合紧密，造型秀丽、精致。圈足外底有三个圆形支烧痕。此碗为五代耀州窑上乘之作。

The bowl has a five-lobed rim with grooves down the exterior wall dividing the body into five petal-like segments. The deep slanting sides tapers towards a broad base resting on a slightly splayed ring foot. Both the interior and exterior are evenly covered with a lustrous and smooth green glaze. The body is thin and hard and the grayish paste sintered well with the glaze. The base enclosed by the ring foot has three circular spur marks. This bowl is a fine example of Yaozhou ware from the Five Dynasties period.

338

白釉弦纹罐

五代

公元 907—960 年

高：16.5 厘米

口径：15 厘米

底径：12 厘米

White-glazed jar with grooved design

Five Dynasties

907 – 960 C.E.

Height: 16.5 cm

Mouth diameter: 15 cm

Base diameter: 12 cm

口大而外撇，唇缘较薄，平底，圈足略微外撇。肩上刻两道清晰弦纹。器身内外施白釉，器外釉不及底，颈部和弦纹聚釉处釉色白中泛青和闪黄，釉面开细碎纹片。罐身可见泪釉痕，呈浅牙黄色。底露胎，胎质洁白、细腻，胎体较薄。造型丰满、端庄大气，极具美感。

The jar has a wide mouth with flared rim and thin lip, a bulbous belly and a slightly splayed ring foot enclosing a flat base. Two distinct grooves encircle the shoulders. The interior and exterior are covered with a white glaze that stops short of the foot on the outside. The glaze is suffused with tiny crackles and has a greenish or yellowish tint around the neck and where it pools along the grooves. There are ivory glaze streaks around the body. The unglazed base reveals a white paste that is thin and refined. The jar is noted for its rounded contours, robust shape and majestic presence.

339

白瓷枕

五代

公元 907—960 年

定窑

高：9.6 厘米

阔：12.1 厘米

长：15.8 厘米

Headrest with white glaze

Five Dynasties

907 – 960 C.E.

Ding kilns

Height: 9.6 cm

Width: 12.1 cm

Length: 15.8 cm

长方形，后高前低，上阔下窄，四角批削成凹棱，平底，底偏中处开气孔一个。枕边缘略低于枕面。枕面中部依外形饰一亚字纹饰，纹饰略高于枕面，与枕面四周凹棱相呼应，使光素枕面平添优雅。底露胎，胎薄洁白、细滑、坚致。器身施乳白釉，釉色纯净，可见数处艾黄色聚釉点。正面近底处两侧可见用手拿着器物蘸釉时留下的手指痕。

The rectangular headrest is higher at the back and lower in the front, wider at the top and narrower at the base and has concave beveled edges down the four corners. The trapezoidal top has a central panel with indented corners. The unglazed base reveals a hard, dense, refined and immaculate white paste. There is a ventilation hole near the center of the flat base. The headrest is covered with a creamy white glaze with a high degree of purity. The glaze appears yellowish in several spots where it accumulates. Finger marks left by the potter from dip glazing are visible on the front wall near the base.

340

葵瓣口碗

五代

公元 907—960 年

邢窑

高：5.5 厘米

口径：14.8 厘米

底径：6.2 厘米

Bowl with foliate rim

Five Dynasties

907 – 960 C.E.

Xing kilns

Height: 5.5 cm

Mouth diameter: 14.8 cm

Base diameter: 6.2 cm

五瓣葵花口，腹壁较深，底足宽大，圈足较矮。胎体薄、洁白、细腻，有粉质感。施釉较薄，釉色白中闪青，聚釉处呈青蓝色。

五代时使用漏斗状匣钵装烧法，窑炉烧木柴，器物在还原焰气氛中烧成，釉色是纯白或白中闪青。入宋以后，柴窑改为煤窑，器物在氧化焰中烧成，釉色白中泛黄。

The bowl has a foliate rim with five indentations, deep sides and a broad and rather low ring foot. The vessel is covered with a green-tinted white glaze that takes on a bluish tint where it pools. The immaculate white paste is thin and refined and has a powdery touch.

Kilns were still fuelled by firewood during the Five Dynasties period. White wares were placed inside saggars and fired in a reduction atmosphere, resulting in a pure white glaze or a white glaze with a greenish tint. By the Song dynasty, due to the exhaustion of firewood, coal was used. Since kilns fuelled by coal produced a weaker fire, the wares were fired in an oxidized atmosphere, causing the white glaze to take on a yellowish shade.

341

白釉唇口碗

五代

公元 907—960 年

定窑

高：8.1 厘米

口径：21.2 厘米

底径：11.4 厘米

White-glazed bowl with hollow lip

Five Dynasties

907 – 960 C.E.

Ding kilns

Height: 8.1 cm

Mouth diameter: 21.2 cm

Base diameter: 11.4 cm

唇口，口下渐敛到底，圈足宽大。胎质细腻、坚硬，叩之发出清越金属声。器内外施白釉，外壁施釉不到底，圈足和外底无釉，露出洁白胎骨。釉色雪白、纯正、润泽，白度高，无开片纹，碗外壁可见泪釉痕。底足有支烧时残留的砂粒。

唇口是为了防止坯体在高温烧制过程中出现变形，在器物成形时将碗口翻折过来黏合而成。一般来说，宽唇者多为空心，是将口缘翻卷而成；窄唇者多为实心，是成型时挤压过力而致。

此碗当为河北曲阳涧磁村、北镇村及野北村、燕川村一带生产的典型器物。

The bowl has a lipped mouth and sides that slant towards the base. The interior and exterior are covered with a white glaze that stops short of the foot on the outside. The snow-white glaze is pure, smooth and without any crackles. Glaze streaks are found around the exterior wall. The ring-foot and the base are unglazed, revealing a hard, refined and immaculate white paste.

The body gives a clear metallic sound when knocked with the knuckles. The rather broad ring-foot enclosed a base adhered with kiln grit from the fireclay spacers.

The lipped mouth was a design to reinforce the rim, thus preventing the vessel from warping when fired to a high temperature. In the process of shaping the vessel, the rim was flipped out and adhered to the body. Generally speaking, broad lips are mostly hollow like a tube while narrow lips are mostly solid due to compression.

The present bowl is a typical example of Ding ware from the areas around Jiancicun, Beizhencun, Yebeicun and Yanchuancun in Quyang, Hebei province.

白釉长颈执壶

五代

公元 907—960 年

定窑

高：19.8 厘米

底径：6.9 厘米

White-glazed ewer with slender cylindrical neck

Five Dynasties

907 – 960 C.E.

Ding kilns

Height: 19.8 cm

Base diameter: 6.9 cm

花形口，长圆筒形直颈，长柄自口边伸出，直落与肩腹部相接。下半部呈球状，上有明显旋削痕。肩上饰凸弦纹两道。底呈矮玉璧形，近边处有支烧痕三处，中间凹入处有不规则形釉块，其余部分露胎，露胎处有褐红色斑点。胎洁白、细腻、质坚硬，叩之声音清越。体薄，壶口薄处只有约 1 毫米厚。通体施白釉，釉薄而均匀，明亮润泽，下腹和底足聚釉处呈浅绿色。

本品造型与浇相类，应是浇花或盛酒、茶、油等的用具。

The entire vessel is coated with a thin and even layer of white glaze with a lustrous and smooth surface. Where the glaze accumulates around the lower belly and the foot, it takes on a greenish shade. Under the foliate mouth is a slender cylindrical neck. A long handle joins the mouth and the upper belly. Distinct scraping marks are found around the lower part of the globular belly. Two indented lines encircle the shoulders. The base in the shape of a jade-disc has three spur marks around its edge and irregular patches of glaze in the recessed center. The unglazed area reveals some brownish red speckles. The pure white paste is hard and refined, and gives a clear sound when knocked with the knuckles. The body is thin and the thinnest part of the mouth rim measures approximately 1mm.

Since this ewer is shaped like a watering pot, it was probably used for watering plants or storing wine, tea or oil.

343

青白釉盖罐

五代

公元 907—960 年

景德镇窑

高：21.6 厘米

底径：9.7 厘米

Lidded jar with *qingbai* glaze

Five Dynasties

907 – 960 C.E.

Jingdezhen kilns

Height: 21.6 cm

Base diameter: 9.7 cm

直颈，丰肩，下腹部内收，宽圈足微外撇，底内凹。附花蒂纽盖。胎质极雪白、细腻、坚硬。器身内外施青白釉，釉薄、均匀、晶莹、亮泽，聚釉处呈青蓝色。外底部有一圈呈火石红色的垫烧残留物。此瓶造型工整、端庄，代表了五代青白瓷烧造工艺的新高度。这样高品质的器物，说明景德镇早于宋代就已能烧制出精美的青白瓷。

The jar has a straight neck, bold shoulders and a lower belly that tapers towards a recessed base enclosed by a slightly splayed ring foot. The lid is surmounted by a floral knob. Both the interior and exterior of the vessel, including the base and the underside of the lid, are coated with a thin and even layer of lustrous *qingbai* glaze that appears bluish where it accumulates. The snow white paste is hard and refined. The base has a circular fireclay mark of burnt orange color. This jar shows that the kilns at Jingdezhen were already capable of producing fine *qingbai* wares before the Song dynasty.

白釉十二菱花口盘

南唐

公元 937—975 年

高： 4 厘米

口径： 13.6 厘米

底径： 7.5 厘米

Twelve-lobed dish with white glaze

Southern Tang dynasty

937 – 975 C.E.

Height: 4 cm

Mouth diameter: 13.6 cm

Base diameter: 7.5 cm

敞口，十二菱瓣口分成四组，如绽开的花。圈足与盘分开制作，较高，外墙稍外撇，内墙内斜，可见旋坯痕。足端较圆，有黏沙。胎细白，质较坚致，稍厚。内外壁施白釉，釉白、莹润、有泪釉痕，聚釉处微泛青灰，无开片。底部一半被足外壁流下的釉覆盖。

本品造型优雅、釉色润亮，胎、釉和工艺都不亚于五代和北宋的定窑产品，是南方窑口早期烧制的高水平白瓷的代表。南方烧白瓷的窑口被陆续发现，部分以往被认为是定窑的器物应是该等南方窑场所出。

1950 年江苏南京南唐后主李昪墓出土有相似的器物。

The dish has a wide mouth in the form of a blooming flower with twelve lobes divided into four segments. It has a rather hard and dense white body. Both the interior and exterior are covered with a smooth and lustrous white glaze with streaks but no crackles. The glaze shows a bluish gray tint where it accumulates. The white paste is finely grained and a bit thick. The rather tall and splayed ring foot is a separate application. Wheel marks are visible along the slanting interior wall. There are sand particles adhering to the rounded foot rim. Half of the base is covered with the glaze running down from the exterior wall.

This dish is noted for its elegant shape and lustrous glaze. Its paste, glaze and workmanship are comparable to Ding ware of the Five Dynasties and Song periods. It is an early and fine example of white ware produced in the southern kilns. As more examples of white ware are discovered from southern kiln sites, some white wares that had previously been attributed to the Ding kilns are in fact from southern China.

A similar artifact was unearthed in 1950 from the tomb of Li Bian the last ruler of the Southern Tang dynasty in Nanjing, Jiangsu province.

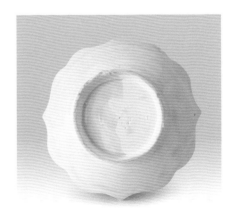

345

白釉海棠盘

南唐

公元 937—975 年

高：3.6 厘米

口：14.1 厘米 × 9 厘米

底：7.8 厘米 × 4.8 厘米

Begonia-shaped dish with white glaze

Southern Tang dynasty

937 – 975 C.E.

Height: 3.6 cm

Mouth: 14.1 cm × 9 cm

Base: 7.8 cm × 4.8 cm

敞口，海棠花口形。口缘长侧各起棱口四个，依棱口位置下压凹棱纹到近底，呈外凹内凸的八瓣花口。在盘内壁和盘心交接处，依口缘海棠花瓣的形状起凸棱八个。圈足与盘分开制作，外撇，足端黏沙。胎白微泛灰，质坚硬而薄，口缘部分只有 1.5—2 毫米厚，盘壁透光。施白釉，釉泛灰，布黑色点。8 倍显微镜下见不到气泡。圈足内壁和底无釉，砂底，有刷纹，见残留白色化妆土。盘心留有弧形垫烧条残痕。

此器仿自唐代流行的金银器式样。

The dish has a wide mouth and a lobed rim in the shape of an eight-petalled begonia flower. The white paste shows a grayish tint and the body is hard and thin. The rim has a thickness of only 1.5–2 mm. The wall of the dish is translucent. The white glaze takes on a grayish shade and has many black dots. No air bubbles are visible under 8x magnification. The splayed ring foot is a separate application. The foot rim is adhered with sand particles. The outside

is partly unglazed. Brush marks and traces of white slip are found on the unglazed base. A ridge highlights the floral shape of the base on the inside. Arched fireclay marks are found in the middle of the dish.

The dish was modeled after the metal ware of the Tang dynasty.

346

白釉五棱碟

南唐

公元 937—975 年

高：2.6 厘米

口径：13.2 厘米

底径：6.8 厘米

Five-lobed dish with white glaze

Southern Tang dynasty

937 – 975 C.E.

Height: 2.6 cm

Mouth diameter: 13.2 cm

Base diameter: 6.8 cm

口缘微外撇，等距压出五个弧形棱口。圈足内壁向内倾斜成 45 度，留有旋坯痕。足端较圆，足底无釉，露白色胎。胎不平滑，呈砂底状。内、外壁施白釉到足外缘，无开片。施釉较厚，釉色明亮、润泽、白中泛灰。

The dish has a slightly everted rim with five indentations. Both the interior and exterior are coated with a glaze that stops short of the foot. No crackles are visible. The white glaze appears lucid, rich and glossy and has a grayish tint. The inner foot rim slants towards the base at a 45-degree angle. Wheel marks are discernible around the inside of the ring foot. Traces of slip are found on the unglazed and uneven grit base.

宋辽金元瓷器

Porcelains of the Song, Liao, Jin and Yuan

宋辽金元瓷器：

精炼辉煌

宋代（公元960—1279年）是一个文化教育都很昌盛的时代，宋代瓷器可用"百花齐放""百家争鸣""各擅胜场"来形容。定、汝、官、哥、钧五大名窑及龙泉窑、吉州窑、建窑、耀州窑、磁州窑、景德镇窑、德化窑、潮州窑等著名窑口的产品各领风骚。

宋瓷美学风格近于沉静雅素，不仅重视釉色之美，更追求釉的质感之美。钧瓷的海棠红、玫瑰紫如行云流水，铜红乳光窑变神秘莫测（图录466号）；景德镇的青白瓷质色如美玉（图录403号）；龙泉梅子青釉青翠晶莹，已达到青瓷釉色美之极致（图录438号）；吉州窑独创的木叶贴花装饰（图录452号）以及黑釉玳瑁斑奇妙无穷（图录453号）；建窑曜变釉缤纷异常（图录469号）；定窑精细的黑瓷（图录374号）和酱釉瓷（图录375号、376号）翻开了黑瓷艺术的新篇章……宋代成为中国瓷器艺术登峰造极的时代。

辽（公元907—1125年）是由居住在白山黑水的古老民族契丹族建立，其制瓷业基本承袭唐代陶瓷工艺，与北宋中原地区的陶瓷制作工艺属同一系统，产品带有强烈的草原民族特点。瓷窑有辽阳江官屯窑、林东辽上京窑、赤峰缸瓦窑、山西大同青瓷窑、北京龙泉务窑等，生产白瓷、黑瓷、青瓷和茶叶末釉瓷等品种，受定窑、磁州窑影响。图录385号白釉"官"字铭盖壶和387号白釉鸡冠壶，其胎质和修削圈足的方法、釉的配方和施釉方式均与定窑相似。辽代最典型的瓷器首推皮囊壶（又称鸡冠壶），这种壶上部有一块鸡冠子形的突起。早期的皮囊壶是用金属和皮革制作，乘马奔驰时使用。

西夏（公元1038—1227年）亦称大夏，窑址有宁夏灵武的磁窑堡、回民巷等地，瓷器品种有白瓷、黑瓷、茶叶末釉瓷、黄釉瓷、青瓷、褐釉瓷等。西夏瓷粗，胎体含砂，釉质也粗，釉不光润。艺术上受磁州窑影响，刻花、划花、黑釉等装饰也豪放粗犷。图录481号的褐釉划花龟形挂壶是西夏陶瓷的代表作。

金（公元1115—1234年）是由女真族建立的封建王朝，其制瓷工艺前期的基础是辽瓷，后期则在北宋的基础上发展起来。仿定白瓷是此时的高档白瓷（图录390号），比辽白瓷水平高出很多。耀州窑也在此时生产出很优秀的月白色青瓷。金代瓷绘艺术主要表现在以磁州窑为代表的作品上，用笔简练，线条明快。

磁州窑是中国古代北方最大的一个民窑体系，装饰上以划花、剔花和珍珠地最具特色，题材多取自民间生活，生动亲切，情趣浓郁，有很强的感染力。产品以白地黑彩剔花器和瓷枕为最（图录491号）。如虎形枕造型威猛，色彩斑斓，绚丽多彩，是金代的特色产品。磁州窑白地绘黑花的绘画式装饰技法，不仅有着雅俗共赏的魅力，且对后世以青花为代表的彩瓷发展有着深远的影响。而在金代大量烧制的红绿彩瓷，对景德镇元代红绿彩和明清五彩等品种有着直接的影响。

元（公元1206—1368年）时钧瓷、龙泉瓷、青白瓷、白瓷生产扩大，不乏一些优秀产品，但总体来说仍较宋瓷逊色。卵白釉瓷是元代景德镇窑场在宋代青白釉瓷的基础上创烧的一种高温釉瓷，其胎质细密坚实，胎体厚薄适中，但较宋代青白釉瓷稍厚，釉质细腻，釉色白而微青，呈失透状，似鸭蛋色泽，故称卵白。元朝统治者青睐卵白釉瓷，应与"元人尚白"的民族习俗有关。大多数的卵白釉瓷器是不带款的，但无论有款或无款，通常被统称为"枢府器"。而习惯上所指"枢府器"并不一定是元代官府的专用器皿，也有部分外销产品。"枢府"瓷多有印花装饰，题材以云龙和缠枝花为常见，因釉属乳浊釉，故纹饰一般不大清晰（图录 420 号）。

元朝最具代表性的瓷器是景德镇青花瓷和青花
釉里红瓷，本书暂不讨论。

Porcelains of the Song, Liao, Jin and Yuan:

Grand Refinement

The Song dynasty (960 – 1279 C.E.) was a period of remarkable achievements. Song porcelains run the whole gamut of styles and types, each excelling in its own right. The five great kilns were the Ding, Ru, Guan, Ge and Jun kilns. Other leading kilns include Longquan, Jizhou, Jian, Yaozhou, Cizhou, Jingdezhen, Dehua and Chaozhou, etc.

Song porcelains are characterized by their subtle elegance with an emphasis on the color and quality of the glaze. The red opalescent glaze on Jun ware (Cat. No. 466), the *qingbai* glaze on Jingdezhen white ware (Cat. No. 403) are fine examples. The plum-green glaze on Longquan celadons (Cat. No. 438) is deemed the finest of celadon glazes. Skeleton leaf design (Cat. No. 452) with black glaze and tortoiseshell-like spots (Cat. No. 453) are unique of Jizhou ware. The transmutation glaze of Jian ware (Cat. No. 469) is especially resplendent. Black ware (Cat. No. 374) and soy-glazed ware (Cat. Nos. 375, 376) from the Ding kilns helped turn a new page for the development of black wares. It was during the Song period that Chinese porcelains reached the height of its development.

The Liao dynasty (907 – 1125 C.E.) was founded by the Khitan, a nomadic people originated from Northeast China. The porcelain industry of the Liao dynasty was a continuation of the Tang ceramic tradition and belonged to the same ceramic production system as those in the Northern Song but with their own distinct nomadic features. The major porcelain kilns include the Gangguantun kilns in Liaoyang, the Lindong kilns and the Daguantun kilns in Liaoning; the Gangwa kilns in Chifeng, Inner Mongolia; the Huairen kilns, the Datong kilns and the Hunyuan kilns in Shanxi; and the

Longquanwu kilns in Beijing. Their white ware, black ware, celadons and tea-dust glazed ware were influenced by Ding and Cizhou wares. Both the white-glazed ewer with the character "*Guan*" on the lid (Cat. No. 385) and the white-glazed cockscomb ewer (Cat. No. 387) are very similar to Ding ware in terms of the quality of their paste, the foot-trimming and the formula and application of the glaze. The leather-pouch ewer, also known as "cockscomb ewer" is the most representative example of Liao ware.

During the Xixia regime (1038 – 1227 C.E.), known as Bactria in the West, porcelains were made in the kilns of Ciyaobao and Huiminxiang in Lingwu, Ningxia. Glazed wares include white, black, tea-dust green, yellow, green and brown wares. The paste of Xixia ware is rather sandy while the glaze is coarse and matte. The influence of Cizhou ware is apparent. Xixia black ware with sgraffito decorations is particularly bold and rustic. The brown-glazed tortoise-shaped flask with incised decoration (Cat. No. 481) is a fine example.

The Jin dynasty (1115 – 1234 C.E.) was founded by an ethnic group called Jurchen. Early Jin porcelain was a continuation of the Liao ceramic tradition while later production was developed and expanded from that of the Northern Song. Ding-style white ware of the Jin period is known for its superb quality (Cat. No. 390), which greatly surpassed Liao white ware. The Yaozhou kilns also produced very fine moon-white glazed celadons during the Jin period. Painted decorations are a characteristic feature of Jin ware, appearing mainly on Cizhou wares. Another representative example of Jin porcelain is the tiger-shaped headrest.

The Cizhou kilns formed the largest private kiln system in ancient northern China. The majority of Cizhou wares are decorated with black sgrafitto pattern against a white ground (Cat. No. 491). Cizhou-type black-on-white porcelains characterized by painterly decorative motifs suited both refined and popular tastes, but also had profound influence on later polychrome porcelains such as blue-and-white ware. Porcelains with red and green painted decorations produced in large numbers during the Jin dynasty had direct influence on Yuan red and green painted porcelains and Qing *wucai* ware made in Jingdezhen.

During the Yuan dynasty (1206–1368 C.E.), the output of Jun wares, Longquan wares, *qingbai* wares and white wares increased. Despite the production of some very fine examples, Yuan porcelains on the whole was less sophisticated than Song porcelains. *Luanbai*, or "egg-white" glaze, is a high-fired glaze invented during this time by the Jingdezhen kilns based on the *qingbai* glaze of the Song dynasty. Its fine, dense paste of moderate thickness is only slightly thicker than that of Song *qingbai* glaze. The white glaze with a greenish tint is lustrous, smooth and translucent, resembling the shell of a duck's egg, hence the name. The Yuan rulers' preference for *luanbai*-glazed porcelain is probably related to the Mongol people's traditional preference for the color white. The majority of *luanbai*-glazed porcelains do not carry a mark. Whether marked or unmarked, they have been referred to as *shufu* ware ("privy council" ware), a type of Yuan dynasty official white ware noted for their elegant shape, dense and refined paste, thick and lustrous glaze, neatly trimmed foot and exquisite craftsmanship. Vessels called "*shufu* wares" were not necessarily exclusive for government use in the Yuan dynasty. Some were made for export. *Shufu* porcelains were precious vessels of its time. Most *shufu* wares are decorated with molded design such as dragon amid clouds or floral scrolls. Since *shufu* glaze is somewhat opaque, the decorative motifs are usually hard to make out (Cat. No. 420).

The finest Yuan wares are the blue-and-white and underglazed red wares from Jingdezhen, which are beyond the scope of this catalogue.

青釉莲瓣纹水盂

北宋

公元 960—1127 年

越窑

高：8.4 厘米

底径：6.6 厘米

Celadon jar with lotus motif

Northern Song dynasty

960 – 1127 C.E.

Yue kilns

Height: 8.4 cm

Base diameter: 6.6 cm

敛口，口缘置弦纹一周，圆腹，圈足外卷成金杯足形。罐体满刻五层仰莲纹，第四层莲瓣纹中央微起竖棱。浅灰色胎，胎较薄，质坚细。全器内外满施青釉，釉面光滑，呈浅青绿色，气泡细密、分布均匀，但在莲瓣纹边缘聚釉处可见较大粒和排列较疏的气泡。釉无开片纹。外底有残留垫圈一周。

金杯足形流行于唐代至北宋早期，为当时贵族上层人士使用的金杯的足形（附图 12）。

浙江慈溪市博物馆收藏有与本品相似的器物。

本品经热释光测定最后烧制年代距今800±160 年。

The jar has an incurved and grooved mouth, a globular belly and a ring foot with spreading rim commonly found on contemporaneous gold cups. The body is densely carved with five layers of overlapping lotus petals. The pale grayish white paste is hard, refined and relatively thin. The interior and exterior of the vessel are covered with a lustrous greenish glaze with tiny air bubbles. More loosely spaced and larger air bubbles appear along the edges of the lotus petals where the glaze pools. No crackles are found. Fireclay marks are visible around the base.

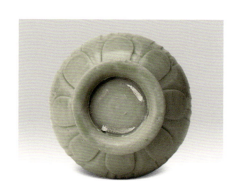

The foot is modeled after those on the gold cups commonly used by the aristocrats and the elites during the Tang to early Northern Song period (Fig. 12).

A similar jar is in the collection of the Cixi Municipal Museum in Zhejiang.

Thermoluminescence test shows that the last firing date of this piece was 800±160 years before present.

附图 12 西安何家村出土刻花金碗（唐）

Fig. 12 Gold bowl with engraved design unearthed at Hejiacun in Xi'an (Tang dynasty)

348

"太平戊寅"铭青釉盘

北宋

公元 978 年

越窑

高：3.6 厘米

口径：14.3 厘米

底径：7.3 厘米

Celadon dish with "*Taiping Wuyin*" mark

Northern Song dynasty

978 C.E.

Yue kilns

Height: 3.6 cm

Mouth diameter: 14.3 cm

Base diameter: 7.3 cm

侈口，浅腹，口以下渐敛，圈足微外撇。口缘细薄，给人轻巧之感。施深橄榄色青釉，釉层薄而均匀、洁净。器表光素，无纹饰。全器裹釉支烧，外底留有支烧垫饼残渣一圈。底刻"太平戊寅"四字。"太平戊寅"为北宋太平兴国三年，即公元 978 年，该年吴越国降宋。

The dish has a wide mouth and shallow sides that narrow to a slightly splayed ring foot. The entire surface including the base is coated with a thin and even layer of refined olive-colored celadon glaze. The dish is neatly shaped and the surface undecorated. The thin rim imparts a sense of gracefulness. The base bears a round of fireclay marks. The center of the base is carved with four characters "*Taiping wuyin*", a year mark denoting the 3rd year of the Taipingxingguo period (978 C.E.) of King Qian Shu of Wuyue. It was in this year that the Wuyue State surrendered to the Song dynasty.

349

青釉印花鸟盒

北宋

公元 960—1127 年

越窑

高：5.8 厘米

阔：14.2 厘米

Celadon box with bird-and-flower design

Northern Song dynasty

960 – 1127 C.E.

Yue kilns

Height: 5.8 cm

Width: 14.2 cm

圆盒，子母口，矮直腹。小平底，微向内凹。盖面微鼓，面、肩间饰弦纹三周。盖面印相对牡丹花两朵，四周满布枝叶、相互缠绕，两只长尾凤鸟反方向相对，在枝叶中飞翔。盖肩刻卷草纹带一周。灰胎，质坚、细滑。除子母口外，全器内外施满釉，釉薄均匀，釉色青绿。底足内四周见垫饼支烧痕，中心部位有缩釉现象。

瓷盒在唐代已出现，主要用于盛装香料、女士化妆用品和药物等。

The slightly domed lid is held in place by the inset rim of the circular box. The shoulders of the lid are incised by three rounds of indented lines. The top is carved with two facing peonies borne on entwining stems and scrolling leaves alternating with two long-tailed phoenixes flying amid foliage. The shoulders are carved with a band of scrolling tendrils. The small flat base is slightly recessed. The gray paste is hard and refined. Except for the rabbeted rim, the entire vessel is covered with a thin and even layer of greenish glaze. Fireclay marks are found around the base and retraction of glaze is visible in the center.

Ceramic boxes were made since the Tang dynasty, mainly for holding scented ingredients, cosmetics and medicines.

青釉划花八棱执壶连温碗

北宋

公元 960—1127 年

越窑

高：23 厘米（壶），13.6 厘米（碗），
　　26 厘米（壶加碗）

阔（碗）：18.3 厘米

Celadon octagonal ewer and warming bowl with incised motifs

Northern Song dynasty

960 – 1127 C.E.

Yue kilns

Height: 23 cm (ewer), 13.6 cm (warmer),
　　　　26 cm (overall)

Width (warmer): 18.3cm

温碗身起十棱，棱间的十面平坦，刻上升的云纹，云尾尖细而弯曲。足外撇，也起十棱，每棱间的面上镂空一个倒置心形。胎灰白色，体薄，质坚致、细滑。全身施灰青釉，底上有一圈多块垫烧痕。

壶身起八棱，棱间的面内凹，刻划重瓣蕉叶纹。流六棱，柄由双条拼合。颈起八棱，与盖的八棱相合。盖纽呈宝珠状，俗称宝顶，下有两级，再下内收直落起八棱，棱间每面镂空成一个倒置心形。全身包括底及足部施灰青色釉，施釉薄而均匀。底上有一圈分成多块的垫烧痕。

The ewer has an octagonal body with eight ribs down the sides and overlapping banana leaf motif incised on the facets between the ribs. The spout with six facets is set on the shoulders opposite a two-strand loop handle that connects the shoulders to the upper belly. The octagonal neck also has ribs mirroring those on the lid. The eight-sided lid pierced with an inverted heart-shaped opening on each facet is surmounted by a pearl-shaped finial. The entire surface including the base and the foot is covered with a thin and even layer of grayish green glaze. The base has a round of interrupted fireclay marks.

The warmer is in the shape of a decagonal bowl with ten flat facets, each incised with ascending clouds with pointed and curling tails. The entire surface is coated with a grayish green glaze. The base has a round of fireclay marks. Each of the ten facets of the splayed foot is pierced with an inverted heart-shaped opening. The grayish white paste is thin, hard, smooth and refined. Both the ewer and the warmer have distinct and sharp edges between the facets.

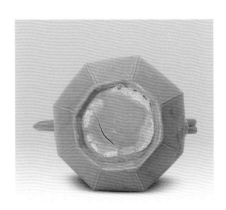

素胎多角瓶

北宋

公元 960—1127 年

高：69.2 厘米

底径：15 厘米

Unglazed lidded jar with horn design

Northern Song dynasty

960 – 1127 C.E.

Height: 69.2 cm

Base diameter: 15 cm

口卷缘、短颈外撇。瓶身作弧形五层状，上小下大，每层环列五只菱角状角，角顶上穿一小孔，角与瓶体相连处四周戳印圆圈。每层均满刻金钱纹和花卉纹。瓶下腹部围以仰莲纹，下挂垂帐纹饰。底座以覆莲纹作饰。僧帽状盖立在像倒置高足杯的覆莲瓣纹盖座上。浅灰白胎，坚硬。器身不施釉，呈紫褐色，但盖座胫部上端四周有蘸釉，器身也多处蘸釉，釉呈青黄色，满布细碎片纹。盖、瓶合烧，盖足缘上和器身肩部残留的垫饼痕相吻合，故盖、身胎色一致。

本品挺拔高大、造型优美、构思巧妙、制作精细、刀工利落、纹饰丰富、庄严华贵，是艺术价值极高的佛教文物。

浙江金华地区宋墓出土有这类器物。

The jar has a rolling rim, a flared short neck and a five-tiered body. There are five horns on each tier and each column. The tip of each horn is perforated with a small hole, and the junction between the horn and the body is impressed with a ring of circlets. The spaces between the horns are incised with coin and floral motifs. The upper part of the lotus plinth is decorated with overlapping lotus petals and the lower part inverted lotus petals. The edge of the upper plinth is decorated with an overhanging scallop edge. The lid looks like a monk's cap resting on an inverted lotus plinth. The recessed base of the jar reveals a grayish white paste with a high degree of hardness. Except for splashes of greenish yellow glaze with small crackles around the stem of the lid and some areas on the body, the vessel is basically bare of glaze, exposing a purplish brown paste. The lid was placed on the body during firing, as evidenced by the matching fireclay marks around the shoulders of the body and the rim of the lid. Since the lid and the body were fired together, they are consistent in color.

This jar is noted for its beautiful shape, monumental size, exquisite workmanship and rich decorations. This artifact is of significant artistic importance.

Similar vessels have been unearthed from Song tombs near Jinhua, Zhejiang province.

352

青釉 "建中靖国元年" 铭
多角瓶

北宋

公元 1101 年

高：41.3 厘米

底径：10.5 厘米

Celadon lidded jar with horn design and inscription

Northern Song dynasty

1101 C.E.

Height: 41.3 cm

Base diameter: 10.5 cm

鼓形器体，塔形盖。盖为宝珠顶，饰花边两道。器身均匀竖排四行凸乳丁，每行五颗，靠尖部有一小孔，烧制时用于排气。乳丁间用褐彩书 "千秋万岁，五谷仓库，年年常满，子孙代代，富贵也。建中靖国元年九月日谨题" 行书字样。灰色胎，坚硬。内、外壁施青灰色釉，釉中泛蓝，有剥落。底平，底边微向内敛，露胎外呈褐色。

中国古人对于子孙众多、香火绵延以及财富、地位的追求，在本品和图录 353 号均有体现。本品和图录 353 号应为福建窑口烧制。

The jar has a drum-like body and a pagoda-shaped lid. Each row is decorated with four horns and each column five. The pointed tip of each horn is perforated with a small hole for the air inside the vessel to escape during firing. The spaces between the columns are inscribed in semi-cursive script as follows: "May the granary be packed with the Five Grains for a thousand autumns and ten thousand years, and the posterity enjoy wealth and honor from generation to generation. Written on an [auspicious] day in the 9th month of the 1st year of the Jianzhongjingguo period (1101 C.E.)." The two-tiered lid is surmounted by a pearl knob and decorated with a foliate rim. The grayish paste has a high degree of hardness. Both the interior and exterior are covered with a greenish gray glaze with a bluish tint. Some flaking of glaze is visible. The rim of the flat base curves in slightly. The unglazed area reveals a paste of brown color.

This jar and Cat. No. 353 are from the Fujian kilns.

353

青釉"崇宁元年"铭多角瓶

北宋

公元 1102 年

高：39 厘米

底径：10.2 厘米

Celadon lidded jar with horn design and inscription

Northern Song dynasty

1102 C.E.

Height: 39 cm

Base diameter: 10.2 cm

本品与图录 352 号外形和结构相似，只是用褐彩书"千秋万岁、五谷仓库、年年常满、子孙日见、大富贵也、谨题。崇宁元年十二月日"行书字样。

本品与图录 352 号均属重要的断代文物，器身文字除表明器物的用途和烧造年代外，对研究民风习俗有莫大帮助。

This jar is similar in shape and structure to the last, Cat. No. 352. The vessel is inscribed in semi-cursive script as follows: "May the granary be packed with Five Grains every year for a thousand autumns and ten thousand years, the posterity thrive and enjoy great wealth and honor. Written on an [auspicious] day in the 12th month of the 1st year of the Chongning period (1102 C.E.)."

Both this jar and Cat. No. 352 are important dated historic artifacts. Apart from confirming the function and the dating of the vessel, the inscription is also an excellent reference for studying the customs of the period.

青釉宝塔形多嘴谷仓

北宋

公元 906—1127 年

高：49 厘米

Celadon jar with horn design and pagoda-shaped lid

Northern Song

906 – 1127 C.E.

Height: 49 cm

器身分为五层，上小下大，每层环列五个角形嘴。盖作楼阁式，顶为宝珠状。灰胎，胎粗糙、疏松。釉呈青绿色。

这种器形始于唐代晚期，流行于五代，多见于长江以南地区。

1978 年福建顺昌宋墓出土有相似器物，现藏福建博物院。

The body of the jar is divided into five tiers, narrower at the top and wider at the bottom. Each tier and each column has five horn-like protuberances. The lid is fashioned as a pagoda surmounted by a pearl-shaped finial. The grayish paste is coarse and porous. The glaze is grassy green in color.

Vessels of this shape first appeared in the late Tang period and were prevalent during the Five Dynasties mostly in regions south of the Changjiang River.

A similar vessel was unearthed in 1978 from a Song tomb in Shunchang, Fujian province. It is now in the collection of the Fujian Museum.

355

青釉酒壶

宋

公元 960—1279 年

高：12.2 厘米

底径：5 厘米

Celadon wine pot

Song dynasty

960 – 1279 C.E.

Height: 12.2 cm

Base diameter: 5 cm

洗口、束颈、实圆饼状足，足心微内凹。颈中部和肩各起弦纹一道。肩腹前后饰长流和曲状把手，左右两侧平贴圆筒形系各一，用于穿带。胎灰白，质坚。施青釉，施釉均匀，釉面满布土渗白点。釉不及底，釉底缘与胎交接处呈褐红色。足露胎，呈浅褐色。

The pot has a basin-shaped mouth and a constricted neck. A rib runs around the mid-section of the neck, and another encircles the shoulders. A handle arches from the lower shoulders up to the mouth while a spout rises from the opposite side. Halfway between the spout and the handle on the shoulders is a pair of tubular lugs used for tying a rope to the vessel. The surface of the vessel is covered with an even layer of celadon glaze with white inclusions. The glaze stops short of the base. The paste along the bottom edge of the glaze appears brownish red. The disc-like solid foot has a base with a slightly recessed center. The grayish white paste is hard. The unglazed foot revealed a paste burnt to a light brown color.

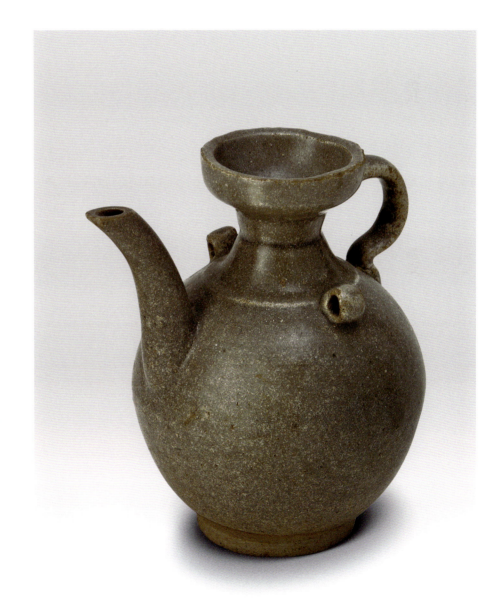

356

青釉菊瓣纹天鸡壶

宋

公元 960—1279 年

高：21.2 厘米

底径：7.7 厘米

Celadon jar with rooster-shaped mouth and chrysanthemum motif

Song dynasty

960 – 1279 C.E.

Height: 21.2 cm

Base diameter: 7.7 cm

壶口堆塑一只头向前伸、翅膀和尾平伸向后、身体丰满、正在疾走的雄鸡，鸡背部开注水口。壶颈上饰弦纹四道。圆腹，腹下渐敛，圈足露胎，微外撇。肩、腹间刻弦纹两周，上下满刻菊瓣纹。胎灰白，稍疏松。施青釉，底足无釉。本品纹饰简洁，但不失华美，且动感十足。

The mouth of the jar is in the shape of a rooster. The neck of the jar is encompassed by four grooves. The rounded belly tapers smoothly towards a ring foot. Two grooves encircle the body at the belly, above and below which are densely overlapping chrysanthemum petals. The grayish white paste is rather porous. The entire surface except the splayed ring foot and the base is coated with celadon glaze.

357

褐釉钱库

北宋

公元 1107 年

高：42 厘米

底径：11 厘米

Brown-glazed lidded cash holder

Northern Song dynasty

1107 C.E.

Height: 42 cm

Base diameter: 11 cm

侈缘，鼓腹平底。碗形盖，顶塑立鸟。口缘下刻菱形纹带，罐腹上下和盖中部贴附加堆纹各一周。腹一侧置门一道，上附门环。门两侧贴门神各一，分持武器朝向左右，左方门神下体可清楚见阴刻男性器官。两门神旁堆贴飞龙各一，朝门口方向飞去。胎灰色，较粗糙、坚硬。盖内侧墨书"饶氏二十一娘钱库"和"宋大□□□丁亥岁闰十月二日葬"。经查证，丁亥年为北宋大观元年，即公元 1107 年。

通常这类罐称"魂瓶"或"骨灰罐"，以前一般认为是墓主人魂魄归依所在。出土的东吴、西晋堆塑瓶内常发现有稻谷和铜钱，个别瓶的颈部刻有"东仓""西库"铭文，故有理由相信此类罐应称为"钱库"，内载金钱和稻谷等显示财富的物品。中国以农立国，除金银珠宝外，在"钱库"内放入稻米也是合理的。此罐的铭文为研究此类器物的用途提供了依据。

中国古代有按叔伯兄弟间婴孩出生的次序来作名的习俗，即通常所谓的大排行。此"饶氏二十一娘"很可能是在同宗、同辈出生的孩子中排行二十一。

The jar has a flared rim, a swelling belly and a flat base. A bird perches on top of the lid in the shape of an inverted bowl.

A ridge with irregular notches runs around the lid, the upper and the lower part of the belly. Below the mouth is a band of lozenge-shaped decoration. One side of the belly features a door with a ring knocker, flanked by a pair of door guardians with weapons in hand pointing in opposing directions. The guardian on the left is depicted with male genitalia. Next to the guardians is a pair of appliqué dragons facing towards the door. The grayish paste is rather hard and coarse. The underside of the lid is inscribed as follows: "Cash holder of Lady Twenty-First of the Rao family" and "Buried on the 2nd day of the 10th leap month of the year *dinghai* in the Da… period of the Song dynasty". Research confirms that the year *dinghai* correspond to the 1st year of the Daguan period or 1107 C.E.

Vessels of this style were usually regarded as mortuary urns for holding the ashes of the dead and thus referred to as "soul urns" or "cinerary urns" in China. They were believed to contain the souls of the dead. However, grains and copper cashes have been found in funerary urns unearthed from Eastern Wu and Western Jin tombs with characters like "Eastern storage" or "Western treasury" carved on them. Therefore, this kind of jars should more accurately be called "cash holders". Cash, grains and other items of value were stored inside these vessels. Since China is traditionally an agrarian society, to put grains into the cash holders alongside jewelry and cash is logical. The dated inscription on this jar is an excellent reference for studying the dating and usage of this kind of vessels.

It was common practice in ancient China to name newborn babies according to their seniority among siblings or paternal cousins. This Lady Twenty-First was perhaps the twenty-first baby born in the same generation within the extended Rao family.

青釉筒形谷仓

南宋

公元 1127—1279 年

将乐窑

高：36 厘米

底径：10 厘米

Celadon granary jar with barrel-shaped body

Southern Song dynasty

1127 – 1279 C.E.

Jiangle kilns

Height: 36 cm

Base diameter: 10 cm

宝珠顶，颈肩间置三个如意状竖耳，肩部饰堆纹一周，以双股凸弦纹将肩、腹明显分界。仓身为上宽下窄的圆筒形，外壁有三条立柱。腹部设有上下两层门，上层门敞开，下层门闭合，有门框。门口左上方贴一云状纹饰，下方贴乳突两枚。上层门上下门框中部拱起，置放谷物、金钱等后可用一小木块堵塞敞开的门，再用一小木条穿过上下拱孔封盖起来。胎灰白，质细滑。通体施青釉，釉色泛黄，釉不到底，釉面满布细碎纹片。

将乐窑位于福建将乐县境内，产青釉和青白釉瓷器，两宋时为烧制擂茶器皿的窑口。

The domed lid is surmounted by a pearl knob supported by three *ruyi*-shaped upright lugs. A round of appliqué design encircles the shoulders. The body of the vessel is in the shape of a barrel with a wide mouth and a narrow base. A double groove divides the shoulders from the belly. The belly features two framed doors, one on top of the other. The lower door is solid while the upper one is carved open.

The top and bottom edges of the upper door are decorated with a ledge with a loop in the center. After grains and cash are inserted into the jar through this opening, a small board can be placed over it and than bolted up by passing a rod through the two loops. Three pillars are featured on the outer wall of the granary. The upper left edge of the door is decorated with an appliqué cloud motif. The lower door has two appliqué studs. The grayish white paste is fine and smooth. The entire vessel except the area near the foot is covered with a crackled celadon glaze with a yellowish tint.

The Jiangle kilns were located in Jiangle county in Fujian. Production included celadon and *qingbai*-glazed porcelain. Tea utensils used for grinding tea leaves were made here during the Northern and Southern Song periods.

359

青釉杯连托

宋

公元 960—1279 年

将乐窑

通高：11.7 厘米

底径（托）：8.7 厘米

Celadon cup with stand

Song dynasty

960 – 1279 C.E.

Jiangle kilns

Overall height : 11.7 cm

Base diameter (stand): 8.7 cm

托座为梯形高足，托身饰波浪扁带纹一
圈，中央竖扁圆形杯托座。杯托座四周
满饰竖弦线纹，底部周边贴仰莲花瓣一
周。杯体外压竖棱六道，棱外凹内凸。
胎质灰白，稍疏松。全器外壁施青釉，
釉色灰青深沉。托底、杯足和杯底无釉。
本品造型别致、线条优雅、杯、托上下
结合、既美观又实用。

The stand is fashioned as a foliate tray with
an upright wavy border supported by a
stem with a stepped profile. The center of
the tray is furnished with a compressed
circular seat with fluted design over the
shoulders and a base of appliqué lotus
petals. The cup is placed on top of the
seat. The exterior wall of the six-lobed cup
is impressed with six vertical grooves to
mirror the six ridges running down the
interior wall. The grayish white paste is
relatively porous. Except for the base of
the stand, and the foot and base of the cup,
the entire vessel is covered with a deep
grayish green celadon glaze. The two-part
structure of the stand makes the vessel
both functional and decorative.

360

青白釉卷草纹碗

南宋

公元 1127—1279 年

景德镇窑

高：5.8 厘米

口径：18.7 厘米

底径：5.8 厘米

Qingbai-glazed bowl with molded tendrils

Southern Song dynasty

1127 – 1279 C.E.

Jingdezhen kilns

Height: 5.8 cm

Mouth diameter: 18.7 cm

Base diameter: 5.8 cm

撇口，浅腹，矮圈足。碗缘原镶有银扣边，已腐烂脱落，但在碗缘仍可见银扣的残留物。内壁满印双勾卷草纹，边缘围以变形回纹，内心饰狮子立金钱纹饰。外壁光素无纹。灰白胎，胎体轻薄，芒口覆烧。碗内外包括圈足施青白釉，釉薄均匀，泛青黄色。本品纹饰清晰流畅，繁复细腻，具浮雕效果，为同类器物之佳品。

The bowl has a flared mouth, shallow sides and a low ring foot. The silver mount over the rim has come off but remnants of the mount can still be seen along the rim. The interior is densely decorated with molded tendril scrolls with double outlines. A stylized fret border runs below the interior mouth rim. The interior center is decorated with a lion standing on a coin. The exterior wall is plain. The grayish white paste is thin and lightweight. The entire vessel including the ring foot is covered with a thin and even layer of *qingbai* glaze. The unglazed mouth rim suggests that the bowl was fired upside down in the kiln. The molded motifs are

distinct and fluid in line and elaborate and minute in detail with relief-like effects. This bowl is the finest of its kind.

361

青白釉莲瓣纹碗

南宋

公元 1127—1279 年

景德镇窑

高：6.7 厘米

口径：17 厘米

底径：6.8 厘米

Qingbai-glazed bowl with carved lotus petals

Southern Song dynasty

1127 – 1279 C.E.

Jingdezhen kilns

Height: 6.7 cm

Mouth diameter: 17 cm

Base diameter: 6.8 cm

敞口，圈足。内壁光素无纹。外壁满刻仰莲瓣纹，刀法工整有力，纹饰简单庄严。浅灰色胎，质较疏松，胎轻体薄。施青白釉，釉色泛淡青黄色，釉薄而均匀，满布开片纹。底足内外无釉，露胎处呈火石红色，外底可见一圈支烧垫饼痕。

The bowl has a wide mouth and a ring foot. The interior is devoid of decorative motif. The exterior wall is neatly and crisply carved with overlapping lotus petals. The light gray paste is thin, lightweight and relatively porous. The vessel is covered with a thin and even layer of pale green crackled glaze. The inner and outer sides of the foot are unglazed. The unglazed base revealed a biscuit of burnt orange color. A round of fireclay marks is visible on the base.

青釉灯

宋

公元 960—1279 年

耀州窑

高：13 厘米

阔：12.5 厘米

底径：7.5 厘米

Celadon lamp

Song dynasty

960 – 1279 C.E.

Yaozhou kilns

Height: 13 cm

Width: 12.5 cm

Base diameter: 7.5 cm

口缘宽大向外斜翻，如倒置浅碟状。腹部收束，满刻直纹，刀工凌厉、工整、古拙有力。茎部起阶梯状凸棱两圈。底座呈高台状、中空、底足外撇。灯内外施淡青釉，釉色莹润、均匀。座及器底露胎，胎浅灰色，质坚而薄。本品造型别致，精巧秀丽，为宋耀州窑的典型作品。

耀州窑创烧于唐而终于元，有 700 多年历史。唐代烧制三彩、白釉、黑釉、青釉等。五代以烧青釉为主，器物在造型、釉色、纹饰上明显受越窑影响。宋代以烧青釉为主，其次烧酱釉、黑釉与白釉。同时或稍晚仿烧耀州青瓷的有河南临汝窑、宜阳窑、宝丰窑、新安城关窑、钧台窑、内乡大窑店窑以及广东西村窑、广西永福窑等，形成了一个与越窑面貌、风格有别的北方青瓷窑系。

The lamp has a broad overhanging rim that slopes gently outward like an inverted dish. The slightly concave sides of the body are carved with vertical ribs imparting a sense of archaic elegance. Two prominent ridges encircle the stem to create a stepped profile. The pedestal has a splayed foot and a hollow body. Except for the pedestal and its underside, the entire surface including the interior is covered with an even layer of smooth and lustrous pale green glaze. The grayish paste is thin and hard. This lamp is noted for its unique shape, exquisite workmanship and elegant design. It is a representative example of Yaozhou ware from the Song dynasty.

The Yaozhou kilns started operation in the Tang dynasty and ended in the Yuan dynasty for a period of over seven centuries. During the Tang dynasty, *sancai* ware, white ware, black ware and celadon were produced. The Five Dynasties kilns mainly produced celadon wares whose shape, glaze color and decorative motifs were obviously influenced by Yue ware. During the Song dynasty, celadons were still the main product followed by soy glaze, black glaze and white glaze wares. Contemporaneous or later kilns producing Yaozhou-style wares include the Linru kilns, the Yiyang kilns, the Baofeng kilns, the Xin'an Chengguan kilns, the Juntai kilns and the Neixiang Dayaodian kilns, all located in Henan, as well as the Xicun kilns in Guangdong and the Yongfu kilns in Guangxi.

363

青釉菊纹碗

宋

公元 960—1279 年

耀州窑

高：5.9 厘米

口径：12.6 厘米

底径：3.6 厘米

Celadon bowl with chrysanthemum motifs

Song dynasty

960 – 1279 C.E.

Yaozhou kilns

Height: 5.9 cm

Mouth diameter: 12.6 cm

Base diameter: 3.6 cm

敞口，深腹，圈足。内壁印缠枝菊花，以一根枝叶绕成三个 "S" 形，把六朵菊花连在一起。碗心饰团菊纹，印纹清晰深錾，具浮雕效果。外壁刻斜直线纹。灰白胎，烧结程度好，坚硬致密。内外壁和外底心施青釉，釉色柔润。足粘窑渣，圈足底呈淡褐黄色。

The bowl has a wide mouth, deep sides and a ring foot. The interior wall is molded with six chrysanthemum blossoms borne on a scrolling stem to form three connected S-shapes. The center of the bowl features a chrysanthemum roundel. The molded motifs are deeply outlined and their edges sharply defined with relief-like effects. The exterior wall is carved with oblique striations. The interior and exterior as well as the space enclosed by the ring foot on the base are covered with a smooth and lustrous celadon glaze, which sintered well with the hard grayish white paste. The foot is adhered with kiln dregs. The unglazed foot rim appears pale brownish yellow in color.

364

青釉鱼水纹碗

宋

公元 960—1279 年

耀州窑

高：6 厘米

口径：13 厘米

底径：3.7 厘米

Celadon bowl with fish and wave motif

Song dynasty

960 – 1279 C.E.

Yaozhou kilns

Height: 6 cm

Mouth diameter: 13 cm

Base diameter: 3.7 cm

侈口薄唇，口以下收敛，小底，圈足。
内壁模印海水波涛纹，有戏水游鱼四尾、
水虫一只，碗心饰另一体形较大的水虫
纹，印纹清晰流畅，鱼纹和虫纹形象生动。
外壁满刻菊纹线。灰白胎，质坚、细滑。
口外施青釉，釉色纯正青翠、润泽。外
底心施釉，底足露胎，内边缘粘有沙泥。

The bowl has a wide mouth with thin
lip, tapering sides, a small base and a ring
foot. The exterior wall is carved with
chrysanthemum petal motif while the
interior is molded with four fish and an
aquatic insect amid corrugated waves. The
center is adorned with a larger aquatic
insect. The grayish white paste is hard
and refined. The entire surface including
the interior is covered with a rich and
smooth layer of green glaze. The foot rim
is unglazed but the base enclosed by it is
glazed. The inner rim is adhered with kiln
grit.

365

青釉 "天知美禄" 铭碗

金

公元 1115—1234 年

耀州窑

高：5.9 厘米

口径：13.7 厘米

底径：4.3 厘米

Celadon bowl with foliate mouth and inscription

Jin dynasty

1115 – 1234 C.E.

Yaozhou kilns

Height: 5.9 cm

Mouth diameter: 13.7 cm

Base diameter: 4.3 cm

菱花口、六组尖、圆花菱相间、圈足。内、外口缘下分别刻弦纹一道和三道。碗内印上下相接的一把莲，四周饰水波纹和一圈花卉纹，碗心刻 "天知美禄" 四字。外壁满刻牡丹花纹。内外施青釉，釉层较薄，釉色青中带微黄。足露酱黄釉。此碗外形优美，碗内印花清晰、精细、流畅。

在陕西耀州窑窑址曾发掘很多带有 "天" 字和 "美" 字的碎片，但未能发现其他字，故当时并不清楚是什么意思。

北宋著名画家张择端所绘《清明上河图》中有一家大酒店，彩旗上标着 "新酒" 二字，门前写的是 "天之美禄" 四字，形容酒之美味。明李时珍在《本草纲目》中也写道："酒，天之美禄也。"

The bowl has a barbed foliate rim highlighted by a grooved border on the inner edge. Three rounds of indented lines encircle the wall under the outer rim. The interior wall is molded with two opposing lotus bouquets against a ground of waves. A band of floral motif runs around the periphery of the bouquets. The center is carved with four characters "*Tianzhi meilu*". The bowl is lavishly carved with lotus design. The ring foot is covered with soy yellow glaze while the rest of the body is coated with a thin layer of greenish celadon glaze with a yellowish tint. This bowl is beautifully shaped and the decoration distinct, exquisite and fluently rendered.

Many potsherds inscribed with the characters "*tian*" and "*mei*" have been unearthed from Yaozhou kilns sites in Shaanxi. Since no potsherds bearing the other two characters (*zhi* and *lu*) were found in the past, the full meaning of the inscription remained unconfirmed.

In the famous Northern Song painting, *Qingming shanghetu* (Along the River during the Qingming Festival) by Zhang Zeduan, there is a large wine shop with the two characters "*Xinjiu*" (new wine) inscribed on its colorful banner. Written next to the shop entrance are the four characters "*Tianzhi meilu*", which can be interpreted as "Delicious bonus from Heaven" to describe the deliciousness of the wine. In his *Bencaogangmu* (Compendium of Materia Medica), Li Shizhen, a pharmacologist of the Ming dynasty writes, "Wine, delicious bonus from Heaven (*Tianzhi meilu*)." Together, they shed some light on the possible meaning of the phrase.

青釉花鸟纹碗

金

公元 1115—1234 年

耀州窑

高：8 厘米

口径：24.2 厘米

底径：8.1 厘米

Celadon bowl with bird-and-flower motif

Jin dynasty

1115 – 1234 C.E.

Yaozhou kilns

Height: 8 cm

Mouth diameter: 24.2 cm

Base diameter: 8.1 cm

敞口，浅腹，圈足。内壁印双线纹六条，将碗壁均分为六等格，上下分别以一圈水波纹线和双弦线将各格相连，格内交错印水波鸭纹和牡丹花纹。碗心刮釉一圈，呈褐黄色，内印六叶团花。外壁口缘下饰弦纹一道，下满刻直线菊瓣纹到底足。灰胎，胎薄，质坚。施青釉，釉色青中带绿，釉薄均匀。此碗造型秀丽，印纹清晰、流畅，水鸭形象生动逼真，展翅翘尾欲飞离水面，无论釉色还是纹饰均异常精细。

The bowl has a wide mouth and shallow sides that taper to a ring foot. The interior wall is molded with six equally sized decorative panels divided by double lines and linked by wavy lines at the top and bottom. The panels are alternately decorated with duck amid wave motif and peony spray. The center of the bowl features a molded floral medallion within an unglazed ring of yellowish brown color. An indented line runs under the outer rim, below which is a chrysanthemum petal motif represented by closely spaced vertical lines rising from the foot. The grayish paste is thin and hard. The entire bowl is covered with a thin and even layer of yellowish green celadon glaze.

青釉莲花纹碗

金

公元 1115—1234 年

耀州窑

高：7 厘米

口径：18.7 厘米

底径：6 厘米

Celadon bowl with lotus design

Jin dynasty

1115 – 1234 C.E.

Yaozhou kilns

Height: 7 cm

Mouth diameter: 18.7 cm

Base diameter: 6 cm

敞口，卷唇，口以下收敛，圈足。内壁口缘下饰弦纹一周，下刻一盛开的卷叶莲花。刀工简练、流畅，刻纹清晰。外壁光素，口缘下有凸弦纹一周。胎灰色，坚硬致密。除圈足底部外，全器内外施青釉，釉厚处呈青绿色，釉薄处呈黄绿色。釉面玻璃质感强，滋润明亮。本品具有明显的金代特色。

The bowl has a wide mouth with a rolling lip that hangs slightly over the outer rim and a ring foot. A groove runs around the interior wall below the rim. The area enclosed by the groove is carved with a lotus blooming amid curly leaves. The carving shows terseness, sweeping fluidity and distinct outlines. Apart from a ridge below the outer rim, the exterior wall is devoid of decorative motif. The grayish paste is hard and dense. The entire vessel except the base of the ring foot is covered with a celadon glaze that appears grassy green where it accumulates and yellowish where it runs thin. The glaze has a lucid, smooth and highly vitreous surface. The bowl is characteristic of Jin celadons.

月白釉婴戏莲纹碗

金

公元 1115—1234 年

耀州窑

高：15.2 厘米

口径：20.7 厘米

底径：6.1 厘米

Bowl with child and lotus motif in moon-white glaze

Jin dynasty

1115 – 1234 C.E.

Yaozhou kilns

Height: 15.2 cm

Mouth diameter: 20.7 cm

Base diameter: 6.1 cm

敞口，口以下渐收敛，圈足。内壁刻缠枝莲花纹，婴孩戏于其间，刀锋深邃，纹饰清晰、流畅，婴孩活泼可爱。外壁口缘下饰弦纹一周，余光素无纹。胎灰白，质坚、细滑。器体外施月白釉，有泪釉痕，釉色白中略闪青，温润如月白色。

月白釉瓷是金代耀州窑的新品种。

The bowl has a wide mouth and sides that narrow to a small ring foot. The interior is carved in relief with a child playing amid lotus scrolls. The carving is deep, precise and fluent. The exterior is plain except for an indented line below the mouth rim. The grayish white paste is hard and refined. The entire bowl is covered with a smooth moon-white glaze with a greenish tint. Glaze streaks are visible on the surface.

Moon-white glaze was a Yaozhou invention during the Jin dynasty.

黑釉酱边兔毫碗

宋

公元 960—1279 年

耀州窑

高：4.7 厘米

口径：16.4 厘米

底径：5.4 厘米

Black-glazed "hare's fur" bowl with soy-red rim

Song dynasty

960 – 1279 C.E.

Yaozhou kilns

Height: 4.7 cm

Mouth diameter: 16.4 cm

Base diameter: 5.4 cm

碗口作七葵花瓣状，口以下内收，圈足外墙高、内墙矮，露胎，圈足与腹下交界处有一涩圈。内壁口缘下约 2.5 厘米处置凹弦纹一周，凹弦下方施黑釉，有细长兔毫纹由碗心向外射出；凹弦上方饰酱红釉，红、黑分界明显。外壁口缘下饰约 1.8 厘米宽的酱红釉带，其下施黑釉不及底，釉厚处呈纯黑色，红、黑分界不如内壁清晰。胎呈浅褐色，胎质较坚硬，露胎处布满褐色斑点。

黑釉的呈色剂为氧化亚铁，当其含量在 8% 左右，器物烧成后呈赤褐色。如果釉厚度达到 1.5 毫米左右，而还原火焰又足够，釉色就会呈现纯黑，并发出美丽的光泽。控制釉的成分和温度，令酱釉、黑釉同时出现在一件器物上且分界清晰，是十分困难的。本品红、黑对比强烈，分界明显，极为难得。

The bowl has a foliate rim with seven indentations. A groove runs around the interior of the bowl approximately 2.5 cm below the rim. The area within is coated with black glaze with long and fine streaks resembling hare's fur radiating from the groove. The area above the groove is glazed soy red. The edge between the two glazes is distinct. The outer wall is similarly glazed; a band of soy red glaze (1.8 cm wide) covers the outer rim while the area below is coated with a black glaze that stops short of the foot. The glaze appears jet black along the thick welt. The boundary between the two glazes is less distinct than that on the interior wall. The sides of the bowl taper from under the mouth rim towards an unglazed ring foot that appears taller on the outside and shorter on the inside. The light brown paste is relatively hard and dense; brown speckles are found on the unglazed areas.

The colorant of black glaze is ferrous oxide. When there is around 8 percent of ferrous oxide in the glaze, the color will take on a reddish brown hue. The glaze would need to be at least 1.5 mm thick and fired in a reduction atmosphere in order to achieve a jet black glaze with a beautiful luster. Also, the glaze composition and firing temperature would have to be just right to achieve such a clear demarcation between the soy and black glaze.

酱釉"夜明珠"铭油灯

宋

公元 960—1279 年

耀州窑

高：5.1 厘米

长：9.2 厘米

**Soy-glazed oil lamp with
"*Yemingzhu*" mark**

Song dynasty

960 – 1279 C.E.

Yaozhou kilns

Height: 5.1 cm

Length: 9.2 cm

圆口，短颈，广肩，腹急折到底，圈足。肩、腹间置三角形流一个，相对侧贴半圆形把手，把手边饰乳丁状物，下方反印"夜明珠"三个字；上方有不规则小凸点七颗，排列如北斗七星，象征光明。胎断面呈浅灰白色，质坚、细滑。内外壁施酱釉，呈酱褐色。釉厚而均匀，柔润亮泽，釉不透光。底露胎，留有绳切割旋纹，露胎处有浅褐色护胎釉。

夜明珠是指晚上能自行发光的一种经加工的矿石，地质学家推测其为萤石的可能性较大。

The vessel has a circular mouth, a short neck, broad shoulders that make an angular turn to join the belly and a ring foot. A triangular spout is set between the shoulders and the belly opposite a semicircular handle with stud design along the border. The inner surface of the handle is engraved with a mirror image of three characters "*Yemingzhu*" or "pearl that glows in the dark" and seven irregularly arranged dots representing the Seven Stars of the Northern Dipper. The chipped foot reveals a hard and refined grayish white paste. The interior and exterior are covered with a thick and even layer of opaque soy brown glaze with a smooth and lustrous surface. Marks from removing the form from the wheel with a cord are visible on the unglazed base. The paste is coated with light brown slip.

"*Yemingzhu*" refers to a kind of reconstituted mineral that is self-luminous in the dark. Geologists surmised that the mineral is probably fluorite.

371

黑釉铁斑碗

金

公元 1115—1234 年

耀州窑

高：4.7 厘米

口径：15.1 厘米

底径：4.6 厘米

Black-glazed bowl with ferruginous splashes

Jin dynasty

1115 – 1234 C.E.

Yaozhou kilns

Height: 4.7 cm

Mouth diameter: 15.1 cm

Base diameter: 4.6 cm

敞口、口微外折、小圈足、底足和底露胎。灰白胎，质坚致密，叩之声音清越。碗内外施黑釉，釉色黝黑、明亮。碗内壁满布褐色斑纹，斑纹流畅自如，其中两条斑纹过墙流到碗外壁。斑纹上留有金属结晶物，闪闪生光。釉厚，外壁下方黑釉遮盖不到之处可见一层酱黄色底釉。本品在黝黑的底色上配以充满动感的褐斑纹，像一盛开的鲜花，形成动与静、黑与褐的对比，使简单的色彩变得优雅悦目，表现出工匠的灵巧心思以及火与土的魔力，是耀州窑黑瓷的优秀作品。

本品经热释光测定最后烧制年代距今850—650 年。

The bowl has a wide mouth with slightly everted rim and a small ring foot. The foot and the base are unglazed. The grayish white paste is hard and dense. The interior and exterior surfaces are covered with a lustrous jet-black glaze. Brown splashes with fluid outlines are found extensively on the inside. Residues of crystalized metal shimmer on the surface. Two of these splashes run over the rim onto the exterior wall. The glaze is thickly applied.

It stops short of the lower part of the exterior wall, revealing a paste coated with soy yellow slip. It gives a clear sound when struck. The brown splashes against a jet-black ground in the form of a blooming flower creates a sharp contrast between motion and stillness. This bowl is a fine example of Yaozhou black ware.

Thermoluminescence test shows that the last firing date of this piece was 850 to 650 years before present.

372

黑釉酱边碗

金

公元 1115—1234 年

耀州窑

高：4.8 厘米

口径：13.8 厘米

Black glazed bowl with soy-red rim

Jin dynasty

1115 – 1234 C.E.

Yaozhou kilns

Height: 4.8 cm

Mouth diameter: 13.8 cm

敞口，口缘外侈，腹急收到底，小圈足。
灰胎，颇细腻，质坚，胎薄。内外施黑色釉，
碗内口缘呈酱色，下有褐青色兔毫纹，
碗心为漆黑色。外壁光素无纹，施釉不均。
圈足底无釉，底心施釉，足底留有垫烧
时的石英砂粒。

本品应为耀州窑仿烧建窑兔毫盏。

The bowl has a wide mouth with flared
rim and sides that taper to a small ring
foot. The grayish paste is hard, thin and
rather refined in texture. Both the interior
and exterior are covered with black glaze.
The inner rim is coated with a soy glaze
and the area below a brownish green glaze
with "hare's fur" streaks radiating from the
mouth rim. The exterior wall is devoid of
decorative motif and the glaze is unevenly
applied. The foot rim is unglazed but the
area within is covered with glaze. The base
is adhered with quartz sand particles used
as spacers during firing.

This bowl is a Yaozhou imitation of the
"hare's fur" bowls from the Jianyao kilns.

373

柿红釉素身碗

金

公元 1115—1234 年

耀州窑

高：7.5 厘米

口径：18.1 厘米

底径：6.1 厘米

Persimmon-glazed bowl

Jin dynasty

1115 – 1234 C.E.

Yaozhou kilns

Height: 7.5 cm

Mouth diameter: 18.1 cm

Base diameter: 6.1 cm

敞口，口缘下微内凹，圆腹，浅圈足。碗心有五组呈放射状的黑弦线纹饰。胎浅褐色，细滑。内外施柿红色酱釉，釉色均匀，晶莹润滑，明亮照人。釉不及底足，底露胎，修刮工整。

柿红釉属酱色釉的一种，是以氧化铁为着色剂的高温釉，由于铁含量的不同和烧造时对温度控制不一，也会产生柿黄或芝麻酱等不同的釉色。

The bowl has a wide mouth with a slight constriction under its rim, rounded sides and a shallow ring foot. The center of the bowl has five groups of tiny black streaks in radiating form. The light brown paste is smooth and refined. An even layer of smooth and glossy persimmon red glaze covers the entire interior but stops short of the foot on the outside. The unglazed base is neatly trimmed.

Persimmon glaze is a type of soy glaze. It is a high-fired glaze using iron as colorant. The variation of iron content and firing temperature results in a range of hues ranging from persimmon yellow to sesame black.

374

黑釉碗

宋

公元 960—1279 年

定窑

高：6 厘米

口径：19.1 厘米

底径：4.5 厘米

Conical bowl with black glaze

Song dynasty

960 – 1279 C.E.

Ding kilns

Height: 6 cm

Mouth diameter: 19.1 cm

Base diameter: 4.5 cm

口阔大，足小，呈斗笠形。胎白，细滑，微带米黄色。除底足外满施黑釉，色黝黑、肥润、亮泽，满布细小棕眼，开大纹片。口缘釉薄处呈褐红色，外壁有泪釉痕。外壁与底足交界处刮釉一圈，圈足和底有土浆痕。

黑定从质地上可分为两类：一类是中心窑场生产的精细高档黑瓷，白胎，质地精细，胎壁很薄，露胎处没有粗大的轮旋纹和粗大砂粒，釉层均匀光滑。另一类是黑釉粗瓷，器物粗厚，釉色偏褐。1992 年辽宁省朝阳市西上台辽墓出土一件与本品相似但较小的黑釉斗笠碗。

本品经热释光检定最后烧制年代距今 800—600 年。

The bowl is in the shape of an inverted cone with a wide mouth and a small foot. The fine-grained white paste has a yellowish tint. The entire vessel except the base is covered with a glossy and lustrous jet-black glaze with large crackles and small pinholes. A reddish brown color comes through the thin glaze along the mouth rim. Glaze streaks are found around the exterior wall. The glaze around the junction between the lower belly and the foot has been scraped clean. Splashes of slip are found around the ring foot and on the base.

As far as the quality of the paste is concerned, black Ding ware comes in two types. The first type consists of fine quality black ware produced in the major kilns, characterized by a fine-grained white paste, a thin body, a smooth and even glaze and the absence of conspicuous wheel marks and coarse sand particles on unglazed areas. The second type consists of coarse black ware with a thick body and a dark brown glaze. A black-glazed conical bowl similar to the present piece but smaller in size was unearthed in 1992 from a Liao tomb in Shangtai west of Zhaoyang, Liaoning province.

Thermoluminescence test shows that the last firing date of this piece was around 800 to 600 years before present.

酱釉梅瓶

北宋

公元 960—1127 年

定窑

高：24 厘米

口径：6.6 厘米

底径：7.5 厘米

Meiping vase with soy glaze

Northern Song dynasty

960 – 1127 C.E.

Ding kilns

Height: 24 cm

Mouth diameter: 6.6 cm

Base diameter: 7.5 cm

小口、翻缘圆唇、直颈、肩和上腹圆鼓、下腹较瘦、小平底。矮圈足，内侧留有垫烧砂粒残渣，底有釉。胎色洁白、细腻。施酱釉，釉层薄，釉面均匀、光亮而平整，芝麻酱色调很重，黑色中带柿红色。本器釉色明丽、造型优美、稳重大方、制作规整、刻意求精，无繁杂的附加装饰，仅以明丽的釉色和变化的弧线构成柔和、挺拔、秀丽、匀称的瓶体，符合宋人清逸典雅的审美情趣。这类瓶以白釉居多，柿釉较少。在色釉瓷器仍以青为尚的宋代，这件酱釉瓶可谓十分珍贵的上乘之作。

紫定是北宋和金代定窑瓷器中的酱釉瓷，酱釉为芝麻酱色、褐红色、赭色和柿色釉的通称。明曹昭《格古要论》说"紫定色紫"，其紫色实际是芝麻酱色而发红色调的颜色，本品即文献中所称的"紫定"。曲阳涧磁村一带定窑遗址出土紫定瓷片的数量很少，说明当时生产数量不多，品种也少。

1974 年江苏镇江北宋章岷墓出土的一对紫定瓶造型、釉色和本品相近。

The vase has a small mouth with out-rolling lip, a straight neck, rounded shoulders, a bulbous upper belly and a lower belly that tapers towards a small flat base enclosed by a low ring foot with sand particles adhering to its inner edge. The white paste is immaculate and refined. The entire vessel including the base is covered with a thin and even layer of sesame black soy glaze with a touch of persimmon red. The surface is smooth and glossy. Elaborate decorations are absent but the beautiful glaze color and elegant shape conform to the aesthetics of the Song dynasty. This type of vase is usually glazed white; persimmon ones are more rare. As green is the predominant color of Song ceramics, this soy-glazed vase is particularly rare and unusual.

"Purple Ding" ware falls within the category of brown Ding ware of the Northern Song and Jin periods. In his *Gegu yaolun* (Essential Criteria of Antiquities), the Ming scholar Cao Zhao writes that purple Ding ware is purplish in color. "Purplish" in fact refers to the reddish tint of the sesame black soy glaze, as exemplified by the present piece. Only a small amount of purple Ding potsherds has been unearthed from Jiancicun and surrounding area in Quyang, suggesting that these vessels were produced in limited quantity and variety.

A pair of "Purple Ding" vases similar to the present piece in shape, structure and glaze color was unearthed in 1974 from the Northern Song tomb of Zhang Min in Zhenjiang, Jiangsu province.

376

紫定渣斗

宋

公元 960—1279 年

定窑

高：7.2 厘米

口径：15.2 厘米

底径：4.7 厘米

"Purple Ding" spittoon with soy glaze

Song dynasty

960 – 1279 C.E.

Ding kilns

Height: 7.2 cm

Mouth diameter: 15.2 cm

Base diameter: 4.7 cm

口外撇，短颈，扁圆腹，圈足。通体光素无纹饰。胎质洁白、润滑、致密，胎体细薄，口缘薄处只有约 1.5 毫米厚。体外施柿色釉至近圈足处，足墙内和内底有沾釉，露胎处可见拉坯旋纹痕和土渍残留物。口缘内侧施柿釉，扁圆腹内罩透明釉，透明釉下可见细密的所谓"竹丝刷纹"修刮痕。柿釉内隐约闪现酱黑色斑点，颈、腹间和下腹、圈足间聚釉处有酱黑色纹线。本品造型优雅、制作精巧，为紫定器极品。

本品碗内心留有小支钉四枚，呈四方形排列，四方形中心有圆柱形残留物。有可能是利用柱状体抵着器物底部最厚之处，以四支钉轻轻支着胎体，减少薄胎器物的变形概率。也有可能只是为了承托另一器物同烧，增加产量。

The bowl has a flared plate-shaped mouth, a short neck, a rounded belly and a ring foot. The entire surface is devoid of decorative motif. The white paste is immaculate, refined, dense and thin. The thinnest part of the mouth measures approximately 1.5 mm in thickness. A persimmon red glaze covers the exterior of the vessel and stops short of the foot. The interior edge of the foot rim and half of the base are also glazed. Wheel marks and fireclay marks are visible on the unglazed areas. The inside of the mouth is also covered with persimmon red glaze but the rest of the interior is coated with a transparent glaze. Fine marks left by bamboo fiber scrapers are visible under the glaze. Soy black speckles are faintly visible in the persimmon red glaze. A soy black line runs around the ring foot and the junction between the neck and the belly. This elegantly shaped and exquisitely crafted vessel falls within the highest grade of "Purple Ding", a type of soy-glazed ware produced at the Ding kilns. Soy glaze is a generic term for sesame black, reddish brown, ochre and persimmon red glazes.

In the center of the bowl are four small spurs with a cylindrical object in the

middle. Using a cylindrical spacer to support the thickest part of the vessel while the spurs remain in limited contact would prevent thinly potted vessels from warping during firing. However, it is also possible that the spacer was used to support another vessel stacked on top of the present vessel, a means often used to increase production.

377

白釉花瓣口碗

宋

公元 960—1279 年

高：5.4 厘米

口径：18.2 厘米

底径：5.8 厘米

White-glazed bowl with foliate rim

Song dynasty

960 – 1279 C.E.

Height: 5.4 cm

Mouth diameter: 18.2 cm

Base diameter: 5.8 cm

六瓣荷花形口，瓣尖高出碗缘，圈足内高外矮。碗心浅刻盛开荷花，围以双圈弦纹。胎色洁白，质细腻，胎体薄而均匀，透光性强。全器内外满覆白釉，釉薄、晶莹光亮，釉色偏淡青色，如青白釉色，外壁可见泪釉痕。圈足底平切，露胎，圈足内墙粘有白色砂粒垫烧残渣。本品造型清秀，釉色雅素。

The mouth of the bowl is fashioned as a six-petalled lotus. The ring foot is taller on the outside and shorter on the inside. The center is carved with a blooming lotus inside double circular frames. The white paste is pure and refined. The thin and translucent body is even in thickness. The entire bowl is covered with a thin and lustrous white glaze with a *qingbai*-like greenish tint. Glaze streaks are found around the exterior. The flat foot rim is unglazed. Remnants of quartz sand particles are found on the inside of the foot.

378

白釉莲瓣盏托

北宋

公元 960—1127 年

定窑

高：9.5 厘米

阔：16.5 厘米

White-glazed bowl stand with lotus petal motifs

Northern Song dynasty

960 – 1127 C.E.

Ding kilns

Height: 9.5 cm

Width: 16.5 cm

碗托呈高底座状。托身呈六瓣口浅碗形，中立倒置杯状盘托，上刻覆莲花瓣纹。足外撇，内中空到托身，饰花形孔三个。胎洁白细腻，质坚。器内外施乳白色釉，釉色晶莹柔润，聚釉处呈湖水绿色。圈足底无釉，足底边和器底内壁粘有许多细小石英砂粒。这样大的碗托在北宋定窑遗物中颇为少见。

The bowl stand has a splayed foot in the form of a high pedestal with a hollow interior connected to the inside of the stand. The sides of the pedestal are pierced with three floral shapes. The tray has a foliate mouth with six indentations, enclosing a stand resembling an inverted cup with sides decorated with inverted lotus petals. The pure white paste is hard and refined. The interior and exterior of the entire vessel are covered with a lustrous and creamy white glaze that takes on a lake green color where it accumulates. The foot rim and the area within the ring foot are unglazed. The foot rim and the inner side of the foot are adhered with many fine quartz sand particles. Bowl stands of this size are quite rare among Ding wares of the Northern Song period.

白釉葵瓣口碗

北宋

公元 960—1127 年

定窑

高：6.4 厘米

口径：17.3 厘米

底径：6 厘米

White-glazed bowl with foliate rim

Northern Song dynasty

960 – 1127 C.E.

Ding kilns

Height: 6.4 cm

Mouth diameter: 17.3 cm

Base diameter: 6 cm

五瓣葵花口，碗内棱骨微凸，碗身约 45 度角斜出，腹壁较深，圈足微外撇，足外边缘斜削一圈。胎体薄，坚致，白净，带粉质感。釉色洁白，釉面光亮、莹润，釉薄处可见胎上的轮旋痕。外壁有因釉层流动而出现的泪釉痕，呈浅青黄色。内外光素无纹，施釉不到底，底露胎，留有支烧石英砂粒。本品具明显的北宋初期定窑白瓷特色，造型优美，制作精细，比例和谐，温文素雅，体现了宋代文人的审美情趣，是优秀的北宋定窑作品。

The bowl has a foliate rim with five notches. A faintly raised ridge runs down the interior wall from below each notch. The wall tapers at a 45-degree angle to a slightly splayed ring foot with a beveled outer rim. The white paste is thin, immaculate and refined. The pure white glaze appears smooth and glossy. Glaze streaks appear along the sides. Wheel marks are visible under the thin glaze. The unglazed base is adhered with quartz sand particles used as spacers during firing. The features of this bowl are characteristic of early Northern Song white Ding ware. This bowl is noted for its simple elegance and conforms to the aesthetic preferences of the Song literati.

This bowl is a fine example of Ding ware from the Northern Song period.

380

白釉"李"字铭盘

宋

公元 960—1279 年

定窑

高：2.8 厘米

口径：13.8 厘米

底径：5.8 厘米

White-glazed dish with *"Li"* mark

Song dynasty

960 – 1279 C.E.

Ding kilns

Height: 2.8 cm

Mouth diameter: 13.8 cm

Base diameter: 5.8 cm

口缘无釉，口下斜收到底，矮圈足。内壁心印盛开的牡丹花，围以弦纹一道。外壁光素无纹。胎质洁白致密。除口缘和外底小部分外，全器覆以白釉，釉面无开片纹，有泪釉痕。外底刻"李"字，字体流畅有力，少部分被釉遮盖。

"李"字可能是制作本品的工匠姓氏，也可能是订烧者的姓氏。

The dish has an unglazed mouth rim and sides that taper towards a low ring foot. Except for the mouth rim and a small part of the base, the entire vessel is covered with a white glaze with no crackles. Glaze streaks appear along the sides. The exterior is plain while the center of the dish is molded with a blooming peony within a grooved frame. The base is incised with the character *"Li"* rendered in vigorous and fluid strokes. Parts of the character are obscured by the glaze. The white paste is dense and pure in tone.

"Li" could either be the surname of the potter who made this dish or the person who commissioned it.

381

白釉"官"字铭碗

北宋

公元 960—1127 年

定窑

高：7.1 厘米

口径：18.9 厘米

White-glazed bowl with *"Guan"* mark

Northern Song dynasty

960–1127 C.E.

Ding kilns

Height: 7.1 cm

Mouth diameter: 18.9 cm

本品与藏品 379 号外形相似，是北宋早期遗物，本来是烧制给皇室使用的器物。外底刻有"官"字铭，笔法自然流畅，是标准"官"字款写法之一。外底圈足内墙残留有垫烧时使用的石英砂粒。

本品在烧制过程中，因温度过高使器物釉面沸腾而出现气泡，气泡表面还留有爆破形成的裂痕。如果温度更高，釉面会变成暗黄色甚至褐黑色，胎体也有可能膨胀破裂。可见当时烧制工艺仍未成熟，成品率低。

This bowl belonging to the early Northern Song period is similar in shape to Cat. No. 379. The base is incised with the character *"Guan"* or "official" indicating that the vessel was made for imperial use. The *"guan"* mark is fluently executed; the writing style recognizable among the standard *"guan"* marks.

Blisters are visible on the surface of the glaze. This is due to firing at too high of a temperature which caused the glaze to boil and the air bubbles to burst. If the kiln temperature had risen any further, the glaze could have turned dark yellow or even dark brown and the paste would rupture due to over-expansion. This shows that the firing technique, in particular the control of firing temperature, was not yet well mastered. The inner wall of the ring foot is adhered with quartz sand particles.

382

白釉印花执壶

北宋

公元 960—1127 年

定窑

高：25.4 厘米

底径：9.8 厘米

White-glazed ewer with molded decoration

Northern Song dynasty

960 – 1127 C.E.

Ding kilns

Height: 25.4 cm

Base diameter: 9.8 cm

直口，长颈，折肩圆腹，底收敛，圈足。肩上一侧贴六棱形长流，相对侧颈、腹间饰曲柄，柄上满印卷草纹，印纹清晰流畅。颈上置圆形台阶状盖，上贴宝珠形纽，侧面有孔两个，用于穿带。胎洁白细滑，质坚。施白釉，釉色白中闪黄，光亮，肥润。底足满釉，盖内露胎。器身可见泪釉痕。造型端庄秀丽。

The ewer has a straight mouth above a long neck, angular shoulders and sides that tapers to a ring foot. A strap handle with molded foliage scrolls connects the neck to the shoulders opposite a hexagonal-shaped spout. The circular lid with a pair of holes on the side and a stepped profile above the neck is surmounted by a pearl-shaped knob. The spotless white paste is hard and refined. The entire surface including the foot and the base is coated with a soft and lustrous glaze with a yellowish tint. The underside of the lid is bare of glaze. Glaze streaks are found on the body.

383

白釉折腰刻花盘

金

公元 1115—1234 年

定窑

高：5 厘米

口径：20 厘米

底径：6.5 厘米

White-glazed dish with angular profile and floral design

Jin dynasty

1115 – 1234 C.E.

Ding kilns

Height: 5 cm

Mouth diameter: 20 cm

Base diameter: 6.5 cm

六出棱口，折腰，矮圈足。覆烧，口缘无釉。外壁无纹，盘内刻萱草纹，纹饰简练生动，刻工流畅有力。胎质坚硬，洁白细滑。内外施白釉，釉色莹润，呈象牙黄色。釉中气泡排列细密，釉面无开片纹，外壁留有泪釉痕。外底小部分无釉遮盖。折腰盘为宋金两代定窑代表性器物之一。

The dish has a foliate rim with six notches, an angular turn down the sides, and a low ring foot. The unglazed rim indicates that the dish was fired upside down. The exterior is plain while the interior is carved with tendril motif. The pure white paste is hard and refined. Both the interior and exterior are covered with a smooth and lustrous glaze of ivory color. The glaze is suffused with tiny bubbles and glaze streaks are found on the exterior wall. No crackles are found on the surface of the glaze. A small part of the base is bare of glaze. Dishes with angular waists are among the representative examples of Ding ware from the Song and Jin dynasties.

384

白釉鱼莲纹碗

金

公元 1115—1234 年

定窑

高：6 厘米

口径：16.5 厘米

底径：5.4 厘米

White-glazed bowl with fish and lotus design

Jin dynasty

1115 – 1234 C.E.

Ding kilns

Height: 6 cm

Mouth diameter: 16.5 cm

Base diameter: 5.4 cm

口微外撇，素口覆烧。碗心印水纹和花果纹。内壁印莲叶、莲花和莲蓬纹，纹间有鳜鱼四尾，在水里畅游、翻腾、生动活泼。外壁光素无纹。胎体薄，洁白细滑、致密、透光。碗内外和圈足施泛牙黄白釉，外壁有泪釉痕。本品烧制工艺、纹饰和施釉方法均与宋代定窑相同，是金代定窑的优秀作品。

The bowl has a slightly flared mouth with an unglazed rim as a result of being fired upside down. The exterior wall is plain while the center of the bowl is molded with flowers and fruits amid waves. The interior wall is molded with four fish swimming amid lotus blossoms and leaves. The pure white paste is thin, refined, smooth, dense and translucent. The entire bowl including the ring foot is covered with an ivory-tinted white glaze. Glaze streaks are found along the outer wall. This bowl is comparable to Ding ware from the Song dynasty in terms of crafting technique, decorative motif and glaze application. It is a fine example of Ding ware from the Jin dynasty.

385

白釉 "官" 字铭盖壶

金

公元 1115—1234 年

定窑

高：19.3 厘米

底径：9.8 厘米

White-glazed lidded ewer with "*Guan*" mark

Jin dynasty

1115 – 1234 C.E.

Ding kilns

Height: 19.3 cm

Base diameter: 9.8 cm

葫芦形纽盖、直口、鼓腹、大圈足，圈足微外撇。带式曲状把手，直流微曲，肩下起凸弦纹一周。胎白致密，叩击时发出清越的金属声。器外壁施白釉，釉色泛浅灰，有泪釉痕。釉面无开片纹。内外圈足露胎，底部刻 "官" 字，字体刚劲有力。

内蒙古赤峰市辽代应历九年（公元 959 年）驸马赠卫国王夫妇墓出土与本品相似的执壶，但无 "官" 字铭。

The ewer has a double-gourd shaped lid, a straight mouth, a bulbous belly and a slightly splayed broad ring foot. A slightly curved spout is set on the shoulders opposite a strap handle that connects the mouth to the shoulders. A ridge runs around the lower part of shoulders. The fine, dense paste gives a metallic sound when struck. The exterior of the vessel is covered with a white glaze with a pale gray tint. There are glaze streaks but no crackles. Both the inside and outside of the ring foot are unglazed. The base is incised with the character "*Guan*" or "official" in vigorous strokes.

An ewer of similar shape but without the "*guan*" mark was unearthed from a Liao tomb in Chifeng city in Inner Mongolia. The tomb is dated to the 9th year of the Yingli period (959 C.E.) of the Liao dynasty. It belonged to the consort of a Liao princess. He was conferred the title of Prince of Zengweiguo.

386

白釉莲瓣纹瓶

辽

公元 907—1125 年

江官屯窑

高：17.7 厘米

底径：7.3 厘米

White-glazed vase with lotus motif

Liao dynasty

907 – 1125 C.E.

Jiangguantun kilns

Height: 17.7 cm

Base diameter: 7.3 cm

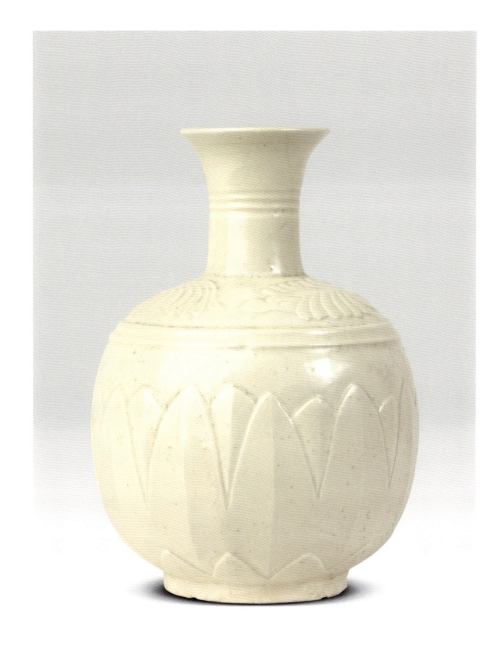

侈口，长颈、丰肩、圆腹、圈足。足内凹，露胎。颈饰弦纹三周、肩饰菊叶纹两组、腹部刻仰莲纹三层，以凸弦纹两道相间。胎细白、较疏松。釉透明、色白、泛黄、尤以聚釉处为甚。造型秀丽、匀称、刻工精细，富立体感，制作工艺与定窑相似。

北宋时期，契丹多次入侵中原地区，并曾一度占领定州，俘获甚众，其中应有来自定州窑区的陶瓷工匠。辽白瓷不论胎土、造型、釉色、制作均模仿定窑，其胎釉与邢窑、定窑极为相似。

The vase has a fine-grained and rather porous white paste, a flared mouth, a long neck resting on broad shoulders and a bulbous belly that tapers to a ring foot enclosing a recessed base. The entire surface except the base is coated with a transparent white glaze with a yellowish tint, especially where the glaze accumulates. The neck is decorated with three rounds of grooves and the shoulders encircled by two groups of chrysanthemum petals. Two ridges encompass the body between the shoulders and the belly. The lower half of the body is carved in relief with three layers of upward-facing lotus petals. The craftsmanship is comparable to that of Ding ware.

During the Northern Song period, the Khitan (Liao) troops repeatedly encroached on the Central Plain. For a time, they also occupied Dingzhou and captured their civilians some of whom were probably skilled craftsmen. The paste, shape, glaze color and production process of Liao white ware are modeled after Ding ware. The glaze is remarkably similar to that of Xing and Ding ware.

白釉"千"字铭马蹬壶

辽

公元 907—1125 年

高：26 厘米

阔：20.7 厘米 × 18.2 厘米

White-glazed stirrup flask with "*Qian*" mark

Liao dynasty

907 – 1125 C.E.

Height: 26 cm

Width: 20.7 cm × 18.2 cm

壶体扁圆，筒状衣褶形小口，上贴带状条花纹饰。曲形提梁，末端后伸作尾。胎色洁白，胎质坚细。施白釉，聚釉处呈浅灰色。有泪釉痕和不明显的细开片纹。腹下部见明显修刮痕。底平、微内凹，露胎，上刻"千"字铭一个。造型别致，较为少见。

马蹬壶为皮囊壶的一种，以其形似马蹬而得名，辽人称之"马盂"。《辽史·兵卫志》："辽国兵制，凡民年十五以上，五十以下，隶兵籍。每正军一名，马三匹，打草谷、守营铺家丁各一人。人铁甲九事、马鞯、辔、马甲铁，视其力；弓四、箭四百、长短枪、錉镍、斧、钺、小旗、锤、锥、火刀石、马盂、秒一斗。秒袋、搭钩、毡伞各一，縻马绳二百尺，皆自备。"考古发掘的辽人墓葬，皮囊壶常与马鞍、马蹬等马具一起出土，秒袋、绳索可能已腐烂。

1981 年北京西郊辽韩佚墓出土一件越窑青釉划花水注，器底刻有"永"字。此类器底刻字的器物，很可能是辽君主赏赐给王公大臣之物。

The flask has a flattened round body with a small pleated mouth encircled by a ribbon-like appliqué design. Over the mouth is an overhead handle with a protruding end. The entire vessel is coated with white glaze with glaze streaks and tiny crackles. The glaze appears grayish blue where it accumulates. Trimming marks are clearly visible on the lower section. The paste is pure white, hard and refined. The unglazed and slightly recessed base is engraved with the Chinese character "*Qian*" or "thousand". The shape of this flask is quite rare.

Stirrup flasks is a type of leather pouch flasks that resemble stirrups. The Khitan called them *mayu* (horse flask). In the "Military System" chapter of *Liao shi* (History of the Liao), it states that: According to the military service system of Liao, men between age fifteen and fifty are required to enlist in the army. Every regular soldier will be given three horses, one forage gatherer, one tent watchman and one servant, nine armor suits, bridle, saddle cloth and horse armor, depending on the load-bearing ability. The following are to be provided by the soldier himself: four bows, four hundred arrows, long and short spears, staff, axe, small flag, hammer and awl, flint, horse-flask, noodle stirrer, bag for holding fried noodles, blanket, umbrella and horse rein with a length of 200 *chi* (Chinese foot). Leather pouch flasks are often found alongside saddles and stirrups in Liao tombs.

A Yue celadon ewer with incised motifs was unearthed in 1981 from the tomb of Han Yi of the Liao dynasty in the western suburb of Beijing. The base of the ewer is incised with the Chinese character "*Yong*" or "forever". Similar vessels with Chinese characters marked on the base are likely to be objects bestowed by Liao emperors upon their officials.

388

白釉鸡冠壶

辽

公元 907—1125 年

缸瓦窑

高：23.5 厘米

阔：16.5 厘米

底径：11.2 厘米

White-glazed "cockscomb" flask

Liao dynasty

907 – 1125 C.E.

Gangwa kilns

Height: 23.5 cm

Width: 16.5 cm

Base diameter:11.2 cm

附图 13　西安何家村出土舞马衔杯银壶（唐）

Fig. 13 Silver leather-pouch ewer with dancing horse motif, and silver cup connected by chain, unearthed at Hejiacun in Xi'an (Tang dynasty)

壶体呈扁状，体肥硕，矮圈足。一侧为直立的管状小口，口微外撇。另一侧为鸡冠状扁片，中间有孔，便于系绳。壶侧及近底部饰模仿皮制水壶的缝接痕，接痕边棱凸起。胎白、细滑，质坚。体外满施白釉，晶莹、润泽，开不明显纹片，有泪釉痕，聚釉处呈浅绿色。底露胎，足缘内侧留有垫烧时的砂粒。

鸡冠壶模仿契丹族生活中各种皮囊容器烧造，以其形似鸡冠而得名，亦称皮囊壶（附图 13）。皮囊壶早期壶身较短，下部肥硕；中期以后壶身增高，缝合痕逐渐消失。

1954 年赤峰辽驸马墓出土有相似器物，现藏内蒙古博物院。

The flask has a flattened body with an upright tubular mouth and a flange enclosed by a raised border and pierced with a hole and a ring foot. The pouch-shaped body is outlined by pronounced seams modeled after a leather prototype. The white paste is refined, smooth and hard. The entire surface is covered with a lustrous and smooth white glaze with glaze streaks and crackles. The glaze appears greenish where it accumulates. The base is bare of glaze and the inner edge of the foot is adhered with kiln grit from the fireclay spacers.

These flasks are modeled after leather pouches used by the Khitan people of the Liao dynasty. Hence, it is also called "leather pouch flask". They are also referred to as "cockscomb" flasks because of the resemblance of some of their lug handles to cockscombs (Fig. 13). Early examples are short and stout while later ones are more slender and have no seams.

A similar flask was unearthed in 1954 from the tomb of the consort of a Liao princess. It is now in the collection of the Inner Mongolia Museum.

389

白釉花口水注

辽

公元 907—1125 年

高：29 厘米

底径：8.4 厘米

White-glazed ewer with foliate mouth

Liao dynasty

907 – 1125 C.E.

Height: 29 cm

Base diameter: 8.4 cm

花瓣口，漏斗形细长颈，颈呈竹节状，斜肩，肩上塑短流，肩、腹交界处起凸弦纹一道，深腹，下腹缓慢收缩到底。矮圈足，稍外撇。灰白色胎，胎质较粗糙。器身敷乳白色化妆土，再上透明釉，釉不到底。器体可见明显轮旋纹。造型饱满，线条优美，具有契丹民族风格。

The ewer has a foliate mouth, a funnel-shaped slender neck, sloping shoulders and a deep belly that tapers toward a slightly splayed low ring foot. The grayish white glaze is rather coarse in texture. The surface of the vessel is coated with a white slip under a transparent glaze that stops short of the foot. Distinct wheel marks are visible around the body. This ewer is characteristic of the vessels used by the Khitan people of the Liao dynasty.

390

白釉玉壶春瓶

金

公元 1115—1234 年

霍窑

高：30.1 厘米

口径：6.4 厘米

底径：7.3 厘米

Yuhuchun vase with white glaze

Jin dynasty

1115 – 1234 C.E.

Huo kilns

Height: 30.1 cm

Mouth diameter: 6.4 cm

Base diameter: 7.3 cm

喇叭口、细长颈、垂腹、圈足略外撇，足底内壁微内斜。胎薄、洁白、质坚、细腻。施纯白釉，釉薄而均匀。釉色晶莹、柔润，口缘下与圈足聚釉处呈牙黄色，足底内无釉。全器可见旋纹痕。本品线条优美、清秀别致，为霍窑器物中的佼佼者。

霍窑窑址在山西霍县，属定窑体系，以烧白瓷为主，为金至清代瓷窑。

玉壶春瓶于唐朝就已经出现，由于造型优美而深受人们喜爱。

The vase has a trumpet-shaped mouth, a slender neck, a pear-shaped body, a slightly splayed ring foot and a base with beveled edge. The pure white paste is hard and refined. The vessel is evenly coated with a smooth, lustrous and glossy white glaze. The glaze takes on an ivory shade where it accumulates underneath the mouth rim and around the foot. The base is bare of glaze. Wheel marks are visible throughout. This vase is one of the finest examples of Huo ware.

The Huo kilns are located in Huo county in Shanxi. They belonged to the Ding-type kilns which produced mainly white porcelains from the Jin to the Qing dynasties.

The *yuhuchun* vase appeared as early as the Tang dynasty.

青白釉十二辰神像

宋

公元 960—1279 年

景德镇窑系

高：19.6—22.5 厘米

Twelve *qingbai* zodiac figurines

Song dynasty

960 – 1279 C.E.

Jingdezhen-type kilns

Height: 19.6 – 22.5 cm

俑人穿袍服、戴冠立于圆饼形底板上，分别手抱代表十二生肖的鼠、牛、虎、兔、龙、蛇、马、羊、猴、鸡、狗及猪。胎白，质坚。满施青白釉，并饰以褐斑彩纹。体中空，座底置气孔。人物头冠正中刻一"王"字。此类像制作时先模印粗坯，再经雕刻及雕塑而成。

据清赵翼《陔馀丛考》考证，十二相属之说起于东汉。古时术数家用十二种动物来配十二地支，子为鼠、丑为牛、寅为虎、卯为兔、辰为龙、巳为蛇、午为马、未为羊、申为猴、酉为鸡、戌为狗、亥为猪，后以人生在某年就肖某物，有关记录见于东汉王充《论衡》的《物势》篇和《言毒》篇。

关于生肖的器物，唐代有红陶人身兽首形象，宋时则用人物捧抱动物来代表。生肖俑做明器用，多放置于墓室四壁的小龛内。

The figurines portray twelve men wearing long robes standing on circular plinths. Each figurine is holding one of the twelve zodiac animals designating the year in which a person is born. These animals are recognizably the rat, ox, tiger, rabbit, dragon, snake, horse, goat, monkey, rooster, dog and pig. The white paste is hard. The figurines are coated with a bluish white *qingbai* glaze embellished with brown splashes. The interiors are hollow and vents are found on the bottom. The center front of their caps is inscribed with the character "*Wang*". The figurines are shaped by molding while details are carved out or applied afterwards.

According to Zhao Yi's *Gaiyu congkao* (Comprehensive Miscellaneous Investigations) written during the Qing period, the duodecimal cycle was first introduced during the Eastern Han period. Twelve animals were used to designate the twelve "Earthy Branches"— rat for *zi*, ox for *chou*, tiger for *yin*, rabbit for *mao*, dragon for *chen*, snake for *si*, horse for *wu*, goat for *wei*, monkey for *shen*, rooster for *you*, dog for *xu* and pig for *hai*. Each person is associated with a particular animal according to the year of his or her birth. Records of this are found in the chapters "*Wushi*" (The Nature of Things) and "*Yandu*" (On Poison) in *Lunheng* (Balanced Enquiries) written by the Eastern Han scholar Wang Chong.

Red earthenware figurines with zodiac animal heads can be found in the Tang dynasty. This is replaced by human figures holding an animal in their hands during the Song period. These figurines are used as burial objects and placed in the side niches of the tomb chamber.

392

青白釉褐斑两头蛇

宋

公元 960—1279 年

景德镇窑

高：17 厘米

底：5.2 厘米 × 4.8 厘米

Twin-headed pottery snake with *qingbai* glaze

Song dynasty

960 – 1279 C.E.

Jingdezhen kilns

Height: 17 cm

Base: 5.2 cm × 4.8 cm

两头蛇即一身二人首的蛇。本品蛇身所附两"尊者"头部一上一下，与常见的平躺、两头左右昂起的一类不同，造型奇特，类似图腾柱的设计。胎细白。通体施青白釉，缀以褐斑，釉开细碎片纹。类似釉色的器物在江西省景德镇湖田和珠山有出土。座底无釉，部分呈火石红色。底无通气孔。

两头蛇据说常二首争食，自相噬咬，是蛇中的畸形品种。有说法认为看见两头蛇不吉。汉贾谊《新书·春秋》有载："（孙叔敖）泣而对曰：'今吾见两头蛇，恐去死无日矣。'"人首蛇俑有说是伏羲和女娲的形象，和墓葬的生肖俑作用相同，用于驱魔辟邪，可能也有生育传继、延绵不绝的含义。在希腊神话中有蛇发女妖（Gorgons），头发由多条小蛇组成，见到她们的人会变成石头。

"尊者"是佛教中的尊称，意为圣者。

The snake is uniquely shaped with an upright body supporting two human heads resembling the Arhats in Buddhism. The two heads are stacked which differs significantly from the horizontal snakes with twin heads. The design is very unusual and resembles a totem pole. The white paste is fine in grain. The entire surface of the snake is covered with a *qingbai* glaze with brown speckles and tiny crackles. The stand is unglazed, revealing a burnt orange color. No ventilation holes are found on the base. Objects with similar glaze color have been uncovered from kiln sites at Hutian and Zhushan in Jingdezhen.

According to legend, twin-headed snakes are anomalies among snakes and they would attack each other for food. Others say that snakes with human heads are the embodiment of Fuxi and Nuwa, the mythological ancestors of all Chinese. Like zodiac tomb figurines, they are used to cast out demons and evil spirits and protect the tombs from plunder. They may also be symbols of fecundity and eternity. Greek mythology tells of the story of the three Gorgon sisters who had snakes for hair and when looked at, could turn the beholder into stone. Twin-headed snakes were considered an evil omen in ancient China. The Han scholar, Jia Yi, in the "*Chunqiu*"(Spring and Autumn) chapter of *Xinshu* (New Writings), tells of a man named Sun Shu'ao who cried and told others that he will probably die soon after seeing a twin-headed snake.

Arhats are the enlightened ones in Buddhism.

393

青白釉扑伏俑

宋

公元 960—1279 年

景德镇窑

长：13.2 厘米（跪状），14.4 厘米（卧状）

Kneeling and prostrating figurines in *qingbai* glaze

Song dynasty

960 – 1279 C.E.

Jingdezhen-type kilns

Length: 13.2 cm (kneeling figure),

　　　　14.4 cm (prostrating figure)

其一跪姿，双手持笏，身体后倾、举头仰观，感应天意；另一身体俯卧，头向侧面，伏耳静听，探索地府动静，守卫墓主人灵魂。

此对俑无论造型、釉色、褐斑和胎质都与图录 391 号器物相同，故推论当属于同一组明器俑。除十二生肖俑、跪拜俑外，此一时期还有文武官俑、人首鱼等陪葬器物。

The kneeling figurine is leaning his body backward and clasping a ritual tablet in his hands to receive divine revelations from Heaven. The prostrating figurine has his head turned sideways listening attentively to the goings-on in the netherworld. They are guarding the soul of their master to make sure that the latter could enjoy eternal peace.

Since they are very similar to Cat. No. 391 in shape, paste, glaze color and speckles, they could belonged to the same group of mortuary objects. Besides figurines representing the twelve zodiac animals, other burial objects also include figurines of civil and martial officers and fish with human head, etc.

394

青白釉鸳鸯油灯

宋

公元 960—1279 年

景德镇窑

高：14.1 厘米

底：15.6 厘米 ×11.1 厘米

Qingbai-glazed oil lamp with mandarin ducks

Song dynasty

960 – 1279 C.E.

Jingdezhen kilns

Height: 14.1 cm

Base: 15.6 cm × 11.1 cm

底板两端呈弧形，左、右贴昂首翘尾鸳鸯各一。鸳鸯间置莲花，上托浅盘形油灯，中立一锥形管，管底开两孔，用以穿放灯芯。粉白胎、细滑、稍疏松。全器施青白釉，均匀、色微黄、明亮，聚釉处呈淡青色，胎釉结合紧密，无开片纹。布纹底板无釉。鸳鸯为印模，贴到底板上再堆塑翅膀、挂上颈圈、贴花、刻羽毛和脸部，造型新颖有趣。

中国古人视鸳鸯为爱情的象征。《古今注》说鸳鸯为鸟类，雌雄未尝分离，人得其一，另一必思而死，故曰匹鸟。陶瓷装饰的鸳鸯皆成双成对出现，且多与莲花相配，习称鸳鸯戏莲纹。

On the slab are two mandarin ducks with heads and tails raised. Between them is a lotus supporting an oil lamp in the shape of a shallow dish. In the middle of the dish rises a tube with two holes at its base for securing a wick. The narrow ends of the base slab are slightly convex. The powdery white paste is refined and porous. The entire piece is evenly coated with a lustrous *qingbai* glaze that appears bluish where it pools. The glaze sintered well with the paste and no crackles are found. The unglazed base is impressed with textile motif. The ducks were made by molding and then attached onto the slabs. Then the wings, chokers and quatrefoils were applied to their bodies while plumage and facial features were carved out.

Mandarin ducks are symbols of conjugal love in China. It was said in the ancient text *Gujinzhu* (Notes to Things Old and New) that these birds always come in pairs and never part from each other; if one of them was taken away, its mate would die of lovesickness. Thus, they are also called "couple birds". Mandarin ducks always appear in pairs as decorations on ceramics and are often portrayed amid lotus pond, a motif commonly known as "mandarin ducks playing amid lotus".

青白釉双狮如意枕

宋

公元 960—1279 年

景德镇窑

高：11 厘米

底：17.4 厘米 × 11 厘米

Qingbai-glazed lion-shaped headrest with *ruyi*-shaped top

Song dynasty

960 – 1279 C.E.

Jingdezhen kilns

Height: 11 cm

Base: 17.4 cm × 11 cm

本品胎质、釉色和塑造工艺均与本图录 394 号相近。底板左右相反方向置卧狮各一，双狮间竖一圆柱体，上托如意形枕面。枕面微向前倾，上印莲花纹。此枕做工精细，造型新颖别致，狮张口、舌上卷、獠牙、竖耳、凸眼、头微昂、利爪弯曲、鬃毛微竖，像守护着酣睡中的主人。

狮子的艺术形象最初出现在汉代，并随着佛教兴盛而流行。狮子的梵语音为"辟邪"，故被视为祥瑞之兽。佛经说释迦诞生时作狮子吼，群兽慑服，又认为"佛为人中狮子"。

This headrest is similar in paste, glaze color and crafting technique to Cat. No. 394. They are likely to have been produced around the same period and at the same kiln. This headrest features two lions crouching in opposite directions on a base slab. The cylindrical pillar between them supports a forward-sloping *ruyi*-shaped top decorated with molded lotus motif. The lions have a slightly raised head, gaping mouth, rolling tongue, protruding fangs, pricked ears, bulging eyes, hook-like sharp claws and curled mane. They are the guardians of their sleeping master.

Lions first appeared as decoration during the Han period and became popular with the rise of Buddhism. They are also referred to as *pixie* ("to ward off evil spirits"). Thus, lion is a symbol of good omen. According to Buddhist texts, Sakyamuni roared like a lion when he was born. It is also said that Buddha is a lion among humans.

青白釉瓜棱盒

北宋

公元 960—1127 年

景德镇窑

高：13.1 厘米

阔：10.2 厘米

底径：6.3 厘米

Qingbai-glazed box with lobed body

Northern Song dynasty

960 – 1127 C.E.

Jingdezhen kilns

Height: 13.1 cm

Width: 10.2 cm

Base diameter: 6.3 cm

子母口，底平。盖体高耸，与盒体形状大小相同。盖顶较平，印圆形花蕊纹，衬以十二瓣菊瓣，如绽开之菊花。盒腹下部内收成半圆形瓜棱底边，与器身相配。胎白，质坚。器表釉面青白光润，透明度好，满布土蚀白点。器内和底露胎。全器棱面线条清晰流畅，一气呵成，器形仿自唐、宋漆器（附图 14）。

宋代饮茶、斗茶之风兴盛，先将茶叶碾成粉，装入此类盒中。

The lid of the box is nearly identical in shape and height to the body. The twelve-lobed sides converge at the molded stamen motif centered on the relatively flat top of the domed lid to resemble a blooming chrysanthemum. The white paste is smooth, refined and hard. The surface of the vessel is coated with a highly translucent and lustrous *qingbai* glaze suffused with numerous white inclusions. The lower part of the body has a well-defined edge and a semi-spherical twelve-lobed base. The interior and the bottom of the box are unglazed. The box is modeled after the lacquerware from the Tang and Song dynasties (Fig. 14).

Tea drinking and tea contests became widely popular during the Song period. Tea leaves are grinded into powder and stored inside these type of boxes.

附图 14　江苏常州出土朱漆戗金莲瓣式人物花卉纹盒（南宋）

Fig. 14　Red-lacquered box with gold-filled figural and floral motifs, unearthed in Changzhou, Jiangsu (Southern Song dynasty)

青白釉薄胎碗

北宋

公元 960—1127 年

景德镇窑（湖田）

高：7.5 厘米

口径：15.4 厘米

底径：5.3 厘米

Bowl with a thin body in *qingbai* glaze

Northern Song dynasty

960 – 1127 C.E.

Jingdezhen kilns (Hutian)

Height: 7.5 cm

Mouth diameter: 15.4 cm

Base diameter: 5.3 cm

碗口外撇，高圈足。碗心印团菊纹，其余光素无纹饰。胎洁白细腻，胎质致密，胎体轻薄如脱胎瓷，最薄处不足 1 毫米。外满施青白釉，釉薄均匀，青中泛白和白中显青，明亮肥润，积釉处釉色较青绿。底露胎，留褐红色垫饼支烧残渣，此碗造型秀丽，胎釉达"青如天、明如镜、薄如纸、声如磬"的地步，在青白釉瓷器中甚少见。宋代的青白釉器不仅达到了越窑青瓷"如玉如冰"的程度，而且质感更好，几与玉器无别。

The bowl has a flared mouth and a high ring foot. Apart from the chrysanthemum motif impressed in the center, the bowl is devoid of decoration. The spotless white paste is refined, dense and as thin as "boneless" porcelain. The thinnest part measures less than 1 mm. Both the interior and exterior are coated with an even layer of lustrous *qingbai* glaze. The glaze appears bluish green where the glaze accumulates. Reddish brown fireclay residues are visible on the unglazed base. *Qingbai* wares have been described as "blue as sky, bright as mirror, thin as paper, and its sound as pleasant as that of a chime stone". This bowl is a rarity among *qingbai* ware. *Qingbai* ware of the Song dynasty is comparable to Yue celadon, which was said to be "like jade, like ice". The porcelaneous body is almost indistinguishable from jade.

398

青白釉堆花盒

宋

公元 960—1279 年

景德镇窑（湖田）

高：5.5 厘米

阔：12 厘米

底径：9.8 厘米

Qingbai-glazed cosmetic box with sculpted decorations

Song dynasty

960 – 1279 C.E.

Jingdezhen kilns (Hutian)

Height: 5.5 cm

Width: 12 cm

Base diameter: 9.8 cm

八瓣瓜棱形，光素无纹。内附三个小碟，可分储粉黛、胭脂和香料等，其中一个为菱边。中央堆贴一盛开的荷花，三条莲茎自花底伸出，把三碟分隔开来。一茎末附一小鸟，一茎末附待放花苞，另一茎末附荷叶一片，排列有序。盖内中央施釉，近口缘处周围无釉。底平无釉，露出洁白胎身，胎质细腻。釉色干净明亮，娇艳欲滴，炉火恰可。底边有垫烧痕，呈棕黑色，中央有"吴家盒子记"阳文长方楷书印。底内外及盖面施浅青色釉。盖和盒体边缘分别有竖直划痕一道，当是用于校准盖的位置。

本品造型优美，应是受金银器影响。宋代江西制盒业兴盛，各个作坊竞为新巧，著名作坊有"段""许""汪""朱""徐""陈""程""蔡"等十余家，尤以"吴"家为最。本品是这类盒中的精品。

The eight-lobed circular box is devoid of decorative motifs. Inside the box are three tiny dishes including one with serrated edges for holding face powder, rouge and scented ingredients. Carved in the round in the center is a blooming lotus with three stems. The tips of the stems respectively support a little bird, a lotus bud and a lotus leaf. The inside of the lid is glazed but the area around the rim is bare. The flat base of the box is unglazed, exposing a paste of very fine texture. The glaze is pure, bright and exceedingly beautiful in tone. Dark brown residues adhered around the base. The center of the base has a rectangular seal with raised characters "box made by the Wu family" in regular script. Both the interior and exterior of the box are coated with a pale blue glaze. A vertical match line at the joint indicates the exact location of where the lid should fit on the box.

This box is probably influenced by metal ware. During the Song dynasty, ceramic boxes were widely made in Jiangxi. The major workshops include: Duan, Hsu, Wang, Zhu, Xu, Chen, Cheng, Cai and Wu. This box is the finest among its kind.

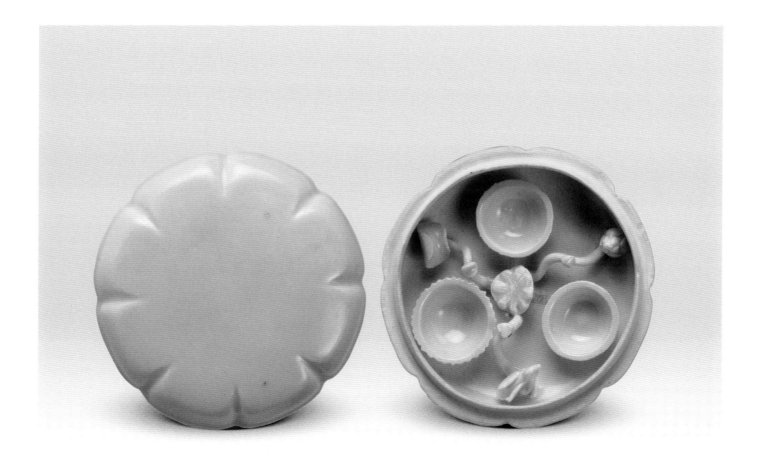

399

青白釉浅盘一对

宋

公元 960—1279 年

景德镇窑（湖田）

高：2.1 厘米

口径：11.9 厘米

Pair of saucers with *qingbai* glaze

Song dynasty

960 – 1279 C.E.

Jingdezhen kilns (Hutian)

Height: 2.1 cm

Mouth diameter: 11.9 cm

六瓣菊花形口，口缘微外侈，底平。全器光素无纹。胎白细腻，薄胎，透光性强。外施青白釉，釉色青绿，釉面光亮，施釉均匀，无开片纹。底呈褐红色，周边留有垫烧残渣。底墨书"新宅"两字，其一字体清晰，另一依稀可见。

Each saucer has a six-lobed and slightly flared chrysanthemum-shaped mouth and a flat base. The entire vessel except the base is devoid of decorative motifs. The paste is thin, refined and translucent. The exterior wall is evenly covered with a lustrous greenish glaze with no crackles. The brownish red base is adhered with a ring of fireclay residues and inscribed in ink with the two characters *"Xinzhai"* ("new residence"). The characters are legible on one saucer but only faintly visible on the other.

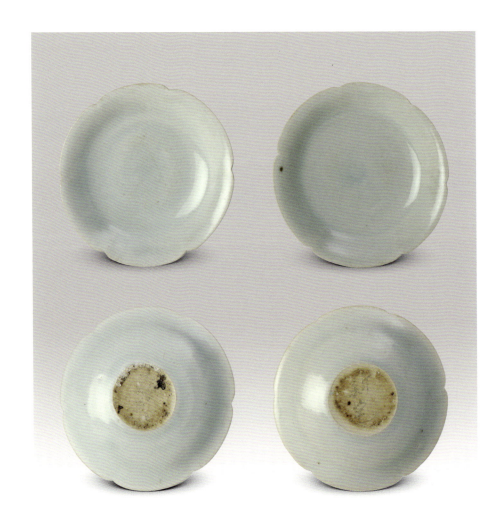

400

青白釉瓜棱碗一对

宋

公元 960—1279 年

景德镇窑（湖田）

高：5.5 厘米

口径：12.6 厘米

Pair of *qingbai*-glazed bowls with foliate rim

Song dynasty

960 – 1279 C.E.

Jingdezhen kilns (Hutian)

Height: 5.5 cm

Mouth diameter: 12.6 cm

口缘外侈，呈六瓣菊花形，腹部起棱六道，圈足较高。胎薄、洁白、质坚、透光性强。全器施青白釉，釉面莹润光滑，聚釉处呈湖水翠绿色。圈足内墙和底部中央留有垫烧残渣和垫烧痕。本品造型优美，釉色青翠。

Each bowl has a flared mouth with six notches to simulate a chrysanthemum flower. The ring foot is rather tall. The pure white paste is thin, hard and translucent. The entire vessel is covered with a smooth and lustrous glaze that appears lake green where it accumulates. The inner wall of the ring foot and the base are adhered with fireclay marks and residues.

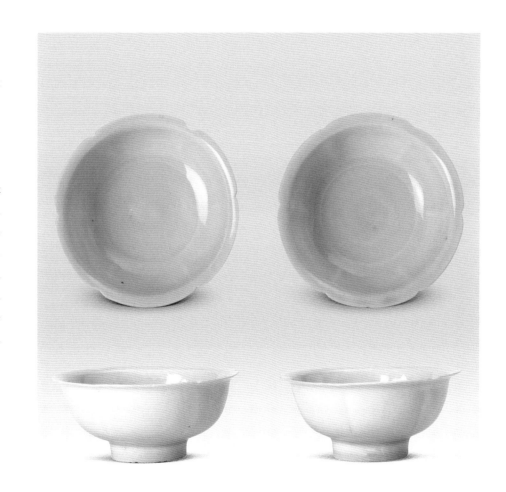

401

青白釉二十四棱碟

宋

公元 960—1279 年

景德镇窑（湖田）

高：2.4 厘米

口径：11.4 厘米

底径：3.5 厘米

Qingbai-glazed dish with foliate rim

Song dynasty

960 – 1279 C.E.

Jingdezhen kilns (Hutian)

Height: 2.4 cm

Mouth diameter: 11.4 cm

Base diameter: 3.5 cm

口缘外折，成二十四出菊瓣形。内壁起凸棱二十四条，与菊瓣相对，瓣内凹外凸。胎白，质坚细密，胎薄，透光性强。釉色白中泛青绿，施釉均匀。圈足近乎平坦，边缘四周留有垫烧残渣。足底露胎，呈火石红色。本品造型精美，釉色青翠可爱，菊花瓣式样简洁生动。

The dish has an everted rim with twenty-four lobes to simulate a chrysanthemum flower. The sides are similarly lobed, accentuated by ribs down the interior wall and grooves down the exterior wall. The white paste is thin, hard, dense and translucent. The evenly applied white glaze shows a greenish tint. The ring foot is adhered with fireclay marks and residues. The unglazed base shows a burnt orange color.

402

青白釉雕瓷香熏

北宋

公元 960—1127 年

景德镇窑

高：7.9 厘米

底径：4.9 厘米

Qingbai-glazed censer with openwork design

Northern Song dynasty

960 – 1127 C.E.

Jingdezhen kilns

Height: 7.9 cm

Base diameter: 4.9 cm

子母口、盖与器身均为半球状，下接台形圈足。盖顶中心有圆孔，孔外透雕圆形、水滴形和葵形网孔。腹部饰弦纹一道。胎薄、洁白细腻、质坚。内外施釉、釉色淡青、莹润、有开片纹。足内有圆形垫烧痕。本品造型秀丽、小巧玲珑、制作精巧。

The lidded censer is supported by a pedestal ring foot. The top of the lid is pierced with rings of circles, teardrop and heart shapes in openwork. A groove encircles the mid-section of the belly. The pure white paste is refined, thin and hard. Both the interior and exterior are covered with a lustrous pale green *qingbai* glaze with crackles. The inside of the foot shows a ring of fireclay marks. The censer is noted for its elegant shape, exquisite design and meticulous craftsmanship.

403

青白釉刻花注碗

宋

公元 960—1279 年

景德镇窑（湖田）

高：13.2 厘米

口径：16.2 厘米

底径：9.9 厘米

Bowl with carved floral motif in *qingbai* glaze

Song dynasty

960 – 1279 C.E.

Jingdezhen kilns (Hutian)

Height: 13.2 cm

Mouth diameter: 16.2 cm

Base diameter: 9.9 cm

六瓣葵花形口，与腹体六道凹竖纹相应，颈外撇，高圈足。外壁竖纹间满刻缠枝花纹，纹饰清晰，生动流畅。胎质洁白，坚致。内外施青白釉，釉色明澈温润，釉汁肥美丰厚，葱翠如玉，聚釉处色泽更为浓郁，美妙至极。内底有支烧钉痕。外底露胎，留有一圈垫烧痕迹，呈灰白色。本品造型稳重，古朴中显灵秀，粗犷中见雅致，纹饰、胎、釉完全合乎宋人的审美情趣，为宋代青白瓷精品。

The bowl has a flared neck and a mouth rim impressed with six notches. Spur marks are found inside the bowl. The unglazed base enclosed by the tall ring foot bears a round of grayish white fireclay marks. The spaces in between the grooves on the exterior wall are lavishly carved with floral scrolls. The paste is white and hard. Both the interior and exterior are coated with a translucent greenish glaze as lustrous and smooth as jade. The color appears deeper in tone where the glaze pools. This bowl is a fine example of *qingbai* ware from the Song dynasty.

404

青白釉刻莲花纹球状注子

宋

公元 960—1279 年

景德镇窑（湖田）

高：16 厘米

底径：8.6 厘米

Ewer with carved lotus in *qingbai* glaze

Song dynasty

960 – 1279 C.E.

Jingdezhen kilns (Hutian)

Height: 16 cm

Base diameter: 8.6 cm

器呈球形，直颈短而细，带盖，盖直壁、顶面隆起，平底，足极浅，足底微内凹，整体造型圆浑饱满。短流下有一乳丁，条形扁柄下亦有乳丁。肩刻莲瓣纹，与盖上旋涡式瓣纹相呼应。器身刻盛开莲花数朵，衬以卷曲叶纹。胎白、坚致、细腻。器身及盖施青白釉，釉色青翠，聚釉处呈翠绿色，釉无开片纹。底边缘上残留垫烧痕五个，呈褐色。本品刻工流畅利落，造型秀丽挺拔，是宋代青白瓷精品。

The ewer has a spherical body with a small mouth and a short straight neck. The cylindrical lid has a slightly domed top. The foot is very shallow and the flat base is slightly recessed. The lower end of the strap handle and the short spout are decorated with a circular protuberance. The lotus petals carved around the shoulders mirror that of the whirling motif on top of the lid. The body is engraved with a few blooming lotuses amid scrolling foliage. The white paste is hard and refined. The entire surface including the lid is coated with a *qingbai* glaze that appears green where it pools. No crackles are found. Five brown fireclay marks are visible around the edge of the base. This is a fine example of *qingbai* ware from the Song dynasty.

405

青白釉注子温碗

宋

公元 960—1279 年

景德镇窑

高：21.4 厘米（壶）、14.5 厘米（碗）

　　　24.5 厘米（壶加碗）

底径：8.4 厘米（壶）、9.5 厘米（碗）

Ewer and warming bowl in *qingbai* glaze

Song dynasty

960 – 1279 C.E.

Jingdezhen kilns

Height: 21.4 cm (ewer), 14.5 cm (warmer)

　　　24.5 cm (overall)

Base diameter: 8.4 cm (ewer), 9.5 cm (warmer)

注子直口，斜肩，圆腹，圈足，配狮形纽盖。圆管流上细下粗，上部向外曲张，流略高于注口。流相对侧置扁平弓形柄。注碗侈口折缘，唇缘尖薄，深腹，口缘和腹皆成六瓣瓜体形。碗内底有支钉痕，外底有垫圈残留痕迹。注子肩部和碗身饰气泡纹，如热水中气泡徐徐上升。通体施青白釉，釉色青中泛灰白，釉面有明显片纹，满布土蚀白点。注子置于碗内，则温碗折缘处刚好与注子肩部相齐。

注子、温碗为盛酒和温酒的配套酒具。饮酒前先将盛满酒的注子置于温碗中，温碗中置热水用于温酒。此套酒具的造型、纹饰、胎釉都处理得很成功，且历经千年仍保留完整，十分难得。

The ewer has a straight mouth, sloping shoulders, a rounded belly and a ring foot. The tubular spout rises slightly above the ewer. A bow-shaped strap handle is affixed to the opposite side. The lid is surmounted by a knob in the shape of a lion. The warmer has a thin and flared rim that joins the deep belly at an angle. Both the mouth and the body of the warmer are six-lobed. Spur marks are found inside the bowl and fireclay marks are visible around the outer base. The exterior of the bowl and the shoulders of the ewer are engraved with spirals evoking the bubbles rising slowly in the boiling water. The entire vessel is coated with a crackled bluish white glaze with a grayish tint and numerous white inclusions. When the ewer is placed inside the warmer, its shoulders are leveled with the angular turn below the mouth of the warmer.

The ewer and the bowl form a wine set. The hot water inside the bowl would keep the ewer and the wine inside warm for serving. The intactness of the wine set makes it an absolute rarity.

406

青白釉兽面壶

北宋

公元 960—1127 年

闽清窑

高：23.6 厘米

底径：8.3 厘米

Qingbai-glazed ewer with animal head spout

Northern Song dynasty

960 – 1127 C.E.

Minqing kilns

Height: 23.6 cm

Base diameter: 8.3 cm

直口，长颈，上饰竹节弦纹。斜肩，腹中部鼓出，圈足。器身一侧饰一兽面长流，兽首大鼻、凸眼、高角、长嘴、翘耳。流相对一侧附带形柄，上接壶口，下贴腹。身置凸棱六条，把壶身分为六等份，间刻花卉纹。盖带一小纽，盖内露胎。胎白，较疏松。施青白釉，釉色带白。胎釉结合不牢，有剥釉现象。本品造型新颖，有很高的艺术水平。

闽清窑在福建闽清县城北，是宋元时期瓷窑，主烧青白瓷。

The ewer has a straight mouth, a long neck with nodular rings, steep shoulders, a bulged lower belly and a ring foot. The long spout is carved with an animal face. On the opposite side is a strap handle that connects the belly to the mouth. The body is divided into six equal segments by six vertical ribs. The spaces in between are engraved with floral motif. The lid is furnished with a small knob. The exterior surface of the vessel is covered with a *qingbai* glaze. The white paste is rather porous. Flaking is visible in some areas.

The Minqing kiln sites are located north of Minqing, Fujian province. They produced mainly *qingbai* porcelains during the Song and Yuan dynasties.

407

青白釉兽首纹壶

北宋

公元 960—1127 年

闽清窑

高：23.9 厘米

底径：7.6 厘米

Qingbai-glazed ewer with animal head spout

Northern Song dynasty

960 – 1127 C.E.

Minqing kilns

Height: 23.9 cm

Base diameter: 7.6 cm

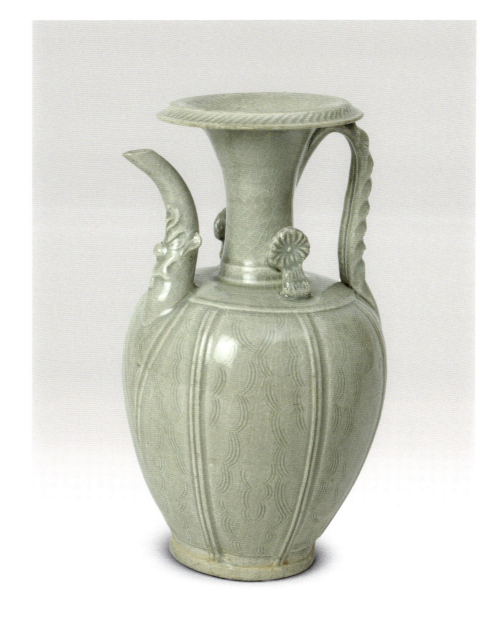

喇叭形口，唇缘尖薄，上饰斜线纹。高颈，平肩，圆腹下敛。肩置弦线一周，以双股竖棱线把器腹分成八部分，并以棱线为主叶脉满刻弧形叶纹。肩腹间置兽首流，流细长弯曲，嘴尖、兽睁眼、大鼻、合嘴、高角、翘耳。流相对侧塑耙齿状宽带柄、连接口缘和肩腹。流和柄下端各刻叶纹一道。肩另两侧贴花形竖耳一对，靠在颈底部两道凸弦线上。胎灰白，质稍疏松。施青白釉，釉色青中泛黄，均匀明亮，全器满布冰裂纹片。釉不到足底。造型新颖，纹饰华丽。

福州市湖东路曾出土一件类似器物，现藏福州市博物馆。

The ewer has a trumpet-shaped mouth with a sharp, thin rim decorated with short oblique lines, a long neck, flat shoulders and a swelling belly. A ridge encompasses the shoulders. From this ridge eight groups of double ribs descend to the foot, dividing the belly into eight segments. The double ribs represent the midribs of leaves and the spaces in between them are incised with continuous arcs to denote the veins. The long and curved spout rising from the shoulders is carved with the face of an animal with a prominent nose, bulging eyes, pursed lips, tall horns and protruding ears. Arching between the mouth and the shoulders on the other side is a broad loop handle with serrate design. A leaf design is engraved under the spout and the handle. Halfway between the spout and the handle on each side is a flower-shaped upright lug. The grayish white paste is relatively porous. The entire surface except around the foot is covered with an even layer of *qingbai* glaze with a yellowish tint and ice crackles.

A similar vessel was unearthed from Hudonglu, Fuzhou, Fujian province. It is now in the collection of the Fuzhou Municipal Museum.

青白釉洗口瓜棱壶
北宋
公元 960—1127 年
景德镇窑
高：16.9 厘米
底径：7.4 厘米

Qingbai-glazed ewer with cup-shaped mouth and lobed body
Song dynasty
960 – 1127 C.E.
Jingdezhen kilns
Height: 16.9 cm
Base diameter: 7.4 cm

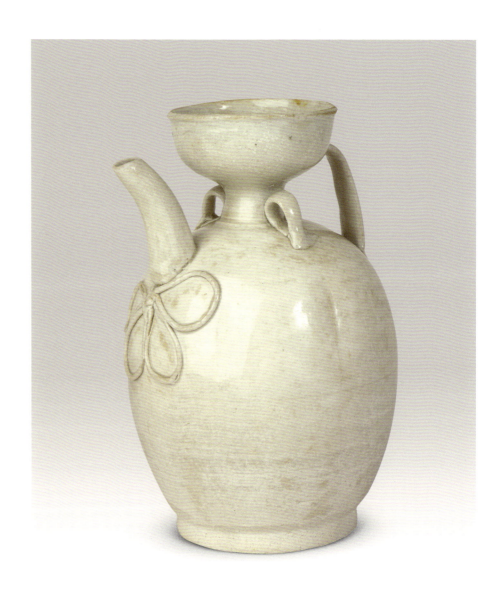

洗口带唇边，短细直颈，丰肩，瓜棱腹，圈足。管状长流，扁带形曲把饰凸弦纹，肩部两侧置对称双系。流下堆贴蝴蝶形花饰。施白釉，釉面光亮，釉层较薄，釉色偏青，釉面有土蚀白斑点。施釉不到底，底部露出白胎，胎颇细滑。

1972 年江西景德镇市北宋治平二年（公元 1065 年）舒氏墓出土有相似器物，现藏景德镇中国陶瓷博物馆。

The vessel has a cup-shaped mouth with lipped rim, a short straight neck, bold shoulders, a lobed body and a ring foot. The strap handle is decorated with rib motif while the long spout is tubular in shape. A loop lug is set between the handle and the spout on both sides. The area below the spout is adorned with an appliqué butterfly-like floral design. The vessel is covered with a thin and lustrous white glaze with a greenish tint and some white inclusions. The glaze stops short of the foot. The base is unglazed, revealing a rather smooth and refined white paste.

A similar vessel was unearthed in 1972 from the tomb of Madam Shu in Jingdezhen, dated to the 2nd year of the Zhiping period (1065 C.E.) of the Northern Song dynasty. It is now in the collection of the Jingdezhen China Ceramics Museum.

409

青白釉瓜棱执壶

宋

公元 960—1279 年

景德镇窑

高：25 厘米

底径：10 厘米

Qingbai-glazed ewer with lobed body

Song dynasty

960 – 1279 C.E.

Jingdezhen kilns

Height: 25 cm

Base diameter: 10 cm

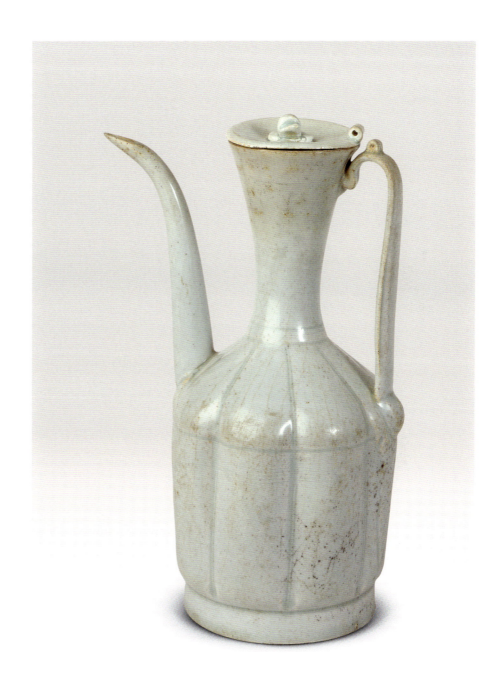

喇叭状口，折肩、深腹、肩腹呈八瓣瓜棱形，宽大圈足。口部有扁平状盖，盖中央贴瓜蒂状纽、盖边一侧饰圆管状小系一个。肩置尖嘴弯曲长流，相对一侧附扁平带形柄，柄端饰圆管状小系一个，与盖上小系相对，以便用绳相系。流下方和柄下端各模印尖长叶纹一个。胎骨洁白细滑，质坚。施青白釉，聚釉处釉色发深。底露胎，留垫饼残渣一圈，呈黄褐色。造型稳重端庄、线条流畅优雅。

The ewer has a trumpet-shaped mouth, angular shoulders, an eight-lobed belly and a broad ring foot. A tall, curved spout is set on the shoulders opposite a strap handle whose upper end is affixed with a small tubular device. The lower end of the spout and the handle are molded with an elongated leaf design with a pointed tip. The flat lid is surmounted by a knob in the shape of a gourd with a stem. The lid can be attached to the handle by tying one end of a rope to the tubular device on the lid and the other end to the device on top of the strap handle. The pure white paste is smooth, refined and hard. The vessel is covered with a *qingbai* glaze that appears deeper in tone where it pools. The unglazed base shows a ring of yellowish brown fireclay marks.

410

青白釉刻花八方壶

宋

公元 960—1279 年

景德镇窑

高：19.5 厘米

底径：8.4 厘米

Octagonal ewer with floral design under *qingbai* glaze

Song dynasty

960 – 1279 C.E.

Jingdezhen kilns

Height: 19.5 cm

Base diameter: 8.4 cm

颈高且粗，广斜折肩，圆球腹，颈、肩、腹均作八棱形，底平。口带八棱状盖，盖顶贴花蒂系，棱端贴小圆系。肩置平嘴尖流，相对一侧贴扁带状曲柄，柄端饰小圆系，与盖上小系相对应，用于系绳。肩和腹满刻花卉纹。胎白、细腻、质坚。釉白而泛青、釉色清澈透亮。底露胎，留垫烧残渣。

江西省博物馆收藏有相似器物。

The ewer has a tall, wide neck on broad shoulders that meets the bulbous belly at an angle. The body of the ewer is divided into eight facets from the mouth rim to the foot rim. A spout with pointed tip and a leveled mouth is set on the shoulders opposite a strap handle. A loop knob is affixed to the top of the octagonal lid. The lid can be attached to the handle by tying one end of a rope to the tubular device on the lid and the other end to the device on top of the strap handle. The shoulders and belly are densely carved with floral design. The white paste is hard and refined. The lustrous clear white glaze shows a greenish tint. Fireclay residues are found around the unglazed flat base.

A similar vessel is in the collection of the Jiangxi Provincial Museum.

411

青白釉剔犀云纹瓶

宋

公元 960—1279 年

景德镇窑（湖田）

高：15.7 厘米

口径：8.3 厘米

底径：8.6 厘米

Vase with carved cloud motif under *qingbai* glaze

Song dynasty

960 – 1279 C.E.

Jingdezhen kilns (Hutian)

Height: 15.7 cm

Mouth diameter: 8.3 cm

Base diameter: 8.6 cm

大口，圆唇微外撇，直颈，鼓腹，圆饼状圈足，足缘内壁向底心倾斜。颈、肩、腹部满刻云纹，用深而宽的斜向刀剔出胎土而成，刀法纯熟。肩有凹弦纹两道，近腹底处饰凸弦纹一周。肩一侧贴三环耳系一对。胎质洁白、质坚细腻。除外足底外，全器内外施青白色釉，釉色柔和、明澈温润。凸棱釉薄处色淡，刻花刀锋用力处和圈足部釉厚处色浓，如青翠的美玉。外壁釉面满布气泡。外足底留有垫烧残渣，呈火石红色。

此瓶造型甚为特别，双系集中在一侧。从圈足扁而阔大、以及近底处置一周凸弦纹来看，此瓶当为挂瓶。环耳系用于穿绳，圆饼形阔大圈足用于固定绳子，而下腹底的凸弦纹则防止绳子向上移动。

The vase has a wide mouth with rounded and slightly flared lip, a straight neck, bold shoulders, a bulging belly and a splayed ring foot. The neck, shoulders and belly are densely carved with cloud spirals. A carving tool with a broad blade has been used to cut into the surface at an oblique angle. Two grooves encircle the shoulders.

A pair of closely positioned three-looped lugs is attached to one side of the shoulder. The white paste is hard and refined. The greenish glaze is as lustrous and smooth as jade. The glaze runs thin and appears lighter over the rib and raised motifs. Since the carving is cut deep into the surface, the glaze that pools along the grooves appears much deeper in color. The glaze on the interior of the vase is suffused with bubbles. The base shows traces of fireclay marks.

The position of the loop lugs on one side is unique. Judging from the broad ring foot and rib above the foot, this vase was designed for hanging.

412

青白釉缠枝莲花荷口瓶

宋

公元 960—1279 年

景德镇窑

高：24.5 厘米

口径：13.5 厘米

底径：10.7 厘米

Qingbai-glazed foliate-mouth vase

Song dynasty

960 – 1279 C.E.

Jingdezhen kilns

Height: 24.5 cm

Mouth diameter: 13.5 cm

Base diameter: 10.7 cm

直颈，口缘外翻成八瓣荷花形，瓣口内起棱骨，颈刻尖叶纹。丰肩、圆鼓腹，足为覆盘形。瓶身刻缠枝莲花纹。外壁和颈内侧施青白釉，兼覆盖足部，釉色淡雅，聚釉处泛湖水绿色，无开片纹，有粉白点蚀痕。底无釉，露出洁白胎骨，有垫烧痕一圈，呈灰褐色。

高规格的荷口瓶发现不多，如本品这般体形较大、造型华丽、纹饰丰富且保持完整的更是十分稀少。

The vase has a foliate rim mouth with eight petals. A rib runs down each petal on the inner side of the mouth. The neck is carved with a band of upward pointing leaves. The rounded shoulders and the bulbous belly are densely carved with lotus scrolls. The foot is like an inverted dish. The inside of the mouth and the entire exterior surface including the foot are coated with a *qingbai* glaze of a very delicate tone. A bluish green color appears where the glaze pools. No crackles are found but white inclusions are visible in the glaze. The base is bare of glaze, exposing a white paste bearing a round of grayish brown fireclay marks.

Vases with foliate rim mouth of such refined quality are exceedingly rare.

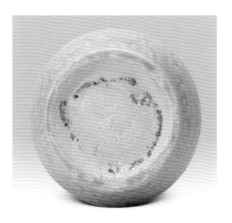

413

青白釉八瓜棱瓶

宋

公元 960—1279 年

繁昌窑

高：15.3 厘米

底径：4 厘米

Eight-lobed lidded jar with *qingbai* glaze

Song dynasty

960 – 1279 C.E.

Fanchang kilns

Height: 15.3 cm

Base diameter: 4 cm

长直颈，斜肩，瓜棱形腹，隐圈足。扁圆拱形盖。肩部饰对称圆系四个，腹部以双弦纹分隔为八部分。浅灰白胎，质坚。施青白釉，釉色白中泛灰，聚釉处呈淡青绿色。釉质光亮，透明度高，釉面满布土蚀的灰白点。釉不到底。底露胎，内墙有一圈垫烧痕。本品做工精细，线条优美，从胎土和釉色来看应为繁昌窑所出。

繁昌窑窑址在安徽繁昌县城南郊和西郊，为宋代窑场，主要生产青白瓷。

The jar has a long straight neck, slanting shoulders, an eight-lobed gourd-shaped body and a hidden ring foot. The body is divided into lobes by double grooves. Four equally spaced loop lugs are set around the shoulders. The pale grayish white paste is hard. The vessel is covered with a *qingbai* glaze with a grayish tint, which takes on a pale greenish shade where it accumulates. The glossy and highly translucent glaze is suffused with grayish white inclusions and stops short of the base on the outside. The base is unglazed. A ring of fireclay residues is found around the inner wall of the foot. The paste and glaze color suggest that this jar was produced at the Fanchang kilns.

The Fanchang kiln sites are located around the Southern and Western suburbs of Fanchang, Anhui province. They produced *qingbai* wares during the Song dynasty.

414

青白釉十二生肖堆塑瓶一对

南宋

公元 1127—1279 年

景德镇窑

高：61.4 厘米、59.3 厘米

底径：11.3 厘米、11 厘米

**Pair of *qingbai*-glazed lidded jars
with twelve cyclical animals**

Southern Song dynasty

1127 – 1279 C.E.

Jingdezhen kilns

Height: 61.4 cm, 59.3 cm

Base diameter: 11.3 cm, 11 cm

直口、短颈、椭圆腹、圈足外撇，瓶体秀长。笠帽式竹节纹盖。盖顶高耸挺拔，上立一振翅欲飞的小鸟。颈和上腹饰堆贴纹各一周、颈周堆塑青龙、白虎、朱雀、玄武和如意纹，瓶体上腹四周堆贴代表十二生肖的立像，下腹部满刻牡丹花纹，寓天地长久之意，为陪葬之用。灰白胎，稍粗，质较疏松。施青白釉，釉色青中带灰黄，满开片纹，上有土蚀白点。此对堆塑瓶造型别致，雕琢细腻，刀法流畅有力，集塑、模印及刀刻于一身，为同类瓶中的精品。

Each jar has a straight mouth rising from a short neck, an ovoid belly and a slightly splayed ring foot. The tip of the nodular spire surmounting the lid features a bird with spreading wings. The neck of the jar is surrounded by a round of sculpted animals, recognizably the Azure Dragon, White Tiger, Scarlet Bird and Black Tortoise, and a number of *ruyi*-shaped motifs. Around the upper belly are twelve figurines wearing wide-sleeved long robes with animal heads representing the twelve zodiac animals. The rest of the jar is densely carved with peony scrolls symbolizing eternity. This vessel was a funerary object. The grayish white paste is rather coarse and porous. The entire surface is coated with *qingbai* glaze with a grayish yellow tint. Crackles and white inclusions are visible in the glaze. This pair of jars is the finest among its kind.

415

青白釉缠枝花纹经瓶

南宋

公元 1127—1279 年

景德镇窑（湖田）

高：23.8 厘米

口径：3.5 厘米

底径：7.8 厘米

***Jingping* vase with carved floral motif in *qingbai* glaze**

Southern Song dynasty

1127 – 1279 C.E.

Jingdezhen kilns (Hutian)

Height: 23.8 cm

Mouth diameter: 3.5 cm

Base diameter: 7.8 cm

小口，短颈，丰肩，肩以下渐敛。颈饰凸弦纹一道，肩和足底上各刻弦纹两周。瓶身满刻缠枝花纹，并衬以浅细的篦纹地。灰白色胎，质坚、细腻。内外施青白釉，釉色明亮，莹润如玉，积釉处呈湖水绿色。隐圈足，圈足内外无釉处呈火石红色。底部留有垫饼残渣。本品刻工深邃、犀利流畅，是青白瓷刻花工艺的代表。

经瓶是宋人对酒瓶的一种特殊称呼。其时经学发达，从皇帝到士大夫都提倡讲经，而每次讲经活动都要准备一瓶酒，讲经结束用来招待讲师，故为“经瓶”。今人多称“梅瓶”，乃源自民国许之衡《饮流斋说瓷》中“口径之小，仅与梅之瘦骨相称，故名梅瓶”之说。

本品经热释光测定最后烧制年代距今约800 年。

1991 年四川省遂宁市金鱼村窖藏出土有相似器物。

The vase has a small mouth above a short neck, bold shoulders and a deep body. A rib encircles the neck while double ribs encompass the shoulders and the area above the foot. The body of the vase is densely carved with peony scrolls against a ground of splint motif. The grayish white paste is hard and refined. The *qingbai* glaze is bright and smooth as jade. The color appears bluish green where the glaze accumulates. The hidden ring foot is unglazed, revealing a burnt orange color. The base is scarred by fireclay marks. This vase is a rarity among *qingbai* ware with carved decorations.

Jingping is the name given to a kind of wine bottle used during the Song period. Lectures given on the Confucian Classics were prevalent during this time and advocated by the emperor and the scholar-officials. As it was customary to serve a bottle of wine to the lecturer after the talk, the bottle was called *jingping* ("classics bottle"). However, they are more commonly referred to as *meiping* ("plum blossom vase"). In his book *Yinliuzhai shuoci* (Remarks on Porcelain from Different Aspects), Xu Zhiheng explains that the mouth diameter of these vase is as tiny as the slender branches of plum blossoms, hence the name *meiping*.

Thermoluminescence test shows that the last firing date of this piece was around 800 years before present.

A similar vessel was unearthed in 1991 from a cache at Jinyu village, Suining, Sichuan province.

416

青白釉净瓶

南宋

公元 1127—1279 年

景德镇窑

高：29.2 厘米

底径：9.1 厘米

Kundika with *qingbai* glaze

Southern Song dynasty

1127 – 1279 C.E.

Jingdezhen kilns

Height: 29.2 cm

Base diameter: 9.1 cm

长颈，溜肩，圆腹，圈足。颈、肩和腹、足分界明显。颈中部有一凸托轮，将颈分成两段。口缘和凸缘四周镶有三角纹的银扣，银扣是在器物烧制完成后镶上，以示珍贵。胎白，质较轻。施青白釉，釉色青中泛蓝，满布开片纹。圈足内底较浅，圈足与内底间有一大圈垫烧残留物，呈浅灰黑色。

净瓶为僧侣"十八物"之一，游方时随身携带以储水或净手用。瓷质净瓶流行于唐、宋、辽时期，入清以后成为朝廷赐给西藏高僧插花供佛之物。

本品经热释光测定最后烧制年代距今900—700 年。

The flask has a long neck, steep shoulders, a rounded belly and a ring foot. The border between the neck and the belly is clearly defined. A broad ledge encircles the middle part of the neck, dividing the latter into two sections. The silver mount encircling the mouth rim and the ledge are decorated with triangular patterns. The white paste is lightweight. The bluish green *qingbai* glaze is covered with fine crackles. The ring foot is rather shallow on the inside. Grayish black fireclay marks adhered between the ring foot and the base.

The *kundika* is one of the "Eighteen Objects" which a mendicant Buddhist monk had to carry. It stores water for drinking or washing. Porcelain *kundika* are prevalent during the Tang, Song and Liao periods. During the Qing dynasty, the court would bestow these on Tibetan monks to be used as altar ware.

Thermoluminescence test shows that the last firing date of this piece was 900 to 700 years before present.

青白釉四灵雕瓷瓶

南宋

公元 1127—1279 年

景德镇窑

高：36 厘米

底径：11 厘米

Qingbai-glazed jar sculpted with the Four Divinities

Southern Song dynasty

1127 – 1279 C.E.

Jingdezhen kilns

Height: 36 cm

Base diameter: 11 cm

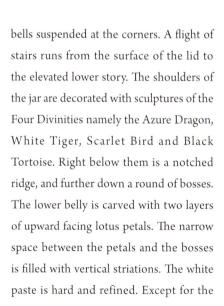

直颈、斜肩、圆腹、底足微外撇。口上带塔形盖，盖面饰莲瓣状凸弦线，上塑两层楼阁，屋檐四角饰挂铃。首层四周围以栏杆，内置圈椅一张。上层挂吊钟一个。阁和盖面以楼梯相连。瓶肩四周雕塑青龙、白虎、朱雀、玄武四灵像，下贴堆纹和乳丁纹各一周。下腹四周刻双仰莲花纹，间饰直纹。胎质坚致、洁白细腻。除瓶的颈、腹为素胎外，其余部分间施青白釉，瓶身内部亦满施青白釉。釉呈淡青白色、偏灰、带开片纹。底足较厚、外底露胎、留垫圈痕。

整件器物充满浓厚的宗教色彩，寓意灵魂经天梯而达极乐世界，造型新颖别致，构思巧妙、做工精细、堆塑技艺高超，是不可多得的艺术珍品。

本品经热释光测定最后烧制年代为距今 800—600 年。

The jar has a straight neck, steep shoulders and a lid in the form of a two-storied tower. The lower story has parapets around its periphery and an armchair with a U-shaped crest rail inside. The upper story has a bell hung from its ceiling. The eaves protruding from each story have aeolian bells suspended at the corners. A flight of stairs runs from the surface of the lid to the elevated lower story. The shoulders of the jar are decorated with sculptures of the Four Divinities namely the Azure Dragon, White Tiger, Scarlet Bird and Black Tortoise. Right below them is a notched ridge, and further down a round of bosses. The lower belly is carved with two layers of upward facing lotus petals. The narrow space between the petals and the bosses is filled with vertical striations. The white paste is hard and refined. Except for the neck and the belly, which are bare of glaze, the rest of the vessel including all sculpted elements is partially covered with *qingbai* glaze. The interior of the urn is fully coated with a pale green crackled *qingbai* glaze with a grayish tint. The foot is rather thick and slightly splayed. The base is unglazed and bears a round of fireclay marks. This jar is a rarity among rarities.

Thermoluminescence test shows that the last firing date of this piece was 800 to 600 years before present.

418

青白釉弦纹贴花盖盒

南宋

公元 1127—1279 年

景德镇窑

高：9.2 厘米

底径：7 厘米

Qingbai-glazed box with grooves and appliqué design

Southern Song dynasty

1127 – 1279 C.E.

Jingdezhen kilns

Height: 9.2 cm

Base diameter: 7 cm

盒直壁，子口，腹壁下折到底。拱形盖母口，盖面堆贴连枝团花三，顶有凸弦纹两周。盖和盒腹饰相间的弦纹和瓦纹五道。胎白，质较疏松。盒内外壁和盖面施青白釉，釉层明亮，聚釉处呈色翠绿，釉面满布开片纹。圈足外深内浅，足内墙斜向外底，足底有火石红色垫饼痕。造型稳重秀丽，端庄大方。

The box has straight sides and a lower belly that tapers to the foot. The domed lid is decorated with a group of appliqué flowers with scrolling stems. A double-grooved circle adorns the top of the lid. The sides of the lid and box are decorated with ridges. The white paste is rather porous. The interior and exterior of the box as well as the top surface of the lid are covered with a lustrous and crackled *qingbai* glaze that appears bright green where it pools. The ring foot has a taller outer side, a shorter inner side and a beveled inner rim. The base is scarred by a circular fireclay mark burnt to an orange color.

419

卵白釉三供

元

公元 1206—1368 年

景德镇窑

高：21.1 厘米（座加瓶），8.1 厘米（炉）

底阔：6.8 厘米（座），6.8 厘米（炉）

Group of vases and censer in *luanbai* glaze

Yuan dynasty

1206 – 1368 C.E.

Jingdezhen kilns

Height: 21.1 cm (overall),

       8.1 cm (censer)

Base width: 6.8 cm (stand),

       6.8 cm (censer)

由两个六瓣蒜头瓶和六边形座以及一个香炉组成。胎白、坚硬、胎体较厚重。外壁施卵白釉，釉色白中泛青，釉层细薄均匀。内壁无釉。器下连座是元代瓷器流行的造型风格。

本品是供桌或祭坛上最为普遍的陈设用器，儒释道三教都使用。可用于烧香插花、祭祖、祀天、供养诸佛菩萨以及众鬼神。

The group comprises two garlic-mouthed vases on hexagonal pedestals and a censer. All pieces are fabricated from a hard and rather heavy white paste. The exterior walls are covered with a thin, even layer of *luanbai* ("egg-white") glaze with a greenish tint. The interior walls are unglazed. Vessels furnished with pedestals are prevalent during the Yuan dynasty.

The present set is the most commonly seen furnishings on altar tables associated with Buddhist, Daoist and Confucian rituals. They are used for the burning of incense and the display of flowers during offerings.

420

"枢府"铭印花碗

元

公元 1206—1368 年

景德镇窑

高：8 厘米

口径：16.8 厘米

底径：6.2 厘米

Luanbai-glazed bowl with *"Shufu"* mark and floral design

Yuan dynasty

1206 – 1368 C.E.

Jingdezhen kilns

Height: 8 cm

Mouth diameter: 16.8 cm

Base diameter: 6.2 cm

撇口，圆腹，小圈足。内壁口缘下印卷草纹一周，在卷草纹空隙间一侧直印阳文"枢"字，相对一侧印"府"字。碗心饰团菊一朵。外壁光素无纹。胎白，质坚，较厚重。施卵白釉，釉汁匀净纯厚。圈足底无釉，露胎处呈浅黄褐色，留有支烧砂粒。

元朝政府设枢密院，主掌军事和宫廷禁卫等事务。有"枢府"字样的卵白瓷应为元朝枢密院订烧的瓷器，故又称"枢府窑器"或"枢府瓷"。明王佐增补《新增格古要论》下卷《古器论》"古饶器"条记载："元朝烧小足印花者，内有'枢府'字者高。"

The bowl has a flared mouth, rounded sides and a small ring foot. The interior wall below the mouth rim is molded with tendril motif. The two characters *"Shu"* and *"Fu"* are molded in relief amid the tendrils on opposing sides. The center

of the bowl features a chrysanthemum roundel. The exterior wall is plain. The white paste is hard and heavy. The bowl is covered with an even layer of smooth *luanbai* glaze. The base is unglazed, revealing a pale yellowish brown paste.

Shumiyuan (*"shufu"*) or "Privy Council" was set up by the Yuan court to take charge of military affairs and the imperial guards. *Luanbai* porcelains with *"shufu"* mark are vessels commissioned by this Council. They were also referred to as *"shufu* ware" or *"shufu* porcelain". In the *"Guqilin"* chapter (Ancient Raozhou Wares) of *Xinzeng geguyaolun* (Newly Augmented Essential Criteria of Antiquities), the Ming scholar Wang Zuozeng writes, "Vessels with small foot and molded design were made during the Yuan dynasty. Those with 'shufu' mark are considered superior".

421

卵白釉印花碗连座

元

公元 1206—1368 年

景德镇窑

高：9.2 厘米（碗），7.9 厘米（座），

    15.3 厘米（碗加座）

口径：20.3 厘米（碗），8.1 厘米（座）

底径：6.2 厘米（碗），8.1 厘米（座）

Luanbai-glazed bowl with molded floral design and stand

Yuan dynasty

1206 – 1368 C.E.

Jingdezhen kilns

Height: 9.2 cm (bowl), 7.9 cm (stand),

    15.3cm (overall)

Mouth diameter: 20.3 cm (bowl),

          8.1 cm (stand)

Base diameter: 6.2 cm (bowl),

          8.1 cm (stand)

碗口微撇，弧壁。圈足厚重，外墙高，内墙极浅，近乎平底。口内缘下方饰回字纹一周。内壁印四时花卉，碗心置团菊纹，绕以一圈弦纹。外壁光素无纹。通体施卵白釉，口缘釉层积聚处呈泛蓝的青绿色，胎釉交界处见火石红色。足底无釉，现浅黄褐色。足底留有支烧砂粒。

座呈圆筒形，底平微内凹，露出洁白胎骨，胎骨较厚重。外壁施卵白釉，光素无纹。口缘和内壁无釉，外口缘下无釉处呈火石红色。

通常小圈足碗均不带座，而本品近乎实足的圈足是刻意把碗的重心降低，以便稳固安放在座上。在本器发现之前，一般人并不知道这类碗是带托座的。

The bowl has a slightly flared mouth, rounded sides and a heavy ring foot. A key-fret border runs below the inner mouth rim. The interior wall is molded with four flowers while the center features a chrysanthemum roundel within a grooved circular frame. The exterior wall is plain. The entire vessel except the base is covered with *luanbai* glaze. The glaze over the mouth rim appears bluish green. The junction between the paste and the glaze shows a burnt orange color. The base is unglazed, revealing a pale yellowish brown paste. The base is adhered with sand particles left by the kiln spacer.

The cylindrical pedestal has a slightly concave base revealing a relatively heavy paste of pure white. The exterior wall is covered with *luanbai* glaze and devoid of decorative motifs. The mouth rim and interior are unglazed. The unglazed area below the exterior mouth rim shows a brick red color.

Bowls with small ring foot usually have no pedestals. Examples with pedestals are quite rare. The almost solid ring foot was purposely designed to lower the center of gravity to allow the bowl to sit stably on the pedestal. It was not previously known that these bowls came furnished with pedestals.

422

青釉"河滨遗范"碗

北宋

公元 960—1127 年

龙泉窑

高：4.6 厘米

口径：13.1 厘米

Celadon bowl with *"Hebin yifan"* mark

Northern Song dynasty

960 – 1127 C.E.

Longquan kilns

Height: 4.6 cm

Mouth diameter: 13.1 cm

敞口，弧腹较浅，口缘有五个下凹花瓣口，内壁相对有五条凸起的竖向线纹，形如花叶的茎脉，口缘下和内底心分别以圆弧线把茎脉相连。内底约圈足位置轻刮胎泥一周，令内底心起一微凸台阶，上印四方图章式"河滨遗范"四字。浅灰色胎，胎质坚硬。施翠青釉，釉色莹润、亮泽。圈足底无釉，胎釉交接处有火石红线。根据胎泥和釉色判断，本品是北宋时期的遗物。

浙江省博物馆收藏有相似的器物。

"河滨遗范"款器物是龙泉窑特有的产品。《史记·五帝本纪》载："舜耕历山，渔雷泽，陶河滨……"《太平寰宇记》曰："河滨在定陶西南十里，即陶丘。"也就是说山东省定陶县城西南为古都遗址。另有一说法，认为舜是远古部落有虞氏的首领，这个部落居于山西永济的蒲州镇，"陶河滨"的"河"指黄河。范为制陶的模范，"河滨遗范"意为舜制陶所遗传的模范。

The bowl has a foliate mouth with five notches. A raised ridge runs down the interior wall from below each notch. The center of the bowl is impressed with a square seal showing the four characters *"Hebin yifan"*. The unglazed base reveals a light gray paste with a high degree of hardness. The bowl is covered with a smooth and glossy celadon glaze. The junction between the paste and glaze shows a line of burnt orange color. The paste and glaze color of this vessel suggest that it is from the Northern Song period.

A similar vessel is in the collection of the Zhejiang Provincial Museum.

Vessels with *"Hebin yifan"* marks are unique products of the Longquan kilns. It was recorded in the *"Wudi"* (Five Mythical Emperors) chapter of *Shiji* (Records of the Grand Historian) that "[Emperor] Shun farmed in Mount Li, fished in Lei Marsh and made pottery in Hebin." According to *Taiping huanyu ji* (Records of the Territory during the Taiping Period [of the Northern Song Dynasty]), "Hebin was located ten *li* (Chinese mile) southwest of Dingtao, [present-day] Taoqiu." The place is said to be the site of an ancient capital southwest of Dingtao county in Shandong. Also, *"hebin"* literally means riverside. Therefore, *"Hebin yifan"* may be referring to a pottery making tradition developed along the shores of the Hebin river.

423

青釉莲瓣纹五管瓶

北宋

公元 960—1127 年

龙泉窑（金村）

高：38.8 厘米

Celadon lidded jar with five spouts

Northern Song dynasty

960 – 1127 C.E.

Longquan kilns (Jincun)

Height: 38.8 cm

莲蓬状盖，外饰覆莲瓣纹，顶有石榴蒂状纽，上承长颈小瓶一个。瓶直口，深腹，圈足稍外撇。肩上安装五支棱状管，管端呈四齿状。腹部刻双瓣仰莲纹到底，瓣内画精细荷叶纹理。瓶盖直口上刻有一椭圆形纹饰，可能寓意通往极乐世界的大门。胎灰白，细腻。全器内外满施淡青色釉，釉面均匀光洁，透着淡淡的青色，如湖水轻盈荡漾。

本品为北宋早期龙泉窑最具代表性的器物，烧制地点在龙泉金村一带。本瓶的装饰涵义丰富："瓶"言"平安"，"莲藕"言"多子"，"石榴蒂"言"多子"，"多棱管""多角"言"多谷"。此外"莲"为佛教圣花，象征圣洁无染的境界，代表着莲花香、净、柔软、可爱四德，使见者能够感到欢喜吉祥。修行净土宗的信徒相信，西方极乐世界是最后皈依处，若得善报，临终时会有观音手持莲花迎接往生极乐世界。

1976 年浙江龙泉市茶丰乡出土有相似器物，现存龙泉青瓷博物馆。

The lid is in the shape of an inverted lotus pod surmounted by a miniature vase with a long neck. The lid is decorated with inverted lotus petal motif. The jar has a straight mouth, a deep belly and a slightly splayed ring foot. Five slightly incurving spouts with serrated tips are set around the shoulders. The body of the jar is carved with multi-layers of double lotus petal motif. The petals are finely incised with vein motif. The side of the lid is carved with an oval shape. It is possible that the opening represents a doorway to Paradise. The grayish white paste is refined in texture. The interior and exterior are covered with a light green celadon glaze that is smooth, lustrous, even where it runs thick.

This ewer is the most representative example of Longquan ware from the early Northern Song period. The kilns were located around Jincun in Longquan. This ewer and its decorative motifs are rich with symbolism. The ewer (*ping*) symbolizes peace (*pingan*); the lotus pod and the persimmon calyx allude to "abundant offsprings"; the tubular protuberances with angular sides and serrate ends signify "abundant grains"; the lotus, an emblem of Buddhism, represents sacredness and the pristine realm. In Buddhism, the lotus has four virtues: scent, purity, softness and loveliness. Followers of the Pure Land Sect of Buddhism believed that the Western Paradise was their ultimate refuge. If they had accumulated enough merits during their lifetime, Avalokitesvara (Guanyin) with lotus in hand would appear before their deathbed and guide them to rebirth in the Western Paradise.

A similar vessel was unearthed in 1976 from Chafengxiang in Longquan, Zhejiang province. It is now in the collection of the Longquan Celadon Museum.

424

青釉牡丹梅瓶

北宋

公元 960—1127 年

龙泉窑

高：38.6 厘米

Celadon *meiping* vase with peony motif

Northern Song dynasty

960 – 1127 C.E.

Longquan kilns

Height: 38.6 cm

高直颈，溜肩，腹渐收到底，圈足外撇。肩左右贴环状耳各一。灰白胎，胎质细腻。施青釉，釉均匀明亮。器身刻相连大牡丹四朵，刀工凌厉、线条流畅、纹饰深邃，浮雕感强。刻划出牡丹雍容华贵、明艳照人、清雅脱俗的独特气质，欣赏价值极高。

The vase has a tall straight neck, rounded shoulders and a belly that tapers to a splayed ring foot. The grayish white paste is refined in texture. The entire surface is covered with an even layer of lustrous celadon glaze. The body is engraved with four large peony sprays with high relief effects.

425

粉青釉长颈瓶

南宋

公元 1127—1279 年

龙泉窑

高：15.1 厘米

口径：6.2 厘米

底径：5.8 厘米

**Long-necked celadon vase with
sea green glaze**

Southern Song dynasty

1127 – 1279 C.E.

Longquan kilns

Height: 15.1 cm

Mouth diameter: 6.2 cm

Base diameter: 5.8 cm

翻沿圆唇，口微侈，长颈，溜肩，圆腹，
圈足。灰白胎，质坚。全器内外施粉青
泛蓝色釉，釉厚，釉色莹润匀净。颈部
有大开片纹。足边露胎呈铁足。全器光
素无纹，温文高雅。

The vase has a flared rim with rounded lip,
a long neck, steep shoulders, a rounded
belly and a ring foot. The interior and
exterior are covered with a sea green glaze
with blue tinge known as "*fenqing*". The
grayish white paste has a high degree
of hardness. The glaze is thick, smooth,
lustrous and even in texture. Large crackles
are found around the neck of the vase. The
unglazed foot rim is dark brown in color,
a feature known as "iron foot". The entire
vessel is devoid of decorative motifs.

426

青釉开片长颈瓶

南宋

公元 1127—1279 年

哥窑

高：14.3 厘米

口径：5.9 厘米

底径：5.5 厘米

Celadon vase with long neck and crackled glaze

Southern Song dynasty

1127 – 1279 C.E.

Ge kilns

Height: 14.3 cm

Mouth diameter: 5.9 cm

Base diameter: 5.5 cm

撇口、长颈、圆腹、矮圈足。圈足上宽下窄。胎质细腻，呈灰黑色。通体内外施米黄色釉，釉质凝厚，足边露胎呈铁足。器体满布金黄色和黑色片纹，大小交织，深浅相间，如金丝铁线。

宋代汝、官、哥窑器物不尚纹饰，而以造型、釉色和开片纹取胜。汝窑和官窑本色细碎开片，哥窑则为大小开片纹相结合，形成独特的装饰风格。

The vase has a flared mouth, a long neck, a rounded belly and a short ring foot. The grayish black paste is refined in texture. The interior and exterior are covered with a rich and thick celadon glaze of rice yellow color. The unglazed foot rim is dark brown in color, a feature known as "iron foot". Dense crackles of varying sizes in contrasting colors of yellowish brown and dark brown known as "golden thread and iron wire" are found all over the glaze.

Decorative motifs are minimal on Ru, Guan and Ge ware of the Song dynasty. Instead, emphasis is placed on the shape, the glaze color and the pattern of the crackles. Ru and Guan wares have tiny crackles. Ge ware has crackles of varying sizes.

427

青釉八棱杯托

南宋

公元 1127—1279 年

龙泉窑（溪口）

高：4.9 厘米（杯），2.4 厘米（托），

5.7 厘米（杯加托）

阔：8.5 厘米（杯），16 厘米（托）

Celadon octagonal-shaped cup and stand

Southern Song dynasty

1127 – 1279 C.E.

Longquan kilns (Xikou)

Height: 4.9 cm (cup), 2.4 cm (stand),

5.7 cm (overall)

Width: 8.5 cm (cup), 16 cm (stand)

由八棱形的杯和托盘组成。杯口平，圈足。托盘口缘宽大、向外伸展，盘内凹，矮圈足。黑胎，胎纯净细腻。施石灰碱釉，釉色呈粉青色调、泛蓝，杯内外和托内壁有开纹片。杯和托盘的口缘和足缘可见多次上釉痕迹。本品制作精巧、造型优美，釉层莹厚，釉色素雅，当为烧制供皇室使用的器物。

The set comprises a cup and a saucer, both of octagonal shape. The cup has a flat mouth and ring foot. The stand has a broad and overhanging rim with a depressed cavity and a short ring foot. The black paste is pure and refined. The entire surface is covered with an alkali-lime glaze with a bluish green tone. Crackles are found on the interior and exterior of the cup as well as the interior of the stand. Repeat application of glaze is evident along the mouth rims and foot rims of the set. It is likely that this set was made for imperial use.

青釉八棱杯托

428

青釉把杯

南宋

公元 1127—1279 年

龙泉窑（溪口）

高：4.9 厘米

口径：9.5 厘米

Celadon cup with handle

Southern Song dynasty

1127 – 1279 C.E.

Longquan kilns (Xikou)

Height: 4.9 cm

Mouth diameter: 9.5 cm

口微内敛，浅腹弧壁，圈足。肩腹一侧附有扁圆柄，柄上覆如意纹挡片。胎体轻巧，做工精美。施粉青釉，釉色泛蓝。釉层醇厚，釉色莹润如玉，开冰裂纹片。口缘和足缘呈紫金土的紫红色，是微生烧所显露出的色调。如过烧，胎会变成灰白色或米黄色；如正烧，胎会变为灰黑或黑色。通常窑工会作微生烧，以获取娇艳柔和、微泛蓝色的粉青色釉。

本品器形沉静雅素，为宋瓷美学风格的代表，应为烧制供皇室使用的器物。

溪口窑是龙泉生产薄胎厚釉黑胎青瓷的主要窑场，由官府指定，产品按官窑器物的式样，以官窑器物所用的物料、工艺技术烧制，供皇室使用。溪口窑黑胎青瓷器物传世极少，完整器物更少。这可能与当时采取"有命则贡，无命则止"的生产方式有关，也可能与元兵攻入临安城后的毁灭性破坏有关。根据上海博物馆陆明华先生在《试述龙泉黑胎青瓷》一文所述，"在 700 多件北京故宫博物院龙泉青瓷藏品中，已知是宋龙泉黑胎青瓷的大约只有五六件，但已发表的只有 1 件；上海博物馆藏龙泉黑胎青瓷只有 4 件；在大英博物馆，能肯定的只有

1 件"（见中国古陶瓷学会：《龙泉窑研究》，故宫出版社，2011 年）。

1972 年浙江湖州市宋墓出土有相似器物，现藏湖州市博物馆。

The cup has a slightly incurved mouth, rounded sides and a ring foot. The mid-section of the belly is furnished with a ring handle, above which is a *ruyi*-shaped tab. The paste is light, delicate and very refined. The cup is covered with a sea green glaze with a blue tinge. The glaze is rich, thick and jade-like and suffused with ice crackles. The mouth rim and foot rim is purplish red in color which is typical of a clay called "*zijintu*" ("purple gold clay"). To achieve this color, the vessel had to be slightly under-fired. Over-firing would result in a grayish white or creamy white color. When the firing temperature is just right, the paste would take on a dark gray or black color.

Judging from the quiet elegance of the cup, it was made for imperial use.

Xikou was a major kiln in Longquan producing black paste celadons with a thin body and thick glaze. These wares were made for imperial use. Their shapes, materials and techniques were stipulated by the imperial court. Extant examples are extremely rare, and intact ones are fewer still. This was probably partly due to the policy known as "send tribute upon receipt of imperial order; stop production when no order is received" that was implemented by the imperial court. In his article, "Tentative Description of Black-Bodied Longquan Celadon", Lu Minghua, Research Director of Shanghai Museum, says, "Of some seven hundred pieces of Longquan celadon in the collection of the Palace Museum, only five to six pieces are known to be Longquan black paste celadon from the Song dynasty, and only one of which was published. Shanghai Museum has only four pieces of Longquan black paste celadon dated to the Song period. The British Museum has only one confirmed example." (The Research of Longquan kiln [China's Ancient Ceramics Institute], Imperial Palace Publishing House, 2011.)

A similar vessel was unearthed in 1972 from a Song tomb in Huzhou, Zhejiang province. It is now in the collection of the Huzhou Municipal Museum.

429

青釉莲瓣纹盅

南宋

公元 1127—1279 年

龙泉窑（溪口）

高：8.2 厘米

口径：13 厘米

Celadon bowl with lotus petal motif

Southern Song dynasty

1127 – 1279 C.E.

Longquan kilns (Xikou)

Height: 8.2 cm

Mouth diameter: 13 cm

敛口，弧形腹，圈足。口缘有多处镶银扣残留物。腹饰仰莲瓣纹，瓣脊起棱。施粉青色釉，釉色泛蓝。釉层肥厚，釉色纯净、润泽。器体内外开冰裂纹片，纹片斑驳交错。口缘和足缘刮釉，露胎处呈紫红色。口缘和圈足外壁可见多层上釉的痕迹。本品应为溪口龙泉窑烧造供皇室使用的器物。

溪口龙泉窑部分器物口缘和足缘都刮釉，是因为烧造时在口缘上放置垫圈，以减少烧造时口缘变形和破裂，提高产量。溪口龙泉窑器物无论制作工艺、釉色处理，还是造型等方面，无不精益求精，产品质量几与官窑类同，甚至某些薄胎厚釉产品较官窑更精巧别致。

1978 年浙江湖州市宋墓出土有相似器物，现藏湖州市博物馆。台北故宫博物院也藏有一件相似器物。

本盅原为一对，20 世纪 90 年代笔者曾在香港一间古玩店见过，当时由于对溪口龙泉窑器物认识不足，加上开价太高，故没有购藏。后在与一位朋友参观一个在香港举办的国际古玩展销会时，于一个英国古玩商摊位再次见到这对盅。这位朋友说，他 10 多年前在国内见过这对盅，当他仍在考虑是否要购买时，物主告诉他已卖出。可见这对盅后来卖来香港，又辗转去了英国。因为这样的渊源，我们决定一齐买下这对盅，每人拿一只。陶瓷器物也有灵性，在适当时间，就算远隔重洋，万水千山，也会再次相遇。这也是收藏乐趣之一。

The bowl has a slightly incurved mouth, rounded sides and a ring foot. The exterior wall is decorated with upright lotus petals, each featuring a raised midrib. The vessel surface is covered with a sea green glaze with a blue tinge. The glaze is thick, lustrous, pure and smooth. The ice crackles on the interior and exterior are highly decorative in effect. The glaze on the mouth rim and foot rim has been scraped away, exposing a purplish red paste. The mouth rim shows traces of a silver mount. Repeat application of glaze is also evident along the edge of the mouth rim and the external foot rim. This bowl was likely made for imperial use.

Some Xikou vessels have both mouth rim and foot rim scraped clean of glaze. A spacer ring is placed over the mouth to prevent the rim from warping and breaking during firing. The quality of Xikou ware is almost on a par with the products of the imperial kilns. Some Xikou pieces with thin paste and thick glaze are even more exquisite than imperial ware.

A similar vessel was unearthed in 1978 from a Song tomb in Huzhou, Zhejiang province. It is now in the collection of the Huzhou Municipal Museum. Another similar vessel is in the collection of the Palace Museum of Taipei.

This bowl is one of a pair. I came across them for the first time in an antique shop in Hong Kong during the 1990s. Since I had little knowledge of Xikou Longquan ware at that time apart from its exorbitant price, I did not acquire it. Some time later, while visiting an international antiques fair in Hong Kong with my friend, I spotted this pair again at a British dealer's booth! My friend told me he first saw these two bowls in Mainland China over a decade ago but they ended up being sold to someone else. My friend and I decided to buy the pair together this time. We then each took one from the pair. It seems that ceramic artifacts also have some kind of intelligence; when the right time comes they will return to look for their desired owners. This is one of the many joys of collecting.

青釉渣斗

南宋

公元 1127—1279 年

龙泉窑

高：7.3 厘米

口径：9 厘米

Celadon spittoon

Southern Song dynasty

1127 – 1279 C.E.

Longquan kilns

Height: 7.3 cm

Mouth diameter: 9 cm

广口外撇、颈微斜、扁圆腹、圈足较高。浅灰胎，胎薄，细腻。施石灰碱釉、釉色呈粉青、泛灰。厚釉，釉色柔润、失透、全器开纹片。胎釉交接处呈浅火石红色。本品造型古朴优雅，应为烧制供宫廷使用的器物。

2002 年浙江丽水市南宋墓出土有相似器物，现存丽水市博物馆。

The vessel has a wide and flared mouth, an oblate belly and a rather tall ring foot. The light gray paste is thin and refined. The surface is covered with a sea green alkali-lime glaze with a grayish tint. The glaze is thick and opaque and the color soft and rich. The entire glazed surface is suffused with crackles. The foot rim shows a burnt orange color. This spittoon was likely made for imperial use.

A similar vessel was unearthed in 2002 from a Southern Song tomb in Lishui, Zhejiang province. It is now in the collection of the Lishui Municipal Museum.

431

黄褐釉渣斗

南宋

公元 1127—1279 年

龙泉窑（大窑）

高：9 厘米

口径：11.4 厘米

Celadon spittoon in yellowish brown glaze

Southern Song dynasty

1127 – 1279 C.E.

Longquan kilns (Dayao)

Height: 9 cm

Mouth diameter: 11.4 cm

口外撇、颈微内斜、扁圆腹、圈足。深紫红色胎。除圈足底边外，全器满施青釉，釉汁醇厚、釉色润泽，满布大小不一的冰裂纹片，清澈透亮，玻璃质感强，呈金黄色、闪闪生辉。口缘四周釉汁下淌，挂釉较薄、呈浅紫红色，圈足底边露胎处呈深紫红色，即所谓"紫口铁足"。龙泉渣斗存世甚少，本品器形古朴典雅、线条流畅、胎体薄、修坯精细，当为烧制供皇室使用的器物。

明陆客《菽园杂记》载："青瓷初出于刘田、去县六十里"。刘田也叫琉田、即今大窑，是龙泉窑的传统制瓷中心。大窑烧制的器物以白胎、灰白胎为主，也有少量黑胎和红砖胎。

The vessel has a flared mouth, a neck with a narrower lower part, an oblate body and a ring foot. The deep purplish red paste is thin and finely trimmed. Except for the foot rim, the entire vessel is covered with a lustrous, smooth and shiny celadon glaze suffused with ice crackles. A light purplish red is shown through the thin glaze around the mouth while a deep purplish red is seen through the unglazed foot rim. These features are referred to as "purple mouth and iron foot". Extant examples of Longquan spittoons are quite scarce. This spittoon was likely made for imperial use.

In *Shuyuan zaji* (Miscellaneous Records from the Bean Garden), the Ming scholar Lu Rong writes, "Celadon ware first came about in Liutian, sixty *li* (Chinese mile) away from this county." Liutian refers to the Dayao kilns, traditionally the porcelain production center of the Longquan kilns. The paste of the majority of porcelains produced in the Dayao kilns is mostly white or grayish white. Examples with black or brick red paste also existed but in small numbers.

432

青釉牡丹花盒

南宋

公元 1127—1279 年

龙泉窑

高：5.6 厘米

阔：12.7 厘米

底径：6.6 厘米

Celadon box with peony design

Southern Song dynasty

1127 – 1279 C.E.

Longquan kilns

Height: 5.6 cm

Width: 12.7 cm

Base diameter: 6.6 cm

扁圆形，子母口，圈足。盖面堆饰牡丹花纹。内底贴三个小盅，其一内心凸起成圆台。浅灰胎，细密，质坚。通体施青色釉，釉色鲜亮，肥厚青翠，娇艳欲滴，清雅迷人，有开片纹。本品造型优美，纹饰秀雅，制作精美，应是大窑龙泉窑生产的珍贵器物。

浙江省龙泉松阳县博物馆藏有与本品相似的器物。

The entire surface of the flattened circular box is covered with a lustrous, smooth, shiny and charming green glaze with crackles. The light gray paste is hard and refined. The top of the cover is decorated with raised peony design. The inset rim of the box holds the lid in place. Three small dishes are attached to the interior of the box. One of them has a circular platform rising from the center. It is a fine example from the Dayao kilns in Longquan.

A similar box is in the collection of the Songyang County Museum in Longquan, Zhejiang province.

433

青釉象纽盖罐

南宋

公元 1127—1279 年

龙泉窑

高：14.1 厘米

Celadon lidded jar with elephant knob

Southern Song dynasty

1127 – 1279 C.E.

Longquan kilns

Height: 14.1 cm

圆饼形盖，上塑立象为纽。筒形身，折肩，近底处微内收。胎细滑，罐口缘和足缘露胎处呈紫红色。罐体内外施粉青釉、釉色均匀，醇厚润泽，无开纹片。器口缘可见盖、罐叠烧残留的痕迹。本品做工细腻，立象生动传神、活泼可爱，当为宫廷订制的器物。

本品寓意"太平有象"。《汉书·王莽传》："天下太平，五谷成熟。""瓶"与"平"同音，"太平有象"即天下太平、五谷丰登的意思，反映了宋朝皇室经历颠沛流亡和被迫南迁后祈求安定的心态。

本品当为盛放香料的器具，名"香宝子"。盖纽上的大象为密宗毗那耶迦形象，毗那耶迦爱香尘，故常被用作香炉、香盒或香宝子盖纽的造型。

2005 年浙江南宋嘉定壬午年（公元 1222 年）李垕妻姜氏墓出土相似器物，现藏丽水市博物馆。

The disc-like lid has a knob in the shape of a standing elephant. The jar has angular shoulders and an almost cylindrical body whose lower part tapers slightly towards the base. The paste is refined. The unglazed mouth rim and foot rim of the jar reveal a purplish red paste. The interior and exterior of the jar are covered with an even layer of sea green glaze with no crackles. The glaze is rich and smooth in texture and subtle in color. The mouth rim shows evidence of the lid being placed over the mouth of the jar during firing. This jar was likely made for imperial use.

Since the word for jar (*ping*) and elephant (*xiang*) are homophonous to "peace" and "sign" in Chinese, together they signify "a sign of peace". It was recorded in the "Biography of Wang Mang" chapter of *Hanshu* (The Book of Han) that "[The nation enjoys] universal peace; the five grains ripen." Therefore, the combined image of a jar with an elephant also represents a bumper harvest.

The present jar is probably a *xiangbaozi* ("incense treasure case"), a type of incense container. The elephant on top of the lid represents the elephant-head deity Vinayaka in the pantheon of esoteric Buddhism. Since this deity loves incense dust, the elephant was often used to adorn censers and incense boxes.

A similar vessel was unearthed in 2005 from the tomb of Madam Jiang, wife of Li Hou, in Zhejiang. The tomb is dated to the *Renwu* year (1222 C.E.) of the Jiading period of the Southern Song dynasty. The vessel is now in the collection of the Lishui Municipal Museum.

434

青釉弦纹樽式炉

南宋

公元 1127—1279 年

龙泉窑

高：6 厘米

Celadon *zun* tripod censer with ribbed design

Southern Song dynasty

1127 – 1279 C.E.

Longquan kilns

Height: 6 cm

直口微外侈，平唇内折，筒腹，底向内平收，下贴扁平垂云足三个。器身饰三组凸棱线，棱线釉薄处呈白色。施梅子青色釉，釉色莹润、青翠、娇嫩可人。腹底中部有圆饼状足一个，足微内凹，露灰白胎，胎质坚硬，胎与腹底部釉交接处呈火石红色。

樽原为古代酒器（图录 160 号）。樽式炉始于宋，汝窑、定窑、龙泉窑均有烧造，是香炉的一种。

The vessel has a slightly flared straight mouth with a flat and inward overhanging rim. The cylindrical body makes an angular turn at the base. Three legs with molded cloud design are attached along the edge of the base. The vessel is covered with a lustrous and shiny plum green glaze. The exterior wall is decorated with three groups of ribs. The glaze appears white where it runs thin along the ribs. The underside of the body has a disc-like foot with a slightly receding rim. The grayish white paste is hard. The unglazed foot rim shows a burnt orange color.

Zun was an ancient wine vessel (Cat. No. 160). Celadon *zun* first appeared in the Song dynasty and were produced at the Ru, Ding and Longquan kilns. They are a type of censers.

435

青釉鬲式炉

南宋

公元 1127—1279 年

龙泉窑（大窑）

高：7 厘米

Celadon *li* tripod censer

Southern Song dynasty

1127 – 1279 C.E.

Longquan kilns (Dayao)

Height: 7 cm

圆口、平缘外卷、颈较高、扁圆腹。肩周起凸弦纹一道，腹下置三实足，三足相靠较近。腹足间凸起竖棱三道。灰白胎，细腻，质坚。施粉青色釉，釉色泛蓝，颈上和腹底聚釉处泛蓝更明显。釉色均匀，釉层肥润醇厚，全器内外开冰裂纹片。足底露胎处呈火石红色。本品体形娇小，釉色明静雅素、令人爱不释手，是用手把玩之物。

鬲炉腹足间的棱线，釉薄处呈白色，俗称"出筋"，是一种装饰手法。釉面上的纹片也是美化器物的一种手法，令素雅的器物更为柔和。

The censer has a circular mouth with a flat and out-rolling rim, a rather tall neck and a compressed bulbous belly supported by three solid legs. Three evenly spaced vertical flanges descend from the belly to the top of the feet. The grayish white paste is hard and refined. The vessel is covered with a sea green glaze with a blue tinge, which is particularly obvious around the neck and on the underside of the belly where the glaze accumulates. The glaze is even in tone, rich and lustrous in texture, and suffused with ice crackles. The unglazed foot rim shows a burnt orange color. This vessel is meant to be handled and held between the hands.

The glaze appears white where it runs thin along the vertical flanges. This decorative technique is known as "*chujin*".

436

青釉兽耳簋式炉

南宋

公元 1127—1279 年

龙泉窑（大窑）

高：7.5 厘米

底径：6.5 厘米

Celadon *gui* censer with animal-shaped handles

Southern Song dynasty

1127 – 1279 C.E.

Longquan kilns (Dayao)

Height: 7.5 cm

Base diameter: 6.5 cm

口缘微外侈，垂肩，腹外鼓，高圈足。腹部对称装双兽耳。香灰胎，胎薄致密。釉呈粉青色，釉色均匀，泛蓝。釉层醇厚，明澈温润，葱翠如玉。釉无开纹片。足缘无釉处呈朱红色。此器仿商周青铜簋造型，古拙端庄，制作精细，符合宋瓷沉静雅素的美学风格，应为烧制供皇室使用的器物。

The censer has an everted mouth, steep shoulders, a bulged lower belly and a tall ring foot. A pair of animal-shaped handles flanks the belly. The ash gray paste is thin and dense. The sea green glaze with a blue tinge is even, lustrous, and smooth with no crackles. The green hue is comparable to that of jade. The foot rim is unglazed, revealing a cinnabar red paste. This censer is modeled after the bronze *gui* censers of the Shang and Zhou dynasty. This censer was likely made for imperial use.

粉青七弦瓶

南宋

公元 1127—1279 年

龙泉窑（大窑）

高：17 厘米

底径：6.8 厘米

**Seven-ribbed celadon vase in
sea green glaze**

Southern Song dynasty

1127 – 1279 C.E.

Longquan kilns (Dayao)

Height: 17 cm

Base diameter: 6.8 cm

盘口，细长颈，斜肩，鼓腹，圈足。颈肩部饰凸弦纹如竹节，故名 "竹节瓶"，又由于通常有弦纹七道，坊间又称 "七弦瓶"。灰白胎，质坚、细腻。通体施粉青色釉，青中泛柔和的粉蓝色，色泽均匀，文静雅素。本品器体拔挺，造型秀丽，釉色可媲美上品的汝窑器物，极为珍贵，应为烧制供皇室使用的器物。

在南宋，七弦瓶是龙泉窑高档器物，存世数量不多，如本品般质量之高的更是凤毛麟角。

1991 年四川省遂宁市金鱼村窖藏出土有相似器物。

The vase has a plate-shaped mouth above a slender neck, steep shoulders, a swelling belly and a ring foot. Since the ribs encircling the neck and the shoulders resemble the internodes of bamboo, vases of this shape are also called "bamboo-node vase". As there are usually seven ribs on the body, another name for it is "seven-ribbed vase". The grayish white paste is hard and refined. The entire surface of the vessel is covered with a bluish green glaze. The glaze is even, smooth and lustrous as jade. This type of vessels was greatly sought after by the Song literati. The glaze color is comparable to the finest Ru ware.

This vase was likely made for imperial use.

The seven-ribbed vase was a high-end product of the Southern Song dynasty. Extant examples are scarce and ones that are as fine as the present piece are exceedingly rare.

A similar vessel was unearthed in 1991 from a cache at Jinyu village, Suining, Sichuan province.

梅子青弦纹净瓶

南宋

公元 1127—1279 年

龙泉窑（大窑）

高：29.2 厘米

口径：3.7 厘米

底径：7.8 厘米

Celadon *kundika* in plum green glaze

Southern Song dynasty

1127 – 1279 C.E.

Longquan kilns (Dayao)

Height: 29.2 cm

Mouth diameter: 3.7 cm

Base diameter: 7.8 cm

直口，长颈，肩和上腹丰满，下腹缓慢收束，底内凹。颈的长度几与瓶身相同，上出一凸托轮，将颈分成两部分，使瓶体形同"吉"字，故俗称"大吉瓶"。全器光素无纹，只在肩上饰弦纹两道、近底处饰弦纹一周。浅灰胎，胎细滑、坚致。除足缘外，通体施梅子青色釉，釉色肥厚、明澈温润、葱翠如玉。口部隐现灰紫色，圈足底无釉处呈黑褐色，即"紫口铁足"。本品稳重典雅、线条简洁、酣畅流利、神完气足，当为烧制供皇室使用的器物。

此种瓶式样始烧于南宋，但同类南宋器物留存极少。清乾隆时期的藏草瓶很可能吸收了此种瓶的外形式样。

在理学盛行的宋代，人们追求美学上的质朴无华和平淡自然的情趣韵味，反对矫揉造作和装饰雕琢。因而宋瓷讲究细洁净润、色调单纯、趣味高雅，表现为对神、趣、韵、味的追求和彼此的协调，与近代奉行的简约美是一致的。这些都在本品中有所体现。

The vase has a straight mouth, a long cylindrical neck, rounded shoulders, a swelling upper belly and a narrow lower belly that tapers towards a base with a recessed center. The neck measures nearly as long as the body. A disc-shaped ledge divides the neck into two sections. Since the shape of the vase is similar to that of the Chinese character *ji*, meaning "lucky" or "auspicious", this type of vase is also referred to as "*daji* (great luck) vase". Except for two grooves around the shoulders and a third one near the foot, the body is without decoration. The light gray paste is hard and refined. The entire vessel except the foot rim is covered with a lustrous plum green celadon glaze. The glaze over the mouth rim appears thin. A grayish purple color is shown through the thin glaze, a feature known as "purple mouth". The unglazed foot rim appears dark brown, a feature referred to as "iron foot". This vase was likely made for imperial use.

This type of vases was first produced in the Southern Song dynasty but extant examples are exceedingly rare. The "herb vase" or "*benba* pot" that is prevalent during the Qianlong period of the Qing dynasty probably derived its shape from this type of vases.

This vase is a fine example of Song aesthetics, which emphasized simplicity and elegance.

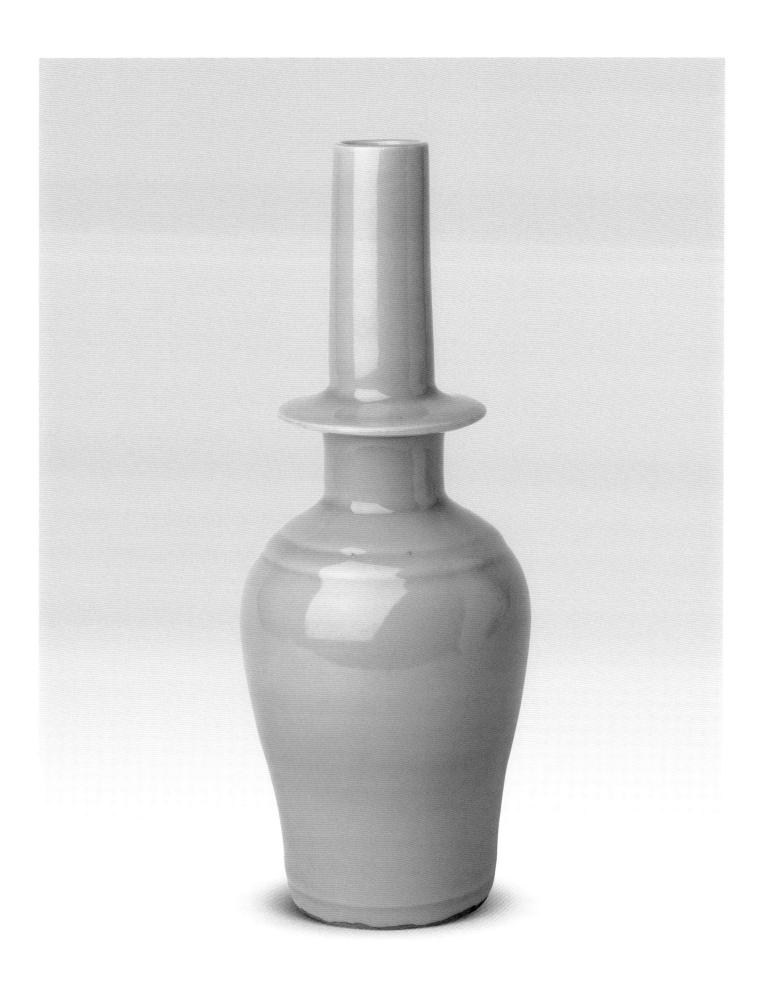

439

青釉莲瓣纹碗

南宋

公元 1127—1279 年

龙泉窑

高：8 厘米

口径：16.5 厘米

Celadon bowl with lotus petal motif

Southern Song dynasty

1127 – 1279 C.E.

Longquan kilns

Height: 8 cm

Mouth diameter: 16.5 cm

敞口、弧腹、小圈足微内敛。外壁刻莲瓣纹，莲瓣中脊挺拔，呈凸棱状。灰白胎，胎薄，细腻。施粉青色釉，釉层肥厚，莹润如玉，青翠可人。全器内外开纹片。圈足缘露胎，胎与釉结合处有火石红色。宋代龙泉窑留存的碗数量较多，但如本品般线条流畅、釉色鲜亮、制作精细且保存完整的不多。

1974 年浙江省衢州市南宋咸淳十年（公元 1274 年）史绳祖夫妇墓出土有相似器物，现藏衢州市博物馆。

The bowl has a wide mouth, slightly rounded sides and a small ring foot with a slightly receding rim. The exterior wall is carved with lotus petal motif. The grayish white paste is thin and refined. The entire vessel is covered with a crackled sea green glaze. The foot rim is bare of glaze and shows a burnt orange color.

A similar vessel was unearthed in 1974 from the tomb of Shi Shengzu and his wife in Quzhou, Zhejiang province. The tomb is dated to the 10th year of the Xianchun period of the Southern Song dynasty (1274 C.E.). The vessel is now in the collection of the Quzhou Municipal Museum.

440

青釉莲纹盘

南宋

公元 1127—1279 年

龙泉窑

高：4.2 厘米

口径：16.2 厘米

**Celadon dish with lotus
petal motif**

Southern Song dynasty

1127 – 1279 C.E.

Longquan kilns

Height: 4.2 cm

Mouth diameter: 16.2 cm

敞口、弧腹、圈足。内壁近底处刻一周凹弦纹，底心微上凸。外壁四周刻仰莲瓣纹。胎灰白、细腻。除圈足缘外，全器施梅子青色釉，釉层肥厚。圈足露釉处呈淡朱红色。器身内外开纹片。精工细作、釉色莹润，青葱可爱。

The dish has a wide mouth, rounded sides and a ring foot. A groove runs around the interior near the bottom, encompassing a slightly raised center. The exterior wall is decorated by lotus motif. The grayish white paste is refined in texture. The entire dish except the foot rim is covered with a rich and lustrous plum green glaze. The foot rim is unglazed, revealing a light cinnabar red paste. The glaze is suffused with crackles.

441

青釉粉青水洗

南宋

公元 1127—1279 年

龙泉窑

高：4.4 厘米

口径：13.8 厘米

底径：7.8 厘米

Celadon brush washer in sea green glaze

Southern Song dynasty

1127 – 1279 C.E.

Longquan kilns

Height: 4.4 cm

Mouth diameter: 13.8 cm

Base diameter: 7.8 cm

口微外侈，口以下渐收敛，折底，圈足阔而矮。足边薄而规整，露胎，呈灰黑色。全器内外施泛蓝色的粉青釉，釉厚，釉色纯正均匀，素净无纹。

龙泉器胎色主要可分为白胎和黑胎两大类，以白胎为主，约占总数九成以上。

The vessel has a slightly flared mouth and sides that taper gently downward and make an angular turn before joining a broad, low ring foot. The edge of the foot rim is thin and neatly trimmed, exposing a dark gray paste. The entire vessel is covered with a bluish green glaze. The glaze is thick, even and flawless.

Longquan ware comes in two major types: white paste and black paste. White paste is prevalent and accounts for over ninety percent of the artifacts.

青釉蔗段洗

南宋

公元 1127—1279 年

龙泉窑

高：3.4 厘米

口径：11.1 厘米

Celadon basin with sectioned sugarcane motif

Southern Song dynasty

1127 – 1279 C.E.

Longquan kilns

Height: 3.4 cm

Mouth diameter: 11.1 cm

撇口，平唇，上腹微斜，下腹斜收到底，底平、矮扁圆圈足，圈足边缘微起凸棱，与外壁中部凸棱相对应。内壁起凸棱 16 条，口缘呈花口状。外壁由上而下压印凹竖纹 15 道，呈蔗段状。施青釉，釉色翠嫩柔润，全器内外满开纹片。圈足包釉，底露胎，呈褐红色，胎质较厚重。本品造型优美、稳重。

The vessel has a flared mouth with flat lip and slightly flared sides that tapers towards a disc-like ring foot. A raised band runs around the exterior foot rim and the mid-section of the vessel. The concave segments on the interior give the inner mouth rim a lobed profile. The exterior wall is divided into fifteen segments to simulate sectioned sugar canes. The vessel is covered with a soft green celadon glaze with crackles. The foot rim is glazed. The base is unglazed, revealing a brownish red biscuit. The body is relatively thick and heavy.

443

青釉八宝纹公道杯

元

公元 1206—1368 年

龙泉窑

高：8 厘米（杯），3.3 厘米（托），

9.8 厘米（杯加托）

口径：7.8 厘米（杯），16.5 厘米（托）

Celadon "Fair Cup" and stand with Eight Buddhist Treasures

Yuan dynasty

1206 – 1368 C.E.

Longquan kilns

Height: 8 cm (cup), 3.3 cm (saucer),

9.8 cm (overall)

Mouth diameter: 7.8 cm (cup), 16.5 cm (saucer)

托作花瓣形，矮圈足，底稍内凹。中置开口中空拱台，四周饰覆莲瓣纹八个，内印八宝纹饰。杯口外撇，外壁印仰莲花瓣纹四个。杯内中央立一老翁，手中拿着一只酒杯，应为酒仙李白。老翁底部有一孔及管道通到杯体外底部。胎灰白、细腻，坚致。除圈足底缘外，器内外满施青绿色釉。

相传此器用于斗酒，每次倒酒时，多余的酒会通过杯底部之孔道流入托上拱形器内，每次杯内盛载的酒量均相同，故叫"公道杯"。定窑和青白瓷也有类似器物，目前所知全套完整的龙泉窑公道杯仅此一套。

八宝纹饰始见于元代，也叫八吉祥纹，包括法轮、法螺、宝伞、白盖、莲花、宝瓶、金鱼和盘长结，为藏传佛教的吉祥象征。

The cup-stand has a floral-shaped mouth and a slightly recessed base. The center features a domed platform with a circular opening at the top and the Eight Buddhist Treasures within eight lotus petals molded around the sides. The cup has a flared mouth. The exterior wall is decorated with four lotus petals. The figurine of an old man, probably the drunkard-poet Li Bo, rises from the center of the cup. Underneath the figurine is a hole connected by a duct to the outside of the cup. The grayish white paste is hard and refined. Both the interior and exterior of the cup and stand are covered with a bluish green celadon glaze.

Legend has it that this type of cup was specially designed for wine drinking contests. When wine is poured into the cup, excess wine will flow into the domed center of the stand through the hole at the base. The cup will thus maintain the same amount of wine every time, and every drinker will drink an equal portion of it. Hence, it is also called a "fair cup". Similar vessels are found among Ding ware and *qingbai* ware. This is the only known example of a complete set of "fair cup" from the Longquan kilns.

The Eight Buddhist Treasures or the Eight Auspicious Emblems consist of: a wheel, a conch shell, a parasol, a victory banner, lotus flowers, a treasure vase, a pair of fish, and an endless knot.

444

青釉贯耳瓶一对

元

公元 1206—1368 年

龙泉窑

高：17.6 厘米，17.8 厘米

底径：5.1 厘米，5.1 厘米

Pair of celadon vases with tubular handles

Yuan dynasty

1206 – 1368 C.E.

Longquan kilns

Height: 17.6 cm, 17.8 cm

Base diameter: 5.1 cm, 5.1 cm

小口，细长颈，溜肩，扁圆腹，圈足外撇。口缘下有约 8 毫米宽的唇，颈中部起弦纹三道，弦纹两侧贴贯耳各一。其中一瓶贯耳并不对称，应为烧制中耳下滑形成的颇特别之"错体"，下滑处露胎并可见下滑痕。肩腹交界处以弦纹一道分隔。全器内外施橄榄色青釉，青翠可爱。釉厚、均匀，可见明显土蚀痕。其中一瓶腹部有大开片纹。圈足底边露胎呈褐色，外底中央微隆。

Each vase has a small mouth, a slender long neck, slanting shoulders, a compressed rounded belly and a slightly flared ring foot. The mouth has a lip that is approximately 8mm wide. The midsection of the neck is encompassed by three grooves and flanked by a pair of tubular handles. One of the handles had slid down the neck during firing. The paste is exposed along the slid mark. Another groove marks the border between the shoulders and the belly. The interior and exterior of both vases are covered with a celadon glaze of olive green color. The glaze is thick, lustrous, even in tone and has visible earth encrustations. One of the pair has extensive crackles on the belly. The unglazed foot rims of both vases are brown in color. The base enclosed by the foot rim is slightly convex.

445

青釉环耳瓶

元

公元 1206—1368 年

龙泉窑

高：16 厘米

底径：6.8 厘米

Celadon bottle with ring-handles

Yuan dynasty

1206 – 1368 C.E.

Longquan kilns

Height: 16 cm

Base diameter: 6.8 cm

口外翻成喇叭状，长直颈，圆桶形腹微向底收，矮圈足。颈两侧贴兽耳各一，上挂环耳。除圈足外，内外满施梅子青釉，釉厚、莹润。外底中部微凸。胎体坚硬，圈足露胎处呈深紫红色。颈上、下各有弦纹两条，下腹近底处一条弦纹作饰。造型优美，为元代龙泉窑精品。

The bottle has a trumpet-shaped everted mouth, a long straight neck and a cylindrical belly that tapers towards a low ring foot. The opposing sides of the neck are each decorated with an appliqué animal-shaped ring handle. The exterior and interior of the vessel except the ring foot is covered with a thick, smooth and lustrous plum-green glaze. The center of the base is slightly domed. The paste is hard and shows a deep purplish-red color where it is left unglazed near the foot rim. Two grooves encircle each of the upper and lower parts of the neck, and one near the bottom. This vessel is a fine example of Longquan ware from the Yuan dynasty.

446

青釉出筋罐

元

公元 1206—1368 年

龙泉窑

高：23.2 厘米

底径：20.8 厘米

Celadon jar with fluted body

Yuan dynasty

1206 – 1368 C.E.

Longquan kilns

Height: 23.2 cm

Base diameter: 20.8 cm

大口，直唇，圆肩，扁鼓腹，圈足。外壁饰菊瓣形凸筋，筋条宽窄随器壁弧度大小而改变。灰白胎，质坚致。器内外施橄榄色青釉，釉面肥厚、滋润、均匀。口缘和圈足露胎，呈火石红色泽。底部厚重，向内隆起，应是器体完成后再套入向内凸起的底部，此为元代大罐器底构造的特征。

The jar has a large mouth with an upright lip, rounded shoulders, a compressed rounded belly and a ring foot. The exterior wall is decorated with fluted design resembling chrysanthemum petals. The widths of the ridges vary with the curvature of the wall. The grayish white paste is very refined. The interior of the jar is covered with an olive green celadon glaze. The glaze is thick, lustrous, smooth and even in tone. The unglazed mouth and foot rim shows a burnt orange color. The thick base bulges up from the bottom. The body and the base were made separately and then attached. This is a distinct feature of the larger vessels from the Yuan dynasty.

447

青釉带座瓶

元

公元 1206—1368 年

龙泉窑

高：14.6 厘米

Celadon vase with stand

Yuan dynasty

1206 – 1368 C.E.

Longquan kilns

Height: 14.6 cm

瓶小口外撇、束颈、丰肩、肩以下渐收、肩腹间饰弦纹两道、足微外撇。瓶底中央微外凸。瓶置于圆几形器座上。器座口外撇、束颈、颈周饰圆孔三个、底置座足五只。浅灰胎、质坚、细腻。除足缘外、全器内外满施青釉、釉呈青褐色、明亮、玻璃质感重、满布开片纹。器物造型雅致、小器大样、带元代大型器的气魄。

本品足缘露胎处现较深的褐红色、而器物棱边凸出部分和釉薄处也呈褐红色、这是在坯体上先上一层褐色底釉再上青釉、刻意令釉色加深。这种青褐色龙泉青瓷、俗称黄龙泉及鹅皮黄釉。带座器为元代流行风格。

The vase has a flared small mouth above a constricted neck, bold shoulders, tapering sides, a splayed foot and a slightly convex base. Two grooves run around the widest diameter. The stand is in the shape of a circular low table with flared top, constricted neck and five legs. Three circular holes are perforated around the neck. The light gray paste is hard and refined. Except for the foot rim, the interior and exterior of the vase and stand are covered with a rich and lustrous green glaze with a greenish and yellowish brown tint. Crackles are found on the surface of the glaze. Despite its diminutive size, the vase has the grandeur of a much larger Yuan vessel.

The unglazed foot rim appears deep reddish brown. The body has been coated with a brownish slip underneath the celadon glaze to give it a deeper tone. A reddish brown color shows through the ribs and edges where the glaze runs thin. This type of Longquan celadon is commonly called "yellow Longquan" or "goose skin yellow ware". Vase with stand is a design feature that is popular during the Yuan dynasty.

448

青釉菱口折腰盘

元

公元 1206—1368 年

龙泉窑

高：3.6 厘米

口径：11.8 厘米

底径：6 厘米

Celadon dish with angular sides

Yuan dynasty

1206 – 1368 C.E.

Longquan kilns

Height: 3.6 cm

Mouth diameter: 11.8 cm

Base diameter: 6 cm

口外侈，十一菱瓣口分成五组，如绽开的花。折腰急收到底足。胎体较厚。器内外和足缘施鹅皮黄釉，釉莹厚，无开片纹。可能由于烧造时炉内温度高低不一，其中一侧釉色呈橄榄绿色。内壁划缠枝花纹，盘心光素无纹。外壁上下分饰莲花纹和莲瓣纹一周。外底露胎，呈褐红色，可见旋纹痕，中央微向外凸出。

The dish has a flared mouth with an eleven-lobed rim featuring five barbs. The sides take an angular turn before tapering rapidly towards the base. The body is relatively thick. The interior and exterior of the dish including the foot rim are covered with a thick and lustrous "goose-skin" yellow glaze. No crackles are visible on the surface. Possibly due to unstable firing temperatures, the glaze appears olive green on one side. The interior wall is incised with floral scrolls while the bottom is plain. The upper and lower parts of the exterior wall are respectively decorated with a frieze of lotus blossoms and lotus petals. Wheel marks are found on an unglazed base that appears brownish red. The center of the base bulges out slightly.

449

褐斑撇口瓶

元

公元 1206—1368 年

龙泉窑

高：16.5 厘米

口径：6.7 厘米

底径：4.8 厘米

Celadon vase with trumpet mouth and brown splashes

Yuan dynasty

1206 – 1368 C.E.

Longquan kilns

Height: 16.5 cm

Mouth diameter: 6.7 cm

Base diameter: 4.8 cm

喇叭口、长颈、斜肩、鼓腹、上腹圆鼓、下腹向内斜收成束腹状。凹圈足、外底心微凸。颈、肩饰弦纹各一道。浅黄色胎、细滑、胎骨较厚重。器内外壁施青绿色釉、釉面满布开片纹。口缘、颈、肩和腹上饰大小不等的褐色斑彩、深浅对比、装饰性较强。足缘无釉、呈火石红色。

青瓷饰褐斑盛行于东晋时期的江浙一带、自南朝中断达八百年之久、至元代才被龙泉窑恢复和发展。目前龙泉窑窑址发现五百多处、约五分之四是元代的、其中有青釉褐斑工艺的很少、此件撇口瓶是研究元代龙泉窑工艺的代表性作品。

本品经热释光检测其最后烧制年代距今约 600 年。

The vase has a trumpet-shaped mouth, a long neck, sloping shoulders, a bulbous upper belly, a concave lower belly and a hidden ring foot enclosing a slightly convex base. A rib runs respectively around the neck and the shoulders. The pale yellow paste is refined. Both the interior and exterior are covered with a bluish green celadon glaze with crackles.

The irregularly sized dark brown patches on the mouth, the neck, the shoulders and the belly contrast sharply with the greenish glaze, creating a highly decorative effect. The unglazed foot rim shows a burnt orange color.

Celadon vases with brown splashes are prevalent around the Zhejiang region during the Eastern Jin dynasty but then vanished for the next eight hundred years. The Yuan dynasty saw the revival and development of these vases at the Longquan kilns. Over five hundred kiln sites have been found in Longquan, four-fifths of which operated during the Yuan dynasty. Very few of them produced celadon with brown splashes. This vase is a

representative example of Longquan ware from the Yuan period.

Thermoluminescence test shows that the last firing date of this piece was around 600 years before present.

450

黑釉玳瑁斑纹盏

宋

公元 960—1279 年

涂山窑

高：5.3 厘米

口径：11 厘米

Black-glazed bowl with mottled tortoiseshell pattern

Song dynasty

960 – 1279 C.E.

Tushan kilns

Height: 5.3 cm

Mouth diameter: 11 cm

敞口，腹壁微收到底，小圈足。内心有涩圈一个。胎粉白，细滑，胎体轻薄。内外施褐黑色釉，釉上泼洒金黄色玳瑁斑作饰，釉色温润。釉不及底，腹下与圈足交接无釉处平削一周，圈足内缘留有修坯切削口。器物造型饱满，制作精细，玳瑁斑如散落在宇宙中五彩缤纷的星云，白色的涩圈如恒星在漆黑苍穹中运行留下的轨迹，装饰效果强烈。涩圈本是为增加产量叠烧器物产生的，但本品的涩圈表面平滑，在粉白的胎上并无叠烧痕迹，应是一种美化器物的装饰手段。

涂山窑遗址在重庆市，产品以茶盏为大宗，以玳瑁纹盏为最。遗存数量不多，特点为器内心留有涩圈，圈足内墙有刮削圈足时留下的切口。本品是涂山窑的代表作。

The bowl has a wide mouth and sides that taper gently towards a small ring foot. The center of the bowl bears an unglazed ring. The pinkish white paste is refined and smooth. The body is light and thin. The interior and exterior are covered with a dark brown glaze lavishly mottled with golden yellow tortoiseshell pattern. The smooth and lustrous glaze stops short of the base on the outside. The unglazed junction between the lower belly and the ring foot has been scraped clean. Trimming mark is visible around the inner rim of the ring foot. Usually, the ring inside the bowl is a tell-tale sign of stacked firing. However, the unglazed ring inside the present bowl shows no sign of stacked firing on its smooth pinkish white surface, indicating that it has been used as a decorative element.

The Tushan kilns were located in Chongqing city. Tea bowls, mostly with mottled tortoiseshell patterns, constitute the majority of the finds. Extant examples are few. Unglazed rings and trimming marks on the inner wall of the ring foot are distinct features of Tushan wares. This bowl is a representative example of Tushan ware.

451

黑釉褐斑斗笠盏

南宋

公元 1127—1279 年

吉州窑

高：4.3 厘米

口径：14 厘米

Black-glazed conical bowl with brown mottling

Southern Song dynasty

1127 – 1279 C.E.

Jizhou kilns

Height: 4.3 cm

Mouth diameter: 14 cm

敞口，斜直壁，圈足细小而矮。内心有小圆突。足露胎，胎灰白色，胎体细薄，颇细腻。器身内外壁在黑釉上泼洒许多浅黄褐色斑点，与黑釉相映生辉，斑斓绚丽。本品体形秀丽，做工精细，色泽柔润，釉色对比分明，为吉州窑上乘之作。

The bowl has a wide mouth, conical sides and a small, low ring foot. The interior center has a small circular protuberance. The unglazed foot rim reveals a grayish white paste that is thin and refined. The interior and exterior are covered with a black glaze mottled with pale yellowish brown pattern. This bowl is a fine example of Jizhou ware.

452

黑釉叶纹碗

南宋

公元 1127—1279 年

吉州窑

高：6.1 厘米

口径：15.6 厘米

底径：5.1 厘米

Black-glazed bowl with leaf decoration

Southern Song dynasty

1127 – 1279 C.E.

Jizhou kilns

Height: 6.1 cm

Mouth diameter: 15.6 cm

Base diameter: 5.1 cm

敞口，斜腹壁，矮圈足。胎浅黄，质稍粗、疏松。施黑釉，釉色明亮柔润，釉不到底足。碗内贴一经腐蚀处理的桑叶作装饰，呈褐黄色，茎和叶脉纹理清晰可见，与周围的黑色对比鲜明，衬托出叶纹之瑰丽。碗经两次施釉，第二次上釉后经高温一次烧成，在外壁下腹部黑釉层下可见一层浅色的底釉。叶纹碗是吉州窑高档产品，如本品般叶纹完整、清晰、艳丽的十分稀少。

1962 年江西南昌出土有相似器物，现藏江西省博物馆。

The bowl has a wide mouth and slanting sides that taper towards a low ring foot. The yellowish paste looks rather porous. The entire vessel except the foot is covered with a jet-black glaze with a soft luster. The center of the bowl is decorated with a gossamer imprint of a yellowish brown mulberry leaf. The midrib and veins are clearly visible. The leaf design looks exceedingly beautiful against the black ground. The body has been glazed twice before firing. After glaze was applied for a second time, the piece was fired to a high temperature. The pale glaze underneath the black glaze is exposed around the lower belly. Bowls with skeleton leaf design were top of the line products from the Jizhou kilns. Examples that are as fine as the present piece are very rare.

A similar vessel was unearthed in 1962 from Nanchang, Jiangxi province. It is now in the collection of the Jiangxi Provincial Museum.

453

玳瑁斑纹盏

南宋

公元 1127—1279 年

吉州窑

高：3.9 厘米

口径：14.1 厘米

底径：4.1 厘米

Shallow bowl with mottled tortoiseshell pattern

Southern Song dynasty

1127 – 1279 C.E.

Jizhou kilns

Height: 3.9 cm

Mouth diameter: 14.1 cm

Base diameter: 4.1 cm

口缘微斜向上，浅腹，矮圈足。盏心在圈足位置压弦纹一道。胎灰白，较疏松。施黑釉，外壁釉到腹中部。黑釉上满布黄褐色的玳瑁斑纹。

The bowl has a slightly incurving mouth, shallow sides and a low ring foot. The center of the bowl is adorned with a groove that is the exact outline of the ring foot below. The grayish white paste is relatively porous. The entire interior and the upper two-thirds of the exterior are covered with a black glaze mottled with yellowish brown speckles.

454

玳瑁斑纹盏

南宋

公元 1127—1279 年

吉州窑

高：6.1 厘米

口径：12.9 厘米

底径：3.5 厘米

Black-glazed bowl with mottled tortoiseshell pattern

Southern Song dynasty

1127 – 1279 C.E.

Jizhou kilns

Height: 6.1 cm

Mouth diameter: 12.9 cm

Base diameter: 3.5 cm

敞口，外口缘下有微凸棱，腹较深，小圈足。内外施黑釉，上满挂酱、黄、乳白等色交织混合的玳瑁釉。开细纹片、色彩瑰丽，釉面润泽。底足露胎无釉、胎浅黄、质疏松、稍粗。从露胎处看为两次施釉。

玳瑁釉为江西吉州窑代表性品种之一，它是在黑色釉面上施以不规则的黄褐色斑块，烧制过程中由于釉的流动形成玳瑁状的斑纹。

The bowl has a wide mouth with a slightly raised rib below the exterior mouth rim and rather steep sides that tapers to a small ring foot. Both the interior and exterior are covered with "tortoiseshell glaze", a black glaze lavishly mottled with intermingled reddish brown, yellow and milky white patterns. Crackles are found on the surface of the lustrous and smooth glaze. The light yellow paste is rather coarse and porous. The unglazed area suggest that the bowl had been glazed twice.

This type of bowls is one of the representative examples of Jizhou ware from Jiangxi province. Speckles of yellowish-brown glaze are applied arbitrarily onto the black glaze to create such an effect. During firing, the glazes melt and run into each other to result in a color scheme similar to that of tortoiseshell.

455

玳瑁斑折肩罐

元

公元 1206—1368 年

吉州窑

高：18.1 厘米

口径：7 厘米

底径：9.6 厘米

Black-glazed jar with mottled tortoiseshell pattern

Yuan dynasty

1206 – 1368 C.E.

Jizhou kilns

Height: 18.1 cm

Mouth diameter: 7 cm

Base diameter: 9.6 cm

口缘外撇、短颈、折肩。底平、微内凹、露胎。胎浅褐色，质轻体薄。施黑色釉，再在黑釉上随意点画黄褐斑，呈玳瑁斑纹。腹近底处无釉。黑釉深沉、明亮润泽。玳瑁斑纹呈金黄色，分布均匀，极具装饰效果。玳瑁斑上开片纹，但黑釉上无纹片。吉州窑玳瑁釉烧制成功者多是碗、杯类，瓶、罐器物很少。

The jar has an everted mouth rim, a short neck and angular shoulders. The slightly recessed flat base is unglazed. The area around the foot is also bare of glaze, revealing the brownish paste of the thin body. The body is covered with a black glaze freely splashed with golden brown speckles in imitation of mottled tortoiseshell. The golden yellow mottling is distributed evenly throughout the vessel. Crackles are found on the yellowish brown speckles but not on the black glaze. Black wares with tortoiseshell pattern from the Jizhou kilns are mainly bowls and cups. Jars like the present piece are exceedingly rare.

456

双凤纹盏

南宋

公元 1127—1279 年

吉州窑

高：4.7 厘米

口径：15.2 厘米

底径：2.9 厘米

Black-glazed conical bowl with phoenix design

Southern Song dynasty

1127 – 1279 C.E.

Jizhou kilns

Height: 4.7 cm

Mouth diameter: 15.2 cm

Base diameter: 2.9 cm

敞口，斜壁小足，具宋代斗笠碗的典型特征。器内壁饰双凤和梅花两支。碗心内凹，饰梅花一朵。浅黄色胎，较疏松和粗糙。施褐黄色窑变釉，纹样生动。外壁黑地上有白褐色斑点至足底部。

剪纸贴花装饰是吉州窑最具特色的地方装饰技法。制作时，先在坯体上施一层含铁量高的釉，贴上各种图案的剪纸后再施一层含铁量低的釉，经一段时间后，揭掉剪纸后高温烧制，即在色彩斑斓的浅褐色窑变釉地上呈现出酱黑色的剪纸纹饰。宋代流行饮饼茶，茶叶店常将当地民间剪纸图案印在茶叶包装纸或茶饼上作为装饰。吉州窑烧瓷工匠用娴熟的技巧将这些剪纸图案烧在黑瓷茶碗上，使普通黑瓷得以美化，产生了意想不到的艺术效果。

The bowl has a wide mouth, slanting sides and a small foot. Its shape typically resembles the conical "bamboo-hat bowl" of the Song dynasty. The yellow paste is rather coarse and porous. Its interior wall is resist-decorated with two phoenixes and two plum blossoms reserved in brown against a transmuted amber ground. A third plum blossom adorns the slightly domed center. A black glaze with white and brown speckles covers the exterior wall down to the foot rim.

Paper-cut design is the most characteristic decorative feature of Jizhou ware. To produce such a design, a glaze with high iron content is first applied onto the surface and then paper cuttings of desired shapes are placed on top. Next, the entire surface is coated with a second layer of glaze with lower iron content. The paper shapes are then removed after some time and the vessel is fired to a high temperature. The shapes will then appear dark brown against a brownish, variegated and transmuted ground. Tea prepared from tea leaves compressed into blocks is a beverage enjoyed by all during the Song period. Folk paper-cut designs are printed on the wrapping paper or directly onto the compressed tea as decorations.

黑釉凤纹碗

南宋

公元 1127—1279 年

吉州窑

高：6.8 厘米

口径：16 厘米

**Black-glazed bowl with
phoenix motif**

Southern Song dynasty

1127 – 1279 C.E.

Jizhou kilns

Height: 6.8 cm

Mouth diameter: 16 cm

敞口，圆唇，腹斜收到底，小圈足。碗
心起一圈弦纹。内壁贴三只黑色飞凤，
碗周有三团一丝丝、乳白泛蓝的纹饰，
如火焰由碗心喷出，寓意凤凰涅槃、
浴火重生。胎淡灰色，颇疏松。碗内
施褐黄色釉。外壁上半部施黑褐色釉，
上泼洒褐黄色斑纹。外壁下半部和圈
足露胎，可见刮削修坯痕迹。

相传凤凰鸟每五百年自焚为灰烬，再从
灰烬中重生，循环不已，成为永生。火
凤凰象征重生，代表脱出困境、获得新生。

The bowl has a wide mouth with rounded
lip and sides slanting towards a small ring
foot. A groove encircles the center of the
bowl. The interior wall is decorated with
three black phoenixes, partitioned by three
clusters of blue-tinted milky white streaks
resembling blazing flames. The phoenixes'
mouths are wide open, alluding to the
legend of phoenixes burning themselves
to ashes in order to be reborn. The light
gray paste is rather porous. The upper
part of the exterior wall is covered with a
dark brown glaze with brownish yellow
mottling while the interior is coated with
a brownish yellow glaze. The lower half
of the exterior wall and the ring foot are
unglazed; trimming and scraping marks
are visible.

In Chinese mythology, the phoenix self-
immolates, burns to ashes and then
regenerates every five hundred years,
attaining eternity through this endless
cycle of rebirth. "Fire phoenix" is a symbol
of resurrection and new life.

458

黑釉黄褐斑纹碗

南宋

公元 1127—1279 年

吉州窑

高：7.2 厘米

口径：15.7 厘米

Black-glazed bowl with yellowish brown mottling

Southern Song dynasty

1127 – 1279 C.E.

Jizhou kilns

Height: 7.2 cm

Mouth diameter: 15.7 cm

敞口、圆唇、口缘下微内凹、腹斜收到底、小圈足。碗心微凸，围以一周弦纹。圈足无釉，足内墙向内倾斜，底足边缘斜削一周。灰白胎，质坚。施黑釉，内外壁刷褐黄微泛蓝的斑带纹，斑纹苍劲有力、挥洒自如，褐黄釉与黑色底釉产生的艳丽曜变色彩显得格外迷人。

The bowl has a wide mouth with rounded lip, a slightly constricted band below the exterior mouth rim and slightly convex sides tapering to a small ring foot. The center of the bowl features a small circular protuberance, surrounded by a narrow groove. The ring foot is unglazed. The grayish white paste is hard. The entire surface is covered with a black glaze. The interior wall is freely splashed with yellowish brown glaze with a bluish tint.

459

黑釉花卉盏

南宋

公元 1127—1279 年

吉州窑

高：4.3 厘米

口径：13.6 厘米

底径：3.5 厘米

Black-glazed bowl with floral design

Southern Song dynasty

1127 – 1279 C.E.

Jizhou kilns

Height: 4.3 cm

Mouth diameter: 13.6 cm

Base diameter: 3.5 cm

敞口，斜腹壁，矮圈足。施黑釉，底足无釉。内底心饰一玳瑁釉斑块。内壁画梅花数枝，画工流畅，纹样生动，白、蓝、褐色的梅花衬托在黝黑的盏壁上分外美观。外底墨书一"王"字。

The bowl has a wide mouth and sides slanting towards a low ring foot. The entire vessel except the foot and the base is glazed black. The center is decorated with a patch of tortoiseshell pattern and the wall with several plum blossom sprigs. The white, blue and brown hues of the floral patterns look particularly painterly against the black ground. The base is inscribed with the character "*Wang*".

460

黑釉剔花梅瓶

南宋

公元 1127—1279 年

吉州窑

高：20 厘米

底径：7.6 厘米

Black-glazed prunus-decorated *meiping*

Southern Song dynasty

1127 – 1279 C.E

Jizhou kilns

Height: 20 cm

Base diameter: 7.6 cm

口微敛，圆唇，瓶颈上端较细、下端较粗、丰肩，腹体盈满，中腹以下缓慢收束，凹圈足。胎质灰白，坚硬，细腻。除内壁及器底外，通体施釉，釉色莹润，色黑如漆，布开片纹。器身两侧剔折枝梅花各一枝，刀法流畅，意趣盎然。花纹处露胎呈淡黄色，花蕊用褐彩勾画，装饰效果很强。通常此类瓶釉大多干涩或有脱釉，本品釉色莹润、釉面保存完整、实属少见。

1972 年江西吉安吉州窑出土有相似器物，现藏江西省博物馆。

The vase has a small mouth with rounded rim, a neck with a narrower upper part, bold shoulders and a belly that tapers towards a ring foot enclosing a recessed base. The grayish white paste is hard and refined. Except for the interior and the base, the entire vase is covered with a glossy, crackled, jet-black glaze. It is decorated with a prunus branch reserved in the biscuit by means of paper cuts with details painted in black. The glaze of this type of vase usually appears matte. Vases

with such a clarity of glaze and intactness are rare.

A similar vessel was unearthed in 1972 from the Jizhou kilns in Ji'an, Jiangxi province. It is now in the collection of the Jiangxi Provincial Museum.

461

褐彩梅鹊瓶一对

南宋

公元 1127—1279 年

吉州窑

高：16.6 厘米，16.8 厘米

底径：5.3 厘米、5.2 厘米

Pair of brown-glazed vases painted with plum blossoms and magpies

Southern Song dynasty

1127 – 1279 C.E.

Jizhou kilns

Height: 16.6 cm, 16.8 cm

Base diameter: 5.3 cm, 5.2 cm

小口，口缘微外撇，长颈，斜肩鼓腹，矮圈足。器身一面绘折枝梅花，上立一只喜鹊；另一面置竹、梅各一枝；其他两侧各饰蝶两只。胎灰白色，体厚重，底部露胎。喜鹊、梅、蝶先用褐釉画出，然后剔出纹样，露出胎体之后罩一层透明釉烧成。笔法精细、流畅有力。花鸟形态逼真，由于施釉厚而具立体感。

1979 年江西九江出土有相似器物，现藏九江市博物馆。

Each vase has a small and slightly flared mouth, a slender neck, steep shoulders, a bulbous belly and a low ring foot. The body of the vase is thickly potted; the paste is white in color and the base unglazed. The body is painted in brown on one side with a magpie standing on a branch of plum blossom and on the other side with a bamboo tree and another branch of plum blossom. Two butterflies appear between these two groups of painted decorations. The magpies, plum blossoms and butterflies are then highlighted by scratching through the brown glaze to reveal the color below followed by a layer of transparent glaze before firing.

A similar vessel was unearthed in 1979 from Jiujiang, Jiangxi province. It is now in the collection of the Jiujiang Municipal Museum.

462

褐彩题字茶盏

宋

公元 960—1279 年

吉州窑

高：4.5 厘米

口径：11.6 厘米

底径：3.8 厘米

Tea-bowl with brown inscription

Song dynasty

960 – 1279 C.E.

Jizhou kilns

Height: 4.5 cm

Mouth diameter: 11.6 cm

Base diameter: 3.8 cm

口微外撇、斜腹壁、圈足。口缘下起棱、外凹内凸、凸棱可防止茶水外溢。胎白、质坚。碗内及口缘施白釉，碗内褐釉书"雀舌先春"四字。碗外施褐釉、釉不及底和足。白色的底足、褐色的碗腹和白色的口缘、白色的内壁、褐色的字、形成了鲜明的对比。

"雀舌"是茶叶的一种，形容茶叶的形状小巧似雀舌。"雀舌先春"四字表明该碗是茶具。

The bowl has a slightly flared mouth and sides that slant towards a small ring foot. The rib running around the interior mouth rim is a design used to prevent tea from spilling out. The white paste has a high degree of hardness. The interior of the bowl and the outer mouth rim are glazed white. The inside is inscribed in brown with the four characters "*Queshe xianchun*" ("the bird's tongue announces the approach of spring"). The exterior is glazed brown while the foot and the base are bare. The brown color of the exterior wall and the inscription forms a delightful contrast with the white color of the

interior, the mouth rim, the foot and the base. "Bird's tongue" is the name of a type of tea, suggesting the fineness of the tea

leaves. The four characters indicate that this bowl was used for serving tea.

463

金彩龙纹瓶一对

元

公元 1206—1368 年

吉州窑

高：14 厘米，14 厘米

底径：5 厘米，5 厘米

Pair of vases with gilded dragon design

Yuan dynasty

1206 – 1368 C.E.

Jizhou kilns

Height: 14 cm, 14 cm

Base diameter: 5 cm, 5 cm

侈口双缘、长颈、斜肩、下腹较鼓出、圈足稍高。颈肩上下置凹凸弦线各一组，两组弦线之间釉层刮去，刻同向龙纹和云纹，纹样以外的地被剔去，使纹样稍高于地，剔地处再满刻斜线纹，立体感强，极具浅浮雕效果。底足刻凹弦纹带一周，与口缘凹纹带相呼应。胎呈灰白色，质坚、细滑。施白釉，微泛青，开细碎纹片。口缘、底足和颈肩间凹纹带施褐色底釉，再在上面贴金箔，惜颈肩间金箔多已脱落。

根据窑址考古资料显示，吉州窑生产陶瓷品种很多，但青白瓷数量很少，应属高档产品。此外吉州窑瓷器的金彩装饰多用在黑瓷上，青白瓷上施金彩实属罕见。本品很可能为元朝皇室使用之器物，弥足珍贵。

Each vase has a wide mouth with double rims, a long neck, steep shoulders, a bulged lower belly and a rather tall ring foot. A frieze bounded by a groove and a rib on its upper and lower borders runs around the area between the neck and the shoulders. The glaze on the frieze has been scraped clean and the area is carved with two dragons amid clouds in low relief against a planed ground filled with oblique striations. The groove around the foot mirrors the one around the mouth. The grayish white paste is smooth and refined. The surface is covered with a white glaze with a greenish tint. Tiny crackles are found on the surface. A layer of slip had been coated onto the frieze and other decorative bands before gold leaves were applied onto the surface. Unfortunately, the gilding on the frieze has mostly come off.

This pair of vases is valued for two reasons: First, Jizhou kilns yielded a wide range of ceramics but very few *qingbai* wares. Secondly, most gilded Jizhou wares are black wares; *qingbai* ones with gilded decoration like this pair are exceedingly rare. These were likely made for imperial use.

金彩龙纹瓶一对

464

月白釉浅盘

宋

公元 960—1279 年

钧窑

高：3 厘米

口径：14.7 厘米

底径：5.2 厘米

"Jun" dish in moon white glaze

Song dynasty

960 – 1279 C.E.

Jun kilns

Height: 3 cm

Mouth diameter: 14.7 cm

Base diameter: 5.2 cm

紫口，盘面浅扁，矮圈足。灰胎，质坚，胎骨较厚重。足缘无釉，呈褐红色。全器内外施月白釉，施釉均匀，釉面凝厚滋润。凝视之，令人有宁静愉悦的感觉，正是宋代文人士大夫阶层所追求的审美情趣。

The dish has a "purple mouth", a flattened body with very shallow sides and a low ring foot. The gray paste is hard, thick and heavy. The unglazed foot rim appears brownish red. The entire dish is evenly coated with a rich and lustrous "moon white" glaze.

465

天蓝霜斑鸡心碗

宋

公元 960—1279 年

钧窑

高：9.5 厘米

口径：15.6 厘米

底径：5.4 厘米

"Jun" chicken heart-shaped bowl with frosty speckles

Song dynasty

960 – 1279 C.E.

Jun kilns

Height: 9.5 cm

Mouth diameter: 15.6 cm

Base diameter: 5.4 cm

口微敛、深腹、弧状腹壁，呈鸡心形。胎灰白，异常细腻。满施乳浊状釉，釉层肥厚，呈天蓝色。内外壁较均匀地散布乳白色霜斑，好像在蔚蓝的天空上飘浮着徐徐下落的霜雪，十分有意趣。足底内壁微倾向碗心，底心施釉。圈足露胎，呈褐红色。本品造型秀丽、色彩淡雅、霜斑装饰在钧窑器物中较为罕见。

The "chicken heart" bowl derives its name from its slightly incurved mouth and deep convex sides that resemble a chicken heart. The grayish white paste is very refined. Both the interior and exterior are covered with a thick layer of opalescent sky blue glaze evenly distributed with frosty speckles like snow falling slowly from a clear blue sky. The inner wall of the ring foot slants slightly. The base is glazed. The unglazed ring foot is reddish brown in color. The bowl is elegant in shape and delicate in tone. Frosty speckles are quite unusual on Jun ware.

天蓝大碗

金

公元 1115—1234 年

钧窑

高：10.2 厘米

口径：22.7 厘米

底径：6.5 厘米

Large "Jun" bowl with sky blue glaze

Jin dynasty

1115 – 1234 C.E.

Jun kilns

Height: 10.2 cm

Mouth diameter: 22.7 cm

Base diameter: 6.5 cm

口微敛，弧状腹，圈足，外底中央微向外隆起。胎呈灰白色，胎体较薄，叩之声音清越。器身内外施天蓝色釉，釉层肥厚，釉色明艳，清澈可爱。足底和足缘内侧露胎。

The bowl has a slightly constricted mouth, rounded sides and a ring foot. The center of the base is slightly convex. The base and foot rim are unglazed, revealing a grayish white paste with a rather thin body, which gives a pleasant sound when struck. The entire vessel except the base and foot rim is coated with a "sky blue" glaze. The glaze is thick, lustrous, even in tone and highly translucent.

467

天蓝紫斑盏托

金

公元 1115—1234 年

钧窑

高：4.4 厘米（杯）、3.3 厘米（托），
　　 6 厘米（杯加托）

口径：8.6 厘米（杯），14.9 厘米（托）

"Jun" cup and saucer with purple splashes

Jin dynasty

1115 – 1234 C.E.

Jun kilns

Height: 4.4 cm (cup), 3.3 cm (saucer),
　　　　 6 cm (overall)

Mouth diameter: 8.6 cm (cup),
　　　　　　　　 14.9 cm (saucer)

盏、托口微敛。圈足无釉、露胎处呈浅黄色，可见轮旋纹。托胎较厚重。内外施天蓝釉，缀以紫红斑块，仿佛绚丽的彩霞飘浮在蓝蓝的天空。釉色凝厚滋润、清新雅淡、有开片纹。口缘釉薄处为酱黄色，足部胎釉交接处呈褐红色。钧窑盏和托成套的器物较少，带紫蓝斑的更少。

Both the cup and saucer have a slightly incurved mouth. The cup has an unglazed ring foot exposing a yellowish paste with wheel marks. The saucer is more thickly potted. The entire set is covered with a crackled sky blue glaze with purple splashes like rosy clouds drifting across blue skies. The glaze is rich, thick and smooth. The glaze runs thin along the rims and gives a soy yellow color. The unglazed foot rim shows a reddish brown color. Cup and saucer sets are quite rare among Jun ware and rarer still are sets with purple splashes.

468

天蓝紫斑盘一对

金

公元 1115—1234 年

钧窑

高：3.6 厘米，3.7 厘米

口径：13.1 厘米，12.6 厘米

底径：5.5 厘米，5.3 厘米

**Pair of "Jun" dishes with
purple splashes**

Jin dynasty

1115 – 1234 C.E.

Jun kilns

Height: 3.6 cm, 3.7 cm

Mouth diameter: 13.1 cm, 12.6 cm

Base diameter: 5.5 cm, 5.3 cm

紫口，口缘外撇，盘面扁平，圈足。外壁口缘下有蚯蚓走泥纹。灰白胎，质稍粗，较疏松。器身内外施天蓝釉，盘内各有一大块紫红斑。圈足和外底无釉，呈浅褐红色。圈足修整规矩。

Each dish has a "purple mouth" with flared rim, a flat bottom and a ring foot. Fine lines resembling the tracks left by a crawling earthworm on wet earth are visible around the mouth below the exterior rim. The grayish white paste is rather coarse and porous. The entire dish except the ring foot and the base is covered with a "sky blue" glaze with a large purplish red patch on the upper face and underside of the dish. The unglazed ring foot and base is brownish red in color. The foot rim is neatly trimmed.

469

黑釉小盏

南宋

公元 1127—1279 年

建窑

高：3.6 厘米

口径：9 厘米

Small bowl in black glaze

Southern Song dynasty

1127 – 1279 C.E.

Jian kilns

Height: 3.6 cm

Mouth diameter: 9 cm

口缘粗圆，斜腹。紫黑色胎，胎体粗糙坚硬、厚重。内外壁施黑釉，釉不及底，釉厚、色黑如漆。口缘内外侧微现褐色兔毫。外壁脚线积釉处堆成釉泪。

建窑小盏留存不多，应为喝酒用的酒杯。

The bowl has a thick rounded mouth and convex sides slanting towards the base. The purplish back paste is hard, coarse, thick and heavy. The interior and exterior are thickly covered with a jet-black glaze. The glaze stops short of the foot on the outside. "Hare's fur" streaks are visible around the inner and outer mouth rim. The glaze congeals in welts above the foot around the exterior wall.

Extant examples of small bowls from the Jian kilns are rare. They were probably used as wine cups.

470

黑釉曜变碗

宋

公元 960—1279 年

建窑

高：6.7 厘米

口径：12.5 厘米

底径：4.2 厘米

Black-glazed bowl with transmuted speckles

Song dynasty

960 – 1279 C.E.

Jian kilns

Height: 6.7 cm

Mouth diameter: 12.5 cm

Base diameter: 4.2 cm

束口，敛腹，浅圈足。外口缘边微内斜，碗口顶部呈尖削形。胎体坚实厚重，呈铁黑色。通体黑釉，垂釉近足，在漆黑光亮的釉面上满布绿松石和银灰色彩晕，既似苍茫夜空中的繁星闪烁，又似节日之夜怒放的烟花，美不胜收。

曜变釉，又称"耀变"，自"窑变"一词转化而来，其黑釉中铁的结晶体围以彩晕，变化多端。曜变盏存世鲜见，传世品仅见日本四件藏品，均被列为国宝。明谢肇淛《五杂组》载："传闻初开窑时，必用童男女各一人，活取其血祭之，故精气所结，凝为怪耳。近来禁不用人祭，故无复窑变。"日本文献《能阿弥相传集》载："曜，天下稀物也，釉色如豹皮，建盏中之上也。"另一日本文献《君台观左右帐记》载："建盏之无上品也，天下稀有之物。"

本品经热释光测定最后烧制年代距今1000—800 年。

The bowl has a concave indentation below the mouth rim and a shallow ring foot. The mouth has a higher outer edge and a lower inner edge, forming a blade-like rim. The body is thick and sturdy, and the paste appears iron-black. The entire vessel is covered with a black glaze that congeals in welts above the foot. Dazzling turquoise and silvery gray speckles are visible all over the glossy black glaze, resembling a star-studded night sky or firecrackers exploding on a festive night. The effect is extremely striking.

In ancient China, this fascinating glaze effect was referred to as *yaobian* ("kiln transmutation"). The ferruginous crystals in the black glaze are encircled by colorful halos producing a variegated color scheme. Extant examples of bowls with speckled transmuted glaze are exceedingly rare. The only four known pieces in Japan have been kept as national treasures. In his book *Wuzazu* (Fivefold Miscellany), the Ming scholar Xie Zhaozhe writes, "Legend has it that before a kiln started operation, blood taken from a maiden and a virgin boy was used as sacrifice. The vital essence produced by their blood would cause very strange glaze effects. Since no more human blood was used in recent years, no more *yaobian* occurred." This particular glaze effect is also mentioned in some ancient Japanese texts. It was recorded in *Noami sodenshu* (Collection of Remarks by Noami) that "wares with *yao[bian]* effect are extreme rarities. The glaze color is like leopard skin. They are the best of all Jian tea bowls." According to the *Kundaikan Sochoki* (A Catalogue of Shogun Ashikaga Yoshimasa's Treasures), another famous book from Japan, these wares are described as "the finest of all Jian tea bowls and extreme rarities of the world."

Thermoluminescence test shows that the last firing date of this piece was 1000 to 800 years before present.

"供御" 铭褐黑兔毫盏

南宋

公元 1127—1279 年

建窑

高：6.7 厘米

口径：12.8 厘米

Black-glazed "hare's fur" tea bowl with "*Gongyu*" mark

Southern Song dynasty

1127 – 1279 C.E.

Jian kilns

Height: 6.7 cm

Mouth diameter: 12.8 cm

束口，斜弧腹，小圈足，矮足墙。口缘下为指沟纹，胎体较薄。足底刻 "供御" 两字。紫红色胎，表面颇细滑。施黑色釉，釉层凝厚，釉色莹润。釉不及底，外壁脚线聚釉成釉泪。口缘因釉层薄呈紫褐色，器体内外在黑色釉上满布褐、黑色放射状兔毫纹。

宋《宣和遗事》记载，政和二年（公元 1112 年），宋徽宗 "以惠山泉、建溪异毫盏烹新贡太平嘉瑞茶，赐蔡京饮之"。近年，建窑遗址出土了许多刻有 "供御" "进盏" 铭文的茶盏残底，可与史料互为印证。

本品经热释光检测最后烧制年代距今 900—700 年。

The bowl has a constricted mouth with concave indentation below the rim. The convex sides slant towards a small ring foot with a low wall. The body is relatively thin, and the purplish red paste is rather refined and smooth. The base is carved with the two characters "*Gongyu*" ("for imperial use"). The bowl is neatly shaped and the overall black glaze is thick, rich, lustrous and smooth. The glaze stops short of the foot and congeals in welts along its lower edge. A purplish brown color shows through the mouth rim where the glaze runs thin. The black glaze on the interior and exterior is richly mottled with brown and black streaks of "hare's fur".

It was recorded in *Xuanhe yishi* (Unrecorded Events during the Xuanhe Reign) that: In the 2nd year of the Zhenghe period (1112 C.E.) of the Northern Song dynasty, Emperor Huizong offered his favorite minister, Cai Jing, the newly submitted tribute tea known as "*Taiping jiarui*" ("peace and auspicious omens"), which was brewed with spring water from Mount Hui and served in a "hare's fur" bowl from Jianxi. Many fragments of tea bowls with "*Gongyu*" and "*Jinzhan*" marks have been unearthed from the Jian kilns in recent years.

Thermoluminescence test shows that the last firing date of this piece was 900 to 700 years before present.

472

黑釉褐蓝鸟羽斑纹盏

南宋

公元 1127—1279 年

建窑

高：6.7 厘米

口径：12 厘米

Black-glazed tea bowl with partridge feather glaze

Southern Song dynasty

1127 – 1279 C.E.

Jian kilns

Height: 6.7 cm

Mouth diameter: 12 cm

敛口，口缘下为指沟纹，斜弧腹。外口缘边微内斜，口顶部呈尖削状。褐黑胎，胎硬。施黑色釉，釉肥厚，色漆黑。内外壁满布铁结晶在黑釉中曜变的由上而下的褐色和蓝白色条纹、斑点，像雀鸟胸前羽毛的色泽。修胎精细、盏形规整。

The bowl has a constricted mouth, concave indentation below the rim and rounded sides. The outer rim is beveled to give a sharp edge. The brownish black paste has a high degree of hardness. The paste of the mouth rim is thin and sharp. The jet-black glaze is rich and thick. The glaze on the interior and exterior of the bowl is covered with brown and bluish white speckles as a result of the transmutation of crystalline iron in the black glaze. The radiating pattern resembles the colorful feathers of a partridge.

473

褐釉黑斑点碗

宋

公元 960—1279 年

建窑

高：6.9 厘米

口径：13.3 厘米

底径：4.3 厘米

Brown-glazed tea bowl with black spots

Song dynasty

960 – 1279 C.E.

Jian kilns

Height: 6.9 cm

Mouth diameter: 13.3 cm

Base diameter: 4.3 cm

敞口，口缘下为指沟纹，圈足外深内浅，近似实足。碗内外施褐釉，再以黑斑点为饰。外壁黑斑点较大，分两排；内壁斑点较小，分三排。碗心以六个黑色斑点组成一朵梅花为饰。口缘下一周呈深褐色，像金属镶嵌口，别有一番韵味。外壁无釉处露紫黑色胎，胎坚硬，古朴厚重。

The bowl has a wide mouth with concave indentation below the rim. The almost solid ring foot has a higher outer wall and a shorter inner wall. The interior and exterior of the bowl are coated with a brown glaze adorned with black dots. The dots on the exterior are larger in size and arranged in two rows. Those around the interior are smaller and arranged in three rows. The center of the bowl features a plum blossom made up of six dots. The dark brown border below the mouth rim resembles a metal mount. The unglazed area on the exterior of the bowl revealed a purplish black paste.

474

黑釉葵口盂

辽

公元 907—1125 年

缸瓦窑

高：8.6 厘米

口径：11.5 厘米

底径：5 厘米

Black-glazed water jar with foliate mouth

Liao dynasty

907 – 1125 C.E.

Gangwa kilns

Height: 8.6 cm

Mouth diameter: 11.5 cm

Base diameter: 5 cm

十一瓣葵花形口，折缘，钵形腹，圈足微外撇。口上葵花口外翻，像一盛开的花蕾。胎薄，洁白，细腻。器身内外施黑釉，均不到底，黝黑、明亮、柔润，釉上微泛蓝。釉开细纹片，口缘薄釉处呈褐黄色。底足露胎，露胎处有明显轮旋痕，尤以内腹为甚。造型秀丽、端庄、高雅。

The water dropper has an eleven-lobed foliate mouth that rises from the bowl-shaped body at an angle. The ring foot is slightly splayed. The white paste is immaculate and refined. Both the interior and exterior walls are covered with a bright and smooth jet-black glaze with a bluish tint. Small crackles are found on the surface. The glaze stops short of the base on both sides. An amber color comes through the thin glaze along the mouth rim. The unglazed areas, particularly around the interior wall, show visible wheel marks.

475

黑釉瓜棱白筋罐

金

公元 1115—1234 年

磁州窑系

高：11.6 厘米

阔：13.1 厘米

底径：6 厘米

Black-glazed ribbed jar

Jin dynasty

1115 – 1234 C.E.

Cizhou-type kilns

Height: 11.6 cm

Width: 13.1 cm

Base diameter: 6 cm

短直颈、圆腹、圈足，造型饱满。罐身满饰瓜棱状凸筋纹，棱边高耸、锐利、气势不凡。胎白、细滑、质坚。颈上不施釉，圈足露胎。罐体内外施黑釉，釉厚处黝黑、黑中泛红，釉薄处呈褐黄色，棱边浅黄白色。近底处有垂釉现象。釉色晶莹、润泽、深浅对比鲜明、风格独特。

本品精巧玲珑，黑釉质细温润，是磁州窑系高档产品，十分难得。

The gourd-shaped jar has a short straight neck and a globular belly resting on a ring foot. The mouth and the ring foot are bare of glaze. The white paste is hard and refined. The body is decorated with sharply defined vertical ribs formed by trails of white slip and covered with a lustrous black glaze that picks up different tones on the vessel, namely jet-black with a red tint where it accumulates, yellowish brown where it runs thin and pale yellow along the edge of the ribs. A thick welt of glaze congeals above the foot.

This jar was a top of the line product from the Cizhou-type kilns.

476

黑釉铁锈斑金瓜壶

宋

公元 960—1279 年

磁州窑系

高：17 厘米

底径：6.7 厘米

Squash-shaped ewer with russet splashes in black glaze

Song dynasty

960 – 1279 C.E.

Cizhou-type kilns

Height: 17 cm

Base diameter: 6.7 cm

小口，斜肩，七瓣瓜棱腹，圈足。口、腹间贴"品"字形三股柄，两侧股端向左右延伸呈蔓藤状攀于肩上，中间股端卷曲在柄顶成小圆结。柄对称侧置折流，流脊呈尖角状。壶带圆锥形盖，上饰蒂形曲钮。盖下方接一圆形管，上置一向上斜凸的闩，经壶口上之凹位旋到壶上，把盖扣紧。盖是放在壶口上一起烧造的，盖和壶口上可见完全吻合的黏烧釉痕。胎白，质细薄，较坚硬。全器外壁施黑色釉，釉色漆黑发亮，满布褐红色斑纹，上有铁的结晶体，熠熠生辉，斑驳绚烂。器内壁、外底和盖内无釉，内壁见细密轮旋痕。本品造工精巧，外形秀丽，色彩明艳动人，为不可多得之器物。

本品经热释光测定最后烧制年代距今1000—800 年。

This ewer has a small mouth, steep shoulders and a seven-lobed squash-shaped body resting on a ring foot. A spout with a ridge along its upper edge is set on the shoulders opposite a three-strand vine-like handle that connects the belly to the mouth. The conical lid is furnished with a stem knob. The lid has a hook-like protuberance on its underside, which can be slotted through a notch on the rim of the ewer and turned to lock it into place. The lid was placed on top of the mouth during firing as evidenced by the traces of glaze on both the mouth and the edge of the lid. The refined white paste has a relatively high degree of hardness. The body is covered in a glossy black glaze decorated with russet splashes running down the sides. The base and the inside of the ewer as well as the interior of the lid are unglazed. Closely spaced wheel marks are visible around the inner wall. The vessel is noted for its exquisite workmanship, elegant appearance and resplendent color scheme. It is a rarity among rarities.

Thermoluminescence test shows that the last firing date of this piece was 1000 to 800 years before present.

477

油滴褐斑纹碗

宋

公元 960—1279 年

高：8.5 厘米

口径：19 厘米

底径：5.7 厘米

Black-glazed bowl with brown splashes and oil spots

Song dynasty

960 – 1279 C.E.

Height: 8.5 cm

Mouth diameter: 19 cm

Base diameter: 5.7 cm

敞口，圆唇，内口缘下向内折，深腹，浅圈足。胎灰白，质坚而厚重。施釉两次，首施酱釉，再施纯黑釉，内壁满釉，外壁黑釉只达口缘下 2—3 厘米处。釉厚，黑釉明显高于酱釉，釉层滋润、明亮，表面均匀散布大小不一的银褐斑点。碗内壁饰五团银褐斑块，如在漆黑苍穹中满布银光闪闪的星星及巨大的星云。黝黑、银白、褐红相互映衬，粗犷豪迈。

斑纹如此清晰、釉色如此美丽的油滴碗实属少见，从碗的造型、胎和釉色看，当为河南瓷窑的产品。

美国纽约大都会博物馆收藏有相似器物。

The bowl has a wide mouth with rounded rim, deep sides and a low ring foot. The grayish white paste is thick and hard. Two layers of glaze have been applied; a black glaze superimposed on a soy glaze. The black glaze covers the entire interior of the bowl and 2–3 cm below the mouth rim on the outside. It is bright and smooth, and so thick that it rises in low relief from the soy-glazed ground. The surface is evenly distributed with silvery and brownish spots of different sizes. Five silvery brown patches are visible on the interior wall. Examples with such resplendent oil-spot effects are very rare.

The form, paste and glaze color suggest that the bowl was produced in Henan.

A similar vessel is in the collection of the Metropolitan Museum of Art in New York, USA.

478

黑釉褐斑白边碗

宋

公元 960—1279 年

磁州窑

高：7.7 厘米

口径：17.5 厘米

底径：4.4 厘米

Black-glazed bowl with brown patches and white rim

Song dynasty

960 – 1279 C.E.

Cizhou kilns

Height: 7.7 cm

Mouth diameter: 17.5 cm

Base diameter: 4.4 cm

侈口，上腹宽肥，往下缓慢收束，小底，圈足。内壁口缘下微凸。釉不到底，露胎处呈浅褐黄色，质稍粗。碗内外施黑釉，口缘一周施白釉。碗内饰三角状褐斑纹五块，碗外布蓝色条状纹。釉色油润明亮，黑、褐色衬托相宜。

The bowl has a flared mouth and a wide upper belly that tapers gradually towards a small base supported by a ring foot. A slightly raised rib runs below the inner mouth rim. The glaze stops short of the foot exposing a relatively coarse paste of light brownish yellow color. The mouth rim is glazed white while the interior and exterior are glazed black. The interior of the bowl is decorated with five brown triangular patches. The exterior is covered with blue streaks. The glaze appears smooth and glossy.

黑釉白边碗

金

公元 1115—1234 年

怀仁窑

高：7.8 厘米

口径：14.7 厘米

底径：5 厘米

Black-glazed bowl with white rim

Jin dynasty

1115 – 1234 C.E.

Huairen kilns

Height: 7.8 cm

Mouth diameter: 14.7 cm

Base diameter: 5 cm

敞口，腹较深，圈足。胎微黄，细滑、坚致。口缘饰一周白釉带，内缘带宽于外缘带，釉色洁白。腹施黑釉不及底。黑、白釉分界整齐，交界处呈黄褐和蓝色斑纹，腹下和底足露胎处施黑褐色护胎釉。日本称此种碗为"白覆轮"。

黑釉瓷在宋代得到发展似与漆器的普遍应用有很大关系，部分黑釉瓷显然是仿漆器而作，黑釉白边即仿自银扣漆器。用两种对比鲜明的色彩来作装饰，或黑釉白口，或白釉黑口，打破了单一釉色，别具一格。目前发现烧黑釉白口碗的有登封窑、禹县窑、临城窑、定窑、磁州窑、介休窑等窑。南方窑场也有烧造，但白釉不如北方纯正。

怀仁窑窑址在山西怀仁县，始烧于金代，历元、明两代。

本品经热释光测定最后烧制年代距今约800 年。

The bowl has a wide mouth, rather deep sides and a ring foot. The pale yellow paste is refined. The mouth is coated with a band of white glaze, which appears broader on the inside and narrower on the outside. The edge between the white border and the black glaze is neatly demarcated. Amber and blue splashes appear below the border. The unglazed lower belly, foot and base are coated with dark brown slip. They are called "white-rimmed *temmoku*" in Japan.

The prevalence of black ware during the Song dynasty seems to be linked to the widespread use of lacquerware. Some were purposely made in imitation of lacquerware. The white rim was meant to imitate the silver mount on some of the lacquerware. Black-glazed bowls with white rims have been unearthed from the Dengfeng kilns, the Yuxian kilns, the Lincheng kilns, the Ding kilns, the Cizhou kilns and the Jiexiu kilns in northern China. Kiln sites in southern China also yielded this type of bowls but their white glaze is not as white as the northern ones.

The Huairen kilns are located in Huairen, Shanxi province. They started production during the Jin dynasty and continued to operate through the Yuan and Ming periods.

Thermoluminescence test shows that the last firing date of this piece was around 800 years before present.

480

褐釉星纹碗

宋

公元 960—1279 年

登封窑

高：5 厘米

口径：16.7 厘米

Brown-glazed bowl with star motif

Song dynasty

960 – 1279 C.E.

Dengfeng kilns

Height: 5 cm

Mouth diameter: 16.7cm

口微外侈，斜腹内收到底。圈足与腹底交接处平刮一圈，刮面棱边规整锐利，圈足微外撇，足缘斜削一周。圈足内墙倾斜约 45 度角，内墙与内底交接处刮弦线一道。浅灰色胎，细滑，胎体厚重。内外壁施白色化妆土，外壁化妆土只到腹部约三分之二处。内外壁化妆土上各画五道圆弧线，弧边到口缘间填黑褐色釉，形成两个如五角星的弧状图案。内壁碗心画一朵五瓣梅花。黑褐和白色对比鲜明，趣味益然。本品制作精美，修坯规整，画工精准，装饰新颖，为登封窑珍贵遗物。

鲁山窑和河南其他窑口也产这类器物，但从胎体、修坯来看，本品应为登封窑器物。

The bowl has a slightly flared mouth and sides that slant towards the base. The border between the ring foot and the lower extremity of the exterior wall has been scraped clean to give a sharp edge. The slightly splayed ring foot has a beveled outer rim and an inner wall that inclines at a 45-degree angle. The junction between the top of the inner wall and the base is demarcated by a groove. The light gray paste is refined and the body thick and heavy. The entire interior and the upper two-thirds of the exterior wall are dressed with white slip and decorated with a scalloped border. The center of the bowl is further decorated with a five-petalled plum blossom.

Although this type of vessel was also produced at the Lushan kilns and other kilns in Henan, the paste and trimming technique of this bowl suggest that it was a product of the Dengfeng kilns.

481

褐釉划花龟形挂壶

西夏

公元 1038—1227 年

灵武窑

高：9.4 厘米

阔：27 厘米

Brown-glazed tortoise-shaped flask with incised decoration

Xixia period

1038 – 1227 C.E.

Lingwu kilns

Height: 9.4 cm

Width: 27 cm

壶体扁圆、流斜口、台唇、短颈。体周挖凹槽，上置四带状曲耳，上下对称，凹槽用于固定穿带，曲耳防止带子滑出。壶身正面划牡丹花一朵，体边绕以连枝纹三组，间饰弦纹两道。灰白胎、质坚。通体施褐釉，釉色光润。此壶装饰花纹清晰明快、简单而粗犷，给人以自由奔放的感觉；扁体造型、形似乌龟，适合出行背带。

龟自古以来被视为祥瑞之物，人们认为神龟千岁而灵、能传递天意、预卜吉凶。

The flask has a spout-like mouth, a short neck, a flattened body with a deep groove along the sides and two pairs of symmetrically positioned tubular lugs straddling the groove. The lugs allow a rope to pass through while the groove holds the rope in place. The upper face of the flask is incised with a peony within a frame of double lines surrounded by three groups of floral scrolls. The grayish white paste has a high degree of hardness. The entire surface is coated with a lustrous brown glaze. This unique tortoise-shaped flask was designed for traveling.

Since ancient times, tortoises have been revered as a symbol of good omen. The ancient Chinese believed that the thousand-year-old tortoise has the ability to deliver messages from Heaven, foretell fortune and exorcise evils.

黑釉龟形 "夜明珠" 铭油灯

宋

公元 960—1279 年

高：10.2 厘米

阔（连头尾）：21.7 厘米

Black-glazed tortoise-shaped oil lamp with inscription

Song dynasty

960 – 1279 C.E.

Height: 10.2 cm

Overall width: 21.7 cm

口平，广肩，腹体呈扁圆形，下腹急收，小平底。肩上饰一龟头，昂首向上，张口，口通内腹，额上及颔下各贴一眼。一上一下的龟眼，示意灯光向天地间照射。龟头相对一侧置圆形筒状尾。另两侧于肩腹交界处各安桥形横系一对，用于系绳，以悬挂油灯。胎灰白，质坚。除外壁下腹和底外，全器内外施光亮黑色釉，釉薄处呈浅褐色，微开片，四周可见灰蓝色窑变釉。下腹有褐釉行书 "夜明珠" 三字，字间以点分隔。

本品造型和工艺颇特别，先用旋盘造出底、腹，肩部则用泥条盘筑而成，再用刀在肩部四周做出凹凸交错的龟甲。龟头及尾也用此法成型，再贴到肩上，故头、尾均表现出龟体的皱褶。器身肩内壁可见一条条的盘筑泥条，内心中央留有灰蓝色窑变釉两大滴。"夜明珠" 三字说明器物是用于照明，字体清丽精到，让我们欣赏到纯正的宋人书法。这是一件普通的民间用瓷，但做工如此巧妙，工匠的艺术创造力令人钦佩。

耀州窑有生产柿红釉油灯，柄上模印 "夜明珠" 字样，见图录 370 号。

The oil lamp has a flat mouth, broad shoulders and a compressed belly that tapers drastically towards a small flat base. A tortoise head protrudes from the shoulders. Its open mouth is connected to the cavity of the lamp. It has an eye on its forehead and another under its chin. A cylindrical tail appears on the other side. There are four bridge-shaped angular lugs, two in the front and two in the back. The lamp can be suspended on its flat side by tying a rope to each of the four lugs. The grayish white paste has a high degree of hardness. Except for the lower belly and the base, the entire vessel including the interior is coated with a glossy black glaze with some crackles. The glaze appears light brown where it runs thin. Grayish blue splashes as a result of kiln transmutation are found around the body. The lower belly is written in brown with the three characters "*Yemingzhu*" or "luminous pearl"; each character is separated by a dot.

This lamp is noted for its unique shape and potting method. The base and belly of the vessel were thrown on a wheel. Then, rings of clay were coiled on the belly to complete the upper section. Grooves were scraped out around the shoulders to create the corrugated tortoiseshell motif. The wrinkles on the tortoise's head and tail were worked out using a similar technique. Coils of clay are clearly visible inside the shoulders. Two large drops of grayish blue transmuted glaze are left inside the vessel. The inscription indicates that the vessel was used as a lamp.

The Yaozhou kilns also produced oil lamps in persimmon red glaze with "*Yemingzhu*" mark on the handles (Cat. No. 370).

黑釉龟形 "夜明珠" 铭油灯

483

黑釉铁锈斑纹执壶

宋

公元 960—1279 年

磁州窑系

高：16.9 厘米

Black-glazed ewer with russet splashes

Song dynasty

960 – 1279 C.E.

Cizhou-type kilns

Height: 16.9 cm

直口、溜肩、瓜棱腹微收到底、底平露胎、底边缘斜削一周。肩置斜口弧形流，对称侧立扁条形鋬手连接颈腹部。胎薄、色灰白、质坚。施黑釉、釉乌黑、釉层凝厚莹润。外壁黑釉上泼洒许多浅褐色斑块、黑褐相间、斑斓绚丽、相互辉映。本品造型饱满、稳重敦实、根据胎土和釉色判断、当为河南或山西窑口烧制。

本品经热释光检测最后烧造年代距今 900—700 年。

The ewer has a straight mouth, rounded shoulders and a lobed body that tapers gently towards an unglazed flat base with a beveled edge. From the shoulder rises a curved spout with slanting mouth. A strap handle connects the neck and the upper belly on the opposite side. The grayish white paste is thin and hard. The jet-black glaze is thick, glossy and smooth. The body is decorated with light brown splashes of various tones that contrast sharply against the black glaze. The paste and glaze color suggest that this piece was made by a kiln located either in Henan or Shanxi.

Thermoluminescence test shows that the last firing date of this piece was 900 to 700 years before present.

484

黑釉双耳出筋罐

金

公元 1115—1234 年

磁州窑系

高：24.2 厘米

底径：9.3 厘米

Black-glazed ribbed jar

Jin dynasty

1115 – 1234 C.E.

Cizhou-type kilns

Height: 24.2 cm

Base diameter: 9.3 cm

直口，卷缘，肩腹丰盈，满饰凸白筋，圈足较小。颈部贴系两个，上刻叶脉状阴纹。灰白色胎，胎质坚硬。内外施釉，器外施黑釉不到底，器内和腹下施酱色釉。黑釉明亮、油润、泛蓝色牛毛纹。白筋是用白泥浆在胎体上堆出来的，高温焙烧时，黑釉汁向低洼处流动聚积，凸筋处因釉薄而露出白色。本品造型端庄而有气势，是金代磁州窑系的优秀之作。

The jar has a straight mouth with rolling rim, rounded shoulders, a bulbous belly with vertical white ribs and a small ring foot. A pair of loop lugs incised with leaf-vein motif flanks the neck. The grayish white paste has a high degree of hardness. A glossy and lustrous black glaze with ox-fur streaks in blue covers the entire jar but stops well short of the base. Thick white slip is used to create the ribs on the body before black glaze is applied onto the vessel surface. When the jar is fired to a high temperature, the glaze runs off the ribs and gathers in the low-lying areas, thus allowing the color of the raised white slip to show through. This vessel is a fine example of Cizhou ware from the Jin dynasty.

485

褐釉剔花酒罐

金

公元 1115—1234 年

磁州窑系

高：36 厘米

底径：15 厘米

Brown-glazed wine jar with sgraffito decoration

Jin dynasty

1115 – 1234 C.E.

Cizhou-type kilns

Height: 36 cm

Base diameter: 15 cm

小口，短颈，台唇，丰肩，圆鼓腹，底平，中部内凹。肩、腹各饰双弦纹两组。腹两侧分别刻 "酒中曾得道" "花里遇神先"，余部刻划四组牡丹纹，间以花叶纹。肩饰卷叶纹一周，剔地。灰白胎，细滑。通体施黑褐釉，釉质光亮、均匀。本品造型圆浑优美，纹饰豪放，线条简练。从刻字可知为盛酒之用。剔花为先在器物表面施釉或化妆土，并刻划出花纹，然后将花纹部分或纹样以外的釉层或化妆土层剔去，露出胎体，再罩以透明釉。器物烧成后，釉色、化妆土色与胎地形成强烈对比，花纹具浅浮雕感。

"花里遇神先" 中 "先" 是 "仙" 的错别字，工匠文化水平可能不高，但思想活泼有趣，令人遐想，使我们体会到了收藏的乐趣。

The jar has a small mouth with a carinated rim, a short neck, plump shoulders, a bulbous belly and a flat base. Two groups of indented lines encompass the shoulders and another two groups run around the lower belly. Inscribed on the two sides is a couplet that reads, "Attain the Way from the wine; encounter an immortal amid the flowers." The body is adorned with four peonies surrounded by foliage. A frieze featuring leafy scrolls against a planed ground encircles the shoulders. The grayish white paste is refined. The entire surface is coated with an even layer of lustrous dark brown glaze. The couplet suggests that this jar was used as a wine container.

Sgraffito is a decorative technique that involves covering the vessel with a layer of glaze or slip of contrasting color. Then, the decoration is scratched out or cut through the glaze or slip to reveal the paste underneath. A clear glaze is applied onto the surface before firing. The result has the effect of bas-relief.

486

珍珠地刻花鸟梅瓶

金

公元 1115—1234 年

登封窑

高：37.5 厘米

底径：10.2 厘米

Meiping vase with bird and quatrefoil motif and ring-matted ground

Jin dynasty

1115 – 1234 C.E.

Dengfeng kilns

Height: 37.5 cm

Base diameter: 10.2 cm

小口外翻，短颈、丰肩、长圆腹，肩以下渐收，矮圈足。肩周刻戏水天鹅四只，生动活泼。腹刻四瓣金钱花，下饰三叶草纹，上、下以弦纹带相间。花鸟纹之外满戳珍珠纹为地。胎灰白色，质稍粗。胎上施白色化妆土，釉色白中微泛黄。瓶内和底足露胎无釉。

珍珠地划花工艺借鉴了唐代金银器的錾花工艺，晚唐时兴起于河南密县西关窑，盛于北宋河南、河北、山西等地，现已发现采用此装饰技法的有河南密县、登封、鲁山、宝丰、修武、新安，河北磁州，山西交城、介休、河津等地窑场。其工艺是在呈色较深的器胎上施一层薄薄的白色化妆土，然后在上面划出装饰纹样，以细金属管在纹样以外的空隙戳印出珍珠般的小圆圈，再罩一层透明釉进行烧制。

登封窑在今河南登封曲河，始烧于晚唐，下限到元代。登封窑以烧白瓷为主，兼烧黑瓷，其白釉珍珠地划花最具特色。

日本东京国立博物馆收藏有外形和纹饰与本品相似的器物，只是肩上刻划的是花卉而非天鹅。

本品经热释光测定最后烧制年代距今约 900 年。

The vase has a small mouth surrounded by a flared apron above a short neck, rounded shoulders and an ovoid belly that tapers gently towards a low ring foot. The shoulders feature four swans frolicking in water. The upper and mid belly are engraved with stylized quatrefoils formed by interlocking coin motifs bounded by double-lined borders. Below that is a band of trefoils. All motifs are presented against a ring-matted ground. The grayish white paste is relatively coarse. A layer of white slip is applied under a white glaze with a yellowish tint. The interior of the vase and the base are unglazed.

Ring-matting is a decorative technique inspired by the repoussé decorations on Tang metal ware. It was produced at the Xiguan kilns in Mixian (Henan province) during the late Tang period and flourished in Henan, Hebei and Shanxi during the Northern Song dynasty. Kilns known to use this decorative technique are found in Mixian, Dengfeng, Lushan, Baofeng, Xiuwu, Xin'an in Henan; Cizhou in Hebei; and Jiaocheng, Jiexiu and Hejin in Shanxi. The production procedures involve first coating the relatively dark body with a thin layer of white slip before decorative motifs are outlined by scratching through the slip. Then, a tiny metal tube with a circular end is used to impress circlets onto the spaces between the motifs. Finally, the vessel is coated with a clear glaze before firing.

The Dengfeng kilns are located near present-day Dengfengqu River in Henan province. Production started in the late Tang period and continued until the Yuan dynasty. It produced mainly white wares but also some black wares. Among these, white ware with incised motifs on a ring-matted ground is the most characteristic.

A vessel of similar shape but with floral motifs incised on the shoulders is in the collection of the Tokyo National Museum.

Thermoluminescence test shows that the last firing date of this piece was around 900 years before present.

487

珍珠地刻花鸳鸯纹枕

北宋

公元 960—1127 年

新安城关窑

高：13.3 厘米

长：27.5 厘米

Headrest with mandarin ducks and ring-matted ground

Northern Song dynasty

960 – 1127 C.E.

Chengguan kilns (Xin'an)

Height: 13.3 cm

Length: 27.5 cm

枕面饰珍珠地纹，纹饰排列细密整齐，刻划同向飞驰的鸳鸯两只，鸳鸯四周饰云气纹七朵，周边刻卷草纹。枕四侧刻牡丹纹，剔地。背面顶部中央置通气孔一个。胎黄褐色，质细腻。釉微黄而透明。胎与釉之间施白色化妆土。本品枕面纹饰刻划细腻流畅，动感十足，四侧花纹刚劲有力，是城关窑的优秀作品。

瓷枕是古代的寝具，始创于隋代，流行于唐、宋、元间。

新安城关窑遗址在河南新安城关，也称新安窑和城关窑，经宋、金、元三代。

The top of the headrest is decorated with two mandarin ducks flying in the same direction amid seven cloud-heads against a ring-matted ground within a frame of tendril scrolls. The vertical sides of the headrest are carved with peony design against a planed ground. The back is pierced with a hole for air to escape during firing. The yellowish brown paste is refined. The paste was coated with white slip before glaze was applied. The transparent glaze has a yellowish tint.

Porcelain headrests were first introduced

in the Sui dynasty and became popular during the Tang, Song and Yuan dynasties.

The Chengguan kilns, also known as

Xin'an kilns, are located in Chengguan in Xin'an, Henan province. The kilns operated from the Song through the Jin and Yuan dynasties.

白地黑花枕

金

公元 1209 年

介休窑

高：12 厘米

长：23.6 厘米

White-glazed headrest with painted floral design

Jin dynasty

1209 C.E.

Jiexiu kilns

Height: 12 cm

Length: 23.6 cm

腰圆形。枕面以黑彩绘画卷叶纹，虽寥寥数笔，却生气益然。近底一侧置气孔一个。枕底墨书"大安元年""马"和"七月十日置"等字、"马"字后有一花押。胎色黄白，质地坚硬。施白色化妆土，釉面呈乳白色，底无釉。大安元年年号有公元 1075 年西夏惠宗赵秉常、公元 1085 年辽道宗耶律洪基和公元 1209 年金代卫绍王完颜永济，按该枕胎土和釉色来看，定为金代较可靠。

花押是代替签名的一种签署样式，带有艺术性。

介休窑在山西介休洪山镇，创烧于北宋，经金、元、明、清，有八九百年历史。宋时以烧白瓷为主，兼烧黑釉、褐釉、白地黑花等品种。

The kidney-shaped headrest is decorated with scrolling foliage painted in black. There is a ventilation hole on one side near the bottom. The base is inscribed, "Bought by Ma on the 4th day of the 10th month of the 1st year of the Da'an period", followed by a *huaya* (a symbol or mark used in place of a signature). The yellowish paste is hard and dense. Except for the base, the entire surface is coated with white slip. Three emperors are known to have adopted the reign title Da'an. Thus, the 1st year of the Da'an period could be 1075 C.E. (Emperor Huizong [Zhao Bingchang] of Xixia regime), 1085 C.E. (Emperor Daozong [Yelu Hongji] of Liao dynasty) or 1209 C.E. (Emperor Weishaowang [Wanyan Yongji] of Jin dynasty). Since the paste and glaze color of this headrest are inconsistent with those of Xixia or Liao ware, this headrest should be dated to the Jin period.

A *huaya* is made up of illegible characters, images or signs used in place of a signature to conceal a person's identity.

The Jiexiu kilns are located in Hongshanzhen in Jiexiu, Shanxi province. Production started in the Northern Song period and continued through the Jin, Yuan, Ming and Qing dynasties, spanning a period of almost nine hundred years. It produced mainly white wares during the Song period but black, brown and black-on-white wares were also produced at the same time.

诗文腰形枕

元

公元 1206—1368 年

平阳窑

高：10.7 厘米

长：31 厘米

Kidney-shaped headrest with inscription

Yuan dynasty

1206 – 1368 C.E.

Pingyang kilns

Height: 10.7 cm

Length: 31 cm

枕呈腰形，枕面出檐。腰形框内刻"为争三寸气，白了少年头"。平底，气孔开在背部左上方。灰白胎，质较疏松。枕面先施白色化妆土，再覆以浅黄色透明釉，釉面开细碎纹片。侧面和底部施酱釉。

宋金时期陶、瓷枕流行题写通俗的词句与民谚，反映中下阶层人民的感情，起激励、警醒的作用。

平阳窑在山西平阳，始烧于宋代。据孟耀虎先生所著《磁枕玄珠》一书（山西古籍出版社，2014 年），他认为从平阳窑发现的资料看，这类器物定为元代比较恰当。

The kidney-shaped headrest has a top with overhanging edges. The kidney-shaped central panel is inscribed with two lines, "In order to strive for three-*cun* (Chinese inch) of credit, the hair on the young head turns white." The ventilation hole is located on the back of the headrest. The grayish white paste is relatively porous. The top of the headrest was applied with a white slip under a pale yellow glaze. Tiny crackles are found all over the glazed surface. The vertical sides and the flat base of the headrest are covered with soy glaze.

During the Song and Jin dynasties, it was fashionable to inscribe lines of popular sayings and proverbs onto headrests.

The Pingyang kilns are located in Pingyang, Shanxi province. Production started in the Song dynasty. In Meng Yaohu's *Cizhen xuanzhu* (About Ceramic Headrests, Shanxi gu ji Publishing House, 2014), he concludes that this type of vessel should be dated to the Yuan dynasty based on the archaeological data obtained from the Pingyang kilns.

490

白地褐彩文字枕

金

公元 1115—1234 年

磁州窑系

高：11 厘米

长：44 厘米

Headrest with brown-on-white motif and inscription

Jin dynasty

1115 – 1234 C.E.

Cizhou-type kilns

Height: 11 cm

Length: 44 cm

长八方形枕，枕面出檐，底平。气孔在枕右侧正中。枕面正中剔长方形框，填褐色彩，以白彩书唐人赵嘏《长安秋望》七言律诗之颔联："残星几点雁横塞，长笛一声人倚楼"，两端绘褐彩花卉各一组。灰白胎。除枕底外，施白色化妆土并覆以牙黄色釉。

本品应为山西晋南器物。

The top of the octagonal headrest has overhanging edges. The ventilation hole is located on the right wall of the pillow. The top features a rectangular panel coated with brown slip and inscribed in white with a couplet taken from the Tang scholar Zhao Gu's poem *Chang'an qiuwang* (Autumn Scene of Chang'an): "The wild geese fly across the borderlands in vanishing starlight; someone plays the flute in a mansion." Two groups of floral design painted in brown slip flanks the central panel. The paste is grayish white. The entire piece except the flat base is coated with white slip under an ivory-colored glaze.

This vessel is likely to be from southern Shanxi.

491

白地填黑婴戏莲纹枕

金

公元 1115—1234 年

磁州窑系

高：12 厘米

长：44 厘米

Headrest with black-on-white child and lotus motifs

Jin dynasty

1115 – 1234 C.E.

Cizhou-type kilns

Height: 12 cm

Length: 44 cm

枕成八方形，枕面出檐，前侧面有一通气孔。枕面以两组弦线分为三部分，中饰如意形开光，内刻"太子玩莲"纹饰，小孩面目丰满、憨态可掬；两端各刻花卉二。周边光素无纹，素底，底呈浅褐红色。胎浅灰白色，细滑、较坚硬。除枕底外，其他部位胎面施一层洁白的化妆土。采用白地填黑工艺，将开光内和两端纹饰外的白色化妆土剔去，露出胎地，再在胎地上填以黑彩，最后罩上一层透明釉进行烧制。布局上大量留白，白釉洁白，黑釉漆黑、色调对比强烈，釉面滋润莹亮，开细碎纹片。该枕刻工流畅、线条刚劲，纹饰生动传神，粗犷中显精细，是十分优秀的作品。

根据造型、胎、釉和绘画手法来看，本品当为山西晋南器物。据孟耀虎先生所著《磁枕玄珠》一书（山西古籍出版社，2014 年），他认为山西枕头镇和河津北部一带可能是烧造这类高水平瓷枕的窑场所在。

The top of the octagonal headrest has overhanging edges. There is a ventilation hole to the right of the front wall. The top has three decorative zones partitioned by double lines. The center features the "child playing amid lotus" motif within a *ruyi*-shaped cartouche, flanked by two flowers on each side. The sidewalls are undecorated. The unglazed base has fired to a pale reddish brown color. The grayish white paste is refined and rather hard. Except for the base, the entire surface is coated with white slip. The white slip within the decorative panel was scraped away and replaced by a black slip to obtain a white-on-black design with large areas reserved in white. The top and the vertical sides are then coated with a transparent glaze before firing. The crackled glaze appears smooth and glossy.

The shape, paste, glaze and painting style of this headrest suggest that it was produced in southern Shanxi. In Meng Yaohu's *Cizhen xuanzhu* (About Ceramic Headrests, Shanxi gu ji Publishing House, 2014), he concludes that this type of headrest was made in the kilns around Shentouzhen and northern Hejin in Shanxi.

492

褐斑双首蛇

宋

公元 960—1279 年

磁州窑系

高：5.4 厘米

长：19.5 厘米

Double-headed snake with brown stripes

Song dynasty

960 – 1279 C.E.

Cizhou-type kilns

Height: 5.4 cm

Length: 19.5 cm

蛇身蜷曲，两首朝相反方向，平卧。人首五官生动、夸张，眉粗大而弯，耳宽且长，长度几达头部的一半。蛇身呈黄褐色，以褐彩纹带十一道作饰。胎灰白、厚重、坚硬。

The snake has a twisted body laid sideways and two human heads facing in opposite directions. The heads are featured with thick arched eyebrows and long broad ears. The yellowish brown body is painted with eleven brown stripes. The grayish white paste is hard, thick and heavy.

493

孩儿枕

金

公元 1115—1234 年

长治窑

高（连头）：15.8 厘米

长：43 厘米

Headrest in the shape of a child

Jin dynasty

1115 – 1234 C.E.

Changzhi kilns

Overall height : 15.8 cm

Length: 43 cm

女孩侧卧，背作枕面，枕面前低后高、枕体中空，在头侧壁置气孔一个。灰黄色胎、质坚、细腻。器体先满施白色化妆土，然后施赭黄釉于躯体和双臂，用黑彩勾勒人物头面、服饰轮廓，并在枕面上绘花草、在人物衣领及花草蒂部饰以白粉点，最后罩透明釉。底露胎无釉。女孩五官端正，面貌丰满、讨人喜欢，彩绘用笔自然流畅，生意益然，整体具有自然质朴、清新活泼的生活气息。

This headrest is fashioned as a girl lying on her side. The top of the headrest is lower in the front and higher at the back. The hole on the side allows air to escape during firing. The grayish yellow paste is hard and refined. First, the entire surface except the base is coated with white slip. Next, the body and arms of the girl are decorated with amber glaze while the details are highlighted in black. The girl's collar and the stamens of the flowers are further adorned with dots of white slip. A layer of clear glaze is applied over the entire surface.

虎形枕

金

公元 1115—1234 年

长治窑

高：12 厘米

底：38.4 厘米

Tiger-shaped headrest

Jin dynasty

1115 – 1234 C.E.

Changzhi kilns

Height: 12 cm

Length: 38.4 cm

枕作卧虎状，虎背为枕面，前低后高，呈腰圆形。在白釉作地的枕面上以赭黄、黑釉绘戏水鸳鸯一对，并以赭黄、黑和灰黄色釉画山石一座，四周饰黑彩翠竹、芦苇和飞雁，竹叶轮廓以刀刻出。虎张口，獠牙，怒目外凸，两个鼻孔与虎体内部相通。虎爪前伸微曲，合于颌下。虎尾随枕底弧线自然弯曲，盘于身侧。虎身模仿虎皮的黄地黑色条纹，色彩斑驳，眼、眉、耳、嘴和尾端以白釉点缀。底无釉。胎浅黄，细滑。施化妆土。

枕面虽着笔不多却显得生意盎然，野趣横生，把秋天的景致展现无遗，显示出一种粗犷不羁、自由奔放的艺术特色，是金代长治窑的代表作。虎形枕代表了这一时期的艺术水平，本枕无论造型、装饰和釉色都堪称典型，特别是枕面上以赭黄、黑和灰黄绞釉绘画的山石，色彩混合流畅，如大理石花纹，其表现方法在金代器物上少见。

这类枕在山西地区磁州窑系遗址中常见。上海博物馆收藏有同类虎形枕，枕面绘湖上水鸟，天空大雁结队高飞，枕底墨书"大定二年（公元 1162 年）六月二十二日□□"铭。

The headrest is in the shape of a crouching tiger with a kidney-shaped top panel. The panel is painted with mandarin ducks, a pair of wild geese, mountain rocks, bamboo and reeds in a palette of amber, grayish yellow and black on top of a layer of white slip. The outlines of the bamboo leaves are accentuated by incised lines. Two holes, which are the nostrils, allow air to escape during firing and are connected to the cavity of the headrest. The patterned fur is painted with black stripes against a yellow ground. The tiger's eyes, eyebrows, ears, mouth and the tip of its tail are highlighted in white. The base is unglazed but coated with white slip. The pale yellow paste is very refined.

The overall painting depicts an early autumnal scene. The brushwork is free and spontaneous. This headrest is a representative example of Changzhi ware from the Jin dynasty. Tiger-shaped headrests represent the height of artistic achievements of this period.

The decorative technique of marbling the mountain rocks with swirling streaks of amber, grayish yellow and black is rare among Jin ware.

Headrests of this kind can be found among the finds from the Cizhou kilns in Shanxi. A similar headrest at the Shanghai Museum has a top panel painted with birds and a flock of wild geese. Its base bears an inscription but the last two characters are illegible. The inscription reads, "The 22nd day of the 6th month XX of the 2nd year of the Dading period (1162 C.E.)."

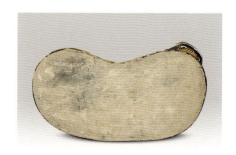

495

三彩"承安三年"铭孔雀竹石茱萸纹长方枕

金

公元 1198 年

磁州窑系

高：13.3 厘米

长：37.9 厘米

Sancai headrest with dated inscription

Jin dynasty

1198 C.E.

Cizhou-type kilns

Height: 13.3 cm

Length: 37.9 cm

枕呈长方形，微弧，气孔在背侧上方正中。胎黄白色。全器施白色化妆土，在枕面刻孔雀、竹石和茱萸纹，填以褐、绿彩，两端饰以叶纹。以孔雀竹石配茱萸花，意为"辟邪长寿"。枕面周边和枕四侧施绿釉，釉不到底，底平露胎。枕底墨书"春前有雨花开早，秋后无霜叶落池（迟）"和"承安三年，记"。枕面背侧亦有墨书"承安三年，记马丞记笔"字样。查承安三年为金章宗完颜璟的年号（公元 1198 年）。在枕底的上下方和左侧露胎处尚有墨书花押或符篆。

本品经热释光测定最后烧制年代距今 800—600 年。

The headrest is in the shape of a rectangular block with slightly arched sides. There is a ventilation hole on the back wall. The yellowish white paste is exposed on the rest of the walls and the unglazed flat base. The entire surface is coated with white slip. The top of the headrest features a panel carved with peacock, bamboo, rocks and sprays of dogwood, highlighted in brown and green. The central panel with foliage is set within green borders. The vertical sides are covered partially in green glaze. The base is inscribed in ink, "Flowers bloom early when rain comes ahead of spring; leaves fall into the ponds when there is [still] no frost after autumn" and followed by "written in the 3rd year of the Cheng'an period". The rear wall of the headrest also has an inscription that reads, "3rd year of the Cheng'an period; signed by Machengji". Cheng'an was the reign title of Emperor Zhangzong (Wanyan Jing) of the Jin dynasty. The 3rd year of Cheng'an period corresponds to 1198 C.E. *Huaya* signs appear above and below the inscription on the base and on the unglazed surface of the left wall.

Peacock and dogwood together symbolize longevity and good fortune.

Thermoluminescence test shows that the last firing date of this piece was 800 to 600 years before present.

狮子戏球风景枕

元

公元 1206—1368 年

磁州窑

高：15.7 厘米

长：40.7 厘米

Headrest painted with lion and landscape scenes

Yuan dynasty

1206 – 1368 C.E.

Cizhou kilns

Height: 15.7 cm

Length: 40.7 cm

枕长方形，枕面出檐，前低后高，两端微翘。顶和正、侧面置菱形开光。顶面绘一飞奔中的狮子在戏球。正面画山水，文人泛舟江上，远处雁群在空中列队飞翔。两侧及枕后壁饰牡丹花纹。开光和枕边之间填以花卉纹。胎浅褐色，质细滑，施化妆土。底无釉，上印"古相张家造"戳记。本品构图巧妙，画面形象生动，线条流畅，动静得宜，是融造型艺术和绘画艺术为一体的工艺美术佳作。

磁州窑白地黑花工艺是陶瓷装饰方法由用刀刻划花转变为用笔画花彩绘的一个重要标志，把中国传统绘画的笔墨技巧运用到瓷器的装饰上，达到了水墨画般的艺术效果。

The top has overhanging edges, up-curved sides and a forward-slanting face. Begonia-shaped cartouche enclosing decorations painted in brown adorns the top, the front wall and the two sidewalls. Within the top cartouche is a running lion. The painting on the front wall depicts a beautiful landscape with a fishing boat drifting in the waters in the near ground and a flock of wild geese flying in the distance. The sides and the back are decorated with peonies. The spaces between each cartouche and the edges of the headrest are filled with floral motifs. The rectangular headrest has a fine and smooth brownish paste coated with white slip. The unglazed base is stamped with the mark *"Guxiang Zhangjia zao"* (Made by the Zhang family of Guxiang). This headrest is a synthesis of figurative and painterly techniques.

Cizhou ware with black-on-white design is a breakthrough in ceramic history because of the application of traditional brush stroke technique to the surfaces of ceramic wares.

497

褐釉蓝白斑如意虎枕

元

公元 1206—1368 年

高：15.9 厘米

长：26.3 厘米

Tiger-shaped headrest with blue and white splashes in brown glaze

Yuan dynasty

1206 – 1368 C.E.

Height: 15.9 cm

Length: 26.3 cm

虎合嘴，闭眼，尾放股上，前、后足屈曲卧于地上，闭目养神。左、右虎耳各置一镂孔。背托如意枕，高台，枕面两端微翘，前低后高，周边依外形饰弦纹一周。胎灰黑，细滑，厚重 a。器体在褐色底釉上满施蓝、白釉，釉厚，交融流淌。底平，施褐色护胎釉，底面上满布白色贝壳残留物。

根据釉色、胎体、造型和烧成温度判断，本品有可能是广东阳江窑产品。

本品经热释光测定最后烧制年代距今约 700 年。

The headrest is fashioned as a crouching tiger with closed eyes, gaping mouth, its tail resting on its backside and forelimbs and hind legs tucked under the body. A hole is found on each ear. From its back rises a *ruyi*-shaped platform with a concave top surface that pitches gently towards the front. An indented line runs around the edge of the platform to form a frame. The dark gray paste is refined and the body is thick and heavy. The entire surface is covered with a thick layer of brown glaze intermingled with lavish blue and white splashes. The brown-slipped flat base is covered with white shell residues .

The paste, glaze color, shape and firing temperature of this headrest suggest that it was produced at the Yangjiang kilns in Guangdong.

Thermoluminescence test shows that the last firing date of this piece was about 700 years before present.

498

红绿彩划花盘

金

公元 1115—1234 年

长治窑

高：5.9 厘米

口径：15.4 厘米

底径：5.3 厘米

Bowl with red and green painted floral design

Jin dynasty

1115 – 1234 C.E.

Changzhi kilns

Height: 5.9 cm

Mouth diameter: 15.4 cm

Base diameter: 5.3 cm

敞口，斜腹，圈足。内外施白色化妆土，再覆以白釉。碗内壁以红绿彩绘画花卉，四周以弦纹和绿彩点缀。外壁腹下部和圈足无釉，露胎处呈浅黄褐色。圈足底可见五个垫饼支烧残留物。

由于金代红绿彩釉是以低温烧成，故较易脱落。

长治窑在山西长治八义镇，所以也名八义窑，以白釉红绿彩品种最具特色，为晋东南地区金代瓷窑。

The vessel has a wide mouth and rounded sides that taper to a ring foot. The interior and the upper part of exterior are coated with white slip under a layer of white glaze. The center is decorated with floral design painted in red and green, surrounded by concentric bands highlighted with green dots. The lower exterior wall and ring foot are unglazed, revealing a pale yellowish brown paste. Residues of five spur marks are found on the base.

Since the red and green painted wares of the Jin dynasty were fired at a low temperature, the colors are prone to flaking.

The Changzhi kilns are located in Bayizhen, Changzhi, Shanxi province. Thus, they are also called the Bayi kilns. They operated in eastern Shanxi during the Jin dynasty. White-glazed ware with red and green painting is the most representative example of Changzhi ware.

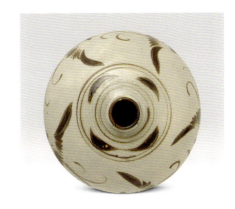

褐彩飞凤小口瓶

元

公元 1206—1368 年

磁州窑系

高：20.6 厘米

口径：3.6 厘米

底径：10.3 厘米

Small-mouthed jar with phoenixes painted in brown

Yuan dynasty

1206 – 1368 C.E.

Cizhou-type kilns

Height: 20.6 cm

Mouth diameter: 3.6 cm

Base diameter: 10.3 cm

圆唇、小口、丰肩、圆鼓腹、凹底。肩、腹饰三组双线弦纹。肩绘飘浮的褐彩羽毛四根。腹周绘展翅飞翔中褐彩凤鸟五只，首尾相逐。浅褐胎，质坚、细滑。器体外壁施化妆土，再罩透明釉、釉色莹润。底露胎，器底修刮规整。口缘和器内满施黑褐釉。本品体形圆浑饱满、各部分比例适中、构图简单、主题突出、色调对比分明、美感益然、表现出豪放潇洒的艺术风格。这类造型的器物宋、金、元皆有生产，此瓶釉色灰白，黑釉浅淡发褐，花纹松散，应是元代产品。

The jar has a small mouth with carinated rim, plump shoulders, a swelling belly and a recessed base. Two groups of double grooves run around the shoulders and the third encircles the lower belly. Four feathers in brown decorate the shoulders. The body is painted in brown with five phoenixes flying in a line with outstretched wings. The brownish paste is hard and refined. The painting is executed between a white-slipped surface and a transparent glaze with a soft luster. The unglazed base is neatly trimmed. The mouth rim and the entire interior of the jar are glazed dark brown. This type of jar was produced throughout the Song, Jin and Yuan dynasties. The grayish tone of the white glaze, the brownish tint of the black glaze and the looseness of the paint suggest that this jar is a product of the Yuan dynasty.

白釉红绿彩俑一组十三件

金

公元 1115—1234 年

磁州窑系

高：11.8—17.8 厘米

Group of thirteen figurines with red and green painted decorations

Jin dynasty

1115 – 1234 C.E.

Cizhou-type kilns

Height: 11.8 – 17.8 cm

判官俑一个、仕女俑八个、小童俑一个、骑马俑两个、马一只，仕女有坐，有立，有抱小孩的，有持花瓶的，有拿食物的……而判官则打开宗卷，作裁决状。胎白，较疏松。

白釉红绿彩是北方磁州窑系所创，即在已烧成的瓷器釉面上用红、绿、黄、黑等彩料描绘花纹，然后再入炉以 800℃左右的温度烘烧，使彩料烧结在釉面上。白釉红绿彩的创烧在中国陶瓷史上具有重大的意义，其釉面上彩绘的方法为后来彩瓷的发展开了先河。

White ware with red and green painted decorations was an invention of the Cizhou-type kilns in northern China. Designs were painted in colors such as red, green, yellow and black on the surface of fired porcelain before the piece was fired for a second time to around 800℃. The emergence of white-glazed ware with red and green painting is significant in Chinese ceramic history. Over-glazed painting is instrumental to the development of polychrome porcelain of later periods.

The group of thirteen figurines is made up of one magistrate, eight women, one child, two riders on horseback and one horse. The figures are either in standing or seated positions; one is cuddling a child and some holding a vase or food. The magistrate is holding a document in his hands. The white paste is relatively porous.

致　谢

在五十载收藏历程中，承蒙不少学者、专家和友人对本堂藏品提出许多宝贵意见，包括，但不限于：故宫博物院耿宝昌先生，每次到香港都来看我堂新购藏品并提出意见，替本堂2003年版和本版图录撰写序言，令图录增色不少；前西雅图艺术博物馆馆长倪密女士，给我堂机会借出200多件藏品在西雅图亚洲艺术博物馆连续展出五年，并替本堂2003年版图录撰写序言；故宫博物院陈华莎女士，提出许多有关收藏的意见，并对本堂图录的出版给予了大力协助。前上海博物馆副馆长汪庆正先生（已殁），指导如何完善和提升我堂收藏系列；前西雅图亚洲艺术博物馆中国艺术部主任许杰先生（现美国旧金山亚洲艺术博物馆馆长和首席执行官），协助我堂五年借展顺利进行；沐文堂主人关善明先生替我堂辨认陶瓷器上的印章文字，并在很多方面提供了帮助；前香港中文大学文物馆馆长林业强先生，提出改进收藏的意见，并协助修改2003年版图录说明；上海博物馆副馆长陈克伦先生，解答有关陶瓷问题，并协助到库房研究非展出器物；上海博物馆陶瓷研究部主任陆明华先生，提点有关陶瓷器真伪的问题；香港佳士德有限公司高级副总裁和中国瓷器及艺术品部国际总监安蓓蕾女士和前香港佳士德有限公司董事总经理林华田先生，对我堂借给西雅图亚洲艺术博物馆的200多件展品进行估价；前南京博物院院长徐湖平先生，协助到库房研究非展出器物；河北省文物出境鉴定组穆青先生，分析定窑器物真伪；山西省文物鉴定站主持孟耀虎先生，讲解山西省陶瓷窑口和瓷枕断代，并带我参观博物馆和私人藏家藏品；浙江省博物馆王屹峰先生，带我参观、访问浙江省内博物馆和私人藏家藏品，不厌其烦解答我方提出的问题，并对本堂所藏原始青瓷提出了许多宝贵意见；香港中科研发有限公司梁燕玲小姐和曾恩赐先生，讲解以热释光进行年代测定的原理和方法，并协助进行本堂藏品的鉴定、分析；香港中文大学文物修复主任窦雄斌先生，替我堂藏品作电子显微镜造像和文物修复；前香港中文大学文物馆游学华先生，替我堂修改2003年版图录中文内容；美国玛利亚·桃丝女士，对2003年版图录的英文部分复核。

此外还有本书责任编辑谷艳雪和王媛女士，对文稿内容、器物时代编排等提出很多宝贵意见，并提议"藏美"的中文书名。复旦大学文物与博物馆学系教授沈岳明、郑建明先生审阅了书稿。杭州南宋官窑博物馆馆长邓禾颖女士、浙江省博物馆陶瓷部主任沈琼华女士、浙江大学教授周少华先生、复旦大学文物与博物馆学系教授刘朝晖先生、前河北邢窑博物馆馆长张志忠先生、深圳博物馆副馆长郭学雷先生、北京大学考古文博学院教授秦大树先生和李伯谦先生、深圳市文物考古鉴定所所长任志录先生，以及吴继远先生、林利民先生等等亦提供了许多帮助。

谨此，对以上各位专家和所有为本版图录的编写和出版提供帮助的人士，表示至诚的、衷心的感谢。同时，也要向我的家人，特别是向我太太致歉，多年来我把营商以外的时间都花在收藏上，疏于对你们的照顾，借此良机，也要向你们说一声感谢，没有你们的支持和体谅，这个"博物馆"是不可能收藏起来的。最后，不能不提我的女儿，在本图录的构思、设计、插图和出版上，给予了我极大的帮助，一并致谢。

李曇鸣
九如堂
2018年11月

Acknowledgements

During my fifty-plus years of collecting, I have had the privilege of getting to know, learning from and relying on many significant friends who have made this journey possible and meaningful:

I would like to thank Geng Baochang of the Palace Museum in Beijing who distinguished the two Jiurutang catalogues with his forewords, evaluated newly acquired artifacts, gave advice without hesitations and graced us with his presence at the Seattle Asian Art Museum for the Jiurutang exhibition. Mimi Gardner Gates, former Director of the Seattle Art Museum, gave us the opportunity to showcase over two hundred works of art from the Jiurutang Collection at the Seattle Asian Art Museum for a consecutive five-year period and honored the 2003 catalogue with her foreword. Chen Huasha, former Specialist of the Palace Museum in Beijing, gave invaluable advice on the collection. Wang Qingzheng, former Deputy Director of Shanghai Museum, gave guidance on shaping and refining the collection. Jay Xu, former Curator of Chinese Art at the Seattle Art Museum (currently Director and CEO of the Asian Art Museum in San Francisco) ensured the smooth operation of the five-year loan at the Seattle Asian Art Museum. Simon Kwan of the Muwen Tang Collection helped identify Chinese characters on seal marks and offered his help in many areas of his expertise. Prof. Peter Lam, former Director of the Art Museum of the Chinese University of Hong Kong, gave advice on refining the collection and helped amend the catalogue entries. Chen Kelun, Deputy Director of Shanghai Museum, personally arranged for us to see many of the rare objects behind the museum vault. Lu Minghua, head of Ceramic Department at Shanghai Museum, gave advice on the authentication of Chinese ceramics. Pola Antebi, SVP and International Director of Chinese Ceramics and Works of Art at Christie's Hong Kong, and Anthony H.T. Lin, former Chairman of Christie's Asia, helped appraise over two hundred items from the Jiurutang Collection before they went on loan to the Seattle Asian Art Museum. Xu Huping, former Director of the Nanjing Museum, organized visits to see many of the hidden treasures behind the museum vault. Mu Qing, Director of the Cultural Relics Appraisal and Authentication Centre of Hebei, helped analyze and authenticate Ding wares. Meng Yaohu, Director of the Cultural Relics Appraisal and Authentication Centre of Shanxi Province, elucidated in detail the history of the kilns in Shanxi and the dating of porcelain headrests and arranged for us to visit many public and private collections. Wang Yifeng of the Zhejiang Provincial Museum organized private viewings of public and private museums and collections and offered his opinions on the subject of proto-celadons. Y.K. Leung and Y.C. Tsang of C-Link R&D Ltd. authenticated items by thermoluminescence analysis. Gary Ning, Conservator at the Chinese University of Hong Kong, conducted electron microscopic imaging analysis and restoration works. H.W. Yau of the Art Museum of the Chinese University of Hong Kong helped edit the Chinese text for the 2003 catalogue. Marian Toy of New York proofread the English text of the 2003 catalogue.

My gratitude also goes to the following individuals: our editor, Ms. Gu Yanxue, and Ms. Wang Yuan of the Cultural Relics Press for their many valuable opinions on the content of the catalogue and the chronological arrangement of the items, as well as their suggestions for the Chinese title of this catalogue. Prof. Shen Yueming and Zheng Jianming of the Department of Museology and Cultural Relics at Fudan University proofread the draft of this book. Deng Heying of the Southern Song Dynasty Guan Ware Museum in Hangzhou; Shen Qionghua, Director of Ceramics Department at the Zhejiang Provincial Museum; Prof. Zhou Shaohua of the Zhejiang University; Prof. Liu Chaohui of the Department of Museology and Cultural Relics at Fudan University; Zhang Zhizhong, former Director of the Xingyao Museum in Hebei; Guo Xuelei, Deputy Director of the Shenzhen Museum; Prof. Qin Dashu and Prof. Li Boqian of the School of Archaeology and Museology at Peking University; Ren Zhilu, Director of the Shenzhen Institute of Cultural Relics and Archaeology; K.Y. Ng and Simon Lam.

A special word of thanks goes to my daughters, who have contributed tremendously to the concept, design, editing, translation, proofreading, researching and illustrations of this catalogue. Finally, I would like to thank my family and in particular my wife for their tremendous support and encouragement without which this "museum" collection would never have been possible. Their efforts and understanding allowed me to realize my dream.

Lee Lurk Ming
The Jiurutang Collection
November 2018

年 表

Chronology

新石器时代	约 10000 年 — 4000 年前	**Neolithic Period**	c.10000 years - 4000 years ago
五帝	约前 30 世纪初—约前 21 世纪初	**Five Emperors Period**	c. 30th - 21st century B.C.E.
夏	约公元前 2070 —前 1600 年	**Xia Dynasty**	c.2070 - 1600 B.C.E.
商	公元前 1600 —前 1046 年	**Shang Dynasty**	1600 - 1046 B.C.E.

周 公元前 1046 —前 256 年

  西周 公元前 1046 —前 771 年

  东周 公元前 770 —前 256 年

      春秋 公元前 770 —前 476 年

      战国 公元前 475 —前 221 年

Zhou Dynasty 1046 - 256 B.C.E.

  Western Zhou 1046 - 771 B.C.E.

  Eastern Zhou 770 - 256 B.C.E.

      Spring and Autumn Period 770 - 476 B.C.E.

      Warring States Period 475 - 221 B.C.E.

秦 公元前 221 —前 206 年   **Qin Dynasty** 221- 206 B.C.E.

汉 公元前 206 —公元 220 年

  西汉 公元前 206 年—公元 8 年

  新朝 公元 9 年 — 23 年

  玄汉 公元 23 — 25 年

  东汉 公元 25 — 220 年

Han Dynasty 206 B.C.E.- 220 C.E.

  Western Han 206 B.C.E.- 8 C.E.

  Xin Mang 9 - 23 C.E.

  Xuan Han 23 - 25 C.E.

  Eastern Han 25 - 220 C.E.

三国 公元 220 — 280 年

  魏 公元 220 — 265 年

  蜀汉 公元 221 — 263 年

  吴 公元 222 — 280 年

Three Kingdoms Period 220 - 280 C.E.

  Wei 220 - 265 C.E.

  Shu Han 221 - 263 C.E.

  Wu 222 - 280 C.E.

晋 公元 265 — 420 年

  西晋 公元 265 — 317 年

  东晋 公元 317 — 420 年

Jin Dynasty 265 - 420 C.E.

  Western Jin Dynasty 265 - 317 C.E.

  Eastern Jin Dynasty 317 - 420 C.E.

南北朝　公元 420 — 589 年

　　南朝　公元 420 — 589 年

　　　　　宋　　　公元 420 — 479 年

　　　　　齐　　　公元 479 — 502 年

　　　　　梁　　　公元 502 — 557 年

　　　　　陈　　　公元 557 — 589 年

　　北朝　公元 386 — 581 年

　　　　　北魏　公元 386 — 534 年

　　　　　东魏　公元 534 — 550 年

　　　　　北齐　公元 550 — 577 年

　　　　　西魏　公元 535 — 556 年

　　　　　北周　公元 557 — 581 年

隋　　公元 581 — 618 年

唐　　公元 618 — 907 年

五代　公元 907 — 960 年

宋　　公元 960 — 1279 年

　　北宋　公元 960 — 1127 年

　　南宋　公元 1127 — 1279 年

辽　　公元 907 — 1125 年

西夏　公元 1038 — 1227 年

金　　公元 1115 — 1234 年

元　　公元 1206 — 1368 年

Northern and Southern Dynasties　　420 - 589 C.E.

　　Southern Dynasties　　420 - 589 C.E.

　　　　Song　　420 - 479 C.E.

　　　　Qi　　479 - 502 C.E.

　　　　Liang　　502 - 557 C.E.

　　　　Chen　　557 - 589 C.E.

　　Northern Dynasties　　386 - 581 C.E.

　　　　Northern Wei　　386 - 534 C.E.

　　　　Eastern Wei　　534 - 550 C.E.

　　　　Northern Qi　　550 - 577 C.E.

　　　　Western Wei　　535 - 556 C.E.

　　　　Northern Zhou　　557 - 581 C.E.

Sui Dynasty　　581 - 618 C.E.

Tang Dynasty　　618 - 907 C.E.

Five Dynasties　　907 - 960 C.E.

Song Dynasty　　960 - 1279 C.E.

　　Northern Song　　960 - 1127 C.E.

　　Southern Song　　1127 - 1279 C.E.

Liao Dynasty　　907 - 1125 C.E.

Xixia Period　　1038 - 1227 C.E.

Jin Dynasty　　1115 - 1234 C.E.

Yuan Dynasty　　1206 - 1368 C.E.